Nuclear Apartheid

THE QUEST FOR

AMERICAN ATOMIC SUPREMACY

FROM WORLD WAR II

TO THE PRESENT

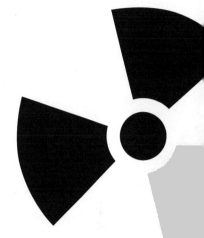

Nuclear
Apartheid

SHANE J. MADDOCK   *The University of North Carolina Press Chapel Hill*

Library of Congress Cataloging-in-Publication Data
Maddock, Shane J.
Nuclear apartheid : the quest for American atomic supremacy from
World War II to the present / Shane J. Maddock.
p. cm. Includes bibliographical references and index.
ISBN 978-0-8078-3355-1 (cloth : alk. paper)

1. Nuclear weapons—Government policy—United States—History. 2. Nuclear arms control—United States—History. 3. Nuclear nonproliferation—United States—History. 4. Nuclear weapons—Government policy—Developing countries—History. 5. Nuclear arms control—Developing countries—History. 6. Nuclear nonproliferation—Developing countries—History. 7. United States—Foreign relations—Developing countries. 8. Developing countries—Foreign relations—United States. I. Title.
JZ5645.M33 2010
327.1′7470973—dc22
2009032361

14 13 12 11 10   5 4 3 2 1

TO MY PARENTS, *Michael Maddock and Sandra Jacobson*

Contents

Preface

In 1998, South African president Nelson Mandela urged the world to ponder a question of profound importance, one that demanded attention from even the most ardent defenders of nuclear might: Why does the world "need" nuclear weapons "anyway." An attraction to "the threat of brute force" offered one explanation, Mandela theorized.[1] But subtler imperatives were also at work. For over sixty years, the United States has reserved the right to brandish nuclear weapons while denying them to states deemed unworthy, irrational, and uncivilized. The result, this hero in South Africa's victory over white supremacy suggested, intensified power disparities between the Western powers and their former colonies, formalizing a global regime of nuclear inequality that benefited North Atlantic Treaty Organization allies, and later Israel, while perpetuating the relative military disempowerment of Asia, Africa, and Latin America. Years prior, another commentator, Indian diplomat V. M. Trivedi, had similarly observed that the nuclear weapons club mirrored political and racial divisions in the global arena, dubbing the system "nuclear weapons apartheid."[2]

This history of the U.S.-Soviet arms race is the first to explore the evolution and persistence of nuclear apartheid from World War II through the present. It does so by focusing on American nonproliferation policy in the context of U.S.-Soviet relations and of Washington's persistent emphasis on maintaining nuclear primacy and global supremacy. Drawing on previously classified sources from U.S. and international archives, this work begins with the discovery of fission in 1939 and ends with George W. Bush's policies toward "nuclear rogues." Since 1945, the United States has worked diligently to preserve its nuclear supremacy. Harry S. Truman proclaimed a U.S. atomic monopoly devoid of any mention of Anglo-American wartime agreements and collaboration. He quickly initiated efforts to ensure that America remained the world's sole nuclear power for the foreseeable future. After the Soviet Union and Great Britain entered the nuclear ranks, in 1949 and 1952, respectively, Truman and his successors sought out other means to preserve U.S. dominance. Two solutions emerged — one technological and the other diplomatic. Truman authorized development of the hydrogen bomb while working to make the British program dependent on U.S. aid and influence. This strategy anticipated the efforts of the 1950s to restrict European nuclear development via "nuclear sharing." Moscow toyed with the same approach to China before cutting ties in 1959.

Beginning in the late 1940s, decolonization laid the groundwork for nuclear apartheid. The United States and the Soviet Union both exploited the promise of nuclear power to woo new states into their respective Cold War camps. Moscow and Washington remained unconcerned over potential proliferation effects because both trusted in their own ability to guard against diversion of nuclear materials and doubted that scientists in developing countries could fabricate sophisticated weapons. As the 1950s gave way to the 1960s, however, worries about nuclear proliferation grew. President John F. Kennedy and Soviet premier Nikita Khrushchev each placed increasing emphasis on nonproliferation and both sought a comprehensive test ban and a formal agreement to impede the spread of nuclear weapons. During the 1960s, the superpowers flirted with preemptive military action to roll back Chinese proliferation. Yet nuclear sharing remained a competing policy course. Divisions within the U.S. government and suspicions among European allies and recently decolonized nations that a nonproliferation agreement would relegate them to a permanently subordinate position helped delay the conclusion of the Nuclear Nonproliferation Treaty until 1968. This agreement codified nuclear apartheid, leaving in place three types of nuclear states: the five recognized nuclear powers (the United States, Britain, China, France, and the Soviet Union), NATO and Warsaw Pact allies with access to nuclear weapons but not ownership, and a large class of non-nuclear states who renounced their right to go nuclear.

Chapter 1 surveys major themes and key elements in the evolution of nuclear apartheid. Chapter 2 examines the development of nuclear weapons during World War II and early efforts to control their spread. Chapter 3 studies the origins and failure of America's first nonproliferation proposal, the Baruch Plan, and the Truman administration's abandonment of nonproliferation from 1949 to 1953. Chapters 4 and 5 trace Eisenhower's nonproliferation policy and the evolution of nuclear apartheid. Ike sought a nuclear test ban agreement to slow the spread of nuclear weapons while promoting Atoms for Peace and NATO nuclear-sharing arrangements that greatly increased proliferation dangers. During these years, a clear distinction was being made between Western countries that could be trusted with nuclear weapons and "little" countries that presumably could not. Chapters 6 and 7 explain why John F. Kennedy placed a greater emphasis on controlling proliferation. These chapters also detail why he settled for a limited test ban treaty when both a comprehensive testing agreement and an accord on nuclear proliferation seemed within reach. Chapters 8 and 9 examine why Lyndon Johnson aborted much of the progress made during the Kennedy years and why he nonetheless succeeded in concluding the Nuclear Nonproliferation Treaty in 1968. Chapter 10 tracks the persistence of nuclear apartheid from 1970 to 2008.

A book of this scope could not have been written and researched without generous financial assistance. The University of Connecticut funded my preliminary research. The John F. Kennedy Library Foundation, the Harry S. Truman Library Institute, the Eisenhower World Affairs Institute, the Herbert Hoover Presidential Library Association, and the Lyndon Baines Johnson Foundation all provided research and travel grants. The Institute for the Study of World Politics and the U.S. Arms Control and Disarmament Agency supported my early research and writing. Completion of this manuscript was greatly aided by professional development grants from Stonehill College and a sabbatical leave in 2006. Provost Katie Conboy and Dean of the Faculty Joseph Favazza have fostered an exciting intellectual environment that allows Stonehill faculty to thrive as scholars and teachers.

Numerous individuals took time from their busy schedules to offer me advice and stimulate my thinking, including Douglas Selvage, Lawrence Wittner, Thomas Schwartz, Frank Costigliola, and David Alan Rosenberg. Vladislav Zubok provided me with a paper on the Baruch Plan negotiations that cast a revealing light on Soviet attitudes toward the proposal. Warren Kimball sent me his interpretation of FDR's thinking on the bomb's role in the postwar world. Alan Greb offered encouragement and sent me the valuable publications of the Nuclear History Project at the University of Maryland's Center for Security Studies.

I deeply appreciate the help and guidance provided by the staffs of the following libraries and archives: National Archives, Library of Congress, National Security Archive, John F. Kennedy Library, Lyndon Baines Johnson Library, Herbert Hoover Library, Dwight D. Eisenhower Library, Harry S. Truman Library, Amherst College Library, Sterling Memorial Library (Yale),

Seeley Mudd Library (Princeton), Swarthmore College Peace Collection, British Public Record Office, Homer Babbidge Library (Connecticut), and MacPháidín Library (Stonehill). I especially thank the Interlibrary Loan Departments at the University of Connecticut and Stonehill College for procuring numerous secondary sources and Peter Alison, the Babbidge Library's history bibliographer, who acquired the important microfiche collection *U.S. Nuclear Non-Proliferation Policy, 1945–1991*, which greatly aided my research. Other archivists who made important contributions to this work include David Haight (Eisenhower Library), William Massa (Yale), Carol Briley (Truman Library), and William Burr (National Security Archive), a talented scholar who gave generously of his time during my visit to the National Security Archive offices and continued to send me important documents after I had left.

Colleagues, friends, and family offered crucial aid. Through numerous debates and conversations, Edmund S. Wehrle provided encouragement and help on individual chapters and insight into American attitudes toward Chinese nuclear weapons. The late A. William Hoglund pushed me to take my analysis to another level, and his keen editor's eye made each chapter stronger. J. Garry Clifford improved this book in countless ways through his encyclopedic knowledge of various archives, his proffered notes on Grenville Clark, and his multiple readings of the entire text. His candid and insightful comments on how to enliven and sharpen my argument proved invaluable. Thomas G. Paterson's contribution to this study shines through on every page. He is a rare combination of brilliant historian, thoughtful and attentive mentor, and good friend. He never doubted the significance of this project, even when the author at times began to wonder if he had taken on an impossible task.

My colleagues in the history department at Stonehill College were always willing to exchange ideas, offer encouragement, and share a good laugh. Thanks to all, but especially to the department chair during my first years, Ed McCarron. My former colleague LeeAnna Keith thoughtfully shared photocopies of her research at the Johnson presidential library. Charles Grench, my editor at the University of North Carolina Press, gave me timely advice and quiet encouragement. He and the excellent staff in Chapel Hill, especially Katy O'Brien, Tema Larter, and Paula Wald, made revising this manuscript for publication a true pleasure. The two readers for the press, Paul Boyer and Peter Kuznick, provided crucial advice on how to improve this work for publication.

My wife, Deborah Kisatsky, has made me a better historian through our running scholarly dialogue. She took time away from her own work to hear my ideas, read my prose, and share documents that she uncovered. Even through the most stressful times, she provided consistent intellectual and emotional support. Our children, Emily Rose and Benjamin Quinn, provided inspiration for the future and needed respites from the grind of writing. Hopefully the world they inherit will learn from the mistakes of the past.

This study is dedicated to my parents, Michael Maddock and Sandra Jacobson, who from my earliest days taught me to love learning and value education.

Abbreviations

ACDA
Arms Control and Disarmament Agency

AEC
Atomic Energy Commission

ANF
Atlantic Nuclear Force

CIA
Central Intelligence Agency

EEC
European Economic Community

ENDC
Eighteen-Nation Disarmament Committee

FBI
Federal Bureau of Investigation

GAC
General Advisory Committee

IAEA
International Atomic Energy Agency

ICBM
intercontinental ballistic missile

IRBM
intermediate range ballistic missile

JCAE
Joint Committee on Atomic Energy

LTBT
Limited Test Ban Treaty

MLF
multilateral force

MRBM
medium range ballistic missile

NATO
North Atlantic Treaty Organization

NPT
Nuclear Nonproliferation Treaty

NSC
National Security Council

PAL
permissive action link

PNE
peaceful nuclear explosive

PRC
People's Republic of China

SALT
strategic arms limitation talks

SANE
Committee for a Sane Nuclear Policy

UN
United Nations

UNAEC
United Nations Atomic Energy Commission

USSR
Union of Soviet Socialist Republics

WMD
weapon of mass destruction

Nuclear Apartheid

The Ideal Number of

Nuclear Weapons States Is One

NUCLEAR NONPROLIFERATION &

THE QUEST FOR AMERICAN ATOMIC SUPREMACY

Rejecting the stigma shadowing nuclear weapons in the early 1950s, Secretary of State John Foster Dulles declared: "In the past higher civilizations have always maintained their place against lower civilizations by devising more effective weapons." A half century later, President Bill Clinton promised to help other "civilized nations" acquire missile defense technology to protect against nuclear violence by "irresponsible" states and allied "terrorists." Comments such as these expose a deep-seated ideology that infused U.S. nuclear policy in general and U.S. nonproliferation policy in particular during the Cold War and beyond.[1] The primary tenets remained consistent from the beginning of the nuclear age—some states could be trusted with nuclear weapons and some could not. An atomic hierarchy emerged, first in the imagination of U.S. policymakers, then in political reality, that mirrored power inequities in the global system. This nuclear regime positioned Washington at the top, followed by its NATO allies and, later, Israel, with the postcolonial world consigned to the bottom. An Indian diplomat rightly labeled the system "nuclear apartheid."[2]

This book is the first to make nuclear apartheid its central theme and demonstrate its impact on U.S. nuclear policy at home and abroad. It does so by studying U.S. policymakers' ideological outlook and the mythic conception of America's past that nurtured atomic inequality and established the United States as the most legitimate nuclear power. Even U.S. leaders who sincerely desired to stem proliferation could not break free from the presumptions of national superiority that fostered nuclear discrimination. At its heart rested a variant of American exceptionalism that envisioned the United States as outside the normal constraints of a combative world system, therefore exempting Washington from most of the arguments used to dissuade other countries from acquiring nuclear arms. As William Appleman Williams once noted, even self-professed internationalists saw America as a "world unto itself," proffering U.S. solutions for all while ignoring lessons that other countries could teach.[3]

Such beliefs clearly made up only one element in the complex matrix of influences shaping U.S. nonproliferation proposals, which included alliance politics, U.S.-Soviet rivalry, decolonization, and fears of all-out nuclear war. Yet ideology's importance should not be understated, for, as one scholar has noted, a country's national security policy functions to protect domestic "core values" from outside threats. Core values help policymakers ascertain external challenges because "fears of foreign threats are a consequence of both real dangers in the external environment and ideological precepts, cultural symbols, and mistaken images."[4] In the case of the United States, racial and gender hierarchies, republican principles, and a nearly limitless faith in the power of technology merged and overlapped with perceived material interests, such as access to markets and natural resources, to provide a map for interpreting military and other threats. The end result was a foreign policy that referenced democratic ideals to advance U.S. hegemonic power and a nuclear policy that falsely presumed American moral and political guardianship over atomic technology. Both ultimately undercut the professed U.S. goal of nuclear containment.

This ends-means disjunction has not been fully visible to scholars or to the educated public. From the end of World War II to the present, U.S. policymakers have vocally opposed the spread of nuclear weapons. Nuclear nonproliferation efforts stemmed from a perceived need to eliminate or reduce the threat of a nuclear attack on the United States and its allies and to prevent the apocalyptic scenario of a nuclear war. But official nonproliferation efforts also served a deeper imperative — to maintain a uniquely powerful position for Washington within the international system. The North Atlantic Treaty Organization (NATO), the primary postwar American alliance, itself had its roots in a U.S. desire to define a common Western identity in the aftermath of

World War II as well as to establish a bulwark against potential Soviet military threats. Preventing proliferation within NATO functioned to preserve U.S. hegemony in both a Realist and a Gramscian sense, eliminating competing power centers within the alliance and impeding the growth of a new and rival strategic culture.[5]

National security and hegemonic goals were used to justify selective proliferation — the controlled spread of U.S.-owned nuclear weapons to trusted allies in order to offset the military strength of the Soviet Union and its Eastern European clients. Presidents from Harry Truman to Ronald Reagan pursued selective proliferation during the Cold War, even as Congress sought to limit its implementation. Many legislators believed that fewer nuclear powers reduced the risk of nuclear war for all humankind. Others thought that American nuclear preeminence could reduce U.S. defense obligations to Western European countries and rebuild the faith in "Fortress America" that had been demolished with Japan's attack on Pearl Harbor. The result of this executive-legislative rivalry was a further weakening of a nonproliferation policy that was already riven by ideological and political contradiction. As a result, the U.S. government actively facilitated Britain's nuclear ambitions (1952) while failing to prevent France (1960) and China (1964) from acquiring nuclear technology.

The dual attraction and repulsion of U.S. leaders to nuclear weapons were already evident during World War II, when policymakers contemplated the bomb's role in the postwar world. Some advocated banning, as poison gas had been after the previous world war. Others envisioned an "ace in the hole" that could restore a sense of U.S. invulnerability that had been lost by the attack on Pearl Harbor. As the wartime alliance with Moscow chilled, banning the bomb appeared chimerical to President Harry Truman and most key policymakers. Those who objected to the dominant view quickly exited the administration.

Dissent outside the government became the next target. Former secretary of war Henry Stimson, among others, published official justifications for the atomic bombings, which employed questionable statistics to rationalize hundreds of thousands of Japanese civilian deaths. U.S. occupation authorities confiscated photographs and home movies that depicted the horrible aftermath of the bombings and kept them hidden for over two decades. These actions enabled fabrication of an official, public narrative — an atomic catechism of sorts — that portrayed the United States as righteous in using the bomb in 1945 and in maintaining proprietorship over it during ensuing decades. The central tenet of this canon was that the United States had reluctantly used atomic bombs against a savage and irrational enemy. These weapons had saved lives and ended the war more quickly than if they had not been used. Once Americans discovered the bombs' terrible destructive power, they resolved that such devastation should never occur again. Truman then generously proposed international control of the bomb, which Moscow rejected because it already harbored ambitions toward world domination. Washington therefore resolved to maintain nuclear supremacy to keep the communist hordes in check while remaining poised to eliminate the nuclear scourge once international stability returned. As for fears of nuclear power running amok, U.S. leaders assured the public that nuclear fission ultimately would prove to be a technological boon—limitless energy produced in totally safe nuclear reactors. Underpinning all these claims lay the presumption that only Americans had the wisdom, courage, and intellect to possess and use atomic power.[6]

Several key features of the American postwar domestic environment encouraged this official narrative to flourish. World War II had concentrated tremendous power in the U.S. executive branch, especially in the presidency. Cold War policies continued this trend, beginning with the Hiroshima and Nagasaki bombings in 1945. Congress did create the Joint Committee on Atomic Energy in 1946 to monitor executive action in nuclear affairs, but presidents could invoke national security to shield their activities, and they gained almost unchecked power to brandish nuclear weapons. Once the United States wedded more powerful thermonuclear bombs to ballistic missiles in the late 1950s, one person now had the ability to devastate whole countries with a single command. Yet, for all their real and statutory authority, presidents could not easily pursue policies that deviated from the official script surrounding nuclear weapons and technology. Powerful interests, inside and outside of government, could resist changes large and small. Bureaucratic foot-dragging also could block executive initiatives because presidents could not carry out orders alone, nor could they constantly monitor the entire national security bureaucracy. The Joint Committee on Atomic Energy also jealously guarded its authority in nuclear matters and could inhibit changes it opposed.[7]

A deep faith in U.S. technology joined bureaucratic and political factors in shaping American nuclear policy. Presidents rarely possessed a sophisticated understanding of nuclear physics or weapons engineering. They remained dependent on experts, and they gravitated to advisers who promised quick and easy solutions. Truman embraced Manhattan Project director General Leslie Groves's claim that Washington's atomic monopoly would persist for decades, despite contrary scientific advice that any "atomic secrets" would be difficult to keep, at best. Truman's myopia paved the way for the badly flawed Baruch Plan for international control of the atom and his hasty decision to build the hydrogen bomb. But Truman's successors also succumbed to the lure of technological utopianism. Dwight D. Eisenhower weighed the promise of nuclear reactors as sources of clean and efficient energy, both in the United States and elsewhere, against the danger that plutonium created in such reactors might be diverted to nuclear weapons. Eisenhower and subsequent presidents became captivated by nuclear energy promoters, who hailed the economic and propaganda benefits of nuclear power development, ignoring proliferation dangers. The nonproliferation benefits of a comprehensive nuclear test ban paled beside visions of the technological marvels promised from nuclear testing. Technological utopianism and American exceptionalism also fed claims that the Soviet Union only acquired nuclear know-how by stealing U.S. secrets, and both tropes nourished American fantasies of an impregnable missile defense system.[8]

When domestic critics offered counternarratives of nuclear weapons, they faced an array of obstacles. Dissent surfaced immediately after the Hiroshima and Nagasaki bombings. Some critics, such as former president Herbert Hoover, condemned the policy of unconditional surrender that prevented negotiations with the Japanese, prolonged the war, and forced the use of immoral weapons. Others feared the day that such horrible weapons would be used against Americans. John Hersey's 1946 account, *Hiroshima*, increased antinuclear sentiments and prompted efforts by Stimson and other Truman officials to justify the bomb. By 1949, talk of "peace" stirred up red-baiting attacks against antinuclear organizations. The government and press quickly labeled critics "communist dupes" or "sympathizers." Diplomat George Kennan captured the prevailing view when he depicted the Soviet Union as a mechanistic monstrosity, impervious to reason, responsive only to the law of force. According to such logic, anyone who advised negotiations with the Soviets was not only traitorous, but delusional, even insane. Critics, in turn, lacked crucial masculine qualities, such as courage, toughness, and rationality, as shown in their presumably weak-willed calls for compromise. Gendered characterizations extended to the international sphere. World powers that challenged the American-dominated regime of nuclear power or that rejected U.S. nuclear and other policies risked being categorized as culturally, racially, and intellectually deficient, and therefore as undeserving of American nuclear assistance.

Despite official attempts to suppress dissent, the specter of nuclear apocalypse haunted the Americans. Even before the United States used the bomb, Secretary of War Henry Stimson feared "a Frankenstein which would eat us up." Los Alamos laboratory scientists wondered if the Trinity test in July 1945 might ignite the atmosphere, destroying the world. After World War II, this apocalyptic narrative helped push Truman to express public support for international control of atomic energy. The enduring public fear of nuclear extinction became a common theme in science fiction films about giant mutant ants (*Them!*), irradiated monsters from outer space (*The Thing*), and aliens warning about nuclear destruction (*The Day the Earth Stood Still*). The television drama *The Twilight Zone* and the novel and film *On the Beach* helped inspire renewed antinuclear activism in the 1950s and 1960s. In the 1980s, films like *The Day After* and *Testament* vividly raised awareness of the devastation of nuclear war and introduced the world to the specter of nuclear winter—a frigid world encircled by clouds of smoke and debris shutting out the sun's light.[9]

Dissent also surfaced abroad. The atomic bomb had come to symbolize American hegemony during the early Cold War, but by the 1950s its persistence in the world served to erode Washington's self-image as the world's only legitimate nuclear power. As France, Britain, and Germany recovered from the devastation of World War II, they grew restless under U.S. leadership and embraced the neo-imperial idiom that equated nuclear weapons with national greatness. Britain took the lead in constructing an independent nuclear deterrent. Washington initially treated Britain as an exceptional case, its vital role in wartime development of the bomb having earned it the right to develop a small nuclear force. France's Charles de Gaulle rejected such claims, believing that the Anglo-Americans sought permanently to subdue the continental European powers. He hoped a French nuclear arsenal would simultaneously break the U.S. stranglehold on alliance decision making and restore French international grandeur. U.S. policymakers pressed de Gaulle to abandon his nuclear ambitions, to no avail.

Washington's emphasis then switched to Germany. Policymakers feared that if Bonn felt discriminated against within the alliance system the world would witness resurgent German nationalism and European conflict. Some policymakers advocated a multilateral nonproliferation agreement that would leave the U.S.-Soviet nuclear arms race largely untouched. But many resisted, fearing it would seem as if the two superpowers had colluded to keep their allies nuclear-free. An agreement that "banned the bomb," even for only a select group of nations, might stigmatize the U.S. nuclear arsenal, making all such weapons appear illegitimate. Washington should instead "share" nuclear weapons with Germany and any other interested European allies under NATO arrangements. From 1960 onward, competing factions within the U.S. national security bureaucracy debated the relative merits of nuclear sharing and a nonproliferation agreement. Several presidents failed to resolve the debate, pursuing both goals simultaneously. This merry-go-round paralyzed U.S. nonproliferation policy from 1960 to 1968.

The paralysis proved crucial. During the 1960s, a host of newly independent states emerged in Africa and Asia. Many new nations looked to China to lead an African-Asian bloc to oppose the troubled European imperialist powers. Beijing had been Moscow's most important ally in the 1950s and had demanded nuclear aid from Moscow after Washington allowed Britain to develop the bomb. The two communist giants split in the 1960s, but the Soviets could not stuff the nuclear genie back into the bottle. In 1964, China tested its own bomb, and the context within which U.S. policymakers evaluated nonproliferation changed dramatically. The most likely proliferators remained countries friendly to Washington. But Beijing had proven that poorer, less technologically developed nations could also develop nuclear weapons. Newly decolonized countries, such as India and South Africa, could cite the Chinese example to justify a quest for nuclear weapons, even though most of their people still lived in squalid conditions. Washington feared, in the words of the nuclear strategist Herman Kahn, that "a Hottentot" might produce nuclear weapons by 1969.[10] The realization that no permanent barrier existed to proliferation, along with racial conceptions of African and Asian peoples as less capable of responsible nuclear development, led to a more concerted effort to conclude a nonproliferation agreement.

Nonproliferation negotiations between the two superpowers, however, ignored important international realities. U.S. and Soviet hegemony had to weather assaults on two fronts—within their alliance systems and from newly decolonized countries. France and China had distanced themselves from arms control agreements, denigrating them as a superpower condominium over the rest of the world. Many African and Asian countries had joined the nonaligned movement to protest the bipolar ordering of international relations. In this global environment, a successful nonproliferation agreement could emerge only from truly multilateral negotiations in which all powers participated on relatively equal footing.

Beginning in 1962, Moscow and Washington went through the pretense of conducting international nonproliferation talks at the Eighteen-Nation Disarmament Committee, but substantive discussions occurred behind closed doors on a bilateral basis. The Nuclear Nonproliferation Treaty (NPT) that emerged in 1968 required no sacrifice from the two superpowers. Under the terms of the NPT, nuclear weapons states pledged only to refrain from transferring nuclear weapons to other powers—something none intended to do even in the absence of a treaty. Non-nuclear nations, however, had to forgo a strategic asset that had been portrayed as an absolute weapon ever since 1945. More important, the accord left nuclear weapons in the hands of countries (Britain, France, and China) that could not claim the unique status of the superpowers. What distinguished China from India, or France from Germany or Sweden? As the Swedish Nobel laureate Alva Myrdal observed, "It should have been recognized from the outset that if there are tenable arguments for some lesser powers in favor of possessing nuclear weapons, such must be equally applicable to others."[11] The only way to address every nation's security concerns would have been to establish a timetable for nuclear disarmament simultaneous with the non-nuclear powers' signing of the NPT. But neither the United States nor the Soviet Union would give up its nuclear arsenal. The superpowers produced a treaty in 1968 that proved unacceptable to many near-nuclear nations, most notably Israel, South Africa, Argentina, Pakistan, and India.

The NPT thus proved an empty victory. Its ratification ushered in another wave of U.S. equivocation toward nuclear proliferation. Many policymakers argued that because proliferation appeared inevitable, the United States must adopt a more flexible attitude toward independent nuclear arsenals or risk alienating such important allies and neutrals as India, Japan, and Israel. When India and Israel acquired atomic weapons capabilities in the 1970s, neither drew protests from Washington. Inconsistency in U.S. policy enabled the perception to flourish that nuclear weapons offered a route to respect on the international stage, while nonproliferation and disarmament provided few benefits and limited security.

To understand the failures of nuclear nonproliferation efforts from 1955 to the present, one needs to "take off the Cold War lens" and acknowledge that very early in the postwar period U.S. policymakers saw decolonization as a dangerous phenomenon that overlapped with but was also distinct from the Cold War. By 1975, the CIA recognized that nonproliferation and other nuclear issues "are often colored by an overlay of North-South tensions." Yet, three decades later, one scholar thought it "ironic" that although the nonproliferation and limited test ban treaties "influenced but marginally" the superpower arms race, "they turned out to be the only major arms control agreements of the Cold War era" that survived. Viewed outside the Cold War context, the apparent irony disappears. Both agreements worked as planned: They sought to preserve the superpowers' nuclear arsenals while constraining the ability of presumed outsiders to join the nuclear club. Though endorsed by many who sought to control the arms race, these agreements codified nuclear apartheid, allowing a select group of Western allied states to retain genocidal weapons in perpetuity, while others, many of them former colonies, renounced their intention to possess such weapons. Yet some postcolonial powers refused to acquiesce to such a system, and by the 1980s many African and Asian leaders shared the sentiments of Libyan president Muammar Gadhafi, who in 1987 asserted that "we should be like the Chinese—poor and riding donkeys, but respected and possessing an atom bomb."[12]

The end of the Cold War held promise both for nuclear disarmament and for nonproliferation. But old patterns reasserted themselves, and addendums to the nuclear catechism claimed that atomic weapons made Moscow behave and that they had won the Cold War for Washington. As William Appleman Williams had argued, U.S. hegemonic aspirations predated 1945 and would outlive the U.S.-Soviet confrontation. The United States still insisted that other countries follow America's example in all vital matters. Even without a perceived communist threat, Washington suffered from "superpower syndrome"—the belief that it could control and dominate the world simply because it had the right to. Rules that applied to other states did not apply to it. In the early twenty-first century, U.S. leaders preached nonproliferation, and policymakers believed that "the ideal number of nuclear-weapons states is one." Truman's ghost still haunted Washington; nonproliferation and disarmament still languished.[13]

Too Stupid Even for
the Funny Papers

THE MYTH OF THE AMERICAN ATOMIC

MONOPOLY, 1939–1945

In September 1945, nuclear physicist James Franck warned President Harry S. Truman that "the idea that there exists a secret formula [for the atomic bomb] which can be guarded in its entirety" should be dismissed "as too stupid even for the movies and the funny papers." The president ignored this warning and soon pledged publicly that the United States would hold its atomic monopoly as "a sacred trust" until "world cooperation for peace" achieved "a state of perfection." Truman's breezy confidence in U.S. atomic secrecy typified early American nuclear policy. He and other U.S. policymakers, including Truman's predecessor, Franklin D. Roosevelt, disregarded warnings from well-informed atomic scientists that America's nuclear secrets could not be kept forever. Political and military leaders dismissed such physicists as starry-eyed idealists, but events soon exposed policymakers as the deluded ones. Beneath their hubristic policy initiatives and public pronouncements lay a deeply engrained faith in U.S. technological prowess, a science fiction–inspired belief in superweapons, and a historical amnesia regarding how American fears of other states, especially Nazi Germany, acquiring atomic bombs had spurred the U.S. nuclear program. Faith in the U.S. atomic monopoly had led FDR and then Truman to waste opportunities to conclude a nonproliferation agreement at a time when enforcement would have been less complicated and before the growing Cold War rivalry between Washington and Moscow made such a treaty much more difficult to negotiate.[1]

"The Wrong End of the Telescope"

Indulging in the stereotype of scientists as eccentrics, President Roosevelt once quipped that he "had little sympathy with Copernicus," who had "looked through the right end of the telescope, thus greatly magnifying his problems. I use the wrong end of the telescope and it makes things much easier to bear." In assessing the threat of nuclear proliferation, Roosevelt actually used both ends of the telescope. He initially used the magnifying lens when he inadvertently exaggerated the threat of a German atomic bomb. But he viewed the danger of postwar nuclear proliferation through the wrong end, minimizing and pushing it into the distance. Roosevelt's successor, Truman, exacerbated these errors. Both men ignored ample data that wartime contingencies had led to the Anglo-American monopoly in 1945. Foreign and foreign-born scientists had made every major discovery leading to the development of the atomic bomb. In 1905, Albert Einstein, a German-born Swiss citizen, first put forth the theory that matter could be transformed into energy. Enrico Fermi, an Italian, discovered that uranium reacted to neutron bombardment in 1934, and in 1938 German chemists Otto Hahn and Fritz Strassmann discovered that rather than absorbing the neutron the uranium nuclei had actually become a lighter element. They announced their discovery of nuclear fission in January 1939.[2]

The discovery of fission brought a flurry of scientific activity. In 1939 alone, scientists throughout the world published approximately 100 articles on the topic and initiated numerous research projects. In summer 1940, Soviet scientists Georgii Flerov and Konstantin Petrzhak confirmed experimentally that some uranium nuclei "split" naturally without neutron bombardment. French scientists under the direction of Frédéric Joliot-Curie quickly established the world's leading nuclear program, albeit one focused on the development of nuclear power plants, not nuclear explosives. French scientists likely would have achieved the first uranium chain reaction but for the Nazi invasion of France in June 1940. The rapid diffusion of nuclear knowledge reflected the interwar flourishing of "scientific internationalism," whose proponents advocated the open publication of experimental and theoretical findings in order to advance humanity's understanding of the universe. Many hoped, especially after the atomic bomb became a reality, that contacts among scientists could bridge barriers to international peace and cooperation.

Knowledge of fission's possible military and civilian applications had already infused the scientific community years before the United States ever produced a functioning nuclear reactor or an atomic bomb. The proliferation of nuclear knowledge via both publication and a mass exodus to Great Britain and the United States of scientists fleeing Nazi persecution inaugurated the Anglo-American nuclear effort. The émigrés employed throughout the Manhattan Project ironically helped germinate the myth of an American atomic monopoly. Yet, in the initial stages of the European "brain drain," the United States still lagged behind Britain in atomic energy research. In March 1940, Otto Frisch and Rudolph Peierls, two refugee German physicists, informed the British government that a crash program could produce an atomic bomb in only two years. The Peierls-Frisch memorandum led directly to the establishment of the Maud Committee to study the possibility of constructing an atomic bomb. Hans Halban and Lew Kowarski, two French scientists fleeing from the victorious Germans, lent further urgency to the effort when they reported that a controlled nuclear chain reaction could occur in natural uranium.

Scientists in other countries reached similar conclusions. In 1940, Soviet physicists Iuli Khariton and Iakov Zel'dovich collaborated on several papers that suggested that uranium could be used to create a bomb. But the Soviet government and the scientific community each viewed the other with suspicion, and even a subsequent memorandum by Khariton and Zel'dovich stressing the destructive potential of an atomic weapon did not galvanize a Soviet atomic bomb project as the Peierls-Frisch memorandum had done in Britain.

In the United States, early attempts to alert the government about incipient nuclear dangers also met with little success. In March, Fermi, who had fled fascist Italy and accepted a position at Columbia University, demonstrated to a group of U.S. Navy scientists and officers how a uranium chain reaction could be used to make a bomb. But the physicist could not break through the suspicious natures of the military officers, who regarded him as a "wop." That summer, Leo Szilard, a Hungarian émigré who worked with Fermi, approached his former teacher Albert Einstein and asked him to alert President Roosevelt to the danger that the Nazis might already be seeking an atomic weapon. Feeling little urgency, Roosevelt sent Einstein's letter to a low-level bureaucrat, who established a perfunctory study group on a uranium bomb. American interest in atomic weapons did not intensify until fall 1941 when

Vannevar Bush, the head of the U.S. National Defense Research Committee, brought the Maud Committee's final report to Roosevelt's attention. The arguments of pragmatic British officials proved more persuasive than those of émigré nuclear physicists. On October 9, 1941, Roosevelt authorized an expanded American nuclear research program.[3]

The United States thus came belatedly to the first phase of the atomic arms race. By late 1941, French, Japanese, Soviet, German, and British scientists had all started on the path toward nuclear weapons. Why, then, did only the Anglo-American effort produce a bomb by 1945? Unlike other powers in the arms race, the United States had tremendous financial resources at its command, and neither air attack nor invasion posed a serious threat. In addition, as the 1940s began, U.S. physics research achieved parity with the rest of the world. The migration of first-rate physicists from Europe enhanced this trend. Without this influx of scientific talent and the wartime disruption of other countries' nuclear programs, the United States likely would not have developed atomic weapons first. Steeped in postwar triumphalism, American leaders failed to acknowledge the importance of temporary wartime advantages when they based U.S. postwar atomic energy policy on the assumption of a secure nuclear monopoly.

Taming the British and Freezing Out the Soviets

Throughout the war years, the United States, Britain, and the Soviet Union treated each other as both allies and adversaries. In the realm of nuclear policy, a competitive relationship prevailed. Initially FDR sought nuclear ties with London. His proposal for an atomic partnership would also help cement an Anglo-American alliance to police the world, the presumed best hope for postwar global peace and stability. But the British, given their early lead in uranium research, saw few benefits in collaboration. London also worried about leaks to the enemy from a partner not yet at war and without adequate security procedures in place. By summer 1942, however, British officials sought to embrace the Americans. They realized that the large industrial and scientific infrastructure needed to produce an atomic bomb would be extremely vulnerable to air attack if located in the British Isles. If Britain wished to produce atomic weapons, it would need to construct plants in Canada—or enter into full partnership with the United States. Attempting to salvage the British program, British prime minister Winston Churchill told Roosevelt that the American and British atomic energy programs should "work together on equal terms, and share the results, if any, equally between us."

The two leaders reached an oral understanding on this issue, but they never told their subordinates to move beyond the limited information sharing that they had previously approved.[4]

Confusion became panic upon Churchill's return to Britain. Sir John Anderson, the prime minister's chief adviser on Britain's atomic bomb project (code-named Tube Alloys), warned Churchill that the United Kingdom had fallen dangerously behind the United States. Only collaboration with the Americans could prevent the empire's being shut off completely from war-time access to atomic weapons. The two allies must conclude a partnership agreement in 1942 or early 1943 while the British still had a significant contribution to make. Washington's desire for cooperation, however, had faded. Because the U.S. project had surged ahead of Britain's, FDR's chief science adviser, Vannevar Bush, and his deputy, James Conant, believed that American interests would be better served by going it alone. Conant argued that the United States already shouldered the majority of the burden and that a joint effort might compromise U.S. security. Because the British had expressed no intention of producing atomic weapons during the war, no military rationale justified collaboration.

Recent news that Britain had signed an alliance with the Soviets pushed both Bush and Roosevelt to endorse Conant's recommendations. FDR, already reticent about sharing atomic information with Stalin, worried that London might feel treaty bound to share such data with Moscow. In late 1942 and early 1943, as the bomb's potential capabilities became clearer, Roosevelt reformulated his thoughts on the postwar peace. His new strategic vision reinforced his distrust of Britain and Russia as atomic partners. In late 1942 and early 1943, Red Army successes against the Wehrmacht convinced him that the Soviets, not the British, would join the United States as one of the two dominant powers after the war. The president envisioned four policemen — the United States, Great Britain, the Soviet Union, and China — as bulwarks of the postwar peace. Smaller states would be disarmed, and the four great powers would manage their traditional spheres of influence. Roosevelt, however, viewed both the Soviet Union and China as immature powers that would have to be educated to act responsibly on the world stage.

The Soviets particularly worried the president. He hoped to control their aggressiveness by enveloping them in an international political and economic system that fostered prosperity and security for all. Roosevelt believed that the multilateral United Nations (UN) and the Bretton Woods system would transform the Soviet Union into a guardian of the status quo. But he knew this process would take time. Roosevelt thought nuclear weapons might hedge against future Soviet truculence. He elevated atomic secrecy to such prominence in his postwar plans that he risked alienating Britain by disregarding previous promises of full nuclear cooperation. By approving a policy of restricted interchange, FDR supplemented the primary goal of U.S. atomic energy policy—an all-out wartime drive to produce a bomb—with a new emphasis on postwar leverage. If four policemen were keeping the peace, only two (and maybe only one) would have atomic weapons.

In 1943, the British attempted to pry loose American restrictions by arguing that they needed atomic weapons to counterbalance postwar Soviet manpower. Conant and Bush, however, thought collaboration on that basis imprudent. Churchill directly approached FDR, who reversed his subordinates and acceded to the Quebec Agreement on August 19, 1943. This accord largely settled the wartime dispute over the extent of atomic collaboration. In late 1943, Bush, Conant, and Brigadier General Leslie Groves, director of the Manhattan Project, along with their British counterparts, fine-tuned details of the new partnership. The three Americans eked out a tactical victory for their position when they relegated Britain to a junior role in the atomic program, with the United States controlling all the major scientific and technical facilities and retaining physical custody of the bombs. The new arrangement foreshadowed U.S. postwar ambitions as Germany's defeat looked more assured. The United States would be dominant militarily after the war, and much of this strength would rest on its atomic monopoly. Washington felt secure enough in its eventual postwar superiority to toy with denying both of its main wartime allies access to nuclear data, but in the end only Moscow remained shut off from the Manhattan Project.[5]

The Quebec Agreement had profound implications for postwar efforts to control the bomb and for U.S.-Soviet relations in general. The pooling of American and British scientific and technical knowledge belied U.S. officials' subsequent claims of an American monopoly on "atomic know-how." By war's end, the United States, Canada, and Great Britain had jointly participated in the Manhattan Project and gained the scientific and industrial information necessary for the development of atomic weapons. London and Ottawa lacked both the infrastructure and the financial health to produce bombs without making difficult economic choices. But Britain did have ready access to raw materials through the Combined Development Trust, established in June 1944 as a corollary body to the Combined Policy Committee, which coordinated Anglo-American nuclear policy. The trust agreement called for joint development and control of uranium and other fissionable natural elements around the world. Both parties had equal legal claims on the raw materials acquired through the trust's activities, and each provided equal financial support for its operations. Given this level of cooperation and shared knowledge, Britain, and to some degree Canada, needed to be treated as full partners when the U.S. government formulated plans for international control. If not, they had the power to undercut any agreement.[6]

The Quebec Agreement also codified many of Roosevelt's nascent ideas about the bomb's role in international politics. The third article of the accord, which barred communicating information to any third party without mutual consent, proved significant both during and after the war. Not only did this provision require both parties to agree before they even initiated discussions with the Soviets; it violated an existing agreement on atomic research between the British and the Free French, underlining Churchill and Roosevelt's shared conviction that postwar security hinged on wartime atomic secrecy.

FDR's desire to preserve Anglo-American supremacy led him to reject several prescient plans to avert a postwar nuclear arms race. Danish physicist and Nobel laureate Niels Bohr first approached both Churchill and Roosevelt during 1944, proposing to inform the Soviets about the Manhattan Project. Bohr had advocated scientific internationalism as a means to global peace and cooperation. He contended that the unrestricted sharing of information that helped world science to thrive could be duplicated in the military realm. Once this principle gained acceptance, an agreement could be reached to ban nuclear weapons. Bohr's arms control model called for establishing a technical inspection body that monitored atomic research and development and formally distinguished dangerous from safe research activities.

Neither FDR nor Churchill was open to Bohr's ideas. Roosevelt initially avoided meeting with Bohr and sent him to talk to "our friends in London." Even after Bohr succeeded in personally presenting his ideas to the president and prime minister, he merely aroused their suspicion as they dismissed his plan in its totality. In September, at the president's home in Hyde Park, New York, the two leaders signed an aide-mémoire rejecting both the "suggestion that the world should be informed" about the atomic bomb and any effort to negotiate an "international agreement regarding its control and use." Both Churchill and FDR concluded that the Anglo-American monopoly offered them more security than any international control scheme, and, to that end, they decided to extend the U.S.-British atomic alliance into the postwar period. To cap their complete rejection of Bohr's proposals and punctuate their disdain for political amateurs, the president and prime minister directed that "enquiries should be made" regarding Bohr's activities and efforts be put forth to "insure that he is responsible for no leakage of information, particularly to the Russians."[7]

Further illustrating the president's commitment to secrecy, Roosevelt warned Bush and other subordinates that his conversations with Bohr raised important security questions. The president asked how much the Danish scientist knew about the Manhattan Project and demanded assurances that Bohr could be trusted with the information he had acquired at Los Alamos. Yet the president had never mentioned his discussions with Bohr to any of his subordinates prior to this meeting and neglected to inform them of his new agreement with Churchill.

During the same conversation, Bush inferred from the president's offhand remarks about postwar collaboration that he had at least reached an informal understanding with Churchill about the matter. He and Conant, like Bohr, had gradually come to think that an international control commission might be the only way to prevent a nuclear arms race. The science adviser quickly warned Stimson of Roosevelt's designs for a postwar Anglo-American atomic partnership and urged him to persuade Roosevelt that a monopoly could not endure after the war. Once Stimson agreed to discuss the issue with the president, Conant and Bush wrote down their ideas so that Stimson would have detailed arguments to present. They stressed that, before scientists developed major advances in destructive capability, a control agreement needed to be concluded, and they reiterated the impossibility of preserving the Anglo-American monopoly after the war. Nonetheless, they did not recommend an immediate approach to Russia.

Stimson appeared uncertain about their proposals and neglected them for more than two months while he focused on other military issues. When the secretary finally discussed atomic secrecy with the president in late December, the matter had become entangled with the discovery that French scientists working in Canada and Great Britain might have leaked information to the newly installed government in liberated France. Because of the perceived instability of the new government and the fact that the leading French nuclear physicist, Joliot-Curie, maintained membership in the Communist Party, many American officials worried about secrets being shared with the Soviets. After meeting with FDR, Stimson immediately began working to ensure that the British complied with the Quebec Agreement and did not give France any information. The U.S. government also surveilled some French scientists and restricted their foreign travel. In early 1945, Churchill settled the issue for the British when he barred the French government from receiving nuclear data.[8]

In late 1944, Stimson warned Roosevelt about atomic secrecy's potentially deleterious effects on postwar U.S.-Soviet relations. But he also contemplated using atomic energy as a bargaining chip to force the Soviets to liberalize their society. His attraction to the latter course persisted through March 1945. Finally, however, pressure from Conant and Bush following the Yalta Conference persuaded Stimson that the issue of postwar controls needed to be settled. On March 15, Stimson told Roosevelt that only two options existed for postwar atomic energy policy: an attempt at continued Anglo-American monopoly or a proposal for international control "based upon both freedom of science and access." Which policy to pursue needed to be decided prior to the war's end. Roosevelt agreed, without telling anyone which of the two policies he endorsed. In the days preceding Roosevelt's death, Stimson continued the existing policy and worked to preserve the atomic monopoly through the elimination of German bomb project facilities in areas to be controlled by the French and Soviets. The postwar fate of American atomic policy remained in limbo when a new president took office on April 12.[9]

Some scholars argue that Roosevelt's final conversation with Stimson showed that he may have been ready to pursue international control after the war, or at least that he remained undecided on the issue. An FDR-Churchill exchange at Yalta superficially supports this interpretation. During that summit conference, Roosevelt casually suggested that atomic secrets should be shared with Soviet leader Joseph Stalin because if Free French leader Charles de Gaulle knew about the bomb project, "he would certainly double-cross us with Russia." But Roosevelt never seriously considered revealing atomic secrets to Stalin. He simply used this threat to compel Churchill to violate existing British-French military patent agreements. Rather than representing a lost opportunity for cooperation, the exchange illustrates the depths of American and British resolve to preserve their nuclear monopoly.[10]

Costly Myths

Roosevelt's faith in the American nuclear monopoly remains puzzling. General Groves, as early as 1942, informed him that Soviet spies had attempted to penetrate the Manhattan Project. And Groves, after the war, admitted that most of the Manhattan Project's antiespionage measures sought to hinder Soviet infiltration of the project. Some scholars contend that FDR did not react to Soviet espionage because he hoped it might help subvert U.S.-British agreements banning data sharing with third parties. Such speculations fail, given that both Groves and Stimson assured FDR that Soviet spies had not acquired substantial knowledge of the bomb project. The president had no reason to believe that the Soviets had effectively breached atomic security.[11]

Yet Groves's and Stimson's assurances themselves proved unfounded. Despite efforts to deny the Russians atomic secrets, Soviet officials recognized the possibility of atomic weapons as early as the Americans did. On September 25, 1941, a Russian intelligence official in London, either John Cairncross or Donald Maclean, both Soviet "moles" inside the British government and part of the notorious Cambridge Five spy ring, transmitted the Maud Committee report to Moscow. They and their fellow spies — Kim Philby, Anthony Blunt, and Guy Burgess — made sure that the Soviets did not long remain ignorant of Britain's bomb project or of Anglo-American collaboration. Klaus Fuchs, a German émigré scientist with communist sympathies who worked on the British project, also began supplying information to the Soviets in late 1941. He became the Soviets' most valuable atomic spy after being transferred to Los Alamos in late 1943. Because the Soviet Union was struggling desperately to stave off defeat in late 1941 and early 1942, its leaders did not evaluate this intelligence information until March 1942. Suspicious of possible disinformation, Soviet officials consulted physicists, although the scientists were not shown raw intelligence material. After much deliberation, Moscow established a modest project guided by the young physicist Igor Kurchatov in March 1943. Stalin hoped to beat Hitler to the bomb, but he hedged his bets because he feared wasting resources on a hypothetical weapon. The small project he authorized had little potential to produce a weapon during the war, but any progress benefited postwar Soviet struggles for power and influence.

The intelligence material that Kurchatov received helped the Soviets avoid many pitfalls but could not solve the debilitating problem of resources. The Soviets lacked both the capital and the uranium and other raw materials needed to conduct important experiments. The American policy of secrecy may ironically have provided some relief for this problem. The Soviets requested uranium and uranium compounds from the United States on four different occasions in 1943. Groves approved these requests to avoid suspicions within the Soviet Union and the United States. No evidence exists that these materials went to the Soviet bomb project. Uranium compounds are also used to manufacture certain steel alloys and in fact may have been requested for this purpose.

By early 1945, the Soviets had at least four intelligence sources on the Manhattan Project, making a farce of American and British atomic secrecy. Soviet battlefield successes also aided their bomb program. The Red Army captured Czech and eastern German uranium mines and stockpiles, and they kidnapped and recruited experts for service in the Soviet project. Moscow had acquired the ability to rapidly expand its limited program after the war.[12]

Although FDR remained unaware of the extent of Soviet espionage, he did know that Stalin had ample evidence that the Manhattan Project existed. Roosevelt's science advisers had repeatedly warned him that the Anglo-American atomic monopoly was a wartime fluke that would not outlast the end of hostilities. Why then did he put so much stock in the atomic bomb monopoly? And why did he risk his well-documented desire for postwar cooperation with the Soviets by maintaining atomic secrecy? FDR's faith in the nuclear monopoly makes little sense on scientific or political grounds. A number of factors, however, together convinced Roosevelt that the monopoly could last much longer than Conant, Bush, and Bohr claimed.

First, the programs that had inspired the U.S. effort had all stagnated during the war. After the Nazi invasion, French scientists either joined the Anglo-American project or stood on the sidelines. Churchill's own stance on collaboration had changed from diffidence to supplication when the United States surged ahead of Great Britain. By late 1944, moreover, Manhattan Project intelligence efforts had determined that the Germans were still "in kindergarten on [the nuclear] question." Although Germany controlled Europe's only uranium mines, its scientists held misguided theoretical assumptions that left Germany years away from developing a weapon at the time the Nazis surrendered. In 1942, Germany's leading physicist, Werner Heisenberg, told the German government that a bomb could not be produced before the end of the war. Thereafter, the project continued, but with very low priority. U.S. intelligence agents learned the extent of the project's failure in late 1944. By FDR's death, the main emphasis of U.S. atomic energy policy toward Germany lay in preventing the Soviet capture of German nuclear physicists and technicians.[13]

The failure of international wartime nuclear projects, including the Soviet and Japanese programs, about which FDR remained ignorant, became magnified in the war's destructive wake. Roosevelt and other U.S. policymakers based their nuclear nationalism on the assumption that a successful nuclear project would surpass the capabilities of the other major combatants for years to come. Such beliefs proved not entirely incorrect. The Soviets would make major sacrifices to test a bomb by 1949, and the British and the French, though ahead of Moscow and Washington before the war, took until 1952 and 1960, respectively, to test their first bombs.

But FDR's confidence in the atomic monopoly did not rest solely on the ravages of combat. Roosevelt may also have believed he could mollify any Soviet anger about being shut out from nuclear data by presenting it as only a hypothetical weapon that would not affect the European war (as it did not). One scholar notes that the atomic bomb could be lumped with British Spitfires, the Norden bombsight, and American and British code breaking as items withheld from the Soviets because, in the judgment of London and Washington, they would not enhance Moscow's success in the current conflict. Groves, moreover, had persuaded FDR and other leaders that the Combined Development Trust could serve to control all the world's uranium deposits, a feat that Groves believed he had achieved by war's end. Showing a xenophobic disdain for Soviet science and technology, he repeatedly claimed that the Russians would take at least twenty years to reach the level of nuclear development that America had achieved in 1945. By the time the Soviets had caught up, the United States would have a huge advantage in any arms race. Under such circumstances, nuclear proliferation might vex future presidents, but it ranked low on FDR's list of priorities.[14]

Despite Roosevelt's discernible preference for Anglo-American exclusivity, he did not bequeath his successor, Truman, a clearly established nuclear policy. Roosevelt never told any subordinates about his pledge of a postwar U.S.-British alliance, nor did he reveal other aspects of his nuclear thinking to them. When Truman entered office, FDR's policies had set the United States on the path toward a postwar arms race. Still, Roosevelt's unwillingness to formally institutionalize his atomic energy policies left open opportunities for Truman to correct, perpetuate, or exacerbate FDR's errors. Truman threw away Roosevelt's telescope, but he replaced it with nationalistic blinders that obscured nuclear realities even more.

"A Sacred Trust"

Truman took office knowing little about the atomic bomb. During their brief time together, Roosevelt had insulated his vice president from foreign policymaking and had never briefed him on the Manhattan Project. Because of Roosevelt's secretive nature, deteriorating health, distrust of an unfamiliar subordinate, and busy schedule in late 1944 and early 1945, the new president began his term in April 1945 heavily dependent on others to guide him in atomic energy matters. The influence of nuclear nationalists, combined with the new president's scientific and technical ignorance, rendered Truman an even more ardent believer in the importance of U.S. atomic monopoly than his predecessor had been.

After a cabinet meeting on April 12, Secretary of War Henry L. Stimson first informed the president about the Manhattan Project, saying that the United States had "a new explosive" under development "of almost unbelievable destructive power." He then let the matter drop for two weeks. In the days that followed, Truman did receive small bits of information about the bomb project from others. James F. Byrnes, Truman's close friend from his years in the Senate, told the president that the atomic bomb could enable the United States to dictate its own terms after the war. Not until April 25 did Stimson, with Groves's help, inform the president of the project's history and of the likelihood that bombs would be ready for combat use by August 1. Both men glossed over the key role that Britain had played in atomic energy development.[15]

Stimson also attempted to apprise Truman of the bomb's political implications. The war secretary, who had gradually adopted the arms control viewpoint of Conant and Bush, argued that the U.S. atomic monopoly would not last indefinitely, but he balanced this warning with the claim that "no other nation" could create an atomic bomb "for some years." Of the nations capable of duplicating the American project, only Russia could begin development "within the next few years." Stimson stressed that it would be "unrealistic" to proceed with the creation of the UN without appreciating the bomb's revolutionary effects on national security calculations. The postwar peace demanded rigorous international controls on nuclear technology, which in turn required "thorough-going rights of inspection and internal controls" greater than any interwar disarmament scheme. If the United States did not impede the spread of atomic weapons, "modern civilization might be completely destroyed."[16]

Despite the president's and war secretary's shared sense of urgency, Roosevelt's strategy of delayed decision blocked consideration of international control. The tumultuous events of spring 1945 drew both Stimson's and Truman's attention to other wartime matters. Had FDR formulated an international control policy earlier, a plan might have been in place prior to this disorderly period of governmental transition and the European war's end. Truman's delay and hesitation in atomic energy policy stemmed partly from his inexperience with international relations. A "parochial nationalist," both suspicious and ignorant of the outside world, Truman preferred handling domestic issues, leaving subordinates to shape foreign policy. Given his status as an "accidental president," Truman also refrained from changing FDR's policies without strong encouragement from more experienced policy-makers. After Stimson let the issue of international control drop, no one else in the administration pressed the president for a change in policy.[17]

Stimson, Bush, and Conant, however, remained concerned about the bomb's postwar role in international politics. On May 2, Stimson asked the president to authorize an "Interim Committee," so-named to avoid offending congressional sensibilities about the legislative branch's shared responsibility for national security policy. The war secretary proposed that he chair the committee, which was also to include Undersecretary of the Navy Ralph Bard, Assistant Secretary of State William L. Clayton, MIT president Karl Compton, Conant (recently returned to his post as Harvard University's president), Stimson's aide George Harrison, and Bush. Others with knowledge of the bomb project, such as Groves and director of the Los Alamos laboratory J. Robert Oppenheimer, would occasionally attend meetings. Truman acquiesced and followed Stimson's advice to name James F. Byrnes as the president's personal representative. Given Byrnes's ardent nuclear nationalism, Truman and Stimson had thus made a fateful decision for the future of U.S. nuclear nonproliferation policy.

Stimson had chosen Byrnes because of his long friendship with Truman and because of Washington rumors that the South Carolinian would soon replace Edward Stettinius as secretary of state. When these rumors proved true, other members of the Interim Committee came to see Byrnes's statements as presidential policy directives, even though Truman had little hand in formulating the secretary of state designate's opinions. Truman had appointed Byrnes to head the State Department because the president had incorrectly perceived the former Senate majority leader and U.S. Supreme Court justice as an expert on foreign policymaking and FDR's postwar plans. Byrnes had cultivated this reputation after attending the Yalta Conference. Yet Roosevelt had mainly invited Byrnes to win conservative southern Democrats' support for the Yalta accords. FDR let Byrnes know only what he believed necessary to fulfill this function. Except for this brief acquaintance with alliance summitry, the secretary of state nominee had little experience with foreign relations. The Truman-Byrnes team combined strong opinions with deep ignorance on nuclear issues.

Byrnes joined the Interim Committee certain that the bomb could be used to shape the peace. He sought to exploit his position on the committee to ensure his control over postwar atomic energy policy. The new secretary of state quickly came under the sway of Groves, who convinced him that the Soviets' lack of raw materials and technology would prevent them from acquiring the bomb. Byrnes staunchly supported the general's view, even after prominent nuclear physicists presented more reliable data on Soviet capabilities. Leo Szilard and two other scientists from the Manhattan Project's Chicago Laboratory traveled to South Carolina to warn that the Soviets could duplicate the American nuclear project within five years. Byrnes scoffed that Russia had no uranium, a gross and costly misjudgment.

The South Carolinian dismissed their advice because he viewed scientists as out of their element in world politics. He relied on Leslie Groves as his chief adviser on nuclear policy. Groves had a proven record as an administrator and had shepherded the Manhattan Project to success. He also offered a far more comforting vision of the postwar world than did the scientists, who claimed that the U.S. atomic monopoly would neither last nor offer much diplomatic advantage. But the general promised that the United States would retain its atomic bomb monopoly into the next generation. Groves's fervent nuclear nationalism even led him to expunge contrary evidence from the record. During the American occupation of Japan, the general ordered some nuclear research facilities and equipment destroyed, to the chagrin of several scientists and Truman administration officials, who lamented this assault on free scientific inquiry. But Groves seemed bent on eliminating any trace of other programs. He had previously ordered many German facilities destroyed to keep them out of the hands of the advancing Soviet forces.

Yet none of these activities diminished Groves's status in the eyes of Byrnes and Truman. Their faith in the general left the scientists with little leverage against an already entrenched nuclear nationalism. Both the president and the secretary of state had limited formal education and often distrusted more educated people who challenged their assumptions. They preferred Groves, a nuclear autodidact, who relied on common sense and instinct unlike the odd, effete, overly educated egg-headed scientists. The president's and Byrnes's faith in the gruff general reflected a larger cultural pattern dating back to the nineteenth century, in which engineers—practical designers and builders— assumed a special place in the national pantheon while theoretical scientists were viewed as dangerously imbalanced dreamers. When J. Robert Oppenheimer came to the White House and expressed guilt over the destruction of Hiroshima and Nagasaki, the president demanded that the physicist be forever barred from his office. Alluding to the stereotype of intellectuals as lacking normal masculine qualities, he dismissed Oppenheimer as a "crybaby" whom he did not "want anything to do with."[18]

Byrnes trusted Groves so completely that he never questioned the latter's predictions. The secretary simply assumed that the United States could control all existing uranium deposits. Had he attempted to confirm the general's claims, he would have discovered that the Soviets already controlled rich uranium deposits in Czechoslovakia. He and Groves also neglected to consider that further deposits likely would be discovered once demand for uranium increased their value. Because comprehensive geological surveys after the war revealed the element to be "common in the earth's crust to the extent of millions of tons," he had made a serious miscalculation.[19]

Byrnes attended the Interim Committee's next meeting oblivious to these flaws in Groves's arguments. A majority of the committee, including Oppenheimer, Stimson, Bush, and Conant, recommended that an inspection and control system be devised and implemented after the war and that the Soviets be informed about the bomb prior to any postwar settlement. Byrnes killed the idea, fearing that the Soviets would demand the same status as the British. The committee dropped the matter and decided to proceed with preparations for wartime use of the bomb while still attempting to preserve relations with Moscow.

Stimson informed Truman that the panel had decided against informing the Soviet Union about the bomb until it "had been successfully laid on Japan." The committee also recommended that after the war an international control commission with broad inspection rights be proposed in order to halt the spread of atomic weapons. Stimson doubted that the Soviets would agree, but if they refused the United States would still have a comfortable lead in a nuclear arms race. Both men thought that in addition to accepting international control, Stalin would have to cooperate in settling "the Polish, Rumanian, Yugoslavian, and Manchurian problems" before the United States would end its policy of atomic secrecy.[20]

Atomic scientists, however, attempted to shake the consensus forming around a continued atomic monopoly. At the Manhattan Project Chicago Laboratory, James Franck, a German-born physicist, formed a committee on the social and political implications of atomic weapons. The panel's report, drafted by Franck, Szilard, Donald L. Hughes, J. J. Nickson, Eugene Rabinowitch, Joyce C. Stearns, and Glenn T. Seaborg, disputed claims that an atomic monopoly could continue indefinitely and presented a sophisticated argument in favor of international control. Demonstrating that knowledge of nuclear physics and its military applications had been widespread before the war, they pointed out that the Soviets already controlled the Czechoslovakian uranium mines and were rumored to be mining radium on their own territory. The report concluded that American nuclear abstinence offered the only opportunity to prevent proliferation. By forgoing the bomb, the United States could propose an international control agreement unsullied by the use of the weapon against any target. If the American military used the bomb, world opinion would condemn the U.S. action and American offers to ban the weapon would be viewed with great suspicion. The scientists also argued that even if U.S. officials viewed international control as infeasible, the bomb still should not be dropped, because its use would reveal the only real secret: that a bomb could be created from uranium. Once foreign nuclear physicists realized that atomic weapons could be made, the nuclear arms race would begin. Refraining from wartime use would allow the United States to expand its lead before other powers even knew atomic weapons existed. Either way, nonuse of atomic weapons would enhance U.S. security.

James Franck sent the report directly to the war secretary, but neither Stimson nor any members of the Interim Committee read the full report. Oppenheimer and the rest of the scientific advisory panel rejected the report's conclusions, arguing that only a direct attack on a military target would end the war and reveal the bomb's power to the world. The Interim Committee decided to postpone any discussion of international control and other postwar problems until after Truman returned from his summit meeting with Churchill and Stalin in Potsdam, Germany.

Still the Franck report had an effect. The Interim Committee now recommended that if the Soviets appeared cooperative on other issues at Potsdam, they should be informed about the bomb project. Truman wondered what to do if Stalin requested details about the bomb. Stimson advised that the president simply respond that the United States was not "yet prepared to give them." Truman seemed to accept the Interim Committee's advice. But when confronted with Byrnes's and Churchill's opposition to disclosure, he hesitated. The British prime minister insisted that Stalin should only be informed of the bomb's existence. He feared that the bomb would provide Britain's only counterweight to the large Red Army after the war, and he dreaded a world in which Moscow possessed nuclear weapons. Byrnes hoped the bomb would advance American diplomatic and strategic advantages in the postwar world. During the Potsdam Conference, the secretary of state told an aide that U.S.-Soviet ideological differences would prevent them from working out "a long-term program of cooperation." All chances for a productive discussion with Stalin about the bomb evaporated when Stimson witnessed firsthand the violent practices of the Soviet occupation forces. A repulsed Stimson told Truman that the United States should move slowly and carefully before working with Moscow on any atomic control agreements. He, however, still placed such great faith in the bomb's diplomatic utility that he "cut a gay caper" after hearing of the successful bomb test in Alamogordo, New Mexico, on July 16.[21]

News of the successful test profoundly transformed Truman's thinking about atomic weapons. He initially feared that the bomb might be "the fire destruction prophesied in the Euphrates Valley Era after Noah and his fabulous Ark." But he finally concluded that the horrific device could be made "most useful." Grateful that "Hitler's crowd or Stalin's did not discover this atomic bomb," he determined that America's monopoly would allow it to define the postwar peace. Truman's confidence in the bomb's power led him to jettison all proposals to conciliate the Soviets to secure their entry into the war in Asia. Assistant Secretary of War John J. McCloy likened Truman and Churchill to "little boys with big red apples secreted on their persons" following the bomb test. Truman still worried that failure to inform Moscow about the weapon might complicate his postwar Soviet policy. Yet, like some of his subordinates, he saw full disclosure as unwise. The president ultimately sought a halfway measure to protect the United States from the Soviets' charges that their government had not been informed of American plans. At the end of the day's proceedings on July 24, Truman diffidently told Stalin that the United States planned to use a new, incredibly powerful weapon against Japan. Stalin said little but later told his foreign minister, Vyacheslav Molotov, that the Soviet Union would now have to speed up its own project. The scientists' fears about freezing out the Soviets had been realized. Yet the president had chosen to ignore their warnings, instead heeding the anti-Soviet counsel of Stimson, Byrnes, and Churchill and delaying any U.S.-Soviet discussion of the bomb until after the war. Nuclear nationalism had prevailed.[22]

While Truman sailed home in early August 1945, the United States dropped atomic bombs on two Japanese cities, Hiroshima and Nagasaki, devastating both sites and killing and injuring hundreds of thousands. Although the president had not yet arrived in Washington, the White House released a triumphal statement in his name. Truman proclaimed America's victory in the "battle of the laboratories" and in winning "the greatest scientific gamble in history." Truman promised immediate domestic controls on atomic energy, but he made no mention of international control and revealed no concern for proliferation.[23]

Public opinion registered strong support for Truman's decision. Polls indicated that 85 percent of respondents approved of the atomic bombings. But many important opinion shapers appeared less sanguine. *Time* magazine claimed that the war now seemed minor and victory in it "most grimly Pyrrhic." Norman Cousins, editor of the *Saturday Review of Literature*, feared that the bomb had made modern society "obsolete." Apprehensions about atomic weapons came from other prominent journalists and publications, including Edward R. Murrow, the *Chicago Tribune*, and the *New Republic*. Catholic and Protestant religious officials voiced disgust and regret in the wake of the American action. Bishop G. Bromley Oxnam, president of the Federal Council of Churches, and John Foster Dulles, chair of the Council's Commission on a Just and Durable Peace, bemoaned the destruction of Hiroshima and Nagasaki and called for a temporary suspension of air attacks on Japan. The pope's apparent condemnation of the Hiroshima bombing especially worried Truman because he feared it might sour U.S. relations with Catholic countries in Western Europe.[24]

Leaders of religious and secular peace groups also expressed outrage at the U.S. action. A. J. Muste and John Nevin Sayre, who headed the Fellowship of Reconciliation, urged all members of the organization to write the president and Congress to express "moral revulsion" at the attacks. The Fellowship of Reconciliation also advocated nonviolent direct action against atomic bomb factories and government offices as well as strikes, fasts, and penitent marches. Muste told Truman that the United States was morally obligated to remove "this terror from the earth." Two leaders of the Women's International League for Peace and Freedom, Emily Balch and Dorothy Detzer, as well as Dorothy Day, founder of the Catholic Worker Movement, also condemned the attack. Detzer drafted a statement saying that "a civilization which has spawned a Buchenwald, a Pearl Harbor and a Hiroshima is morally diseased." Some Manhattan Project scientists echoed the peace groups' statements about the bombings.[25]

Despite such vocal protests, the apparent agreement with the bombings would seem to have placed Truman on solid ground in formulating postwar atomic energy policy. But scholars have noted that most of the U.S. public paid little attention to international issues, with only about 25 percent well informed about world affairs. Yet that slim minority constituted the "real" foreign policy public, and its judgments had to be given greater weight than mass opinion because of its power to shape popular and political discourse. Truman would have to take into account the informed and literate sector when formulating atomic energy policy after the war.[26]

While Truman assessed the public furor at home, America's wartime allies did not sit idly waiting for the United States to dictate the bomb's role in the postwar world. Following Hiroshima, the Soviet government took steps to ensure that the Anglo-American powers did not long retain their atomic advantage. On August 20, Stalin established a special committee to direct the Soviet atomic bomb project and ordered intensified atomic espionage efforts. Britain's new prime minister, Clement Attlee, also worked to prevent the United States from pushing London aside. After hearing Truman's press release refer to the bomb project in almost exclusively American terms, he urged Truman to join him in jointly announcing U.S.-British intentions to serve as "trustees for humanity" in the atomic realm. The president used Attlee's language in his radio address after the bombing of Nagasaki on August 9. He announced that the United States and Britain would exercise custodianship over atomic energy until proper controls could be found. He gave no further details on what type of controls the United States desired. Attlee applauded the speech and released a similar statement.[27]

Truman's vague reference to a control agreement reflected his nebulous understanding of the science behind the atomic bomb. Earlier that day, he had approved the publication of physicist Henry D. Smyth's official report, titled *Atomic Energy for Military Purposes*. This publication allegedly constituted "the most important single set of disclosures in the history of atomic weapons." It began with an abbreviated history of nuclear physics prior to 1940, acknowledging the major contributions of non-American scientists. Much of the report described the Manhattan Project's primary lines of scientific and technological development, such as the essential roles of uranium isotope 235 and plutonium. Smyth emphasized technical problems that had been particularly difficult to solve, such as isotope separation and purity of materials. But neither the president nor the war secretary read the report prior to its publication. Both men trusted in Conant's and Groves's assurances that it did not reveal information that other nations could use to create atomic weapons. Stimson and Groves anticipated that Smyth's account would set official limits on scientific and technical discussion about the bomb, stifling public cries for more information and neutralizing the protests of the scientists at the Chicago Laboratory. Truman privately hoped that the report would squelch the "crazy tales" of "fake scientists." Conant, however, expected that the report's brief history of pre–Manhattan Project nuclear physics would dispel the myth of an American "atomic secret" for the president himself.[28]

The report failed on all counts. A careful and informed reader could glean vital information concerning the development of atomic weapons. Such prominent physicists as Szilard and Einstein continued to contest the government timetable for Soviet acquisition of atomic weapons. And although

Smyth gave sufficient evidence of American dependence on previous foreign work in nuclear physics, Conant's goal remained unfulfilled because Truman—the person he most needed to dissuade of the atomic secret's reality—never read the report.

Truman's approval of the Smyth report underscored the careless and ill-informed nature of his atomic energy policy. Contemporaries noted the organizational chaos of the early Truman presidency. George M. Elsey, Truman's aide, admitted that the White House was "a pretty damn inefficient place in those first few months of the Truman administration. There's no point in kidding anybody and pretending it was otherwise."[29]

Truman's simplistic ideas about history and science further complicated international control efforts. The president espoused a variant of technological utopianism, a naive belief in the power of technology to ensure lasting peace. Truman had swallowed the deep-seated American fantasy that ultimate weapons could be used to create world peace and world government. As early as 1907, popular magazines, such as *McCall's* and *Collier's*, had published war stories that depicted the United States defeating Japan with airplanes and radioactive weapons. From 1908 to 1941, other magazines and books featured tales of American dictators or scientists using radioactive superweapons to coerce the rest of the world to accept complete disarmament. Truman's correspondence reveals that he avidly read these popular stories. He later indulged himself during a troublesome time in his presidency both at home and abroad by composing a mock memorandum in which he took dictatorial power: "Declare an emergency—call out the troops. Start industry and put anyone to work who wants to work. If any leader interferes, court-martial him. [John L.] Lewis ought to have been shot in 1942, but Franklin didn't have the guts to do it. . . . Adjourn Congress and run the country. Get plenty of Atomic Bombs on hand—drop one on Stalin, put the UN to work, and eventually set up a free world." Although Truman was only blowing off steam, his daydreams tellingly mirrored the science fiction tales of benevolent dictators using superweapons to restore domestic order and world peace. His subsequent faith in America's obligation to maintain an exclusive trusteeship over atomic energy contradicted the advice of Stimson and atomic scientists but conformed to these fantasy tales.[30]

The majority of the U.S. public endorsed the president's atomic energy policy, despite its faulty logic, largely because Americans shared his technological utopianism. Polls showed that 73 percent of the American public wanted the United States to retain exclusive rights to the "atomic secret." Prominent intellectuals also supported this policy, suggesting some administration success in winning over the foreign policy public. Noted philosopher and educator John Dewey, along with other leading citizens of New York City, wrote a letter to the *New York Times* arguing for a permanent U.S. trusteeship over atomic energy. A poll of Congress in September 1945 exposed the pervasiveness of this nationalistic stance. Fifty-five of the sixty-one senators and members of Congress who responded opposed sharing nuclear data with any country. World opinion also apparently favored U.S. trusteeship. Only governments still officially at war with the United States condemned the atomic bombings. Most Western European countries displayed little public discontent with the American atomic monopoly. Great Britain did witness a brief flurry of protest against the bombings, but it quickly died down as the country turned its attention to postwar recovery efforts.[31]

Still, opposition to U.S. atomic energy policy among disarmament advocates intensified. The Chicago scientists recruited other discontented Manhattan Project veterans. Various peace organizations advocated the elimination of atomic bombs. Other eminent and respected public figures also backed international control and world government as solutions to the nuclear threat. World government advocates included U.S. Supreme Court justice Owen Roberts; Grenville Clark, a lawyer and important member of the eastern establishment; University of Chicago chancellor Robert M. Hutchins; businessman Owen D. Young; U.S. senators J. William Fulbright and Claude Pepper; and writers Thomas Mann and E. B. White. The celebrity status of these figures as well as their political clout forced the Truman administration to contend with their criticisms and proposals.

A Discussion "Unworthy of the Subject"

While recuperating from a heart attack in upstate New York, Stimson monitored this public debate and concluded that the United States needed to negotiate a great-power nuclear arms control arrangement with Great Britain and the Soviet Union. But Stimson discovered that Byrnes adamantly opposed any international control agreement. The secretary of state instead "wanted the implicit threat of the bomb in his pocket" while he attended the London Council of Foreign Ministers meeting. Stimson failed to dissuade Byrnes from this belligerent negotiating ploy and instead made a direct approach to the president.[32]

But Stimson undercut his own arguments against "atomic diplomacy" when he submitted his letter of resignation on September 5. The war secretary's imminent departure left the nuclear nationalists without any significant countervailing voice. On September 12, Stimson presented his revised plan for postwar controls to the president. The war secretary still believed that the Soviet Union loomed as a threat to U.S. national security until the Russians liberalized their society. But he had come to realize that the bomb could not be used as a "direct lever" to open up Russia, and efforts to prevent nuclear proliferation could not await reform of the Soviet dictatorship. He instead recommended that the United States advance a proposal for coopera-tion with the Soviet Union and Great Britain on harnessing "atomic power for peaceful and humanitarian purposes." If Moscow accepted this offer, the United States should also seek a ban on weapons research, an agreement to dismantle existing atomic weapons, and a pledge not to use atomic weapons unless all signatories to the agreement agreed otherwise. At no time did Stim-son suggest that the United States share military data on atomic energy with Russia. But he did explicitly warn against working through the newly cre-ated UN. He believed Stalin would scorn negotiations with "small nations who have not demonstrated power or responsibility." Other countries could be brought into these arrangements after the three major powers reached concurrence. As he left, Stimson gave Truman a memorandum from Oppen-heimer and other atomic scientists that supported his arguments.[33]

The war secretary departed the White House certain that the president had agreed with "each statement I made." Truman's assent may not have been genuine. He rarely let powerful, respected men know when he disagreed with them — he often appeared to concur with their proposals when meeting them face-to-face but later pursued the opposite policy. He did, however, offer Stimson the chance to present his views to other administration officials at the war secretary's last full cabinet meeting on September 21.[34]

Stimson quickly began recruiting supporters for his plan. He first con-tacted Undersecretary of State Dean Acheson, who appeared to be "strongly on our side in treatment of Russia." He also approached his chosen succes-sor as secretary of war, Robert Patterson, and persuaded him to abandon his objections to a control agreement with the Soviets. But Stimson faced stiff opposition from Secretary of the Navy James V. Forrestal, who in the words of one scholar "regarded the bomb as a form of private property owned col-lectively by the American people, to be licensed out only to private firms for capitalist purposes." The navy secretary believed that the United States should maintain "exclusive control" of the bomb while delegating authority for its use to the UN. All other countries would then agree not to manufacture their own atomic weapons. Forrestal admitted that the plan required other countries to invest great faith in the United States, "but compared to the risks they would run under any other plan a vote of confidence in the United States would be an act of intelligent self-interest." He had earlier warned that "the Russians, like the Japanese, are essentially Oriental in their thinking" and could not be trusted to uphold nuclear agreements. Forrestal had tapped into a variant of American racial thinking that imagined Asians as "subhuman yet cunning, unfeeling yet boiling inwardly with rage, cowardly and decadent yet capable of great conquests." Put simply, the Soviets stood outside the bounds of Western civilization and could not be counted on to act rationally and honorably. In addition to encountering this strong opposition within the cabinet from Byrnes and Forrestal, Stimson's proposals followed upon revelations about a Soviet atomic espionage ring in the Manhattan Project's Canadian facilities. Many wondered how the Soviets could be trusted to abide by an international control agreement if they had spied on their allies during the war.[35]

Upon close examination, Stimson's last cabinet meeting appears to have been a valedictory event rather than a serious policy discussion. Upon his arrival at the White House on September 21, Truman ushered Stimson into a Rose Garden ceremony honoring the colonel's distinguished government career. Stimson entered the Cabinet Room flushed with emotion from the president's words of praise and exhausted from a long day of celebrations and honors. The president had not made any preparations for a serious discussion of the war secretary's proposals, failing to circulate Stimson's memorandum prior to the meeting and allowing Byrnes, who the president knew opposed international control, to remain in London for the Council of Foreign Ministers' meeting. Acheson, the State Department's representative, had been in office barely three weeks and had received only three days' notice to prepare for the meeting. He later summed up the discussion that day as "unworthy of the subject."[36]

Truman invited "the former secretary of war" to commence discussion of international control. Others in attendance included Forrestal, Acheson, Patterson, Vannevar Bush, Secretary of the Treasury Fred Vinson, Secretary of Commerce Henry A. Wallace, Secretary of Agriculture Clinton Anderson, Attorney General Tom Clark, and Senator Kenneth McKellar, president pro tempore of the U.S. Senate. Stimson spoke extemporaneously, and he emphasized the lack of danger in approaching the Soviets, not the urgency of preventing an arms race. Bush's comments followed the same lines. He did, however, add that without international control Moscow could produce an atomic weapon in five years. Neither man presented a detailed argument for international control. Bush later explained that both he and Stimson "pulled their punches" before the large group. Acheson voiced support for Stimson's proposal and argued that a quid pro quo arrangement in atomic energy matters would help preserve U.S. national security. A majority of the others at the meeting also registered approval, including Wallace and Patterson. Forrestal spearheaded the opposition, reiterating his plan for exclusive U.S. trusteeship over the bomb. Other opponents, such as Anderson, Clark, Vinson, and McKellar, crudely and inaccurately defined Stimson's proposal as giving the bomb to the Soviets. The meeting ultimately reached no clear decision, but Truman did solicit memoranda from the participants, saying that after careful consideration of these written arguments, he would announce his decision.[37]

Although twelve of the eighteen people in attendance fully or partially endorsed Stimson's proposal, the entire meeting accomplished little. The opposition to the war secretary's proposal largely came from the president's closest friends in the administration — Clark, Vinson, Byrnes, and Anderson — who had far more influence on Truman during the early days of his presidency than did Bush, Acheson, or Patterson. Also, prior to the meetings, the president had canvassed the Joint Chiefs of Staff and had learned of their unanimous opposition to sharing atomic energy information with the Soviets. The U.S. embassy staff in Moscow and the FBI also warned the president that the Soviets actively sought to end the American atomic monopoly and should not be trusted with any atomic secrets. By September 1945, moreover, Truman had already rejected Bush and Stimson's argument that the Soviet Union could acquire the bomb within five years, later telling Robert Oppenheimer that Moscow could never duplicate the American accomplishment. Because the president believed that the United States could maintain its atomic dominance indefinitely, he saw no reason to risk divulging any atomic data beyond what had been published in the Smyth report.[38]

But the cabinet officers still went through the motions of presenting their arguments to Truman. Acheson composed the most thoughtful and reasoned argument for Stimson's plan. He concluded that if the great powers did not reach agreement on international control, "there will be no organized peace but only an armed truce."[39] Patterson, Wallace, and the other international control advocates also sent their views to the president, with Wallace enclosing supporting memoranda from atomic scientists, including Szilard, Franck, and Einstein.[40] The opponents of international control largely summarized their cabinet meeting presentations. Anderson probably came the closest to Truman's own viewpoint. He argued: "We know that in the production of the atomic bomb there was a certain element of American mathematical and mechanical genius which has given us the automotive industry, the great development of the telephone industry, and countless other inventive processes which are not always developed in every land, and which seem to be peculiarly the result of long years of mechanization of industry within the United States. I quoted to you those lines from Kipling which suggested that they had copied all they could copy, but they couldn't copy our minds."[41] With the president and his closest confidants embracing this imperial conceit, Stimson's plan had little chance.

Forrestal so feared Stimson's proposal that he spread damaging rumors about it. The navy secretary leaked a distorted account of the cabinet meeting to the press, claiming that Wallace, the bête noire of conservatives in both parties, had been the main champion of sharing atomic secrets with the Soviets. Signaling the pervasiveness of nuclear-nationalist thinking in Congress, key senators immediately expressed disapproval of the "Wallace Plan." Senator Thomas Connally, chair of the Senate Foreign Relations Committee, demanded "complete secrecy" in all atomic matters. Other senators endorsed Forrestal's proposal of a UN-recognized American trusteeship for atomic energy.[42]

Truman privately supported Connally's position, but the issue of international control soon became entwined with the larger issue of presidential authority over atomic energy policy. The Senate had established a Special Committee on Atomic Energy in early October, and it appeared to be staking a claim to its preeminence in atomic energy policy. Debate, moreover, had already begun on a War Department plan for military control of atomic energy. Truman had initially favored this bill but came to realize that its provisions would severely limit executive and civilian control over atomic weapons. The president quickly retreated from the army plan and requested help from other officials in framing his atomic energy proposals.

On October 3, in a speech to Congress, Truman officially announced his atomic energy policy in a hastily composed speech that rescinded his earlier, uninformed support of military dominance in atomic energy matters. The president appended a brief statement about international control, telling Congress that he would soon initiate discussions with Great Britain and Canada. With their cooperation, he would then engage other nations "in an effort to effect agreement on the conditions under which cooperation might replace rivalry in the field of atomic power."[43] Truman had apparently voiced support for international control. But State Department officials had drafted the passages on U.S.-British-Canadian consultations on short notice and with little input from the White House. One of Truman's aides had merely combined the State Department draft with a War Department draft with no eye to framing a consistent policy. Such sloppiness would continue to characterize Truman's words and deeds on atomic energy as he prepared for his meeting with the British and the Canadians.

"A Chapter in *Alice in Wonderland*"

Truman's message to Congress did not rule out a great-power nuclear arrangement along the lines Stimson envisioned. But the president revealed his inchoate thinking on international control during an informal news conference on October 7. While on a fishing trip in Tennessee, the president revealed to reporters that he had embraced the policy of indefinite monopoly that Groves, Forrestal, and Byrnes had advocated. He quickly distinguished scientific theories of nuclear physics that already had become "virtually worldwide knowledge" from engineering "know-how" and the "industrial capacity and resources needed to produce the bomb." The latter, Truman argued, guaranteed long-term American dominance in atomic weaponry. Echoing Clinton Anderson's earlier memo, Truman claimed that the U.S. monopoly rested on the same grounds that enabled Americans to mass-produce automobiles and construct the "greatest long-distance bomber in the world." The president made clear that he would not share atomic "know-how" with anyone, not even the British. The president's comments suggested that only general scientific knowledge would be discussed in forthcoming talks with Great Britain, Canada, and "other countries."[44]

A few days later, Truman revealed even more starkly the depths of his nuclear nationalism. Longtime friend Fyke Farmer, a Missouri attorney, asked the president if his statements in Tennessee meant that a nuclear arms race had begun. Truman conceded that they did, but he avowed a lasting U.S. advantage in this competition. "Maybe we could get world government in a thousand years or something like that," he said, "but it was nothing more than a theory at the present time." The president next told the press that Secretary of State Byrnes would oversee U.S. international control policy upon his return from London. The secretary of state still opposed international control, but his faith in atomic diplomacy had diminished after his unsuccessful attempts to use the bomb as an implicit threat at the London foreign ministers' meeting.[45]

Upon returning to the United States, Byrnes conferred with both Forrestal and Patterson. He warned that no good could come of Truman's proposal to discuss international control. No one on the American side had thoroughly studied the issue, and now danger loomed that Molotov would seek equal status with the British in the Manhattan Project. The issue should have remained dormant until the United States had explored whether a "decent peace" could be concluded. Forrestal chided that the president's statement might bring "increased pressure" from U.S. international control advocates to conclude an agreement quickly and "turn the bomb over to a piece of paper."[46]

The secretary of state continued to stew about Truman's international control offer through early November. He believed international control plans were "childish" in the face of Soviet refusals to let westerners travel in Eastern Europe. If the Soviets banned travel to Romania and Bulgaria, he argued, they surely would oppose the inspection provisions necessary to reach a viable control agreement. In the view of Patterson, Byrnes, and Forrestal, the entire control debate emanated from the ravings of emotionally unstable scientists who knew nothing about international politics.[47]

The secretary of state also objected to consultations with the British and the Canadians. He refused to prepare for the conference with Attlee and Prime Minister Mackenzie King of Canada, scheduled for November 11. Vannevar Bush, with help from Patterson and Groves, ultimately stepped into the vacuum Byrnes created. Bush's final product consisted of both a control plan and a restricted cooperation agreement to replace the wartime partnership. Control of atomic technology should begin with the control of technical and scientific knowledge itself and then expand to consideration of the mechanisms needed to prevent cheating. Any plan should be implemented in stages to ensure that the United States not destroy its atomic weapons before the Soviets proved they could be trusted. The UN should also create a mechanism for international control negotiations. Bush's last-minute efforts to formulate an American proposal left him exasperated. He lamented to Henry Stimson that he had "never participated in anything that was so completely unorganized or so irregular. I have had experiences in the past week that would make a chapter in *Alice In Wonderland*."[48]

Byrnes and Truman delayed accepting Bush's proposal until the opening day of the conference in Washington. Neither the secretary of state nor the president had planned for consultations with the British and Canadians so soon after the initial U.S. offer. But the failure of the London Conference to produce any agreements, combined with public fears about atomic weapons, pressured the Truman administration into making symbolic gestures toward controlling the bomb. A meeting with America's wartime atomic partners served this purpose better than a conference that would include the Soviets, who might demand a share of the atomic data given the British before participating in control negotiations. Forrestal, Bush, and Groves further hoped that these talks would lead to the termination of the postwar Anglo-American nuclear alliance they had long opposed.

When the conference began, the British and Canadian prime ministers accepted Bush's arguments about information sharing and inspection and control. Truman affirmed that the bomb would remain in national hands until "we [are] absolutely sure that the confidence of each nation in the good faith of the other is well founded." Great Britain voiced no objection to a U.S. monopoly as long as the level of Anglo-American cooperation remained high.[49]

The conference's general atmosphere of goodwill began to evaporate when the British raised the subject of Anglo-American collaboration. The British delegation feared that the Truman administration aimed to exclude all other nations, even America's wartime atomic partners, from receiving technical information. But the U.S. negotiators, Bush and Groves, finessed the collaboration issue. They proposed that the Combined Policy Committee and the Combined Development Trust remain in place. If the trust dissolved, prolonged negotiations on how to allocate raw materials could ensue. The new agreement ensured that the United States would continue to receive all the trust's uranium ore. Truman and Byrnes believed the Anglophobic Groves to be an expert on the wartime partnership and allowed him to work out the precise details of the new collaboration agreement. Despite a U.S. pledge of "full and effective cooperation," Groves negotiated a very limited collaboration agreement, promising only to exchange scientific information and share raw materials.[50]

When the three leaders gathered in the Oval Office on November 15 for the reading of the conference's final proclamation, Attlee and King still believed that the wartime agreement remained in effect with only minor modifications. The final text of the Washington Declaration, moreover, made no mention of further discussion with the Soviet Union. Instead, the Anglo-American powers proposed the establishment of a UN commission to study the problem of international control and endorsed Bush's recommendation that any plan should move in discrete stages toward a complete ban on atomic weapons. Truman made no mention of the exact stage at which the United States would halt production of atomic weapons or destroy its existing stockpile. The Soviet ambassador to the United States told his superiors that while the Anglo-Americans still wished to use the bomb to their diplomatic advantage, they also hoped to use the Washington Declaration to dispel accusations that they had aggressively exploited their atomic monopoly.[51]

The declaration calmed few critics of the Truman administration atomic energy policy. Several British and U.S. newspapers criticized the conference for excluding the Soviets from atomic energy discussions and embittering Anglo-American relations with Moscow. Proponents of a continued American monopoly also objected to the statement. Two key members of the Senate Foreign Relations Committee, Arthur Vandenberg and Tom Connally, walked out in protest immediately after Truman finished reading the Washington Declaration. The lack of congressional consultations prior to the signing of new agreements with the British and Canadians and Truman's announcement of American international control policy had left both men offended and irate. Vandenberg demanded that the American monopoly be preserved until all other countries agreed to an international control system that guaranteed the "absolute free and untrammeled right of intimate inspection all around the globe." Others in Congress shared similar nuclear nationalist sentiments. Senator Edwin C. Johnson, a Democrat and erstwhile isolationist on the Special Committee on Atomic Energy, heralded an American opportunity to "compel mankind to adopt the policy of lasting peace." Should the rest of the world resist this effort, it risked being "burned to a crisp."[52] The Washington Conference thus accomplished little, and U.S. atomic energy policy remained unsettled.

Substituting the Carrot for the Stick

Shortly after the Washington Conference, Byrnes changed his attitude toward international control. His inability to use the bomb as an implied threat at the London Conference had persuaded him to abandon that tactic. He now hoped that an offer of an international control agreement and the prospect of collaboration on peaceful uses of atomic technology might elicit Soviet concessions on such outstanding postwar issues as the Far Eastern settlement.

Byrnes cabled Molotov and proposed a conference of foreign ministers' meeting for December. The British Foreign Office expressed dismay at the hasty decision. London agreed that Moscow should be informed of Anglo-American international control policy prior to the UN General Assembly meeting in January. But the British believed that the U.S. and British ambassadors in Moscow could handle such talks. Ernest Bevin, the British foreign secretary, told Byrnes that a December conference could not be adequately prepared and that it was foolish to discuss international control in Moscow when the British, Canadians, and Americans had not even agreed on the specifics. Byrnes swept these objections aside. He perceived the three atomic partners as largely in accord in their atomic energy outlook and thought they could reach an arms control agreement within a few days. It would be more damaging not to discuss the control proposal with the Soviets and to risk their scuttling attempts to establish a UN commission in a fit of pique. The British acquiesced only after Byrnes threatened to visit Moscow alone.[53]

The increasing lack of communication between Truman and his secretary of state on atomic energy issues produced the most daunting obstacle for Byrnes's strategy. In almost a replay of the events leading up to the Washington Conference, Byrnes forged ahead with his international control plans while other issues, such as economic reconversion, commanded the president's attention. In late November, the secretary of state established an informal interdepartmental committee to formulate an international control plan. The panel followed the general outlines of Bush's proposal but superficially seemed more open to Soviet participation in framing UN international control policy. Like all previous government proposals, it sought to maintain the U.S. monopoly until the viability of control had been established. But two features of the proposal incensed other administration officials and members of Congress. First, controls and safeguards appeared last in the list of stages toward a complete ban on military applications of atomic energy. Many opponents excitedly claimed that safeguards and controls had to be in place before the United States should agree to proceed on other aspects of international control. The second offending passage pledged "affirmative action" wherever progress could be made. Critics feared that this clause indicated that Byrnes's desire for an agreement might produce a compromise that threatened U.S. security. Byrnes did give Truman a copy of this proposal, but the president most likely never read it or never fully comprehended its implications.[54]

Several advocates of a continued atomic monopoly did, however. Both Forrestal and Groves immediately protested what they judged to be a dangerously generous plan. The secretary of state did not acknowledge these critics, but he did finally attempt to mend the rift with Senators Connally and Vandenberg. Consulting with them just prior to departing for Moscow, Byrnes outlined his atomic energy plans without offering any specifics. Connally angrily objected to any international control proposal that would end the U.S. atomic monopoly, while Vandenberg labeled the plan "sheer appeasement."[55]

After the secretary of state departed, Vandenberg, Connally, and the members of the Special Committee on Atomic Energy took their grievances to the president. They expressed fear that Byrnes planned to compromise on the inspection issue, especially since he had taken James Conant with him to help establish scientific exchanges with the Soviets. Vandenberg argued that if Byrnes agreed to scientific interchange prior to the creation of safeguards, he would "prematurely give away . . . at least half of all our 'trading stock.'" Truman replied that the secretary of state had no intention of agreeing to atomic cooperation before verification measures had been negotiated. He displayed the "policy directive" under which Byrnes operated. Vandenberg and Connally expressed astonishment when the document duplicated the provisions of the State Department paper to which they had already objected. They explained their worries about the order of stages to the president. Although Truman still doubted their interpretation, he promised Connally that he would contact Byrnes and urge him to revise his proposal.[56]

Acting Secretary of State Dean Acheson cabled the secretary of state in Moscow and informed him that the president wanted all international control proposals sent to Washington for approval before the conference concluded any agreements. Truman also wanted it made clear that the United States would not disclose any information about the bomb until all parties had approved inspection and safeguard provisions. The secretary of state claimed that he did not plan to go beyond the Washington Declaration, which simply called for UN discussions of the matter. When Byrnes later submitted a revised atomic energy proposal to Truman, he made substantial concessions to Vandenberg and Connally. He now sought only to get joint U.S.-Soviet sponsorship of a UN atomic energy commission, and he abandoned hopes of any scientific cooperation prior to an international control accord.[57]

Conant, along with Byrnes's aides and the embassy staff, drafted the new proposal. In his diary, the scientist recorded that most Americans in Moscow agreed that "the Russians cannot accept inspection and the scheme will bog down somewhere as a consequence." But the secretary of state's concessions to his American critics now stirred up trouble with the British delegation. Pleased with the draft Byrnes had initially shown to Connally and Vandenberg, Bevin hoped it demonstrated that "Mr. Byrnes has now realised that the Russians will simply not agree to have the Urals and Siberia roamed over by international surveyors of raw materials" without receiving comprehensive atomic energy data first. When the secretary of state gave the British an information-only copy of the revised proposal, Bevin fumed at what he saw as a unilateral American decision. Some in the British delegation thought the paper an outright rejection of the Washington Declaration and a threat to Britain's status as a nuclear power. George F. Kennan, the U.S. chargé d'affaires in Moscow, privately criticized Byrnes's "direct bad faith" toward the British in his handling of the matter. The secretary saw his atomic energy strategy about to unravel. At Bevin's request, the British and American delegations began private negotiations to reconcile their atomic energy plans.[58]

While the two atomic allies debated international control, the conference itself concentrated on other issues. Byrnes and Bevin did not discuss atomic energy with Molotov until December 22, when the Soviets introduced their own plan. Although both Bevin and Byrnes expressed appreciation of Moscow's willingness to cooperate on establishing UN machinery, the U.S. delegates objected to Soviet plans to place the UN Atomic Energy Commission (UNAEC) under the authority of the Security Council. They feared that the five permanent members' veto power would weaken any international control agreement. Stalin claimed that the Soviets had "accepted nine-tenths of the American proposal" and only asked for this one concession. Byrnes reflected overnight and conceded on the Security Council issue. In return, the Soviets dropped their objection to the U.S. demand that a control agreement be implemented in stages.[59]

The Soviets' agreeing to establish the UNAEC likely rested on pragmatic grounds. Stalin believed that the UN talks sought "pseudo-international mechanisms" to guard the U.S. monopoly and impede the Soviet atomic program. But if the Soviet Union prevented the creation of the UNAEC, the Anglo-American bloc would have gained a clear propaganda victory. The Soviets lost little by agreeing to sponsor the UNAEC, while they gained the chance to use the commission, as they saw it, to expose the cynical aims of the American proposals. A month after the Moscow Conference, Stalin revealed his limited faith in the UNAEC when he ordered Soviet atomic energy research expanded so it would operate "on a Russian scale."[60]

The Americans and the British also demonstrated little confidence in the Moscow agreement. On the same day the foreign ministers agreed to sponsor the UNAEC, the U.S. embassy predicted that the Soviets would soon begin an all-out effort to develop the bomb. As the conference ended, a British diplomat remarked to the American delegation that although inspection had no chance of being accepted "we must act 'as if' [it did]." Conant came away with the impression that Byrnes had embraced international control as a public relations ploy and had little desire to achieve a final agreement with the Soviets.[61]

Whatever Byrnes's actual motives, his conduct at the Moscow Conference had damaged his political standing at home. He had offended key members of the Senate and the Special Committee on Atomic Energy before leaving for the conference. By the time he returned, the secretary had also succeeded in alienating the president. Truman complained that Byrnes had ignored his instructions to clear all atomic energy proposals with him before reaching agreement. The final conference communiqué especially irritated the president. Byrnes seemingly deviated from Truman's insistence that safeguards be in place before scientific interchange began. In the passage on stages, once again scientific interchange appeared first and safeguards last. This apparent insubordination had already aroused the president's temper, but he exploded when he heard the conference's agreements on the radio before he heard them from Byrnes. When the secretary returned to Washington, he discovered that an irreparable breach had opened between him and the president. Truman complained that Byrnes had made too many concessions in Moscow, including on atomic energy. The president had to take the embarrassing step of clarifying his secretary of state's conference communiqué, explaining to the American people that the passage on international control should be taken as a whole and not be seen as listing the stages in the order they would be implemented. Byrnes remained secretary of state for another year, but hereafter his control over atomic energy policy greatly diminished.[62]

Byrnes's downfall stands out as just one incident among many that solidified American nuclear nationalism, the faith that James Franck had so strongly ridiculed in 1945. Despite overwhelming evidence that other countries would eventually be able to produce nuclear weapons, both Roosevelt and Truman clung to the fantasy that America's atomic monopoly could persist for decades. Perhaps the difficulties of the British and German programs, which had provided the impetus for the Manhattan Project, convinced U.S. leaders that they would have time after the war to ponder the dilemma of nuclear proliferation. This confident attitude, combined with their conviction that the bomb offered insurance against Soviet aggressiveness, stifled attempts by Stimson, Bohr, and others to halt nuclear proliferation before it gained momentum. When Truman entered office, the policies that Roosevelt had put in place had set the United States on the path toward a postwar arms race. FDR's failure to forge institutional roots for his atomic energy policies gave Truman the opportunity to reverse his predecessor's errors, had he been better equipped to navigate the rabbit hole of wartime nuclear planning. Truman instead emulated Lewis Carroll's Red Queen in believing three impossible things before breakfast. First, he embraced Leslie Groves's promises of a perpetual monopoly. He then let his mind drift back to the science fiction tales of his youth that depicted benevolent American leaders using superweapons to force the world to abandon war. Last, he swallowed Groves's claims of cornering the world uranium market. Although Stimson, Bush, and Oppenheimer had all argued that many countries knew the scientific principles behind the bomb and could soon produce nuclear weapons if they wished, the threat of nuclear proliferation simply did not exist for Truman. Public fears about the bomb did force him to make gestures toward international control. The president, however, kept his promises of international cooperation limited to scientific interchange, always excluding from discussion other elements of American "atomic know-how." By late 1945, Truman's secretary of state had formulated a new strategy, using the promise of international control to expose Soviet intransigence to the world. But this ploy proved too nuanced for the president, who accused Byrnes of "babying" the Soviets.[63] Truman preferred straightforward assertions of nuclear nationalism to the intricacies of diplomatic intrigue. During 1946, these two visions of nonproliferation would compete to establish policy for the rest of Truman's presidency.

Winning Weapons

A-BOMBS, H-BOMBS, & INTERNATIONAL

CONTROL, 1946–1953

In 1946, Harry Truman swore that the United States would not "throw away our gun until we are sure the rest of the world can't arm against us." By late 1945, many government officials had embraced Truman's belief that weapons rather than treaties ensured U.S. security. They made no pretense of sharing American know-how with the rest of the world. Others, including Secretary of State Byrnes, also wished to preserve the atomic monopoly but feared that the growing chorus of voices urging international control of atomic energy might work to Soviet advantage. With most national security managers fearing communist ideas more than Soviet arms, Washington needed to appear more reasonable and peace loving than Moscow. By going through the motions in the UN, Byrnes and like-minded officials hoped to convince the American and Western European publics that an effective nuclear nonproliferation agreement could not be negotiated with the Soviets. They worked to make the American proposal appear generous and conciliatory while including conditions unacceptable to Moscow. U.S. efforts did succeed in mollifying public opinion, but the president never shared Byrnes's point of view. He would rather that the United States act as the lone sheriff with nuclear six-guns at the ready than as one of FDR's four international policemen. If Washington had allies, they would be subordinates, not equals, and he felt no need to join any charade of nuclear multilateralism. Truman's treatment of the Anglo-American nuclear alliance from 1945 to 1953 made this quite clear. He ultimately decided that "since we can't obtain international control we must be strongest in atomic weapons." Truman then worked to solidify U.S. nuclear superiority with little concern for nonproliferation.[1]

Crafting the Ruse

After returning from the Moscow Conference, Byrnes had little time to set his international control policy in motion. He knew that neither Truman nor such important congressional leaders as Connally and Vandenberg supported his variant of atomic diplomacy. To deflect congressional opposition, in early 1946 Byrnes created a committee on atomic energy to formulate an international control proposal for the UNAEC meetings that summer. His undersecretary, Dean Acheson, chaired the panel, which also included Vannevar Bush, James Conant, Leslie Groves, and former War Department aide John Mc-Cloy. Acheson seemed an odd choice as the point man for Byrnes's strategy. In his last experience with atomic energy policy, he had supported Henry Stimson's 1945 proposal to negotiate bilaterally with the Soviets, and he disdained the UN as too idealistic and unwieldy to serve U.S. national interests. But what Acheson and Byrnes shared was the notion that the Soviets might be made more pliable through positive inducements than through threats.

Acheson hoped that the State Department committee could pull together what he saw as an inchoate U.S. atomic energy policy. Technical knowledge would be key because the success of Byrnes's strategy hinged on the plan at least appearing to be reasonable and practical. Although Acheson respected the committee's members, he feared that only Bush had the expertise to formulate a strong international control proposal. At the committee's first meeting, he proposed creating an advisory board to study several possible plans, ignoring Groves, who protested that he, Conant, and Bush knew more about atomic weapons than any outside consultants.

Acheson selected David E. Lilienthal, head of the Tennessee Valley Authority, to chair the panel because of his experience in government and his familiarity with technical issues. The undersecretary confessed to Lilienthal that the government desperately needed a thorough study of international control to assess how best to deal with Truman's and Byrnes's public and private commitments, which he said had been issued without "the facts nor an understanding of what was involved in the atomic energy issue."[2]

To what degree Lilienthal might have been "in" on the Acheson/Byrnes strategy as he met with the rest of the board is unclear. In any case, the panel, which included Robert Oppenheimer and several industrialists who had worked with the government during the war—Chester Barnard, Harry A. Winne, and Charles Thomas—loomed large in the subsequent debate, for it went beyond its advisory role and contributed most of the ideas that appeared in the committee's final proposal. Oppenheimer became the primary scientific expert for both the Lilienthal board and the Acheson committee. The scientist crafted an arms control scheme that limited the military applications of nuclear technology while promoting such "harmless" applications as radiation treatments and electric power production. Oppenheimer proposed that the UN create an international atomic development authority to control all fissionable raw materials. This agency would conduct research on peaceful applications and disperse uranium and plutonium to individual nations or companies for use in nuclear power plants. He later amended this proposal to allow the body to conduct research on atomic explosives in order to acquire the data needed to inhibit surreptitious weapons production.[3]

Oppenheimer's plan reflected his adherence to the tenets of both technological utopianism and scientific internationalism. He believed that technical means could be devised to track fissionable materials while allowing collaboration on nuclear science's peaceful applications. The United States needed to share its nuclear know-how, he contended, because other nations would resist an agreement that protected the U.S. lead in nuclear technologies while inhibiting progress elsewhere. A plan that stressed inspection and penalties, moreover, would meet hostility in the United States because many provisions would initially apply solely to American facilities. The close links between the research and technology needed to create atomic weapons and reactors necessitated a large force of inspectors to ensure that no military projects took place. Such a nuclear posse would prove intrusive and expensive to maintain. Oppenheimer claimed that his plan would be cheaper and easier to implement because it largely eliminated the need for inspections and appealed to other nations' self-interest by accelerating their acquisition of nuclear technologies. He admitted that his proposal required changes in conventional notions of national sovereignty and international cooperation, but he believed that armies of inspectors would infringe more on national sovereignty than would a development agency.[4]

While Acheson labeled the Lilienthal board's report "a brilliant and profound document," the rest of the State Department group expressed deep reservations. Groves claimed that a raw materials monopoly could be circumvented through the exploitation of low-grade uranium deposits. This critique contradicted his previous claims that the United States could maintain a twenty-year reign as the lone atomic power via control of known uranium deposits. Bush and Conant warned that the plan understated the need for inspection and safeguards. Bush also feared that if the United States gave up its atomic weapons too quickly, the Soviet army would be left in a commanding military position. He repeated his argument of November 1945 that international control should be implemented in stages to test the Soviet Union's and other countries' trustworthiness. Transition stages would also give the U.S. military time to compensate for the loss of atomic weapons. An explicit schedule of stages, moreover, had to be included in the U.S. proposal if the government hoped for support both from the American public and from other nations, who would demand a clear explanation of how and when the agreement would take effect. The Acheson committee thereupon directed the Lilienthal board to revise its proposal to include inspection provisions, an explicit schedule of stages, and clear barriers against cheating.[5]

Caught in the Cold War

The Acheson committee's insistence on strict safeguards and gradual implementation of international control reflected a growing anticommunist outlook within the Truman administration. In late January and February, Stalin and other officials had delivered speeches that appeared openly hostile toward the West. Many U.S. officials feared that this rhetoric signaled imminent Soviet remilitarization and an aggressive foreign policy. George Kennan, the chargé d'affaires at the Moscow embassy, assessed Soviet intentions in a "Long Telegram," which became a guiding document in the emerging superpower rivalry. According to Kennan, permanent peace was impossible with the Soviets, who sought to disrupt Western society and "destroy its traditional way of life." Kennan's pessimism received a sympathetic hearing in Washington, where Secretary of State Byrnes labeled it a "splendid analysis," and Secretary of the Navy Forrestal and the former ambassador to the Soviet Union, W. Averell Harriman, eagerly circulated the document throughout the government. One Truman administration official leaked the telegram to the press in an effort to shape public opinion.[6]

On March 5, former British prime minister Winston Churchill added his voice to the critics of Soviet conduct. In a speech at Fulton, Missouri, with Truman nodding approvingly nearby, Churchill warned that the Russians had constructed an "iron curtain" that cut off Eastern Europe from the outside world and that the Soviets would attempt to expand unless confronted with the West's firm resolve. Although the president later claimed that he had been unaware of the contents of the speech beforehand, in fact he had gone over the speech and endorsed it prior to Churchill's delivery. Soviet provocations further widened the breach with the West. In early March, the Red Army missed a treaty deadline to withdraw from northern Iran. Washington charged Moscow with attempting to create a satellite regime and ordered a UN investigation. The Soviet UN representative walked out of the Security Council in protest. The Iran question created a crisis atmosphere in Washington that lasted into April. At one point, Truman told Harriman that war might be near.

In February and March, the public revelation of the Canadian atomic espionage ring, first discovered in September 1945, gave anti-Soviet critics further ammunition. On February 3, 1946, journalist Drew Pearson announced that a secret government source had told him of the Canadian atomic espionage case. He offered few details, but his report forced Canadian authorities to make arrests before they had concluded their investigation. The source of Pearson's story remains a mystery. But it may have been the same official who provided even more incendiary information to Washington columnist Frank McNaughton: General Leslie Groves. The general told McNaughton that the FBI had discovered another spy ring operating in the United States but had not been able to make any arrests because "state department men" claimed "that to do so would upset our relations with Russia." Groves had leaked this distorted account of Soviet espionage activities in an effort to force a stricter domestic atomic energy law through the Senate. His strategy inflamed a panic about atomic secrecy and fueled the general anti-Soviet climate of opinion.

Acheson shared the growing suspicion of the Soviets. The Iran crisis and Soviet tactics in the Council of Foreign Ministers had convinced him that the Soviet Union would resist the emergence of the United States as the dominant world power. During 1946 and 1947, he gradually developed an approach to U.S.-Soviet relations that he later termed "negotiating from strength." Acheson believed that if the United States took some pronounced risks, even pushing the Soviets to the brink of war, Stalin would "agree to terms consistent with our objectives." A quid pro quo approach had clearly failed and would only fritter away American strength. He rejected discussions that were "mere talk apart from action" because "action is often the best form of negotiations. It affects the environment," which is "likely to determine the outcome" of diplomacy itself. In early 1946, Acheson had just begun formulating this philosophy. But he did give hints of his new outlook. At a party shortly after Churchill's iron curtain speech, he expressed agreement with the former prime minister's assessment of the Soviets. According to Secretary of Commerce Henry Wallace, Acheson said that the United States and Britain should be willing to risk "immediate war with Russia" in order to prevent the Soviets from expanding their influence.[7]

On March 17, amid rising U.S.-Soviet tensions, the Lilienthal board's revised report received a hostile reception from Acheson's committee. Both Bush and Groves rejected its contention that a detailed schedule should not be developed prior to the UN negotiations. Groves insisted that the American negotiator needed a clear plan accounting for what to do "if Russia suddenly dropped out." Conant wanted an explicit U.S. commitment to manufacture bombs until international control reached its final stages. Their demands illustrated how distrust rather than cooperation had become the main theme of the superpower relationship. During the afternoon session, the two groups went over the plan, paragraph by paragraph, but could not reach consensus. The Acheson committee convened a private conference that evening to review the day's proceedings.[8]

The Oppenheimer plan for international ownership and development appeared dead. Acheson's assistant Herbert Marks left the meeting and told Lilienthal that "things looked very bad indeed." The next day, the undersecretary of state informed the board of consultants that his committee still feared that premature disclosure of atomic data might harm U.S. security. An ensuing tense discussion threatened a serious rift between the two panels. But, during a strategic coffee break, small groups of disputants worked out a compromise. When the formal meeting reconvened, Acheson asked whether his committee wished to transmit the report to Byrnes with a letter of approval or send it along with no recommendation. Bush immediately called for a strong letter of endorsement that would include the State Department committee's reservations. Lilienthal termed this sudden reversal "nothing less than a miracle."[9]

Earthly reasons better explain the committee's shift. The specific thinking of the Acheson panel may never be known because no records exist of its private meeting. Still, writings and recollections of participants suggest that many on both the Acheson and the Lilienthal committees seriously doubted that the Soviets would accept international control, especially if it included inspection. When someone suggested as much during the Lilienthal group's deliberations, Herbert Marks blurted out: "Then we'll just destroy them."

Marks's comment reflected a growing consensus that the coercive power of the U.S. monopoly was more important than the particulars of its international control proposal.[10]

Others on the Acheson committee had additional reasons to back the Lilienthal report. Conant, for one, had scaled back his claims for the urgency of international control. His brief contact with Soviet scientists in December 1945 persuaded him that Moscow would need at least fifteen, and perhaps even twenty, years to produce atomic weapons. The Soviets therefore would covet international control as a means to accelerate its acquisition of nuclear technology. The United States, moreover, could reduce the threat from a possible clandestine weapons program in the Soviet Union by continuing to produce bombs until the agreement reached its final stages. Groves's willingness to sign the letter flowed from more pragmatic motives. The general adopted the strategy of the Joint Chiefs of Staff: that is, officially accept the fact that the president had committed the United States to UN negotiations but emphasize the need for stringent safeguards and the inability of inspections to catch cheaters.[11]

Acheson, however, played the key role in winning endorsement of the Lilienthal report. The undersecretary had concluded that the Soviets would not voluntarily accept U.S. demands. The UN international discussions, therefore, offered little prospect of an agreement. But Acheson believed that "occasionally, one had to go through the motions in order to win over popular opinion at home and abroad." The Oppenheimer plan served this purpose well. On the surface, it appeared to be a generous offer to share U.S. atomic technology with the rest of the world. But the inspection provisions would surely prove unacceptable to the Soviets. The resulting breakdown of negotiations in the UNAEC would confirm that the Soviets refused to cooperate with the West and that the United States was justified in maintaining its atomic supremacy. The Oppenheimer scheme's emphasis on atomic development promised to win over world opinion, while the inspection and safeguard provisions helped ensure that U.S. nuclear dominance would endure for fifteen to twenty years. Although Acheson never thought that the plan would be accepted, he believed the United States had to act as if it could. Near the end of his life, Acheson praised both Truman and Abraham Lincoln because they "did things contrary to the baloney that [they] talked." In the undersecretary's view, Wilsonian internationalist rhetoric about disarmament served a public function, but it should never actually underpin American national security policy.[12]

Baruch at the Helm

For Acheson's strategy to succeed, Truman and Byrnes would have to have selected a chief negotiator with enough subtlety to appreciate the unspoken assumptions of the Acheson-Lilienthal report. But the secretary of state and the president evinced more concern for domestic politics than for international opinion. In late February, Byrnes asked Wall Street financier Bernard M. Baruch, his close friend and fellow South Carolinian, to be the U.S. delegate to the UNAEC. Already seventy-six years old and nearly deaf, Baruch had health problems that restricted his ability to attend meetings. As a self-styled adviser to presidents, he had built his reputation working on economic issues, especially inflation, and he lacked diplomatic experience. Baruch nonetheless enjoyed inflated public status as a wise man and had many friends among conservative Democrats and Republicans in Congress (largely earned through generous campaign contributions). By appointing him, Byrnes hoped to defuse congressional hostility toward Truman's atomic energy policy, simmering since the Moscow Conference.[13]

Baruch hesitated to accept. When asked to assess the vice presidential hopefuls at the 1944 Democratic convention, Baruch had called Truman "nine pounds lighter than a toy balloon." The president, in turn, thought Baruch "a conniver." Yet Truman needed Baruch's prestige to build domestic support for the UN negotiations. And the aging financier believed the appointment offered his only chance to put his mark on the postwar settlement. Baruch's quest for fame ultimately trumped his doubts about working for Truman, but he harbored grave doubts about the negotiations. He observed: "If Russia will not permit entree of news men or others, can we believe they will permit any inspection?"[14]

When Truman and Byrnes announced Baruch's nomination on March 18, the media and public generally praised the president's choice. The entire Senate Special Committee on Atomic Energy applauded the nomination, while Senator Arthur Vandenberg, the leading Republican on the Foreign Relations Committee, declared that if Baruch assured him that no atomic data would be disclosed to the UNAEC prior to implementation of safeguards, no hearings on the nomination would be necessary. Most members of the Acheson-Lilienthal group, however, did not share the public's enthusiasm. When Lilienthal heard the news, he felt "quite sick," fearing that the Soviets would read Baruch's appointment as a sign that the United States did not actually desire international cooperation. Bush lambasted Baruch as "the worst qualified man in the country for this job." The chief British delegate to the UNAEC, Alexander Cadogan, concurred, labeling Baruch "dreadful" and "impossible to work with."[15]

Unaware of the Acheson-Lilienthal group's hostility, Baruch set about compiling a staff. He surrounded himself with like-minded conservative aides: Herbert Bayard Swope, a publicist and journalist; John M. Hancock, partner in the Lehman Brothers investment firm; Ferdinand Eberstadt, an investment banker who was close to the anti-Soviet Forrestal; and Fred Searls, a mining engineer. All four men had worked with Baruch so frequently in the past that Lilienthal called them "the old crowd." None had diplomatic experience or nuclear expertise.[16]

No one informed Baruch about the State Department committee's recommendations when he accepted the post. Upon discovering that the document advocated international ownership and development, Baruch complained that if Truman and Byrnes had already approved the study, the UN negotiator served as nothing but a "messenger boy." Two days later, when someone leaked key passages of the Acheson-Lilienthal report to the press, Baruch threatened to resign. If he accepted the UN appointment without assurances that he could revise the report, he would perpetrate a fraud on the American people, who believed that he had responsibility for shaping U.S. atomic energy policy. Truman decided the political costs of Baruch's resignation would be too high. When the financier asked him directly who was in charge of U.S. international control policy, Truman responded, "Hell, you are!"[17]

The conflict over the board of consultants' recommendations, however, ground on. When Byrnes acceded to Acheson's entreaties to publish an official version of the report, Baruch angrily asked the Senate to delay the vote on his nomination. He then wrote a long letter questioning the board of consultants' study. Claiming that the UN Security Council's veto power would hamper the UNAEC, he also warned against the Atomic Development Authority becoming a cumbersome bureaucracy that stifled nuclear entrepreneurship. The Acheson-Lilienthal plan, moreover, lacked reciprocity, compelling the United States to give atomic data to the rest of the world as a "gift" with nothing expected in return. After Byrnes promised that the study could be reworked, Baruch allowed the Senate to confirm his appointment a few days later.[18]

As Baruch feared, many observers viewed the Acheson-Lilienthal report as official U.S. policy. Most commentators praised the report as generous and well crafted, with the *New York Times* calling it a good "starting point." Numerous atomic scientists and peace advocates also voiced their approval. But the report was quickly criticized from the right and the left. The conservative *Chicago Tribune* condemned it as a scheme to give the atomic bomb to the Soviets. Washington journalist I. F. Stone, writing in the left-leaning journal *The Nation*, told readers to ignore the "newspaper hoopla" and closely scrutinize the study. He argued that the report's recommendation that the United States continue stockpiling weapons until international control had proven its effectiveness meant that the plan "might turn out to be a prize phony, a slice of atomic pie in the sky." Apparent popular enthusiasm for the report masked fissures in American opinion. The foreign policy public, which included most journalists and the atomic scientists, favored international control more strongly than did the majority of the U.S. population. Most ordinary Americans did support UN atomic energy negotiations but opposed giving the "atomic secret" to the UN or to any other country. Shallow backing for the Acheson-Lilienthal report gave Baruch sufficient freedom to revise it.[19]

In an April 5 meeting, Oppenheimer attempted to persuade Baruch and his staff to endorse the Acheson-Lilienthal plan. The scientist's presentation, however, only increased the Baruch group's pessimism about the UN negotiations. They feared that the Atomic Development Authority could be the entering wedge for internationalization of various economic activities, which would destroy U.S. capitalism and the American "way of life." The interwar period showed that international cooperation and disarmament could not succeed. Baruch and his aides rejected the founding premise of U.S. atomic energy pronouncements: namely, that international control served American security interests.[20]

Baruch, however, could not openly renounce international control and still remain the chief UNAEC negotiator. Instead, he clandestinely struggled to revise U.S. policy. The Acheson-Lilienthal plan's popularity among opinion leaders meant that he had to proceed carefully or risk alienating the attentive public. He attempted to co-opt members of the Acheson-Lilienthal group, hoping that if an architect of the public policy joined his team he could mute criticism from the left when he reworked the plan. He could then strengthen the inspection, safeguard, and punishment sections in the U.S. proposal, which would enhance support from the right and ensure Soviet refusal.[21]

Baruch immediately contacted all members of the Acheson and Lilienthal panels, but only McCloy and Groves agreed to help. But their offers meant little because they had urged continued military control of the Manhattan Project and thus had roused suspicion among many international control advocates. When Bush, Conant, and Acheson declined to join the UNAEC delegation, Baruch focused on Lilienthal and Oppenheimer. But the Tennessee Valley Authority director declined, certain that Baruch planned to scrap the board of consultants' report. Oppenheimer also refused because he believed Baruch's group had "no hope of agreement" and instead looked to prepare the "American people for a refusal by Russia."[22]

Despite his failure to win over Oppenheimer and Lilienthal, Baruch had gained the trust of the military and of anti-Soviet administration officials. Groves, U.S. Army Chief of Staff Dwight D. Eisenhower, and chief of naval operations Admiral Chester Nimitz agreed to advise and appoint formal military aides to Baruch's staff. Baruch's emphasis on safeguards and punishment also found sympathy with War Secretary Robert Patterson and Senator Brien McMahon, chair of the Senate Special Committee on Atomic Energy.

Acheson emerged as Baruch's most effective opponent. In urging that the UNAEC delegation develop an international atomic agency charter that included "a sound, fair-minded statement of policy and procedure," he stressed that the best approach would lay down a fair plan and "test the good faith of the world." While Acheson did not "reasonably expect general acceptance of any plan we might propose," he feared increased public unrest if the United States did not act on international control within sixty days. Baruch and his staff suspected that Acheson was merely feigning urgency to scuttle their attempt to revise the Oppenheimer plan.[23]

Despite Acheson's admonitions, Baruch's aides advanced their effort to reformulate international control policy. Their revisions transformed the Oppenheimer plan into an obvious propaganda ploy. First, Baruch reshaped the proposal into a program for total disarmament and abolition of war. Such ambitious and utopian schemes only recalled past failures. Numerous countries had endorsed disarmament and the outlawing of war during the interwar period, but the Kellogg-Briand Pact and several disarmament conferences had not prevented World War II. Many commentators later claimed that interwar disarmament efforts had actually invited Nazi aggression.

Second, Baruch changed the Atomic Development Authority's function from "owning" to merely controlling mines and fissionable raw materials. Private companies would manage the uranium and thorium mines because "the Government couldn't operate anything successfully." Baruch and his advisers may have opposed public ownership on principle, but private ownership also served their individual economic interests. Fred Searls, Baruch, and Secretary of State Byrnes all had invested in Newmont Mining Corporation, which specialized in uranium mining.

Third, Baruch's UNAEC delegation proposed initiating a worldwide raw materials survey prior to any agreement on other international control issues.

It hoped to use Soviet compliance as a test of good faith. Most important, the delegation proposed that the UN Security Council veto be repealed to allow "immediate and certain" punishment of any international control violations. Behind this rhetorical flourish lurked a plan to turn the UN into an atomic league of Western nations. Baruch and Searls believed that the clear bias of the U.S. proposal might force the Soviets to withdraw from the UN after the American plan had received majority approval. The United States could then gain UN approval for its trusteeship of atomic weapons, and the UN could be transformed into a U.S.-dominated, anti-Soviet alliance.[24]

With the outlines of their proposal in hand, the Baruch group launched a series of meetings with the veterans of the Acheson-Lilienthal committees to forge consensus on U.S. international control policy. Instead of agreement, however, intensified struggle resulted. The Acheson-Lilienthal group opposed all of Baruch's revisions — the emphasis on punishment, the change to a plan for total disarmament, and the raw materials survey. Schemes to use the raw material survey to test the Soviets' good faith provoked the most consternation. Acheson argued that Soviet refusal would conclusively prove bad faith, while others warned that the survey would actually compromise U.S. security by revealing secret uranium-ore agreements with Belgium and Great Britain. Following a private conversation with Fred Searls, moreover, Lilienthal surmised that the Baruch group hoped to use Soviet intransigence as an argument in favor of preventive war against Moscow.[25]

The bureaucratic intrigue continued as forces deep within the federal government attempted to sabotage the Oppenheimer plan by questioning its supporters' loyalty. On May 29, FBI director J. Edgar Hoover sent a letter to Truman aide George E. Allen describing an espionage ring within the government that sought to give the Soviets data to build their own atomic bomb. The ring also allegedly aimed to convince the American people that the U.S. atomic monopoly eliminated the need for a strong army and navy. Hoover accused eleven government officials and two journalists of wittingly or unwittingly aiding the Soviet effort, including Acheson, State Department aide Herbert Marks, Secretary of Commerce Wallace, former War Department aide John McCloy, radio commentator Raymond Gram Swing, and *Washington Post* reporter Marquis Childs. All the accused had supported international control. Hoover sent his letter the same day that Baruch and Hancock traveled to the capital to present their proposal to Byrnes and Truman and two weeks before the start of UN negotiations. The timing of the accusations suggests that they aimed at undercutting support for the Oppenheimer plan.[26]

Even with this outside help, Baruch had trouble winning approval of his revisions. Although not as hostile as Acheson to Baruch's suggestions, Byrnes reminded the financier that the UN General Assembly had given the UNAEC a very specific mandate. The United States would be ill-advised to move beyond international control to more sweeping disarmament discussions at this late date, while a raw materials survey should be postponed until after the UNAEC had agreed on the general outline of an international control plan. In the face of this opposition, Baruch abandoned his more sweeping changes. But Byrnes found little comfort in success. Fearing that Baruch had failed to understand his own subtle strategy, Byrnes soon complained that Baruch's appointment was "the worst mistake I ever made." The Pentagon proved more sympathetic to the UNAEC delegation's ideas. The Joint Chiefs refrained from endorsing Baruch's plan for an atomic league but did endorse automatic sanctions and retention of the atomic monopoly until international control reached its final stage of implementation.[27]

Emboldened by the military's support, Baruch looked to Truman to settle the dispute between his delegation and the State Department. The president privately had voiced sentiments very similar to Baruch's, telling one foreign policy aide that the United States could not abandon the atomic bomb as long as it remained vulnerable to "outlaw attack." Truman often drew upon America's frontier iconography to depict the United States as the purveyor of civilization to a disorderly world. He freely asserted America's right to regulate world politics, contending that just as "courts must have marshals" and counties need "a sheriff," the United States would need to use its military might, including the atomic bomb, to police the globe. Such thinking did not fade as the Cold War deepened. In 1954, one U.S. Air Force study advocated that American air superiority take control of Soviet skies in order to pressure Moscow to behave according to American dictates. Such a course would be defensive, comparable to the "Wild West," where a man had to carry a gun for protection and could shoot to kill if a rival seemed to be reaching for his gun. Survival in a nuclear world hinged on striking first, before the opponent initiated hostilities. With Truman so steeped in Wild West thinking, it came as no surprise to Acheson and Byrnes that the president quickly and enthusiastically approved Baruch's policy statement.[28]

Unveiling the Baruch Plan

On June 14, Baruch put the bureaucratic battle behind him and ballyhooed his proposal before whirring cameras and a thicket of microphones. He raised his 6′4″ frame to its full height and in a deep, booming voice announced,

"We are here to make a choice between the quick and the dead." He promised an agreement that contained "enforceable sanctions" and not just "pious thoughts." The UNAEC representative also hinted that the United States might demand controls on "bacteriological, biological, [and] gas" weapons, as well as the elimination of war itself, before it would abandon its "winning weapon." General Groves "gleefully" assured other Americans in the auditorium that the Soviets would never accept the American proposal. Winston Churchill observed that the plan's emphasis on inspection aimed at eliciting Soviet rejection: "It is of course only a pretext and if it failed through some Soviet manoeuvre another would have to be found."[29]

Despite its implicit commitment to the U.S. atomic monopoly, the "Baruch Plan" received an overwhelmingly positive response both in the United States and in Western Europe. Over 98 percent of newspaper editorials surveyed by Baruch's staff praised the speech. *New York Times* military affairs correspondent Hanson Baldwin called the proposal "thoughtful, imaginative, and courageous." Other newspapers cheered the plan's magnanimity and ingenuity. Leading world government advocate Grenville Clark hailed the speech as a positive step. Atomic scientists on both sides of the Atlantic also largely supported the proposal. More important, key members of the UNAEC publicly lauded the Baruch Plan, including Canada, Great Britain, France, China, Mexico, and Brazil.[30]

But the U.S. proposal did not escape criticism. Nuclear nationalists and former isolationists in both political parties, including Democratic senator Kenneth McKellar and Republican senator Bourke Hickenlooper, blasted the plan as too generous. The Hearst newspaper chain condemned the "imbecilic" attempt to hand American atomic secrets to "foreign masters." On the other side of the political spectrum, many nuclear pacifists and disarmament advocates argued that the plan needed to go further. The Emergency Committee of Atomic Scientists believed that international control should only be seen as an interim step toward world government, while the Fellowship of Reconciliation argued that the United States had no moral authority to demand concessions from others until it halted production of atomic bombs.[31]

Moscow remained curiously silent. Since the bombings of Hiroshima and Nagasaki, the Soviets had refrained from public comment about atomic weapons. The Moscow Declaration of 1945, which had advocated the establishment of the UNAEC, stood as the Soviet government's only official statement on atomic energy. Yet the U.S. embassy in Moscow claimed that all available evidence suggested that Stalin would reject any plan that required inspection or interfered with the Soviet bomb project. Senator Arthur

Vandenberg, in Paris for the Council of Foreign Ministers meeting, claimed that the UNAEC negotiations were "*the* 'show down' with Moscow" and that rejection of the U.S. proposal would signal that "this will be *two* worlds instead of *one*."[32] After waiting anxiously for the Soviet reaction, later that day Vandenberg had his answer.

On June 19, the Soviet representative to the UNAEC, Andrei Gromyko, proposed that the UNAEC negotiate a treaty banning the production and use of atomic weapons before it moved to the question of verification and enforcement. He offered national self-inspection in place of an international inspection commission, which Moscow rejected as an unacceptable infringement of sovereignty. The UNAEC should coordinate the international exchange of scientific information and receive reports on each nation's atomic energy research activities. The Soviets opposed suspension of the Security Council veto for any reason. Except for the separation of an atomic weapon ban and enforcement provisions into different agreements, the "Gromyko Plan" in many ways conformed to a model international control treaty that the Carnegie Endowment for International Peace had proposed in March 1946. Both proposals resembled previous international agreements to prevent the spread of illegal substances, such as narcotics. But the Soviet plan to ban atomic weapons before negotiating enforcement provisions suggested little faith in the UN talks. The Soviets effectively asked the United States to disarm unilaterally and trust other countries to provide adequate control and enforcement mechanisms. It inverted Washington's demand that other countries prove their trustworthiness before the United States would abandon its atomic monopoly. Each superpower had thus put forth a "cynical" proposal designed to put the onus for international control's failure on its rival.[33]

The incompatibility of the two proposals and the general atmosphere of mutual distrust gave the UNAEC talks "an air of unreality." The meetings soon degenerated into pedantic wrangling over procedural rules and administrative matters. Baruch feared that the impasse in the UNAEC worked to the Soviets' advantage because Moscow had introduced the last proposal and its call for an immediate ban on atomic weapons could be understood by the world public more easily than could the more complex U.S. proposal. The financier proposed reviving his plan for general disarmament, which would mute Moscow's propaganda edge and pressure the Soviets to disband portions of their large army. But Truman, Acheson, and other State Department officials still believed that introduction of a general disarmament proposal would needlessly complicate the UNAEC negotiations and obscure the U.S. position on international control. The UNAEC representative reluctantly accepted these arguments with the proviso that the State Department would counteract Soviet propaganda with increased global publicity for the Baruch Plan.[34]

Baruch's biggest public relations problems, however, stemmed from the Truman administration's uncompromising stance. Two issues became the focus of criticism: the veto and continued production of atomic weapons. Newspaper columnist Walter Lippmann believed that Baruch had obscured stronger U.S. demands, such as inspection and international ownership, by emphasizing the veto and enforcement. If any country violated the international control agreement, war would break out and the UN would likely collapse. The renunciation of the veto would then be reduced to an empty legalism. The veto issue created a split in the foreign policy establishment. Some, including Acheson and Lilienthal, privately joined world government advocates in endorsing Lippmann's position. Others, such as John McCloy and Henry Stimson, found Baruch's position sensible and thought critics should give him time to make his tactics work.[35]

The UNAEC delegation also received criticism for refusing to abandon the U.S. commitment to build bombs until the last stage of the control agreement. Both disarmament advocates and leading religious groups condemned the U.S. policy of uninterrupted atomic weapons development. In private, Oppenheimer argued that the United States could stop bomb production and dismantle all its existing bombs with minimal risk to American national security because the U.S. atomic arsenal in 1946 consisted of only a few partially dismantled plutonium bombs. But the Truman administration could not accept the physicist's argument without revealing the bluff behind the American image of atomic omnipotence. Military analysts believed the United States would need anywhere from twenty to two hundred bombs to win a war with the Soviet Union, a stockpile level not reached until after 1948. Baruch's staff, moreover, thought that the call to halt bomb construction might aid Soviet attempts to turn the American people against atomic weapons and stiffen U.S. public opinion against resumed production after hopes for a nonproliferation agreement had collapsed.[36]

With Gromyko publicly announcing that Moscow could not accept the Baruch proposals "either as a whole or in their separate parts," it was clear that neither superpower actually sought an agreement. The United States wanted to retain its monopoly and the Soviet Union sought a bomb of its own. But the negotiations continued because the Soviets and the Americans viewed the UNAEC talks as a propaganda forum that should not be halted until one rival gained a clear advantage. By late summer, the Soviet UNAEC delegation informed Moscow that it must prolong the talks until it could abandon its strategy of "passive defense" and provide a positive alternative to the U.S. position.[37]

The Death of International Control

Throughout summer and fall 1946, events beyond the UNAEC talks threatened to render the negotiations moot. The Paris Council of Foreign Ministers meeting and the subsequent Paris Peace Conference perpetuated U.S.-Soviet acrimony. Any hint of serious negotiation vanished as both Byrnes and Molotov played to the journalists in the galleries rather than attempting to resolve their disputes over Eastern Europe and a German peace settlement. As tensions between the Soviets and the Americans grew, the UNAEC talks seemed out of step with the anti-Soviet tenor of U.S. policy.[38]

Baruch sensed that both the mood of the administration and public opinion were "running very strongly against the Soviets." Early that summer, Truman had asked his aides Clark Clifford and George Elsey to produce a comprehensive study of U.S.-Soviet relations. The duo's final report showed near-unanimous administration acceptance of Kennan's argument that no permanent settlement could be reached with the Russians. According to the report, the United States should prepare for a long period of international tension in which all other foreign policy considerations were subordinated to the goal of checking Soviet expansion. Clifford and Elsey specifically recommended that the United States "entertain no proposal for disarmament or limitation of arms" as long as the Soviet threat persisted. The president hesitated to make the Clifford report government policy, but its overwhelming acceptance by senior policymakers made continuation of the UNAEC talks appear foolish.[39]

Congressional atomic energy policy also contradicted the goals of the UNAEC negotiations. Throughout 1946, the Senate Special Committee on Atomic Energy worked to pass legislation on domestic control of atomic energy. An early commitment to bring the Manhattan Project under civilian control and encourage scientific openness came under assault in the wake of the Canadian atomic espionage cases. The Atomic Energy Act of 1946, which Truman signed in August, banned the dissemination of nuclear "restricted data" to any foreign nations and called for a new Military Liaison Committee to review the decisions of a civilian Atomic Energy Commission (AEC). The law raised serious questions about U.S. commitment to international control and threatened to make Anglo-American atomic energy cooperation illegal. The Atomic Energy Act reflected a broad congressional commitment to protecting the U.S. atomic monopoly, a sentiment that intensified after the Republican victory in the November 1946 congressional elections. The new law suggested that any international control plan had dim prospects for senatorial ratification.

Despite the widening breach in U.S.-Soviet relations and congressional resistance to international control, the UNAEC talks served U.S. national security calculations. The Truman administration still hoped to use the failure of the negotiations to justify American reliance on atomic weapons as the primary line of defense against Soviet aggression. The UNAEC meetings accordingly had to produce unambiguous evidence both of Russian bad faith and of American willingness to eliminate the threat of nuclear weapons. On several occasions during the talks, Baruch believed that he had accomplished this task. But several setbacks in the summer and fall of 1946 undercut those propaganda objectives, making it necessary to prolong the UNAEC discussions.

The initial public relations gaffe occurred in July when the United States conducted the first postwar atomic bomb tests at the Bikini Atoll in the South Pacific. Just two weeks after the UN talks began, Washington held a widely publicized test of the bomb's effect on naval vessels. The coincidence of the tests with international control talks led many both at home and abroad to charge the Truman administration with trying to intimidate Moscow into accepting the U.S. atomic energy proposal. But all available evidence points to bureaucratic bungling rather than nuclear coercion as the reason for the inopportune scheduling of the event. The results of the test increased the public relations problem. The minor damage to the naval vessels raised serious questions about the bomb's power and usefulness in war. Oppenheimer had warned Truman that the Bikini tests could be misconstrued, and he feared that the test design would not adequately demonstrate the bomb's power. The president, however, dismissed him as a "cry baby."[40]

During July and August, continued Soviet intransigence allowed the United States slowly to regain some of its propaganda edge. But then the *New Yorker* magazine published John Hersey's article "Hiroshima," a lengthy account of six Hiroshima residents' efforts to cope with the bombing's aftermath. "Hiroshima" provoked an overwhelming popular response, spurring a public debate on the morality and necessity of the bombings. Despite the mass approval of the bombings and of U.S. international control policy, James Conant and others in the foreign policy establishment worried that mounting criticism of the bomb decision might adversely affect American atomic energy policy. Conant believed that a respected wartime figure needed to defend the bomb decision to counter Hersey. He soon persuaded both Karl T. Compton, a former Manhattan Project administrator, and Henry Stimson to write articles about the Hiroshima decision, both emphatically depicting it as necessary to end the war and save American lives. Conant edited both pieces so that they presented a single version of the decision-making process, and he made sure that neither contained any references to postwar security calculations. The fallout from the Hersey article had made it imperative that the UNAEC talks continue until antibomb sentiment among the "verbal-minded" citizenry had died down.[41]

After the UNAEC's scientific and technical committee unanimously endorsed the U.S. proposal in mid-September, momentum in the propaganda battle seemed to pass to the Baruch group once again. The UNAEC delegation wondered if it should cut its losses and seek a vote on the U.S. proposal. The vote tally would most likely be ten in favor, with the Poles and Soviets either abstaining or voting against issuing a report. With the Soviets in opposition, the report would go nowhere after it reached the Security Council, but the vote would demonstrate that a clear majority within the UNAEC supported the Baruch Plan. As well, the vote would take advantage of a rare Soviet procedural miscue that had allowed the scientific and technical committee to endorse the technical features of the U.S. proposal without dissent. With this tactical victory in hand, Baruch asked the president and the State Department for permission to terminate the talks. But once again outside events worked against him.[42]

On September 12, 1946, Secretary of Commerce Wallace gave a speech in New York that criticized American policy toward the Soviet Union, including U.S. international control policy. The president had told reporters prior to the speech that he had read and approved Wallace's remarks. When the media depicted the speech as a repudiation of both Byrnes's tactics in Paris and Baruch's in the UNAEC, Truman attempted to retract his previous statement, claiming that he had merely approved Wallace's right to make the speech. The press immediately labeled the president's effort "a clumsy lie." On September 18, the damage to the UNAEC negotiations increased when someone leaked a July 23 letter from Wallace to Truman that compared the Baruch Plan to a rigged poker game. According to Wallace, the proposal obviously intended to preserve the U.S. atomic monopoly and helped fuel "immoral and stupid" threats of preventive war.[43]

Baruch demanded either presidential repudiation of Wallace or a complete retraction from the commerce secretary. If neither occurred, the entire

UNAEC staff would resign. Although the speech angered and embarrassed him, Truman feared alienating the liberal faction of the Democratic Party that Wallace had symbolically led for more than a decade. The president tried to prevent a complete break with the commerce secretary by asking him to refrain from making any foreign policy statements until after the Paris Peace Conference had ended. But this compromise pleased no one, least of all Baruch and Byrnes. Truman requested and received Wallace's resignation after Byrnes convinced the president that Wallace's retention in the cabinet would undermine his authority in the Paris talks. The commerce secretary's removal, however, did not solve Baruch's public relations problem, for Wallace still had not retracted his criticisms of the international control proposal.

After the September setbacks, Baruch and his staff deliberately drew out the UNAEC talks through the month of October. Truman had not answered the financier's written request to terminate the talks, most likely because the president had become embroiled in the Wallace affair soon after receiving Baruch's memorandum. Even though the UNAEC delegation lacked Truman's approval, it looked to bring the international control talks to a climax. Baruch's staff met informally with Assistant Secretary General of the UN Antonin Sobolev, a Soviet diplomat, to probe whether the Soviets would cooperate in bringing the talks to a close. The conference did little but confirm American suspicions that the Soviets sought their own atomic weapons and would resist any outside attempts to block their effort. Sobolev even hinted that if the United States continued to impede Soviet "freedom" in atomic energy matters a war might result.[44]

The Sobolev discussions energized the Baruch group to seek an immediate end to the talks. Baruch phoned the president and sought his approval to put the U.S. proposal to a vote. But this request came too late to stave off yet another propaganda setback. On October 29, Soviet foreign minister Vyacheslav Molotov took the floor of the UN General Assembly and delivered a blistering attack on the Baruch Plan, labeling it a transparent attempt to preserve the American atomic monopoly. He also called for the UNAEC talks to include a discussion of general and complete disarmament. Baruch exploded. He had warned the State Department from the beginning that the United States had left the door open for such a Soviet propaganda maneuver. He blamed Acheson for scuttling his general disarmament proposal.[45]

Acheson, however, thought Baruch had damaged the U.S. position in the UNAEC by emphasizing the veto and enforcement. He reiterated his contention that enforcement provisions meant nothing since violations would lead to the collapse of the treaty anyway. Although the undersecretary believed that the Soviets had rejected the fundamental spirit of the UN and had participated in it only to bend it to their own purposes, he recommended that the United States seek accommodation with the Soviets through that body. As a practical measure, the United States should also ready itself "to lick the hell out of" the Soviets in ten or fifteen years if efforts toward accommodation failed. Despite his pessimism, Acheson opposed Baruch's efforts to push for a UNAEC vote because he believed some Western nations, such as Great Britain, still did not fully support the U.S. proposal and resented Baruch's heavy-handed negotiating style.[46]

Acheson lost this debate. On November 5, Byrnes and Truman gave Baruch the go-ahead to put his plan to a vote. The UNAEC staff labored throughout the month to gain the noncommunist countries' votes and diminish the propaganda value of Molotov's disarmament proposal. Then, on November 13, the UNAEC approved, by a ten-to-two vote, the U.S. proposal to issue a report to the UN Security Council by the end of the year. The Soviets made some conciliatory gestures in hope of continuing the negotiations, but Baruch brushed them aside. The financier felt no sense of urgency to reach agreement since the United States could "get what she wants if she insists on it. After all we've got [the atomic bomb] and they haven't and won't have it for a long time to come." He focused accordingly on keeping the other ten votes in the U.S. fold. While Baruch complained that the British Labour government was "always playing footie-footie with the Russians and Poles," London supported his attempt to end the talks because British officials realized that international control had long since left the realm of real diplomacy. Baruch had to work much harder to secure the French and Canadian votes, but finally the UNAEC voted to approve a majority report, with only the Soviets and the Poles abstaining.[47]

Oppenheimer, who retained informal ties to the UNAEC delegation, had predicted in July how the negotiations would end, claiming that Baruch would take his time and ultimately produce a ten-to-two vote. The Soviets then would use their Security Council veto to keep the report from reaching the General Assembly, which "will be construed by us as a demonstration of Russia's warlike intentions. And this will fit perfectly into the plans of that growing number who want to put the country on a warfooting, first psychologically, then actually." The scientist proved stunningly prescient. Later, in 1947, the Federation of Atomic Scientists, a group that formed to advocate international control, inaugurated the journal *Bulletin of the Atomic Scientists*, featuring its Doomsday Clock. Despondent over the fate of the Baruch Plan, they placed the hands at seven minutes to midnight.[48]

In January 1947, Baruch submitted a resignation letter that advocated continued bomb production and strict unilateral nonproliferation measures. The next month, the Security Council began debate on the UNAEC report. From the start, Gromyko made it clear that the Soviets rejected all the majority recommendations. On March 10, the Security Council voted to send the matter back to the UNAEC, and the process began anew. The United States allowed the UNAEC talks to continue until domestic and world public opinion accepted that no progress could be made. The UNAEC, therefore, stumbled along until the first half of 1949, often returning to topics multiple times. The State Department anxiously sought escape from an "impossible situation."[49]

The UNAEC negotiations dragged on from 1946 to 1949, and the Soviets continued their efforts to create nuclear weapons. On December 25, 1946, just five days before the UNAEC vote on the Baruch Plan, a Soviet experimental nuclear reactor sprang to life. On August 29, 1949, the Soviets tested their first atomic bomb. Truman, dumbfounded by the test, waited nearly a month before announcing that the United States had detected a nuclear explosion in the Soviet Union. The Federation of Atomic Scientists moved its Doomsday Clock to three minutes to midnight. Soviet acquisition of the bomb dealt the fatal blow to the UNAEC and brought the first phase of U.S. nuclear nonproliferation policy to a close.

The earlier impasse in the UNAEC negotiations led to renewed consideration of an international atomic alliance against the Soviets. But both the State and the War Departments ultimately rejected this option. Acheson believed that the weaker powers in the alliance would become a liability during a war, while the military feared that sharing atomic data might lead to leaks of classified information to the Soviets. The Truman administration concluded that retention of the U.S. atomic monopoly would serve national security better than nuclear sharing would. This doctrine of nuclear exclusivity defined the limits of U.S. nuclear nonproliferation policy from 1945 to 1949, until the Soviet nuclear test weakened the executive branch's faith in American atomic unilateralism. But now congressional resistance posed the chief obstacle to nuclear collaboration with other countries.[50]

Battling Congress

With the collapse of the UNAEC negotiations, Congress emphasized unilateral nonproliferation measures, such as export controls and the restricted-data provisions in the Atomic Energy Act of 1946. State Department officials in 1947 had hoped to persuade Congress to restore atomic collaboration with

Great Britain and Canada by revealing the extent of Anglo-American war-time cooperation. But when Acheson admitted that the Quebec Agreement enabled a British veto over U.S. use of the bomb, the Joint Committee on Atomic Energy (JCAE) "erupted in indignation and anger." More important, Senator Hickenlooper, JCAE chairman, and Senator Vandenberg, Foreign Relations Committee chairman, threatened to delay approval of the Marshall Plan until the Truman administration formally abrogated the Quebec accord. Although the State Department succeeded in separating congressional action on the Marshall Plan from the issue of atomic cooperation, the Truman administration had to settle for a restrictive modus vivendi that limited cooperation to areas that Hickenlooper, Vandenberg, and other nuclear nationalists would approve: namely, scientific interchanges that did not directly aid British production of nuclear weapons. But the agreement did allow U.S. access to the British-controlled uranium reserves it coveted. The American and British negotiating teams labeled the new document "an agreement among people who disagree."[51]

After 1947, ambivalence lingered within the Truman administration over whether British manufacture of weapons should be encouraged. In early 1949, AEC and State Department functionaries concluded that the British and American programs should be tightly integrated to maximize the use of resources and manpower. Full and complete exchange of information on all aspects of atomic energy, including weapons data, would be needed to achieve full coordination. But the group's conclusions met stiff resistance. Lewis Strauss, a conservative Republican financier and former rear admiral, voiced the lone dissent on the AEC. Strauss had claimed since 1948 that the British Labour government was "too far to our left" and might give atomic secrets to the Soviets. In early January 1949, the Republican commissioner persuaded the president to end collaboration with the British. The next month, Truman told AEC chairman David Lilienthal that the wartime agreements with Great Britain should be terminated to eliminate the threat of British bombs being captured by the Soviets during a future war. Acheson, however, dissuaded Truman from implementing that order. Instead, the president appointed a special committee of the National Security Council (NSC) to examine U.S.-British cooperation. That body recommended expanded technical collaboration in exchange for a British pledge to locate all its atomic weapon production facilities in North America. Truman, always the follower rather than the leader on nuclear matters, approved this report on March 31.[52]

On July 14, the president and his chief national security advisers presented the case for expanded U.S.-British cooperation to congressional leaders.

Truman painted a broad atomic alliance as the only sensible alternative to failed efforts at international control. But Vandenberg's and Hickenlooper's hostility to nuclear sharing had not diminished. Both senators decried a give-away policy that clearly benefited the British at U.S. expense. The Labour government had no grounds "to demand full participation in the so-called 'know how,'" Vandenberg insisted. Like Strauss, Hickenlooper feared that the British government might give American secrets to the Soviets. He staunchly opposed sharing "our greatest heritage and asset" with anyone.[53]

The July 14 meeting ignited a brouhaha between the Truman adminis-tration and the JCAE. The Republican minority threatened resignation if the State Department pursued negotiations with the British. Acheson cited intelligence estimates that the Soviets would produce a bomb by mid-1951 as the rationale for expanding technical cooperation. But Hickenlooper and Vandenberg dismissed these arguments, warning that the U.S. monopoly's demise would diminish American prestige within the Western alliance. The Truman administration backed down once again. Instead of widening the Anglo-American atomic relationship, the United States worked to extend the modus vivendi beyond its expiration date of December 1949.[54]

The Soviet atomic explosion in September helped quash, in Acheson's words, "a good deal of senatorial nonsense about our priceless secret heri-tage." Although Soviet acquisition of the bomb made the JCAE more ame-nable to Anglo-American atomic collaboration, the committee still did not support unlimited exchange of data. Sir Roger Makins, the chief British negotiator on atomic energy collaboration, warned his colleagues in London that within the U.S. government there existed "perhaps an ill-defined and almost unconscious feeling that atomic energy should remain an American monopoly, both for military and industrial purposes." The British, however, would settle for nothing less than full partnership. They had grown impatient with U.S. efforts to constrain the United Kingdom's atomic energy program. As the talks bogged down, it became apparent that no agreement could be concluded in 1949. As a stopgap, the Americans and British compromised on the allocation of raw materials. The Truman administration had hoped to revive the negotiations in 1950, but revelations that Klaus Fuchs, a British atomic scientist, had spied for the Soviets eliminated any realistic hope of winning JCAE approval of broadened collaboration. The subsequent defec-tions to the Soviet Union of British atomic scientist Bruno Pontecorvo in 1950 and diplomats Guy Burgess and Donald Maclean in 1951 deflated hopes of renewed talks during Truman's presidency.[55]

The repeated attempts to broaden U.S.-British atomic cooperation demonstrated that key factions within the Truman administration had rejected a policy of strict nonproliferation as early as 1947. These voices instead supported selective proliferation, an approach that enabled key U.S. allies to acquire nuclear technology and weapons. But Congress, especially members of the JCAE, refused to jettison the U.S. atomic monopoly. Even after the Soviet atomic test, congressional leaders wanted to preserve American nuclear preeminence. The Truman administration could not overcome both the resistance of the JCAE and the damage of the British spy scandals.

Near the end of Truman's presidency, the inadequacy of U.S. nonproliferation policies became clear. Despite prior American refusals to cooperate with the British nuclear weapons program, the United Kingdom developed an atomic bomb. The Labour government wanted permission to use the American Nevada test site in order to avoid constructing its own costly facilities in Australia, but the Truman administration had to reject the request as violating the restricted-data provisions of the Atomic Energy Act. The United States instead offered to test a bomb for the British under highly restricted conditions that London understandably found unacceptable. A clear metaphor for the myopia of nuclear nationalism, Great Britain tested its first atomic weapon on October 3, 1952, with no Americans present.[56]

Embracing the Arms Race

The United States did not view atomic collaboration with the British as the only means to counteract the Soviet bomb. The Soviet atomic test also prompted U.S. contemplation of more destructive nuclear weapons. Yet the AEC's General Advisory Committee (GAC) and George F. Kennan, director of the State Department's Policy Planning Staff, thought the end to the U.S. monopoly should inspire a new effort to halt the nuclear arms race before it spiraled out of control. Although nuclear expansionists won the policy debate, proponents of limited nuclear arms control planted seeds that germinated in future nonproliferation proposals.

The push to recover the American lead in nuclear technology began immediately after Truman's public announcement of the Soviet test. In mid-October 1949, Truman approved a military request to expand the U.S. atomic stockpile and build additional production facilities for fissionable materials. At the insistence of Lewis Strauss, the GAC simultaneously sought to determine the feasibility of accelerated development of thermonuclear weapons. While the AEC prepared plans to build a "superbomb," Acheson initiated a Policy Planning Staff study of U.S. international control policy. Aware that the U.S. military's dependence on nuclear weapons contradicted American disarmament plans, he warned AEC chairman Lilienthal that "if we keep saying we want the control policy when we don't, we are perhaps fooling others, but we shouldn't commit a fraud upon ourselves." Acheson hoped that Kennan and the rest of the Policy Planning Staff would devise a method for the United States to withdraw its support for the UNAEC majority report with minimal propaganda damage; however, neither the GAC nor Kennan produced the results that Strauss and Acheson desired.[57]

The GAC entered the debate first. The panel unanimously opposed an "all-out" effort to develop the hydrogen bomb, even though members differed on the grounds for their conclusion. Oppenheimer, the GAC chairman, and Conant authored the majority report, which warned that the H-bomb "might become a weapon of genocide" and urged that it "never be produced." Although the majority opinion became the focus of the debate on thermonuclear development, Isidor Rabi's and Enrico Fermi's minority report had greater influence on the future course of U.S. nonproliferation policy. Both scientists condemned the weapon as "an evil thing considered in any light" and recommended that Washington propose an international agreement "not to proceed in the development or construction of weapons of this category." Rabi and Fermi argued that the nuclear fallout and seismic effects of a hydrogen bomb test could be easily detected by existing physical means, eliminating the need for inspection and verification of an H-bomb ban. Thermonuclear research should continue only if the Soviets refused to cooperate.[58]

After the GAC transmitted its report to AEC chairman Lilienthal, the Fermi-Rabi proposal faded from view. The full AEC voted on the advisory panel's report and accepted the majority opinion by a three-to-two vote. But the two commissioners voting in the minority had important political connections. Lewis Strauss enjoyed the confidence of the JCAE's Republican members, and Gordon Dean had once been JCAE chairman Brien McMahon's law partner. After conferring with Dean and Strauss, McMahon entered the debate by vigorously advocating a "crash" hydrogen bomb program. He threatened public opposition from the JCAE if the president failed to pursue thermonuclear weapons aggressively. The Joint Chiefs of Staff and Secretary of Defense Louis Johnson (a "missionary for the H-bomb," according to one journalist) also urged an accelerated hydrogen bomb program.[59]

Truman decided to set aside the AEC decision and appointed a special NSC committee consisting of Lilienthal, Acheson, and Johnson to study the feasibility of thermonuclear weapons. Johnson and Lilienthal had already made their positions clear to the president. Acheson, therefore, held the key vote in determining whether the committee would support the H-bomb. Already inclined to approve an expanded thermonuclear program, Acheson, nonetheless, wanted a clear picture of the weapons' strategic and diplomatic potential before rendering a final decision. He asked his friend Oppenheimer to explain his opposition to the superbomb. Acheson listened attentively but afterward asked a colleague, "How can you persuade a paranoid adversary to disarm 'by example'?" On January 31, 1950, the special committee reported its conclusion to Truman. Acheson and Johnson supported H-bomb development, with Lilienthal still opposed. The president rudely interrupted the AEC chairman's attempt to explain his vote and speedily approved the majority decision. The discussion and Truman's acceptance took a mere seven minutes.[60]

Once the president's decision became public, some disarmament and scientist groups protested, but the majority of the American public rallied behind Truman's policy. One poll revealed that 73 percent of the American people favored all-out development. Public support weakened somewhat after February 2, however, when McMahon astonishingly reversed his private stance, took to the Senate floor, and recommended a five-year, worldwide Marshall Plan in exchange for Soviet agreement on international control of atomic and thermonuclear weapons. McMahon's motivations remain unclear; neither earnest fear of nuclear war nor political opportunism can be eliminated as explanations. Shortly after McMahon's speech, Senator Millard Tydings, chair of the Senate Armed Services Committee, also suggested that Truman convene a world disarmament conference. Polling data, in March, indicated a positive response to these appeals; 69 percent of those questioned favored concluding an international control agreement prior to proceeding with thermonuclear development. Still, 60 percent of the respondents believed that any disarmament negotiations with the Soviets would fail. Truman and Acheson quickly mounted a campaign to discredit the McMahon and Tydings proposals.[61]

The rejection of Kennan's arguments for renewed international control talks foreshadowed the hostility toward the McMahon and Tydings speeches. After the Soviet atomic test, Acheson had charged the Policy Planning Staff with reassessing U.S. international control policy. Kennan sounded out military and scientific opinion on the future course of atomic energy negotiations. No one among those interviewed—the military, the AEC, or veterans of the Acheson-Lilienthal committees—believed that the Soviet government would accept the U.S. proposal. Most advised that the Truman administration should withdraw the Baruch Plan from consideration, warning that its implementation would damage U.S. national security.[62]

When writing the report, however, Kennan largely ignored the views of others inside and outside the government. The sometimes maverick State Department counselor disapproved of the American military's heavy reliance on atomic weapons, arguing that European-based conventional forces constituted a sufficient deterrent to Soviet aggression and allowed the United States to de-emphasize atomic weapons. Kennan also claimed that atomic bombs, because of their destructive power, complicated diplomacy and increased the possibility of another horrific general war. He recommended decreased dependence on nuclear weapons, a newly formulated international control plan more acceptable to the Soviet Union, and increased U.S. conventional strength in Europe. Kennan, in retirement, labeled the paper "one of the most important, if not the most important, of all the documents I ever wrote in government." When Kennan pressed for further consideration of his proposals, Acheson snapped, "If that is your view you ought to resign from the Foreign Service and go out and preach your Quaker gospel, but don't do it within the department."[63]

Despite the vehement rejection of his main conclusions, Kennan anticipated the future course of U.S. nuclear policy when he advised that if Washington remained dependent on atomic weapons, the Truman administration should proceed to "bury the subject of international control as best we can for the present." This tactical advice received implicit acceptance in National Security Council Paper Number 68 (NSC-68). In this document, which depicted the Cold War as a conflict between two competing ideological systems, Policy Planning Staff director Paul H. Nitze ruled out any chance of an enforceable international control agreement.[64]

Acheson would have gladly followed NSC-68's guidance and stifled all discussion of international control, but McMahon's and Tydings's speeches in February inspired renewed public debate. Acheson asked the AEC to examine whether thermonuclear weapons had rendered the Baruch Plan obsolete. At the same time, McMahon's JCAE staff began interviewing Los Alamos laboratory scientists to determine if thermonuclear weapons raised problems for enforcement of an international control agreement. All the scientists believed that political issues posed greater obstacles to nuclear disarmament than did scientific advancements. Before either study had ended, however, Assistant Secretary of State for UN Affairs John Hickerson blundered by testifying to the JCAE that the Baruch Plan provided adequate control measures for hydrogen weapons.[65]

In reality, the hydrogen bomb and nuclear proliferation had greatly complicated hopes for international control. With two countries producing atomic bombs and the British poised to join them, any plan for international control would have to have accounted for all fissionable and thermonuclear materials produced prior to implementation. As bomb stockpiles mounted, the chance of fulfilling the rigid security requirements of the Baruch Plan evaporated. Not even the United States would have countenanced the intrusive inspection and verification measures necessary to provide absolute security from nuclear attack. Production of thermonuclear weapons further complicated chances for a nonproliferation agreement. Hydrogen weapons required only small amounts of fissionable material to ignite a fusion explosion, making it easier to hide plutonium and uranium to manufacture weapons clandestinely.[66]

The near impossibility of implementation did not impede American efforts to flaunt the U.S. international control proposal as a propaganda weapon. On October 24, 1950, Truman met calls for new disarmament negotiations by reviving Baruch's gambit of replacing the UNAEC with a UN Disarmament Commission, which would develop plans for concurrent nuclear and conventional arms control. Truman combined the stalemated international control talks with the equally stalled conventional disarmament negotiations, dooming any chance for agreement. The futility of the UN discussions became readily apparent when attempts to establish the new Disarmament Commission stretched into early 1952.

The Truman administration's approach to UN disarmament negotiations ultimately produced little of substance. Nuclear nonproliferation policy soon became buried amid the long texts of comprehensive disarmament proposals. With the United States engaged in the Korean War and a massive military buildup, American disarmament proposals offered "countermeasures to Soviet propaganda" criticizing U.S. militarism. The new U.S. disarmament plans also sought to correct previous policy by tying an international control accord to progress in conventional arms control. This linkage ensured that the United States would not abdicate its atomic counterweight until the Soviets had reduced their manpower advantage. The State Department rationalized the U.S. military buildup as necessary to "induce" Moscow's acceptance of international control and disarmament. Once again any serious proposal for nonproliferation was sacrificed for propaganda points.[67]

The logical contradiction in a policy aimed at reaching a disarmament agreement by accelerating the arms race did not worry Acheson or other U.S. policymakers because they believed Soviet acceptance of any disarmament program unlikely. At the same time, most policymakers still wanted to produce a realistic outline for genuine negotiations once the Soviet regime collapsed and a new, hopefully more cooperative, regime emerged. During preparations for the UN Disarmament Commission meetings, a few State Department officials understood that technical advancements had made the Baruch Plan obsolete and that international ownership and development required a relaxation of national sovereignty that the United States could no longer even pretend to find acceptable.[68]

Acheson, however, opposed any change in the U.S. international control proposal. Reflecting on his previous experience with the subject, he feared that any revision might spark criticism from Bernard Baruch and his press allies of the entire Truman disarmament effort. Most policymakers also saw international control as inextricably entwined with the larger U.S.-Soviet rivalry. Any arms control agreement required a measure of trust between its signatories because safeguards and verification measures could never be made perfectly reliable. In their minds, no acceptable international control agreement could be designed as long as the Cold War persisted.[69]

The Eleventh-Hour Test Ban Proposal

Because official thinking on nonproliferation had ossified, the only chance for a viable international control proposal lay outside of government. Acheson had resisted efforts to create a disarmament advisory body, but in early 1952, with Truman's consent, he appointed a Panel of Consultants on Disarmament. The new advisory group consisted of Oppenheimer, Bush (now president of the Carnegie Institution of Washington, a private scientific philanthropy), Allen W. Dulles (deputy director of central intelligence), John Dickey (president of Dartmouth College and a former State Department official), and Joseph E. Johnston (president of the Carnegie Endowment for International Peace). Why Acheson acceded to an outside group remains unclear. Some scholars argue that the secretary of state, trained to be "a shrewd, cautious attorney," may have hoped that this group of eminent individuals might endorse existing U.S. policy. The Panel of Consultants ostensibly worked to provide a more fully developed American proposal for the UN Disarmament Commission talks. Yet the group's conclusions remained top secret, and Acheson never communicated the findings to the U.S. delegate to the UN talks, Benjamin V. Cohen.[70]

During the first meetings of the Panel of Consultants, State Department officials did not hide the cynical nature of official disarmament policy. Paul

Nitze informed the panel that the administration worried that "the Soviets might actually do something concrete to reduce tensions which would have the effect of persuading the free world to let down its guard and neglect its armament effort." On May 6, however, Bush changed the tenor of discussions with a proposal to test the Soviets' good faith: a moratorium on thermonuclear testing, which would not require "overt inspection of Soviet territory." But State Department officials feared that a moratorium would undercut U.S. arguments for strict verification and inspection provisions. Bush, undeterred, pushed harder for postponement of the first H-bomb test, scheduled for late 1952. If the test went forward, it might scuttle hopes for a nuclear standstill agreement.[71]

Yet resistance to a test moratorium within the bureaucracy ran deep. On June 6, Nitze contended that a moratorium would force the thermonuclear arms race underground, not end it, warning that "an agreement of that sort might merely lull the gullible and mislead men of hope and goodwill."[72]

The Panel of Consultants nonetheless continued campaigning for a moratorium and a delay of the H-bomb test. They warned that "if the test is conducted, and if it succeeds, we will lose what may be a unique occasion to postpone or avert a world in which both sides pile up constantly larger stockpiles of constantly more powerful weapons." A moratorium would only be a temporary measure to be followed by more comprehensive agreements if the superpowers hoped to halt nuclear escalation and proliferation.[73]

The nuclear standstill question never even reached Truman. Acheson and Secretary of Defense Robert Lovett smothered the proposal at an October 9 meeting of the Special Committee of the NSC. The secretary of state disputed the consultants' contention that the greater destructive force of thermonuclear weapons would persuade the Soviets to accept international control. The Defense Department contended that even the suggestion of a test ban would weaken U.S. national security. Lovett demanded "that any such idea should immediately be put out of mind and that any paper that might exist on the subject should be destroyed."[74]

The intense anticommunist climate of 1952 may have foreordained the rejection of the Panel of Consultants' proposal. During the election campaign, the Republicans charged the Truman administration, especially Acheson, with being "soft" on communism. The congressional crusade to expose any hint of red within the government had reached its zenith, spearheaded by the efforts of Senator Joseph McCarthy, the McCarran committee, and the House Un-American Activities Committee. Lovett worried about the Panel of Consultants' vulnerability to a McCarthyite attack because of Robert

Oppenheimer's many past associations with communists and communist-front organizations.[75]

The test went ahead as scheduled on November 1. At 7:15 A.M., AEC scientists detonated the Mike device, the sky filled with 80 million tons of radioactive debris, and a mushroom cloud covered the horizon for over a hundred miles. The thermonuclear device destroyed Elugelab, the Pacific island on which it rested, leaving only a crater behind. The blast that had shook heaven and earth left U.S. nuclear nonproliferation policy unmoved.

The panel, however, continued its work. Its report criticized the Truman administration as overly committed to a "policy of noncooperation and unilateral decision," which hampered attempts to "undertake any serious efforts to limit the arms race." The panel proposed two major changes in disarmament policy. First, atomic secrecy needed to be relaxed to allow for informed discussion about the arms race. Only through candor could the American people become sufficiently impressed with the need for arms control. Relaxed atomic secrecy within the government would enable more agencies and individuals freely to participate in disarmament debates. Second, the American government should stop introducing new arms control initiatives at the UN because "these proposals seem almost inevitably unreal" and have no hope of Soviet acceptance. The stalemate in the UN Disarmament Commission only intensified Cold War tensions and blocked genuine efforts at disarmament. Confidential, bilateral talks with the Soviets should replace the UN negotiations.[76]

The Truman administration rejected the call for candor. Acheson argued that "a great deal of harm and no good could come from the proposal." If the president revealed the consequences of a hydrogen bomb attack on American cities, Acheson believed that "we would end up with a predicament where the people of the United States would be running around like frightened sheep in the pasture urging all manner of follies upon the Administration."[77]

Truman thus ended his presidency with an incoherent and failed nonproliferation policy. One week after leaving office, he retracted his own statements from 1949 acknowledging the existence of a Soviet bomb and declared that "I am not convinced the Russians have achieved the know-how to put the complicated mechanism together to make an A-Bomb. I am not convinced they have the bomb." After nearly eight years managing atomic energy policy, Truman apparently still nourished the fantasy that only Anglo-American "know-how" could manufacture nuclear weapons. Congressional leaders and the newly installed Eisenhower administration scrambled to prevent the former president's unsupported claims from gaining wider adherence.

Truman's ignorance and arrogance in nuclear matters remained undimmed even as he became a private citizen.[78]

From 1946 to 1953, the United States sought hegemony in nuclear affairs. All of its nonproliferation measures aimed at fulfilling this goal. Truman thus never seriously attempted to conclude a bilateral or multilateral nonproliferation agreement with the Soviets. In its infancy, nuclear technology held great promise for placing limits on atomic weapons before factors of politics, time, or scientific innovation made them much more difficult to eliminate. But this era also witnessed the birth of the Cold War. Each superpower viewed the other with intense suspicion, and neither Truman nor Stalin could afford to give up a "winning weapon." Still, the United States had publicly committed itself to international control. Truman could not disavow these statements without risking widespread disapproval at home and abroad. The Baruch Plan offered a solution. The UNAEC delegation and the State Department designed a proposal that aimed at winning public support while remaining unacceptable to the Soviets. The UNAEC talks achieved this limited goal. Once the Baruch Plan failed, the Truman administration actively sought to share nuclear weapons technology with Great Britain. Only a suspicious Congress prevented the selective relaxation of the unilateral nonproliferation policy then in place. Truman thereafter concentrated on making the United States predominant in nuclear and thermonuclear weapons. Paltry attempts to halt the development of hydrogen bombs received no support in the upper reaches of the government. A few policymakers did appreciate the dangers of nuclear diffusion, and their scuttled initiatives of 1946–53 would be revived later when the U.S. government once again turned an eye toward nonproliferation. Still, squandered opportunities and a markedly more dangerous world stood as the most important legacies of the Truman era.

4

The President in the
Gray Flannel Suit

CONFORMITY, TECHNOLOGICAL UTOPIANISM, &
NONPROLIFERATION, 1953–1956

"Soon even little countries will have a stockpile of these bombs, and then we *will* be in a mess," exclaimed Dwight D. Eisenhower in spring 1954.[1] The president had grown frustrated with his advisers' resistance to a nuclear test ban and other nonproliferation measures. Many administration officials viewed the spread of nuclear weapons as inevitable. They also saw nuclear weapons as the only guarantor of U.S. security and sought technological solutions for both national security and propaganda challenges. Eisenhower's desire to control nuclear weapons did inspire several studies of nonproliferation measures from 1953 to 1956. But because the president refused to impose his views on a resistant bureaucracy, these reviews did little to alter administration policy. Eisenhower's Atoms for Peace proposal actually increased the risk of proliferation. By 1956, multiple converging factors—ignorance of the link between nuclear power and nuclear weapons, Cold War suspicions, internal administrative disagreement, and presidential inefficacy—together subordinated nonproliferation to other American policy goals, namely maintaining NATO unity and winning over nonaligned states with Atoms for Peace aid. Instead of "Happy Days," Eisenhower ushered in a period of happy denial where problems were ignored in public and discussed only behind closed doors.

Chance for Peace?

Although he had little comprehension of the proliferation threat when he took office, the new president had a more nuanced understanding of the nuclear arms race than had his predecessor. As U.S. Army chief of staff (1945–48) and as NATO supreme commander (1951–52), Eisenhower helped supervise the integration of atomic weapons into U.S. strategy. As president, he combined this experience with adherence to the German military thinker Carl von Clausewitz's theories on the interconnection of war and politics. But Clausewitz offered a confusing compass for the nuclear age. Eisenhower feared that if he sustained the high level of defense spending inherited from Truman, it would damage the U.S. economy. A military policy based primarily on nuclear deterrence offered a feasible means to reduce defense spending while ensuring sufficient striking force to deter Soviet aggression. The new president nonetheless worried that large-scale nuclear attack violated the Clausewitzian principle that military victory must serve a clear political purpose. Eisenhower challenged military leaders to imagine the aftermath of a nuclear attack on the Soviet bloc. He observed, "Here would be a great area from the Elbe to Vladivostok and down through Southeast Asia torn up and destroyed, without government, without its communications, just an area of starvation and disaster. I ask you what would the civilized world do about it?"[2]

The president also contended that nuclear armaments posed a greater threat to U.S. than to Soviet security because atomic weapons favored "the side that attacks aggressively and by *surprise*." Since the United States would presumably never initiate an undeclared war, the continued nuclear threat worked to the Soviets' advantage. Nuclear abolition would conversely favor the United States because the Soviet Union could not match its industrial capacity in the event of conventional war. Eisenhower's fears about atomic weapons ultimately compelled him to embrace nuclear disarmament as the third major pillar of his national security policy, along with defense and deterrence. But these three national security approaches did not receive equal emphasis, and the Eisenhower administration achieved few clear disarmament gains.[3]

Eisenhower's thoughtfulness and wariness about nuclear weapons and military spending startled scholars in the 1980s who had been reared on depictions of a bland and disengaged Ike. But notions of Eisenhower as a genius that filled journals in the late twentieth century have also faded. While de-classified records exposed his cunning, they also revealed how it "was errati-cally and sometimes foolishly deployed" by a leader who too often confused "sincere distaste for public bombast with simple cowardice about taking strong stances" and "good intentions with concrete progress." Eisenhower may have been a general, but he would never be mistaken for a charismatic man on horseback. In the age of Sloan Wilson's *The Man in the Gray Flannel Suit* (1955), Eisenhower embraced the culture of conformity and the ethic of groupthink. His envisioned corporate commonwealth thrived on consensus and order, and he seldom challenged the conventional wisdom of the for-eign policy and business establishments. William Whyte's definition of the "organization man" as someone who cared less about his own "creativity than supervising the work of subordinates"—someone who "preferred coopera-tion to open rivalry, managerial efficiency to disruptive debate, the 'practical team player' to the eccentric genius, getting along to getting ahead"—better describes Eisenhower's leadership style than does the popular moniker "hid-den hand presidency." Unwilling to lead, Eisenhower failed to develop an effective nuclear nonproliferation policy from 1953 to 1961. And, like Truman, he did not fully understand the intricacies of nuclear physics and the multiple avenues of potential proliferation.[4]

Eisenhower's ambivalence toward nuclear weapons shaped his early arms control policy and breathed life into the Panel of Consultants' report (still sitting on the Oval Office desk as Truman left office). As the new adminis-tration digested and reworked the group's recommendations, it produced an atomic energy proposal with important implications for U.S. nonprolif-eration policy. Both Eisenhower and Secretary of State John Foster Dulles, however, questioned the panel's recommendation to de-emphasize the UN as a forum for disarmament negotiations, instead embracing Vice President Richard M. Nixon's advice to make a "sensational offer" to the Soviets and "put them on the spot."[5]

The president's contradictory attitudes toward nuclear weapons also colored his reaction to other recommendations of the panel. He readily en-dorsed the group's call for increased nuclear cooperation with NATO allies and a more robust defense against an attack on North America. But its ad-vocacy of public openness and its approach to arms control troubled him. Full disclosure of nuclear dangers might violate the security provisions of the Atomic Energy Act. His experience as president of Columbia University had taught him that scientists—such as Oppenheimer and Bush—had a limited grasp of the need for secrecy. Both men had endorsed the publication of the

Smyth Report, the government account of the Manhattan Project, which he regarded as a serious breach of atomic security. Still, Eisenhower agreed to a "candor" study group composed of staff from the AEC, the Psychological Strategy Board, the CIA, and the Defense and State Departments.

While the ad hoc committee deliberated, the unexpected death of Joseph Stalin on March 5 increased debate about a new approach to Moscow. Prior rumors of Stalin's illness had prompted C. D. Jackson, the special assistant to the president for psychological warfare, to examine how best to exploit the confusion surrounding a period of leadership transition. He argued that the United States should keep Moscow off balance while Eisenhower formulated plans to preempt any possible Soviet peace offensive. Those in the government who believed in "liberation" of the Soviet Union and its satellites thought this an especially propitious moment to aggressively undercut Soviet power. But before any U.S. psywar efforts came to fruition, the new Soviet leader, Georgii M. Malenkov, signaled his willingness to relax Cold War tensions, proclaiming the goal of "peaceful coexistence" between capitalist and communist powers.

Eisenhower dismissed the new regime's stance as a rhetorical ploy. Wanting to gain the propaganda advantage, Jackson urged Ike to accept a summit meeting. But Dulles trumped him with a proposal that scrapped calls for a summit and instead asked for proof of Soviet peaceful intentions through positive steps toward ending the wars in Korea and French Indochina. Eisenhower combined this suggestion with a disarmament proposal recently sent to him by Samuel Lubell, a syndicated columnist and Bernard Baruch's close friend. Lubell's plan emphasized the drain the armaments race placed on world living standards. The president believed that, given the relative poverty of Eastern European and Soviet peoples in comparison to the West, such an approach would provide an effective public relations tool and might actually elicit a positive response from Malenkov.

A month later, Eisenhower delivered his "The Chance for Peace" speech to the American Society of Newspaper Editors. One biographer labeled it Eisenhower's finest speech, albeit "still propaganda." The president stressed that "every gun that is made, every warship launched, every rocket fired signifies, in the final sense, a theft from those who hunger and are not fed, those who are cold and are not clothed." He expressed what seemed to be a deep commitment to ending the arms race and challenged the Soviets to demonstrate their commitment to peace through actions, such as ending the Korean War. Both at home and abroad, commentators reacted positively. But whatever hope Eisenhower had had of using the address to ease U.S.-Soviet tensions evaporated two days later when Dulles delivered to the same group of editors "a business as usual Cold War speech." The differing tones left Malenkov questioning whether Dulles or Eisenhower had expressed the real U.S. position. The secretary of state's speech was severely attacked in the Soviet press, but even the president received brickbats for listing multiple preconditions for initiating negotiations. The Soviets may have also wondered how much stock to place in Eisenhower's peace rhetoric given that he simultaneously sent the People's Republic of China (PRC) nuclear threats to coerce a Korean settlement.[6]

As the diplomatic and propaganda effects of "The Chance for Peace" speech subsided, two disarmament study groups delivered their findings to the NSC. The ad hoc group analyzing the Panel of Consultants' report strongly endorsed a policy of nuclear openness, which it dubbed Operation Candor. But the NSC executive committee on arms regulation adopted the consultants' proposal for stall tactics in the UN Disarmament Commission. Even though both superpowers viewed public disarmament proposals as shams, Eisenhower hesitated to abandon the UN talks because they provided the only existing forum for disarmament negotiations. Yet he nurtured even deeper reservations about a policy of candor. The dilemma hinged on the question of how much and what kind of information could be safely disclosed. The president feared that too much information already had become public, even as he conceded that a free government needed an informed public to function properly. He ordered his aides to draft several "candor" speeches to help him decide whether to deliver some version thereof. Later he told a key aide, "Keep them confused as to fission and fusion." Apparently complete truthfulness about the greater destructive power of thermonuclear weapons could backfire, leading to a collapse of public resolve to counter the communist threat.[7]

By early September, the NSC had postponed Operation Candor. The AEC and the Defense Department questioned its benefits. Dulles reluctantly acceded, despite believing that "the United States was doing itself a great disservice by surrounding atomic weapons with a cloak of silence and mystery. This . . . only adds to the tendency to place these weapons in a category apart from all other weapons and to reinforce the idea that their use was immoral. We tie our own hands with this taboo." During the policy debates, AEC chairman Strauss displayed the same obsessive commitment to atomic secrecy he had demonstrated during his earlier tenure on the commission. Strauss had consistently influenced nuclear policy from 1946 to 1958, beginning with his appointment by Truman as one of the original atomic energy commissioners as a concession to congressional conservatives to counterbalance the first chairman, David Lilienthal, a liberal New Dealer. Whereas Lilienthal was linked with the conservatives' bête noir Franklin Roosevelt, the admiral had long admired Herbert Hoover, beginning with his service as Hoover's aide in the Food Relief Administration during World War I. He then became a wealthy investment banker during the 1920s. During World War II, he entered the navy, rising to the rank of rear admiral, a title he preferred for the rest of his life. Since he never served afloat, critics derisively called him the Tugboat Admiral. At this time, he also drew the attention of a fellow virulent anticommunist and nuclear nationalist, Secretary of the Navy James Forrestal, and worked as his special assistant throughout the war.[8]

During his long stay in government service, Strauss displayed the influence of his two mentors, Hoover and Forrestal. From them, he imbibed a seething hatred of communism, a deep faith in laissez-faire economics, and a conviction that his own diligent guardianship of the nation's security was needed to counteract the softheadedness of liberal policymakers. His unquestioning faith in these precepts led him to mount ruthless campaigns against his political opponents, including his subsequent notorious vendetta against Oppenheimer. The noted physicist found out that if one disagreed with Strauss, he "assumes you're just a fool at first. But if you go on disagreeing with him, he concludes you must be a traitor." During his first term on the AEC, Strauss emerged as one of the staunchest guardians of the so-called nuclear secret. He urged terminating nuclear cooperation with Great Britain and Canada, pushed for expanded intelligence efforts against the Soviet nuclear program, and stridently advocated a hydrogen bomb program. After a brief stint on Wall Street, he eagerly returned in 1953 as Eisenhower's chairman of the AEC and special adviser on atomic energy. From that year until 1958, he once again protected the nuclear arsenal against perceived communist machinations and punished anyone who questioned his policies.[9]

Robert Oppenheimer's connection with the disarmament panel immediately roused Strauss's suspicions. The two had become rivals during the early days of the commission. Oppenheimer, then chair of the GAC, often testified in favor of sharing peaceful nuclear technology with other countries. On one occasion, Strauss opposed the export of radioactive isotopes lest they be used to develop radiological weapons. When the AEC voted in favor of selling them abroad, the rear admiral vigorously dissented. A livid Strauss then leaked negative information on the program to Senator Hickenlooper. During a JCAE investigation of the commission's management practices, Strauss hyperbolically testified that the isotope export program compromised U.S.

national security. Refuting the admiral's testimony, Oppenheimer compared the isotopes' contribution to nuclear weapons development to that of shovels, bottles of beer, and vitamins. This humiliating gibe infuriated Strauss, igniting a feud that still raged in 1953.

Strauss initially saw Oppenheimer as merely arrogant and rude. Once he discovered the scientist's flirtation with radical politics in the 1930s, he decided that the "father of the atomic bomb" posed a major security risk. Strauss thought Oppenheimer's policy of openness might mask an attempt to reveal classified information to the Soviets. The panel's report also angered the admiral because it implicitly accused the government of adopting an "unfairly and stupidly secretive" atomic energy policy. When Oppenheimer published a widely praised declassified version of the panel's findings, Strauss claimed that the reception must have been orchestrated in advance and counterpunched by covertly recruiting *Fortune* magazine columnist Charles J. V. Murphy to write a piece discrediting Oppenheimer.[10]

Strauss actually had little cause for worry because Operation Candor had already developed laryngitis. C. D. Jackson had written several drafts of a speech, but Eisenhower rejected them as leaving "everybody dead on both sides with no hope anywhere." He told Jackson to include some reason for optimism or he would not approve the project. In early September a news leak by columnist Stewart Alsop further wounded the program when it revealed administration plans to use the speech to justify its increased emphasis on nuclear weapons. Faced with resistance from the AEC and the State and Defense Departments, as well as presidential ambivalence, Operation Candor appeared dead in early September 1953.[11]

Atoms for Peace

Operation Candor, however, found new voice on September 10 when Eisenhower proposed creating a UN atomic bank to which the United States and the Soviet Union could commit unspecified amounts of fissionable material designated for peaceful purposes. Precise contributions would be set at levels that the United States could easily handle but would hamper Soviet nuclear development. The policy had to finesse the basic reality that economical nuclear power production could not be developed for at least another decade. Ike sought implementation advice from Strauss. Since taking over the AEC in July 1953, Strauss had persistently downplayed the technical difficulties besetting nuclear power and had attempted to spur research by allowing private utility companies access to government data. To both Eisenhower and the

AEC chair, the government monopoly on atomic power development raised the specter of a publicly owned nuclear energy industry modeled on the Tennessee Valley Authority, a model that smacked of "creeping socialism." Their commitment to privatizing nuclear power quickly exerted its influence on U.S. foreign policy.[12]

When the president asked for an infusion of hope in the draft "Candor" speeches, Strauss quickly proposed peaceful uses. Throughout the summer of 1953, the admiral's informal adviser, Stefan T. Possony, sent him memoranda hyping "the sunny side of the atom." Possony, like Strauss, drank deeply from the well of extreme anticommunism. Throughout the Cold War, he shuttled between positions in military intelligence and conservative academic think tanks, including a stint as the director of international studies at the Hoover Institution at Stanford University. He also joined numerous anticommunist lobbying groups, including the Committee on the Present Danger, the American Security Council, and the U.S. affiliate of the World Anti-Communist League. Responding to Strauss's request for advice, Possony revealed his deep faith in technological utopianism and the U.S. sense of mission, arguing that the president's speech could demonstrate that "the nuclear resource fundamentally is a positive and beneficial force." Rather than focus on American and Soviet stockpiles and destructive capabilities, the Eisenhower administration should explain how nuclear power would eliminate economic scarcity and invalidate the Marxist doctrine of class struggle. Possony's memorandum appealed to Strauss's "almost naive faith" in science, prompting him to jot "good ideas" in its margins.[13]

In early October, Strauss combined Possony's and Eisenhower's proposals to suggest using the atomic pool concept as the cornerstone of a new disarmament plan. All the nuclear powers would cease uranium, thorium, and plutonium production for ten years, with the exception of one plutonium production reactor for research purposes. Restricted production and annual contributions would yield gradual disarmament. This proposal still rested on Eisenhower's intention to establish mandatory contribution levels that would not slow U.S. nuclear development but would hamper the Soviet program. The admiral also proposed a World Atomic Power Administration to control fissionable materials donated from the United States, Great Britain, and the Soviet Union. Any country could utilize these deposits for peaceful purposes.[14]

The plutonium and uranium would be stored underground in inaccessible vaults, "preferably in solution or other inconvenient form, guarded by nuclear eunuchs." Strauss's gendered language reflected a widespread practice among

U.S. policymakers of coding perceived political and military threats in psycho-sexual terms. International "potency" hinged on nuclear strength; only non-nuclear powers ("eunuchs") could be trusted not to sully the atomic "harem" because they had no power to do so and would long remain dependent on Western largesse to develop their own nuclear industries. Strauss also conveyed a double meaning with this language, for these eunuchs not only lacked nuclear armaments — they often espoused neutrality in the Cold War. Strauss implicitly invoked the cultural stereotype of the leading neutral nation, India, and its followers in the nonaligned movement as lacking virility and martial skill — a bias shared by Eisenhower and his advisers, who often referred to the "feminine hypersensitiveness" and "emotional" manner of Indian policy-makers. These characteristics inspired contempt for their military and technological aptitudes and anger toward the neutrals' unwillingness to take sides in the Cold War.[15]

Eisenhower and Jackson immediately recognized that Strauss's proposals offered the means to save Operation Candor as well as the president's atomic pool scheme. Beginning in November, the AEC chairman and the "psywar" adviser used a series of breakfast meetings, dubbed "Operation Wheaties," to combine the candor and atom bank proposals. By month's end, the "Atoms for Peace" proposal had taken its final form. The numerous reworkings of the speech, moreover, transformed Strauss's original plan. Jackson renamed the atomic bank the International Atomic Energy Agency (IAEA) to distinguish the organization from the Atomic Development Authority in the Baruch Plan. The Defense Department made the most substantive change when it deleted all references to a production cutoff of fissionable materials, not wishing to even hint that it might have to halt its nuclear weapons buildup. This final change removed any real disarmament component. Even if nuclear countries made annual deposits to the IAEA, they could simply replace any loss to their stockpiles through increased production. Eisenhower ignored this important revision and penciled into the speech the claim that Atoms for Peace constituted the first step toward nuclear arms control.[16]

Had Eisenhower sincerely desired negotiations with the Soviets, he should have heeded Dulles and opted for confidential, bilateral talks. The president instead aspired to make a stirring speech because he primarily valued Atoms for Peace as a Cold War weapon. Jackson shared that goal. Changing the audience for the speech from the American people to the world community by switching the venue to the UN, Jackson contrived to have the proposal selected as "Story of the Year" by the Associated Press as he promoted Eisenhower for the Nobel Peace Prize. Jackson's technical ignorance of nuclear power further led him to make wild assertions about U.S. abilities to provide immediate benefits to the power-starved areas of the world. He excited people's imaginations at the eventual cost of disillusionment when American promises fizzled.[17]

Strauss chose not to correct his collaborator's mistakes. By exaggerating the benefits of nuclear power, the speech helped the AEC chairman achieve several goals. First, it increased pressure on the JCAE to liberalize the Atomic Energy Act so that private companies could develop nuclear technologies. Second, the new plan voided the Baruch Plan's call for international development of nuclear power. The United States would still aid other countries in the nuclear field, but with a new program that targeted American entrepreneurs as the main agents for spreading nuclear technology around the world, ensuring that private companies reaped the financial benefits from the "peaceful atom." As under Truman's Marshall Plan for Europe and his Point IV program aimed at the developing world, private firms would spread American products around the globe and demonstrate the technological development and prosperity possible under liberal capitalism. Third, the AEC chairman used the atomic pool proposal to diminish the impact of the candor portions of the speech. After Eisenhower delivered the address on December 8, Strauss gloated when the press and public ignored the nuclear revelations in the first three-quarters of the address, contending that the lack of attention vindicated his opposition to Operation Candor.[18]

Although a propaganda success, Atoms for Peace produced unintended consequences. Because neither Jackson nor Strauss possessed sufficient technical knowledge of nuclear physics, they misjudged the potential for nuclear proliferation. Their insistence on secrecy prevented nuclear experts from examining the text and inserting safeguard provisions to prevent the diversion of fissionable material from power plants to military uses. U.S. policymakers ignored the primary finding of previous disarmament studies, namely, that peaceful and military technologies cannot be segregated. Claiming to beat swords into plowshares, the Eisenhower administration ignored the fact that nuclear plowshares could be recast as swords.[19]

When British prime minister Winston Churchill warned the president about the proliferation dangers latent in Atoms for Peace, Eisenhower brushed his worries aside and asserted that the materials and information promised under the plan would not constitute a threat. Blinded by his own faith in U.S. technology, the president made this claim before consulting the scientists on the GAC, whose advice he solicited only after the UN speech. Even then, the GAC neglected the proliferation problem and concentrated on the political benefits of the plan. The administration appeared more concerned with a sudden military seizure of the uranium and plutonium stores than with any gradual diversion of fissionable materials from nuclear reactors into weapons development. The Defense Department, in particular, downgraded the proliferation threat, worrying instead that Atoms for Peace and domestic power development might diminish the amount of uranium and plutonium available for military programs.[20]

Few outside commentators noted the proliferation danger either. Congressional leaders, the press, and foreign governments generally praised Atoms for Peace. Even some American peace groups supported the plan. The speech, however, did receive some criticism. The Indian government characterized its call for an international organization to control nuclear technology as a new variety of colonialism. A few disarmament advocates believed it failed to go far enough and noted its lack of safeguards. Henry D. Smyth, the only nuclear scientist on the AEC, blasted Atoms for Peace as a "thoroughly dishonest proposal" because it ignored proliferation dangers and exaggerated current prospects for nuclear power. Nuclear nationalists sarcastically labeled the plan "Watts for Hottentots" and lambasted it as an ill-conceived government giveaway program.[21]

Nor did the proposal escape further resistance within the government. Strauss himself doubted Atoms for Peace after his adviser Possony excoriated the address as a transparent propaganda ploy rife with the language of appeasement. Strauss then had Possony draft a clarification that avoided mention of disarmament and stressed the plan's reliance on free enterprise to produce the myriad benefits of nuclear power. The Defense Department soon joined Strauss's efforts to eliminate any references to arms control when discussing Atoms for Peace.[22]

Eisenhower and his advisers had stitched together Atoms for Peace from several familiar ideological strands. The United States, fulfilling its world missionary role, would use its status as an exemplar to other nations to advance the fruits of free enterprise and of American scientific genius. As one commentator later put it, "Providence bestowed atomic energy on the United States" and with this gift came a duty to use it for "the common good of all mankind." Atoms for Peace also displayed a strong element of technological utopianism, plunging ahead with the smug assumption that safeguards could be developed to inhibit weapons development before any study had examined the issue. This supposition proved false, and ironclad safeguards against plutonium and uranium diversion proved elusive into the twenty-first century.[23]

The domestic response to the speech meant little as long as the most important audience of the president's speech, the Soviet leadership, responded positively. But the new group in Moscow sent mixed signals. In public, the Soviets vilified the proposal, claiming it did nothing to reduce the threat of nuclear war and labeling Eisenhower's tone "warmongering." In private, Moscow sought to explore U.S. suggestions for confidential, bilateral discussions. The Soviets, however, insisted on linking a complete nuclear weapons ban with Atoms for Peace. While diplomats from both countries groped for an acceptable formula for negotiations, both the Soviet and U.S. governments waged a propaganda battle over the president's proposal. C. D. Jackson continued to tout schemes, such as building a nuclear reactor in Berlin as a demonstration of Western advancement, while the Soviets hammered away at the absence of any concrete disarmament provisions in the U.S. plan.[24]

In late December, Ambassador Charles Bohlen told the Soviets that while the president would entertain any "workable disarmament proposal," the primary goal of the U.S. negotiators would be an agreement on peaceful uses. Moscow accepted U.S. conditions but would not conclude a peaceful uses agreement unless the talks produced progress on disarmament. Although the superpowers had agreed to bilateral discussion of nuclear matters for the first time, their differing goals made another diplomatic stalemate likely.[25]

Twin Explosions: The *Lucky Dragon* and the Test Moratorium

The new administration entered its second year without a coherent nuclear nonproliferation policy. Despite Eisenhower's repudiation of Truman's policies during the 1952 campaign, Ike's approach to nuclear proliferation resembled his predecessor's. Neither Truman nor Eisenhower had a deep understanding of the problem, and each unwisely diminished the U.S. commitment to defuse it. Both presidents also resolved to make the United States predominant in nuclear weapons and sought to develop deliverable thermonuclear weapons with little regard for the way this effort complicated nonproliferation efforts. Eisenhower culminated these trends by proposing Atoms for Peace.

In 1954, two explosions, one thermonuclear and the other diplomatic, awakened American nonproliferation policy from its half-decade slumber. The first blast occurred in the Marshall Islands, a U.S.-administered UN trusteeship. There the AEC detonated its first deliverable hydrogen bomb, code-named *Bravo*, on March 1, 1954. The explosion of fifteen megatons left a crater 250 feet deep and one mile wide in the ocean floor, while the blast's fireball expanded outward for nearly four miles. Radioactive material spread well past the boundaries of the fifty-thousand-square-mile danger zone surrounding the test site, bathing American servicemen, scientists, and the peoples of the Marshall Islands in dangerous radiation. U.S. physicists had estimated a yield of only five megatons, but they had miscalculated the reaction in the bomb core, allowing the experiment to run nearly out of control.

The Eisenhower team downplayed the unexpected results. The AEC simply announced that a minor accident had occurred during a routine nuclear test. But the AEC's public relations campaign collapsed when reports emanated from Japan about a crew of ill fishermen. On March 14, the ironically named Japanese tuna trawler, *Fukuryu Maru* No. 5 (the *Lucky Dragon*), returned to its home port carrying irradiated fish and a crew that exhibited signs of radiation sickness. The American and world public demanded an immediate and full explanation. Eisenhower had hoped to delay any public statements until month's end when AEC chairman Strauss returned from observing the nuclear test series. But, during a press conference on March 24, the president admitted that the explosion's intensity had "surprised and astonished the scientists." Meanwhile, Secretary of State John Foster Dulles received pleas from NATO allies to end the public relations debacle. Dulles warned the AEC chair that the "hysteria" surrounding the *Lucky Dragon* exposure could turn U.S. allies away from NATO and produce "polic[ies] of neutrality and appeasement." Strauss characterized the incident as "grossly exaggerated" by people "who wish we did not have such a weapon and don't care if Russia has it."[26]

Once back in Washington, the AEC chair continued spewing out outrageous accusations. He told Eisenhower's press secretary James Hagerty that the *Lucky Dragon* was probably part of a "Red spy outfit" and implied that the contaminated fish were part of a Soviet plot. He ludicrously exclaimed, "If I were the Reds I would fill the oceans all over the world with radioactive fish. It would be easy to do!" Although less inflammatory, the admiral's statements during a March 31 press conference agitated, rather than soothed, public worries. He assured the American people that fallout posed no health threat and promised that the Marshall Islanders and fishermen would recover fully. Despite ample evidence to the contrary, he also claimed that contamination of the ship had occurred only because it had strayed well within the boundaries of the exclusion zone. If Strauss had stopped there, he might have calmed public opinion. But, during the question period, he stumbled in admitting that a hydrogen bomb could destroy any city, even New York. The next day, headlines across the country featured the admiral's apocalyptic remarks.[27]

The Eisenhower administration also badly mishandled Japan's profound fear and anger over the *Lucky Dragon* crew's plight. This mood helped make the low-budget science fiction film *Gojira* a sensation in 1954 (the film arrived in the United States in 1956, retitled *Godzilla*). Depicting a mutant, rampaging dinosaur roused from his slumber on the ocean floor by U.S. nuclear tests, it served as a powerful allegory for the horrors of nuclear weapons and a forum for anti-American sentiments over the damage that Japan had suffered at the hands of American nuclear bombs. Washington had no clue how to respond. Initial U.S. claims that the incident was orchestrated by Japanese communists to embarrass the West had to be quickly jettisoned in the face of overwhelming evidence to the contrary. Washington next shifted the onus to Japan's emotional instability and atomic psychosis, which allegedly made the Japanese people "pathologically sensitive" to further deaths from nuclear exposure. The Japanese scientists and doctors who had warned against the contaminated fish supply were merely "fuzzy-minded leftists, pacifists, neutralists." The U.S. government had to counteract the increased influence of these naysayers and their supposed allies — "feminists and professional anti-Americans" — and encourage "tougher-minded" Japanese governments that displayed a more rational outlook on nuclear weapons. Such callousness to Japanese sentiments did not fade with the death of one of the fishermen, Kuboyama Aikichi. Some U.S. doctors insisted that Japanese physicians were wrong in attributing the death to radiation exposure, claiming that Kuboyama had died due to jaundice stemming from improper blood transfusions. Washington issued perfunctory apologies and monetary compensation only after it became obvious that the *Lucky Dragon* incident had produced a grave crisis in Japanese-American relations.[28]

The negative publicity intensified when publications around the world ran stories about the potential dangers of fallout and the genocidal implications of thermonuclear war. American opinion fragmented, with some voices clamoring for a test moratorium and others declaring that a large nuclear arsenal protected the United States from the Soviet threat. The U.S. public was clearly worried but never showed any enthusiasm for privately constructed fallout shelters, even in the face of repeated government urgings. The *Bulletin of the Atomic Scientists* did place the hands of the Doomsday Clock at two minutes to midnight — the closest to nuclear Armageddon they would ever be. The international outcry proved more intense and more worrisome. Dulles presciently warned that if Strauss kept "shooting off these big bombs," U.S. allies might demand an immediate nuclear disarmament agreement. Within days, calls for an end to thermonuclear tests sounded around the world. In Britain, the minority Labour Party introduced a resolution supporting a great-power summit to negotiate a test ban, which the Conservatives, led by Prime Minister Winston Churchill, defeated only when they promised to seek such a conference in the near future. In Asia, negative sentiment toward nuclear testing ran even higher, with many voicing consternation that Asian people had suffered most from nuclear weapons. In Japan, 78 percent of the public opposed all nuclear testing under any circumstance, while on April 2, Indian prime minister Jawaharlal Nehru emphatically called for an immediate test moratorium and UN negotiations toward a comprehensive disarmament agreement.[29]

Dulles had seen and heard enough. During an NSC meeting on April 6, he scribbled a note to the president advising the administration to "consider whether we could advantageously agree to Nehru proposal of no further experimental explosions." The moratorium concept gained quick support from UN ambassador Henry Cabot Lodge and the British government, although both thought it better to limit only very large explosions. A public relations victory, not arms control, emerged as the primary motivation of test ban proponents in the Eisenhower administration. The president wanted to get off the defensive and announce a test moratorium. He urged subordinates to complete the technical studies in time for his May commencement address at Columbia University. That April, both Pope Pius XII and noted humanitarian Dr. Albert Schweitzer importuned the United States and the Soviet Union to halt nuclear experiments.[30]

While the Eisenhower administration pondered a moratorium, the United States took a propaganda beating on nuclear testing. Washington attempted to balance the Cold War scales by building on the goodwill engendered by the president's Atoms for Peace proposal. Bilateral negotiations with the Soviets, however, inched forward. Since January 1954, the two powers had exchanged numerous diplomatic notes, and Dulles and Soviet foreign minister Vyacheslav Molotov had talked informally during a Four Power Conference in Berlin. But little of substance had emerged. Some officials worried that a valuable Cold War initiative would be frittered away.

A potentially critical meeting between Dulles and Molotov occurred during the Geneva Conference on Korea and Indochina in May. The secretary of state arrived in Geneva prepared for Soviet objections. Since Eisenhower's speech in December 1953, the Soviets had repeatedly criticized Atoms for Peace for failing to reduce the risk of nuclear war. In Geneva, Dulles worked to deflect Soviet claims that the U.S. plan fell short of Eisenhower's rhetoric, did not reduce nuclear stockpiles, and failed to ban the use of atomic weapons. He vigorously defended Atoms for Peace as a confidence-building measure, which might inspire further progress on disarmament.[31]

Molotov, however, held fast in maintaining that Eisenhower's proposal "might lead to an increase in the amount of materials and bombs" in the hands of other nations. The secretary of state floundered for a reply, ultimately claiming, in direct contradiction to U.S. studies, that Atoms for Peace would actually decrease the amount of fissionable material for weapons use. Both statesmen soon confessed that they lacked the technical knowledge to discuss proliferation dangers associated with peaceful uses, but Molotov refused to retreat from his original position. Soviet scientists had warned their government in early April that disseminating knowledge about nuclear power technology also meant increasing the number of nations capable of producing nuclear weapons. The Eisenhower administration's failure to attend to this obvious danger had now produced diplomatic embarrassment. Faced with Molotov's insistence that U.S. physicists could confirm the Soviet position, Dulles lamely promised to "seek out a scientist to educate him more fully."[32]

Dulles took the Soviet reply at Geneva as a tacit rejection of Atoms for Peace. But he had little time to focus on this setback before the test ban issue commanded his attention. Pressure to limit nuclear experiments mounted on multiple fronts. At Geneva, British foreign minister Anthony Eden told Dulles that scientific opinion in the United Kingdom supported a ban on all tests larger than fifty kilotons. He also hinted that London expected the United States to expand nuclear collaboration in exchange for London's cooperation on a test ban.[33] Britain's quid pro quo would have required the Eisenhower administration to persuade the congressional Republican majority to abandon its nuclear nationalism. Relaxation of the Atomic Energy Act's restricted-data provisions might also have prompted requests for nuclear data from other countries, such as France and West Germany.

Dulles could not dwell on the potential diplomatic and political costs of British support for a test moratorium. Although the U.S. test series ended in May, hostility toward testing increased, convincing Dulles and Eisenhower to consider a U.S. test limitation proposal. At an NSC meeting on May 6, the two leaders argued that a test moratorium might freeze the U.S. lead while providing a "psychological advantage" in the Cold War. Exclaiming, "Everybody seems to think we're skunks, saber-rattlers, and warmongers," Eisenhower backed a test moratorium as a means to reaffirm America's peaceful intentions. But Admiral Strauss and Pentagon officials feared Soviet cheating and did not believe that the United States had a decisive advantage in nuclear technology.[34]

The policy debate in 1954 established the contours of the bureaucratic struggle over a test ban for the remainder of the decade. The AEC, the CIA, and the Defense Department all rejected a test moratorium as undermining U.S. national security. Even Dulles backed away from a test ban after he realized that such a proposal might "boomerang" to the Soviet Union's advantage by allowing Moscow to renew demands to outlaw nuclear weapons or else present a more sweeping test ban agreement. Dulles had little empathy for the world antinuclear movement, arguing that "it was implausible to him why it was moral to kill ten thousand people with ten weapons but immoral to do so with one." The anti–test ban consensus within the bureaucracy led to the curious spectacle of Eisenhower's having to justify his support for a test moratorium during a May 27 NSC meeting. Claiming that the United States could not afford "to take a negative view of this terrible problem," the president reaffirmed his contention that elimination or reduction of nuclear weapons offered the most effective insurance of U.S. security. He argued that, absent control measures, even "little countries" would add them to their arsenals. Strauss snapped back that it would be "quite a long time before little countries" posed a nuclear threat, while Secretary of the Treasury George Humphrey questioned whether Eisenhower "really believed that the Soviets would honor a promise to stop conducting weapons tests." The president nonetheless refused to accept the majority opinion and asked for further examination of the issue.[35]

The new round of studies merely reconfirmed positions taken earlier. Secretary of Defense Charles Wilson effectively summarized the anti–test ban position when he claimed that the propaganda benefits of a test moratorium could not compensate for the potential decline of the U.S. technological advantage, given that the Soviets would inevitably evade the inspection provisions in a test ban treaty. With the national security bureaucracy lining up in opposition to a test ban, Dulles had little trouble composing a unanimous report. Eisenhower relented and endorsed his advisers' rejection of a test moratorium "a hundred percent." The organization man had prevailed.[36]

Going through the Motions

Abandoning the test ban idea also shifted attention away from nonproliferation. Dulles did warn publicly of the proliferation danger, but U.S. policies soon fell into the familiar pattern of selective proliferation. The president continued trying to shrink America's defense budget by increasing its reliance on nuclear weapons. This strategy also expanded NATO's access to nuclear munitions. In late 1953, the United States began stockpiling tactical nuclear weapons in Europe, under nominal American control. The Eisenhower administration simultaneously proposed amending the Atomic Energy Act to allow for expanded technical collaboration with U.S. allies, especially Great Britain.

This proposal met with great resistance in Congress and within the bureaucracy, especially from the Defense Department and the AEC. Faced with a divided NSC, the president moved slowly. He expanded the exchange of information with Great Britain to the limits allowed by the Atomic Energy Act but delayed seeking amendments to the law. London quickly grew impatient. Winston Churchill had hailed Eisenhower's election, knowing that the former general had long advocated increased Anglo-American nuclear collaboration. But Ike in his first year liberalized few restricted-data regulations, and Churchill warned that Britain would accept nothing less than restoration of the wartime nuclear alliance. At the Bermuda Conference, in December 1953, the French also demanded close nuclear ties with the Americans. Eisenhower accordingly asked that the Atomic Energy Act be amended to enable transfer of fissionable material to the IAEA and greater nuclear cooperation with Britain and France. Congressional opposition mushroomed as Senator Bourke Hickenlooper reaffirmed his long-standing opposition to "giving away our atomic secrets to any foreign countries."[37]

Soon both the British and the French governments discussed expanding and linking their own nuclear programs. In summer 1954, Britain told Washington that it had authorized development of a hydrogen bomb, while the French bureaucracy incrementally moved toward its own nuclear capability. In August 1954, after Congress finally approved amendments to the Atomic Energy Act that allowed bilateral peaceful uses and limited military data cooperation, British and French worries actually intensified because the new provisions still barred weapons information. Leaders in both countries also feared that a test ban agreement might relegate them to permanent nuclear inferiority. They hence accelerated their own weapons programs and pursued discussions with other Western European countries to create a regional military organization independent of U.S. influence.[38]

By mid-1954, Eisenhower's nuclear policies were in a muddle, beleaguered on multiple fronts. The Soviets seemed unwilling to cooperate with Atoms for Peace unless it included links to disarmament. International public opinion demanded a test moratorium, which the U.S. bureaucracy adamantly rejected. Congress voiced qualms about encouraging peaceful uses and expanding NATO access to nuclear weapons and data. Each setback seemed to reinforce the others. Allies who had cheered American willingness to share nuclear data in January worried about the consequences of nuclear fallout. When U.S. policy stalled on both nuclear cooperation and test limitation, NATO members questioned the alliance's reliance on nuclear weapons, especially if the United States refused to abandon its thermonuclear monopoly.

Faced with these problems, Eisenhower resorted to nuclear propaganda. National Security Adviser Robert Cutler and UN Ambassador Lodge proposed creating the IAEA without Soviet cooperation. But Dulles wanted one more stab at winning Soviet acceptance. He asked the Soviets for renewed discussion of Atoms for Peace but rejected Molotov's call for a link between peaceful uses and disarmament. "Ways can be devised," Dulles claimed, to prevent diversion of fissionable materials to weapons programs. The secretary, however, still had not consulted scientists on the feasibility of that premise.[39]

The Soviets also ignored their own warnings about the link between proliferation and peaceful uses. In January 1955, Moscow announced that it would provide Eastern European countries and China with nonmilitary nuclear aid in exchange for nuclear raw materials. While the Soviets withheld weapons-grade uranium for use in reactors and required the return of spent fuel for chemical reprocessing, they overlooked the likelihood that dissemination of technical knowledge raised proliferation risks. In the mid-1950s, both superpowers exploited nuclear technology for interalliance purposes with little regard for the strategic consequences.

Eisenhower's impatience forced the secretary of state to push Atoms for Peace forward without awaiting a Soviet reply. The UN propaganda battle over nuclear testing had damaged U.S. prestige, and Atoms for Peace seemed the most promising palliative. Although the United States had prevented any UN action to condemn American testing, both India and the Soviet Union had effectively used the UN General Assembly and the Trusteeship Committee to criticize U.S. nuclear experiments. By moving ahead with Atoms for Peace and using U.S. propaganda to shift world attention to Soviet nuclear testing, the Eisenhower administration hoped to win back the goodwill of the developing world.[40]

With this new impetus, the U.S. bureaucracy reinvigorated its efforts to implement Atoms for Peace. By August 1954, however, opposition from the Soviet Union and the U.S. Congress had whittled down the scope of the project. The Soviet refusal to participate eliminated its utility as a confidence-building measure, while Congress had included provisions within the Atomic Energy Act amendments that reduced the powers and responsibilities of the IAEA. Senator John W. Bricker, a leading Republican on the JCAE and persistent critic of supranational organizations, had revised the executive branch's bill to preserve strict congressional control over fissionable material by requiring congressional approval of all bilateral cooperation agreements. He also stipulated that any treaty creating an IAEA had to conform to existing U.S. restricted-data regulations. These changes effectively killed Eisenhower's plan for an international atomic pool. Strauss had secretly fed Bricker damaging information to sabotage Atoms for Peace. Despite playing a central role in drafting the original proposal, the AEC chair had quickly reversed course and claimed that an atomic pool threatened U.S. control over the world supply of fissionable materials.

The NSC accordingly implemented a less ambitious version of Eisenhower's proposal. Under the new plan, most atomic energy cooperation would take the form of bilateral arrangements, and the IAEA would largely become a clearinghouse and promotional vehicle for industrial applications. Language calling for the return of spent fuel rods to the United States for reprocessing constituted the only nonproliferation measure. In an effort to make the bilateral agreements more attractive, Eisenhower further weakened this safeguard by making U.S.-controlled reprocessing voluntary. The administration thus left open the threat that countries would divert plutonium created in nuclear reactors to weapons purposes. Proliferation concerns receded as the president focused on dispelling the negative publicity that had persisted since the *Bravo* test.[41]

The Soviets, however, blocked an American public relations coup. In late September, Moscow accepted the U.S. offer for further negotiations and recommended publication of all previous diplomatic exchanges on peaceful uses. State Department officials suspected the last as a ploy to raise the specter of nuclear proliferation. Fearful that the Soviets might sabotage any IAEA, U.S. officials could not alienate public opinion by rejecting Soviet offers to negotiate. Washington proposed a meeting of Soviet and American experts to discuss proliferation safeguards. Strauss balked, claiming that a simple solution existed: chemical reprocessing under UN supervision.[42]

U.S. officials again forged ahead before the Soviets could reply. After discussing Atoms for Peace with other countries, they realized that cooperation on peaceful uses would complicate numerous international issues. Sweeping restricted-data regulations had pent up demand in Western Europe and the developing world for nuclear technology and data. But the Western and non-Western countries had very different needs and desires. And the non-European countries that supplied the United States with uranium and other fissionable materials sought greater representation in the Atoms for Peace negotiations and the international agency's controlling bodies. Even if the Soviet Union refused to participate, cooperation on peaceful uses would require lengthier negotiations than first envisioned. Fearing that U.S. pronouncements had dangerously raised hopes, Dulles asked Lodge and UN delegate C. D. Jackson to tone down their rhetoric. When the Soviets officially accepted bilateral talks, however, the propaganda battle quickly flared up again, with both countries courting world opinion as being the authentic advocate of atomic energy cooperation. This jockeying for favor added yet another variable to the negotiations.[43]

The Eisenhower administration had had little time to assess its performance on peaceful cooperation when it became entangled in preparations for the UN Disarmament Subcommittee meeting scheduled for February 1955. The president had ordered a review of U.S. disarmament policy in 1953, but his advisers had failed to agree on a new proposal. The State Department advocated a partial arms control plan, while the Defense Department eschewed real negotiations, favoring a highly detailed comprehensive disarmament scheme designed to place the onus on the Soviet Union for its failure. The bureaucratic deadlock allowed Britain and France to seize the initiative during the 1954 subcommittee meetings. Their support for a test moratorium proposal, however, made it risky to repeat the same scenario at the 1955 sessions. Despite numerous meetings, Eisenhower's advisers produced consensus on only three items: the obsolescence of the Baruch Plan, the improbability of reaching agreement with the Soviets, and the need for a special consultant to knit together competing approaches to U.S. disarmament policy.[44]

The president thereupon selected Harold Stassen as his presidential assistant for disarmament. The former governor of Minnesota already headed the Mutual Security Administration, but this agency was about to be absorbed by the State Department. Although a longtime proponent of disarmament and world government, he seemed a poor choice for the position because he had repeatedly irritated Dulles by treading on the State Department's turf. The secretary of state approved the appointment because he hoped Stassen would become trapped in an administrative cul de sac. But Eisenhower had different motives. Beyond currying favor with moderate Republicans and reinforcing public perceptions of the U.S. commitment to disarmament, the president hoped Stassen could overcome bureaucratic hostility toward innovative arms control proposals. When a *New York Times* editorial labeled Stassen "the Secretary of Peace," Dulles barked out, "What am I? Secretary of War?" This incident deepened the rift between Stassen and Dulles as both competed for presidential approval.[45]

Eisenhower's plans faltered when Stassen took up his duties weeks after the new session of the UN Disarmament Subcommittee began, forcing the U.S. delegation to start without a firm policy in place. The administration paid heavily for this disorganization. The United States needed to use these negotiations to deflect criticism of its opposition to a test ban and to draw attention away from its sponsorship of German rearmament.

Despite its negative repercussions for world opinion, Washington could not reverse itself on German rearmament, a policy it had promoted for nearly six years. Indeed, under heavy pressure from the United States, West German chancellor Konrad Adenauer had "voluntarily" renounced production of nuclear weapons. Bonn effectively became the first state to adopt an official nonproliferation commitment. Yet Dulles and Eisenhower had two key political motives for not emphasizing Germany's nuclear self-restraint. First, Adenauer contended that when he made his public pledge, the secretary had responded with ostentatious gratitude and immediately attenuated the pledge's impact by claiming it was only valid under existing international conditions. To play up the assurance risked exposing its political expediency, not to mention inspiring public cries for all states to follow Bonn's example. As well, if Washington drew attention to the nonproliferation pledge, public scrutiny might focus on U.S. plans to place a NATO stockpile of tactical weapons within West Germany, thereby transforming that new nation into "an atomic powder keg."[46]

German rearmament also complicated attempts to quell public discontent over nuclear testing. Public pressure for a moratorium had intensified throughout 1954 and 1955. Emotions in Japan still ran high in the wake of the *Lucky Dragon* incident, while Europeans and some Americans clamored for more information on fallout dangers. Insistent that testing posed no health threat, Strauss urged a press release that disputed all negative claims and gave positive scientific data on nuclear blast effects. But Dulles opposed it, facing several dilemmas. World opinion demanded information on fallout effects, yet such data might fan public fears and put pressure on the United States to disarm unilaterally. American allies and the mass public urged the Eisenhower administration to make some positive gesture toward test limitation, even though Dulles believed this step would threaten U.S. security. Strauss, moreover, had scheduled another series of tests for spring 1955.[47]

News in February that Great Britain would release a public report on thermonuclear effects inspired U.S. reciprocation. Efforts to deflect media attention from the statement failed when the American press passed over the bulk of the report (which stressed minimal danger from global fallout) and concentrated instead on the chilling claim that an H-bomb explosion could "threaten all life in a state the size of New Jersey." Public fears mounted, pressuring world governments to act.[48]

After this public relations gaffe, the administration sought to mute the public outcry. Dulles approved renewed study of a test moratorium in preparation for the UN Disarmament Subcommittee meetings. Once again, the main question hinged on whether the propaganda benefit of a limitation agreement would outweigh the national security risks and possible technological losses. The guidance given to the U.S. disarmament delegation recommended avoiding the subject altogether, taking no public stand if raised by another participant, and, most important, letting the Soviets take the blame for rejecting test limitation. State Department intelligence estimates, nonetheless, detected a growing desire for nuclear disarmament, especially a test ban, among Europeans and the Japanese. In NATO countries, public and elite opinion registered strong support for neutralism and for the maxim that "no single power, and particularly no non-European power," should have sole responsibility for initiating nuclear war.[49]

Such findings did not reverse bureaucratic opposition to a test ban, nor did anyone on the NSC grasp that neutralist sentiment and discontent with American nuclear preeminence might inspire national nuclear forces in Europe and the rest of the world. In a letter to the president, however, Atomic Energy Commissioner Thomas Murray simplistically contended that a test moratorium would "freeze technology and limit possession to nations now having them." Murray recommended a ban only on large explosions and argued that small experiments provided sufficient insurance for the U.S. technological lead.[50]

Eisenhower used the commissioner's letter to spur another round of test-limitation studies. But few noted the nonproliferation segments of Murray's argument. Strauss set the pattern by disputing his fellow commissioner's claims that small detonations could provide sufficient nuclear data and warning that a "cynical and treacherous enemy" would surely cheat and use a moratorium to erode America's nuclear deterrent. Qualified support for test limits did emerge in the lower levels of the State Department, but senior officials rejected Murray's proposal. This intransigence allowed the Soviets to seize the initiative at the UN Disarmament Subcommittee meetings by introducing an arms control plan on May 10 that accepted many previous Western proposals and incorporated an immediate halt to testing. "Publication of the Russian disarmament manifesto today," Lodge wrote to Dulles, "makes me feel like the man who was lying on the New York Central track, knowing that the express was about to come through — and stays there and is run over." Lodge's warnings to get off the defensive on the test ban issue had gone unheeded. By permitting Britain and France to stake out the Western position in the subcommittee, the Eisenhower administration had forged no clear position on many of the Soviet proposals. An outright rejection might squander opportunities to reduce international tensions and would surely rebound to the Soviets' advantage in the court of world opinion. If the U.S. delegation negotiated further, however, it risked making uninformed and dangerous concessions. After a week of fumbling and delay, the United States pushed for a recess until June. Eisenhower's team had to ascertain whether the Soviets had made serious concessions on disarmament. Although Harold Stassen thought the proposal might be sincere, State Department analysts dismissed the plan as just another Cold War maneuver.[51]

Scholars of Soviet nuclear policy largely agree with Stassen. By 1955, Nikita S. Khrushchev, first secretary of the Communist Party, had replaced Georgii Malenkov as the dominant figure in the Soviet hierarchy. Malenkov's desire to reduce international tensions and diminish the risk of nuclear war remained central Soviet goals. The USSR's May 10 plan sought to slow the arms race in order to accelerate consumer production. Khrushchev and other Soviet leaders also wanted to impede German rearmament. But American leaders squandered this opportunity for disarmament because they would not jettison their Cold War suspicions. They searched for their own propaganda weapon rather than common ground with Moscow. Some U.S. policymakers, including Dulles and Charles Wilson, believed that the arms race actually served American security goals because the U.S. economy could outproduce the Soviets. The secretary of state used sports metaphors to deflect disarmament proposals, contending that the United States was "prepared to run a mile in competition with another runner whose distance suddenly appears to be a quarter mile." Why call off the race at the quarter-mile mark and let the Soviets off the hook? If Washington pressed the full distance, however, Moscow would have to surrender to American superiority or spend itself into financial ruin.[52]

Still, the Eisenhower administration had to answer the cries within the UN for progress on limiting nuclear testing. Even prior to the Soviet proposal, U.S. officials realized they would face another wave of test moratorium resolutions during the 1955 UN General Assembly meetings. Lodge proposed a preemptive U.S. resolution authorizing a UN scientific study to investigate the health effects of fallout. Strauss won another bureaucratic battle when he extracted promises that no restricted data would be shared with other countries, making the UN committee merely a clearinghouse for independent national studies of radiation effects. Yet the wall of secrecy surrounding nuclear fallout did not extend to corporate America. Eastman Kodak Company, for instance, received bulletins on the geographic location and intensity of fallout from nuclear tests in Nevada so that it could avoid damage to its film products—a courtesy not extended to the UN or to U.S. citizens downwind from the explosions.[53]

To mute nuclear fears, the Eisenhower administration pushed forward with Atoms for Peace. Although devoid of disarmament effects, this program did refute claims that nuclear technology provided no economic or social benefits. The United States also emphasized peaceful uses to woo newly decolonized nations into the Western camp. But peaceful uses scored few immediate propaganda points. The negotiations to establish the IAEA moved slowly, the Soviets continued to be coy about their participation, and U.S. technology proved incapable of fulfilling all the president's promises of December 1953. Bilateral cooperation treaties often amounted to paper promises because nuclear power production remained expensive and inefficient.[54]

The Rise and Fall of Harold Stassen

Stassen took up his post with great fanfare, but the glitter quickly faded. Dulles resented his acting as a free agent and cultivating the image of "secretary of peace." Stassen did win Eisenhower's support for a July 1955 summit conference with the Soviet leadership. Yet none of Stassen's ideas made it to the conference table in Geneva. He recommended disavowing the Baruch Plan and offered a nuclear standstill agreement as a replacement. He also warned that if the major powers did not progress on arms control, within ten years other countries would obtain nuclear weapons, including Canada, France, Japan, the PRC, West Germany, India, and Argentina. But he hedged on a strict commitment to nonproliferation, arguing that small nuclear forces might offer "an essential counterpoise to a growing USSR nuclear weapons threat."[55]

The rest of the NSC rejected Stassen's arguments. This continued hostility toward disarmament irked Eisenhower. If they rejected arms control, "why they did not counsel that we go to war at once with the Soviet Union?" Eisenhower nonetheless left for Geneva without a disarmament proposal. He instead offered the Soviets a plan for mutual aerial inspection divorced from arms limitation, later dubbed "Open Skies."[56]

Although Soviet premier Khrushchev rejected Open Skies as a "bald espionage plot," the new emphasis on inspection allowed Eisenhower to skirt outright rejection of the Soviets' May 10 proposals. Such tactics, however, incurred costs. The United States remained vulnerable to charges that it had rejected a test moratorium, further alienating skeptics and neutral nations.[57]

Given the cloudy future of Open Skies, Stassen needed a new U.S. disarmament plan. He emphasized nonproliferation because he feared reducing the American nuclear arsenal and believed that only the United States could be trusted with nuclear weapons. From November 1955 until the UN Disarmament Subcommittee meetings began in March 1956, dubious bureaucrats wrangled over the Stassen plan. Stassen had failed to make clear that he envisioned both a test ban and the diversion of nuclear materials to peaceful uses as nonproliferation measures. His heavy emphasis on peaceful uses as a vehicle to inhibit nuclear dissemination held little promise because the Eisenhower administration had not yet determined what safeguards to include in the Atoms for Peace program. The AEC, moreover, still viewed the IAEA as a multinational promotional agency for the nuclear energy industry, a function in tension with Stassen's plans to use that body to enforce a "no-weapons" pledge from any nation that drew on its materials and expertise. Within such a context, a test ban emerged as the only viable means to check proliferation. Even that suggestion quickly disappeared, however, in the face of vigorous opposition from the AEC and the Pentagon. Strauss argued that even a temporary moratorium would compromise "the virility of our research program." The Pentagon contended that nuclear proliferation could not be prevented and that acquisition of nuclear weapons by countries such as France and Japan would actually enhance U.S. security. Hopes of using the IAEA to advance nonproliferation also collapsed when both Strauss and Dulles objected to a "no-weapons" provision in the organization's charter. Stassen's meager proposal after months of study and preparation left Eisenhower underwhelmed with "the mountain which labored and came forth with a mouse."[58]

Stassen's failure had far-reaching implications. In 1955, nuclear proliferation had already acquired dangerous momentum. After Washington threatened to use its nuclear weapons to force the PRC to accept Taiwan's control of the islands of Jinmen (Quemoy) and Mazu (Matsu) in winter 1954–55, Chinese leaders decided to pursue their own nuclear weapons capability. The danger of Chinese proliferation intensified later in 1955 after the Soviet Union began aiding Chinese nuclear weapons research and promised to transfer a completed nuclear bomb by decade's end. France joined the Soviets in exacerbating the threat of nuclear dissemination. In 1955, while the French initiated their own weapons research, they also began supplying Israel with nuclear data. A close relationship between the two programs persisted into the 1960s.[59]

The United States also inadvertently spurred proliferation by promoting peaceful uses even after two technical studies, one by a multilateral safeguard conference, another by a U.S. government panel, concluded that no means existed to prevent diversion of fissionable materials to weapons purposes. Washington, in turn, negotiated bilateral cooperation agreements under very liberal terms. The head of the U.S. delegation to the international safeguards conference, nuclear scientist Isidor Rabi, warned that control measures needed to be devised prior to constructing U.S. reactors overseas or "even a country like India . . . would go into the weapons business." Although not directly contributing to a country's weapons program, peaceful uses aid allowed other countries to shift resources from civilian to military programs. Given resistance from India and other nonaligned countries, the Eisenhower administration failed to demand rigid safeguards in the IAEA charter. It then proceeded throughout the 1950s to provide India with nuclear materials, resources that later enabled New Delhi to produce nuclear weapons.[60]

The United States also encouraged European proliferation by helping create a European atomic energy organization, EURATOM. The Eisenhower administration viewed European atomic energy cooperation as crucial to the region's political and economic integration and ignored its implications for nuclear dissemination. EURATOM aroused some opposition from State Department officials, who urged a quid pro quo for atomic energy cooperation, and from Strauss, who labeled the plan socialistic. France, however, quickly quashed a proposed "no-weapons" pledge.[61]

Unable or unwilling to enact rigorous safeguards, the United States formed a cartel of uranium-producing countries in the hope of managing the trade in fissionable materials. But the composition of this Western Suppliers Group, which included the United Kingdom, Canada, South Africa, France, Belgium, Australia, and Portugal, ensured its failure as a nonproliferation measure. France and South Africa not only sought to produce their own nuclear weapons but also aided Israel's program. More important, the group excluded the Soviet Union, the PRC, and Czechoslovakia, three major uranium producers.

Besides enabling proliferation through nuclear power production, the

Eisenhower administration pursued expanded NATO access to atomic weapons. The president vigorously advocated relaxed restrictions on sharing nuclear data with allies and sought to persuade NATO states to incorporate tactical nuclear weapons into their "conventional" war plans. As part of its attempt to "normalize" atomic weapons, the Eisenhower administration also deployed nuclear artillery and bombs in West Germany under very loose controls.

As the UN subcommittee meetings approached, Stassen, Eisenhower, and Dulles patched together a disarmament proposal that blended Open Skies, U.S. and Soviet donations of fissionable materials for use in power reactors, and a commitment from both superpowers to stockpile all future fissionable production for uses other than "explosive weapons." Strauss had demanded changes to the original plan, which had called for cutting output to levels needed for "peaceful purposes." He feared such promises would cripple the U.S. nuclear industry and might also prevent the U.S. Navy from developing nuclear propulsion reactors. The AEC chair, as usual, won this argument, and the infelicitous phrase "explosive weapons" found its way into the U.S. plan.[62]

When Stassen revealed the new proposal to the British and French, they immediately criticized it for not addressing public demands for test limitation. Within the American government, opposition to a test moratorium remained tenacious. The JCAE, the AEC, Dulles, and even Stassen agreed that limiting tests prior to a comprehensive disarmament accord would dangerously compromise U.S. security. Earlier that year, during a state visit, British prime minister Anthony Eden had discussed test limitation with Eisenhower and other American officials and they had decided that both countries needed to continue testing. The British, however, expressed greater willingness to publicly support a moratorium in order to mute protests. The French had also hoped Washington would change its stance on test limitation. Despite such polite entreaties and evidence of increasing popular animosity toward testing both at home and abroad, the Eisenhower administration remained implacably opposed to a test moratorium.[63]

American intransigence threatened to open a breach among the Western allies. In consultations prior to the formal UN subcommittee meetings, both the British and the French delegations made clear that domestic politics required them to include a test ban in their proposals. France and Great Britain worked to persuade the United States that its plan would not effectively counter Soviet propaganda. But the Eisenhower administration rejected the French and British view of the subcommittee as merely a public relations gimmick and feared that Paris and London had failed to anticipate the consequences if the Soviets accepted their proposals.[64]

Press coverage of the Western divisions doomed the London meetings before they began. During the early sessions, the Soviets appeared content with scoring rhetorical points and probing the splits in Western attitudes. But during Khrushchev's and Soviet premier Nikolai Bulganin's April 1956 state visit to Britain, Stassen tried to draw the Soviet leaders into a substantive discussion of disarmament, with emphasis on the danger of nuclear proliferation. Khrushchev agreed that "it may be true" that many other countries would soon have the bomb but asked, "What can be done about it?" Stassen construed this noncommittal response as meaning that the Soviets might cooperate with the West in stemming the nuclear tide. But the British claimed that the Soviet leader showed no appreciation of the "fourth-country problem." After prodding by London, Khrushchev casually suggested that perhaps a test ban would help ease proliferation concerns. Both the United States and Great Britain had previously dismissed a test ban as inadequate protection against nuclear diffusion, especially because the Soviets had proposed only a thermonuclear test moratorium. Despite the obvious differences between the U.S. and Soviet attitudes toward proliferation, Stassen believed that possible "common ground" could be discovered.[65]

Upon returning to Washington, Stassen eliminated the haziness of his earlier proposal. He enumerated specific nonproliferation and selective proliferation measures designed to maintain U.S. control over Western nuclear policy: limitations on production of fissionable material; creation of both a small UN nuclear weapons force, dubbed "Atoms for Police," and an elite NATO group armed with tactical weapons and atomic bombs; a comprehensive U.S.-British nuclear alliance; gradual transfer of previously produced fissionable material to peaceful purposes; and a nuclear test ban. He also added the stricture that the United States would endorse these measures only after the implementation of a proven inspection system. Although more detailed than his earlier plan, Stassen's ideas still lacked the support of careful technical studies. The only staff work consisted of a two-page checklist of reasons why countries might or might not abstain from producing nuclear weapons. The paper largely identified proliferation motives outside direct U.S. control, such as internal political and economic constraints and psychological factors. But the report also suggested two means to inhibit uncontrolled nuclear dissemination that allowed for U.S. action — namely, supplying allies with American nuclear weapons and creating multilateral nuclear arsenals under UN or collective security arrangements. Stassen's muddled thinking failed to apprehend that from Moscow's perspective such initiatives resembled proliferation, not arms control.[66]

The new plan immediately drew fire from the AEC and the Pentagon. The Joint Chiefs of Staff rejected a test ban, while Strauss dismissed Stassen's claims of a "fourth-country problem" as overly speculative. He held that a deadline to cut off fissionable material production should be established only after extensive study had ascertained the number of nuclear weapons necessary to ensure continuing U.S. military superiority. He also urged including the PRC in any arms control agreement to ensure that the Soviets did not use their Chinese allies to evade inspection. Chinese participation would surely ensnare Stassen in the complex political and diplomatic tangle of U.S. non-recognition policy toward the Beijing regime. But this time Strauss's delaying tactics did not persuade the president to abandon Stassen's new proposals.[67]

Politics Derail Disarmament

Just as the policy debate heated up, the disarmament adviser became distracted by Republican Party factional intrigue. Eisenhower had decided to run again, despite his health problems, largely because he believed that only he and Dulles could be trusted to manage U.S. foreign policy. The president's personal popularity seemed to assure his reelection, but some moderate Republicans feared that Vice President Richard Nixon would hurt the party's chances of winning control of Congress. Stassen took it upon himself in late July to call a press conference wherein he publicly asked Nixon to withdraw from consideration, boldly proposing Massachusetts governor Christian Herter as a substitute. The announcement provoked a backlash from congressional Republicans, who defended the vice president and called for Stassen's resignation. Eisenhower, however, refused to endorse or condemn either man. He instead asked his disarmament adviser to take a leave of absence until after the Republican convention. Stassen's rivals hoped that in the interim his new proposal would be discarded, allowing disarmament planning to "start from scratch."[68]

The June 29 proposals, however, did not go away. The State Department bolstered Stassen's ideas by endorsing a one-year unilateral test moratorium, a public relations measure designed to swing world opinion in U.S. favor. Upon his return, Stassen arranged a September 11 meeting to discuss both the June 29 plan and the State Department proposal. Strauss discovered the State Department's new test ban stance shortly before the disarmament meeting and frantically urged Dulles to stifle its discussion. The secretary of state, in turn, warned Stassen that nuclear testing had become a sticky political issue that should be deferred until after the election. When the meeting convened at the White House that afternoon, Strauss, Joint Chiefs of Staff chairman Admiral Arthur W. Radford, and Dulles all rejected the July 1, 1957, deadline as "unrealistic." Radford urged continued testing and production of fissionable material until the United States had accumulated large nuclear weapons stockpiles at "various places all over the world."[69]

An impatient Eisenhower interjected: "We could sit and find obstacles to the plan without end." Doing nothing no longer sufficed, the president argued, because soon the economic costs of the arms race and the spread of nuclear weapons would pose a greater threat to U.S. security than did the Soviets. He also brushed aside Strauss's claims that the United States could never stop testing, warning that the "rising concern of people everywhere" required action on a moratorium. But Eisenhower's suspicions of the Soviets tempered his support for arms control and prompted him to acquiesce that no action could occur until an inspection system was in place. The president once again deferred decision on Stassen's proposals and demanded that there be a clear consensus before the issue was raised again.[70]

Although the presidential campaign delayed further nonproliferation policy debate until late November, the general trend within the government favored restrictions on nuclear dissemination. After an Atoms for Peace progress report in late September, Stassen and Treasury Secretary George Humphrey expressed fear that the program could encourage proliferation. During the ensuing discussion, the AEC chair and the disarmament adviser reversed their usual roles; Stassen questioned the adequacy of safeguards while Strauss defended them as sound. The AEC chair and other proponents of peaceful uses continued to discount the "fourth-country problem" and emphasized the propaganda and potential economic benefits of Atoms for Peace. The United States, meanwhile, continued technical aid to countries that harbored known nuclear ambitions, such as France, Israel, India, and Japan.[71]

In October, presidential politics again disrupted momentum toward nonproliferation and the test ban. Throughout 1956, nuclear testing had slowly become a partisan issue. The Democrat-controlled Senate Foreign Relations Committee's disarmament subcommittee hearings increasingly focused on the feasibility of a moratorium. The hearings also offered an important public forum for test limit proponents, such as AEC commissioner Thomas Murray. In April, Adlai Stevenson, prospective candidate for the Democratic presidential nomination, advocated a unilateral halt to thermonuclear tests.

Stevenson's speech prompted criticism from Eisenhower and the press but also drew praise from scientists, pacifists, and religious organizations. Some State Department officials suggested privately briefing Stevenson on the test ban issue to persuade him to keep silent in the future, but Dulles objected, and Stevenson soon abandoned the issue of his own volition.[72]

Through the summer of 1956, domestic politics still exerted less pressure for a test moratorium than did U.S. allies and world public opinion. In June 1956, because of its own domestic outcry against testing, the British government lent public support to test limitation outside of a comprehensive disarmament agreement. London's announcement left the United States as the only nuclear power opposing a test ban as a separate measure. Eisenhower privately contemplated a proposal to halt tests as soon as the Soviets did, but Strauss countered that it was imperative to conduct experiments whenever a new scientific principle needed to be examined. Still, the Eisenhower administration seemed capable of weathering the international storm. The British had changed their position largely for domestic political reasons, and UN delegates who also condemned the U.S. position in the UN General Assembly expressed sympathy in private.[73]

As the presidential race heated up, the two leading Democratic advocates of a test ban, Murray and Stevenson, renewed their criticism of the Eisenhower administration's nuclear policies. In August, Murray urged the president to halt large thermonuclear tests and instead to emphasize the development of tactical weapons. Strauss dismissed Murray's arguments as a politically motivated attempt to embarrass the administration. In a September speech to the American Legion, Stevenson, now the Democratic nominee, repeated his call for a test moratorium. The response illustrated the prevalent tendency in American political culture to link intellectuals and effeminacy with Cold War dissent. During his 1952 and 1956 presidential campaigns, critics labeled Stevenson as "soft" and as an "egghead," equating his call for a test moratorium with proposals to ban the bomb, when it more accurately fell into the arms control category. In the wake of the 1952 campaign, one political commentator contended that the previously neutral term "egghead" had been redefined to refer to "a person of spurious intellectual pretensions, often a professor or the protégé of a professor. Fundamentally superficial. Overemotional and feminine in reactions to any problem. Supercilious and surfeited with conceit and contempt for the experience of more sound and able men. Essentially confused in thought and immersed in a mixture of sentimentality and violent evangelism. . . . An anemic bleeding heart." The *New York Daily News* took its attacks on Stevenson further. Calling him "Adelaide," mocking his voice as "fruity," the paper dismissed Stevenson's supporters as "typical Harvard lace-cuff liberals," "lace-panty diplomats," and "pompadoured lap dogs" who wailed "in perfumed anguish" at McCarthy's accusations and on occasion "'giggled' about their own anti-Communism." Stevenson's call for a test moratorium during the 1956 campaign prompted further criticism. Vice President Richard Nixon, whose "manly explanation of his financial affairs" in his 1952 "Checkers" speech garnered praise from the *New York Daily News*, quickly lambasted Stevenson's proposal as "naive and dangerous." Initially silent while Nixon and former New York governor Thomas Dewey ridiculed Stevenson's proposal, the president reversed course and blasted a unilateral moratorium on large tests as a "theatrical national gesture." Stevenson struck back, observing that Pope Pius XII, the British government, various church groups, and Thomas Murray supported his position. This exchange catapulted nuclear testing into a central campaign issue, with Stevenson and the administration both accusing each other of risking American lives and national security.[74]

The Soviets soon turned this debate into an international issue by obliquely praising Stevenson in a letter critical of Eisenhower's test ban policy. Nikolai Bulganin's message prompted cries that Moscow had meddled in American politics and provided fodder for Strauss's claim that the entire test ban campaign was a communist plot. During the remainder of the campaign, Stevenson endured criticism from the press and political pundits that he was Moscow's candidate, with only 24 percent of Americans favoring his test moratorium proposal. Eisenhower, however, labored to keep his hands free on the test ban issue. Late in the campaign, as Dulles prepared a statement on fallout, the president told him to make it "so factual as to be uninteresting." Eisenhower also notified Strauss that after the election he would no longer tolerate stonewalling tactics on test limitation.[75]

Despite such efforts, events outside the president's control worked against arms control and a test moratorium. U.S. relations with France and Great Britain, already frosty on disarmament matters, grew even more frigid after Eisenhower opposed British attempts to seize the Suez Canal. The U.S.-Soviet chill in the wake of Bulganin's October letter deepened after the Red Army invaded Hungary in November 1956. The political rancor of the presidential campaign and Stassen's diminished position in the administration after his "Dump Nixon" efforts further undermined prospects for international nonproliferation measures. All these factors conspired to diminish Eisenhower's electoral triumph on November 6.

The president could not feel satisfied with his first term's arms control record, especially on nuclear proliferation and test limitation. From 1953 onward, Eisenhower persistently voiced his desire to control testing and inhibit the spread of nuclear weapons. And in 1956, the president soberly conceded to his advisers that "we may find we have failed to do things that would have made the difference between mutual destruction and survival." Yet, faced with his subordinates' intransigence, Ike hesitated to defy the bureaucratic consensus. Stevenson exploited this inaction in the 1956 campaign. By the end of his first term, the president's dream of harnessing atomic energy for peaceful purposes had lost its luster, largely because existing technology could not live up to American rhetoric, and the lack of safeguards allowed fissionable material to be diverted to military uses.[76]

Eisenhower's darkening mood might have dimmed further had he known how costly his failures had become. Because of the arms control deadlock, France, Israel, and the PRC all advanced significantly toward attaining nuclear weapons. Eisenhower's cabinet of conservative millionaires attacked test ban proponents as naive dreamers. But, in retrospect, it was the gray-flanneled bureaucrats who were out of touch with reality, their bland exteriors masking tortured thinking and emotional anxieties. Anticommunist paranoia led Eisenhower's men to believe that all Americans were literally "better dead than red," prompting them to resist efforts to prevent proliferation and nuclear war. Political and technological hubris fostered a climate wherein numerous states intensified efforts to join the nuclear ranks, and wherein the incipient nuclear arms race threatened to spiral out of control.

Seeking a Silver Bullet

NONPROLIFERATION, THE TEST BAN, &

NUCLEAR SHARING, 1957–1960

In April 1957, Dwight D. Eisenhower averred that the Soviets had "more to gain from preventing the spread of atomic weapons to fourth countries than do we." That belief shaped U.S. policy throughout Eisenhower's second term. The United States sought to control, not prevent, proliferation within the Western alliance, choosing which countries acquired nuclear weapons and making those allies dependent on American technology and data. Eisenhower valued NATO solidarity more than nonproliferation and displayed a willingness to attenuate U.S. nuclear hegemony in order to strengthen its dominance within the alliance more broadly. He gambled that Soviet fears of nuclear diffusion would render Moscow pliant in arms control negotiations. Worldwide protests against atmospheric testing helped elevate the test ban as Eisenhower's primary arms control goal. During disarmament talks, the United States probed Soviet willingness to concede on verification and inspection in exchange for a nonproliferation accord. Both goals foundered on U.S. bureaucratic discord and renewed U.S.-Soviet acrimony following the U-2 spy plane incident. Absent arms control, the Eisenhower administration decided that sharing nuclear technology and data would sate Western alliance appetites for national nuclear forces. When President Charles de Gaulle's insistence on an independent French nuclear arsenal scuttled the first nuclear-sharing proposals, Eisenhower responded by proposing a multilateral force

(MLF) under NATO command. The MLF exemplified the oxymoronic belief in American policy circles that increasing access to nuclear weapons would inhibit their spread, and that technological quick fixes could better ensure U.S. security than diplomatic agreements could.[1]

"Worse Than Suez"

In early 1957, the United States faced strained relations with Great Britain and France following the Suez crisis. Repairing alliance ties directly affected nonproliferation policy. Forced withdrawal from Egyptian territory under threat from both the United States and the Soviet Union fed Great Britain and France's desire to reinvigorate their eclipsed great-power status by expanding their respective nuclear programs. Washington thereafter pursued a "schizophrenic" or "*divide et impera*" policy, encouraging the British while condemning the French. Attempting to control Britain's program through a tightly coordinated Anglo-American nuclear alliance, Washington simultaneously tried to nip the French program in the bud in order to contain "the neutralist dangers of a Third Force" in Europe and inhibit France from acting irresponsibly to save its collapsing colonial empire. These conflicting attitudes toward the two independent European nuclear programs shaped Western consultations prior to and during the London UN Disarmament Subcommittee meetings in March 1957.[2]

Eisenhower and his disarmament adviser, Harold Stassen, hoped that easier access to nuclear data and technology might salve post-Suez Britain's wounded pride. Nuclear sharing might also wean London away from the emerging Franco-British-German bloc in the Western European Union and encourage its support of U.S. arms control positions. In January, the president dismissed objections within the national security bureaucracy and approved an agreement to exchange data on nuclear submarines with the British. More important, he also offered intermediate range ballistic missiles (IRBMs) under a unique arrangement that gave the British control over the delivery vehicles and the United States control over the warheads. This agreement stretched to its limits the Atomic Energy Act's prohibition against transferring nuclear weapons to other powers. U.S. possession of the "key to the warhead cupboard" provided the only American veto over missile use.[3]

Already hints of greater cooperation had inspired London to distance itself from Paris and Bonn and embrace the U.S. position on test limitation and proliferation. At the Bermuda Conference of 1957, British prime minister

Harold Macmillan and Eisenhower had agreed that without arms control "atomic weapons might come into the hands of irresponsible countries." John Foster Dulles, too, worried that a world without checks against proliferation might "enable a dictator" to acquire a nuclear capability sufficient to "blackmail" other powers. Nonetheless, the Anglo-American powers could only wanly agree "to do very little by way of encouraging or assisting" the French nuclear program. Through the foggy language one thing shone clearly: "Britain had dumped its European allies" in favor of closer relations with Washington and its own national nuclear force.[4]

Despite renewed U.S.-British amity, the UN Disarmament Subcommittee sessions seemed fated to end unproductively. Numerous clouds hung over the proceedings, including the Suez crisis, the Soviet invasion of Hungary, and France's Algerian war. The Bermuda communiqué and new Soviet tests immediately prior to the London meetings also underlined the continuing hostility toward a test ban agreement in both the East and the West. Stassen, however, remained optimistic. He and his staff stood convinced that nuclear diffusion frightened the Soviets. The prospect of nuclear weapons in the hands of the West Germans just might persuade Moscow to compromise on arms control. Yet the plan Stassen took with him to London, already previewed during the UN General Assembly debate in January, provoked little enthusiasm among the Soviet delegates.

Once the Disarmament Subcommittee convened, Stassen and his Soviet counterpart, Valerian Zorin, conducted numerous informal talks, which proved far more productive than the official meetings. In the first formal session, however, Zorin made clear that Moscow would not halt fissionable material production without a total ban on the manufacture and use of nuclear weapons. Soviet rejection of the production cutoff shifted focus to the test ban talks, with the Soviets making a passionate call for an immediate halt to testing. Zorin claimed that compliance with a test ban could be easily verified because "we can immediately detect the explosion of any atomic bomb anywhere."[5]

The Soviet emphasis on a test ban to control proliferation created a dilemma for Stassen. Zorin offered progress in controlling a danger he had championed in intergovernmental debates since 1955, but U.S. policy explicitly rejected a separate test ban agreement. The Western allies' opinions and policies also complicated any discussion of a testing halt. France adamantly opposed a separate test ban agreement as fostering two classes of powers — nuclear "haves" and nuclear "have-nots." The Bermuda communiqué, moreover, had committed both the United States and Great Britain to rejecting a test ban outside a comprehensive disarmament agreement. Other U.S. allies nonetheless wanted substantive reduction of tests for domestic political reasons. Such public clamor seemed to be growing, not subsiding. Japan, Canada, and Norway had already called for registration of nuclear tests with the UN. At the London meetings, the Canadian delegation privately urged a test ban prior to the conclusion of a comprehensive disarmament treaty. Japan, Norway, India, and Yugoslavia also publicly called for an end to testing and clamored to testify before the Disarmament Subcommittee. Stassen's instructions, however, allowed only limited and symbolic concessions.

Eager to move forward, Stassen decided to violate the spirit, and possibly the letter, of his instructions in order to gauge Soviet sincerity. In preparation for further meetings with Zorin, Stassen asked for studies of the relationship between test limitation and nuclear proliferation. The disarmament adviser, meanwhile, hinted in both informal and official meetings that test limits apart from a comprehensive disarmament treaty might gain U.S. acceptance. Stassen's activities led Lewis Strauss to demand the latter's recall for compromising U.S. security. Dulles confessed that Stassen had flooded the State Department with more cables than anyone could possibly read, but that the "fourth-country problem" justified taking some risks. Strauss's ex cathedra pronouncements that Washington could do little to prevent proliferation failed to persuade either Stassen or Dulles. Eisenhower approved Stassen's nonproliferation emphasis, hoping that the Soviets' desire to prevent nuclear diffusion "might prove a valuable bargaining point."[6]

Stassen received more good news in London. The British government appeared eager to reach an agreement both on the fourth-country problem and on a test moratorium. Halting tests had become important in British politics. The Bermuda communiqué had set off a parliamentary debate in which the Labour opposition had publicly criticized Macmillan for backing away from a separate test agreement. The Soviets, moreover, seemed intent on more bilateral discussions, especially concerning nonproliferation. After more talks with Zorin, Stassen formulated new proposals. The nonproliferation components included a pledge by all non-nuclear states not to manufacture or use nuclear weapons, a cutoff of fissionable material production, and a twelve-month test moratorium.

Fearing that the plan had become "too grandiose," Dulles again called Stassen home for consultations. The political atmosphere in Washington had changed for the worse. The secretary had attended a NATO meeting in which the allies had badgered him about nuclear arms control. The European partners, with the exception of Bonn, urged negotiation of conventional arms control first. If NATO de-emphasized nuclear weapons, an inordinate amount of power might shift to West Germany because of its economic strength and manpower reserves. Dulles now believed that no arms control agreement could be achieved in 1957 without threatening the alliance.

The interdepartmental study on the connection between test limitation and the fourth-country problem had also exposed deep divisions within the national security bureaucracy. Neither the Defense Department nor the AEC believed that the threat of nuclear proliferation warranted a risky comprehensive test ban. Yet a consensus also emerged that partial testing limitation had little hope of containing proliferation because many nations could allegedly construct primitive nuclear weapons without testing them. The AEC, moreover, likened a twelve-month moratorium to trying to "stop breathing for three hours." If tests were ever suspended, the Pentagon and the AEC feared that public opinion would prevent their resumption.[7]

When he returned to Washington on May 17, Stassen attempted to persuade Dulles, Strauss, and Secretary of Defense Charles E. Wilson that the Soviets genuinely wanted an arms control agreement. He stressed the danger that proliferation posed to U.S. national security. But nothing the disarmament adviser said softened the Pentagon's and AEC's adamant opposition, including evidence that both France and Germany were poised to initiate nuclear weapons programs. The president ultimately interceded. Without an end to the arms race, he argued, the United States would face serious financial problems. In characteristic fashion, however, he then tempered his arms control instincts, warning that any disarmament agreement "should not incur serious risks" to U.S. security.[8]

The president's wary approach allowed the AEC and the Pentagon to water down the nonproliferation features of Stassen's proposals. The Defense Department successfully argued that the fourth-country problem should not be the controlling feature of any U.S. disarmament plan. This policy shift forced Stassen to revise the provision for nuclear abstinence by all non-nuclear powers. Rather than the denuclearized Europe envisioned by the disarmament adviser, the NATO alliance would remain effectively unchanged. Signatories would pledge not to manufacture weapons, but they could still acquire them from a nuclear power and use them independently in the event of war. The production cutoff and transfer of fissionable material to peaceful purposes also underwent revision to enable the nuclear powers to maintain a "very substantial nuclear weapons capability," thus eliminating the proposal's usefulness in convincing France, Germany, and other potential fourth countries that the superpowers would also restrict their nuclear arsenals.[9]

The twelve-month test moratorium emerged relatively unscathed. But without the no-weapons pledge and the fissionable material cutoff to support it, a testing halt seemed unlikely to inhibit nuclear diffusion. Nonproliferation, of course, did not provide the sole motive for the moratorium. The need to respond to public and congressional worries about the fallout danger provided the strongest impetus. Congressional testimony that strontium-90's effects could not be accurately gauged refuted Eisenhower administration claims that atmospheric tests posed little risk. In April, Dr. Albert Schweitzer issued a new appeal to halt testing, which Strauss called "a body blow to the testing program."[10] The British added to this public furor when they tested their first hydrogen bomb on May 15. The Eisenhower administration, moreover, increasingly worried that the test ban campaign had fallen under communist influence and that testing might have to be limited in order to deprive the Soviets of a powerful propaganda weapon.

Still other forces subverted an arms control accord. In May, the Italians and the Germans protested the new U.S. willingness to negotiate with the Soviets, claiming that Washington might sacrifice Western European security interests in order to escape the economic burden of the arms race. Stassen reinforced these fears on May 31 when, without consulting allies or the State Department, he gave Zorin an informal memorandum detailing the new U.S. proposals. A political firestorm immediately broke out on both sides of the Atlantic. The French labeled the action "worse than Suez," clear evidence that European nations needed their own nuclear weapons programs. In London and Bonn, talk of "une bombe européene" also reemerged. In his eagerness to reach agreement with the Soviets, Stassen had inadvertently sabotaged his own initiatives.[11]

Eisenhower fumed about Stassen's "idiotic" actions. Although the informal memorandum largely conformed to the text agreed upon during Stassen's Washington consultations, he had badly embarrassed the administration. A "seriously shaken" Eisenhower contemplated a replacement as Dulles formally reprimanded Stassen and ordered him to ask Zorin to return the talking paper. The uproar over the Zorin-Stassen affair made nuclear dissemination an extremely sensitive issue within the alliance. Dulles revised the U.S. proposal further and removed the explicit no-weapons pledge, hoping that the test ban and fissionable material provisions would suffice as nonproliferation measures.[12]

Muddying the Waters

Turmoil still plagued the London conference. On June 14, Zorin introduced a Soviet counterproposal to Stassen's informal memorandum. Offering a two- to three-year moratorium on testing, rather than just one, Moscow for the first time accepted on-site inspections. London and Paris ironically displayed a willingness to moderate their previous opposition to a comprehensive test ban. While Dulles tried to escape the diplomatic eddy in which Stassen had stranded the administration, Eisenhower muddied the waters further by implying during a press conference that he might drop the linkage between a test moratorium and an end to fissionable material production. Such a policy shift would have rendered a test ban nearly useless as a nonproliferation measure. But Eisenhower seemed to view a moratorium primarily as a means to quell public agitation and as a stepping-stone toward more significant arms control measures. France, however, would sign a test ban treaty only if it restricted the superpowers' ability to produce nuclear weapons. Dulles scrambled to correct the president's miscue, contending that the press had misunderstood Eisenhower's statements.

Strauss used this turmoil to reopen the issue of a test moratorium. Although Eisenhower hoped to end atmospheric testing, he also wished to avoid the appearance of kowtowing to public pressure. With protests against tests ever increasing, the Eisenhower administration sought to undercut the influence of the antinuclear movement both through attacks on individual members and with blanket condemnations. Allegations of communist influence quickly emerged to smear test ban activists. Many scientists and nuclear pacifists who warned of the health dangers of nuclear tests suffered whispering campaigns about their Cold War loyalties. Albert Schweitzer, Norman Cousins, physicist Ralph Lapp, geneticist Hermann Muller, physicist Leo Szilard, and chemist Linus Pauling became targets of FBI and CIA investigations, as well as journalistic innuendo. Government officials routinely dismissed pacifist and liberal antinuclear groups, such as the Committee for a Sane Nuclear Policy (SANE), as well-meaning but dangerous communist dupes. Antinuclear organizations also became subjects of FBI inquiries and congressional investigations. Eisenhower claimed in 1957 that the test ban protests seemed "like an almost organized affair," implying communist infiltration of the antinuclear movement. On a television interview program in 1958, Strauss charged that behind the test ban agitation lurked "a kernel of very intelligent, deliberate propaganda. I can't put my finger on it—I can't identify it. But we see that a great deal of money is being spent on it."[13]

If arms control proponents were not stigmatized as disloyal, they were dismissed as "impractical." Strauss fumed that scientists tended to meddle in international politics, where "the prestige which they enjoy as scientists gives their political views a weight beyond their real worth." Yet although scientists proved "as frequently wrong as other men," they were "apt to be wrong in more critical areas and where the damage from being wrong is more irreparable." Eisenhower publicly chided scientists in the test ban movement as straying outside "their own field of competence." Such comments tapped into the anti-intellectualism of American culture. Even Eisenhower, the erstwhile president of Columbia University, too easily depicted intellectuals as disconnected from reality. He joked publicly that an intellectual was "a man who takes more words than are necessary to tell more than he knows." During the 1960 campaign, he praised Nixon and his running mate Henry Cabot Lodge for not learning "their lessons merely out of books."[14]

Strauss exploited divisions within the scientific community to again play "Ike like a violin." He brought key nuclear scientists Ernest Lawrence and Edward Teller to Washington to testify before Congress and to meet with the president. Teller and Lawrence, both in public and in their private meeting with Eisenhower, called a test moratorium a "crime against humanity" because it prevented development of a "clean bomb" that eliminated 90 percent of the fallout. The prospect of fallout-free weapons obviously affected Eisenhower's thinking. A few days later, he told the press that it might serve American security interests if the Soviets also developed clean bombs. Lawrence and Teller, meanwhile, deftly persuaded many powerful senators and representatives to express doubts about the U.S. disarmament proposal. Dulles soon informed Stassen that both Congress and the president now questioned the wisdom of a test ban. Transfixed by the prospect of a technological "silver bullet" to ease public anxiety about nuclear fallout, the secretary of state and the president decided to slow the pace of moratorium negotiations. A jubilant Strauss sent a letter, praising Teller's and Lawrence's performances.[15]

By early 1957, government efforts to manage U.S. public opinion seemed to be successful. Most Americans now opposed a unilateral halt in testing — 60 percent of those surveyed supported a multilateral test ban if accompanied by proper safeguards. During the summer and fall of 1957, however, antinuclear agitation gained coherence. In the United States, SANE emerged as a vehicle for liberal disarmament advocates, while the Committee for Non-Violent Action brought together numerous radical disarmament advocates. In Great Britain, the Campaign for Nuclear Disarmament and the Direct

Action Committee against Nuclear War became the voices of liberal and radical protest, respectively.[16]

This growing antinuclear strength suggested that talk of clean bombs would not quell public discontent. Eisenhower seemed willing to talk with nuclear pacifists. But Strauss feared that legitimizing test ban proponents through dialogue would signal a lack of confidence in the AEC and its atomic scientists. AEC scientists ironically fueled antinuclear agitation when they reported that continued testing would cause more leukemia deaths and some genetic damage in the world population. Such effects seemed small when expressed as percentages but would be "large in absolute terms." The outcry would have been even greater had the U.S. public known that much of the data resulted from secret AEC human experiments and clandestine body snatchings of corpses and stillborn fetuses—a project given the perverse title of Operation Sunshine.[17]

Eisenhower and Dulles understood that prolonging the London meetings would enhance Soviet propaganda opportunities. Allied distrust of Stassen also hampered the negotiations. In late July, the president sent Dulles to London to take command of the talks. The move calmed West Germany and other distressed allies but signaled that Stassen no longer spoke for the United States. Premier Khrushchev, who had survived a Kremlin coup in June through the last-minute support of the military, lost faith in the UN talks and sought a summit meeting to bridge the gap between the American and Soviet positions. Dulles, however, believed that Khrushchev's new political debt to the military foreclosed even the slim chance for arms control that might have existed earlier. By September 6, all delegates agreed to recess the subcommittee session. It never reconvened.

Stassen and Dulles waged a pitched bureaucratic battle over the contours of American nonproliferation policy. Stassen wanted U.S. policy to allow the negotiation of a two-year test moratorium separate from any other measures, with the possible exception of a trial inspection zone in Europe. The probability of a French nuclear test within the next two years made it vital to conclude an agreement to inhibit proliferation. Nonetheless, as always, he could not explain how test suspension alone would halt nuclear diffusion. Nor did he have any plan to ensure French compliance with the ban. Stassen's proposal provoked unanimous opposition from the national security bureaucracy. While Dulles urged continued talks with the Soviets, the Pentagon and the AEC rejected a test ban divorced from other measures.

Throughout the waning months of 1957, Eisenhower gradually inched toward a separate test ban agreement. Calls for test limitation continued unabated among U.S. allies, neutral countries, and the mass public. Strauss and his staff still tried to smear the antinuclear movement as communist controlled or manipulated, but Eisenhower proved less persuaded by Strauss than he had been in the past. The president feared being "crucified on a cross of atoms" if he continued testing. In late October, the atomic scientist Isidor Rabi, a friend of Eisenhower's dating from his days at Columbia University, ridiculed Teller's and Lawrence's promises of clean weapons and dismissed fears of Soviet cheating. Rabi insisted that an immediate test moratorium would actually "freeze" the U.S. lead in atomic armaments because the Soviets needed further tests to correct a "fatal flaw" in their thermonuclear warheads. Strauss lamely insinuated that Rabi had a personal vendetta against Teller but failed to shake the president's confidence in his longtime friend. Pressure from such key legislative leaders as Senator Hubert Humphrey and Representative Chet Holifield also indicated that test limitation could resurface as an election issue in 1958 and 1960. Eisenhower thought a separate test ban treaty feasible if the Atomic Energy Act could be amended to allow nuclear collaboration with U.S. allies, and he instructed Dulles to run the idea past the British and the French.[18]

Even as a test ban's prospects brightened, Stassen grew discouraged and resigned in February 1958. After his departure, officials paid lip service to a test halt as an obstacle to nuclear diffusion, but few believed it sufficient to control the problem. One intelligence estimate suggested that even a comprehensive disarmament scheme would only slow proliferation temporarily. The emphasis in the test ban negotiations shifted to quieting public protests, opening up the Soviet Union to Western inspection, and preserving the American lead in the nuclear arms race. The burden of preventing proliferation thus shifted to unilateral measures, especially the logically paradoxical policy of nuclear sharing.[19]

Sharing Weapons and Preserving Hegemony

The Eisenhower administration consistently sought to expand NATO access to nuclear weapons. During his first term, the president had deployed hundreds of tactical nuclear weapons in West Germany, nominally under U.S. control. But the Atomic Energy Act prevented a comprehensive program of selective proliferation among the NATO countries, and the JCAE jealously guarded American atomic secrets. To its members, nuclear weapons formed the linchpin of U.S. world leadership, and such power should not be squandered. Events in the fall of 1957, however, helped create a more receptive atmosphere for nuclear sharing.

On October 4, 1957, the Soviets launched Sputnik I, the first artificial earth satellite. The achievement sparked fears that the West had fallen dangerously behind in science and technology. More important, Sputnik raised the specter of Soviet superiority in nuclear-delivery vehicles because missile and space technology went hand in hand. Cries of a "missile gap" produced the blue-ribbon Gaither committee on deterrence and survival in the nuclear age, whose final chairman, Robert Sprague, advocated either preventive war or a "hot" negotiation, whereby Washington threatened to attack Moscow unless it accepted U.S. arms control proposals. If the United States did not ensure its nuclear preeminence it would have to "place reliance in God to find a solution." Similar fears persuaded many on the JCAE that the United States should seek to offset Soviet intercontinental ballistic missiles (ICBMs). Because operational U.S. ICBMs would not be ready for several years, the basing of intermediate range missiles in Europe offered a quick solution.[20]

Before Sputnik, Eisenhower had had limited success with nuclear sharing, but afterward political pressure from U.S. allies to relax nuclear restrictions increased. The president had used the Thor missile deal of March 1957 with Britain as a trial balloon. Yet the arrangement bogged down shortly after the Bermuda conference because of problems with bilateral controls and finances. During 1957, Eisenhower tried to soothe British discontent over the delay by exchanging data on nuclear submarine technology without awaiting congressional approval. Administration officials also hinted that a test ban agreement might restore Anglo-American nuclear cooperation to its wartime levels.

The German and French desire for nuclear weapons posed the central problem. Despite discussions at Bermuda, neither Britain nor the United States had a clearly defined policy on how to approach Franco-German nuclear ambitions. If they appeared too hostile, NATO might splinter and a neutral bloc in Western Europe might form. But an independent French nuclear force or a Franco-German nuclear force also could spur nationalist impulses throughout Western Europe. The problem gained urgency in late 1957 and early 1958 as France and Germany began a brief "nuclear flirtation." French, German, and, at times, Italian defense officials discussed fashioning a Western European arms consortium that produced both nuclear and conventional weapons. Prior to his resignation, Stassen had warned that if Washington did nothing, Paris and possibly Bonn could possess as many as "50 [atomic] bombs in 1960."[21]

Dulles proposed managing nuclear weapons under the NATO umbrella, gambling that such an arrangement would not arouse Moscow's fears. Eisenhower also pushed to revise U.S. restricted-data provisions, publicly labeling the Atomic Energy Act "a deplorable incident in American history." With the JCAE seemingly amenable to change, the administration officially requested amendments to allow greater nuclear sharing within NATO and with Britain. Although Strauss still opposed full nuclear cooperation, Eisenhower quashed his objections and pushed for unrestricted nuclear sharing with London.[22]

The Anglo-American nuclear rapprochement temporarily suspended Britain's nuclear dalliance with France and Germany and became one component of the Eisenhower administration's larger effort to stifle European atomic ambitions. A new policy took shape amid the preparations for the NATO heads of government meeting scheduled for late 1957. Eisenhower proposed a NATO IRBM force, an enlarged stockpile of tactical nuclear weapons, and the pooling of military data. He also sought new amendments to the Atomic Energy Act that would facilitate nuclear data sharing and training of European troops to use nuclear weapons. Still, the IRBMs alone might not clinch the deal. The early Thor and Jupiter missiles were slow to their targets and highly vulnerable to attack, inviting Soviet strikes. A promise of nuclear submarine data and a commitment eventually to replace first-generation missiles with more sophisticated weapons sweetened the offer to the Europeans.

The new NATO nuclear policy possibly solved two problems: NATO susceptibility to Soviet missile attacks and the potential for European proliferation. Dulles told the JCAE that the proposals would be acceptable to "those allies who presently" could develop nuclear weapons and that it might persuade them not to seek "an independent nuclear capability. That is what we want to check." This policy reflected Eisenhower's new belief that trying to stop proliferation among industrially advanced countries was like "sitting on the beach waiting for the rising tide to stop."[23]

Toward "little countries," however, Ike had a very different attitude. He perceived "a great difference between NATO countries and other countries" and imagined "nothing worse than permitting Israel or Egypt to have a nuclear capability, as they might easily set out to destroy one another." This central assumption with its Eurocentric bias was a continuing theme throughout U.S. nonproliferation policy well into the twenty-first century. The West presumably could manage nuclear munitions with sobriety and restraint during crises. But the rest of the world could not. In parallel fashion, Eisenhower's first secretary of defense, Charles E. Wilson, warned against trading "firearms with the Indians." A child of the Kansas plains and an avid reader of pulp

Westerns, Eisenhower recognized the folly of equipping a "savage" foe with advanced weaponry. Deterrence only worked when both sides viewed their security dilemma responsibly and rationally. In U.S. eyes, Asian, African, and Latin American states lacked the full capacity for reason and so could not be trusted.[24]

The United States also viewed nuclear dissemination through the economic lens of comparative advantage. The administration sought to make it more financially attractive for Europeans to acquire weapons from the United States than to develop them independently, thereby retaining U.S. leverage over European arsenals. Eisenhower, however, did not want to aid countries that had no potential for contributing to proliferation, backing "giving nuclear information to allies who could afford to make nuclear weapons" on their own but not to those who could not. The Soviet Union, however, viewed American policy as dangerously hastening West German acquisition of nuclear weapons. The Eastern bloc therefore attempted to forestall nuclear sharing through an alternative nonproliferation proposal, the Rapacki Plan. In October 1957, during the UN General Assembly meeting, Polish foreign minister Adam Rapacki called for a nuclear-free zone in Central Europe, composed of Poland, Czechoslovakia, and East and West Germany. The proposal received little attention until George F. Kennan, during a series of highly publicized radio lectures in Great Britain, similarly advocated removal of all nuclear weapons from Europe and the creation of a neutral, unified Germany. Kennan thought it self-evident that the introduction of nuclear weapons into Europe would needlessly complicate the Cold War by making any settlement of the German problem dependent on nuclear disarmament.[25]

Eisenhower, Macmillan, and the U.S. ambassador to Poland, Jacob Beam, initially thought that the Rapacki Plan might offer some advantages for the West by fostering tension within the Warsaw Pact. But Kennan's call for "disengagement" seemed to strike at the heart of NATO's function of "dual containment"—that is, curtailing both Soviet and German power. The Rapacki Plan and disengagement ignited criticism from a host of sources, including Dean Acheson, James Conant, French strategic analyst Raymond Aron, Harvard political scientist Henry Kissinger, and the West German government. Acheson faulted Kennan's "mystical attitude" toward power relationships. Others worried that disengagement would make NATO "a paper organization." The public uproar helped the Eisenhower administration debunk suggestions for "denuclearizing" Europe.[26]

Although some scholars cite rejection of the Rapacki Plan as "one of the most fundamental errors of Western policy in the postwar period," the proposal contained several flaws from the U.S. and West German perspectives. On the surface, the benefits to the West seem clear. Moscow would open Poland, Czechoslovakia, and East Germany to Western inspection and control in return for preventing U.S. nuclear sharing with West Germany. Acceptance of the nuclear-free zone also would have achieved the American and British goal of inhibiting German proliferation. But the Rapacki Plan did not address the German reunification issue and implicitly required the recognition of East German sovereignty, a point upon which the Adenauer government would not budge. Bonn also resisted attempts to block acquisition of nuclear weapons and prolong its second-class status within NATO. The Eisenhower administration feared that if it forced the Rapacki Plan on West Germany, the Adenauer government might withdraw from NATO and advocate a Franco-German neutralist bloc in Western Europe. Disengagement itself would have required a new NATO strategy. The alliance's war plans called for the immediate use of nuclear weapons after the initiation of hostilities. Abandoning this strategy would have subverted the entire purpose of NATO.[27]

As the Rapacki Plan faded, critics of nuclear sharing emerged within the U.S. government. Gerard C. Smith, director of the State Department Policy Planning Staff, warned that the IRBM deployment would actually provide incentive for independent nuclear capabilities so as to eliminate the U.S. veto on warhead use. Loose IRBM control measures might also increase the chance for accidental nuclear war. Lewis Strauss and some Defense officials also argued that nuclear sharing might prompt leaks of restricted data to the Soviets.

Congressional hearings elicited similar concerns. Nuclear nationalists on the JCAE such as Bourke Hickenlooper and Richard Russell feared leaks, while such liberals as Clinton Anderson and Chet Holifield worried about giving Europeans "nuclear do-it-yourself kits." In June 1958, the administration accepted compromise language that restored Anglo-American cooperation but prevented most other countries, especially France, from receiving highly sensitive nuclear data. Yet IRBM deployment and expansion of the tactical weapons stockpile escaped unscathed from the JCAE review. The administration's promise of loose controls over the NATO nuclear stockpile left the United States with "titular possession only" of the warheads and rendered meaningless Congress's intended limits on nuclear sharing.[28]

New Atomic Energy Act amendments cleared the way for a test moratorium by allowing nuclear cooperation with Britain. The test ban had stalled in January when Eisenhower rejected Stassen's final proposal. During early

1958, the administration had taken a beating in world public opinion because of its atmospheric test series and its resistance to the Rapacki Plan. In March, Dulles suggested that a unilateral moratorium for the rest of Eisenhower's term might be the only means to deflect criticism. Rejecting Dulles at first, Ike reiterated his willingness to seek a test moratorium if Congress passed the Atomic Energy Act amendments. Eisenhower had notified the AEC and Pentagon that technical arguments would not dissuade him from ending atmospheric testing. Public pressure had reached a point where the only way to prevent America's "moral isolation" lay in a test ban. By May, Eisenhower had decided not to order any more tests during his administration. He kept this decision secret primarily to avoid rousing the British, who would not accept a test ban until the Anglo-American alliance was restored. The antinuclear movement had unknowingly scored a major victory, but at a high price. Largely because of public pressure, the government decided to seek a moratorium divorced from any other nonproliferation measures. The United States thus became more committed to nuclear sharing as a means to inhibit independent nuclear weapons programs. Although the leaders of SANE recognized the danger of the new NATO nuclear policy, their efforts to defeat the amendments to the Atomic Energy Act paled in comparison to the time, effort, and publicity they gave to their antitesting campaign.[29]

Eisenhower's decision of March 24 not to announce an end to American tests also incurred immediate costs. Just days after the president declined to approve a unilateral moratorium, the Soviets announced one of their own, gaining a tremendous propaganda advantage. In the wake of the Soviet initiative, Dulles again lobbied the president to suspend testing for the remainder of his administration, and Eisenhower finally committed himself to a test moratorium once Congress passed the Atomic Energy Act amendments. He also sent Khrushchev a series of letters resulting in a multilateral conference of experts that convened in July to study the technical requirements of an inspection and verification system to monitor test ban compliance. Strauss still refused to relent, but with his term on the AEC expiring at the end of June 1958, the admiral had lost much of his influence. Rather than reappoint him as chairman, the president slyly offered him the top post at the Commerce Department.

Confronting de Gaulle

By July 1958, the most vociferous critic of a test ban had left his national security post, Congress had just passed the Atomic Energy Act amendments, and the Geneva conference of experts had convened. The prospects for a test moratorium looked favorable. But nuclear sharing, the other component of U.S. nonproliferation policy, met trouble. When Eisenhower had first presented the new nuclear-sharing policy to NATO in December, it had appeared to be a great success. Most observers ignored the fact that the United States could not produce IRBMs in large numbers until late 1958 and focused instead on the alleged "missile gap" and the increased responsibility given to the allies in nuclear matters.

France immediately gave cause for concern. Although Paris seemed willing to accept IRBM bases and a tactical-weapons stockpile on its soil, it also remained intent on obtaining an independent nuclear force. When Charles de Gaulle came to power in France in June 1958, the challenge to American leadership in NATO intensified. He immediately refused to allow any U.S. nuclear weapons in France unless the French military had unchecked authority over their use. Committed to restoring France as Western Europe's preeminent power, de Gaulle would not countenance any nuclear arrangements functionally inferior to the Anglo-American nuclear alliance, and he expressed indignation that Washington refused to share with Paris "what a thousand Soviet corporals already know."[30]

Eisenhower harbored some sympathy toward France's quest. The president nonetheless drew the line at treating de Gaulle "like God." In 1958, little possibility existed that the JCAE would revise the Atomic Energy Act to appease Paris. In the first bilateral discussions with de Gaulle in July, Dulles explained that American policy aimed to discourage independent nuclear forces because proliferation would destabilize both the international system and the Western alliance while complicating arms control negotiations. Given France's political instability since World War II, the JCAE could not elevate Paris to the same level as London in nuclear affairs. If de Gaulle established a healthy political environment in France, the JCAE might reverse its earlier decision.[31]

The general clearly found Dulles's presentation disingenuous. All countries pursue nationalist policies to increase their world stature, he said. At times, leaders attempted to obscure selfish motivations: Khrushchev hid behind Marxism, and the United States hid behind "the American Congress." Although Dulles did not fire back at de Gaulle while in France, he showed less circumspection in Washington, feminizing the general's resistance to nuclear sharing as "playing hard to get." The secretary refused to "get down" on his "knees" and "beg" Paris to embrace the U.S. proposal.[32]

De Gaulle's vision of French resurgence sent disruptive ripples through the Western alliance. Upon ascending to power, the general immediately terminated the exploratory talks with Bonn on nuclear energy cooperation. He refused to allow any other nation to have a hand in determining France's nuclear course. These actions led the West Germans to turn against their prospective nuclear collaborators. Spurned, Adenauer sowed suspicions among U.S. policymakers that the French might turn to the Soviets for nuclear aid. West German defense minister Franz Josef Strauss called on incipient nuclear powers to pledge publicly not to produce atomic weapons in order to bring "moral pressure" on other would-be proliferators. By November, West Germany had balanced these explicit and implicit condemnations of the French program with a secret request for American IRBMs. But Washington had to tread lightly down this path, for nuclear missiles in West German hands might provoke both Soviet and European fears.[33]

The prospect of a bomb in Bonn impelled Khrushchev to act. In November, he issued an ultimatum to the West, vowing to sign a separate peace treaty with East Germany, thus terminating American, British, and French occupation rights in the western sectors of Berlin. Khrushchev viewed that divided city as "the testicles of the West. Every time I want to make the West scream, I squeeze on Berlin." In 1958, he perceived an overall German settlement that barred both Bonn and East Berlin from acquiring nuclear weapons as within his grasp. The United States lamely defended its nuclear-sharing policies against charges of proliferation by saying that the warheads remained American. But to the Soviets, who owned the bullets mattered less than who pressed the trigger. Moscow had initially attempted to use the Rapacki Plan to head off German proliferation. When that failed, the Soviets resorted to ultimatums.[34]

The United States stood fast on Berlin but compromised on the nuclear question. NATO commander Lauris Norstad informed the State Department that no military basis existed for placing IRBMs in West Germany, and Dulles, embroiled in the Berlin crisis, contended that current political conditions precluded nuclear sharing with Bonn. But in order to salve complaints that NATO nuclear-sharing policies discriminated against West Germany, Washington included Bonn among the powers slated to manufacture second-generation IRBMs for the NATO stockpile, using U.S. blueprints.

By early 1959, the nuclear-sharing proposal, despite early acclaim, had yielded more negative than positive outcomes for NATO unity and U.S. security. France refused to cooperate, the other NATO countries balked at German participation, and because many feared either Soviet reprisal or domestic political problems, only Italy and Turkey actually received IRBMs under the program. Eisenhower, moreover, killed plans to send missiles to Greece, claiming that nuclear weapons so close to Soviet territory would be too provocative. He told his advisers: "If Mexico or Cuba had been penetrated by the Communists, and then began getting arms and missiles from them, we would be bound to look on such developments with the gravest concern and in fact [I think] it would be imperative for us to take positive action, even offensive military action." Why missiles in Turkey did not prompt the same consideration remains unclear. One scholar suggests that the contradictory policies toward Greece and Turkey illustrated Eisenhower's superficial attention to the IRBM program and his weak control over its implementation. In any case, these early IRBMs, soon obsolescent because of improved missile technology, offered meager gains. Nuclear sharing instead helped set in motion the Berlin crisis, the most serious threat to European peace since 1948–49. The failures of the December 1957 nuclear-sharing proposals left Eisenhower groping for a means to counter European nuclear ambitions.[35]

The Test Ban Battle

After a promising beginning in July 1958, the test ban negotiations also stumbled. The Soviet Union had stunned the State Department when it accepted the president's proposal for a technical conference. Because of the brief period allotted to prepare for the meetings, the U.S. team had harbored some uncertainty about the aims of the Geneva conference. The two superpowers also sparred over whether the meeting signaled a commitment to end tests regardless of the experts' findings. When Eisenhower refused to prejudice the results of the conference with such a promise, many analysts feared the Soviets would not attend. France further complicated matters by refusing to participate in any arms control talks that discriminated against nonnuclear powers. In the end, both Khrushchev and de Gaulle sent scientists to the conference, albeit in the French case with strict instructions to oppose a separate test ban agreement.

Despite these distractions, the Conference of Experts produced a consensus report. It recommended creation of 180 detection stations to be located on both U.S. and Soviet territory and won Soviet acceptance of on-site inspections. American scientists estimated that the monitoring system could detect atmospheric tests as low as one kiloton and underground tests above five kilotons. Given the complicated technical questions, the conference's success surprised many observers. Both groups of scientists included individuals who had worked hard to reach a compromise. Strauss, in one of his last acts as AEC chairman, pushed to add Edward Teller to the U.S. delegation as a way of blocking agreement. Public and congressional opposition forced him to withdraw the nomination and substitute Ernest Lawrence, a former test ban opponent newly intent on limiting nuclear tests. As the American scientists prepared to leave for Geneva, Strauss warned Lawrence to "never let yourself forget that [the Soviet scientists] are the envoys of men who are cold-blooded murderers."[36]

The admiral thus fired the first shot in his campaign to sabotage U.S.-Soviet moratorium talks. As Soviet willingness to devise a verification system became clear, the president told his advisers that if "full technical agreement" emerged from the Conference of Experts, the weight of argument would swing in favor of a cessation of tests. Moscow's approval of on-site inspections and scientific inspection posts on its territory deprived test ban opponents of their timeworn tactic of dismissing disarmament plans for lack of verification and control measures. With the president now committed to ending tests, the AEC and Defense Department undertook "intense efforts to salvage at least underground tests." Opponents still claimed that the Soviets would cheat and challenged the technical adequacies of the Geneva system. Because underground and atmospheric tests could not be detected below a certain threshold, the United States should not approve a ban on low-yield tests. Test ban advocates, meanwhile, urged only reasonable deterrents to cheating, contending that a joint research program among the signatories could correct any defects. Proponents argued that anything less than a comprehensive test ban could not quell public concerns nor meet the demands of nonaligned countries.[37]

Competing visions of technological utopianism clashed in the testing debate. Opponents viewed the test ban as blocking imminent improvements in nuclear technology necessary to preserve U.S. security. But these same people denied that continued research could provide adequate verification and control. Test ban advocates believed that weapons research had reached the point of diminishing returns, while the relatively new and unexplored processes of test detection offered nearly limitless possibilities for improvement. Convinced that the existing American nuclear arsenal provided sufficient security and that the pace of the arms race needed to slow, Eisenhower nonetheless fretted about the Geneva system's inability to detect high-altitude and underground tests. He thus wavered, sometimes endorsing continued underground tests and other times supporting a complete test ban.

In August, moratorium opponents lost the first battle. Despite spirited arguments against a testing halt by new AEC chairman John McCone and

Deputy Secretary of Defense Donald Quarles, Eisenhower proposed a one-year moratorium and negotiations to make the ban permanent, both of which would begin on October 31. The president and the secretary of state deemed the moratorium necessary to restore "U.S. prestige and influence." Eisenhower's announcement had the desired effect. Even SANE's executive council pondered whether to declare its work accomplished and close shop, although most members agreed that much still needed to be done on the arms control front. Public hopes continued to soar after Khrushchev quickly accepted Eisenhower's proposal for talks.[38]

That optimism, however, proved premature as the negotiations soon sputtered. The British balked at Eisenhower's sudden decision to halt tests. Only after receiving assurances regarding crucial data on warhead design did they agree formally to endorse the moratorium and test ban negotiations. Eisenhower ignored de Gaulle's objections to a test ban, hoping that the French would voluntarily halt testing once they had achieved their own nuclear capability or after the JCAE allowed the United States to provide them with nuclear data.

Bureaucratic jockeying also threatened the talks. All three nuclear powers appeased their domestic nuclear establishments by conducting a flurry of last-minute tests. When the Soviets continued to test past the October 31 deadline, Dulles feared that the talks were doomed. Because the Soviets violated the initial moratorium agreement, Eisenhower announced that the United States was no longer bound by its terms, even though he had no intentions of resuming testing. The unrelated Soviet Berlin ultimatum and the renewed crisis over Chinese offshore islands also placed the talks in jeopardy.

The conference still convened on schedule but immediately deadlocked when Moscow insisted on a test ban treaty before starting negotiations on verification and control measures. After weeks of debate, Moscow finally agreed to discuss verification first, saving the conference from breaking up over the agenda. The delay allowed the AEC to analyze data from the underground tests conducted in September and October, which exposed the inadequacy of the Geneva seismic monitoring system. In January, Washington's presentation of the new technical findings to the Soviets "spread a pall over the negotiations from which they never recovered." Eisenhower lamented his lost opportunity. Had he announced a test moratorium two years earlier when he had first wished to do so, the onus for a failed permanent ban would have rested on Moscow. Because he had heeded the Pentagon and AEC's technical arguments against a moratorium, Khrushchev had successfully cast the United States in the role of obstructionist.[39]

Neither the Soviets nor the Americans wanted the talks to break down. Washington could not afford the public outcry, and Moscow now viewed a test ban as the best means to contain nuclear proliferation. Although these differing motives prevented adjournment, they also complicated any chance for agreement. Seeking primarily a propaganda victory, the United States proposed a ban on atmospheric tests only. Such a measure would calm public fears of fallout but do little to inhibit nuclear diffusion. Khrushchev, however, rejected an atmospheric ban as "a dishonest deal," insisting instead on a comprehensive ban. London concurred. Facing strong political pressure to conclude a testing agreement, Prime Minister Macmillan feared electoral defeat should he support the president's limited ban. Thinking that the British should play the Greeks (the diplomats and scholars) to the Americans' Romans (the imperialists and generals), Macmillan soon traveled to Moscow to attempt to break the superpower deadlock over Berlin and the test negotiations. Distressed by the new American data, the Soviets had retreated from their acceptance of on-site inspections. Macmillan proposed a quota on on-site inspections, thereby decreasing the chance that any power would use them primarily for espionage purposes. Khrushchev accepted this compromise, as did Eisenhower, despite initially dismissing Macmillan's proposal as "silly." Bowing to both British and Soviet demands, the United States renewed its public commitment to a comprehensive test ban, although in private Eisenhower saw the safest course in a limited treaty banning only those tests that could be detected by the Geneva system.[40]

The president's faltering commitment to a comprehensive ban invigorated opponents and attracted important new participants. John McCone, a California businessman who had made sizable contributions to Eisenhower's campaigns, had replaced Lewis Strauss as chairman of the AEC in July 1958. Like Strauss, McCone distrusted the Soviets and believed they would inevitably violate any arms control agreement. The new AEC chairman cultivated better relations with Congress than had his predecessor, but he had less influence with the president, in part because he too became notorious for leaking information to the press. Test ban proponents also experienced a changing of the guard when John Foster Dulles, ill with cancer, resigned in April 1959. Eisenhower appointed Dulles's deputy, Christian Herter, as secretary of state. Like Dulles, Herter supported a test ban, but he had neither his predecessor's forceful personality nor the unquestioned trust of the president.

Opponents had a much easier time presenting their case to Eisenhower now that Dulles could not contradict them. Some argued that the PRC must be included in any monitoring system, but Eisenhower refused to let the U.S.

policy of nonrecognition derail the negotiations. Attacking the technical capabilities of the Geneva monitoring system proved the most effective tactic. Any means to evade detection became fair game no matter how elaborate or impractical. Opponents charged that experiments at high altitude, in outer space, or in huge man-made caverns offered ways to evade the detection system. First, they argued that the Geneva system needed to be extended to high-altitude tests. When the Soviets agreed to technical talks on that issue, they switched their emphasis to outer space and seismic decoupling. Seismic decoupling raised serious questions about the ability to police an underground test ban. In theory, a country could construct enormous caverns, which would act like soundproofed rooms to muffle the explosion and cause seismographs to record a weaker nuclear explosion than actually occurred.

Presidential science adviser James Killian, a former president of MIT, disputed these arguments. He noted that evading the Geneva system through the use of outer-space tests and seismic decoupling would be tremendously expensive and could be discovered through traditional intelligence methods, such as clandestine overflights. But the nuclear nationalists at the AEC and the Pentagon nonetheless scored a victory as Eisenhower ordered studies of both seismic decoupling and outer-space tests. These reports ultimately persuaded him that "it would be much worth our while to abandon efforts to control underground tests." A disgusted and wearied Killian resigned in July. A scientist opposing the test ban later gloated to Killian that "whatever advances might be made in detection technology, the West Coast group led by Teller would find a technical way to circumvent or discredit them." As long as the blinkered president insisted on using technical, rather than political, justifications for a test ban, these relentless opponents would continue to scuttle any treaty.[41]

Killian's resignation brought a new protagonist into the test ban debate, George Kistiakowsky, Manhattan Project veteran and former Harvard physics professor. Taking a more aggressive approach than Killian, the new science adviser poked holes in the test ban opponents' arguments, showing that their so-called remedies complicated negotiations while offering no greater security from cheating. He urged a return to the original goal of a comprehensive test ban, using the Geneva system as the basis for verification and control. The Conference of Experts had proposed a monitoring regime capable of deterring cheaters even if it could not detect every test. These arguments persuaded the president to extend the moratorium until January 1960. Although Eisenhower thought a comprehensive treaty unlikely, he feared defeat in the court of public opinion if he abandoned this goal too quickly. Washington returned to Geneva with a proposal for renewed technical talks on inspection and seismic detection. Moscow, however, refused to deviate from the Conference of Experts' report.

From Camp David to the Paris Summit—Hope and Failure

The deadlock began to loosen after Khrushchev visited the United States in September 1959. Meetings between Khrushchev and Eisenhower helped thaw international tensions and identified areas where the superpowers could cooperate, including nonproliferation. While touring the United States, Khrushchev alluded to proliferation dangers and told Ambassador Lodge that "we have a common interest" in "an orderly world." The Soviet premier's concern regarding nuclear proliferation had deepened during the previous year. In June 1959, Sino-Soviet ties had strained over Beijing's willingness to risk nuclear war to recapture Taiwan. Khrushchev increasingly viewed the USSR-PRC military alliance as one-sided, and in 1959 he terminated the Sino-Soviet nuclear cooperation arrangements.[42]

During September 1959, the U.S. government continued to underestimate the Sino-Soviet schism and predicted that Soviet nuclear missiles would be based in China by 1962 or 1963. Although aware that Khrushchev dreaded European proliferation, Eisenhower failed to appreciate the extent of his fears over Asia. The cagey Soviet premier, moreover, neglected to communicate his position on nuclear proliferation to Eisenhower during their private meetings. Still, Khrushchev's hints to Lodge and his UN disarmament speech helped inspire another round of U.S. nonproliferation studies. In October, U.S. ambassador to the Soviet Union Llewellyn Thompson provided further impetus when he stressed to Eisenhower that Khrushchev wanted disarmament and a test ban primarily to bar nuclear weapons from China and West Germany.[43]

Other events also renewed American interest in a nonproliferation arrangement. The NATO nuclear-sharing proposal had not dimmed European nuclear ambitions, and neutral nations also seemed to support nonproliferation measures. In September, Ireland introduced a UN resolution calling for a multilateral treaty barring nuclear diffusion. That same month, the United States and the Soviet Union agreed to revive arms control talks in the Ten-Nation Disarmament Conference where East and West would enjoy equal representation. But continued bureaucratic infighting left Washington with no new proposals when the conference convened.

Eisenhower then shifted his sights to the upcoming summit with France,

Great Britain, and the Soviet Union. The Soviet premier's willingness to talk civilly during his visit had impressed the president. Since September, more-over, the Soviets had pushed back their deadline for a Berlin settlement. The president hoped for progress on multiple fronts, including bans on nuclear tests and fissionable material production and possibly an agreement not to transfer nuclear weapons to other powers except during war.

In the months before the meeting, Eisenhower and Khrushchev exchanged numerous letters discussing proliferation in Europe. When the Soviet premier protested U.S. nuclear-sharing policies, especially potential German access to IRBMs, Eisenhower countered that "states with a major industrial capability" would not remain satisfied if they lacked nuclear weapons "for their own defense." Ike defended nuclear sharing as a viable means to satisfy nuclear hunger while curbing independent nuclear forces in Europe. He suggested that Washington and Moscow together inhibit proliferation by agreeing to control testing, safeguard peaceful uses, and end production of fissionable materials. Khrushchev would only concede to a test ban agreement, seeing it as the most promising means to halt nuclear diffusion. As early as their first meeting in 1955, Khrushchev demonstrated that he understood the emotional and strategic appeal of a test ban better than Ike, remarking that "we get your dust, you get our dust, the winds blow, and nobody's safe."[44]

Despite these differences, Eisenhower clearly saw nonproliferation as an area in which Moscow and Washington might reach accord in Paris. The president in February had protected a fissionable material cutoff proposal from AEC and Pentagon attacks. The Defense Department argued that con-tinued production of uranium-235 and plutonium was needed to produce warheads for antiaircraft and antiballistic missiles. Eisenhower admitted that such applications would enhance national defense but contended that a cut-off offered even greater benefits. The Eisenhower administration later won British and French approval for the proposal during consultations leading up to the summit. Along with a test ban, the idea became the centerpiece of the U.S. talking paper on disarmament, raising the possibility that Paris could lay the groundwork for a first-step nonproliferation agreement. Others shared Eisenhower's optimism. The *Bulletin of the Atomic Scientists*, buoyed by public support for a test ban and the upcoming Paris summit, moved the hands of the Doomsday Clock back to seven minutes to midnight.[45]

On May 1, 1960, the promise of Paris exploded in the skies over Sverdlovsk when Soviet antiaircraft batteries brought down a U-2 spy plane piloted by Gary Francis Powers. Although the Soviet Union had known of American espionage flights for some time, a U.S. spy mission just weeks before the summit made détente look wrongheaded and threatened Khrushchev's standing in the Presidium. The Soviet premier scrambled to save the summit by suggesting that the flights had not been ordered by Eisenhower but were a plot by American militarists to scuttle East-West rapprochement. The president, however, undercut Khrushchev's arguments when he took personal responsibility for the u-2 missions. Pressed by Kremlin hard-liners, Khrushchev in Paris vituperatively demanded an apology from Eisenhower, a promise to discontinue u-2 flights, and punishment of those responsible for the espionage mission before he would participate in the summit. The president refused: "He was damned if he was going to be the only one at the conference to raise his hand and promise never to do again something that everybody else was doing." The summit collapsed, and with it any chance for a nonproliferation agreement. The United States continued pressing for a fissionable material cutoff in the Ten-Nation Disarmament Conference, but in June the Soviets walked out to protest the u-2 affair.[46]

Moscow, however, did not abandon the test ban talks. The spirit of cooperation fostered by Khrushchev's visit had also infused the Geneva negotiations. In October 1959, the Soviets had accepted a new American proposal to discuss on-site inspection requirements and the detection problem. Despite pressure from the Defense Department and the AEC to resume underground testing, Eisenhower viewed these talks as a means to construct an acceptable inspection system for a comprehensive treaty, not as an excuse to table a limited agreement. Kistiakowsky and Herter expressed elation, which quickly deflated when Eisenhower had difficulty finding a top scientist to head the U.S. delegation. Several scientists refused appointment because they feared being used to scuttle a test ban. The Eisenhower administration also learned that jeremiads about verification defects by Teller and other opponents had eliminated any chance of achieving the two-thirds Senate majority needed to ratify a comprehensive treaty.[47]

When the technical conference opened, the Soviets delivered the final deathblow by ridiculing American seismic data and attacking the integrity of the U.S. delegation. Eisenhower thereupon decided to press for a threshold treaty that banned all but underground tests below 4.75 on the Richter scale. Test ban opponents had successfully discredited the Geneva system with their arguments of seismic decoupling, notwithstanding Kistiakowsky's quip that likened their scenarios to "proposing nuclear tests on the other side of the sun."[48]

Despite success in the bureaucratic struggle, the test ban's enemies faced a public increasingly anxious about fallout. A flurry of cultural products during the late 1950s tapped into public fears about radiation and nuclear war. The beat poet Allen Ginsberg's "Howl" (1955–56) referenced "Los Alamos," "monstrous bombs," and "sexless clouds of hydrogen." Another Ginsberg poem, "America" (1956), angrily told the United States "to go fuck yourself with your atom bomb." Pat Frank's novel *Alas Babylon* (1959) and Walter Miller's book *Canticle for Leibowitz* (1959) depicted a world after a devastating nuclear war. Frank condemned the suicidal obsessions of other writers and portrayed a rural Florida town "determined to build a new and better world on the ruins of the old." In Miller's more pessimistic vision, however, a new Dark Age engulfs the world. Pious monks preserve scientific knowledge for future generations despite their premonition that it will be used to build another wicked, secular society. Their fears prove legitimate, and civilization's rebirth prefaces yet another nuclear holocaust. These two tales proved popular, but 1959 brought even more powerful rejoinders to the government's reassuring rhetoric.[49]

In December 1959, officials on the NSC staff and the AEC bristled at *On the Beach*, the film adaptation of Nevil Shute's 1957 novel about the aftermath of a nuclear war that killed everyone in the Northern Hemisphere. The book and film trace the travails of a group in Australia anticipating the arrival of radioactive clouds that will extinguish all humanity. Lambasting the film's "extreme pacifist and 'Ban the Bomb' propaganda," the NSC's Carl Harr persuaded the cabinet to instruct U.S. missions abroad to discredit the film's overly emotional treatment of nuclear war and to stress that "fallout radiation diminishes so rapidly that it would be inconceivable for people a long distance away to be killed by fallout from a nuclear conflict." But five months later, the film's government critics emerged red-faced from an NSC meeting on the immediate consequences of nuclear war. Eisenhower concluded that "no one would want to live in the Northern Hemisphere" and lamented that an official report on the consequences of nuclear war had ignored the long-term effects of fallout. The best John McCone could manage in the AEC's defense was an admission that "while fallout effects were undoubtedly serious" they "would not be as bad as that portrayed in . . . 'On the Beach.'" He then contradicted himself by observing that "after 5,000 megatons" of nuclear explosions "it no longer mattered what target was hit because a lethal blanket of fallout would be produced regardless of the target." The growing public disquiet ultimately kept the test ban alive and forced the administration to defend its threshold proposal as the first step toward a comprehensive testing halt and not the abandonment of that goal.[50]

In February 1960, the United States submitted its threshold proposal to the Soviets. Washington sought to demonstrate its commitment to a complete testing halt by offering to conduct joint seismic research to improve the detection system. After a month of debate, the Soviets agreed to negotiate the treaty and conduct joint experiments to improve the monitoring system if the Americans accepted a four- to five-year testing moratorium. Despite pressure from the British to agree, Eisenhower could not legally bind his successor unless the moratorium provisions were included in the treaty. Because congressional opponents would kill any treaty that included an unpoliced testing halt, the president offered a counterproposal that included a one- to two-year moratorium as a side agreement.

The American desire to use nuclear explosives in the seismic research program also complicated the negotiations. The Soviets rejected this suggestion as a veiled attempt to resume weapons research — a correct assessment, given that the U.S. testing grounds would have contained devices to measure weapons effects. The Eisenhower team tried to quiet Soviet objections by using old gun-type weapons assemblies for the seismic improvement program. The JCAE, however, balked at letting Moscow see even these antiquated weapons designs, insisting on reciprocal disclosure of nuclear data. After the U-2 incident chilled U.S.-Soviet relations, the deadlock tightened. In November, Republican presidential candidate Richard M. Nixon's defeat in the general election seemed to foreclose progress, and the talks recessed until after John F. Kennedy's inauguration. When McCone and the Defense Department lobbied to resume underground testing, Eisenhower refused. He would neither place the onus for the talks' failure on the United States nor present his successor with a fait accompli.[51]

The MLF Quick Fix

The failure of both the disarmament and the test ban negotiations left nuclear sharing as the only surviving element in U.S. nonproliferation policy. But this approach did nothing to stem the spread of nuclear weapons outside of Europe. China's quest for nuclear weapons had only intensified with the Sino-Soviet schism. U.S. intelligence analysts predicted that Beijing would acquire an independent nuclear capability by 1963 or 1964. The introduction of nuclear weapons into East Asia would likely inspire other atomic energy programs, especially in Taiwan and Japan. Asia's strategic picture became more complex when both the Soviets and the French reported that India had begun using peaceful uses technology to produce weapons.[52] The Indian bomb project gained impetus from Indo-Chinese rivalry, beginning with a series of border disputes in September 1959. In 1960, Kenneth Nichols, Manhattan Project veteran and then Westinghouse executive, witnessed Homi Bhabha, chair of the Indian Atomic Energy Commission, boasting to Indian prime minister Nehru that he could produce atomic bombs in about one year.[53] If India developed nuclear weapons, its regional foe Pakistan would surely follow.

The "Nth-country problem," as some commentators dubbed proliferation, loomed even more ominously. The United States feared a Middle Eastern arms race in which the United Arab Republic, which included Egypt and Syria, sought nuclear weapons—a frightening prospect given evidence late in Eisenhower's term of an Israeli nuclear weapons program in the Negev Desert. The United States responded noncommittally to Israel's claim that the facilities in question aimed only at peaceful research, though most officials privately believed that Tel Aviv sought a weapons capability. But the obvious inability of nuclear sharing to anticipate or prevent such developments failed to inspire serious consideration of alternative policies.

After the medium range ballistic missile (MRBM) proposals of 1957 failed to appease French and German nuclear ambitions, some U.S. officials contemplated multilateral control of nuclear weapons as the best solution for the Nth-country problem in Europe. Until this idea won acceptance in late 1959, the Eisenhower administration pressed Adenauer and de Gaulle to accept nuclear warheads under a bilateral arrangement, albeit with little success. Bonn insisted that U.S. reluctance to place IRBMs on German soil relegated West Germany to an inferior position within NATO. U.S. allies, however, objected to West German access to anything other than tactical weapons. De Gaulle, moreover, refused to allow American or NATO control over nuclear weapons on French soil, although he did accept such arrangements for French forces based in Germany.

Eisenhower increasingly found restrictions on nuclear aid to France both foolish and frustrating. He unsuccessfully sought a compromise in the face of de Gaulle's intransigence and the JCAE's unwillingness to conclude a nuclear alliance with any country other than Britain. He complained that de Gaulle had a "Messiah complex, picturing himself as a cross between Napoleon and Joan of Arc," and griped that inflexible U.S. laws forced "other countries to become nuclear powers." After France detonated its first nuclear bomb in February 1960, the president and McCone continued trying to bind the French nuclear program to the United States through increased nuclear sharing, to no avail.[54]

Unable to resolve the French problem, the Eisenhower administration focused on quenching Bonn's thirst for nuclear weaponry. In late 1959, the concept of corporate control took center stage after NATO commander Lauris Norstad and Secretary of Defense Thomas Gates advocated a land-based NATO IRBM force under multilateral oversight as the best alternative to European proliferation. Under this plan, NATO would become the fourth nuclear power. But the State Department believed that IRBMs on German soil might unduly provoke the Soviets and quickly offered an alternative to the Norstad and Gates proposal. Robert Bowie, former head of the State Department Policy Planning Staff, helped devise a new corporate-control proposal while serving as outside consultant. Bowie advocated a sea-based missile force under multilateral control. The missiles and warheads would be provided by the United States but would come under the physical control of mixed-manned NATO forces. Eisenhower endorsed the idea, believing it would help build an esprit de corps within the alliance. Once again, a technological chimera had mesmerized the president.

European reaction proved mixed. According to France, the proposal's timing seemed designed to complicate its parliamentary debate on funding for a missile force. The British publicly supported the initiative but in private characterized corporate control as unnecessary because most NATO members had no desire for nuclear weapons. Germany and some smaller NATO countries, however, eagerly embraced the idea. After the Eisenhower administration publicly unveiled the MLF proposal in December, the Soviets blasted it as a scheme to aid German militarists. Yet Eisenhower introduced the program so late in his term that decisions about how to respond to European and Soviet criticisms fell to the incoming Kennedy administration. President Eisenhower had refrained from tying his successor's hands on the test ban issue, but he had failed to show the same restraint on nuclear sharing.[55]

Despite Eisenhower's desire to control the arms race, he left office having done more to encourage nuclear proliferation than to prevent it. In part, this failure stemmed from a cavalier attitude toward proliferation within NATO and an inability to understand the myriad ways weapons data could be acquired, including so-called peaceful uses. Eisenhower viewed proliferation exclusively from an American perspective and failed to consider how the possession of nuclear weapons by certain countries, such as Germany and China, would threaten others. The president pushed forward with nuclear-sharing policies despite their negative effect on U.S.-Soviet relations, and he repeatedly squandered opportunities to conclude a nonproliferation agreement with the Soviets. Although Eisenhower supported a test ban treaty, he divorced the measure from other nonproliferation measures in order to reap a public relations victory. Technological quick fixes to proliferation problems pushed multilateral diplomacy into the background. The Eisenhower administration's most imaginative nonproliferation plan, the MLF, epitomized the hoped-for technological silver bullet. But it actually would have expanded nuclear weapons access to more countries — a fitting epitaph for Eisenhower's convoluted thinking on the Nth-country conundrum.

Tests and Toughness

JFK'S FALSE START ON THE PROLIFERATION

QUESTION, 1961–1962

"Courage," John F. Kennedy claimed, stood as the "most admirable of human virtues." As a senator, Kennedy lent his name to *Profiles in Courage*, a ghostwritten paean to politicians who bravely resisted popular pressure to compromise their "ethics," "integrity," and "morality." Principle proved more important to these leaders than did political success. While campaigning for president, Kennedy invoked their virtuous examples, portraying himself as a war hero and a "tough-minded" leader. In practice, JFK proved far more attuned to his electoral fortunes than to his private convictions. While senator, he had warned "of a nuclear holocaust being initiated for irrational reasons by a fanatic or a demagogue" should nuclear proliferation continue unchecked. As president, he made clear that the demagogue he most feared ruled in Beijing. The Soviets also hoped to impede Chinese, as well as West German, access to the bomb. Yet Kennedy and Khrushchev faced domestic critics, especially in their own defense establishments, who did not support a modus vivendi to contain proliferation. Unwilling to sacrifice his political standing for an agreement with Moscow, Kennedy resorted to false machismo and a traditional positions-of-strength policy, including a massive military buildup, and he resumed nuclear testing, all undercutting his arms control goals. By spring 1962, the prospects of a nonproliferation agreement seemed dimmer than at any other point since 1958.[1]

Kennedy entered office publicly and personally committed to a test ban and nonproliferation. After his friend Senator Clinton Anderson persuaded him that it would benefit national security, Kennedy had supported Democratic nominee Adlai Stevenson's call for a test moratorium in 1956. Three years later, a series of conversations with his close friend British diplomat David Ormsby-Gore strengthened his desire to curb testing and proliferation. That same year, Kennedy publicly condemned nuclear proliferation and argued that a test ban would place a major obstacle in the path of potential nuclear powers. This conviction did not fade during the 1960 presidential campaign. After his election, Kennedy instructed his staff to study how best to halt both European and Chinese proliferation. Secretary of State Christian Herter also warned him that Israel and India had shown signs of initiating nuclear weapons programs and advised the new administration to seek inspection and control of each country's nuclear facilities.

Shortly after the November election, Khrushchev attempted to assess Kennedy's commitment to nonproliferation. The Soviet embassy in Washington depicted Kennedy as "a typical pragmatist" with no firm convictions. This personality profile noted Kennedy's willingness to negotiate with Moscow, especially on arms control, but warned that the new president believed that the arms race would continue until the United States had reclaimed its "position of strength" throughout the world. Despite this guarded assessment, Khrushchev sent a wave of emissaries to sound out the incoming administration's attitudes toward détente and disarmament. Soviet ambassador Mikhail Menshikov visited Adlai Stevenson, who many thought would be the next secretary of state, and informed him that Moscow had "high hopes" for a test ban treaty.[2]

Others close to Kennedy also received private assurances that Khrushchev wanted to improve U.S.-Soviet relations and negotiate nonproliferation measures. Walt W. Rostow and W. Averell Harriman, both of whom would hold numerous foreign policy positions in the Kennedy and Johnson administrations, became convinced that the Soviets urgently sought arms control. In late 1960, Rostow met with Soviet scientists and bureaucrats during two conferences, one in the United States and the other in the Soviet Union, organized by private nuclear disarmament groups. To his surprise, Moscow's representatives seemed serious about arms control. Harriman emerged as the most frequent contact for Khrushchev's emissaries. Menshikov and other

Soviet officials left Harriman with the impression that Moscow desired arms control agreements both to release economic resources for consumer production and to diminish the threat of German and Chinese proliferation.

These initial hopes for détente soon faded. Kennedy's major foreign policy appointments signaled a tough public line with Moscow. The new president bypassed Harriman, Stevenson, and Chester Bowles, a foreign policy adviser during the campaign, all of whom had advocated reducing Cold War tensions. Kennedy instead appointed Dean Rusk, a veteran of Truman's State Department, as secretary of state. For the other national security posts, the president selected Republicans: Robert S. McNamara as secretary of defense, McGeorge Bundy as national security affairs adviser, and John J. McCloy as disarmament adviser. Kennedy also retained Allen Dulles as CIA director. None of these appointments suggested changes from Truman and Eisenhower nuclear policies. Khrushchev likened McCloy's appointment as arms control czar to sending "a goat to guard the cabbage patch."[3]

More important, Kennedy and Khrushchev both made strident Cold War speeches in January 1961. Khrushchev, on the defensive within the Kremlin since the Paris summit fiasco in May 1960, addressed an international gathering of communist propagandists and ideologists and called for uncompromising support for wars of national liberation. Experienced observers of Soviet politics credited the speech's heated language to Sino-Soviet rivalry over the allegiances of newly decolonized countries. But Kennedy, insecure after a razor-thin victory in the November election, fearful of renewed McCarthyism, and sensitive to America's tenuous status in the developing world, dubbed it "one of the most important speeches of the decade." His own inaugural address vowed to "pay any price, bear any burden, meet any hardship, support any friend, oppose any foe" in confrontation with Soviet communism. His State of the Union message reinforced this rhetoric with concrete proposals for a massive nuclear buildup.[4]

Neither leader perceived a disjunction between his public statements and his private assurances to his counterpart that he sought accommodation. Each used inflamed rhetoric to address constituencies within his own country or alliance system and apparently gave little regard to how his rival would interpret his pronouncements. Yet each also viewed the remarks of the other with great suspicion and thought that they displayed more accurately the real intentions of the respective governments than had private communications in November and December. Both men continued privately to seek improvement in U.S.-Soviet relations, but each came to believe that a public stance of toughness would more successfully bring his opponent to heel than would words of compromise. Their tough public positions also insulated each from charges of concessions made in the face of heated rhetoric.

With increased Cold War tensions as a backdrop, Kennedy resisted pressure to resume nuclear testing during his early presidency. Eisenhower had maintained the voluntary moratorium through January 1961 to provide flexibility to his successor. But in meetings before he left office, Eisenhower had urged Kennedy to resume testing. The JCAE and other influential members of Congress also pressed the president to end the moratorium before attempting to reach agreement with the Soviets. Although Kennedy received a national intelligence estimate that recommended against breaking the moratorium, the rejection of its conclusions by military intelligence analysts revealed the deep hostility of the Joint Chiefs of Staff to the testing halt.

Despite opposition from the military and Congress, Kennedy kept his campaign promise to refrain from nuclear testing until he had made a good faith effort to conclude a testing accord. In his first press conference, he reiterated his desire for a test ban treaty, promising to create a study group to reevaluate the U.S. position. This committee, led by John McCloy, pored over all the official records and transcripts of the Geneva talks. After reviewing the record, JFK became convinced that Eisenhower had frittered away a grand opportunity for a test ban in 1960.

In early March, when Kennedy met with key advisers to hammer out the U.S. position for the test ban talks, he still had much to learn about the styles and strengths of his arms control team. He lacked prior experience with any of his top foreign policy advisers. One aide joked that the cabinet contained "nine strangers and a brother." This unfamiliarity complicated Geneva preparations, restraining the flow and candor of discussion. The end product hardly mapped out a "new frontier" in arms control policy. The Kennedy proposals duplicated Eisenhower's in many details, including a call for twenty on-site inspections and continued underground tests below a seismic signal of 4.75 on the Richter scale. The basic conservatism of Kennedy's test ban policy stemmed in part from his conviction that factors other than the U.S. proposals, primarily the U-2 incident, had prevented a test ban treaty in 1960. If the American position had seemed basically acceptable to the Soviets, no reason existed to change it. But the limited outcome of these policy discussions also reflected the confident personalities and Cold War beliefs of the men who surrounded Kennedy.[5]

The president had bragged to one journalist that "nothing beats brains" (to which Dean Acheson retorted that "brains are no substitute for judgment"), and the media quickly labeled the new administration "the best and the brightest." Kennedy policymakers did have impressive credentials. Most had roots in the eastern establishment, had attended elite prep schools and Ivy League universities, and enjoyed many Wall Street connections. Henry Stimson and Dean Acheson functioned as their intellectual godfathers, instilling a sense of global noblesse oblige alongside a cold-blooded view of world politics.[6]

Though a southerner, Secretary of State Dean Rusk had been inducted into this political fraternity as assistant secretary of state for Far Eastern affairs under Acheson. After leaving government, he solidified his establishment credentials as president of the Rockefeller Foundation. Believing that communications between the president and the secretary of state should be utterly confidential, he hesitated to talk about sensitive subjects on the telephone and sometimes remained silent during large meetings. His willingness to act the "dumb dodo" led many to underestimate his working relationship with Kennedy; it also irked the president, who wanted Rusk to be more forceful. McGeorge Bundy mocked Rusk's tendency toward caution, quipping to reporters that Rusk had once asked that the room be cleared so that he and Kennedy could speak in private. When everyone had gone, the president asked Rusk what he had to say, and the secretary replied, "Well, if there weren't so many of us in the room. . . ." With characteristic prudence, Rusk wanted to guard against the tendency for democracies to "disarm at the drop of a hat." But he supported a test ban as long as the treaty guaranteed reliable inspection and control.[7]

Others in the administration shared Rusk's establishment credentials and his lukewarm attitude toward arms control negotiations. Presidential disarmament adviser John J. McCloy and national security adviser McGeorge Bundy had developed their establishment connections via Henry Stimson. McCloy had served Stimson at the War Department during World War II and had helped shape Truman's international control policy as a member of the Acheson-Lilienthal Committee. In the 1950s, he functioned as an informal adviser to Eisenhower and also served as chairman of the Chase Bank and the Council on Foreign Relations. McCloy advocated disarmament but thought the benefits of a test ban treaty were primarily psychological.

McGeorge Bundy imbibed his worldview both from Stimson and from Acheson. Bundy's father had been a Stimson aide, and later McGeorge helped write Stimson's memoirs. When he subsequently helped Acheson with his writings, he learned that "the United States was the locomotive at the head of mankind, and the rest of the world the caboose." The bright, arrogant Bundy had spent the 1950s at Harvard University and had served as dean of Harvard College before Kennedy recruited him. He proved an accomplished synthesizer and sifter of information—and was so close to the president that one commentator dubbed him "Harry Hopkins with hand grenades." But his brusque, self-assured manner affronted many people. Liberal Republican and disarmament advocate Grenville Clark dismissed Bundy as "a plain ordinary stinker," while one diplomat later remarked that the NSC adviser had "a very tactical sense of the truth." Skeptical of military arguments against the test ban, Bundy also harbored suspicions about the Soviets' reliability and intentions.[8]

Secretary of Defense Robert McNamara had the most tenuous links to the establishment and the least experience in government. A graduate of Harvard Business School, McNamara had served as an Army Air Corps logistics analyst during World War II, and after the war he became one of the "whiz kids" who revamped Ford Motor Company. He had become president of Ford shortly before moving to the Pentagon. McNamara tended to view every problem as quantifiable, and he preferred hard data to the esoteric impressions of the professional diplomat. Paul Nitze, his assistant secretary for international security affairs, filled in gaps in McNamara's knowledge of foreign affairs. A veteran of the Truman White House, Nitze also had firm roots in the establishment. McNamara initially gave tenuous support to nonproliferation efforts, but, heeding Nitze's advice, he regarded a test ban as insufficient to control proliferation.

By temperament and experience, Kennedy's advisers tended to be cautious and pragmatic, schooled in the Achesonian approach that emphasized building "situations of strength" around the world. The president made it clear that he wanted advisers who had both "*cojones*" (testicles) and "brains" in the right combination—men who knew "that the real division" was "not between left and right" but "between hard and soft." He and his "action intellectuals" arrived in Washington primed "to prove their muscle." They recognized the danger of nuclear war but wished not to appear to be appeasing the Soviets. A few members of the administration actually viewed arms control in the same threatening light "as the Soviet Union or Red China." Kennedy's national security team embraced an ethic of toughness that constrained the president's desire and ability to negotiate a nonproliferation accord.[9]

Even before the Geneva talks resumed, ominous signs appeared. McCloy seemed wary about putting his full prestige behind the test ban negotiations, making only tepid arguments before Congress for the arms control and non-proliferation aspects of a treaty. His real passion focused on renewing comprehensive disarmament negotiations and establishing the U.S. Arms Control and Disarmament Agency. McCloy's understated approach to the test ban talks magnified growing congressional and military discontent with the test moratorium. The Joint Chiefs of Staff believed a comprehensive test ban treaty put U.S. security at risk and wanted immediate resumption of nuclear testing. The differences in presidential and military opinion fueled the growing antagonism between civilian officials within the Kennedy administration and the Joint Chiefs. Chair of the Joint Chiefs Lyman L. Lemnitzer believed that Kennedy was mistaken and misguided regarding U.S. nuclear strategy. General Curtis LeMay, U.S. Air Force chief of staff, later recalled the Kennedy administration as "the most egotistical people that I ever saw in my life. . . . They had no respect for the military at all." The JCAE and the armed services committees in both houses of Congress also voiced growing skepticism about the prospects and desirability of a test ban. Official hostility compounded public attacks on the test ban negotiations from conservative journalists and former government officials, such as Lewis Strauss.[10]

Had the Soviets appeared eager to conclude an agreement, Kennedy might have shrugged off the dissenters. But the burgeoning Sino-Soviet split and the failure of Khrushchev's détente strategy had inspired a shift toward a publicly more anti-Western foreign policy. In March, U.S. ambassador to the Soviet Union Llewellyn Thompson warned Kennedy that the new climate offered little chance for progress. Contradictory news arrived on March 20, the day before the negotiations began. Alexander Fomin, the chief KGB operative in Washington, informed a *Washington Post* editor that a compromise might be reached on the inspection issue.

But the hope Fomin inspired proved false. On the opening day of the Geneva talks, Semyon K. Tsarapkin, the chief Soviet delegate, put forth new Soviet proposals that included a call for the creation of a three-person executive, or troika, for the test ban control commission. The new control arrangement would give each country a veto over inspection. The United States rejected this system as merely the facade of verification with no real assurances against cheating. Tsarapkin further inflamed the growing East-West hostility when he charged the United States and Great Britain with encouraging French nuclear tests and possibly deriving data from these experiments. Absurd on the surface because of France's seemingly crude weapon design, these accusations proved prescient in light of U.S. plans. In August 1961, Washington clandestinely monitored French tests in the hope of acquiring intelligence on the *force de frappe*. Whether a stab in the dark or based on hard data, Moscow's accusation underlined its fear that Washington could not manage its alliance partners.

As talks continued, Soviet intransigence puzzled Kennedy and his aides. Both McCloy and U.S. ambassador to the UN Adlai Stevenson attempted to uncover Soviet motivations during Soviet foreign minister Andrei Gromyko's visit to the UN. Neither man, however, succeeded in prying loose more than general assertions that Moscow gravely doubted the sincerity of U.S. arms control proposals. The United States did not give up hope. Arthur Dean, a Wall Street lawyer appointed chief U.S. negotiator on the recommendation of his friend John McCloy, probed for any willingness on Tsarapkin's part to make concessions. Dean speculated that Moscow stalled, awaiting some credible excuse, such as a French atmospheric test, to walk out of the talks.

The Geneva deadlock intensified calls to resume U.S. testing. Congressional critics, former Eisenhower administration officials, and conservative commentators dug up Kennedy's campaign promise to end the moratorium if the Soviets proved intransigent. The AEC and the Pentagon joined the public calls to resume testing. The Joint Chiefs of Staff, too, backed test resumption to aid antiballistic missile development and to advance neutron bomb research (an enhanced radiation weapon with minimal fallout and blast effects designed to kill people and to not damage buildings or roads). Dissenting from a CIA report that the Soviets continued to observe the moratorium, the Joint Chiefs presented circumstantial evidence of Soviet cheating. They capped their arguments by suggesting that public outrage could be limited if the United States tested clandestinely (a tactic that U.S. officials always argued that only Moscow would use).

Civilian officials backed the military position. Secretary of Defense McNamara and his chief deputy, Roswell Gilpatric, endorsed the Joint Chiefs' arguments for further tests, with McNamara stressing that "power is essential, but inferiority is tragic." McCloy also recommended ending the moratorium, arguing that the United States needed to demonstrate the will to test. The new AEC chairman, Glenn T. Seaborg, proved less active in the test ban debate. As a scientist, not a politician like his predecessors, he believed his responsibility lay in providing technical information on test requirements and potential weapons innovations. He usually allowed others to debate the proper balance between political and scientific considerations. Lewis Strauss and John McCone, although now private citizens, rushed to fill the vacuum left by Seaborg. Both in public and in private, they lobbied for resumption of testing. They found a receptive audience among the nuclear hawks in the Democratic Party, especially Senators Henry "Scoop" Jackson, Albert Gore Sr., and Thomas Dodd.[11]

Kennedy resisted hawkish calls to end the moratorium. He gave the military and political arguments a thorough hearing, but he remained unconvinced that the technologies the Pentagon coveted fulfilled urgent national security requirements. An NSC staffer summarized the White House attitude toward the new nuclear weapons technologies: "Sure they would be swell, but is there an important need for them?" The president still hoped that if the Soviets "feared proliferation enough," some chance existed for a test ban agreement in 1961.[12]

Kennedy's own worries about proliferation had increased since his inauguration. Carl Kaysen, an NSC staff member, recounted: "There were two subjects that you could get the President started on and he'd talk for hours. One was the gold standard and the other was nonproliferation." In early 1961, the nuclear ambitions of Israel and China seemed to pose the greatest threat to international stability. As intelligence estimates warned that Chinese acquisition of nuclear weapons could come sometime between 1962 and 1965, Kennedy became obsessed with the possibility of a Chinese nuclear arsenal. He warned that "the Chicom nuclear explosion" would likely be "the most significant and worst event of the 1960s." The world would be far worse off, he argued, "if the Chinese dominated the Communist movement, because they believe in war as the means of bringing about the Communist world. Mr. Khrushchev's means are destructive, but he believes that peaceful coexistence and support of these wars of liberation . . . will bring about our defeat." Beneath Kennedy's strategic rationale lurked racist assumptions about the "yellow peril" and the flawed belief that Asian peoples valued human life less than Westerners did. Kennedy counseled one French official that "the Chinese would be perfectly prepared to sacrifice hundreds of millions of their own lives" to achieve their goals. PRC leader Mao Ze-dong reinforced Kennedy's prejudices by bombastically alluding to nuclear war — as in 1957, when he told a gathering of world communists not to fear atomic destruction because eventually the "years will pass and we'll get to work producing more babies than ever before." Khrushchev shared Kennedy's contempt for the Chinese. He dismissed Beijing as "typically Oriental" and, on one occasion, accused Mao of "sticking a needle up [my] ass." By the 1960s, Khrushchev could no longer "view China through the eager and innocent eyes of a child. . . . China was China, and the Chinese were acting in increasingly strange ways."[13]

Israeli proliferation also worried U.S. policymakers because even the rumor of Tel Aviv's acquisition of nuclear weapons might spark a war or accelerate a regional nuclear arms race in the context of combustible Middle East politics. When Kennedy first heard about the Dimona reactor and its plutonium production capabilities, he called it "highly distressing." Congressional apprehensions about Israeli proliferation also prodded the new administration to action. Senator Bourke Hickenlooper, in an executive session of the Senate Foreign Relations Committee, blasted Tel Aviv for "just lying to us like horse thieves about this thing." Throughout 1961, the JCAE and the Senate Foreign Relations Committee pressed the State Department for information about the Dimona reactor and Israeli intentions. Kennedy officially accepted Prime Minister David Ben-Gurion's assurances that his government had no plans to produce nuclear weapons, but he had substantial evidence to the contrary. Behind the scenes, the president and his aides continued to monitor the Dimona reactor and to push for international inspection and safeguards on all Israeli nuclear activities. In the face of Ben-Gurion's resistance to opening up the Israeli facilities, the Kennedy administration attempted to bribe Tel Aviv with sophisticated conventional weapons. These policies sought to delay a Middle East nuclear arms race long enough for an arms control arrangement to be implemented.[14]

NATO Troubles

Kennedy also opposed proliferation within NATO. In late 1960, Paul Nitze, the head of Kennedy's transition team on national security policy, monitored the MLF negotiations and consulted with British, German, and French leaders on other nuclear-sharing issues. The Eisenhower administration had urged JFK to endorse its ideas, but the new president reserved judgment. Adding to his NATO troubles, Kennedy rejected massive retaliation, which emphasized nuclear over conventional forces, prompting continental rumblings. Europeans feared that Kennedy's new U.S. strategy of "flexible response," which called for a conventional buildup and a higher threshold for the use of tactical nuclear weapons, suggested a U.S. desire to fight a local war in Europe without obliterating New York or Moscow. The MLF added to this anxiety because Eisenhower's proposal had called for Europeans to shoulder most of the cost to alleviate the American balance-of-payments problem. Some

Europeans perceived an implicit threat to pull U.S. forces out of Europe if the other NATO countries did not agree to bear a greater military and financial burden. The desire for national nuclear forces became intertwined with these suspicions about the U.S. role in NATO. French and German nuclear ambitions became prime targets of Kennedy's nonproliferation policy, as they had been of Eisenhower's. Charles de Gaulle's nuclear program posed the major challenge to U.S. dominance in the Western alliance. Yet in 1960, German defense minister Franz Josef Strauss trumpeted Bonn's discontent when he complained about subordinating West German "foot soldiers" to "American atomic knights."[15]

In January 1961, the State Department advised Kennedy that, despite the need to curb European proliferation, it would be "impossible to draw that line where it is at the moment." Because national nuclear forces in Europe appeared inevitable, Washington needed to steer the process on a course most favorable to the United States. The department rejected the MLF as a means to this end because the force's ability to threaten Soviet targets implied a continuing reliance on massive retaliation. Instead, the United States should seek to create a joint grand deterrent placing all Western nuclear forces, including U.S. strategic weapons, under multilateral control. Such an arrangement could be better integrated with a strategy of flexible response and would help reduce the strain that the U.S. nuclear buildup had placed on the domestic economy. Kennedy, however, thought that schemes to control French and German proliferation via nuclear sharing could enable NATO allies to embroil the United States in a nuclear war against its will.[16]

Congress also complicated Kennedy's policy toward European proliferation. In late 1960 and early 1961, JCAE members had investigated command and control of U.S. nuclear weapons based in Europe. They came away convinced that the vaunted "two-key" control system amounted to "just a lot of nonsense." During secret hearings, Senator Stuart Symington argued that during a crisis a European general could "always knock our man in the head and fire the missile." Evidence also emerged that an enterprising British officer had substituted a screwdriver for the U.S. key during a Thor missile test. JFK shared some of these fears, and in April 1961, he initiated a study of how to prevent unauthorized use of the NATO nuclear stockpile.[17]

Control of the NATO arsenal, nonetheless, did not directly address the problem of French and German nuclear ambitions. Kennedy's European policy concentrated on containing a resurgent West Germany and sought "to make it impossible for the Germans to develop an independent nuclear capacity." After France's nuclear test in 1960, Bonn remained the last non-nuclear power among the leading NATO nations, prompting Undersecretary of State George Ball to warn against a "revival of the inter-war German psychosis" and Harvard professor Henry Kissinger, a part-time adviser, to label West Germany a "candidate for a nervous breakdown." The architects of the New Frontier, primarily junior officers from World War II, interpreted European politics through the lens of the 1930s and the 1940s. They feared that if U.S. and NATO policies relegated Germany to an artificially inferior position, its leaders might take a nationalist turn, either becoming a neutral force in world politics and playing the two superpowers off one another or else allying with the Soviet Union in order to achieve reunification.[18]

France's challenge to U.S. hegemony grew more threatening because of its potential effects on German nationalism. Kennedy's team worried that de Gaulle's call for a more limited role for the United States in Europe might spawn Franco-German nuclear collaboration. Even if the Germans and French did not conclude an alliance, de Gaulle's *force de frappe* might inspire Bonn to seek its own nuclear arsenal. Secretary Rusk warned that an independent German nuclear force or a joint Franco-German effort "would shake NATO to its foundations." Confronted with a nascent nuclear Germany, moreover, Moscow might preemptively precipitate a third world war. Kennedy's emphasis on flexible response, thus, pushed Bonn toward a stronger bilateral relationship with France by feeding German fears that the United States would abandon NATO.[19]

The MLF Merry-Go-Round

After rejecting the early State Department recommendation of a joint grand deterrent, Kennedy continued seeking a way to limit European proliferation while preserving NATO's function of dual Soviet–West German containment. He received conflicting advice on the best course to follow. Some State Department analysts, dubbed the "theologians" by their adversaries, opposed the French nuclear deterrent and sought to use the MLF along with the Common Market to forge a united Europe. They contended that if the United States supplied the hardware and data for the MLF, it could require a veto over its use. A politically integrated Europe might eventually emerge, and the U.S. veto might be repealed, though such a regime would take years, perhaps decades, to emerge. The United States in the interim would have to preserve its options by fending off de Gaulle's demand for a tripartite French, British, and American directorate to manage Western policy in Europe and the world.

NSC staff "pragmatists" opposed the theologians' vision of a united Europe under American management. They preferred a less ambitious strategy in which the United States would let the Europeans take the lead on European integration, including the MLF. Others also took a dim view of the MLF. NATO commander General Lauris Norstad believed Polaris submarines should remain solely under American control and advocated a land-based MRBM solution to NATO's nuclear problem. Secretary McNamara and his deputy Nitze wanted NATO unity but opposed any European nuclear force, whether national or multilateral, which decentralized control of the Western nuclear deterrent. Nitze curtly dismissed the MLF as a "gimmick." After fielding French requests for nuclear aid, U.S. ambassador to France James Gavin also rejected the MLF and advocated an expanded bilateral nuclear relationship with Paris as the best means to contain de Gaulle's plan for an independent Europe. Some argued that U.S. aid to France would eventually provide the same "element of control that our cooperation with the British has given us."[20]

These bureaucratic divisions accentuated Kennedy's own intellectual restlessness and impatience. Dean Rusk once complained that "you could never get President Kennedy to think beyond what he had to do at nine o'clock tomorrow morning." JFK wanted both quick decisions and options. Administrative chaos and reactive policies often resulted, as in the Bay of Pigs fiasco of April 1961. Determined never to suffer such public embarrassment again, Kennedy asked McGeorge Bundy to recommend improvements in the policymaking process. "I hope you'll be in a good mood when you read this," warned Bundy as he laid the bulk of the blame squarely on the president: "We can't get you to sit still. . . . Right now it is so hard to get to you with anything urgent and immediate that about half the papers and reports you personally ask for are never shown to you because by the time you are available you have clearly lost interest in them." Kennedy's lack of administrative acumen left the government without a well-developed nonproliferation policy, especially toward Europe. The president established clear positions on neither NATO nuclear sharing nor independent deterrents, thereby confusing allied leaders and souring U.S.-European ties.[21]

Kennedy turned to an elder statesman, Dean Acheson, for advice, asking the former secretary of state to review NATO policy. As early as December 1960 Acheson had confided to Dirk U. Stikker, a Dutch diplomat and incoming NATO secretary-general, that the MLF's only purpose was to "prevent de Gaulle from doing something very foolish." Acheson's final report in April 1961, however, provided ambiguous advice on nonproliferation and nuclear sharing. He opposed independent nuclear forces, urging the administration to discourage French proliferation and even suggesting that Britain should be persuaded to phase out its nuclear program. Acheson framed the "dilemma" quite starkly: "If we helped the French, the Germans would insist on equal treatment. If we did not and the French persisted, they could only succeed by calling in the Germans." But he offered no means to roll back or prevent proliferation in NATO, rejecting the MLF as a solution until all NATO countries had achieved their conventional buildup targets. Acheson also insisted that NATO have tactical and strategic nuclear weapons at its disposal, albeit with a U.S. veto over their use. In the end, Washington should "drag out a multilateral proposal and let the Europeans wrestle with it a while until they saw all the bugs in it and decided that they'd be better off to leave the nuclear forces to us."[22]

Despite its haziness, Kennedy gravitated to Acheson's "pragmatic" solution. He de-emphasized the MLF while making clear that the United States still wanted a multilateral solution to NATO nuclear requirements. In a speech to the Canadian parliament in May, the president proclaimed U.S. support for a seaborne mixed-manned force. But he also offered Acheson's caveat that the United States would only move forward on this initiative after conventional force goals had been fulfilled. He placed the burden of determining the MLF's feasibility on European shoulders. Kennedy's Ottawa speech aimed at more than offering a solution to NATO's nuclear worries. He hoped that by making all U.S. nuclear aid contingent on the creation of a multilateral deterrent, he could pressure France and Britain to contribute their national nuclear forces to a NATO nuclear command. Should they fail to surrender unilateral control over their weapons, the United States would starve their programs by withholding technical and financial aid. Paris and London would be forced to decide whether to commit massive expenditures to modernize their delivery systems or cling to obsolete and ineffective deterrents.[23]

Confronting de Gaulle and Khrushchev

While visiting Europe in May and June, Kennedy pressed both de Gaulle and Khrushchev to cooperate with U.S. nonproliferation policy. On the surface, the trip to Paris appeared to be a great success, with John and Jackie's visit provoking great acclaim among the French people and press. In private, de Gaulle proved immune to the Kennedy charm. Although he conceded that the disadvantages of German proliferation would be "far greater than the advantages," the general did not find Kennedy's arguments against the French deterrent or European proliferation persuasive, claiming that only a few countries could afford nuclear weapons and that Germany could not legally possess them because of its antinuclear pledge made at the signing of the Western European Union Treaty. De Gaulle also dismissed the MLF proposal, claiming that "no one believes that any country will place its atomic weapons in the hands of others." He found the U.S. insistence on a veto on the MLF's use as "quite normal" but unsatisfactory to France, which needed its own nuclear deterrent to preserve its national identity. While France might only deploy one-tenth the striking power of the Soviet Union, it would have enough strength to "tear off an arm," which might cause Moscow to hesitate before attacking. After the visit, de Gaulle dismissed the conversations as confirming Kennedy's attachment to "previous bad habits." Thereafter France's commitment to its nuclear program waxed while its allegiance to NATO waned. Though appreciating the general's discretion in not airing their differences publicly, the president complained that de Gaulle cared only for his country's "selfish interests."[24]

Kennedy next flew to Vienna for meetings with Khrushchev. His brother Robert had received assurances from a Soviet military intelligence operative, Georgi Bolshakov, that the Soviet premier was ready to make concessions on a test ban treaty. The summit also offered a unique opportunity to talk candidly about Chinese and German proliferation. Kennedy hoped to persuade Khrushchev that he would go the "last mile" to end nuclear testing and stop Chinese acquisition of nuclear weapons.[25]

In preparation for the summit, JFK immersed himself in policy papers and analyses of Khrushchev's personality. After a week of studying his adversary, Kennedy exclaimed, "He's smart," and "He's tough!" But the president also concluded that Khrushchev would probably negotiate rather than go to war over Berlin or other Cold War flashpoints. Although some State Department analysts also believed that Khrushchev sought détente to contain both Germany and China, Rusk doubted the permanence of the Sino-Soviet split, suspecting that the two communist powers could bridge their differences and leave the United States dangerously exposed. The secretary's views did not dissuade Kennedy from going to Vienna intent on reaching at least a modus vivendi on nonproliferation—an implicit quid pro quo on banning Chinese and German access to nuclear weapons.[26]

Khrushchev also had high hopes for the Vienna summit, in part because he thought JFK politically weak after the Bay of Pigs fiasco. Bolshakov's promises about Soviet flexibility regarding the test ban, however, proved false. The Kennedys believed the military intelligence officer to be Khrushchev's personal representative in the Soviet embassy, but he did not have the premier's personal confidence nor had he independent authority to negotiate.

He could only transmit messages from JFK, and the information he gave in return often proved inaccurate. Llewellyn Thompson, the U.S. ambassador in Moscow, consistently provided better guidance on Khrushchev's thinking, but the contempt for the Foreign Service that Kennedy had imbibed from his father initially blinded him to Thompson's virtues. At Vienna, the Soviet premier and Gromyko both proved intransigent on the test ban, refusing more than three on-site inspections. Their only concession was a promise not to break the moratorium first. When Kennedy raised the need to conclude a test ban before the world contained "ten or even fifteen nuclear powers," Khrushchev dismissed the treaty's nonproliferation capabilities as merely theoretical. Only general and complete disarmament would stop proliferation. But Kennedy cited the Chinese proverb that a "thousand-mile journey begins with one step." Khrushchev bristled, observing that "the President apparently knew the Chinese very well but that he too knew them quite well." With the subject of China closed off and Khrushchev unresponsive to nonproliferation arguments, conversation focused on Berlin. To Khrushchev, Kennedy appeared even more rigid on the "German question" than Eisenhower had two years before. Frustrated and angry, the premier vowed to sign a peace treaty with East Germany by year's end. Kennedy had hoped to leave Vienna with a test ban treaty agreement, at least in principle. Instead, he journeyed home alarmed that war might be imminent.[27]

Reversals

A new Berlin crisis preoccupied Kennedy back in Washington, but nonproliferation and testing did not disappear from view. The president wrongly suspected that Chinese pressure had caused the Soviets to abandon their test ban effort. The main question for the United States now became how to disengage from the Geneva talks on nuclear testing without stirring up discontent among neutrals and antinuclear activists. Kennedy pondered Llewellyn Thompson's suggestion to revive Eisenhower's plan for an atmospheric test ban. If the Soviets rejected it, the United States had a pretext to terminate the talks. A presidentially authorized study also examined the risks of a continued moratorium. When a special ad hoc panel on nuclear testing, chaired by nuclear scientist Wolfgang Panofsky, concluded that no urgent technical reasons for testing existed, the Pentagon vigorously dissented, arguing that both a neutron bomb and antiballistic missile technology constituted vital defense needs.

Buttressed by the Panofsky report, Kennedy chose to weather criticism from test ban opponents and make one last attempt to compromise with the Soviets. He took a calculated political gamble. Dwight Eisenhower, Dean Acheson, and John McCloy all advocated ending the moratorium, although only Eisenhower had voiced his views publicly. Opinion polls, moreover, showed that 55 percent of the American people supported resuming testing, a product of public pressing by Lewis Strauss, John McCone, and such congressional hawks as Thomas Dodd. But even proponents of the test ban believed the moratorium was doomed. Some commentators argued that the moratorium encouraged proliferation by fostering an image of U.S. weakness and creating doubt about whether Washington would honor its alliance commitments in a future confrontation with Moscow.

The president nonetheless thought the key to Cold War victory lay in cultivating the allegiance of the developing world. Because unilateral resumption might hurt the U.S. position in the UN, he sought some clear scientific or military justification for renewed testing. The technical arguments of the Joint Chiefs of Staff offered insufficient evidence that a delay in nuclear testing threatened national security. The president hence played a waiting game, privately believing that "we should clearly resume testing soon" while hoping to find a solution to the "UN problem." He did order the Defense Department and the AEC to begin preparing a new series of underground tests, but he believed he needed six months to persuade world opinion to accept U.S. testing. When both McNamara and Seaborg argued that the United States could test underground in less than six months, he had them withdraw their studies so that he could claim that the delay rested on technical, not political, grounds.[28]

Kennedy's motives behind not ending the test ban talks were not entirely cynical. He still believed that common ground existed between the United States and the Soviet Union on arms control. In addition to continuing the moratorium, he refrained from retaliating for Khrushchev's Berlin ultimatum by canceling bilateral talks on disarmament. He also continued working to establish an arms control and disarmament agency independent from the State Department. Although the Berlin crisis enveloped these efforts in an atmosphere of pessimism, both met with a degree of success.

In late June, Kennedy submitted to Congress his proposal for a U.S. Arms Control and Disarmament Agency. In July and August, the war crisis atmosphere over Berlin placed that legislation in jeopardy, but Kennedy strongly supported the bill and McCloy and his staff lobbied strenuously against congressional opposition. The legislation ultimately passed with comfortable margins in both houses, and in late September Kennedy signed the bill into law.

McCloy, meanwhile, had also initiated a new round of bilateral discussions with Moscow on general disarmament. Reviving the Ten-Nation Disarmament Conference provided the ostensible reason for these talks, which commenced in June 1961, but they also offered the superpowers a forum for reducing Cold War tensions and controlling proliferation. Because of the Berlin crisis, McCloy entered the meetings with very conservative goals: winning the propaganda battle and preventing transfer of the test ban negotiations into the general disarmament talks. But the first two rounds of these discussions produced little progress. McCloy's trip to the Soviet Union in July only provided another occasion for Khrushchev to bluster and issue threats about Berlin. Out of the tug and pull of these talks, McCloy formulated the general outline of a nonproliferation agreement: a pledge by all the nuclear powers not to transfer control of nuclear weapons to other states and a reciprocal promise from non-nuclear countries not to accept nuclear weapons. A form of limited world government, a concept McCloy had borrowed from Grenville Clark and Harvard law professor Louis Sohn, would administer the control and inspection provisions of the agreement.

Any satisfaction Kennedy felt about the small successes of his disarmament policy quickly evaporated. On August 13, Soviet troops sealed the border between East and West Berlin to stop the flow of East Germans fleeing from communist rule. At first the president reacted with relief, privately calling a wall "a hell of a lot better than a war." Within days, however, his failure to take aggressive action against the barrier inspired charges of appeasement at home and abroad. French and German critics saw Kennedy's acquiescence as proof that U.S. nuclear assurances were unreliable. Khrushchev, like Kennedy, had to navigate between various political forces within his own government and alliance system. The premier approved the wall to avoid a military confrontation between East German and NATO forces that might trigger Soviet intervention. Under pressure from the East German regime and hardliners at home to act, he had tried to buy time by warning that Kennedy was "a lightweight" unable to control his own government. If the Soviets pushed Kennedy too far, they risked war.[29]

Kennedy's measured response to the wall did not strengthen Khrushchev's moderate flank but instead inspired calls for increased pressure on the West. On August 28, U.S. intelligence intercepted Soviet military signals that nuclear tests might be imminent. "Fucked again!" Kennedy exclaimed on hearing the news. As in June, when Bolshakov had promised progress on a test ban, Kennedy had taken at face value Khrushchev's assurances that he would not test first. Soviet testing put the president, already staggering in the aftermath of the Berlin Wall, on very precarious political footing. When the Soviets tested on August 31, Kennedy stared at the CIA report and cursed: "The bastards. That fucking liar." To have tested in late August, the Soviets must have begun preparations in May, several weeks before Khrushchev promised at Vienna that he would not break the moratorium. The test resumption appeared even more insulting and internationally disruptive because it occurred only a day after Arthur Dean had presented a new U.S. proposal at Geneva.[30]

In the anger of the moment, Kennedy wanted to order immediate resumption of U.S. underground tests. When some aides recommended delaying tests in order to exploit the propaganda edge offered by Soviet actions, he scoffed, "What are you? Peaceniks? They just kicked me in the nuts. I'm supposed to say that's okay?" But further arguments from UN ambassador Stevenson and Edward R. Murrow, director of the U.S. Information Agency, convinced Kennedy that restraint might work to his advantage. He decided to offer the Soviets an unpoliced atmospheric test ban if they ended their experiments by September 9. When Khrushchev immediately rejected the offer, Kennedy concluded that he had no choice but to announce resumption of underground testing on September 5. The Geneva talks recessed a few days later. Ambassador Stevenson made another case for courting world opinion. But the president brushed his objections aside: "I don't hear of any windows being broken because of the Soviet decision. The neutrals have been terrible."[31]

With the test talks in limbo and the Berlin crisis forestalling U.S.-Soviet cooperation on nonproliferation, Kennedy explored other avenues to controlling proliferation. In July, he had authorized Project Pacifica, a study of the long-term implications of Chinese proliferation for both Asia and NATO. The State Department Policy Planning Staff also formulated alternate methods of reducing the impact of a Chinese nuclear test. Reflecting the continuing fascination of the diplomatic corps with selective proliferation, George McGhee of the State Department Policy Planning Staff suggested that it might be in U.S. interest to use covert technical aid to ensure that India rather than China became the first Asian nuclear power. Considering that intelligence estimates warned that a Chinese nuclear explosion could come anytime from 1961 to 1963, McGhee's plan would have required a massive infusion of money and technical aid to the Indian program. Rusk and ambassador to India John Kenneth Galbraith killed the idea. During 1961, Rusk emerged as the most ardent supporter of Kennedy's nonproliferation policy within the administration. He warned subordinates that "to assist some other country, even for important political or psychological reasons, would start us down a jungle path from which I see no exit."[32]

Kennedy had also flirted with increased nuclear sharing during the Berlin crisis. In early July, he asked Rusk, McNamara, and Secretary of the Treasury Douglas Dillon to explore how best to exploit increased superpower tension to win European approval of the MLF. Although the president remained ambivalent about the scheme, the MLF appeared to be the minimum needed to assuage NATO discontent. As well, the Berlin confrontation had intensified U.S. efforts to build up NATO conventional forces, which in turn had inspired further European doubts about American willingness to use nuclear weapons. With sentiment in favor of land-based MRBMs still strong, JFK grasped at the MLF as a less-destabilizing and less-provocative alternative. The renewed interest in nuclear sharing stemmed partly from the momentum of U.S. military preparations in the summer and fall of 1961. Determined to improve the U.S. defense posture and maintain NATO unity, the Kennedy administration forged closer nuclear ties with France, promising consultations on nuclear weapons use and signing a limited nuclear cooperation agreement. Washington also sought emergency authority to stockpile nuclear weapons in France.

As Berlin tensions diminished, so did Kennedy's interest in the MLF. The United States reverted to its policy of emphasizing conventional force requirements, invoking the MLF largely to deflect calls for land-based MRBMs. But American openness to nuclear sharing during the Berlin crisis raised hopes in France of a full nuclear alliance, prompting Ambassador Gavin to argue again for more substantive French nuclear aid. His recommendations, however, provoked strong opposition from Washington and the U.S. NATO military command, and Kennedy reaffirmed his personal hostility to national nuclear forces. By December 1961, the many sudden shifts and mixed messages of U.S. policy had left many Europeans scratching their heads.

A Foolish Inconsistency

The Kennedy administration had developed an oscillating pattern of toughness and conciliation that U.S. allies and the Soviets both found difficult to interpret. By mid-September 1961, the president had retreated from his confrontational stance of the summer and again sought a modus vivendi with Khrushchev. The Berlin crisis and resumed testing had set off a series of briefings that reinforced Kennedy's conviction that the nuclear arms race needed to be corralled. After Air Force general Thomas Powers briefed him on U.S. nuclear war plans, JFK sighed, "And we call ourselves the human race." Searching for a way to pull back from the brink, he used his first UN speech to signal a new mood. On September 25, he challenged Moscow to a "peace race" in a stirring address that laid out U.S. disarmament goals, including nonproliferation.[33]

In the weeks prior to the speech, Khrushchev had projected a more conciliatory attitude, using secret channels to request negotiations on Berlin and instructing his disarmament delegate to reach agreement with McCloy on principles regarding general disarmament. Khrushchev also initiated clandestine correspondence with the president. Having temporarily placated his domestic hard-liners with more assertive action, the Soviet premier felt free to pursue détente once again. Although Kennedy displayed more reticence than did his Soviet counterpart, these early letters eased tensions and prompted some discussion of nonproliferation in the Berlin talks that began in late September.

Since July, the Kennedy administration had suspected that a Central European nuclear-free zone or a more sweeping nonproliferation agreement might be a prerequisite to a Berlin settlement. Rusk, therefore, anticipated that Gromyko would revive the Rapacki Plan during discussions. While hesitant about commitments that impinged on German sovereignty, the secretary admitted that both superpowers had a strong national interest in halting proliferation. Gromyko boldly stated that any Berlin treaty must guarantee that West Germany would not gain control over nuclear weapons. Although the Soviet Union and the United States appeared closer on the proliferation issue, other Soviet conditions for a Berlin settlement prevented substantial gains.

The Rusk-Gromyko meetings nonetheless gave Kennedy enough hope for a negotiated agreement that he began preparing the American public and U.S. allies for improved relations with the Soviet Union. In November, the president, on a speaking tour of western states, claimed that the United States must demonstrate its "national maturity" and "accept the fact that negotiations are not a contest spelling victory or defeat." He also met with West German chancellor Adenauer to assess his reaction to a Berlin agreement and a possible German nonproliferation pledge. Kennedy and the elderly German leader already had an icy relationship. Many U.S. policymakers found Adenauer's constant need for reassurance annoying and childish, while the chancellor questioned Kennedy's loyalty to NATO and his willingness to provide assertive leadership for the Western alliance. Their testy conversations in November 1961 even resulted in the burning of minutes from one heated meeting to expunge them from the official record.[34]

After Kennedy's UN speech and the Rusk-Gromyko talks, Adenauer ridiculed U.S. disengagement from Germany and scoffed at "nonsense about atom-free zones." JFK assured him that the United States did not wish to place Bonn in an inferior military position within NATO. But the president also stressed his commitment to nonproliferation. During Adenauer's subsequent Washington visit, Kennedy turned the tables and conveyed his concern that Bonn might be tempted to neutralize Germany or ally with the Soviets in exchange for reunification. This chilly exchange prompted a tense discussion of German nuclear ambitions. Adenauer claimed that Bonn had no intention of seeking nuclear weapons. But his reminder of the conditional nature of West Germany's pledge not to manufacture atomic bombs and his insistence that NATO needed the ability to use nuclear weapons independent of a U.S. veto forced the Kennedy administration to renew its efforts to use the MLF as a substitute for national nuclear forces. Kennedy nonetheless still preferred a global nonproliferation agreement that blocked German access to nuclear weapons. In an interview with Khrushchev's son-in-law Alexei Adzhubei, an editor with the Soviet newspaper *Izvestiia*, he assured the Soviets that they had nothing to fear from Bonn because it had no nuclear weapons and no ground forces outside the NATO system. The president conceded that "if Germany developed an atomic capacity of its own, if it developed many missiles or a strong national army that threatened war, then I could understand your concern and I would share it."[35]

This expression of U.S.-Soviet common interests did not prevent organizational failures in late 1961 and early 1962 from wasting the initial promise of the Rusk-Gromyko talks. Bureaucratic divisions hobbled attempts to build a clear strategy at home, while Western European fears of a superpower agreement at their expense did the same abroad. Kennedy sought to hold out the possibility of an MLF arrangement in order to placate U.S. allies long enough to buy time to see if the Berlin negotiations would bear fruit. He still hoped to prevent both European and Chinese proliferation. But to succeed, this policy needed to be communicated clearly to the bureaucracy and rigorously coordinated by either the White House or the State Department. Because Kennedy eschewed the consensus-building, formal policy apparatus of the Eisenhower years, many of his subordinates remained uninformed of his multilayered nonproliferation tactics and aims.

As the United States prepared for the NATO ministerial meetings in

December 1961, the MLF continued to be clouded in uncertainty. McNamara and the Defense Department emphasized the need to fulfill the conventional force levels that the "flexible response" strategy required, and they did not want to distract the alliance with a nuclear-sharing proposal that served no military purpose. The State Department, NATO ambassador Thomas Finletter, and the NSC staff, however, believed that allied unity necessitated a restatement of both American willingness to help create a NATO nuclear force and its opposition to independent deterrents. The United States arrived at the NATO meeting voicing the ambiguous policy first set down by Kennedy in his Ottawa speech in May: Washington opposed national nuclear forces and would only provide technical and financial support to multinational efforts. Responsibility for financing the MLF rested in European hands. As the meetings unfolded, West German discontent with existing nuclear policy dispelled any U.S. illusions that the nuclear-sharing issue could be finessed. Kennedy could not simply increase American pressure for the MLF because both Great Britain and France expressed hostility to the initiative, rightly suspecting that the United States was manipulating them to phase out their national deterrents.

Facing a dilemma, Kennedy resumed his favored tactic of pursuing contradictory options simultaneously. In January 1962, he pressed de Gaulle to abandon his nuclear efforts by candidly discussing U.S. fears that the *force de frappe* would compel Germany to pursue nuclear weapons. De Gaulle imperiously refused to debate the merits of U.S. nonproliferation policy and pointedly reminded Kennedy that France had more to fear from Germany than did the United States. This exchange left little hope that U.S. arguments would prove effective. The British and German proliferation problems also seemed insoluble. Macmillan's White Paper on Defence endorsed the continuance of Great Britain's national nuclear deterrent into the 1970s. JFK immediately reminded the British prime minister that, during their last meeting, Macmillan had agreed that proliferation needed to be halted. Now Britain's public commitment to an independent deterrent would surely make Paris and Bonn more intransigent about their own nuclear ambitions. During early 1962, moreover, German defense minister Franz Josef Strauss continued calling for the creation of a NATO MRBM force and advocating greater NATO independence in the targeting and use of nuclear weapons.

To Kennedy, preventing German proliferation took priority over any other NATO objectives. Given French and British hostility to the MLF, he thought of abandoning the scheme and offering France nuclear aid in return for its cooperation in NATO and its help in the larger nonproliferation effort. He also continued to fear that U.S. resistance to the *force de frappe* might drive Paris to forge a nuclear alliance with Bonn. To forestall this contingency, and in the hope of using French military purchases to offset U.S. balance-of-payments problems, Kennedy allowed Assistant Secretary of Defense Nitze to send out feelers to French military officials about a deal on nuclear cooperation. Despite State Department opposition, Kennedy gave Nitze permission to proffer nuclear aid during the balance-of-payments negotiations. When the French envoy, General Gaston Lavaud, brought Washington a "shopping list" that included numerous items beneficial to the French nuclear program, Nitze inquired as to whether France would be willing to play a more cooperative role in NATO in return for American largesse. Lavaud's instructions limited him to discussing military purchases, and he agreed only to communicate Nitze's offer to Paris. By the time the French responded, news of the first conversation had leaked to the State Department and the JCAE, and both erupted against any nuclear-sharing arrangement. Kennedy had to withdraw the offer and reiterate U.S. hostility to the French nuclear effort. In so doing, the president accelerated the downward spiral of U.S.-French relations. The inconstancy and hesitancy that typified Kennedy's foreign policy brought up fears that the only lightly experienced president was in over his head.[36]

Toeing the "Tough" Line

U.S. nonproliferation policy lay in shambles. The test ban talks had resumed in November but achieved little. The United States and the Soviet Union used the Geneva meetings primarily to denounce each other's testing programs. In December, Semyon K. Tsarapkin, the Soviet negotiator, confided to Arthur Dean that "in view of the present tensions in the world, there is no possibility whatsoever of any further negotiations on the nuclear test ban agreement." The negotiations finally collapsed at the end of January 1962. Despite his skepticism toward multilateral talks, Kennedy acquiesced to Khrushchev's earlier demand that the test ban be folded into the broader disarmament talks slated to begin in March.[37]

As long as the talks remained deadlocked, Kennedy had to contend with enormous political pressure to authorize atmospheric tests from nuclear nationalists in the Pentagon, the AEC, and Congress. He hesitated because he still found the technical arguments weak and unlikely to defuse protests from neutrals and antinuclear activists. In November, he did authorize preparations for atmospheric tests. But he insisted that they not begin until April and not before he had fully studied their scope and necessity. Kennedy also weathered criticism for both the underground tests and the atmospheric preparations from antinuclear groups, such as Women Strike for Peace, SANE, and the Student Peace Union. Yet the Kennedy administration did not exhibit the strident antagonism toward nuclear pacifists that its predecessors had. Mc-Cloy, Carl Kaysen of the NSC staff, and other U.S. officials maintained contact with disarmament advocates and showed respect for their viewpoints, although Kennedy himself displayed less openness to the test ban movement than did his subordinates, in part because he still resented the fact that Soviet tests had received less international criticism than had U.S. resumption. Kennedy's penchant for toughness also dissuaded him from openly embracing the antitest movement. At times, he even disparaged antinuclear activists in mocking tones, snorting that the Harvard faculty who protested nuclear testing had also believed that "the Chinese communists" were just "agrarian reformers." Washington's lukewarm attitude toward the antinuclear movement echoed among close European allies. West Germany, France, and Great Britain harassed, arrested, and intimidated antinuclear groups. While Moscow kept a lid on homegrown protests, Khrushchev did try to cultivate amicable ties to such Western antinuclear activists as Linus Pauling and Leo Szilard. He even grudgingly allowed the protest voyage of *Everyman III*—a demonstration explicitly aimed at Soviet nuclear testing—to dock in Leningrad. Washington, Moscow, and London, moreover, looked to the Pugwash conferences that convened scientists from both East and West as forums from which to glean innovative technological ideas capable of breaking the testing and verification deadlock. Still, Kennedy believed he had less to fear from antinuclear activists than from the pronuclear lobby because opinion polls showed support for testing.[38]

A growing unease, however, simmered beneath the quiescent public surface. Kennedy's call for enhanced civil defense measures in his Berlin crisis speech of July 1961 sparked an increasingly surreal debate about civilian deaths in a nuclear war. The mainstream press consistently backed the president's campaign for private fallout shelters, while more obscure forums discussed preparations to weather a nuclear strike, including the viability of shelters for cows. Amid cries of "better dead than red," commentators also contemplated the morality of shooting neighbors and strangers who tried to enter one's backyard shelter. Few families built shelters, however, and shallow public support for testing could evaporate if nuclear fears continued to grow.[39]

In 1962, the most effective lobbying against atmospheric testing came from Great Britain rather than from the United States. Wanting to avoid further uproar in the UN over U.S. testing and looking to prevent resurgent protest against nuclear fallout, Kennedy decided that neither the Nevada testing site nor the Enewetak test facility, located in a UN trust territory, could host atmospheric testing. He therefore asked Prime Minister Macmillan if the United States could use Christmas Island, a small outpost in the South Pacific that the United Kingdom and Australia controlled. Macmillan had to contend with a much more active and influential antinuclear movement. Since September, he had tried to secure a British veto over U.S. tests in the hope of alleviating his domestic political problem, prompting Bundy to warn the president: "This is dirty pool." But Kennedy also had some leverage in these negotiations because the British military wanted to use the Nevada site's underground test facilities. The two leaders sparred over Christmas Island throughout winter 1961–62, with Kennedy seeking unfettered use of the island and Macmillan lobbying for British participation in determining the scope and duration of testing. They reached an implicit compromise under which the United States acquired use of Christmas Island while the Western powers entered the Eighteen-Nation Disarmament Committee (ENDC) in March with a new test ban offer designed to be more acceptable to the Soviets. Kennedy refused to halt testing during the negotiations, believing that the United States needed to maintain the pace of the arms race in order to force concessions from Moscow.[40]

Macmillan's warning that renewed testing would scuttle resolution of the Nth-country problem did disturb Kennedy. In January, the usually unflappable prime minister had emotionally declared in a letter to the president that resumed atmospheric testing would hasten the day when "dictators, reactionaries, revolutionaries, [and] madmen" acquired the bomb and triggered nuclear war "by error or folly or insanity." Although the State Department dismissed the letter as "emotional blackmail," the president once again reevaluated his nuclear policies, especially after his longtime friend and confidant, British ambassador to the United States David Ormsby-Gore, repeated Macmillan's points. Skepticism toward the scope of the AEC and Pentagon testing proposals and a willingness to entertain arguments against test resumption emerged as the first signs of Kennedy's doubts and reconsiderations. He nonetheless still believed that he had to display his toughness to the American public in order to blunt the effect of right-wing attacks on his national security policy.[41]

The Berlin crisis and the resumption of Soviet nuclear testing had inspired a wave of conservative claims that U.S. military strength lagged behind Moscow's. At a White House luncheon in fall 1961, E. M. Dealey, the publisher of the *Dallas Morning News*, lambasted the administration as "a weak sister" and claimed that rather than emerging as a "man on horseback" during the country's moment of maximum danger, the president appeared to be "riding Caroline's tricycle." Infuriated, Kennedy decided to end questioning of both his and the nation's potency by directing Deputy Defense Secretary Roswell Gilpatric to give a speech divulging the massive nuclear superiority of the United States. The president had campaigned on charges of a "missile gap," claiming that Eisenhower had let U.S. military strength deteriorate. But early in his presidency, he learned that the "gap" actually favored the United States. For domestic political reasons, however, he kept this information secret and forged ahead with a missile-building program that even some Pentagon officials found excessive. On October 21, 1961, Gilpatric's speech dispelled any doubt about which nation prevailed in the arms race. He claimed that the United States had "tens of thousands" of nuclear weapons and hundreds of intercontinental delivery vehicles at a time when the Soviets possessed no more than a handful of weapons capable of striking North America. JFK succeeded in quieting fears of American weakness, but he shocked the Soviets with startling information about U.S. intelligence-gathering capabilities, badly damaging Khrushchev's domestic political status. Since gaining power in the 1950s, the Soviet premier had attempted to divert resources from defense to domestic needs. The Gilpatric revelations strengthened the Soviet military's bargaining power at the October party congress and provoked an embarrassing defeat for Khrushchev's reform program. In the wake of these setbacks, Khrushchev unambiguously signaled that U.S. toughness would not generate new Soviet concessions. On October 31, 1961, he approved detonation of the largest nuclear explosive in history, a fifty-megaton blast.[42]

In early 1962, Kennedy worried more about appearing weak to his domestic and foreign rivals than about being unduly provocative. Although he kept the testing program brief and personally approved each experiment, he finally determined that he could not delay atmospheric testing any longer. Pentagon and AEC arguments that the latest Soviet tests had produced important advances in antiballistic missile technology overcame his personal ambivalence toward increased fallout and an accelerated arms race. Kennedy did publicly promise to cancel the tests if substantial progress toward a Berlin settlement or a test ban treaty developed before the series began in mid-April. But no one believed this political gesture would inspire Soviet acquiescence. The president had been the last senior policymaker to endorse atmospheric testing, yet few of his subordinates or associates apparently knew how deep his reservations went. When *Washington Post* editor Ben Bradlee inquired whether anyone in the administration had qualms about the test resumption, Kennedy barked, "I suppose if you grabbed Adlai by the nuts, he might object." Wanting to seem resolute in public, the president privately reformulated his arms control policy in the hope that informal discussions during the ENDC talks or the Berlin negotiations might yield an agreement.[43]

The ENDC and the Berlin Talks

The Eighteen-Nation Disarmament Committee first convened in early 1962 and quickly emerged as the primary forum for U.S.-Soviet arms control talks. This new body had been devised during the negotiations between presidential arms control adviser McCloy and Soviet UN ambassador Valerian Zorin in fall 1961. McCloy and Zorin had agreed on general principles for disarmament that seemed largely propagandistic but did contain Moscow's first acceptance of the right of unrestricted inspection. When the UN General Assembly endorsed these principles, it paved the way for the general disarmament talks. In December, the United States and the Soviet Union built on this renewed interest and created a new negotiating body, the ENDC, consisting of five NATO countries, five Warsaw Pact countries, and eight neutrals.

The McCloy-Zorin principles contained no specific arms control proposals, largely because the Joint Chiefs of Staff protested McCloy's failure to link progress on testing with other nuclear disarmament proposals and because President Kennedy labeled the projected sharp cuts in nuclear stockpiles "too radical." McCloy resigned in October, frustrated with the administration's wavering support for arms control and unwilling to work further with Rusk, whom he considered unremittingly hostile to disarmament. But McCloy's efforts in the Zorin talks, along with the president's disarmament speech to the General Assembly, did inspire a revealing UN debate on nonproliferation. Both Ireland and Sweden introduced resolutions calling for international cooperation to stop the spread of nuclear weapons. Washington had pressured the Irish delegation not to seek a ban on nuclear-sharing arrangements. But the Swedish resolution explicitly aimed to prevent the superpowers from sharing nuclear weapons with allies. The debate became mired in semantics, with the Irish delegation proposing a ban on transferring "control" of nuclear weapons and the Swedish representatives contending that the superpowers should not give "custody" of nuclear weapons to other powers. The United States lobbied heavily for the Irish version, claiming that Western nuclear-sharing measures allowed Washington to retain control over its nuclear arsenal. The Kennedy administration achieved a stalemate in the General Assembly, with both the Swedish and the Irish drafts passing by substantial margins.[44]

JFK realized that the MLF could also complicate nonproliferation discussions at the ENDC. Although he decided to include a nonproliferation proposal in the U.S. disarmament plan, he instructed the delegation not to debate the issue during the formal sessions. Because of the political sensitivity of the MLF, Kennedy restricted discussion of nonproliferation to the bilateral talks between Rusk and Gromyko on Berlin. Rusk had developed a full understanding of the complexities of the president's nonproliferation policy and knew that NATO unity had to be weighed against any Soviet offer to contain nuclear dissemination.

The Berlin discussion added a third negotiating track to U.S. nonproliferation efforts, along with the ENDC test ban talks and NATO consideration of the MLF. Both Kennedy and Rusk believed that the superpower confrontation in Germany could pry loose Soviet concessions on nonproliferation. Rusk told French and British officials that Moscow might "feel that if tension mounts it would be difficult to withhold nuclear weapons from the Germans." The secretary of state renewed the Berlin negotiations in March when he and Gromyko traveled to Geneva to open the ENDC meetings. In his briefcase, Rusk carried a draft modus vivendi with a global nuclear nondiffusion clause, indicating that Kennedy sought to use a Berlin settlement as leverage for concessions on nonproliferation. The linkage of Berlin to other issues worried Bonn officials, who feared that a violation of the nondiffusion arrangement or other unrelated items might provide a Soviet excuse to abrogate the entire settlement. State Department officials viewed the ancillary agreements in the opposite light, believing that they would enhance Moscow's commitment to the Berlin accord. To calm Adenauer's worries that Washington had revived the Rapacki Plan, Rusk also assured Bonn that the United States would not settle for a nonproliferation arrangement that singled out the two Germanys. A West German official seeking to scuttle the talks leaked two American position papers to the Bonn press corps, leading Washington to protest a "flagrant breach of diplomatic usage."[45]

Bonn had little to fear, for the Rusk-Gromyko meetings failed. Because Washington remained satisfied with the status quo in Berlin, it sought Soviet concessions, such as a global nonproliferation treaty, in return for an agreement to adjust its occupation rights. Moscow, however, did not want Germany linked to global issues that might further delay a settlement. The Soviets advocated a German nuclear-free zone apart from a more comprehensive treaty, while remaining open to a more sweeping nondiffusion accord. Gromyko also informed Rusk that any treaty, whether aimed solely at Germany or at the entire international community, would have to bar the creation of the MLF. Although the Soviets and the Americans still had much work to do, the absence of an outright Soviet rejection of a modus vivendi imparted an unusual degree of optimism.

The Berlin talks offered Kennedy a promising opportunity to devise an overarching and consistent nonproliferation strategy. Since the inception of his presidency, Kennedy had expressed his intent to halt, or at least inhibit, proliferation. But at no point had he authorized a comprehensive study of U.S. nuclear policy and its effects on the spread of nuclear weapons in order to eliminate any contradictory aspects. He instead vacillated between strict and selective nonproliferation policies. In spring 1962, numerous examples of this inconsistency surfaced, including the Lavaud mission, the Berlin modus vivendi, and the continuation of nuclear-sharing policies. In the space of seven days in March, Nitze had offered General Lavaud aid for the French nuclear program, Rusk had suggested to Gromyko that a nondiffusion agreement would benefit both powers, Kennedy had contemplated abandoning the MLF, and the NSC had approved arrangements to disperse thermonuclear warheads to NATO countries and endorsed other nuclear-sharing agreements.

Kennedy approved the continued dispersal of tactical nuclear weapons to NATO forces because of the development of permissive action links (PALS). These devices, which were eventually placed on all NATO nuclear weapons, required the input of a special code to arm the nuclear warhead. PALS reduced the risk of accidental or unauthorized firings but did not eliminate such dangers altogether. Like any technical device, the electronic locks could fail, or they could be disabled by a particularly ardent NATO officer. During a crisis, tactical weapons would be released to field commanders along with the codes. PALS, therefore, provided security during periods of international calm but became less useful during those very episodes that raised fears of an unintentional spiral toward nuclear war.

JFK versus Europe

After Rusk returned from Geneva, Kennedy did attempt to reconcile aspects of his nonproliferation policy. But he continued to work on a case-by-case basis that sowed confusion and contradiction. In March, the president made his first efforts to untangle his nuclear policy. During a discussion of the MLF, he wondered to Secretary of Defense McNamara and other officials whether the administration was "pouring our money into the ocean . . . in order to satisfy a political need whose use was dubious." He believed the MLF addressed German and French nuclear ambitions but left the other NATO powers uninterested. The United States could ultimately expend a great deal of political capital and discover that a NATO nuclear force functioning under a U.S. veto would do nothing to check the growth of national nuclear deterrents. Robert Bowie, an informal consultant to the administration and the original architect of the MLF, disagreed. He admitted that the force did not fulfill any military needs, but he believed its political functions to be vital. The United States had to envision France *after* de Gaulle. French public opinion appeared divided on the *force de frappe*, and if the United States provided an alternative, the general's successors might abandon the French deterrent. McNamara reluctantly endorsed Bowie's political rationale, and Kennedy decided to let the plan stand.[46]

The president's open questioning of the MLF coincided with McNamara's fitful awakening to the dangers of proliferation. Up to March 1962, Kennedy and Rusk had been the primary advocates of strict nonproliferation. But McNamara's qualified support of the MLF in March served as a harbinger of his gradual conversion into a nonproliferation proponent. Since entering office, he had grown disenchanted with existing nuclear war plans. Kennedy and Bundy shared his contempt for the Joint Chiefs' targeting and firing schemes, viewing them as the antithesis of strategy. Bundy sneered that "military planners who calculate that we will win if only we can kill 100 million Russians while they are killing 30 million Americans are living in a total dreamland." In spring 1962, McNamara's efforts to impart control and flexibility to U.S. war plans converged with the administration's goal of eliminating and discouraging the growth of national nuclear forces within NATO. In 1961, when he first contemplated revision of U.S. nuclear strategy, he toyed with minimum deterrence, which looked to deploy only as many nuclear weapons as were needed to discourage a Soviet attack. But such a strategy would actually encourage European proliferation by providing a justification for limited British and French national deterrents.[47]

A new school of nuclear strategists who saw proliferation as a threat to nuclear deterrence convinced him that arms control should be used to control the bilateral nuclear arms race rather than to end or retard it. Nonproliferation, in other words, could help keep arms competition manageable and predictable. Washington had to persuade Europeans that U.S. nuclear forces provided sufficient striking power for NATO and were best used under a system of centralized command and control. McNamara decided that a counterforce, or no-cities, strategy offered both flexibility and a check on European nuclear ambitions.

Under counterforce targeting, U.S. nuclear weapons would be aimed at Soviet military sites rather than at cities. Urban areas would be spared in the first strike so that they could serve as hostages in a threatened second strike. Such a policy placed a premium on having a large and varied arsenal of nuclear weapons to hit targets with great precision. This rationale proved to be an empty abstraction because military installations tended to be near cities. Military planners included the anticipated civilian casualties in their calculations as "collateral damage" or "bonus effects." If counterforce became the accepted NATO strategy, small nuclear forces would add little to Western war-fighting ability and might even detract from it by striking cities and undercutting the second half of the war plan.

The military eagerly adopted the new doctrine partly because it offered incentives for continuing to expand defense budgets — every time the Soviets deployed new missiles or built new bases, the United States would have to build nuclear delivery vehicles to hit the additional targets. But the Joint Chiefs still valued NATO unity over nonproliferation and condemned the administration's hostility toward the French nuclear program. In April, General Maxwell Taylor argued vigorously for a selective proliferation policy to resolve NATO disagreements, contending that France should receive unlimited technical assistance in return for its cooperation in the alliance. Kennedy nonetheless concluded that cooperation with de Gaulle promised few gains and instructed Ambassador Gavin to cease all conversations with the French about nuclear cooperation to avoid inflaming the dispute. When the president rejected Taylor's recommendations, the general or someone sympathetic to his views leaked to the press U.S. consideration of aid to the French program, implying that cooperation might be imminent. Yet another round of confusion and denials ensued, bad omens for the forthcoming U.S. nonproliferation initiatives.

Taylor's attempt to co-opt the French *force de frappe* coincided with McNamara's plans to unveil the new U.S. counterforce strategy to NATO. By early 1962, the secretary had circulated the new strategic principles within the U.S. government, but he had not made a formal announcement to the allies or to the American public. Some McNamara intimates doubted the usefulness of a dramatic speech promulgating counterforce principles. The secretary and the president, however, had grown frustrated with more subtle approaches to educating Europeans about the need for central command and control over Western nuclear forces. Earlier in the year, U.S. officials had met with French, German, and NATO officials and had briefed them on American nuclear strength and the justifications for integrated control over the Western deterrent. But these conversations had not tempered German and French nuclear ambitions. Impatient, Kennedy told McNamara to deliver a forceful presentation of U.S. attitudes on nuclear strategy at the NATO ministerial meeting in Athens, Greece.

Preparations for the Athens meeting also required a review of U.S. policy toward the MLF. Debate within the administration became both acrimonious and public, leading to hostile European press reports and fostering skepticism toward McNamara's arguments. Although Kennedy failed to take command of this debate, he created the illusion of a clear U.S. nonproliferation policy. In March, the NSC staff proposed that the United States voice continued support for the MLF, while stressing the importance of conventional strength and the need for Europeans to lead in forging any new NATO nuclear arrangement. In place of vigorous advocacy of the MLF, the U.S. delegation should suggest broadening allied participation in Western nuclear strategy through the creation of a new information program and a planning board. Washington would also ask NATO to help draft clear guidelines about when the United States would fire its nuclear weapons in defense of Europe. The NSC paper seemed to endorse a shift from "hardware" quick fixes to political solutions for alliance problems.

The White House proposals soon came under fire from both military officials and NATO capitals. The Joint Chiefs and the U.S. military command in Europe opposed the new information programs and the use of Polaris submarines as the building blocks for the MLF. The dominant strain of thought in military circles viewed land-based MRBMs as the best solution for NATO nuclear needs. When Kennedy's military opponents and their European allies learned that the president had killed any chance for a land-based force, reports appeared in European newspapers chastising Washington for reneging on its promise to make NATO an independent nuclear power.

These press reports produced the first crack in what would soon widen into a deep rupture in U.S.-NATO relations. Upon being briefed on the new nuclear policy, the U.S. ambassador to Italy warned that rumors of plans to eliminate land-based MRBMs could foment controversy in Rome, especially after the Italian parliament had only reluctantly accepted Jupiter missiles during the Eisenhower administration. The most scathing critique of U.S. policy came from France. The French political commentator Raymond Aron, in a discussion with a U.S. Defense Department official, labeled American policy toward French and European nuclear weapons "absurd." The U.S. government concentrated solely on technical questions and ignored the political realities in Europe, needlessly squandering the scientific and economic assets that the region could contribute to Western defense. He also contended that the Soviet Union and the United States had implicitly agreed to deny nuclear weapons to other powers and to limit the next war to Central Europe. Coming from a respected intellectual and political figure who had often criticized de Gaulle in the past, Aron's charges carried great weight. Some U.S. officials argued that if moderate French opinion had turned so strongly against the United States, a revision of American nonproliferation policy might be necessary. These fears intensified after the West German government expressed hostility to a nondiffusion clause in the Berlin modus vivendi lest Washington sneak a commitment to a Central European nuclear-free zone into the fine print of the agreement. Faced with this outcry, Kennedy officials braced for a full-scale allied revolt on the eve of the NATO conference.[48]

In the final policy meetings prior to the Athens meeting, the State Department nonproliferation advocates came out on top. Rusk provided the most consistent voice against deviating from a strict nonproliferation stance. He advocated further retreat from the tepid endorsement of the MLF that Kennedy had made earlier, stressing that it had no military utility and should not distract from the conventional buildup. McNamara and Taylor rejoined that although nonproliferation served American long-term interests, Washington could not afford to alienate de Gaulle at such a crucial point in the Cold War. The president should bow to the inevitable and aid the *force de frappe*. Rusk countered that all available evidence indicated that aiding de Gaulle would serve only to speed his break with NATO and scuttle any chance that the MLF would dissuade Bonn from seeking nuclear weapons. The pendulum had swung so far in the direction of a strict nonproliferation policy that both Bundy and the State Department urged a retreat from the Anglo-American nuclear alliance. Rusk labeled the renewal of the special nuclear relationship "a mistake," fearing that so long as London retained its nuclear deterrent it served as "a standing goad to the French to follow suit."[49]

Kennedy sided with Rusk in every dispute. He ignored the Joint Chiefs' qualms about information sharing and endorsed the earmarking of the entire American Polaris submarine fleet for NATO use as a substitute for a mixed-manned force. The president's opposition to aiding the French also appeared unaltered during the preparations for the Athens meetings. Implicit in JFK's approval of Rusk's arguments lay further backpedaling from the MLF. After Athens, Washington would not actively promote the force and would instead only agree to cooperate with Europe toward its creation and deployment.

Kennedy and the State Department hoped that including the NATO allies in strategy formulation, committing the Polaris fleet to Europe, and creating guidelines for U.S. nuclear retaliation for an attack on Europe would eliminate the need for a NATO missile force.

Still, beneath this unusual display of decisiveness and clarity lurked JFK's familiar muddled thinking. At the last minute, he decided not to announce his new position on the MLF at the NATO conference, instead leaving it implicit in Rusk's and McNamara's presentations. Several NATO nuclear policies, moreover, still risked encouraging proliferation. The new information program could potentially disseminate data in Europe that might be useful in pursuing an independent nuclear program, and U.S. tactical weapons policies continued to place nuclear weapons in the hands of local commanders in Europe. More important, after the Athens meeting began, Kennedy allowed McNamara to offer jet tankers to Paris, which would increase the striking distance of French nuclear bombers.

Rusk himself undercut U.S. nonproliferation policy. He informed the German and Canadian foreign ministers that American opposition to the *force de frappe* did not stem solely from resistance to the spread of nuclear weapons, citing as other reasons France's unstable political atmosphere, de Gaulle's deviance from European integration along the lines advocated by Washington, his contempt toward NATO and the UN, his uncooperative behavior regarding disarmament and the Berlin negotiations, and his implicit goal of breaking from the Western alliance and pursuing an independent foreign policy. The secretary's subordinates immediately protested that he had made U.S. nonproliferation policy appear as if it rested on expediency rather than on the inherent danger of a world riddled with nuclear powers. Rusk brushed aside this criticism, claiming his remarks merely reinforced McNamara's speech on the new counterforce strategy.

Against all of these reversals, contradictions, and qualifications, the secretary of defense delivered his Athens presentation. McNamara carefully and forcefully explained the new strategy, stressing that it provided flexibility and prevented a hasty escalation to nuclear war. Most important in terms of U.S. nonproliferation policy, he asserted that America's nuclear arsenal offered sufficient firepower for the entire alliance, and he criticized weak national forces as liabilities that only invited preemptive strikes during crises. The Europeans initially seemed to appreciate the newfound candor concerning U.S. nuclear strength and strategic concepts, a reaction that changed once they returned to their capitals and reflected on the possible consequences of his pronouncements. Still, the allies' relatively placid demeanors during the

NATO conference allowed Rusk to trumpet the meeting as the most productive in the administration's tenure. He believed that it had paved the way for smooth U.S.-NATO relations in the future, possibly even with the French. Within days the illusion of success faded. By summer 1962, both the NATO and Geneva avenues of U.S. nonproliferation appeared to have reached dead ends.

In January 1961, when Kennedy entered office, he committed his administration to ending nuclear testing and impeding proliferation. The convoluted nonproliferation policy he had inherited from Eisenhower hampered his ability to achieve these goals, but he continued to press for their fulfillment. Khrushchev, moreover, had grasped at signs of compromise emanating from Washington and signaled his own willingness to negotiate. But JFK demonstrated more concern for his shaky domestic political status after a narrow election victory than for reaching agreement with Khrushchev. He lacked the very political courage to pursue unpopular policies that he had touted while a senator, fearing that setbacks in Cuba, Berlin, and the test talks made him look weak. Although he did pursue negotiations with the Soviets, he used a massive increase in defense spending and test resumption to defuse domestic critics and to demonstrate to Khrushchev that he could not be bullied. This obsession with toughness and political image damaged whatever goodwill he had inspired from Moscow. While desiring a U.S.-Soviet modus vivendi, Kennedy succeeded only in increasing Cold War tensions. Khrushchev also oscillated between confrontation and conciliation in a desperate effort to maintain control over the Soviet government and its military allies. The always-mercurial leader became increasingly difficult to gauge as both a potential opponent and a bargaining partner. Although both Kennedy and Khrushchev still hoped for détente by summer 1962, a nonproliferation agreement seemed more unlikely than at any other point since the test ban negotiations had begun in 1958. Still, the nuclear issue would not fade away. The world public feared nuclear testing. And allies pressured the superpowers to allow either equal access and control of nuclear weapons or a general disarmament agreement to eliminate the exclusive nuclear club. In the summer of 1962, the United States and the Soviet Union both faced serious challenges to nuclear hegemony at home and abroad.

Too Big to Spank

JFK, NUCLEAR HEGEMONY, & THE LIMITED
TEST BAN TREATY, 1962–1963

"Personally, I am haunted by the feeling that by 1970 . . . there may be ten nuclear powers instead of four, and by 1975, fifteen or twenty," President John F. Kennedy confessed in March 1963. After becoming president, Kennedy sought but failed to achieve a nonproliferation treaty because of Cold War suspicion, domestic political vulnerability, and a penchant for toughness. By 1962, nuclear proliferation loomed as a powerful symbol of declining superpower hegemony. The nuclear world was no longer bilateral, and that frightened JFK. Both the United States and the Soviet Union had to placate allies who resented the superpowers' nuclear hegemony. Kennedy worried lest Washington land "on the outside looking in" at Western Europe, leading him to flirt with nuclear sharing to maintain alliance unity. Soviet premier Nikita Khrushchev largely resisted U.S. efforts to ally against the Chinese nuclear program because he still wished to heal the rift in the communist world. Still, a nonproliferation agreement seemed a real possibility by late 1962 because, following the Cuban Missile Crisis, both Kennedy and Khrushchev feared the consequences of nuclear anarchy. But resistance from Britain, France, and West Germany impeded a nonproliferation agreement and a comprehensive test ban. In the end, because nonproliferation continued to be subordinated to alliance relationships and Cold War competition, Kennedy and Khrushchev succeeded only in producing a weak arms control agreement: the Limited Test Ban Treaty.[1]

European Woes

In early May 1962, the Kennedy administration confronted a hostile allied reaction to McNamara's counterforce strategy. Kennedy grew livid after columnists C. L. Sulzberger and Joseph Alsop wrote pieces condemning U.S. policy toward France as misguided and divisive, especially on nuclear issues. Kennedy and most Washington insiders recognized that Sulzberger's column actually represented a reply from de Gaulle. The French leader had fed the *New York Times* journalist a steady diet of exclusive interviews since returning to power in 1958, particularly when he wanted to make a point outside official channels. Kennedy's anger had not dimmed when he hosted a dinner for the French minister for cultural affairs, André Malraux. Confronting Malraux, the president snapped that de Gaulle seemed to prefer a Europe without the United States. The United States felt like "a man carrying a 200-pound sack of potatoes, and other people not carrying a similar load, at least in potatoes, keep telling us how to carry the burden." Malraux retorted that while the president "was carrying the potatoes, others had their own burdens."[2]

After Malraux's visit, the U.S.-French animosity deepened. Previously behind-the-scenes disputes broke into the public arena. De Gaulle accused the United States of imperious leadership that threatened to turn Europe into a mere protectorate. In his opinion, "it would suffice for Western Europe to know that if war were to start it could rely on [the United States]." Kennedy fired back that Europe could not expect both America's "military presence and our diplomatic absence." If a Paris-Bonn axis attempted to dominate European affairs, the United States would have to abandon its NATO commitments. Conversations between Rusk and French ambassador Hervé Alphand failed to smooth over Franco-American divisions, leaving Rusk convinced that de Gaulle was "a devil with horns and a tail."[3]

The rift with France constituted the most prominent problem in U.S.-European relations. Kennedy still sought to de-emphasize the MLF and replace it with closer consultations on nuclear strategy. When U.S. officials consulted Bonn, however, they discovered substantial support for a multilateral nuclear force along with a deep suspicion of American attempts to link a nonproliferation clause with a Berlin settlement. Any attempt to revise the U.S. position on the MLF, therefore, risked angering the Germans and driving Bonn closer to Paris.

Britain's decision to seek membership in the European Economic Community (EEC, also known as the Common Market) further vexed alliance politics. Because many supporters viewed the customs union as the first stage of Western Europe's complete political and economic unification, its members looked askance at London's continuing special relationship with the United States. If Kennedy withdrew his promise to make NATO a nuclear power, critics might claim that the Anglo-Americans had constructed a condominium on nuclear defense issues. Reliable French sources, moreover, indicated that if Britain expected de Gaulle's approval for its Common Market membership, London would have to form a new Anglo-French-German nuclear cabal. Prime Minister Macmillan secretly contemplated dangling nuclear cooperation in front of de Gaulle to win his support. Given the delicate nature of the Common Market negotiations, the British implored the Americans to remain quiet on nuclear issues, to no avail.

In mid-June, first NATO ambassador Thomas Finletter and then Secretary of Defense McNamara made speeches that additionally strained the Western alliance. Finletter's speech came at his own urging. He had been working faithfully to fulfill Kennedy's instructions to prepare a European initiative on the MLF. By June 1962, his efforts had produced limited success. He wanted to make a formal statement stressing U.S. support for the MLF. But JFK insisted that no military requirement existed for the MLF or any MRBM force; that the United States would not support anything but a seaborne, mixed-manned project; that Europe would have to pay the majority of the cost; and, finally, that the United States offered the MLF as but one possible way to satisfy NATO's nuclear desires but did not demand its creation. Kennedy admitted that the chances for European acceptance of the MLF on U.S. terms were "low at present." Finletter reluctantly conveyed Kennedy's views to the alliance despite his fears that it would kill the project.[4]

The NATO allies had had no time to digest Finletter's presentation when, the next day, McNamara gave them more to chew on in his commencement address at the University of Michigan. Since his return from Athens, McNamara had wanted to give a declassified version of his counterforce speech to educate both the American public and the Soviets about the strategy. Kennedy worried that McNamara's language about weak national forces might further inflame the French and that the references to American nuclear superiority might provoke Soviet charges of missile rattling. The president swallowed his doubts and permitted the speech with some minor changes. McGeorge Bundy, however, warned that no amount of revision would completely defuse the French problem, for de Gaulle viewed nuclear weapons as "the most potent status symbol since African colonies went out of fashion." More important, because the classified Athens speech had already raised de Gaulle's hackles, a public attack on weak nuclear forces would only enrage the general and irritate the British. McNamara lamely calculated that because Paris and London had heard the speech once and had not officially protested, a public address held no danger. As one commentator aptly observed, both the Athens and the Ann Arbor speeches constituted "the pure product of strategic thinking" — "intelligent and brilliant, logical and synthetic, but also cold and disembodied — and, more or less consciously, politically maladroit."[5]

The cumulative impact of the Finletter and McNamara presentations could not have been worse. Finletter's diffident discussion of the MLF sparked criticism from all quarters, including from the NATO commander, General Lauris Norstad. The French and the Germans openly accused the United States of seeking to dominate Europe, with German defense minister Franz Josef Strauss dismissing McNamara and his aides as "eggheads" and "desk warriors." Dirk Stikker, the secretary-general of NATO, voiced his own irritation and warned of rising anti-American and anti-NATO sentiment in key European countries. British prime minister Macmillan labeled McNamara's speech an "ill-disguised attack upon the determination of Britain." The British press berated this "crippling blow to the UK's independent nuclear deterrent" and claimed that McNamara lacked "the qualities of a statesman." The Defense Department clumsily denied that the speech's arguments applied to Britain, contradicting the Athens guidelines that sought to eliminate the British deterrent. By absolving the British, the Pentagon essentially admitted that the French had been the main target of McNamara's criticisms, further aggravating that already tense relationship. Even with the Defense Department's qualifications, Macmillan had to endure the embarrassing spectacle of answering questions in Parliament about whether Britain had an "interdependent," rather than completely separate, deterrent. He sniffed that he could not be held responsible for the statements of the U.S. secretary of defense.[6]

Angered and disappointed, Macmillan reached toward de Gaulle, hinting that cooperation might be necessary to guard against U.S. designs on their national nuclear forces. But the prime minister hesitated to break completely with the Americans as de Gaulle demanded. Macmillan instead played a double game, withholding information from both Washington and Paris. He played the powers off of one another to finagle a trilateral nuclear complex that preserved the British deterrent, maintained the Anglo-American nuclear partnership, and won British entry into the EEC. In the end, the Foreign Office's opposition temporarily blocked nuclear cooperation with the

French, but Macmillan continued to hold this potential negotiating gambit in reserve as the vote on British Common Market membership moved closer. De Gaulle, on the other hand, publicly stressed the uncertainty of the U.S. nuclear commitment and contrasted it with the *force de frappe*, "the beginning of a European force."[7]

Ambassadors or Psychoanalysts?

The imbroglio over nuclear issues expanded the scope of Rusk's previously scheduled trip to Europe. The secretary had originally planned to visit Paris to patch up U.S.-French relations. He instead confronted the full fury of the entire NATO alliance. Despite the president and Rusk's conviction that a NATO nuclear force served no military purpose, the secretary of state, in another switch, decided to recant Finletter's presentation and revive the president's MLF proposal of May 1961. Rusk stressed the political importance of the collective nuclear force and claimed that the NATO ambassador had sought merely to impress upon the alliance that the MRBM requirement did not have to be pursued with any urgency. Although the smaller powers, including the Netherlands and Belgium, quickly voiced their support, the British, German, and French representatives remained silent.

The bilateral discussions with French officials fared even worse. The two sides continued to assert their national positions with no signs of potential compromise. Both de Gaulle and French foreign minister Maurice Couve de Murville criticized the bilateral negotiations on Berlin, believing them a manifestation of American hegemonic pretensions. They also derided U.S. arguments against nuclear proliferation. Couve de Murville scoffed that nothing could stop the spread of nuclear weapons and speculated that soon Israel, Sweden, China, and India would produce their own bombs. U.S. nuclear policies toward NATO inspired the most venomous responses. The foreign minister dismissed the Athens program, the MLF, and NATO consultations and guidelines as "nothing new" because they left American nuclear dominance undisturbed. De Gaulle displayed even greater candor with a blunt, fundamental question. Observing that the United States and the Soviet Union seemed intent on deciding Europe's fate in bilateral discussions, and given McNamara's claims of Washington's overwhelming nuclear superiority, he asked rhetorically, "Why should there be an alliance?" Rusk blasted back that if France targeted its nuclear weapons independently, Washington would aim some weapons at the *force de frappe* to prevent Paris from sparking an all-out war between the Soviets and the West.[8]

Rusk pursued a different tack when he traveled to Bonn. Rather than sell U.S. policies with reasoned arguments, he lectured the Germans as if they were schoolchildren. Emphasizing Washington's long-standing commitment to nonproliferation, he remarked that not all governments were ready to handle the responsibility of unilateral control of nuclear weapons. Rusk said, "Frankly[,] . . . when we send envoys to some capitals, we are doubtful whether to send an Ambassador or a psychoanalyst. These weapons are not toys." But he reassured the Germans that the MLF still represented a viable initiative, even though Washington wanted its allies to be realistic about its costs and complications. When Adenauer lobbied for a land-based MRBM force, Rusk contended that political and military conditions had changed since Norstad first proposed the idea. The United States, therefore, would not provide financial or political support for such a venture. The West German government, in turn, opposed a nonproliferation clause in any Berlin settlement—language that would leave Bonn "a second class" or "third class" power. Rusk proved less rigid on the last point. Because the Soviets had not proved accommodating, the timing might be right to shift the discussion to the ENDC. He warned, however, that this course also carried risks because the neutrals might ally with the Soviets to oppose the MLF.[9]

The trip imbued the secretary with a deep pessimism about U.S. efforts to contain European proliferation. Because de Gaulle's motivation for nuclear weapons stemmed from "primarily psychological and subjective" motives, rational arguments had little potential to dissuade de Gaulle from creating a *force de frappe*. The general had successfully entwined the nuclear issue into French conceptions of nationhood, which made it likely that the program would continue after the French leader left office. Rusk's visit to Bonn also convinced him that only the MLF would counter cries for a German deterrent, and he dismissed British arguments that NATO consultations and guidelines on the use of nuclear weapons could take the place of hardware for the Germans.[10]

In the wake of the Finletter and McNamara speeches, the Kennedy administration also discovered that General Norstad had run out of patience. He had never endorsed counterforce targeting or a seaborne MLF, but McNamara and Finletter's maladroit handling of NATO pushed him toward open defiance of the new policies. Trips to the United States to iron out differences provoked open conflict over Norstad's belief that he served NATO and not the United States. Norstad ultimately resigned at Kennedy's request. But the general did not go quietly. During his farewell tour of NATO capitals, he continued to carp at the administration, sowing more confusion by urging that NATO develop an independent nuclear deterrent. The Kennedy administration, not wishing to foment a full-scale political controversy, remained silent, even though some officials privately faulted the general for acting like a "proconsul in Outer Gaul."[11]

Norstad's removal alone could not ease the strains that had developed in the alliance. Charles Bohlen, Rusk's special adviser, drafted a long memorandum charting a new course after the summer's setbacks. Calling proliferation the "biggest single political issue" facing NATO, he argued that national nuclear ambitions reflected Europeans' resentment of their dependence on the United States during the immediate postwar period. Western Europe, especially France, looked to nuclear weapons to shake off American dominance. To avoid further embarrassments, Bohlen recommended a joint State-Defense study group to formulate a coordinated strategy so that policy on proliferation and Britain's Common Market membership did not become hopelessly entangled. Such a policy, however, had to recognize that the United States could not block French proliferation without mortally wounding the alliance. German ambitions also had to be addressed by the MLF or some other cooperative scheme that would ease other countries' fears of unilateral control by Bonn. In a veiled critique of McNamara's speech, Bohlen urged the silencing of calls for centralized control of the Western nuclear arsenal because Europeans perceived these arguments as a mere fig leaf for continued U.S. hegemony.[12]

Kennedy put aside his own doubts about the MLF and adopted aspects of Bohlen's suggestions. He still believed that U.S. interests would be better served if the force never came into being, but he did not want to stir up more discontent within NATO. He chose a waiting game until a better strategy to satisfy European nuclear desires could be devised. In summer 1962, the president commissioned an internal study of the MLF's feasibility and costs. He also sent Gerard Smith, his special representative on the MLF and a consultant to the State Department Policy Planning Staff, and Admiral John Lee to European capitals to brief officials on American plans, which called for the mixed-manning of Polaris submarines or twenty-five missile-bearing surface ships. Until October, the president's new approach seemed successful. The MLF appeared to be on a timetable that did not create political complications, and the Smith-Lee mission received favorable reviews in West Germany, Belgium, and Italy, notwithstanding British and French skepticism.

The strategy soon unraveled. The Joint Chiefs of Staff's hostility to the use of Polaris submarines in the MLF could not be overcome. The only option now appeared to be a fleet of twenty-five surface ships, each with eight Polaris missiles aboard. McNamara opposed the scheme lest it scuttle the conventional buildup required to implement flexible response. In a series of State-Defense policy conferences, he claimed that European support for the plan was illusory, arguing that the Smith-Lee mission had oversold the MLF by not stressing that surface ships were the only options, downplaying the costs, and not making it clear that U.S. funding would come only after all NATO countries had met their conventional force requirements. Rusk leapt to Smith and Lee's defense, contending that they had adhered to their instructions. But he agreed that the Europeans might not support the MLF if they gave careful attention to all American preconditions. In the face of McNamara's opposition, the nuclear-sharing scheme appeared dead. In the fall of 1962, the question of how to appease European nuclear ambitions once again went searching for an answer.

Resuscitating the Test Ban Talks

NATO did not constitute the only venue for U.S.-European tensions. In spring 1962, Washington and London jousted over the Western position in the ENDC talks, especially the test ban. France also showed its disdain for U.S. policy by boycotting the disarmament negotiations, and Canada began collaborating with the eight neutral members of the conference more than it did with its NATO allies. The Kennedy administration ignored French and German uncooperativeness and concentrated on bringing U.S. and British policies into line. London seemed to have a distinct advantage in this debate because, at Kennedy's request, David Ormsby-Gore had been appointed British ambassador to the United States in October 1961. The president had deep admiration for his longtime friend and professed to trust him as "I would my own Cabinet."[13]

Ormsby-Gore emerged as Britain's point man in its efforts to revise the Western test ban position. In early March, he called for the elimination of the 4.75 seismic threshold in order to make the Western draft a comprehensive test ban. He also urged reduced requirements for inspection and verification. The Kennedy administration initially treated these proposals warily, fearing the appearance of retreat in the face of Soviet firmness. Many officials in the Defense Department and the AEC also worried about opening up dangerous opportunities for Soviet cheating. Proponents of the British position, however, could point to Washington's own difficulties in experimenting underground as evidence that evading the monitoring system would be much more difficult than originally suspected.[14]

Intent on making the test ban a nonproliferation measure, the president proposed dropping the threshold requirement to make the U.S. draft a comprehensive ban. The AEC and the new CIA director, John McCone, protested, but Kennedy remained unmoved. He did, however, satisfy congressional hawks and the anti–test ban faction in the bureaucracy by inserting a demand for on-site inspection for clandestine preparations. Still smarting from the abrupt resumption of Soviet testing, the president would not be duped again.

The British and the Soviets took a dim view of the new U.S. proposals. London applauded U.S. flexibility on the threshold issue but contended that controls against clandestine test preparations would needlessly complicate the negotiations. Macmillan and his science advisers actually wanted to abandon inspection posts on Soviet territory. They wanted to rely on national means of inspection and replace a fixed quota of on-site inspections with a sliding scale dependent on the number of suspicious events detected. British scientists scorned "inspection for inspection's sake." Despite Moscow's appreciation for the U.S. concession on the threshold, the Berlin crisis and the breakdown of the moratorium prompted the Soviets to take a less conciliatory position in the test negotiations. Eschewing compromise, Khrushchev withdrew his previous offer of three on-site inspections, claiming that national means of detection provided sufficient assurance against violations. These arguments about inspections floated in an air of unreality. Would U.S. hawks really have accepted an agreement that allowed Soviet inspection teams to roam freely throughout the American countryside? Viewed within a Cold War context, on-site inspection demands appeared to be designed to kill a test ban, not strengthen it.[15]

If the Soviets continued to reject inspection, Kennedy concluded that further discussion of the test ban would be useless. He first wanted to draw out the Soviets in order to get their absolute refusal to compromise on inspection into the official record. Under British pressure to postpone the U.S. atmospheric tests scheduled for April 1962, he conceded to a joint message to Khrushchev laying out the Western position and disavowing any intent to use inspection for espionage purposes. When the Soviets rejected their entreaties, both JFK and Macmillan resigned themselves to resumed U.S. atmospheric tests, and they accused Moscow of using the American experiments to justify another Soviet series, which had long been planned. The president opted for a brief round of tests to satisfy congressional critics, the AEC, and the Joint Chiefs and hoped that after the Soviets completed their experiments an agreement could be negotiated.

With negotiations stalled, the Kennedy administration received constant reminders of the political and strategic need for test ban and nonproliferation agreements. U.S. and Soviet atmospheric testing revitalized the test ban movement. SANE ran the most successful newspaper advertisement in its history, which featured noted pediatrician Dr. Benjamin Spock warning of the risk fallout posed to future generations. Other groups also organized letter-writing and petition campaigns, and radical pacifists conducted nonviolent protests. But mainstream liberal agitation for arms control had declined amid congressional red-baiting and the ongoing Berlin crisis. In the cultural realm, novels such as Joseph Heller's *Catch-22* and Ken Kesey's *One Flew Over the Cuckoo's Nest,* along with Bob Dylan's protest songs, "Masters of War" and "Let Me Die in My Footsteps," elicited flickers of the dissent against the Cold War that would erupt later in the 1960s. But in spring 1962, most Americans supported atmospheric testing and a hard-line stance against the Soviets. The relatively subdued reaction of neutrals to the American tests also relieved international political pressure to conclude a treaty. By late summer, Kennedy tossed aside speculation that an unpoliced atmospheric ban would produce calls to halt all tests, claiming that "he felt no pressure for a moratorium." Public opinion, then, had a mixed effect on U.S. policy. Renewed protests, combined with the agitation of congressional hawks, reinforced the president's determination not to agitate either the left or the right on the testing issue. Kennedy also realized that the neutrals could renew their pressure for disarmament. UN ambassador Stevenson persistently reminded the president of international opinion, stressing signs in the General Assembly of continued antitesting sentiment and a strong commitment to nuclear nonproliferation. In the months ahead, the United States appeared cooperative on all nuclear disarmament issues, including regional denuclearized zones in Latin America and Africa.[16]

In the end, strategic calculations and alliance politics proved more influential. When Kennedy met with Macmillan in April 1962, both agreed that their governments should formulate a new test ban proposal after the Soviets and the Americans had concluded their test series. Keeping up the pressure for more concessions from Washington, Macmillan also expressed frustration that the West kept squandering opportunities, especially because "we could have had an agreement some years back on what we are offering now." Macmillan subsequently played on JFK's well-known preoccupation with proliferation, claiming that a comprehensive test ban offered the only way to check the spread of nuclear weapons. The U.S.-British talks failed to produce any real change in the American proposal, although both sides did agree that when the ENDC resumed they would lay the groundwork for both a complete test ban and a more limited agreement that exempted all underground tests.[17]

The prospects for a successful agreement increased a few days later. On July 7, the Defense Department released data from its seismic research program that revealed new techniques for detecting underground explosions and showed that far fewer earthquakes in the Soviet Union could be mistaken for nuclear tests than previously estimated. These findings suggested that the United States could eliminate its demand for monitoring stations inside the Soviet Union and reduce its requested quota for on-site inspections. Before the Kennedy administration could fully evaluate this new information, the chief test ban negotiator, Arthur Dean, blurted out during an impromptu news conference that such changes were under consideration. This gaffe created a stir in the ENDC and in Washington, where government officials scrambled to put together a new position that guarded U.S. security and Kennedy's standing against critics who called him "soft."

The new data emerged amid heightened attention to the proliferation issue. In July, the new Soviet ambassador to the United States, Anatoly Dobrynin, signaled Moscow's continued interest in nonproliferation. But he also questioned whether the MLF and rumors of a nuclear alliance with France indicated retreat from prior U.S. positions. Later that month, Gromyko offered Rusk possible compromise language, suggesting simply that the treaty ban the "direct or indirect" transfer of nuclear weapons to other powers. Admitting the suggestion's potential, Rusk sought confirmation that Moscow would not interpret the treaty as barring the MLF. These Soviet feelers and disturbing new information about the Chinese and Israeli nuclear programs combined to reenergize American efforts to conclude nonproliferation and test ban treaties.[18]

In late July, the Kennedy administration held a flurry of meetings to reevaluate U.S. arms control policy in light of the new technical data and changed political circumstances. In the first discussions, on July 26, William C. Foster, a Republican businessman and former deputy secretary of defense, represented the new Arms Control and Disarmament Agency (ACDA). A forceful advocate of a comprehensive test ban treaty and a nonproliferation agreement, he believed that the U.S. delegation should introduce a comprehensive treaty in the ENDC. If the Soviets refused to compromise on on-site inspection and international monitoring stations, the United States should seek a limited test ban allowing underground explosions. In light of Soviet interest in halting proliferation, Rusk proposed moving forward simultaneously with an atmospheric test ban and some form of nontransfer agreement. But others opposed dropping a comprehensive ban too quickly and urged seeking maximum goals on both fronts. McNamara and Seaborg formed the moderate camp, arguing that a total testing halt would best serve the United States if it could be verified. But they also claimed that Washington had insufficient information to arrive at a final decision. They thus proposed studies of various scenarios, including comprehensive and limited test ban agreements, a nonproliferation accord, and an unrestricted arms race. Dean created the greatest stir when he contended that the air force had suppressed the new seismic data "for over a year." Conceding that the administration had had the information earlier but did not realize its implication until early July, Bundy snorted, "Maybe we were dumb, but we weren't corrupt."[19]

The "best and brightest" then took their arguments to JFK. Rusk stressed that any new proposal would face resistance from congressional leaders, who opposed any concessions to the Soviets while they continued to test nuclear weapons. After hearing all the arguments for comprehensive, limited, and nonproliferation treaties, Kennedy concluded that the danger of proliferation, especially the prospect of Israeli and Chinese nuclear arsenals, offset any danger of Soviet cheating. He mused that the administration "should go to Congress with this argument." The president contemplated a multi-track policy, which featured atmospheric and comprehensive test ban proposals, separate discussions of nonproliferation, and continued American tests pending a treaty. But he refrained from a final decision until he received more information on the merits of each treaty and more data on the dangers of proliferation.[20]

Kennedy's advisers provided the information he sought. A comprehensive test ban treaty, according to both the Pentagon and the ACDA, would most benefit U.S. security. A complete testing halt would freeze the American lead in nuclear technology, especially in tactical weapons, and it would offer the most effective check against proliferation. The Defense Department also stressed that while a comprehensive test ban constituted a necessary but insufficient measure against proliferation, a limited treaty would not impede or significantly increase the costs of a rudimentary nuclear capability. The Pentagon suggested that a full test ban could precipitate a permanent U.S.-Soviet effort to police nuclear proliferation, first in China and then in the rest of the world. Without a test ban, the cost of nuclear weapons would decline and the availability of technical knowledge would expand greatly, heightening the proliferation danger.

The ACDA, however, feared it premature to alter the U.S. test ban proposal. Unless the administration began a public education program, the Senate would defeat any treaty with more lenient inspection provisions. Foster also stressed that experts had not yet determined how many monitoring stations and on-site inspections could be cut without undue risk of Soviet cheating. Although the comprehensive ban provided the greatest benefit, it also carried the greatest risk of successful clandestine tests. After assessing all the arguments, Kennedy decided on a limited treaty while simultaneously probing Soviet attitudes toward a nonproliferation accord outside the ENDC. Inhibiting the spread of nuclear weapons still had too many implications for NATO relations to be discussed candidly with neutrals present.

The British thought the new American proposals too cautious. Arthur Dean had raised high expectations with his careless remarks about the new data, but he failed to follow up with specifics on how inspection and verification could be simplified. London grew frustrated with Kennedy's refusal to embrace a comprehensive ban with limited inspection. But the president explained that he "could not get five votes" in the Senate for the treaty language the British advocated. He wanted to wait to introduce a new draft until after Dean had explored Soviet attitudes toward on-site inspection and international monitoring stations. Faced with British threats to dissent publicly if the United States did not soon revise its comprehensive test ban language, Kennedy acquiesced in late August 1962 and allowed the American and British delegations to present both comprehensive and limited test ban draft treaties. In an Anglo-American compromise, the comprehensive test ban treaty left the number of inspections and monitoring stations to be determined by later negotiations with the Soviets.[21]

Although the Soviet representative to the ENDC immediately rejected the two proposals, Khrushchev later sent a private message to Kennedy agreeing to sign a limited test ban treaty if both sides continued working for a comprehensive agreement. But he also added two other conditions: The French must comply with the agreement, and the United States and the Soviet Union should observe a moratorium on underground tests while negotiations proceeded. Kennedy thought the new opening promising, but Macmillan feared that it contained tricky demands, especially the question of French compliance. Not dissuaded, Kennedy pushed forward. He and Khrushchev set a target date of January 1, 1963, for signing a limited test ban treaty. Except for some sparring over Chinese accession and debate over whether automatic seismic recorders, so-called black boxes, could replace manned monitoring stations, the negotiations went smoothly, and the superpowers seemed on track to sign a treaty when Khrushchev attended the UN General Assembly meeting in November 1962.[22]

The nonproliferation discussion also inspired optimism. In early August, Rusk conveyed a private message to Gromyko, warning that twenty countries might achieve a nuclear weapons capability in the next several years. He suggested that Washington and Moscow craft a compromise that would be acceptable to U.S. allies and not threaten the MLF. The Soviets, however, still preferred a separate agreement limiting German acquisition of nuclear weapons prior to negotiating a general nonproliferation accord. Rusk recognized that Gromyko wanted to contain Germany, but the United States most feared mainland China and thought both superpowers should work to prevent Israel and Egypt from acquiring nuclear weapons.[23]

Two weeks later, Moscow agreed to drop its demand for a separate nonproliferation agreement for the two Germanys but still wanted to prohibit transfer of nuclear weapons to non-nuclear countries through military alliance arrangements, such as the MLF. Rusk believed that with further discussions the American and Soviet positions could be reconciled. The main task would be convincing the NATO allies to cooperate with a nonproliferation arrangement. Although the Joint Chiefs of Staff still opposed a nonproliferation agreement, Kennedy decided to push forward with the preliminary discussions and drafted letters to Adenauer, Macmillan, and de Gaulle, asking their opinions. Kennedy also told Khrushchev that he hoped that they could announce their agreement in principle on nonproliferation before the UN General Assembly meeting recessed.

For a nonproliferation accord to succeed, JFK had to withstand firm resistance from the Joint Chiefs and the CIA. Although civilians in the Pentagon supported a nondiffusion treaty, they believed that other controversial military budget issues precluded another bureaucratic battle with the military brass in late 1962. In the familiar tropes of nuclear nationalism, the Joint Chiefs complained that the proposed agreement aided Soviet efforts to gain disarmament without inspection and played into the hands of the communist campaign to weaken NATO unity by raising fears of U.S. nuclear hegemony. They also contended that because nuclear proliferation appeared inevitable the United States should not forgo nuclear alliance relationships that could possibly strengthen Western defense. The CIA reinforced these arguments, contending that a U.S.-Soviet agreement would have a negligible effect on

China's nuclear aspirations. According to its study, the high cost of a nuclear arsenal would provide a stronger deterrent to proliferation than would a treaty.

McNamara, dissenting from his own department's report, concluded that on balance such an accord would benefit more than threaten U.S. security by slowing the rate of diffusion within both the Western and the Eastern blocs. Soviet unwillingness to supply nuclear weapons to its allies seemed stable in the short term, but these policies might change by the 1970s and 1980s when the proliferation threat would be even greater. A treaty would provide greater overall international stability by inhibiting a nuclear arms race between smaller and developing countries and by reducing Soviet fears of German revanchists. If handled clumsily, an agreement could damage U.S.-NATO relations and further complicate a Berlin settlement, but rather than abandoning efforts to contain proliferation, the administration should proceed cautiously. Kennedy accepted McNamara's advice and opted for exploratory talks with the Soviets before engaging France and other allies. Still, American efforts to conclude test ban and nonproliferation treaties had shown progress in the last half of 1962. A limited test ban appeared only months away, and a nonproliferation accord now seemed within reach.[24]

"Now We Can Swat Your Ass"

On October 14, these gains proved ephemeral. A U-2 spy plane discovered Soviet nuclear missile sites in Cuba. When McGeorge Bundy told Kennedy of the CIA findings two days later, the president exclaimed of Khrushchev, "He can't do that to me!" Later that day, Robert Kennedy examined the photographs through a magnifying glass, hissing, "Shit, shit, shit." For thirteen days, the administration remained transfixed over how to remove the MRBMs from Cuba. JFK blurted out that he could not fathom Khrushchev's motive for building the missile sites: "It's just as if we suddenly began to put a major number of MRBMs in Turkey." Bundy pointed out that the United States had committed that very provocation in 1961. By raising the issue, Kennedy had pulled back the curtain of unconscious hypocrisy, revealing the double standard of U.S. nuclear-sharing policy. The president did not dwell on this issue when formulating his response to the Soviet action. On October 22, after ruling out both diplomacy and a military strike, Kennedy went on television to demand the immediate removal of the missiles and announce a naval quarantine of Cuba. He had eschewed readily available diplomatic channels for a public ultimatum.[25]

The world teetered on the brink of nuclear holocaust. Khrushchev initially bristled at the effrontery of American threats and refused to yield. Kennedy proved equally intransigent. But after a few days, the Soviet premier sent a confused, at times rambling, letter that offered the outlines of a possible settlement. He suggested that the Soviet Union would remove its missiles and other offensive weapons in exchange for an American pledge not to invade Cuba and the end of the quarantine. But before Kennedy responded, he received a new public message from Khrushchev that added the removal of Jupiter missiles from Turkey to the mix. The president and his advisers had discussed trading the Jupiters for the Cuban missiles in the days prior to Khrushchev's latest letter. But Rusk and others feared that should Washington remove the weapons under pressure, Europeans' worst fears about U.S. reliability would be confirmed. Kennedy finally decided to accept the conditions in the first letter and ignore the Jupiter missiles in his public response.

The president nonetheless feared that Khrushchev would insist on a quid pro quo. Upon Rusk's urging, he instructed his brother Robert to meet with Dobrynin and tell him that if the Jupiters posed an obstacle to agreement, the president would offer personal assurances that they would be removed within four to five months after the Soviets pulled their MRBMs out of Cuba. Kennedy, however, could not agree publicly to link the Jupiters to a Cuban settlement because such an act, he believed, would mortally damage the NATO alliance. Had Khrushchev demanded a formal linkage of the Turkish and Cuban missiles, Kennedy had prepared another plan to avoid the appearance of kowtowing to Moscow's demands. He had instructed Rusk to contact the undersecretary of the UN, Andrew Cordier, and ask him to prepare a missile trade proposal for UN secretary-general U Thant to be revealed only upon a confidential request from the United States. This public quid pro quo would have meant acceding to a UN proposal rather than to a Soviet demand and could have been more easily defended to both the American public and the NATO allies. Kennedy ultimately did not have to choose the "Cordier ploy" because Khrushchev accepted the informal arrangement. When the Soviet premier attempted to get the agreement on the Jupiter missiles in writing, Robert Kennedy refused, claiming it would prove too embarrassing to the president. Khrushchev accepted this justification for secrecy, and both sides moved forward with the settlement.[26]

Both the origin and the resolution of the Cuban Missile Crisis profoundly impacted U.S. and Soviet nonproliferation policy. Although Khrushchev had multiple motives for placing missiles in Cuba, including deterring a U.S. invasion of Cuba and redressing the strategic imbalance between the superpowers, he also wanted to give Americans "a little bit of their own medicine" by placing nuclear weapons close to their country. He would show them that "it's been a long time since you could spank us like a little boy—now we can swat your ass." Both Kennedy and Eisenhower had privately confessed that the Soviets had legitimate security concerns about the Jupiter missiles in Turkey. But neither had taken steps to remove the weapons prior to the crisis. The Cuban confrontation illustrated the dangers of placing nuclear missiles in an area likely to antagonize one's principal rival, especially if the conventional balance of power favored the threatened party. Former Soviet policymakers revealed years later that Khrushchev sent tactical nuclear weapons to Cuba and may have given Soviet commanders permission to use them if attacked. Had Kennedy listened to his Joint Chiefs of Staff and authorized air strikes and an invasion, the crisis would likely have escalated to thermonuclear war. Selective proliferation, much like unmoderated nuclear proliferation, had proved to be dangerously destabilizing. Yet the MLF theologians remained unfazed, advocating a Mediterranean MLF, composed of Turkish, Italian, Greek, and U.S. sailors, to replace the Jupiters withdrawn from Italy and Turkey.[27]

Following the crisis, the Warsaw Pact instituted command-and-control policies to ensure that tactical weapons could only be fired after high-level authorization from Moscow. The Kennedy administration also accelerated plans to place PALs on all NATO tactical weapons and rejected Adenauer's renewed appeal for West Germany to acquire unrestricted control over the nuclear weapons deployed on its soil. The Cuban Missile Crisis also revealed the dangers of nuclear alliances for smaller powers. Western and Eastern Europeans remained powerless as the superpowers decided the world's fate in an area far away. The confrontation, therefore, strengthened support for de Gaulle's arguments about U.S. hegemony and led some Warsaw Pact countries, such as Romania, to pull away from the Soviet Union.

Postcrisis Optimism

The crisis initially inspired a renewed interest in arms control in both the United States and the Soviet Union. In their letters establishing the public terms of the settlement, Kennedy and Khrushchev reiterated their commitment to arms control, especially a test ban and nonproliferation. But neither leader seemed willing to compromise. Khrushchev still denied any need for on-site inspection. Unable to speak publicly of Kennedy's most strategically significant concession, the Soviet premier could not afford to appear to retreat from his past position — especially given stinging Chinese rebukes of his alleged cowardice and Kremlin snickering that he had "shitted in his pants" during the confrontation. Kennedy conversely basked in the glow of victory. He avoided publicly rubbing Moscow's nose in "defeat" but privately boasted that he had "cut [Khrushchev's] balls off." This macho attitude shaped the U.S. stance in the ensuing test ban talks. Walt W. Rostow, head of the State Department Policy Planning Staff, later explained that Kennedy "had set Khrushchev on his behind. The only way that Khrushchev became a nice, clean-cut kid — interested in the test ban — was by making it clear to him that nuclear blackmail wouldn't work." Although the two leaders expressed continued desire to conclude an agreement, the United States and the Soviet Union had already retreated from their commitment to sign a limited treaty by January 1, 1963.[28]

The two superpowers explored cooperation on nonproliferation, as well as a test ban, in the wake of the Caribbean confrontation. The desire to avoid a repeat crisis added momentum to efforts to create a Latin American denuclearized zone. Although Kennedy supported the Brazilian resolution in the UN, France warned that a favorable vote on the proposal might legitimize Soviet attempts to denuclearize Central Europe, possibly delinking U.S. and European security concerns. Washington dismissed Paris's warning as another shot in their war of words. But Paris may have been more attuned to superpower thinking than the Kennedy administration cared to admit. The Cuban Missile Crisis, especially the downing of an American U-2 over Cuba and Cuban leader Fidel Castro's secret request for a Soviet preemptive strike against the United States, had exposed the reality that proliferation could drag both Moscow and Washington into a nuclear war that neither wanted.

Postcrisis public statements emanating from Beijing also highlighted fears that the PRC might act irresponsibly if it possessed nuclear weapons. Rusk and Bundy argued that the United States urgently needed test ban and nonproliferation agreements to contain Chinese proliferation. Bundy also hinted that if arms control failed the administration should consider a military option against Beijing.[29]

The new U.S.-Soviet dialogue flowed through multiple channels. Kennedy seemed intent on exploiting every opportunity for a test ban or nonproliferation agreement. He utilized Norman Cousins, editor of the *Saturday Review* and a prominent member of SANE, to deliver a message to Khrushchev expressing the president's deep desire to end the Cold War. NSC staff member Carl Kaysen also encouraged Leo Szilard, a former Manhattan Project scientist and disarmament advocate, to pursue the "Angels Project," designed to convene nongovernmental arms control experts from both the United States and the Soviet Union to craft a reasonable disarmament plan. Khrushchev accepted the use of informal channels to float trial balloons. He expressed support for the Angels Project and told Cousins to inform Kennedy that he desired a test ban and wished to keep nuclear weapons from "spreading all over the world." Poland's delegation to the UN also alluded to the communist bloc's desire for arms control during private conversations with the well-connected Washington columnist Walter Lippmann.[30]

Although these informal discussions did not constitute a negotiating forum, they did establish a climate of cooperation. The Kennedy administration and the Soviet government discussed nuclear testing in both bilateral talks and the ENDC. But neither channel produced a treaty acceptable to both superpowers. The ENDC meetings began with much optimism. The UN General Assembly, over both U.S. and Soviet abstentions, had passed a resolution calling for an end to all nuclear tests by January 1, 1963. Washington and Moscow's failure to kill the resolution and their willingness to suspend atmospheric testing during the talks seemed to augur progress. But the issues of inspection and verification still divided Washington and Moscow. Khrushchev insisted that any partial ban include a halt on other experiments, while Kennedy rejected a moratorium without assurances against further Soviet surprise test series. The two sides moved slightly closer on seismic stations ("black boxes"), agreeing that they would allow a reduction in total inspections and elimination of manned stations. Moscow, however, claimed that these devices could substitute for all on-site inspections, a contention vigorously disputed even by American test ban proponents. The neutrals offered a compromise proposal, but Moscow refused to accept even minimal inspections. The talks recessed on December 20 without fulfilling the UN mandate. Retreating from earlier commitments to suspend nuclear experiments during the talks, the Soviets reverted to earlier patterns of Cold War gamesmanship when they resumed atmospheric testing on December 13.

The day before the Geneva talks recessed, however, Khrushchev indicated willingness to compromise. Still rejecting the scientific justifications for unlimited on-site inspections, the Soviet premier agreed to an annual quota of two to three. The president felt "exhilarated," but he found confusing Khrushchev's claim that American officials had already endorsed the principle of limited inspections. Kennedy's willingness to allow a plethora of informal discussions and his inattention to staff work had fed the misunderstanding. Both Arthur Dean and Jerome Wiesner, the president's science adviser, had communicated to the Soviets their private views that Washington would accept minimal inspections. Wiesner had also told the president that only three inspections might suffice. But the ACDA claimed that no fewer than seven inspections had to be mandated if the administration hoped for congressional approval.[31]

The president reiterated to Khrushchev the U.S. requirement of eight to ten inspections. The exchange did prompt a series of bilateral discussions aimed at producing a number acceptable to both powers. But American policymakers wrongly expected Moscow to be agreeable, following the Cuban Missile Crisis. On February 1, the Soviets refused to accede to Kennedy's demands, with Khrushchev sputtering that when "you hold out a finger to" Americans, "they chop off the whole hand." Talks broke down, and Washington resumed testing that month, sounding the death knell for a speedy test ban. Arthur Dean's resignation as the chief negotiator emerged as the only substantive outcome of the resuscitated test talks.[32]

Efforts at a nontransfer agreement had paralleled the test ban negotiations. In November, Rusk renewed U.S. attempts to win allied adherence to a nonproliferation agreement, under the assumption that the Cuban Missile Crisis had not changed the Soviet position. After brief consultation with Dobrynin, he packed a draft nontransfer agreement in his briefcase when he traveled to the NATO ministerial meeting in December. Stressing the administration's elevated interest in blocking Chinese nuclear ambitions and Washington's continued commitment to the MLF, Rusk urged the French, Germans, and British to endorse the U.S. draft. London accepted the American proposal, Bonn agreed to comply if Beijing also signed, and Paris said it would study the document. Given U.S.-French animosity, Rusk felt "slightly encouraged that we had not had oracular rejection from Paris." Kennedy had high hopes for nonproliferation talks with the Soviets and the Europeans, especially after CIA reconnaissance satellites revealed that the Chinese had constructed a nuclear test site at Lop Nor in the isolated northwestern part of their territory. A consensus emerged in the government that even if the Chinese refused to cooperate with a nonproliferation agreement, Beijing's intransigence would at least serve to isolate it diplomatically.[33]

Skybolt

Alliance politics again complicated U.S. nonproliferation efforts just as they inched toward success. NATO had rallied around Washington during the Cuban Missile Crisis, but the confrontation raised new doubts. Many Europeans feared that the superpowers would conclude a nonproliferation agreement hostile to the national interests of both NATO and Warsaw Pact countries. In British and French policy circles, these sentiments took on more substance because of McNamara's critique of small nuclear forces in June 1962. The October crisis had further underlined the inherent dangers of nuclear proliferation, increasing American opposition to both London's and Paris's nuclear deterrents.

Allied suspicions of American nuclear hegemony helped turn a McNamara budgetary decision into the most severe test of alliance unity since the Suez crisis. The controversy stemmed from Eisenhower's agreement to help Britain modernize its deterrent via an air-launched ballistic missile, dubbed Skybolt. In return, Washington received the right to base U.S. nuclear submarines in British ports. In 1960, however, Skybolt remained an untested concept not ready for deployment until mid-decade. As early as July 1960, the missile's future seemed in question when the President's Science Advisory Committee warned of technical problems that might warrant cancellation. A transnational alliance between the British and the American air forces kept the weapon alive until 1962, when McNamara deemed Skybolt "a pile of junk." To avoid arousing Skybolt proponents on both sides of the Atlantic before its death became a fait accompli, the defense secretary kept his decision secret until the last possible moment. He dropped hints to the British that the weapon's future might be bleak, but U.S. warnings of cancellation had become an annual event and were easily ignored. In December, McNamara told British defense minister Peter Thorneycroft that Skybolt was dead, inspiring accusations that Americans had used deception to pressure Britain into abandoning its independent deterrent. Some U.S. officials, especially in the State Department, indeed harbored hopes that cancellation would help kill Britain's nuclear force. An infuriated Macmillan leaked a report suggesting that McNamara had cancelled Skybolt for political reasons and not for its technical failures.[34]

Kennedy desperately sought to avoid a breach with Britain, especially given continued frostiness in U.S.-French relations. Rusk agreed that the United States needed "*somebody* to talk to in the world. . . . We can't talk to DeGaulle . . . or Adenauer." State Department officials had worried from the beginning that Skybolt's cancellation could precipitate the Macmillan government's collapse. But McNamara ignored their recommendation to consult with the British, rather than merely inform them of the decision. By charging ahead, Washington risked driving London into the arms of Paris. Skybolt jumped to the top of the agenda for a summit with Macmillan scheduled for December at Nassau (the Bahamas). The prime minister meanwhile conferred with de

Gaulle in France. This conference ostensibly sought to smooth British entry into the Common Market. With the Skybolt crisis in full flower, however, the general eagerly seized the opportunity to attempt to entice Macmillan into an Anglo-French nuclear relationship. But while the prime minister proffered cooperation on submarine delivery systems, he resisted any "unholy alliance," fearing it might rupture U.S.-British relations beyond repair. Macmillan suffered a double blow when it became clear that de Gaulle would retaliate by blocking British entry into the Common Market.[35]

Washington had suspected that de Gaulle would make nuclear cooperation a condition of Britain's joining the EEC. Kennedy, therefore, realized that he might have to outbid France at the Nassau meeting. The Americans opened the summit hoping to buy time. Kennedy would initially propose joint study of alternatives to Skybolt, and if Macmillan demurred, he would suggest as fallback proposals independent British development of the weapon or U.S. sale of Polaris missiles to London.

The Polaris option sparked heated opposition from the MLF theologians. When a Pentagon official first raised the possibility of offering London Polaris missiles, they reacted as if he had "called Christ an atheist in a room full of bishops." With de Gaulle's veto of British entry into the EEC almost inevitable, the prime minister desperately needed a victory on Skybolt. He had told Thorneycroft that they had to show the Americans that "we are not 'soft,'" especially since the Kennedy administration "rather admire[s] a 'tough' attitude." During the first meeting, he heatedly lectured the president on Britain's contributions to the Manhattan Project and demanded an immediate replacement for Skybolt — a "bride" he no longer wished to marry now that her "virginity" was "doubtful."[36]

Kennedy assuaged Macmillan's anger but only at a heavy price for U.S. nonproliferation policy. He agreed to provide Polaris missiles on the condition that British submarines be assigned to NATO defense and possibly integrated into the MLF upon its creation. Macmillan, in turn, extracted an agreement from Washington that Britain could withdraw its nuclear deterrent from NATO in a "time of national emergency." This arrangement became confused when the American delegation agreed to include a provision for a NATO multinational nuclear force, which would consist of national nuclear forces committed to European defense under unified command. The Kennedy administration interpreted this proposal as duplicating a previous Macmillan plan to control the dispersal of tactical nuclear weapons to individual NATO nations. The British, however, read the language as referring to the proper arrangement for the commitment of their Polaris submarines to the alliance.[37]

De Gaulle's long shadow loomed over Nassau. Washington and London had hoped that Britain's entry into the Common Market would be the first step toward a "greater Europe," which would channel French energies onto a less nationalistic path. An offer of Polaris missiles to Britain might scuttle hopes that France would approve London's entry into the EEC. Kennedy, therefore, offered de Gaulle the same conditions as Macmillan. But the United States also had to avoid alienating the Germans and the Italians, who might consider the Nassau proposal discriminatory. Bonn and Rome believed Skybolt would only extend the life of the British deterrent to 1969, while Polaris would keep London in the nuclear club for at least two decades. Washington assured them that the new agreements would lead to the integration of all European national nuclear forces into the MLF, a point also stressed in the final negotiations with London.[38]

Despite American enticements, de Gaulle oscillated between a "cool" to an overwhelmingly hostile attitude toward the Nassau agreements. On first hearing of the Anglo-American Polaris accord, he flew "into a tremendously violent temper" and denounced the British as "betraying Europe" and "no longer worthy of being considered a free country." The U.S. offer to France gave him pause until he studied the details. The State and Defense Departments had already warned that if Paris interpreted the American language, "under the same conditions," literally, the Polaris offer would be unacceptable to France. London had its own submarines and warheads and only needed missiles. Although Kennedy knew that Paris needed more help, he did not want to supplement his offer until de Gaulle reacted to the first proposals, primarily because moving beyond the wording of the Nassau agreement would require complex maneuvering with Congress. But the general did not want to dicker with the Americans and concluded that Kennedy sought to trap France in protracted negotiations until it had no resort but to join the MLF. On January 14, he delivered his verdict on Nassau, blasting both Washington and London while rejecting the Polaris arrangement and British membership in the Common Market. To make matters worse, Paris and Bonn announced a new bilateral security alliance just one week later — an agreement many in Washington feared would lead to nuclear cooperation between the two states. De Gaulle once wrote that "to be great is to sustain a great quarrel" — at that moment he must have felt flush with grandeur.[39]

The "general's thunderbolts" shook London, Moscow, and Washington. With a single statement, de Gaulle exploded hopes for Kennedy's "Grand Design" and raised the specter of a Europe independent of either bloc. The Soviets reacted with equal horror. Washington could be expected to contain

French and German nationalist ambitions, but a Western Europe dominated by Paris and Bonn, armed with nuclear weapons, could be a dangerously destabilizing force. The United States, moreover, might be tempted to give West Germany nuclear weapons to keep it in the American fold. Both superpowers braced themselves for the aftershocks of the Gaullist blast. Macmillan told Kennedy that de Gaulle had gone "absolutely crazy," willing to do anything to be "the cock on a small dung hill instead of having two cocks on a larger one." JFK wondered if de Gaulle's actions were meant "to run us out of Europe by means of a deal with the Russians." He feared that in such a case "the Germans would go with the French." Some administration officials asked what "the children would look like" in "a marriage of a known" (Germany) and an "unknown" (de Gaulle).[40]

Chasing Genies

Within days of the French actions, Kennedy told his NSC that because Western Europe had recovered from the devastation of World War II and no longer depended on U.S. economic assistance, it had become "less subject to our influence." Tying waning economic leverage to nuclear proliferation, the president observed that "if the French and other European powers acquire a nuclear capability they would be in a position to be entirely independent and we might be on the outside looking in. We must exploit our military and political position to ensure that our economic interests are protected" and "squeeze Europe" back into line with U.S. preferences. The president also blustered that he would "haul out" of Europe if France and Germany cooperated on nuclear weapons. These tough words hid the fact that Washington stayed in "Europe not because the Europeans want us there but because we believe our presence there is essential to the defense of the U.S." U.S. hegemony in Europe depended on Bonn staying in its camp. Threats and the MLF became the main weapons against a Franco-German bloc. Former secretary of state Dean Acheson scolded one German official that Bonn's assurances about the Franco-German treaty's intent indicated that Adenauer either thought Washington "stupid" or else constituted an admission of "duplicitous" dealings with de Gaulle. Washington's pressures succeeded, prompting Adenauer's own party to repudiate his Gaullist policies. The West German Bundestag added a preamble to the Franco-German treaty pledging Bonn's loyalty to NATO and support for British entry into the EEC. In the end, the German Foreign Office concluded it better to deal with "a strong and distant hegemon than a weak and nearby one." De Gaulle mused that treaties seemed to last no longer than "roses or young girls." As the fear of Bonn's emulating Paris began to fade, so did the president's support for the NATO nuclear force. During the briefings for the MLF negotiating team in February, he contended that "the British were not for it, the French were clearly against it, and the Italians did not have a deep-seated interest in it. The Germans reportedly were interested, but once they realized how little they were getting for their money, they might look at it differently." Kennedy would not stick with the MLF too long if it appeared to be a losing issue, and he "saw little advantage" in "making Europe less dependent on us." Convinced that Europeans became "psychotic" when not full participants in policymaking, however, he directed his advisers to formulate alternative multilateral solutions to the NATO nuclear problem.[41]

The president's pessimism regarding the MLF proved prophetic. Admiral Hyman Rickover, the father of the U.S. nuclear navy, used his sway with Congress to preempt even the slimmest possibility that Polaris submarines would be part of the MLF. Both the Italians and the Germans viewed a NATO nuclear force composed of surface ships as a transparently second-rate system, and the British thought the entire concept of a mixed-manned force, whether surface ships or submarines, an absurd contrivance. One German journalist labeled the scheme an "egg-laying wooly milk pig"—a monstrosity borne of the futile effort to please all parties. Yet State Department Europeanists, led by Undersecretary of State George W. Ball, championed the scheme so fervently that it became impossible to kill. Ball saw the MLF as crucial to encouraging European integration after de Gaulle had vetoed British membership in the Common Market. Washington had to take the lead in advancing a united Europe since Bonn was "just emerging from a long adolescence under stern parental guidance" and no other European powers had the needed wealth and power. The strength with which Ball and the other theologians supported the MLF brought Kennedy to the brink of a preliminary agreement during his European tour in June 1963.[42]

Bundy rescued the president at the last moment. In a tightly argued memorandum, he accused Ball and his subordinates of pressing the case for the MLF "more sharply and against a tighter timetable, at every stage, than either you or the Secretary would have chosen." He blanched at suggestions that the MLF should be created without an explicit U.S. veto. According to Bundy's analysis, the scheme would stir up both the Europeans and the Soviets, and its passage would require the president to expend precious political capital in Congress (where some believed the idea "nutty") for a costly endeavor that filled no military need. Because two administrations had endorsed the policy, the United States could not suddenly disavow the plan, but a preliminary agreement during the president's European visit should be abandoned and replaced with exploratory talks. If the Europeans acquired a clear sense of American ambivalence, Bundy argued, the MLF might die a natural death.[43]

Combined with Macmillan's political weakness in the wake of a "sex-for-secrets" spy scandal and the president's own belief that "the whole debate about an atomic force in Europe is really useless, because Berlin is secure and Europe as a whole is well protected," the Bundy memorandum helped put the MLF on the back burner. In the end, Kennedy and Bundy shared Acheson's assessment that "in being exasperated and irritated by the neurotic and irrational conduct of German officials — and often the German public — [we] are making the mistake of a busy parent annoyed by the pressing of a high strung, insecure, but affectionate — almost too affectionate — child. It is a mistake to take what it says literally; and the worst thing to do is to shout at it or slap at it." Because Germany was perceived as childish, Kennedy could discount its worries about becoming a second-class power. The United States could always find some other way to mollify Bonn, and if not, it would simply enforce its parental will on its recalcitrant ward.[44]

The push for NATO nuclear sharing, however, had already dealt a debilitating setback to the U.S.-Soviet nonproliferation talks. In early February, Dobrynin informed Rusk that the Soviets viewed the MLF as a legal smoke-screen for handing nuclear weapons to the Germans. Rusk insisted that the Soviets were "boxing shadows" on the issue because the MLF did not exist and many particulars had not yet been established. State Department officials concluded that Moscow's protests stemmed from deeply ingrained fears of German aggression and did not serve purely propaganda purposes. Although Rusk piqued French interest in an agreement (largely because they also feared independent German acquisition of nuclear weapons), the Soviets still adamantly opposed the MLF. The secretary of state continued meeting with Dobrynin, with little success. The two diplomats developed a friendly relationship, joking and verbally jousting without heated Cold War rhetoric. The Soviet ambassador playfully asked Rusk "if [the United States] wanted the Chinese to be a member of a [Soviet] multilateral force." The secretary later teased Dobrynin about Moscow's contribution to Beijing's nuclear program, claiming that "you have already lost your virginity on this point, and we are still trying to preserve ours." The ambassador laughed at the remark and advised Rusk to repeat it to the earthy Khrushchev. The nonproliferation talks, however, remained stalled.[45]

Kennedy could have had a nonproliferation agreement at any time during spring 1963 had he been willing to abandon the MLF. But the Skybolt debacle had shaken the president and left him wary about another NATO crisis. He did not relent in seeking Soviet acceptance of the scheme, but time was running short to halt proliferation. With bilateral talks stagnant, the United States contemplated unilateral action in the Middle East and China. Kennedy stepped up surveillance of the Israeli and Egyptian nuclear projects and sought information on French designs to build clandestine and overt nuclear ties with Italy and Germany. The president also sent John McCloy to Cairo in the hope of staving off a Middle Eastern nuclear arms race. But Kennedy's prior decision to sell Hawk missiles to Israel came back to haunt him when Egypt's leader Gamal Abdel Nasser defended his missile program on grounds that Tel Aviv already possessed such weapons. Nasser also warned McCloy that concrete proof of an Israeli nuclear program would ignite a "protective war" in the Middle East. McCloy then cancelled his visit to Israel. Washington pressured Tel Aviv to abandon its nuclear aspirations, but to no avail.[46]

Attempts to contain Chinese nuclear ambitions also faced problems. The Joint Chiefs of Staff provided Kennedy with a laundry list of diplomatic and military options designed to persuade or coerce Beijing to abandon its nuclear program. These included attacks by Chinese nationalists, conventional air raids on Chinese nuclear facilities, and the use of tactical nuclear weapons. But ultimately they concluded that a joint U.S.-Soviet campaign held the most promise of success.[47]

The Limited Test Ban Treaty

The need for political trust between Moscow and Washington prior to any nonproliferation regime put added emphasis on a test ban agreement. The ENDC reconvened in February, but the deadlock persisted. The political debate at home, meanwhile, had grown increasingly acrimonious. Lewis Strauss and other nuclear nationalists had fed information to conservative Washington columnist Earl H. Voss, who published an anti–test ban tract titled *Nuclear Ambush: The Test Ban Trap*. Other test ban opponents blasted administration proposals in congressional hearings, and key Democrats, such as Thomas J. Dodd, Henry Jackson, Stuart Symington, and Richard Russell, warned the president that they could not vote for the U.S. treaty draft as written. While Republicans accused Kennedy of considering a "Munich-style agreement" that would strip the United States of "its nuclear shirt," Congress hinted that it might cut the ACDA's budget if it proved too eager to conclude a test ban treaty. Within his administration, Kennedy continued to confront opposition from the Joint Chiefs of Staff and CIA director John McCone. McCone leaked damaging information to congressional committees, conservative newspapers, and Strauss.[48]

The nuclear nationalists tried to appear reasonable by saying that they did not oppose the idea of a treaty, only the language of Kennedy's proposals. But the crux of their critiques suggested that any agreement would be foolish because Moscow could not be trusted. They consistently demanded ironclad inspection provisions, even though neither the Soviets nor the Americans would accept the large number of on-site inspections the test ban critics envisioned. Their proposed verification measures would have been exorbitantly expensive, requiring large inspection teams and a full-time staff. Strauss and McCone almost certainly realized these problems and used them to stymie a test ban.

Despite persistent criticism, Kennedy hesitated to jettison arms control and risk alienating the informed public while giving free rein to Chinese nuclear ambitions. With NATO in turmoil, Kennedy did not want to move too quickly on nuclear testing and arouse additional political furor domestically. But his near obsession with preventing Beijing's acquisition of the bomb kept him committed to a test ban. On several occasions in 1963 he told his advisers that, "in his opinion, the whole reason for having a test ban is related to the Chinese situation. Otherwise, it wouldn't be worth the disruption and fighting with Congress, etc."[49]

Convinced that a desire for a nuclear-free Germany provided common ground on which test ban and nonproliferation agreements could be built, Macmillan also kept badgering the president for concessions so that the Soviets would accept a comprehensive agreement. But Kennedy's advisers believed the timing was poor in early 1963. Khrushchev faced too many problems, both foreign and domestic, for him to engage in the compromises that serious negotiations would require. Rather than pushing for a summit meeting as Macmillan recommended, Kennedy suggested a joint letter to Khrushchev reiterating the Western commitment to ending tests. The president also continued his top secret correspondence with the Soviet premier. This series of letters helped break the logjam. On April 11, 1963, Kennedy proposed sending a personal representative to Moscow to discuss the test ban, nonproliferation, and other matters. He repeated the proposal in a joint letter with Macmillan sent later that month.

Khrushchev initially seemed hostile to the new approach, expressing continued outrage that Kennedy had rejected his offer of three on-site inspections. Later in April, however, his attitude changed. Undersecretary of

State W. Averell Harriman visited Moscow to discuss the Laotian settlement with Khrushchev, and their wide-ranging talks touched on the test ban and the Sino-Soviet split. The two men had met several times before and had developed a frank, if not completely friendly, relationship. Harriman's assertion that the United States and Great Britain honestly desired a test ban seemed to impress the premier, who had come to trust the American diplomat's word. A few days later, Khrushchev accepted Kennedy's offer to convene a meeting of high-level representatives.[50]

Kennedy's strategy also seemed to pay dividends domestically. He had advised his subordinates to get off the defensive and strike back at test ban opponents. In hearings before the JCAE and the Senate Foreign Relations Committee, State Department and ACDA officials advocated the administration's test ban position in the strongest terms. The president used his news conferences to argue for a test ban treaty and against proliferation. In May, Kennedy also pressed McCone to testify in favor of the U.S. test ban position. With intelligence estimates warning of a Chinese nuclear test at any time, Beijing remained the primary impetus for Kennedy's actions. He wanted to use a Moscow meeting to conclude a test ban treaty and forge an anti-Chinese alliance. His advisers' conclusions that a test ban could inhibit, but not prevent, proliferation therefore did not dampen his optimism. He still believed that the test ban could offer the first step toward a jointly enforced nonproliferation agreement.

In June, Kennedy contemplated a bold political gamble. But before moving ahead he once again probed Khrushchev's seriousness about a high-level meeting. When the Soviet premier agreed to a conference in Moscow in mid-July, the president delivered the most ambitious speech of his presidency. On June 10, he addressed the American University commencement exercises, calling for détente between the superpowers and promising not to be the first to resume atmospheric tests. This rhetoric did not constitute a risky instance of public diplomacy, as some have argued. Kennedy had little reason to resort to negotiations through the media when he had already received Khrushchev's agreement to a test ban conference. While the president's peace speech did convey to the Soviets a desire for agreement, it also used the bully pulpit in an attempt to defang hard-line American Cold Warriors and create a congressional climate more hospitable to a comprehensive test ban treaty.

With the United States and the Soviet Union more willing to negotiate seriously, Kennedy moved to build support for his policies within the alliance and within the government. He tried to entice the French by hinting that American nuclear aid might be forthcoming if they signed a test ban treaty.

But Paris remained noncommittal. Kennedy also had limited success with the bureaucracy. The Joint Chiefs continued their blind opposition to a comprehensive test ban. Kennedy might have ordered any other officials either to testify in favor of his policy or to resign. The Joint Chiefs, however, by law had the right and the obligation to present their personal views during congressional inquiries. Without military support, the test ban would surely run into stiff resistance in the Senate. Although tempted at times to dare Congress to reject a test ban, Kennedy realized that such a defeat might prevent further progress on nonproliferation. He opted for caution, still seeking a comprehensive treaty but not compromising any of the previous U.S. positions on inspection and verification.

Kennedy proved successful only with the British. While visiting Europe, he told Macmillan that political constraints prevented him from moving closer to the Soviet position. He nonetheless hoped that Khrushchev's fear of China would make the premier eager for agreement and willing to accept the Western proposal. Skeptical, Macmillan agreed to follow the American lead so long as a treaty seemed likely.

Kennedy had to choose his chief negotiator carefully. John McCloy emerged as the president's first choice because of his experience with disarmament and his previous contacts with Khrushchev. McCloy, however, refused the appointment, claiming that the Sino-Soviet conference scheduled for the same week as the test ban talks would prevent serious negotiations. Harriman became everyone's second choice. Kennedy had chosen an emissary well suited to implement the tactics he envisioned. Harriman understood and could talk candidly with Khrushchev. He also symbolized Soviet-American cooperation because of his service as ambassador to the Soviet Union during World War II. Most important, he shared the president's conviction that the key to détente with the Soviets lay in exploiting the Sino-Soviet split. Although he found the coincidence of the Sino-Soviet negotiations with the test ban talks suspicious, fearing that Khrushchev would try to play Beijing off Washington, he believed that Khrushchev's reaction to Kennedy's peace gestures indicated that a U.S.-Soviet rapprochement lay within reach.

An experienced diplomat, Harriman wanted flexibility in his instructions and bargaining chips to produce substantive agreements with the Soviets. But he thought ACDA and State Department guidelines hopelessly unimaginative and restrictive. In late June, he threatened to resign from the mission if he did not have something to trade. With the president fenced in politically, the United States could not make significant concessions on a comprehensive test ban. A treaty, moreover, would not immediately impact the Chinese nuclear program. Harriman and the president hence concentrated on forging a cooperative military agreement against Beijing's nuclear facilities. After reading through several lengthy studies of the problem, they concluded that nothing short of a surgical air strike would eliminate the Chinese threat. Kennedy believed such a raid "wouldn't be too hard if we could somehow get kind of an anonymous airplane to go over there, take out the Chinese facilities — they've only got a couple — and maybe we could do it, or maybe the Soviet Union could do it." A Soviet official who hinted that Moscow was open to joint action against a nuclear PRC convinced Harriman that Moscow might cooperate in such a venture, or at least not protest if Washington did it.[51]

Because such an act would splinter the world communist movement, Khrushchev needed additional incentives to accept the U.S. proposal. Harriman, never a Kennedy intimate, complained that Washington's misguided voluntary removal of Jupiter missiles from Italy and Turkey eliminated what would have made perfect trading stock for the test ban negotiations. Harriman asked Kennedy if instead he might exchange the NATO nuclear force for Khrushchev's agreement to break with the Chinese. "Of course," the president exclaimed. "It would be a great relief to get rid of that!" But the MLF theologians in the State Department once again mobilized to save their pet project, claiming that it could not be traded away so soon after de Gaulle had sabotaged the U.S. Grand Design for Europe. Kennedy ultimately told Harriman that if Khrushchev appeared cooperative on "the China problem," he could indicate that under "certain circumstances" the United States might give up the MLF. But he should give no "specific assurances" about cancellation. Part of the president's hesitancy to disavow nuclear sharing stemmed from his desire not to close off "giving weapons to France if we so desired." Naively and incredibly, even after the Nassau proposal had blown up in his face, Kennedy still hoped to woo de Gaulle back into full participation in the alliance and win his cooperation with U.S. nonproliferation policy. A bribe still seemed the most efficacious means.[52]

On July 2, 1963, Khrushchev raised the issue of a German settlement in a speech in East Berlin. He proposed a NATO–Warsaw Pact nonaggression treaty and a limited test ban treaty as a package deal. The Soviets clearly wanted a nonaggression treaty to symbolize the success of their peaceful coexistence strategy. A Western commitment to the European status quo combined with a test ban treaty would give Khrushchev valuable ammunition in his ideological battles with the Chinese. Although Kennedy believed that a nonaggression treaty posed no problems for the United States, the West Germans refused to approve any negotiations because they would legitimize the division of Germany, while de Gaulle apprehended the U.S.-Soviet "condominium of the world" he had vowed to prevent. Harriman therefore traveled to Moscow with very little to trade. As fallback positions, he would try to formalize limited intelligence sharing on Chinese nuclear activities and attempt to persuade the Soviets that Beijing's refusal to sign a test ban treaty would violate the Sino-Soviet treaty of alliance. The only grounds for optimism rested on Khrushchev's acceptance of a partial ban. If Harriman could break the link between a nonaggression pact and a testing agreement, he seemed certain of returning home with some type of test limitation accord. JFK wanted him to leave Moscow with at least a test ban, but he had given Harriman detailed instructions for a comprehensive nuclear agreement on proliferation, warhead limits, and constraints on delivery vehicles if the Soviets proved amenable.[53]

Because of the choppy political waters, both domestic and international, Kennedy did not allow Harriman to navigate the Moscow negotiations without guidance. The president instructed his envoy to give detailed accounts of each day's proceedings. Kennedy would then meet with his advisers and instruct the Moscow delegation on how to respond. To keep these exchanges secret, Kennedy created a code word, BAN, that placed the transmissions above top secret classification and restricted their circulation. Upon arriving in Moscow on July 15, Harriman followed the president's guidelines closely, but Khrushchev did not prove to be cooperative. The Soviet premier signaled immediately that a comprehensive test ban was nonnegotiable, and he dismissed the urgency of containing the Chinese nuclear threat, arguing that nuclear weapons would actually moderate Mao's behavior.[54]

Kennedy thought the Soviets' willingness to discuss a limited test ban encouraging, but he "remained convinced that [the] Chinese problem is more serious than Khrushchev's comments in [the] first meeting suggest." He told Harriman to press the question in private meetings and "try to elicit Khrushchev's view of means of limiting or preventing Chinese nuclear development and his willingness either to take Soviet or accept U.S. action aimed in this direction." On July 18, Harriman asked permission to play down further discussions of nonproliferation, warning that the Soviets might use the issue to drag the MLF into the negotiations. Despite the unsuccessful parallel negotiations with the Chinese, the Soviets wanted to avoid aggressive action against Beijing. Khrushchev instead sought a limited test ban treaty to isolate Mao politically, hoping that neutrals would shun China if it refused to cooperate. Kennedy reluctantly resigned himself to achieving only a limited test ban treaty—a major concession in light of his labeling nonproliferation the primary focus of the negotiations prior to the conference. To avoid scuttling even a partial ban, he instructed Harriman to persuade the British to abandon their emphasis on nonproliferation as well.[55]

Once the president agreed to drop nonproliferation, the negotiators made rapid progress toward a treaty banning nuclear tests in the atmosphere, outer space, and underwater. The only major disagreements revolved around a withdrawal clause and the linkage with a nonaggression pact. After the United States and Great Britain promised to initiate NATO discussions on the subject, the Soviets agreed to abandon simultaneous negotiations on a non-aggression accord. The withdrawal clause once again raised the issue of Communist China. The United States, wanting protection against a change in the world balance of power should Beijing acquire nuclear weapons, demanded that its legal right to withdraw from the treaty be recognized formally. The Soviets believed such a clause unnecessary because the right of withdrawal based on changed world conditions already existed under international law. They also claimed that the language of the U.S. draft clearly aimed at provoking Communist China. The two powers worked out compromise language that seemed less insulting to Beijing. By July 25, with these problems cleared away, the three parties initialed an agreed text to the Limited Test Ban Treaty (LTBT). In most of its particulars, the final document followed the draft treaty that the United States and Great Britain had presented at the ENDC in August 1962.[56]

Both the United States and the Soviet Union publicly hailed the test ban conference as a great success. But given what Kennedy and Khrushchev had hoped to accomplish, the meeting fell short. The Soviet premier did not succeed in isolating Mao. France refused to sign, as did several smaller communist countries, including Cuba, North Vietnam, and Albania, allowing Beijing to escape the full onus for reducing the ban's effectiveness. More important, Moscow's attempt to keep the treaty's language from being unduly provocative toward China also failed. Beijing had long suspected that a U.S.-Soviet agreement would seek "to bind China by the hands and feet." After the signing of the LTBT, Beijing labeled the agreement "a dirty fraud," and the schism in the communist bloc gaped even wider. Chinese rhetoric became so heated that Washington began contingency planning to deal with increased political agitation, or even a desperate act of aggression, on the part of Beijing. The degree of worry in the capital became public when Stewart Alsop, an influential columnist and brother of Kennedy intimate Joseph Alsop, wrote in the *Satur-*

day Evening Post that, given "the madness of Mao Tse-Tung," the "president and his inner circle" have concluded "that China must be prevented, by whatever means from becoming a nuclear power." Alsop mused that "a few rather small bangs" would suffice to eliminate the Chinese nuclear threat. In the long term, Kennedy continued to contemplate military action against China's nuclear complex, whether by Washington or by Taiwan with U.S. assistance, evoking the surreal and frightening specter of an Asian Bay of Pigs.[57]

From Kennedy's perspective, the treaty achieved little. Proliferation could continue relatively unimpeded because an agreement that allowed underground tests would not dissuade advanced countries from developing effective bombs. More important, as technology improved, many countries could produce relatively sophisticated weapons via subterranean experiments. Kennedy and Rusk hoped that Khrushchev would pursue further checks on proliferation after the signing of the treaty. But as Harriman had warned, the Soviets refused to discuss nonproliferation as long as the MLF remained an American goal.[58]

The domestic battle over ratification and Kennedy's attempts to placate European allies further reduced the significance of the LTBT. The president worried that he would not get the two-thirds Senate majority needed to approve the treaty. He therefore caved to Senate hawks and the Joint Chiefs with promises to accelerate the underground testing program, undercutting any limits on the pace of the arms race. From 1945 to 1963, the United States had conducted 347 tests; in the nineteen years after the treaty, it conducted 555 tests.

Alliance politics produced the most devastating consequences for U.S. nonproliferation goals. Kennedy continued to seek French adherence to the treaty with nuclear aid, even to the point of providing warheads to Paris. Prior to the Moscow conference, Macmillan offered to circumvent the JCAE objections to a Franco-American nuclear alliance by funneling the aid through London. Kennedy rejected the offer, not wanting any Macmillan–de Gaulle secret deals to undermine U.S. power in Europe. The president had good reason to fear backroom deals. The Nassau agreement had left many in London bitter, especially Thorneycroft. He pressed for abrogation of the Anglo-American nuclear alliance in favor of Anglo-French nuclear cooperation. But Macmillan remained more wary of de Gaulle than he was of Kennedy. None of these stratagems mattered because de Gaulle had no desire to be dependent on, or beholden to, either the United States or Great Britain in the nuclear field, and he scoffed at nonproliferation efforts, believing a nuclear Germany and China inevitable. The only effects of these maneuvers was to reduce Harriman's maneuvering room in Moscow and to push France and China closer toward normalized relations in January 1964 — expressly to challenge Moscow and Washington's "double hegemony."[59]

Germany also posed problems. Even absent a nonaggression pact, Adenauer feared that U.S.-Soviet détente might ossify the status quo of European and German division. Other German politicians labeled the agreement "another Versailles" and "American appeasement." Kennedy and his aides scrambled to reassure Bonn while getting East Germany's signature on the LTBT. In the end, Washington had to reenergize the MLF and even promise the West Germans that it could be pursued as a bilateral measure should Italy and Great Britain refuse to cooperate. By November 1963, the United States and the Soviet Union appeared further apart on nonproliferation than they had been prior to the Cuban Missile Crisis. The LTBT debate and the Skybolt controversy combined to convince the Kennedy administration that Washington and Moscow had lost leverage, creating an international climate in which many countries had grown "too big to spank."[60]

Kennedy had entered office committed to halting the spread of nuclear weapons. But alliance politics, Soviet defensiveness, political cautiousness, administrative ineptness, bureaucratic resistance, and domestic politics prevented him from concluding a nonproliferation agreement during his brief presidency. Many analysts and Kennedy administration policymakers have legitimately touted the LTBT as a significant first step toward the solution of multiple Cold War problems and conflicts, including proliferation. But it also represented the last time the two superpowers could conclude an agreement bilaterally with any hope of the rest of the world acceding to it. The LTBT provided precious little building material for a subsequent nonproliferation agreement, especially as U.S.-Soviet political and nuclear hegemony waned. Kennedy, however, would not make the final push for such an accord. His assassination in November 1963 placed a less experienced and less knowledgeable foreign policy hand in the White House, Lyndon Baines Johnson. The nonproliferation policy that Kennedy bequeathed his vice president appeared clear in its intentions but muddy in its execution. The question that confronted his predecessor would continue to haunt Johnson: Which was more important to the United States, NATO or nonproliferation?

Hunting for Easter Eggs

LBJ, NATO, & NONPROLIFERATION,
1963–1965

Lyndon B. Johnson told one Soviet official that when it came to arms control, Moscow and Washington "were like children hunting for Easter eggs." But the president often forgot that other "children" also needed to join the hunt. By late 1963 when LBJ entered the Oval Office, the superpowers had lost leverage over their respective alliances and the UN General Assembly. Newly decolonized nations increasingly challenged northern dominance over them. In this changing world system, nuclear weapons remained an important symbol of international status. Washington feared the uncontrolled proliferation of weapons within NATO, even as French president Charles de Gaulle questioned the U.S. commitment to Europe and threatened to split the alliance. The MLF prospectively blunted both threats. But the U.S. proposal and the British variant, the Atlantic Nuclear Force (ANF), provoked Moscow's vigorous opposition. As long as a NATO nuclear force remained a possibility, a U.S.-Soviet nonproliferation agreement proved impossible. Yet such a pact offered the best hope of containing the spread of nuclear weapons in Latin America, Africa, and Asia. Unwilling to commit to a strategy, LBJ allowed U.S. nonproliferation efforts to languish during the first phase of his presidency. Neither Chinese acquisition of nuclear weapons in October 1964 nor the recommendations of a presidential task force on proliferation prompted decisiveness. The Easter eggs remained hidden, and they risked being rotten when finally uncovered.[1]

Enter LBJ

The world public had greeted the LTBT with great acclaim, and the *Bulletin of the Atomic Scientists* had pushed back the Doomsday Clock to twelve minutes to midnight. But even before its ratification, in October 1963, hopes for progress on nonproliferation had faded. In the Kennedy administration's last days, Moscow and Washington sought further agreements as they anxiously monitored Beijing's progress toward a nuclear capability. But a nonproliferation treaty required consideration of both allied and nonaligned powers' security needs as well as their cooperation in its enforcement. From the perspective of the non-nuclear powers, a nonproliferation agreement appeared grossly imbalanced — they pledged not to acquire weapons that had come to symbolize major power status, while the superpowers conceded nothing and gained international legitimacy for their large nuclear arsenals.

The U.S. proposal for a NATO multilateral nuclear force also complicated negotiations. Khrushchev wanted a nonproliferation treaty and even toyed with signing an agreement that did not explicitly ban the MLF as long as the United States pledged not to place nuclear weapons under Bonn's "direct command." But after Poland's leader Władsław Gomułka protested vigorously, Khrushchev hesitated, and Soviet foreign minister Andrei Gromyko reaffirmed Moscow's opposition to the MLF. Yet Gromyko hinted to U.S. officials that Moscow might sign a treaty if Washington promised to drop the MLF at some future date. With Bonn demanding access to nuclear weapons as proof of U.S. faith in NATO, the Kennedy and Johnson administrations faced the Hobson's choice of either scuttling progress on nonproliferation or undercutting the Western alliance. In fall 1963, Kennedy pushed forward with preliminary negotiations and technical talks on the feasibility of mixed-manned vessels. But he viewed the MLF as only symbolic reassurance that the United States remained firm in its alliance commitments. Britain, conversely, opposed the NATO force as a needless contrivance. Washington's unwillingness to abandon the scheme paralyzed the nonproliferation talks. Gromyko lamented in October 1967 that the present state of disarmament negotiations "could not be worse." Verbal support for a Latin American denuclearized zone emerged as President Kennedy's last token gesture in favor of nonproliferation.[2]

With Kennedy's assassination, Lyndon B. Johnson assumed the presidency.

Johnson came to the office after twenty-three years in Congress representing Texas. As majority leader of the Senate from 1955 to 1960, this master legislator had amassed considerable power and influence. In 1960, his decision to be Kennedy's running mate surprised everyone, including the newly minted presidential nominee. After nearly three years of tedium as vice president, Johnson faced the daunting task of replacing a martyred leader. He rushed to assure the American people of his commitment to Kennedy's domestic and foreign policies. Part of this process included persuading Kennedy's national security team, Dean Rusk, McGeorge Bundy, and Robert McNamara, to remain in the administration. He professed inexperience in foreign affairs and claimed: "I need your help more than Jack Kennedy did." Johnson also admitted discomfort in dealing with other world leaders, complaining that "foreigners are not like the folks I am used to." At times, he expressed an antipathy toward ungrateful allies, complaining that "everybody treats us like we all used to treat our mother. . . . We just know that she's sweet and good and wonderful and she is going to be kind to us and she'll always know that we came out of her womb and we belong to her and every damned one of them talk to me that way. . . . I just talk to 113 nations and they just screw us to death." His wariness toward international affairs also stemmed from his substantial ego. LBJ wanted to exceed the historical stature of his idol FDR, and he believed the East Coast elite would never give him credit "for anything I do in foreign affairs . . . because I didn't go to Harvard." NATO allies also sensed that, in the words of Britain's U.S. ambassador, Johnson "had no feeling for world affairs and no great interest in them." De Gaulle called LBJ a "cowboy radical" who "doesn't even take the trouble to pretend he's thinking," while Adenauer bluntly pronounced him "stupid."[3]

Despite his acknowledged ignorance of international relations, Johnson insisted on being the dominant personality in his administration. He told one aide that had any president tried to bypass Congress on a major international issue during his stint as majority leader, he would "have torn his balls off." After the president had reached a decision, his subordinates risked his wrath or the famed "Johnson Treatment" if they continued to disagree with him. The treatment began with LBJ crowding his subject, getting nose to nose, and then combining "supplication, accusation, cajolery, exuberance, scorn, tears, complaint, the hint of threat" with "lapel-holding, shoulder massage, elbow and knee grabbing, fingerwagging, and nose thrusting." One victim recalled that after leaving the president's office "you really felt as if a St. Bernard had licked your face for an hour, had pawed you all over."[4]

The president also used humiliation and scorn. He often forced subordinates to accompany him into the men's room, thriving on their obvious discomfort when he relieved himself. One aide remembers Johnson ridiculing McGeorge Bundy as "one of the delicate Kennedyites who came into the bathroom with me and then found it utterly impossible to look at me while I sat there on the toilet. You'd think he had never seen those parts of the body before." Such comments, along with a vaunted desire to have his vice president's "pecker in his pocket" to ensure his loyalty, underscored the president's association of political power, masculinity, and respect with sexual prowess and the male anatomy. To defer to another or to be shown disrespect equaled emasculation, while discomfort with male nudity revealed effeminacy.[5]

Johnson's preoccupation with masculinity infused his conduct of foreign policy. He dismissed his first UN ambassador, Adlai Stevenson, who regularly advocated diplomatic over military solutions to international problems, as "a fruit" who "squats when he pees." Suspecting the State Department of leaking policy decisions to journalists, he wondered whether Joseph McCarthy had been right in claiming that the diplomatic corps was riddled with homosexuals ("a bunch of sissy fellows," he had called them) who were easy prey for blackmailers. When State's violation of presidential orders continued, he asserted "somebody's got something on 'em."[6]

On another occasion, during a policy meeting, Johnson went around the table lambasting all his subordinates for their past failures. Dean Acheson, an informal foreign policy adviser, finally interrupted the president: "You don't pay these men enough to talk to them that way—even with the federal pay raise." LBJ's need to bully his aides inhibited candid and forthright advice. Cowed counselors were ill-suited for the delicate task of balancing NATO obligations against the American desire for nonproliferation. Britain's ambassador to Washington sensed this change, noting "how much less willing McNamara and Bundy, two very prominent and talkative members of the Kennedy administration, are now to express views which might be thought to be at variance with the President's views."[7]

LBJ's past stances on defense and nuclear issues also inspired little optimism. As a young representative from Texas, in 1947, he had scoffed that he had not become "a member of the Atomic Energy Committee to liquidate the atomic bombs and make America the vassal of another power." In subsequent years, he distinguished himself as an advocate of a strong national defense, pushing for a subcommittee on military preparedness in the wake of the Sputnik launch—a forum he used to promote fears of a U.S.-Soviet "missile gap." In many ways, during the 1950s, Johnson symbolized the bipartisan anticommunist foreign policy that oversaw the construction of the national security state. Despite Soviet hints that the Cold War security apparatus, including bloated military budgets and the arms race, could be scaled back, he never abandoned the goal of nuclear superiority. Even had he been more open to arms control, Johnson's natural tendency to seek consensus and build coalitions, acquired during his days as majority leader, suggested that he might not push such goals aggressively in the face of political opposition. LBJ did highlight Goldwater's opposition to the test ban treaty as a campaign issue in 1964 and at times used that pact as "peace demagoguery"—talking about mothers "worried over children drinking contaminated milk" or fearful of birthing "a baby with two heads." In private, Johnson valued the agreement as a means "to affect world opinion." The president, moreover, attended to most foreign policy issues sporadically as he became increasingly preoccupied with the Vietnam War. Nonproliferation advocates could nonetheless cling to a modicum of hope because in 1946, prior to the full onset of the Cold War, Johnson had defended international control of atomic energy, warning that "civilization is going to be wiped out" if the UN failed to check nuclear proliferation. He also hoped to retake the peace issue from the Soviets, complaining after one Khrushchev salvo that "I am tired, by God, of having him be the man who wants peace and I am the guy who wants war."[8] LBJ's retention of Kennedy administration national security personnel, moreover, meant that many aspects of JFK's nonproliferation efforts remained intact.

Theologians in the Pulpit

Although he had reaffirmed the U.S. nonproliferation commitment immediately following Kennedy's assassination, LBJ prioritized NATO unity and bringing the MLF negotiations to a speedy resolution. Khrushchev's flexibility convinced the force's proponents that they could get both the MLF and a nonproliferation treaty if they presented Moscow with a fait accompli. This argument undercut the ACDA and NSC's claim that a European settlement might be possible in late 1963 should Washington abandon the MLF, sign a nondissemination agreement, and agree to normalize Berlin and the division of Germany. Preparations for the annual NATO ministerial meeting had begun prior to JFK's death, and the collective nuclear force figured as an important topic. State Department Atlanticists wanted immediate action to "rebuild the Alliance" and saw the NATO nuclear force as part of that process. The Joint Chiefs also expressed fear that Western European leaders overestimated the strength of the emerging détente with the Soviet Union. The new administration used Kennedy's state funeral to take the temperature of U.S.-European relations. Members of the administration assured European leaders of U.S. resolve to treat threats toward NATO allies as if directed against the United States. The most significant of these meetings occurred with de Gaulle. Johnson suggested a Washington summit meeting for February 1964 in the hope of reducing U.S.-French tensions. But LBJ's observation that "it is easier to knock somebody's barn down than to build one" had little effect on the general, who refused to return to the United States.[9]

The flurry of meetings with European leaders in November presaged renewed efforts by MLF theologians to win congressional and presidential backing for their pet project. Both Walt Rostow, director of the State Department Policy Planning Council, and officials of the State Department European desk urged LBJ to push hard for the MLF. Rostow used language especially attuned to Johnson's unsophisticated understanding of international relations, which flowed out of the 1930s and the "lessons" that American isolationism and appeasement could lay the groundwork for another European war. He portrayed Europe's center as hanging on by a slender thread, especially in Germany, and warned that if the MLF was junked, moderates might collapse, as had happened during the Weimer Republic, giving way to a right-wing, nationalist government with an independent nuclear arsenal. In many respects, Rostow parroted the Bonn oft-invoked specter of "another Versailles leading to another Hitler." The State Department's official briefing, albeit less stark, also portrayed the NATO nuclear force as the only feasible means of keeping Bonn's finger off the nuclear trigger.[10]

Johnson had grown up among German immigrants in the Texas hill country and believed he understood their national character. He once remarked: "If you let the Germans isolate themselves, they will do crazy things." There might be "some 17-year-old right now in Germany who would be a 20-year-old Hitler in another three years." Johnson's quick approval of MLF consultations, thus, hardly came as a surprise. Yet he remained uncertain about the missile force, remarking that "I don't want to bring any more hands on the [nuclear] button than we already got if we can avoid it." McGeorge Bundy urged postponing any agreement until after the 1964 election in order "to avoid getting pinned to a very complex and difficult treaty commitment" during a presidential campaign. Johnson, who consistently viewed foreign policy through the prism of domestic political calculations, needed little encouragement to delay a final decision, especially when Secretary of Defense McNamara warned him that the MLF was not justifiable on military grounds. Keeping his options open, LBJ approved a mixed-manned experiment on a non-nuclear ship.[11]

This demonstration on the guided missile destroyer *Claude V. Ricketts* lasted eighteen months, from June 1964 to December 1965. Hailed as a success by MLF proponents, it also produced more ammunition for critics. The United States supplied over half the crew, including officers and the captain of the ship. All official business took place in English, and U.S. Navy regulations applied in most cases. Six NATO nations supplied the other half of the crew—West Germany, Italy, Greece, the United Kingdom, the Netherlands, and Turkey. Both the integration of the new crew members and language difficulties inhibited the ship's readiness to join the Sixth Fleet in the Mediterranean. Eventually the ship did make it to the Mediterranean and acquitted itself well, according to naval observers. But political controversy cast a cloud over the European phase of the demonstration. Several NATO countries declined to take part or refused to have the ship dock in their ports, including Belgium and Italy. Press interest remained low, and when stories did appear, they often exposed discontent among the crew. In the *Maltese News*, an American sailor scorned the notion that the demonstration was "a success," and Dutch, German, and British crew members acknowledged divisions between European and U.S. personnel, with one commenting that "an outsider is an outsider, and an American is an American. There are only American rules here and I didn't like it very much." In the end, the *Ricketts* demonstration did little to dispel European worries about U.S. hegemony in NATO, especially over nuclear matters. As one British observer noted, "mixed-manning" seemed "irrelevant" compared with overall "control" of the fleet.[12]

NATO remained split over the MLF. NATO secretary-general Dirk Stikker viewed the proposal as an antidote for de Gaulle's equation of nuclear weapons with great-power status. He also hoped that the NATO nuclear force "would provide a sound solution" for German nuclear desires for "at least a 5–10 year period." The Italian government also embraced the scheme, seeing the MLF as a way to escape its inferior position within NATO. Domestic political divisions nonetheless required a four- to five-month delay before the Italians could present the issue to Parliament. Greece, Turkey, and Germany, the three allies most eager to acquire American MRBMs since the 1950s, enthusiastically supported the MLF. Other countries, such as Belgium and the Netherlands, remained cool, eventually declining to participate but conceding that the MLF best addressed German nuclear ambitions.[13]

France and Great Britain remained the two most resistant allies. The State Department believed that de Gaulle would accede to the MLF "as long as French territory and facilities were not involved." The best course, therefore, would be to ignore French objections and continue to seek the widest support possible among the other NATO allies. Britain, the only other Western European nuclear power, thus assumed greater importance given that the United States expected the Europeans to bear the majority of the cost. Because Greece and Turkey could make only minimal financial contributions, a NATO nuclear force without British participation would become, in reality, a bilateral U.S.-German endeavor. Rusk urged President Johnson to announce his determination to push forward with the MLF whether or not London chose to join—otherwise the British might think that the United States did not care if the project succeeded or failed. The State Department and U.S. officials in the NATO command also conspired to convince the British that the MLF would be militarily justified and effective. The new British prime minister, Sir Alec Douglas-Home, however, could not commit to the MLF until after the British general election later in the year. His government essentially functioned as a caretaker regime after Harold Macmillan resigned in the wake of the Profumo spy/sex scandal. All indications pointed to a Labour Party victory in the next elections, and that party's shadow cabinet opposed both the MLF and retention of the British independent nuclear deterrent.[14]

The domestic MLF debate also caused multiple factions to emerge. At the State Department, European integration proponents, such as Undersecretary of State George Ball, Policy Planning Council director Rostow, and ambassador to NATO Thomas Finletter, pushed hard for the MLF. "Wise men" John J. McCloy and Dean Acheson, who served as informal policy advisers, also joined the State Department theologians in support of the project. These two Cold War stalwarts shed their previous ambivalence toward the MLF because of growing fears that de Gaulle would shatter the NATO alliance and with it the U.S. hegemony in Europe that they had helped to create. Acheson and McCloy soon came to see a nonproliferation agreement in the same threatening light as they did the French leader. From December to April, as LBJ pondered his options on MLF policy, Rostow portrayed the project as a virtual panacea in U.S.-European relations. According to Rostow, the NATO nuclear force would strengthen the allied deterrent by adding variety to the Western nuclear arsenal, accelerate European integration, and keep Germany from joining France in pursuing an independent foreign policy course.[15]

Elsewhere in the administration, a more subdued attitude toward the MLF persisted. The ACDA viewed it as the main stumbling block to a nonproliferation agreement. The NSC staff also voiced skepticism, contending that arguments in favor of the MLF contained a basic flaw. German nuclear ambitions could be contained by a multilateral venture only if such agreement allowed for eventual German control over the weapons. Staffers rejected such a scenario and looked to the MLF to inhibit, or even eliminate, such a likelihood. The scheme presented by Rostow, therefore, would never work because both American and German goals would be thwarted. The NSC staff did not urge scuttling the NATO nuclear force because backing away after such fulsome publicity would have profound negative consequences for U.S.-German relations. They advocated a policy of benign neglect that left the initiative with the squabbling Europeans.[16]

Johnson's three principal advisers, Rusk, Bundy, and McNamara, also remained ambivalent. Bundy believed that "the MLF, both on its merits and by process of elimination, is the best arrangement for the active participation [in nuclear matters] of non-nuclear powers that the American government has been able to devise." Yet, rather than compel the Europeans to accept the project, he would let them draw their own conclusions about the necessity of the force. Rusk also advised caution, recommending quiet conversations with the allies and careful preparations on Capitol Hill. McNamara, moreover, remained unconvinced of the MLF's military utility but resisted jettisoning it without a substitute to rein in European nuclear ambitions.[17]

The debate spilled outside the administration. Former president Eisenhower told Johnson that "he was not as concerned as some about the dangers of proliferation of nuclear weapons to allies" and gave his support. Former vice president Richard Nixon also voiced enthusiastic approval. Congressional leaders, however, seemed indifferent and even hostile, with a few keeping an open mind and many important legislators, such as Senate majority leader Mike Mansfield, Senator Richard Russell (chairman of the Armed Forces Committee), and Senator J. William Fulbright (chairman of the Foreign Relations Committee), opposing the concept. One Senate aide suggested that the MLF had grown too divisive both at home and abroad. He proposed a compromise under which the United States would earmark some of its new Minuteman ICBMs for NATO use. As well, U.S. disarmament groups, such as Women Strike for Peace and SANE, saw the MLF as a dangerous acceleration of nuclear proliferation and the arms race. In January and February, MLF advocates in the State and Defense Departments met with representatives from Women Strike for Peace and with physicist Leo Szilard, the guiding force behind the Council for a Livable World, in an unsuccessful attempt to blunt criticism of the NATO nuclear force.[18]

Undaunted, State Department Atlanticists turned to President Johnson. Impatient with LBJ's indecision, the main MLF proponents (Ball, Rostow, Finletter, and the chief MLF negotiator, Gerard Smith), along with Bundy and ACDA director William Foster, met with the president on April 10 to discuss the NATO nuclear force. The MLF theologians may have stacked the deck by scheduling the meeting at a time when Rusk and McNamara could not attend. Ball portrayed the project as the only way to give the Germans a sense of equality within NATO while still keeping them "on a leash." He lampooned de Gaulle's "force de crap" and dismissed British objections as a smoke screen for their real goal, a veto over American use of nuclear weapons. Finletter also urged the president to stop being "diffident" toward the MLF, claiming that the Europeans would cooperate if Washington vocally supported the project. Breaking with the majority view, Foster interjected, "Mr. President, I feel like a skunk in a garden party, but if you go ahead with the MLF you must recognize it's going to make my chances of negotiating a nonproliferation treaty harder." With other MLF skeptics absent and Bundy taking a neutral stance, the ACDA director's comments carried little weight. Johnson thus decided to push forward with the MLF, aiming to complete an agreement by year's end. He observed that "the Germans have gone off the reservation . . . twice in our lifetime and we've got to be sure that doesn't happen again." He still did not want, however, to "shove the project down the throats of the potential participants."[19]

MLF advocates moved quickly. Ball instructed ambassadors in all NATO capitals to reassure European leaders that Washington sought an agreement by December. Finletter returned to NATO headquarters elated that the study phase had ended and the action phase beckoned. But he worried that LBJ's admonition not to force European acceptance might provoke doubts in some leaders' minds. Ball, acting secretary of state while Rusk toured Southeast Asia, responded sympathetically, instructing ambassadors to use persuasion, but avoid coercion, to attain allied support for the MLF. Rusk, however, exploded when shown Finletter's telegram. He remained convinced that the NATO nuclear force only made sense if the Europeans wanted it. U.S. pressure might boomerang and lead to a loss of American prestige, especially if Britain and Italy could not participate for domestic political reasons. Rusk angrily scolded his undersecretary: "I do not know why we cannot deal with this matter in a businesslike fashion as a constructive worthwhile move without involving it with a second coming of Christ." Rusk's tirade had little effect. On April 20, while the secretary of state continued to tour Asia, Johnson delivered a major foreign policy address in which he pledged his support for the NATO nuclear force. Behind Rusk's pique lay his belief that nuclear-sharing efforts and arms control negotiations should proceed simultaneously. Frustrated with European demands for greater access to nuclear weapons, the secretary lectured subordinates that "our responsibility toward the arms race is to try to prevent this globe from becoming a cinder and we must be forgiven if we try to get on with it even if others are hypnotized by toys and gadgets which they themselves only dimly understand."[20]

Khrushchev's hints of flexibility on the NATO nuclear force stirred up trouble in his own alliance. Warsaw's Gomułka unveiled plans for a nuclear freeze in Central Europe under which Poland, Czechoslovakia, and the two Germanys would cap nuclear weapons on their soil at existing levels. Such a pact would prevent the MLF from docking at West Germany's Baltic ports. Warsaw's proposal flowed from its own security concerns regarding German acquisition of nuclear weapons and its fear that East-West détente might weaken the Soviet-Polish security arrangement. The Johnson administration opposed the plan, lest it provoke West German charges of discrimination while leaving untouched Soviet missiles aimed at Germany. But Washington did not dismiss the proposal out of hand, in part because it hoped to cultivate independent foreign policy maneuvering by Eastern European states. Other nuclear freeze or nuclear-free-zone arrangements also emerged with the express purpose of breaking the stalemate on nuclear proliferation, but these schemes drew opposition from the Joint Chiefs and McNamara. East Germany advocated an agreement between the German states to ban nuclear armaments, nuclear weapons production, and participation in multilateral nuclear arrangements. Because it would have required Bonn to recognize East Germany and called for the removal of U.S. tactical nuclear weapons from West Germany, this plan had no chance of acceptance. The Polish government viewed it as a Soviet-inspired tactic to push its own proposal into the background. Gromyko later lambasted nuclear freeze proposals as reviving the "thick icy frost of cold war." As Foster had predicted, the MLF prevented any progress on nonproliferation because no European state wanted Bonn to have its finger on the nuclear trigger. Still Johnson pressed forward, urging Soviet ambassador Anatoly Dobrynin to keep an open mind about the MLF.[21]

To NPT or Not to NPT

Immediately after becoming president, Johnson approved a new U.S. position in the ENDC. The ACDA, in December 1963, had urged a package of nuclear containment measures, including a nondissemination pledge, a fissionable material production cutoff, expanded international safeguards for sale or transfer of fissionable material for peaceful uses, a comprehensive test ban, destruction of nuclear-delivery vehicles, and a ban on transfer of delivery vehicles to non-nuclear powers. In early January, LBJ endorsed these policies in messages to Congress and the ENDC, and he elaborated on them in a letter to Soviet premier Nikita Khrushchev. The Soviets also came to the ENDC with a package of nuclear containment measures, including nuclear-free zones, a comprehensive test ban treaty, and a nondissemination agreement. But the U.S. delegation operated under instructions that the MLF "will and can be protected," while the Soviets insisted that no progress on arms control could occur until Washington abandoned plans to place nuclear weapons in Bonn's hands.[22]

In early February, Foster tested for areas of compromise in private conversations with Soviet delegate Semyon K. Tsarapkin. Though not exactly a "dialogue of the deaf," the talks produced little progress. Alexei Roshchin, another Soviet diplomat, suggested anew that Moscow would not insist on elimination of the MLF if Washington offered assurances that the NATO nuclear force would not contribute to proliferation. But in the next meeting, Tsarapkin retreated and repeated the standard Soviet claim that the MLF would empower the Germans to spark another world war. He pointedly asked why the United States defended the NATO nuclear force when it had "objected to what amounted to MLF in Cuba [in 1962]."[23]

Foster believed the Soviet positions to be sincere. Rusk, however, suspected that Khrushchev merely sought to complicate U.S. relations with NATO allies. Once the West established the MLF, the Soviets would talk seriously about nonproliferation. He perceived no urgency because neither Washington nor Moscow planned to transfer nuclear weapons to other powers. If the president wanted both an MLF and a nonproliferation agreement, the best strategy was to concentrate on the NATO nuclear force first. Bundy also warned that any multilateral arms control agreement, such as nonproliferation, would come slowly, thereby reinforcing Johnson's inclination to concentrate on the MLF. With no movement on the MLF, the ACDA advocated unilateral nonacquisition pledges by non-nuclear powers as an alternative to a nonproliferation pact. But even this symbolic gesture alienated MLF supporters as unduly complicating NATO nuclear-sharing policies.[24]

Throughout spring and summer 1964, the nonproliferation treaty and the MLF remained in stasis. Despite the Atlanticists' vigorous lobbying efforts, London sidestepped commitments to a NATO nuclear force before the October general elections. Increasingly disenchanted with the nuclear-sharing scheme on nonproliferation grounds, the British objected to transferring launch authority for the MLF to a group of sovereign states, claiming that such devolution clearly constituted proliferation. Washington lamely countered that it wished to impede transfer of control to only "individual" states, not to a group of countries. The Labour Party, still in opposition but highly favored to win the October general election, castigated the MLF as "a military monstrosity" borne of American "artificial dissemination." One presidential aide warned of an embarrassing split with London on the level of the 1962 Skybolt crisis. With French disapproval a certainty, West Germany remained the only frontline NATO power enthusiastic about the MLF. In June 1964, German chancellor Ludwig Erhard met with LBJ and publicly pledged to conclude a nuclear force agreement by the end of the year. Years later, Walt Rostow called the Erhard visit the "high point" of MLF diplomacy.[25]

The theologians' liturgies, however, failed to change congressional opinions. Despite what the NSC staff described as "overselling" and "sheer nonsense" in the State Department's congressional briefing, most legislators retained deep skepticism toward the MLF. Congress gave the issue very low priority, with the JCAE holding one brief session and other Senate and House committees postponing hearings until they had resolved more pressing business. In early September, eight Democratic senators urged LBJ not to conclude an MLF agreement until the proposal had undergone a thorough congressional examination. The next month, Representative Chet Holifield advised waiting until after the new Congress convened in January 1965. Combined with a scathing JCAE critique of the MLF, these letters from Democratic legislators indicated that the nuclear-sharing proposal would undergo rigorous scrutiny if submitted for congressional approval. Congressional critics feared either that the project might undercut arms control efforts or that it might hasten the decline of U.S. hegemony in Europe. Ambassador to Britain David K. E. Bruce concluded that Congress would block any NATO fleet that included a European option or gave non-nuclear nations control over the launching of nuclear weapons.[26]

The fierce debate in Washington did not provoke a similar passion in the general public. Many commentators have observed that the antinuclear movement peaked in 1963 and began its decline the following year. In the wake of the Cuban Missile Crisis and the LTBT, mass attention to nuclear dangers provoked a spate of books and movies that depicted the insanity of nuclear war and the impossibility of controlling every variable in a crisis. While establishment figures trumpeted their alleged ability to "manage" danger, several films of 1964 portrayed the consequences of Cold War extremists acquiring access to nuclear weapons. *Fail-Safe* had appeared as a serialized novel in October 1962 just as the Cuban Missile Crisis made nuclear war a palpable danger. Both the book and the film chronicled a group of Strategic

Air Command pilots who scrambled to confront an apparent Soviet nuclear attack that proved to be a false alarm. All attempts to call the squadron back came to naught, with the lead pilot even dismissing his wife's pleas over his radio as a communist trick. With Moscow's destruction inevitable, the president seals a bargain with the Soviet premier to destroy New York as recompense in order to avoid a larger nuclear war, even though the First Lady is visiting the city. Although this scenario chilled audiences, the president and the Soviet premier appear as reasonable and noble leaders trying to control the chaos spawned by out-of-control technology. Bombs and broken circuits are the villains, not human beings. *Seven Days in May* featured a virtuous president confronting crisis, but this film made human beings the force to be feared. When a liberal president signs an arms control agreement with Moscow, a conservative military cabal decides that politicians are too weak to protect the country and plot a coup. A noble staff officer uncovers their plans and aids the president in foiling them. Earnest and preachy, both *Fail-Safe* and *Seven Days in May* highlighted the zeitgeist of nuclear fear that coursed through LBJ's first year as president.

The third antinuclear movie of 1964, *Dr. Strangelove*, exceeded the other films' cultural impact and artistic achievement. The director and credited co-writer, Stanley Kubrick, used elements that appeared in the other two films: pilots who had advanced past their fail-safe points bearing down on their targets in the Soviet Union and crazed, reactionary generals willing to commit treason to advance their goals. But his tone was darkly satiric, and the suicidal logic of nuclear strategy culminates in the destruction of all human life at the hands of an automated doomsday machine. The film parodies Curtis LeMay, Robert Strange McNamara, Henry Kissinger, former Nazi and later U.S. rocket expert Werner Von Braun, and the American Radical Right, while incorporating more accurate information about nuclear strategy than the typical nuclear film. Kubrick had loosely based the movie on a novel by a former British air force officer as well as his own readings of important nuclear strategists, including RAND veterans Herman Kahn and Albert Wohlstetter. His masterly black comedy exposed the absurdity of nuclear thinking as it had evolved over the preceding twenty years (so that everyone in charge of nuclear weapons embraces insanity, not just the reputed villain of the piece, General Jack D. Ripper), and he mixed in Freudian insights about the links between sex and death. The full title (*Dr. Strangelove, or How I Stopped Worrying and Learned to Love the Bomb*), the purposeful character names (Turgidson, Muffley, DeSadeski), and the startling visual elements in the films (including an eroticized depiction of B-52s being refueled in midair) all drove home the strange and twisted fascination with military firepower. Columbia Pictures found the film so scandalous that it distanced itself from it both before and after its release. Movie critics blanched and many theater seats remained empty. But, in the end, Kubrick had made the most important nuclear film in cinematic history.[27]

Pentagon officials knew that these dissenting films were in the works and labored to blunt their impact. Curtis LeMay personally approved the production of *A Gathering of Eagles* (1963), an uncritical account of the Strategic Air Command that mimicked earlier films such as *Bombers B-52* (1957) and *Strategic Air Command* (1955, with Jimmy Stewart as the heroic and selfless bomber pilot). But LeMay and others in Washington need not have worried. The three cinematic indictments of nuclear war and nuclear warriors appeared just as the antinuclear movement turned its attention to other issues. The Vietnam War and social justice issues commanded American grassroots activism for the rest of the 1960s. *Dr. Strangelove* and the antinuclear movement had to wait until the 1980s for their next moment in the sun, when Ronald Reagan surrounded himself with Albert Wohlstetter's acolytes, Richard Perle and Paul Wolfowitz, and fear of nuclear war surged to the levels of the 1950s and early 1960s. In 1965, Tom Lehrer's "MLF Lullaby" provided one of the few cultural artifacts specifically highlighting public worries about a nuclear Germany. In it, he lampooned the proposed force with black humor:

Once the Germans were warlike and mean
But it couldn't happen again
We taught them a lesson in nineteen eighteen
And they've hardly bothered us since then
So sleep well my darling, the sandman can linger
We know our buddies won't give us the finger
Heil—hail—the Wehrmacht, I mean the Bundeswehr
Hail to our loyal ally
MLF will scare Brezhnev
I hope he's half as scared as I.[28]

The antinuclear movement receded just as the fortunes of the MLF and the nonproliferation treaty plummeted. With a consistent beat of criticism against American nuclear-sharing policies, Moscow insisted in both public and private that a nonproliferation agreement would not be possible until Washington abandoned the MLF. Washington's questions about the Soviet attitude toward Beijing's nuclear program likewise received only evasive answers. One ACDA official observed that confronting a potentially nuclear

China, the Soviet Union had to weigh its national interests against the prospect of alienating the Chinese and eroding Moscow's leadership of the "international communist movement." The different emphases "are quite comparable to the position which the Administration has had to take in connection with the Soviet Union on the one hand and with the United States Senate on the other."[29]

Khrushchev's ability to affect arms control waned along with his position in the Soviet oligarchy. His efforts at détente with Bonn and Washington prompted unease among other members of the Presidium. These fears intensified during summer 1964 when he sent his son-in-law Alexei Adzhubei to Bonn to confer with West German elites, including Chancellor Erhard. Adzhubei made clear that, at least in his eyes, China posed the greatest threat to the Soviet Union. Quaffing beers with Franz Josef Strauss, he blurted out: "We'd just as soon give you Germans a hundred hydrogen bombs, form a corridor through the Soviet Union, and let you mop up the Chinese." The West German press covered Adzhubei's "yellow peril" effusions, and Eastern European intelligence services taped his private conversations. The already-tottering premier could not afford more controversy and disavowed his son-in-law—but too late to rescue the nonproliferation talks.[30]

With neither superpower able to compromise on nonproliferation, their allies took the initiative. London suggested a U.S.-French-British declaration. Washington raised no objections but left to Britain the task of winning French support. As anticipated, Paris brushed aside the proposal, likening it to three sinners attempting to tell others not to sin. After the abortive British gambit, the ACDA pressed to revise the American negotiating position, with little success. Although both the U.S. and the Soviet delegations agreed that only the MLF stood in the way of a nonproliferation agreement, neither group could persuade its superiors to jettison the NATO nuclear force. By the end of summer 1964, nonproliferation remained deadlocked on both the NATO and the Geneva fronts.

The United States instead undertook some unilateral actions to stem nuclear diffusion. In January and April 1964, Johnson reduced American production of enriched uranium and plutonium to signal his seriousness in slowing the arms race. Khrushchev pledged to reciprocate, despite his belief that the measure had little substantive importance for arms control. LBJ implemented the cuts largely for budgetary reasons, remarking that he did not intend to "operate a WPA nuclear project just to provide employment when our needs have been met." Later that year, he announced IAEA inspection of a large American nuclear power reactor, hoping that such a gesture would persuade other countries that inspection did not dilute national sovereignty. Both initiatives had primarily symbolic value and did little to inhibit the arms race or proliferation. Johnson still craved bilateral nuclear agreements. In December, he subjected Soviet foreign minister Andrei Gromyko to the Johnson Treatment, plaintively telling him that in the quest for arms control Moscow and Washington "were like children hunting for Easter eggs, and it was important that both of them searched until they were found."[31]

Confronting Israel and the PRC

Other dissemination threats provoked more than political gestures from the Johnson administration. Johnson initially replicated Kennedy's cautious vigilance toward Israel's nuclear program. Within days of LBJ's ascension to the presidency, AEC chairman Glenn Seaborg warned of Tel Aviv's nuclear ambitions. Yet, despite concerns about an Israeli nuclear arsenal, the United States continued providing Tel Aviv with peaceful nuclear aid, including a reactor for a desalinization project. This relationship ultimately prompted Egyptian president Gamal Abdel Nasser's charge that the United States facilitated Israel's acquisition of nuclear weapons. By spring 1964, both Washington and London had grown fearful of a Middle Eastern nuclear arms race. The Johnson administration primarily blamed Nasser, citing his threatening language toward Israel and his open flirtation with the Soviets.

That summer, Washington pressed both Cairo and Tel Aviv to abstain from nuclear weapons development. In a June 1964 summit meeting, Johnson urged Israeli prime minister Levi Eshkol to open the Dimona reactor to international inspection. LBJ promised modern conventional weapons in exchange for nuclear abstinence. Eshkol ambiguously promised not to be the first to "introduce" nuclear weapons into the Middle East. But he acquiesced only to U.S. inspection of Dimona. The U.S. "visits" to the reactor complex (Israel refused to call them inspections) ultimately provided little information. Tel Aviv kept the time at Dimona short and made sure Americans arrived when workers had all left for the weekend. Despite annual visits from 1964 to 1967, Israel successfully concealed its weapons program from U.S. engineers. The meeting with Eshkol served as the first of a two-pronged diplomatic effort to reassure Nasser and keep him from seeking "a Cuba-type deal with the USSR." Egypt's statements in the ENDC and its support for a nuclear-free zone in Africa seemed to signal a willingness to refrain from acquiring nuclear weapons if Israel also agreed to do so. Johnson sent John Mc-Cloy as a secret emissary to persuade Egypt not to acquire nuclear weapons or develop surface-to-surface missiles. Although Nasser proved willing to talk about the arms problem, McCloy left without an accord.[32]

Despite the Middle East proliferation danger, the Johnson administration had already diverted its attention to East Asia. In August 1964, satellite intelligence indicated that the PRC's test site would be ready for use within two months, and rumors swirled that a Chinese bomb would mark the fifteenth anniversary of Mao's regime. The ACDA also warned that the first Chinese test could occur at any time and urged action to forestall an imminent East Asian arms race that could include the PRC, India, Pakistan, Taiwan, and Japan. Regional rivalries among India, Pakistan, and Beijing emerged as pivotal issues. A Chinese nuclear test might start dominoes tumbling toward a completely nuclearized East Asia. India renewed its pledge not to acquire nuclear weapons that August but reserved the right to reverse its policy if the regional balance of power shifted dramatically.

The United States pondered both diplomatic and military actions. In September 1964, the administration revived Kennedy's proposal to cooperate with Moscow against Beijing's nuclear facilities. Bundy and his NSC staff urged a military or covert operation, even though the State Department argued that the Chinese would act cautiously and not immediately threaten the United States. At the Pentagon, McNamara saw the threat of a nuclear China as greater than North Vietnam, but the Joint Chiefs did not share his views. The president's team ultimately decided against "unprovoked unilateral U.S. military action against Chinese nuclear installations at this time" but reserved the right to take "appropriate military action against Chinese nuclear facilities" should the United States find itself "in military hostilities at any level with the Chinese Communists." With the cycle of escalation already initiated in Vietnam and the historical precedent of the Korean War prominent in most American policymakers' minds, the implications could not have been more startling. Johnson clearly anticipated destroying Beijing's nuclear capability should Chinese forces directly aid the North Vietnamese. One mid-level official at the Defense Department even advocated seizing "any opportunity created say by a major blow-up in [Southeast Asia]" to destroy the PRC's nuclear facilities. Others vigorously dissented, noting that Nasser might use U.S. action to justify attacking Israeli facilities, and the Soviets might "play similar games." Walt Rostow simply disagreed that Beijing would be more dangerous with nuclear weapons, contending that "with nuclear weapons comes caution." His comments presaged a rethinking of U.S. China policy among more perceptive policymakers who questioned Beijing's responsibility for troubles in Vietnam and regarded the PRC's entry into the UN as inevitable and helpful, given that disarmament and nonproliferation efforts had foundered in China's absence. But Rusk and others in the State Department pressed a hard line. Because the Chinese "shrew" could not "be tamed by the application of sweetness and light," U.S. tactics, but not its goals, should change toward Beijing. LBJ sided with Rusk and dismissed discontent with his China policy among newly decolonized nations, snapping that "he did not pay the foreigners at the UN to advise him on foreign policy."[33]

With unilateral U.S. action against the PRC on hold, LBJ did not rule out joint U.S.-Soviet options. Johnson instructed Rusk to contact Soviet ambassador Dobrynin to discuss a possible superpower warning to Beijing, the option of a comprehensive test ban to pressure China, and even an "agreement to cooperate in preventive military action." Available records do not reveal the extent, if any, of the Rusk-Dobrynin talks. Rusk later claimed no recollection of approaching Dobrynin about the matter. When Bundy contacted the Soviet ambassador in September, Dobrynin brushed aside talk of U.S.-Soviet action. Beyond killing many Chinese and provoking moral outrage among African, Asian, and Latin American nations, a preemptive strike against China would have put both LBJ and Khrushchev at risk politically in fall 1964. Johnson, although heavily favored to win, could have endangered his chances in the presidential election had he attacked Beijing. Khrushchev's own political strength had deteriorated, and his rivals succeeded in removing him from power on October 15, 1964. The new leadership cited Khrushchev's decisions to send Adzhubei to Bonn earlier in the year as an example of foreign policy blundering.[34]

Beijing announced its successful test of a nuclear bomb the next day. The Johnson administration had been preparing world opinion for a Chinese test since late September, but the two seismic shifts in the communist world created a crisis atmosphere in Washington. In an official statement, the president downplayed the political and military significance of the Chinese achievement and reiterated the U.S. commitment to nonproliferation. Outside public view, the president convened his top advisers to consider the best response to Khrushchev's ouster and Beijing's new international status. Few policymakers anticipated major shifts in Soviet policy, but some did fear profound propaganda repercussions from the Chinese nuclear test. A nonwhite nation had struck a blow for the developing "South" against the former colonial "North." Even in India, the anti-imperialist implications of the PRC's act received accolades. One journalist contended that the "first fruits of the Chinese nuclear explosion will be psychological and political, rather than military," with one of the most important effects being "the sense of pride that one of [the colonial peoples in the world] has been able to break what has hitherto been a monopoly of the white nations." Beijing further inflamed Washington's worries about revolutionary nationalism in the developing world when it explicitly endorsed nuclear proliferation among "Afro-Asian countries" as the best means to "shake off imperialist control." The neutrals' attitude appeared to be especially contradictory because the Second Conference of Non-Aligned Countries had formally called for nondissemination of nuclear weapons only five days prior to Beijing's nuclear test.[35]

To reassure public opinion, both Johnson and Rusk made denigrating comments about the Chinese achievement. LBJ dismissed Beijing's first nuclear weapon as "crude," noting that the resources would have been better spent raising the Chinese standard of living. He later differentiated between the "serious and sober" nations that had first produced nuclear weapons and the Chinese, who conspicuously lacked those very qualities. The president assured congressional leaders that it would be some time before Mao could threaten the United States with nuclear attack.[36]

Washington sent emissaries to Asian capitals to calm allies and take the pulse of major neutrals. Taiwan and India expressed the most anxiety over Mao's nuclear achievement. Despite its long-standing opposition to nuclear weapons, New Delhi reconsidered its commitment to nonproliferation in the wake of China's test. While Indian prime minister Lal Bahadur Shastri reiterated his country's intention to refrain from acquiring nuclear weapons, some Indian officials confided in private that, as the balance in Asia clearly tilted toward Beijing, New Delhi must seek a nuclear capability. One military official told his American counterpart that Shastri lacked the popularity and "dominant stature" of recently deceased prime minister Jawaharlal Nehru, and, therefore, he would have to appease nationalist nuclear advocates in Parliament. Shastri indeed placed India on its path toward a "peaceful nuclear explosion" shortly after the Chinese test.[37]

Washington had anticipated that India would seek an independent deterrent if China went nuclear. Johnson had earlier in the year established an interdepartmental committee on nuclear weapons capabilities that analyzed the prospect of Indian acquisition. The committee's findings reached Johnson only days before Beijing's first test. Because it considered only bilateral measures, the committee offered an ill-defined program for reinforcing New Delhi's existing nonproliferation commitment. The Johnson administration also decided to offer all Asian non-nuclear powers broad security guarantees against Chinese nuclear attack. The United States took no immediate action, however, even as Pakistan expressed deep concern about New Delhi's nuclear efforts.[38]

Taiwan's president, Jiang Jie-shi (Chiang Kai-shek), conversely, warned that without an immediate military response to Beijing's nuclear ascendancy Mao would control the mainland for decades to come. Most Taiwanese officials paired the bomb test and Khrushchev's ouster and saw the two events as dangerously strengthening Mao's hold over China and increasing his global prestige. In the weeks after the bomb test, Jiang used private entreaties and newspaper editorials to press either for a U.S. strike on Chinese nuclear facilities or for Washington to sponsor a Taiwanese attack, possibly with tactical nuclear weapons. Jiang also urged a full-scale invasion of the mainland before Mao could enhance his nuclear stockpile and delivery system. The Johnson administration did not dismiss such possibilities. As early as April 1964, the State Department Policy Planning Council had contemplated a Nationalist Chinese air attack or an air drop of Nationalist Chinese sabotage teams as a means of eradicating Beijing's nuclear potential. The group eventually rejected both options on logistical grounds. Disillusioned with the U.S. reluctance to act and doubting the effectiveness of the U.S. nuclear umbrella, Jiang soon began his own bomb project.[39]

The Johnson administration still sought Soviet military cooperation against Beijing's nuclear facilities. The change in the Soviet leadership, however, had increased uncertainty about Moscow's attitude toward Chinese nuclear weapons. The new regime seemed intent on repairing its relationship with Mao and refrained from condemning the nuclear test in public. Off the record, some Soviet officials suggested that they could foster international stability by teaching China the proper conduct of a nuclear state. Dobrynin dismissed American fears, saying it would take some time before the PRC became a true nuclear power. The ambassador instead urged greater superpower cooperation on banning all tests. Both nations agreed, however, that Indian security concerns should be allayed lest New Delhi travel down the nuclear path. But they offered Prime Minister Shastri only limited security guarantees.[40]

The Gilpatric Committee—"Explosive as a Nuclear Weapon"

With most short-term military options closed off, the Johnson administration decided that nonproliferation policy needed systematic reassessment. Many disarmament organizations had cited Beijing's nuclear test as proof that a nonproliferation treaty deserved immediate attention. But as one NSC aide warned Bundy, "It is not even clear that the State Department wants a [nonproliferation] agreement." Leaks from the special interdepartmental committee on nuclear proliferation that Johnson had established in August 1964 prompted these worries. The chair of the committee, Llewellyn "Tommy" Thompson, emerged as a persistent and vocal critic of multilateral nonproliferation efforts, calling instead for unilateral and/or intrabloc policies to control the spread of nuclear weapons. The Chinese nuclear test and Khrushchev's ouster exacerbated an existing split over nonproliferation policy between Bundy and his NSC staff and the MLF theologians at the State Department. Bundy pressed Johnson to look beyond the existing bureaucratic fiefdoms and seek a more far-ranging study of possible nonproliferation options, especially methods to blunt the nuclear ambitions of India, Israel, and Sweden. On November 1, 1964, LBJ announced a President's Special Task Force on Nuclear Proliferation. Election-year politics may have hastened the panel's creation. Beset by numerous crises in the month preceding the election, LBJ may have wanted to demonstrate to the American public that he had matters under control. The government had no shortage of groups studying the implications of the Chinese nuclear test for future nuclear proliferation policy (one observer counted no fewer than five panels examining the issue), and there seemed no bureaucratic urgency for another task force.[41]

The creation of the so-called Gilpatric Committee, however, did signal increased presidential attention to nuclear proliferation. The announcement committed Johnson to finding some new approach to the problem or at least indicated a need to place the foreign policy establishment's imprimatur on existing policies. For this task, Johnson assembled an impressive roster of former government and military officials. Roswell Gilpatric, deputy secretary of defense during the Kennedy administration, chaired the task force, which included Arthur Dean (former test ban negotiator), Allen Dulles (former CIA director), George B. Kistiakowsky (Eisenhower's science adviser), Herbert York (former director of the Department of Defense's Research and Engineering Division), John J. McCloy (former presidential assistant for disarmament), and General Alfred M. Gruenther (former military commander of NATO). Cornell University president James Perkins, IBM chairman Arthur K. Watson, and William Webster, president of the New England Electric System, rounded out the group. Gilpatric also recruited skilled and experienced staffers from the NSC and from the State and Defense Departments.

In November, as the special task force took shape, the Thompson panel on nuclear proliferation issued its final report. As expected, it questioned the utility of a nonproliferation treaty and strongly backed the MLF, displaying deep suspicion that Moscow espoused nonproliferation only to sow dissent and confusion within NATO. Much of the text explored the best means to protect the NATO nuclear force from attacks during the upcoming UN General Assembly meeting. More important, Rusk, who had manned the State Department's China desk during the "who lost China" frenzy of the Truman years, abandoned his previous advocacy of nonproliferation now that Beijing had the bomb. He questioned "whether the US should oppose other countries' obtaining nuclear weapons over the next ten years." He "could conceive of situations where the Japanese or Indians might desirably have their own nuclear weapons." Perhaps the best U.S. response might be to create an Asian MLF, especially given that Japan's new prime minister had recently commented that Tokyo "should provide herself some nuclear deterrents." The president's other principal arms control advisers dissented from this view. The ACDA continued to seek some balance between the president's pursuit of the MLF and nonproliferation, while both McNamara and Bundy had soured on the NATO nuclear force and looked to a nonproliferation agreement to provide some international stability. The secretary of defense, however, opposed any nonproliferation treaty that required Washington to extend security guarantees to all non-nuclear powers, labeling such commitments a dangerous overextension of U.S. military resources. In Asia, where no analogue to NATO existed, a collective nuclear organization with Australia and the Philippines as charter members might be the solution. He also toyed with an antiballistic missile system to check Chinese proliferation.[42]

When the Gilpatric Committee held its first meeting on December 1, it immediately became embroiled in the administration's internecine warfare, with the various factions seeking to use the task force's final recommendations to boost their preferred policies. Adrian Fisher, deputy director of the ACDA, warned that "categorical Soviet opposition to the MLF" would block Soviet acceptance of a nonproliferation agreement. ACDA director Foster, moreover, expressly urged abandonment of the NATO nuclear force.[43]

The State Department, however, prioritized nuclear sharing over nonproliferation. Rusk expressed his own ambivalence, contending that "nonproliferation is not the overriding element in US relations with the rest of the world." He rejected energetic efforts to conclude a comprehensive test ban treaty in favor of piecemeal approaches to the proliferation problem, suggesting that an "Asian nuclear defense community, perhaps, with a US nuclear stockpile available for it to draw upon, may be one solution." Most State Department officials believed that bilateral solutions to nuclear dissemination held greater promise than did a multilateral agreement. Thompson asserted that Moscow had no real interest in nonproliferation beyond denying West Germany nuclear weapons. Walt Rostow pooh-poohed a sweeping multilateral agreement, arguing that the unique conditions motivating proliferation in individual countries required varied approaches. Victory in Vietnam would allegedly ease the security worries of noncommunist Asian countries and reduce their desire to take part in proliferation. George Ball emerged as the most forceful critic of a multilateral treaty, arguing that incipient nuclear powers needed something concrete, such as expanded U.S. nuclear protection or American nuclear weapons, in return for their pledge not to acquire weapons. Without such a quid pro quo, any treaty would "probably be no more effective than the Kellogg-Briand Pact" to outlaw war that the United States had co-sponsored in the late 1920s. No agreement, however, should leave West Germans as "second-class citizens" languishing in "a discriminatory state of original sin." Ball praised the MLF/ANF proposal as a means to "roll back" the British forces and urged nuclear sharing in Asia via a nuclear weapons "bank" from which countries threatened by the PRC could draw "when and if required."[44]

As the committee deliberated, its members split over the best means to stem proliferation. Gilpatric concluded that "to make any headway against the further spread of nuclear arms, the MLF must either become a fait accompli, be abandoned, or be shelved indefinitely." He also averred that the Germans had little reason to complain, noting that, with "thousands of tactical nuclear weapons now deployed on German soil for use by both US and FRG [West German] forces," Bonn already wielded a strong hand in nuclear policy. He privately suggested allowing Europeans to decide the fate of a NATO nuclear force but admitted he "would be just as happy if it did not come off."[45]

Gilpatric occupied the committee's middle ground, with other members staking out opposite poles. McCloy was the group's leading MLF advocate. He feared that NATO had lost its guiding purpose and teetered on the brink of dissolution. Although complicating the quest for nonproliferation, a NATO nuclear force might paper over some of the emerging cracks in the alliance. If Johnson abandoned the MLF, the United States risked "losing the Alliance and nonproliferation as well." Like LBJ, McCloy feared that exchanging a NATO nuclear force for a nonproliferation treaty might repeat the mistakes of the 1920s and 1930s by forcing the Germans into an unnaturally subordinate role. Inflamed nationalist sentiment would in turn provoke Bonn's withdrawal from the Western alliance.[46]

Arthur Dean reached contrary conclusions. He frankly argued that U.S. policy should be reexamined from the ground up, suggesting that NATO and the MLF might not guarantee peace in Europe and the wider world and urging disarmament negotiations with Communist China. Efforts to settle European tensions might fizzle, so long as Washington insisted on allied approval of any agreement with Moscow. He asked if his colleagues had "ever thought that the French or Germans might wish to postpone a settlement for reasons which were not in the best interests of the United States."[47]

The committee embraced the spirit of Dean's advice and did not merely assume that existing or previous policies had been wise. The panel examined four alternative programs: selective proliferation; the existing policy of stressing the MLF at the expense of a nonproliferation agreement; energetic efforts to conclude both a comprehensive test ban treaty and a nondissemination treaty; and a "rollback" approach that attempted not only to prevent further nuclear spread but also to reverse previous proliferation (including British and French) via diplomacy or military action. Gilpatric assumed that proliferation was neither desirable nor inevitable. He thus rejected the first two options as giving "lip service" to nonproliferation while either encouraging or merely delaying the rapid expansion of nuclear powers. Even course three seemed inadequate because it ventured only to hold the number of nuclear powers at the existing level for the near term. Gilpatric clearly favored a "rollback" policy that would "take Time by the forelock" but admitted that such an aggressive program "is probably not feasible if only because neither of the great nuclear powers, US or USSR, are ready for strong measures."[48]

Before resigning himself to course three, Gilpatric explored sentiments within the administration toward a "rollback" policy, including destruction of China's nuclear weapons facilities. In mid-December 1964, George Rathjens, a task force staff member, argued that previous studies of preemptive military action had underestimated both the political and the military consequences of Chinese proliferation and suggested that "further consideration of direct action against Chinese nuclear facilities, or at least consideration of exploration of that possibility with the Soviet Union might be warranted." Armed with this memorandum, Gilpatric informed George Ball that "he had been thinking a little about the possibility of direct action to roll back Chinese nuclear-weapons development." Ball dismissed such a possibility in the near term but agreed that "it might appear in a different light if the Chinese were responsible for starting something up at some time in the future." The ever-mercurial McNamara meanwhile had reversed his position on nonproliferation, perhaps under the influence of Deputy Assistant Secretary of Defense for International Security Affairs Henry Rowen, who favored an aggressive nonproliferation policy. While calling rollback "out of the question (except for the United Kingdom)," he came out strongly for course three, endorsing a nonproliferation agreement, a full test ban, and security guarantees for non-nuclear powers.[49]

Finding little support for rollback, Gilpatric steered his panel toward a modified version of course three—with an emphasis on ending nonproliferation's subordination to other national security considerations. At the committee's third meeting, Gilpatric endorsed a more vigorous nonproliferation effort as a means to prevent another "Sarajevo incident." Although some committee members and staffers believed NATO should be Washington's first priority and rejected a more vigorous nonproliferation policy as too risky, Gilpatric concluded that he had enough support to draft the committee's report, which criticized the administration for neglecting nonproliferation in favor of "other, often less important, policies." The emphasis on nuclear sharing, for instance, had caused Washington "to sidetrack and delay" both a non-proliferation treaty and a comprehensive test ban. The report also called for making nuclear weapons less prominent in U.S. strategy. Without explicitly advocating some staff members' arguments for making nuclear weapons illegal except to retaliate against another power's nuclear attack, their argument that Washington had to change its attitude toward nuclear weapons survived. The antihegemonic effects of the PRC's test also received attention in Gilpatric's draft. Staff papers warned that Beijing's bomb could create "a widespread feeling that nuclear weapons, now in the hands of the yellow man, can be in the hands of brown and black men. This attitude may reverberate back to the white countries and speed up spread among them." Amplifying these racial concerns, the draft warned that "any major trend of nuclear capabilities among the populous, non-white nations of the earth would greatly strengthen their hands in attempting to obtain an ever greater share of the earth's wealth and opportunity." Nuclear "rollback" using military force did not seem feasible, but Gilpatric hinted that covert action as well as the UN might function to inhibit and condemn the French and Chinese programs.[50]

Gilpatric's draft inspired heated opposition from McCloy and, somewhat surprisingly, from Dean, both of whom believed that nonproliferation served U.S. interests but feared that hasty abandonment of the MLF might push West Germany "to turn elsewhere in order to get unrealistic USSR promises of cooperation." The two friends argued that the "desirability of nonproliferation may be more instinctive than analytical." Too much emphasis on nondissemination had already led to the "fantastic" assumption that Europeans could resolve the MLF/ANF question on their own, which would only produce "a real triumph for de Gaulle" and "his opposition to collective security." Western unity should take priority over any Asian nuclear threat. McCloy insisted that efforts to deal with "the future of the under-developed countries including the looming menace of the emerging African continent with its Asian overtones is also impaired by every postponement of further steps to unify the West." Dean thought nonproliferation a worthy goal, but "there is no reason to believe that the USSR's politico-ideological objective — communist world domination — has changed." Abandoning the MLF might drive Bonn into the embrace of Paris or Moscow. Dean shared McCloy's disdain for Asia, asserting that "there are no real assurances that if we gave . . . India or Japan nuclear weapons that they will always remain friendly to us or would not form a nuclear alliance against us." White Europeans obviously provoked no such worries.[51]

Seeking unanimity, Gilpatric had his staff revise the committee's report. While still urging greater attention to nonproliferation, it muted support for some of course three. It still endorsed a nonproliferation agreement, a comprehensive test ban, and nuclear-free zones but backpedaled on security guarantees to India and other non-nuclear powers. Actions against the French nuclear program should not be initiated in Washington, notwithstanding possible U.S. support to other parties that did seek action against Paris. China received scant treatment, with an ambiguous call for further study of the problem. The report offered no real changes in overall U.S. nuclear policy except for a vague recommendation "that we avoid giving an exaggerated impression" of nuclear weapons' "importance and utility." The committee also hedged on the MLF, merely suggesting that it should not prevent Washington from immediately pursuing a nonproliferation agreement.[52]

The hopes of even minor revisions in U.S. nonproliferation policy dimmed before the task force formally presented its watered-down conclusions to the president. After seeing an advance copy of the committee's report, Rusk firmly rejected its conclusions, claiming its proposed actions threatened national security and unwisely sacrificed alliance cohesion to arms control goals. LBJ also seemed to convey disinterest in scheduling his meeting with the committee for the morning after his inaugural ball. During that gathering, the facade of unanimity created by Gilpatric crumbled. McCloy spoke at length about needing to preserve the Atlantic alliance system despite U.S. interest in nonproliferation, angering others on the task force who believed he had betrayed the meeting's purpose. Johnson seemed impatient, observing "sardonically that it seemed like the implementation of the committee's report would be 'a very pleasant undertaking.'"[53]

Although McNamara called the document "as good a report done on a short time scale as any I've seen since coming to Washington," Rusk warned, in mixed metaphors, that "the report was as explosive as a nuclear weapon and that its premature disclosure could start the ball rolling in a[n] undesirable manner." The president concurred and restricted the report to the personal use of his select arms control advisers. He ordered that no one mention that the Gilpatric Committee had presented a *written* report. Atomic Energy Commissioner Glenn Seaborg later noted that the secrecy surrounding the task force's findings kept it from being cited in subsequent policy debates. "The time and conscientious effort of distinguished private citizens and a superbly qualified government staff" had been "to a large extent wasted," he lamented. Raymond Garthoff, a committee staff member and a State Department analyst who served on all five bodies studying the implications of the Chinese explosion, concurred that "there were few identifiable concrete results" from the panel's work. The suppression of the committee's report left Gilpatric angry and critical of Rusk's unwillingness to revise U.S. foreign policy.[54]

"I Don't Want to Be a Woodrow Wilson"

Johnson's rejection of the Gilpatric report did not mean complete victory for the MLF faction. In January 1965, the theologians still smarted from a series of setbacks. Johnson's April 1964 decision to seek an MLF treaty by year's end had produced few desirable results. Washington remained on the defensive in the UN and in the ENDC throughout the year, due to unwillingness to compromise on the MLF. The Soviets, moreover, stepped up their criticism of the NATO nuclear force. Although U.S. ambassador to the Soviet Union Foy Kohler claimed that Moscow had merely reacted "in familiar Pavlovian fashion to a Western defense measure," he conceded that the "Soviets are also probably genuinely concerned that the MLF will only hasten the day when [West Germany] becomes a nuclear power." More important, France switched from passive indifference to active opposition. When de Gaulle visited West Germany in July 1964, he criticized the Erhard government's lack of compliance with Franco-German military cooperation agreements and blasted the MLF.[55]

De Gaulle's heightening hostility toward the NATO nuclear force became an issue in German national politics. Konrad Adenauer, Erhard's predecessor and architect of the Franco-German alliance, broke with government policy and called for a review and possible delay of the MLF negotiations. For Erhard, the NATO nuclear force had come to symbolize his struggle to wrest control of West German politics and the Christian Democratic Party from Adenauer and its Gaullist wing. Rather than reducing the German commitment to the MLF, he pressed Johnson to produce a treaty by the end of 1964. The chancellor also recurrently reminded the president of previous assertions that the United States might proceed bilaterally if other NATO countries declined to participate. When West German NATO ambassador Wilhelm Grewe delivered this message to Rusk, he urged coordination and consultation with Bonn on overall nuclear strategy. The secretary of state, however, dispelled any illusions about a U.S.-German nuclear partnership, stating that the United States would consult on atomic matters but would never "give any veto or any control over the U.S. nuclear deterrent to countries who were not taking the same commitments and risks in the world." Johnson's official response emphasized his inability to act on either the MLF or improved nuclear consultation within NATO until after the November election. After the chancellor reluctantly acceded to postponing any treaty until early 1965, LBJ bragged about managing his counterpart, claiming that Erhard "was ready to go in the barn and milk my cows if he could find the teats. There's only one way to deal with Germans. You keep patting them on the head and then every once in a while you kick them in the balls."[56]

The Grewe visit, the Labour Party's victory in the British elections, and de Gaulle's vigorous anti-MLF stance set in motion yet another interdepartmental review of U.S. policy. Ball and Bundy directed the study group, which attempted to reformulate the NATO nuclear force proposal to address the needs and concerns of both the Germans and the British. While Ball reiterated the standard arguments in favor of the MLF, an increasingly skeptical Bundy thought it impeded U.S. efforts at arms control and threatened to tear apart NATO. The new Labour government in London, he claimed, would agree to a compromise in which Britain participated only on a token basis. Unrelenting French criticism of both Washington and Bonn for seeking the MLF threatened to enhance de Gaulle's status in Western Europe and might undo one of the major diplomatic achievements of the postwar era: the Franco-German rapprochement. Even Bonn's support appeared problematic because of the split over the MLF within the ruling party. Also acknowledging the prospect of intense congressional opposition from "a curious collection of liberals, Joint Committee atom-guarders, and neo-isolationists," Bundy recommended "that the U.S. should now arrange to let the MLF sink out of sight." At first, Bundy communicated these views only to Ball, Rusk, and Mc-Namara, none of whom rejected his conclusions out of hand. They claimed that "this is a decision which may well be the right one down the road" but wanted to wait until after British prime minister Harold Wilson's visit in early December before abandoning the missile force. Ball also argued that Washington could not kill the MLF directly but had to guide the Germans toward abandoning the proposal under the guise of studying its feasibility. But his apparent acceptance of Bundy's assessment proved disingenuous. Just days later, Ball told Wilson that if London intended to reject the MLF, "it would be better if [he] cancelled [his] visit," a sly statement issued while he simultaneously goaded Bonn into withholding support for Britain's shaky currency until London committed to the MLF. The British, however, soon received assurances from Washington that Ball, Rostow, and their "co-fanatics in the State Department" had lost influence to Bundy and the NSC staff.[57]

The president did not fully consider the MLF until December 5, just two days before Wilson's arrival. Torn between the fear that doing nothing would inspire German proliferation and the political reality that Congress opposed what his advisers had proposed, Johnson grew livid upon learning the extent of the domestic and international complications surrounding the NATO nuclear force. "I don't want to be a Woodrow Wilson[,] right on principle and fighting for a principle, and unable to achieve it," Johnson wailed. He also blanched at the MLF theologians' hostility to London and solicitousness toward Bonn, bellowing, "Aren't you telling me to kick Mother England out of the door into the cold, while I bring the Kaiser into the sitting room?" Demanding to know what Kennedy's position on the proposal had been, he adjourned the meeting until the next day. Bundy exploited this opening to expose the president to the full case against the MLF, carefully laying out the difficulties with Congress, France, and the Soviet Union and the splits within the military and bureaucracy. In the end, a multilateral nuclear force would require the president to expend enormous time and political capital to achieve a goal that nearly everyone agreed did not constitute a viable end in itself. If the MLF failed to produce what its proponents claimed it would, the president would have risked much and gained nothing. But, Bundy argued, "if you go half steam ahead, there will probably be no MLF, but it will not be your fault alone. . . . There will be plenty of opportunity for debate, discussion and delay, and for gradual and ceremonial burial." Rather than hastily implement an ill-advised and provocative scheme, Johnson's "wisdom, caution, and good judgment will have the praise of liberals, of military men, of the British, of the French, and of many Germans — and you will have the freedom to make a different choice later if you wish." LBJ scoffed, "If Europe isn't for it then the hell with it."[58]

In the meeting on December 6, the president left MLF proponents confused as to what he would say to Prime Minister Wilson, but it soon became clear that he had adopted Bundy's advice to pursue gradual burial of the scheme. He later presciently remarked, "[Wilson will] say no and then we'll shame him a bit and agree that we both have to talk to the Germans." There followed a bravura LBJ performance during Wilson's visit. He immediately took the offensive, criticizing the prime minister for speeches during the campaign and his recent anti-MLF statements in Parliament. Having backed Wilson into a corner, he turned to the MLF issue and relented somewhat, claiming he would not "take an adamant position and had no intention of forcing the matter now." But he warned that unless London and Washington did something to slake the German nuclear thirst, Bonn's national ambitions might again grow unchecked and precipitate World War III. Wilson, who had a reputation for distrusting "Frogs, Wogs, and the Hun," later marveled at LBJ's anti-German sentiments, which seemed "much worse than anything on the Labour backbenches."[59]

The British had arrived in Washington prepared to counter demands that something had to be done to contain German proliferation. Wilson realized that the United States had invested too much energy and prestige in the MLF to disavow it directly. The Labour Party, moreover, had campaigned on a pledge to eliminate the British deterrent. Its slim majority in Parliament, however, did not allow it to take such a drastic step, and Wilson realized that the national nuclear force "had an emotional appeal to the man in the pub." Labour needed a compromise that would mute Conservative criticism, appease Washington, and prevent the party's left wing from accusing the government of giving nuclear weapons to the Germans. The alternative Wilson formulated, named the Atlantic Nuclear Force (ANF), would combine national and multinational nuclear commands and require all non-nuclear members to sign a nonproliferation pledge. Britain would contribute bombers and submarines, the United States would contribute submarines and possibly Minuteman ICBMs, and France would earmark some of its forces for NATO use. A mixed-manned component might make up a unit within the ANF, but a nation could join the NATO nuclear force without participating in the multilateral aspect. Like Johnson did, Wilson hoped that the ANF might kill the MLF slowly and surreptitiously. In attempting to avoid damaging U.S. prestige by not overtly jettisoning an American proposal that had stood since

1960, both London and Washington ignored one of LBJ's favorite adages—
"While you're trying to save face, you'll lose your ass."[60]

Grasping the British proposal as a way out of his policy dilemma, Johnson neither rejected nor accepted the ANF. He agreed instead to combine
the MLF and British proposals if London could convince Bonn and Paris to
accept them. As Bundy later exulted, Washington had put "the ball back in
the European court," and Johnson had positioned himself "as the firm but
patient leader of the Alliance." The president soon codified his new policy in
a National Security Action Memorandum that avoided reference to any timetable for an ANF or MLF agreement and sought "the largest possible consensus among interested allies." Bundy's allies in London dubbed the Johnson-
Wilson summit "Ball's last stand." Even Ambassador Bruce remarked that
"George is out on a limb, which the President may saw off."[61]

London and Bonn now faced long negotiations unlikely to produce agreement. The French immediately recognized Johnson's ploy, noting with approval that "what is acceptable to [the] Germans is anathema to [the] British
and vice versa." Bonn also realized that Washington had ducked its previous
commitment to the MLF and saw itself consigned to a discriminatory position within the Western alliance. Erhard lamented that Washington had effectively delayed any final decision on the MLF until after the German elections
in September 1965, which allowed his opponents to continue using the issue
against him. Rusk dismissed these worries and reiterated the administration's
commitment to a NATO nuclear force; yet he simultaneously approved the
quiet disbanding of the State Department's MLF working group. Having decided to kill the MLF softly, Johnson failed to convey his new policy either to
European allies or to subordinates.[62]

LBJ's rejection of the Gilpatric report and his murky policy toward the
MLF perpetuated the confusion surrounding U.S. nonproliferation policy.
Both arms control advocates and State Department Atlanticists had suffered
setbacks, but both still hoped to continue fighting for their goals. The administration needed clear presidential leadership to determine whether a nondissemination treaty or a NATO nuclear force was the main nonproliferation
policy. But during 1965, as in 1964, Johnson's attention remained fixed on
other political issues, notably escalation of the war in Vietnam. The tug and
pull within the government continued, with little change in any of the factions' arguments. This deadlock also ensured that no progress on either the
MLF/ANF or a nonproliferation treaty could occur.

Despite this lack of a coherent policy, the Johnson administration continued its efforts to prevent Asian and Middle Eastern nuclear arms races.

India remained the focus in Asia. The Shastri government persistently advocated a nonproliferation agreement in the UN General Assembly but faced criticism at home from nationalists who demanded a nuclear arsenal to counterbalance Beijing. Washington wanted India to cultivate neutral backing for nonproliferation but refused to support New Delhi's resolution in the General Assembly because it contained language opposing the MLF. One possibility emerged when an Indian official hinted that U.S. assistance could enable New Delhi to achieve a peaceful nuclear success greater than China's bomb test. The Johnson administration showed interest in such a joint effort but could not agree on what type of project would be most effective. Any hopes of cooperation faded after Johnson canceled a state visit by Shastri, angering the Indian government. When a second Chinese nuclear test occurred on May 14, 1965, the pressure on India increased, and Washington had little diplomatic leverage to counter it. U.S. analysts further warned that other potential Asian nuclear powers existed, including Japan, which already had the capability to create a deliverable nuclear arsenal but faced both constitutional and cultural restraints on military development.

In the Middle East, the United States remained wary of Israel's nuclear program. Throughout the early months of 1965, Washington urged opening the Dimona reactor to regular international inspections to prove that it provided no plutonium for Tel Aviv's military program. If the Israelis had diverted nuclear material from Dimona for a bomb project, U.S. analysts predicted that a test could occur as early as 1968. Israel, in turn, used the possibility of going nuclear as an implied threat every time the United States seemed reluctant to provide more powerful conventional weapons. In the end, the Johnson administration gained little because Tel Aviv only slowed the pace of its covert nuclear program, and Arab countries, especially Egypt, continued to seek ways to counter Israeli proliferation, including nuclear options of their own.

Johnson wished to stifle these regional nuclear arms races before they started, but bilateral diplomacy produced scant results. He therefore briefly revived U.S. efforts to negotiate a nonproliferation agreement with the Soviet Union. The president sought to unveil a new proposal in a speech commemorating the twentieth anniversary of the UN. But the personal and political rivalry between LBJ and Senator Robert Kennedy intervened to kill that new nonproliferation effort. On June 23, 1965, Kennedy gave his first formal speech as a member of the Senate, claiming that controlling the spread of nuclear weapons constituted the "most vital problem facing this nation and the world." His recommendations included a nonproliferation treaty, extension of the LTBT to cover some underground experiments, nuclear-free zones, and a strengthened IAEA—all aspects of the Gilpatric Committee report. The NSC staff member who examined Kennedy's speech concluded that "the overall package appears to be too close to the proposals" in Johnson's UN speech "to be coincidental." Kennedy also seemed extremely familiar with the still closely guarded conclusions of the Gilpatric Committee. Infuriated, Johnson demanded to know who had helped Kennedy with his speech. The president deleted the disarmament items from his UN anniversary speech, roaring, "I don't want one word in there that looks like I'm copying Bobby Kennedy." Lamenting his choice of Gilpatric to head the nonproliferation task force, LBJ buried the committee's report deeper and ordered the ACDA to begin a full review of nonproliferation policy. McGeorge Bundy adroitly assured the president that "in light of the fact that the Gilpatric Committee has not worked out to your satisfaction, I want to be quite sure that our next efforts in this critically important field are along lines you approve."[63]

During Johnson's first several months in office, uncertainty regarding his foreign policy judgment, the haunting specter of interwar mistakes, and deep-rooted wariness of alliance politics all combined to prevent LBJ from constructing a coherent nuclear policy. As a result, both the NATO nuclear force and a nonproliferation agreement remained out of reach. Attempts to compensate for the policy confusion by seeking unilateral and bilateral solutions also proved unsuccessful. Even the Gilpatric Committee failed to move Johnson to prioritize U.S. policy goals. LBJ instead delayed a decision as he concentrated on reelection, his ambitious Great Society reform program, and Vietnam. While he continued to procrastinate, China acquired the bomb and full-blown Middle Eastern and Asian nuclear arms races gathered momentum. The nightmarish scenario of ten to twenty nuclear powers that had so frightened Kennedy moved closer to reality. Declining superpower hegemony meant that any effort to conclude a nonproliferation agreement required assessing the interests of numerous nations—a far more complex task than had confronted JFK when he negotiated the LTBT. Whether LBJ possessed the skill to craft a solution to the nonproliferation problem remained an open question in 1965.

A Treaty to Castrate the Impotent

CODIFYING NUCLEAR APARTHEID, 1965–1970

"If I had a dollar for every time I consulted with the Germans, I'd be a millionaire," snorted President Lyndon Johnson in March 1967. Johnson's anger flared after the Bonn government complained of the superpowers' "atomic complicity" in negotiating a nonproliferation treaty. The president had legitimate reasons to be irritated. During his first years in office, he had been extremely sensitive to Germany's and other allies' security interests, allowing nonproliferation negotiations to be shaped more by alliance politics than by superpower rivalry. Bonn "had written half the treaty," according to Dean Rusk. Moscow and Washington had concluded that nonproliferation enhanced both U.S. and Soviet national security, especially with respect to West Germany and non-Western nations. They envisioned a two-tier system in which their respective alliance partners would have tightly controlled access to nuclear weapons while the rest of the world pledged nuclear abstinence. Newly decolonized nations, however, objected to this system of "nuclear weapons apartheid," demanding that Moscow and Washington cut their nuclear arsenals to offset the sacrifice of non-nuclear nations. The superpowers instead promulgated a nonproliferation agreement that the most significant near-nuclear nations rejected. Conclusion of the NPT became even less meaningful in 1969 when LBJ's successor, Richard Nixon, abandoned all but the most symbolic efforts at enforcement. The NPT that finally took effect in 1970 marked, in the words of one jaded proponent, a "worthless triumph."[1]

Wrestling with Frankenstein's Monster

In summer 1965, Johnson had rejected the Gilpatric Committee's findings. His pique over Robert Kennedy's use of the committee's report to criticize administration nonproliferation policy and his anger that someone had leaked parts of the document to the press played into his decision. Still, William Foster and his subordinates kept revising the U.S. position to make it more acceptable to Moscow. The ACDA director lobbied for popular support of his agency's position with an article in *Foreign Affairs*. His prediction that a weakened alliance would be a necessary cost of an agreement and his hints that the MLF should be abandoned prompted worry both inside and outside of the administration. Yet Foster failed to win a renewed presidential commitment to seek a treaty. Little support ultimately existed for softening the language that allowed nuclear sharing, especially after West Germany insisted that reunification and the MLF's creation needed to precede a treaty. Despite U.S. rejection of Bonn's preconditions, Foster received orders to craft language that "finessed" the MLF issue.[2]

A nonproliferation policy review in summer 1965 buried the Gilpatric report for good. Bundy promised LBJ that the review would "bring the issues up clear and clean where you can see them and hear the arguments of the different parties of interest." Bundy chided the Gilpatric Committee for its overly sanguine assessment that "immediate progress is possible" on nonproliferation, but he sought the review so as to "reaffirm our basic support for the *principle* of non-dissemination and the *principle* of a comprehensive test ban treaty." The NSC staff warned against sweeping Gilpatric's "report under the rug," but in April 1965 the State and Defense Departments vigorously objected when Bundy proposed an extremely watered-down version of the task force's recommendations. In the end, a nonproliferation agreement emerged as the only committee recommendation that survived to the end of the Johnson administration, and that goal predated the committee by four years. The policy review left the muddled, ineffective policy that had been in place since 1963 undisturbed.[3]

A dustup with London prior to the ENDC meetings underscored the Gilpatric report's limited effect on U.S. policy. The British government had pressed for a draft nonproliferation treaty since early 1965. Frustrated with Washington's tepid support, Prime Minister Harold Wilson and his advisers produced their own text. LBJ opposed the British draft because it explicitly forbade the transfer of the MLF to a united Europe. The Johnson administration had dangled the prospect of such a transfer in front of German nationalists to mute their support for de Gaulle's policy of a Europe for Europeans. The Labour government believed that domestic exigencies required keeping nuclear weapons out of German hands. The United States countered with its own draft treaty that left many issues surrounding the MLF unresolved. The British accepted this text as the basis of further discussion, but they made clear that they opposed U.S. claims that transfer of the MLF to European control would not constitute proliferation.

Despite this meager display of alliance unity, Foster presented the first U.S. draft nonproliferation treaty to the ENDC. The text represented five years of effort by both the Kennedy and the Johnson administrations. But it proved anticlimactic. Having refused to consider any treaty that allowed for the MLF's creation, the Soviets rejected the U.S. draft and introduced an alternative that forbade transfer of nuclear weapons to any group or alliance of states. Such language not only banned the MLF but would have required the United States to abandon existing nuclear-sharing policies. The stalemate since 1963 deepened as the Vietnam War chilled U.S.-Soviet exchanges. Public discussions of a nonproliferation treaty became sterile. Britain also found itself shut out from further discussion of the treaty text because Washington now considered London untrustworthy on the subject.[4]

With no prospect for a nonproliferation treaty and increasing evidence that India sought a nuclear arsenal, disarmament advocates focused on extending the Limited Test Ban Treaty. Either a comprehensive test ban or a halfway measure that banned all underground tests that could be detected without on-site inspections offered hopes of blunting proliferation. But the Limited Test Ban Treaty remained controversial. Critics argued that Moscow had already violated the agreement and that the treaty inhibited U.S. efforts to develop high-yield warheads and an antiballistic missile system—areas wherein the Soviets had allegedly overtaken the United States. The Joint Chiefs joined with Llewellyn Thompson, who believed that both Soviet and German agreement to any nonproliferation measures was highly doubtful, and with Rusk, who preferred a simple declaration from non-nuclear states that they would not acquire or produce nuclear weapons. In the end, opponents blocked any compromise regarding on-site inspections. With Moscow insisting that existing verification measures sufficed to police underground testing, the test ban talks remained stalemated.[5]

Nonproliferation advocates hoped to forge some accord around a so-called threshold test ban treaty—an agreement that would ban all nuclear explosions that could be reliably detected without on-site inspections. Although hopes for a comprehensive test ban died quickly, the threshold ban garnered enough support to remain a live option until progress toward a nonproliferation treaty resumed in late 1966. No consensus formed on a threshold test ban, and ultimately it lost support. Moscow was thought likely to counter any U.S. proposal with calls for a moratorium on all tests below the seismic threshold, while opposition from the Joint Chiefs and critics in Congress "would use up more capital than the treaty is worth."[6]

One final testing gambit surfaced: peaceful nuclear explosions. Peaceful uses advocates had long trumpeted the ability of nuclear explosives to shift the course of rivers, level mountains, and aid in canal construction. Even though these nuclear explosions would be indistinguishable from weapons, some officials believed that offering peaceful nuclear explosives (PNEs) to India and other aspiring nuclear powers might forestall them from developing a nuclear capability under the pretext of exploring nonmilitary applications. Washington hesitated to ban PNEs because it still dreamed of a sea-level canal in Panama using nuclear technology. George Ball, who had a penchant for harebrained schemes that put Rube Goldberg to shame, proposed a U.S.-sponsored international PNE consortium to block Indian acquisition of nuclear capability. Moscow agreed to technical talks, but both superpowers lost interest once the nonproliferation treaty deadlock broke. With test bans and PNEs no longer options, ineffectual warnings to New Delhi about costs and wasted resources constituted the only response to Indian nuclear aspirations. One Indian leader likened American counsel to a "smoking parent advising his son not to smoke."[7]

In October 1965, disturbed by nuclear rumblings in Israel and India and frustrated with administrative dithering, Foster told LBJ that an agreement was long overdue and urgent. The ACDA director recommended immediate conclusion of a nonproliferation treaty even if it "would not permit a mixed ownership NATO nuclear force." Although Bundy characterized Foster's argument as "one-sided" and ignorant of "our German problem," most other policymakers had finally turned against the MLF.[8]

The president preferred to let London and Bonn quietly kill the idea, but that strategy had failed to produce results. The Anglo-German negotiations in early 1965 had failed to produce even the rough outlines of agreement, with the British insisting that the ANF be the only subject of negotiation and the Germans reluctant to abandon the work already invested in the MLF proposal. Believing that the British plan saddled Germany with financing

London's outdated bomber fleet, Erhard refused to pay a penny for such "worthless stuff." Former British foreign secretary Patrick Gordon Walker observed that the United States "had killed and buried not only the MLF but the ANF" when it left the Europeans to work out their differences without American intervention. The ANF was "the only fleet that had not been created that torpedoed another fleet that hadn't yet sailed," quipped Franz Josef Strauss. Rusk rejected "complaints about our alleged failure to exercise leadership" when "the critics generally want us to lead the other fellow." He blamed de Gaulle for the impasse, a charge not easily dismissed. France had appeared indifferent to the MLF/ANF proposal until late 1964 (content to dismiss it as a "multilateral farce"), at which time Paris switched tactics and began issuing veiled threats concerning its loyalty to both NATO and the Franco-German alliance. Unrelenting French opposition had forced Erhard to place the ANF issue on ice until after the September 1965 general election. De Gaulle boasted, "The MLF is dead. It is I who killed it." In Britain, some commentators pointed fingers elsewhere, with the *Economist* declaring that "the responsibility lies first with President Johnson."[9]

Despite attempts to bury it, the MLF had resurfaced in September 1965 looking more like its ANF sibling. Erhard had survived his reelection campaign, and he now renewed his attention to nuclear sharing. As long as Bonn's nuclear role in the alliance remained unresolved, neither the United States nor West Germany could undertake other diplomatic initiatives, such as the nonproliferation treaty and the settlement of conflicts with France. Erhard, moreover, had domestic political motives. Nationalist critics in his party had castigated him for risking the Franco-German alliance over the MLF chimera. These critics pinned their hopes on the *force de frappe* becoming an all-European force once integration came to pass. With relations with de Gaulle strained to the breaking point, the MLF's failure might destroy Erhard's ability to mange his party and government.

Johnson, however, faced both domestic and international problems that might snowball if he actively pursued an MLF/ANF agreement. In September 1965, the president told Harlan Cleveland, ambassador to NATO, that "he did not wish to pick a quarrel unnecessarily with the Russians" or "get pinned into any position which would not have Congressional support." The Johnson administration thereupon moved away from a "hardware" solution to the nuclear defense problem and turned to "systems of consultation and staff participation," like the newly initiated NATO Nuclear Planning Group, which offered Germany a "more modest and more practical" nuclear decision-making role. Even George Ball concluded that the MLF no longer offered the best solution to NATO's nuclear defense problem, but he refused to abandon a hardware solution altogether for fear that allies would doubt Washington's commitment to European integration.[10]

Despite the larger role in strategic planning that the NATO Nuclear Planning Group offered Europeans, the State Department continued to advocate at least symbolic American support for a collective nuclear force. Even MLF doubters, such as State Department analyst Martin Hillenbrand, cautioned against precipitous abandonment because "no matter how much tinsel we hang on the tree, the Germans are unlikely to find satisfaction over the long run in any nuclear arrangement which does not involve some actual hardware." Convinced that the NATO nuclear force could proceed without proliferation, the State Department European section argued that a collective force (renamed the North Atlantic Collective Defense Authority to avoid invidious comparisons to the MLF) composed of mixed-manned British bombers, British and U.S. nuclear submarines (possibly mixed-manned), and surface vessels could win congressional support. Such a force might also satisfy German nuclear demands and lead to the elimination of the independent British deterrent. Hillenbrand thought the proposal deeply flawed, but the theologians still had an ally in George Ball, despite his burial of the mixed-manned surface fleet. "A non-proliferation agreement without a German signature will not be worth anything," Ball asserted, whereas "a Soviet Union signature on a non-proliferation agreement is not important other than for ... sentimental reasons" because it was allegedly in Moscow's interest never to give nuclear weapons to other powers. Bonn, however, would refuse to sign without a guarantee of greater nuclear participation. According to Ball's twisted logic, the only way to preserve NATO and have a viable nonproliferation agreement lay in U.S. sponsorship of a collective nuclear force, Soviet objections be damned.[11]

Ball urged LBJ to offer the European desk's proposal to Erhard when he visited Washington in December 1965. The undersecretary played on Johnson's fears of a 1930s redux by portraying a collective nuclear force as the only way "to prevent Germany from becoming once more the prey of its own Teutonic fantasies." Ignore Bonn's efforts to address legitimate security fears, and Washington might face any number of threatening scenarios, including a clandestine German bomb project, a Franco-German nuclear initiative, or a German-Soviet alliance, as the perceived best path to reunification.[12]

Bundy had anticipated Ball's arguments. The MLF, the national security adviser claimed, lacked strong support in both the United States and Europe, and the new State Department proposal would provoke the same hostility as it had previously. Because the plan would surely fail, U.S. sponsorship would "simply prolong a debate which has now grown weary on all sides." The United States must substitute a NATO forum on nuclear matters for hardware. This policy not only would "make [a nonproliferation] treaty easier to get," it would best serve the alliance itself. Should consultations fail to quell German nuclear anxieties, a hardware option could be revived at some later date. Soviet ambassador Dobrynin convinced Bundy, in a private meeting, that Washington "may well be able to make some money with Moscow if we tell them privately before we sink [the MLF] publicly." Dobrynin also persuaded him that the Soviets would accept the new NATO Nuclear Planning Group. If Moscow now acquiesced to existing NATO nuclear-sharing policies, the Johnson administration could resolve the NATO nuclear defense problem and achieve a nuclear nonproliferation agreement.[13]

Johnson had to sort through this contradictory advice and information. The U.S. embassy in Bonn insisted that abandoning the MLF would alienate the Erhard government and hurt the chancellor's standing in domestic politics. Other reports suggested that rejection would play into the hands of de Gaulle and his German devotees, who still loudly advocated a wholly European force. LBJ needed a clearer sense of German and British wishes before he could choose between the Ball and Bundy options. He had little time to decide before both Wilson and Erhard came to Washington in December.

The president also wanted to bypass the bureaucratic and political battles being waged surreptitiously via press leaks. American and European press rumors circulated that the administration had already killed chances for a NATO nuclear force. Henry Owen, deputy chairman of the State Department Policy Planning Council, coaxed John McCloy to counteract the press's "absolute nonsense" about the nonproliferation treaty and the NATO nuclear force. McCloy thereupon charged treaty advocates with an "oversimplification" that associated "all evil with proliferation and all good with nonproliferation."[14]

In the absence of a voluntary retreat from Erhard's previous support for the NATO nuclear force, some Johnson administration officials, including Bundy, Rusk, and McNamara, attempted to send discreet signals that a hardware solution should be scrapped. In one meeting with an Erhard adviser, Kurt Birrenbach, Rusk and McNamara expressed doubt that the Europeans would accept what the United States could reasonably offer. The defense secretary noted that no military requirement existed for the force, it could not serve as an independent deterrent against Soviet missiles, and maintenance of a U.S. veto over firing would give Germany no more control over nuclear weapons than it already possessed. With such flaws, Bonn would simply "be wasting its money." Birrenbach stated archly that "if German desires for greater participation are irrelevant . . . why [are] these proposals . . . made by the United States?" Any hopes for a tacit understanding that allowed the MLF/ANF to die gracefully faded when Erhard gave a speech to the Bundestag calling for its creation. Behind the speech lurked Birrenbach's conversations with MLF proponents, including Dean Acheson and John McCloy, who had persuaded him that "the outlook for . . . a hardware package is excellent." The theologians' zeal then led Erhard, upon Birrenbach's advice, to shed his own ambivalence and reiterate his commitment to a larger nuclear role for West Germany.[15]

With Erhard and Johnson trying to balance multiple political and diplomatic interests, their meeting in late December 1965 took on unusual importance. Since December 1964, Johnson had delegated responsibility for the MLF to his subordinates while he occupied himself with domestic reform and the escalating war in Vietnam. But his administration's internal divisions necessitated a more active presidential role. Johnson's political instincts pushed him to expand consultations and scrap the MLF/ANF option. A hardware solution appeared too politically costly. World opinion would view a NATO nuclear force as proliferation, and any chance for a nonproliferation agreement would likely evaporate. Relations with the Soviet Union and France would also become more strained. Robert Kennedy, moreover, had recently given another speech advocating a nonproliferation treaty. If Johnson pursued a hardware solution at the expense of such an accord, Kennedy "might well have a field day." But if LBJ abandoned a proposal supported by both Eisenhower and JFK, he risked angering NATO allies and fielding criticism from such establishment stalwarts as Acheson and McCloy. Such a decision might help de Gaulle, who would spotlight the collective force's death as proof that the United States would not even grant its European allies symbolic partnership in nuclear matters.[16]

Johnson kicked the MLF/ANF can down the road once again. British prime minister Wilson, whom LBJ once called a "little creep camping on my doorstep," soon arrived in Washington with a means to avoid confronting the Germans. He assured LBJ that London still supported its own ANF proposals, despite British opinion that no military reason existed for a collective nuclear force. If Erhard agreed to substitute the ANF for the previous American plan, Johnson could possibly delay matters as Washington, London, and Bonn worked out the logistics. Postponement would deflect domestic and international criticism and might enable practical problems to arise that prevented implementation of the British plan. The NATO Nuclear Planning Group would be fully established before the allies could move forward with the ANF, and this consultative body alone might satisfy German nuclear ambitions. Despite Bundy's and Foster's warnings that he could no longer stall, the president viewed a do-nothing approach as the least politically damaging option. As Bundy later admitted, Johnson sought to juggle the nuclear-sharing and nonproliferation issues in a way that kept "the Germans on board" and did not "let Bobby get out ahead of him."[17]

During Erhard's subsequent visit, Johnson again displayed his celebrated ability to reach his goal through verbal indirection. Claiming he always put himself in other people's shoes, the president insisted that "he personally was not obsessed by fear about the German people or their attitudes. But he could also understand how the English, for instance, might feel differently." The American, German, and British governments must therefore create a collective nuclear force that served all their national interests but did not revive fears of German aggression in Europe. LBJ also brushed aside German worries about a nonproliferation agreement impeding a NATO nuclear force, remarking that "with regard to non-proliferation he did not see how much could be accomplished as long as the Viet-Nam problem was in the way." To achieve a compromise agreement, Johnson asked what Erhard "needed to take home to his people." Erhard insisted on some form of multilateral nuclear sharing. He presented a draft plan to Johnson, who expressed willingness to hear suggestions from Bonn or London. Having established his empathy for the chancellor's political strength, the president then became confrontational. He claimed that he could not understand why Bonn would take on the expense of a nuclear force when existing U.S. nuclear strength satisfied NATO's deterrent needs, especially if the allies all trusted each other to fulfill their security commitments.[18]

The German proposal had in fact moved some distance toward the ANF, just as the president had hoped. Sending Wilson a copy of Erhard's plan, LBJ admitted that its particulars would vex members of Congress and the British parliament. But he urged an open mind, stressing that "what is essential is a stable and healthy Germany." The president had lobbed the ball back into Wilson's court without arousing domestic critics or angering the Germans. Once again, he instructed his subordinates to let London and Bonn solve their differences "without strong U.S. pressure on either one." LBJ then became "so preoccupied over Vietnam and other problems" that he gave no "further attention to nuclear sharing" until the next crisis.[19]

Despite finessing both allied and domestic critics, Johnson had only prolonged the stalemate. The problems that confounded the administration in 1965 plagued it again in 1966. While the Germans had moved closer to the British, Wilson abandoned even symbolic efforts for a collective nuclear force. The British also resisted the State Department theologians' attempts to eliminate their nuclear force by folding it into NATO. One Foreign Office official remarked that the German feelings of "nuclear nakedness" should not prompt Britain "to undress as well." The inability of Bonn and London to reach agreement alarmed MLF theologians, prompting them to advocate a more active U.S. role in the negotiations. Bundy and Johnson once again had to rein in Ball and the other State Department Atlanticists.[20]

Then news arrived from Germany that revealed that Washington may have gravely miscalculated on nuclear sharing from the outset. Erhard, in early 1966, confided to Henry Kissinger, a sometime Johnson foreign policy consultant and professor at Harvard University, that "the last thing he wanted was for Germany to own nuclear weapons." But the chancellor could not afford to be publicly known "as the man who had rejected a nuclear option for Germany when it was in effect offered to him." Further conversations with German officials persuaded Kissinger that no one outside the German Foreign Office truly supported a NATO nuclear force. The government, however, felt obliged to go along because the MLF theologians had convinced them that the United States viewed it as the best solution to the alliance's nuclear defense problem. The consul of the U.S. Embassy in Bonn backed up Kissinger's assessment, arguing that neither the public nor any major political figure really desired a German nuclear force. Yet no one wanted to denounce the nuclear option, seeing it as a possible bargaining chip for German reunification. By pushing nuclear hardware on the Bonn government when few West Germans wanted a nuclear arsenal, Washington left Erhard little choice but to embrace the scheme lest he fall prey to criticism from the Gaullist wing of his party. The Americans had, in effect, created their own Frankenstein's monster.[21]

NPT Pressures

The realization that the MLF had exacerbated the issue that it had been designed to ameliorate did Johnson little good in early 1966. He could not abandon a NATO nuclear force so soon after agreeing to consider Erhard's proposals. Nonproliferation, moreover, remained a sticky issue with no easy solution. Although both the United States and the Soviet Union had unveiled draft nonproliferation treaties in 1965, they still seemed far apart. Within the

State Department, some officials still suspected that Moscow's objections to the MLF rested not on fears of proliferation but on a desire to roil the internal NATO debate on nuclear sharing. Beyond abandoning a collective nuclear force, Moscow demanded as preconditions for a nonproliferation agreement changes in extant alliance nuclear-sharing policies and a ban on the formation of the NATO Nuclear Planning Group. While the folks at Foggy Bottom viewed Kremlin motives with suspicion, the NSC staff and the ACDA believed the Soviets would compromise on the MLF if it sped conclusion of a treaty. Some Soviet diplomats had hinted that Moscow might sign a nonproliferation agreement if Johnson privately assured them that Germans would never acquire nuclear weapons. The CIA dismissed these feelers as Soviet disinformation meant to divide the Western alliance. Private bilateral talks commenced, but a NATO nuclear force impeded substantive negotiations.[22]

Outside the administration, concern over nuclear proliferation increased. In October 1965, French sources had warned that both Israel and India would "go nuclear" if Moscow and Washington failed to conclude a nondissemination agreement with strong enforcement provisions. Israel had in fact contracted with a French company to produce medium-range missiles for its nuclear warheads. Beijing also provoked international anxiety when it advocated "Afro-Asian" nuclear proliferation as the best means to "shake off imperialist control." In fall 1965, the Chinese comments helped fuel a UN General Assembly debate in which a group of nonaligned countries, including India and Egypt, urged speedy conclusion of a nonproliferation treaty and called for a World Disarmament Conference that included the PRC. If the United States and the Soviet Union could not conclude a nondissemination agreement, they risked being placed on the defensive in both the UN General Assembly and the ENDC. The nonaligned nations' growing support for including Beijing in disarmament negotiations also threatened to increase Communist China's prestige and influence, a development that both Washington and Moscow sought to avoid.[23]

Domestic opinion also favored rapid conclusion of a nonproliferation treaty. A presidential commission on disarmament and international cooperation, which included Roswell Gilpatric, Harold Stassen, and Carl Kaysen, strongly endorsed a nonproliferation agreement and other supporting measures, such as safeguards on peaceful uses and a comprehensive test ban treaty. More important, members of Congress publicly worried about possible Asian and Middle Eastern nuclear arms races. In 1965 and 1966, dissenters in the U.S. Senate and House criticized Johnson's Vietnam policies and his decision to invade the Dominican Republic. This new congressional independence also inspired action on the nonproliferation front. With the help of Adrian Fisher, deputy director of the ACDA, Senator John Pastore of Rhode Island, on January 18, 1966, introduced a congressional resolution that urged more presidential activism to conclude a nonproliferation treaty.[24]

Hopeful signs also emerged from the new ENDC sessions in Geneva, where the Soviets seemed eager for an agreement and willing to compromise on NATO nuclear-sharing policies as long as Washington retained its veto over firing decisions. The Johnson administration responded with amendments to its draft treaty that banned "any action which would cause an increase in the total number of States and associations of States having control of nuclear weapons." The Soviets still insisted that such language would allow the West Germans access to nuclear weapons via NATO and asked for stronger assurances against indirect proliferation. The superpowers had begun to negotiate seriously for the first time in three years. If the Johnson administration could dispose of the MLF/ANF proposal, an agreement might be possible as early as summer 1966.[25]

Sinking the MLF

The final deathblow to the MLF seemed imminent in early 1966. Even U.S. ambassador to West Germany George McGhee, heretofore a firm supporter, recommended the NATO Nuclear Planning Group as an overt substitute for the nuclear force. McNamara's special committee of NATO defense ministers, moreover, reached "consensus on the adequacy of existing strategic nuclear forces," ending the MRBM debate that had initially inspired the MLF.[26]

Still the MLF would not sink. Clinging to conclusions he had reached on the Gilpatric Committee, John McCloy opposed sacrificing NATO for a fatuous nonproliferation treaty. He conspired with George Ball, Henry Owen, and the MLF's intellectual godfather, Robert Bowie, to reenergize U.S. efforts toward a NATO nuclear force, including urging such prominent nonproliferation treaty advocates as Senators John Pastore and Robert Kennedy to abandon their opposition to expanded nuclear sharing.[27]

Another thunderbolt from de Gaulle also struck arms control efforts. His announcement in March 1966 that he would withdraw French forces from NATO's integrated military command exacerbated worries about the alliance. Claiming he did not want "a pissing match with de Gaulle," LBJ refrained from direct attacks. Dean Acheson, who chaired the president's NATO crisis management group, felt no such restraint. He publicly excoriated the French president, likening him "to a recovered patient" who "has finally been built up and had good food and good care, been in a warm house and warm bed and suddenly he says, 'I'm a big man[;] I don't need any more food, no more doctors, no more house, I want to get out in the wind, the ice, and the snow.'" LBJ distanced himself from Acheson, painting him in the press as an anti-Gaullist extremist, contending that "when a man asks you to leave his house, you don't argue; you get your hat and go." Acheson fired back that the president "made the greatest imperial power the world has ever seen kiss de Gaulle's arse." Angered and dismayed at Paris's action, Johnson sought evidence that NATO remained stable before he renewed efforts on nonproliferation and risked sapping the alliance by abandoning a long-promised collective nuclear force. De Gaulle's announcement also ignited internal debate over whether a quick MLF agreement would stabilize the alliance. The *force de frappe* reached operational readiness just weeks before de Gaulle's announcement, confirming fears that European nuclear forces weakened U.S. hegemony. Rusk strongly urged reopening the MLF issue. Ironically, the self-professed friends of Europe who backed the MLF/ANF scheme illogically claimed that without U.S. leadership the Western Europeans "were like inexperienced teenagers who knew what to do once they were told but were incapable of deciding on their own what was right or necessary."[28]

Amid this bureaucratic tussle, MLF advocates gained an important advantage when Walt Rostow assumed the post of special assistant for national security affairs, replacing Bundy, a hitherto formidable opponent of the scheme. Rostow proved Bundy's equal in arrogance and had long numbered among the State Department theologians. His career is striking for both the power and influence he accrued (Averell Harriman dubbed him the "American Rasputin") and for the fact that history has proven his stance on nearly every issue—the MLF, the Soviet Union, Europe, economic modernization, and Vietnam—misguided and harmful. His advocacy of the MLF and Johnson's wariness of alienating Bonn skewed the odds in favor of one final effort to appease Germany's nuclear ambitions. In April, the president authorized two studies on how to solve NATO's nuclear problem, one that assumed creation of a nuclear force and one that did not. The policy review took several months and ultimately left U.S. policy toward nuclear sharing unchanged. The administration decided to make the NATO Nuclear Planning Group a permanent alliance committee with regular meetings and assigned additional nuclear armaments to defend Europe. The issue of a collective force remained open "without prejudice." The Johnson administration proved unwilling to end the zombielike existence of the MLF.[29]

The MLF theologians had once again displayed their uncanny ability to keep their half-dead offspring on life support. Congress, however, proved less patient. The Pastore resolution had spawned JCAE hearings on nonproliferation policy. While Rusk voiced doubts that the Soviets seriously desired an agreement, other administration officials, including McNamara, provided strong national security justifications for cooperating with Moscow. Both the JCAE and the Senate Foreign Relations Committee approved the Pastore resolution and sent it to the full Senate, where, on May 17, 1966, it passed, 84 to 0. Besides demonstrating strong congressional sentiment in favor of a nonproliferation agreement, the Pastore resolution hearings indicated that the JCAE would never agree to repeal the Atomic Energy Act's ban on transfer of U.S. nuclear weapons to other powers. The Joint Chiefs of Staff, moreover, had renewed their opposition to the MLF; their testimony before the Senate's military committees would surely damage the force's chances with those bodies. LBJ's deputy national security adviser, Francis Bator, further confessed that the ANF had no appeal to Bonn, which would have to pay a great deal of money "for essentially non-voting stock in a club" that controlled "a very small fraction" of NATO's strategic force. Germany should learn to make "a virtue out of its non-nuclear status," reducing anxieties in Europe and the Soviet Union.[30]

Johnson did not immediately respond to the Pastore resolution. Already under fire from some in Congress for his conduct of the Vietnam War, the president may have resented their intrusion into another foreign policy matter, especially at a time when alliance politics had grown tense and complicated. A month after the Senate vote, however, Johnson wrote Pastore a laudatory letter that portrayed the resolution as a valuable sign of congressional support.[31]

A concatenation of forces had pushed the president toward a more energetic nonproliferation effort. This switch occurred after ACDA deputy director Adrian Fisher bypassed Rostow, who as national security adviser would have been the proper channel to the president, and presented the ACDA's arguments directly to Bill Moyers, who had recently resigned as press secretary to become a presidential foreign policy aide. Finding a sympathetic ear in the White House proved crucial to winning Johnson's support. LBJ had nurtured a disdain for the ACDA as parochial and regarded its major accomplishment, the LTBT, as wrongheaded. Fisher won two formidable new allies when McNamara and Assistant Defense Secretary John McNaughton also concluded that the MLF must be abandoned to stem nuclear proliferation.

This new alliance gradually persuaded the president that more energetic efforts toward a nonproliferation treaty might help counteract the negative public opinion that the Vietnam War's escalation had generated. While Moyers pressured LBJ, the British lobbied for a change in the draft treaty text that would block German ownership of nuclear weapons until a "fully federate European State" acquired British and French weapons by right of succession. The Soviet Union also softened its attacks on NATO nuclear policies and the new Nuclear Planning Group. In early June 1966, moreover, as U.S. officials again worried that India teetered on the brink of going nuclear, McNamara dashed off a memorandum stating that the time had come to revise U.S. treaty language. McNamara and Johnson's combined interest in changing U.S. treaty language to meet Soviet concerns provided the nonproliferation talks with a clarity of purpose they had previously lacked.[32]

Reminding Moyers of "the Japanese on Guam" who continued to fight "after World War II ended," the MLF theologians refused to surrender. Through summer and fall 1966, they blocked any treaty language that foreclosed an Atlantic or European nuclear force, arguing that even total surrender to Soviet demands would not guarantee an agreement. Treaty opponents and the Joint Chiefs of Staff singled out proposed language barring "physical access" as a potential problem for existing NATO nuclear-sharing arrangements that allowed allied governments to handle, transport, and aim nuclear weapons up to the point where the warhead became armed. The MLF purists considered it axiomatic that proliferation could not be halted because those states most needing to be contained would reject any treaty that "shut them out of the club." Given the inevitability of proliferation, the United States should not "abandon our option to spread nuclear weapons where we consider this necessary."[33]

Although the MLF proponents had successfully blocked language banning physical access, Rusk, responding to Johnson's renewed commitment to a compromise, probed whether the Soviets would accept a simple ban on the "transfer" of nuclear weapons to other powers, hoping that such a broad and ambiguous clause would avoid antagonizing Bonn. Without White House knowledge but with Rusk's approval, Foster instructed Fisher to conduct these talks "ad referendum," a term that indicated that the views expressed did not flow from official instructions and should not be considered binding by either party. Fisher kept these talks secret from all members of the Geneva delegation, even his own staff. The Soviets praised the new spirit of cooperation at Geneva but still insisted on specific language that barred transfer of nuclear weapons to non-nuclear states through alliance arrangements. The nonproliferation talks also received a big boost when Soviet premier Alexei Kosygin publicly declared that although détente with the United States would not be possible while the Vietnam War continued, certain agreements might be reached prior to a relaxation in tension, including a nonproliferation treaty.[34]

Nonproliferation advocates argued that a ban on indirect proliferation through alliance arrangements would place a compromise text within reach during Rusk-Gromyko meetings scheduled for September. Rostow reflexively led the MLF theologians in yet another mad dash to save nuclear sharing. It would not be "wise," he argued, "to sell out major Western or Asian interests to get a nonproliferation agreement with the USSR." But Rostow's contentions, which grossly caricatured Johnson's options as either détente with Russians or appeasement of Germany, did little to halt the momentum. After the president publicly backed U.S.-Soviet cooperation on nonproliferation and NATO disarmament experts proposed elimination of the European option in the U.S. draft text, Rostow attempted to formulate language that would save collective nuclear arrangements by guaranteeing that the United States would always retain its veto over decisions to fire.[35]

Rusk's discussions with Gromyko in September persuaded him that the Soviets would accept nothing less than an explicit ban on indirect proliferation. The superpowers edged closer to agreement as Rusk and Gromyko agreed to co-sponsor a nonproliferation resolution in the UN General Assembly and jointly draft compromise language on nuclear sharing. After several meetings, the U.S.-Soviet negotiations produced language that prohibited transfer of nuclear weapons to non–nuclear weapons states "directly or indirectly, either individually or collectively with other members of a military alliance or group of States." Adrian Fisher admitted that such a treaty eliminated any chance for Germans to "own" nuclear weapons except as a component of a federated European state. But he argued that attempts to preserve the option of a collective nuclear force "would render a non-proliferation treaty non-negotiable."[36]

Nonproliferation proponents would have found it difficult under any circumstances to persuade LBJ to accept this compromise, but late September 1966 proved especially inauspicious. From September 24 to September 27, Erhard met with Johnson to attempt to resolve outstanding issues, including nuclear sharing. The Johnson administration had continued assuring Bonn that the NATO Nuclear Planning Group provided adequate German influence over nuclear policy. But West German leaders insisted that even if McNamara's new committee served their short-term interests they could not permanently abandon the possibility of a collective nuclear force. Arguing that the nuclear option should only be forfeited in exchange for German re-unification, some Germans protested that the nonproliferation treaty nego-tiations elicited "concessions from the wrong side and the wrong address." Erhard had come to Washington politically weakened and facing a tough November election. Although the chancellor admitted that no one held out hope for a hardware solution, he insisted that Bonn have a clear role in NATO nuclear arrangements so long as it lived with the threat of Soviet MRBMS. Erhard's frustration reflected German desire for a larger NATO role than the Nuclear Planning Group provided.[37]

Having no alternative to offer Bonn, Johnson hesitated to hammer the MLF's coffin shut with a nonproliferation treaty. Ball exploited LBJ's fears, again contending that nonproliferation combined with the issue of offset payments (money from Bonn to defray the expense of stationing U.S. sol-diers in Germany) had prompted a potential "crisis in our relations with Ger-many — and hence with Europe." With Erhard's government laboring under the same "malaise" as had sent "an early warning signal in German history on earlier occasions," Johnson could not risk a failed meeting. Once again casting himself as Bonn's psychoanalyst, Ball faulted West Germans for chronically "feeling sorry for themselves." This German penchant for self-pity produced "neuroses" that were "catastrophic for all of us. . . . A neurotic disaffected Germany could be like a loose ship's cannon in a high sea." Others, including Francis Bator at the NSC and Ambassador McGhee in Bonn, argued that LBJ could use reason with Erhard regarding the MLF/ANF proposal. McGhee told Rusk: "Germany stands little hope" of joining a NATO nuclear force and "no hope at all" of acquiring its own nuclear arsenal. Any effort to pro-duce its own weapons would force Washington to "withdraw" from Europe, cause other NATO allies to "disassociate themselves" from Bonn, and prompt a "preemptive attack" from Moscow. Amplifying McGhee's observations, Bator counseled Johnson that it would be better to compromise on the offset issue and take the more worthwhile risk of pressing Bonn to forgo nuclear hardware. Then Washington could truly test Moscow's intentions regarding a nonproliferation treaty. Johnson, however, also had to deal with an increas-ingly fractious Congress, which passed a nonbinding resolution calling for cuts in U.S. forces in Europe. Behind this resolution lay the "emotional posi-tion" that "fat and lazy" Europeans sought to "enjoy their prosperity [under] the protection of an American nuclear shield." There seemed no way to save the summit with Erhard. The Senate would never approve a NATO nuclear force agreement that gave Bonn direct access to nuclear weapons, and it demanded some solution to the dollar drain of U.S. military commitments in Germany, especially in light of Bonn's new economic prowess. Johnson gave Erhard nothing to take back to Germany, and the chancellor's government soon collapsed, charged with being Washington's "whipping boy." The episode underlined LBJ's basic disinterest in Europe by the middle of his presidency. As one French official observed, "Vietnam became Johnson's almost exclusive preoccupation. What he wanted from Europe was not to have to think about it."[38]

Not wanting a deeper crisis with Bonn, Johnson rejected the working group's language at a weekend meeting at Camp David. Summing up his position, LBJ said, "I'm not going to get into the details of drafting, but there are two principles here. One, there can't be any transfer of nuclear weapons. The statutes forbid it. American public opinion forbids it. It's just impossible to even contemplate. The second is, I'm not going to eliminate the possibility of an Atlantic solution — of an alliance solution. I don't want one now and we may not want one in the future but that possibility has to be preserved because it may be necessary to keep the Germans locked in for many reasons." Moyers tried to persuade the president that the working group language would allow the United States to transfer ownership of delivery systems to NATO allies as long as Washington maintained control of the warheads. The Soviets would probably gripe if the United States went forward with such an arrangement, but they might accept it if a treaty already existed, because a collective nuclear force organized in such a fashion would resemble bilateral nuclear-sharing policies already in place. Johnson remained unconvinced and officially rejected the working group language when he met with Gromyko on October 10.[39]

Despite this setback, Gromyko and Rusk instructed their representatives to continue meeting until they produced language acceptable to both countries. Rusk assured Moscow that "a U.S. nuclear weapon" would never be "fired by a German soldier on order of a German government . . . without U.S. consent." To preclude press leaks that might inflame German nationalism following the collapse of Erhard's government, the talks continued ad referendum — they could be disavowed if the need arose. Through October and November 1966, the superpowers sparred over definitions and semantics. The United States concentrated on banning transfers to individual state control, while the Soviet Union demanded an explicit prohibition on transfers to collective entities. At times, both sides vented frustration and expressed fear that the talks would collapse.[40]

"A Versailles of Cosmic Proportions"

Before another opportunity faded, events in Germany helped the superpowers reach agreement on the first two treaty articles. After Erhard's government fell, a new Grand Coalition, including both Christian Democrats and Social Democrats, took power. Following an initial atmosphere of crisis, this new government decided not to insist on either reunification or a hardware solution prior to signing a nonproliferation treaty. With fears of German extremism abating, Washington agreed to accept Soviet treaty language that barred nuclear weapon transfers "directly or indirectly" and forbade relinquishing control "to any recipient whatsoever." The United States still insisted that it would not be bound by the working group language until after it had completed NATO consultations. Foster believed that winning allied concurrence would be relatively easy and that a joint U.S.-Soviet text could greet delegates to the next ENDC session beginning on February 21, 1967.[41]

But the ACDA director proved to be too optimistic. The new German government may have privately forsaken a hardware solution, but it regarded a public commitment to the Soviets as very different from a confidential understanding with its allies. The Germans still worried that the Johnson administration would brush their interests aside to achieve détente and that the nonproliferation treaty would duplicate their experience with the LTBT, which froze them out of the drafting process and left them without input into the final text. While the coalition government approved the draft text in principle in January 1967, rumors about the still-secret text heightened anxieties that Washington had betrayed West Germany by negotiating the treaty behind its back. A split emerged within the new coalition. Foreign Minister and Vice Chancellor Willy Brandt, a Social Democrat, favored a nonproliferation treaty over a collective nuclear force, believing that such a policy would improve Bonn's relations with its Eastern European neighbors. Brandt also told U.S. reporters that he did not want "to act like a girl who constantly has to be reassured by her boyfriend that he still loves her." The Christian Democratic faction within the government, led by Chancellor Kurt Georg Kiesinger and Finance Minister Franz Josef Strauss (both members of the party's Gaullist wing), conversely attacked the treaty, accusing Washington of "atomic complicity" with Moscow and labeling the accord "a Versailles of cosmic proportions."[42]

Yet the United States and West Germany both resisted a full public airing of their differences. After John McCloy asked him if he wished to abandon NATO for a closer relationship with France, Kiesinger contended that he had never meant to suggest that Washington had "any ill purpose in relation to

Germany in seeking a non-proliferation agreement." Johnson cultivated Kiesinger's support for the draft text, expressing sympathy over the stormy political climate in Germany. Upon Ambassador McGhee's advice, the president invited Kiesinger to Washington to discuss the nonproliferation treaty and other divisive issues. U.S. policymakers assured the Germans that the new treaty language would not prevent a United Europe from inheriting French and British nuclear weapons and would not prevent a NATO nuclear force so long as Washington retained ownership and control of the warheads. Bonn, however, doubted that the Soviets would accept these interpretations.[43]

To calm German fears, the Johnson administration submitted to the Soviets a list of nonproliferation treaty interpretations. The document stated that the prohibition on transfer would not affect the dual key nuclear-sharing arrangements that the United States had with its allies, a federated European states' right of succession to nuclear weapon–state status, and the transfer of ownership of nuclear-delivery vehicles. Moscow initially resisted, then expressed willingness to accept the U.S. reading as a private communication, refusing, however, to accept Washington's insistence that these interpretations be made public during Senate hearings on the treaty. The two superpowers, after months of wrangling, decided that they would agree to disagree. Washington would not ask for any Soviet comment on its version, either public or private, and Moscow would not issue a disclaimer when these readings became public during the ratification debates.[44]

With the text of the first two articles settled, the Johnson administration wanted to submit a complete treaty at the next ENDC session. But U.S. disagreements with the Soviets and with U.S. allies blocked early conclusion of the nonproliferation talks. Both the Soviet Union and the United States sought safeguards that gave the IAEA responsibility for ensuring that nonnuclear states did not use their peaceful uses programs for clandestine military purposes. The United States had to tread carefully in this area, however, because Western Europeans refused to place their own peaceful atomic facilities under IAEA inspection. The treaty exempted nuclear weapons states from any international inspection, which meant that France's peaceful uses would not be subject to IAEA supervision even if it chose to sign the treaty. The other members of EURATOM feared that such discriminatory arrangements would endanger the European integration movement. They argued that EURATOM safeguards offered sufficient protection against diversion of nuclear materials. The Soviet Union accurately labeled such arrangements "self-inspection" and refused to accept them.[45]

U.S. efforts to forge a compromise under which EURATOM countries accepted IAEA safeguards "as soon as practicable" collapsed. The Johnson administration then decided to delay the decision on safeguards and submit to the ENDC a partial draft treaty with a blank safeguards article. But the Soviets resisted unveiling the joint text until all articles had been completed. In June 1967, Johnson hoped to break the logjam and open the way for strategic arms reduction talks during a meeting with Kosygin in Glassboro, New Jersey. The CIA assured LBJ that, unlike his more colorful predecessor, Kosygin "will certainly keep his shoes on his feet." The Soviet premier, however, seemed preoccupied with the Middle East—Israel had just conquered large chunks of territory from Moscow's Arab clients. The president complained that "each time I mentioned missiles, Kosygin talked about Arabs and Israelis." The Soviets, on the other hand, believed LBJ's grasp of arms control poor and his performance at the summit "clumsy." In the end, Kosygin agreed to study the possibility of presenting a partial treaty at the ENDC and issued a routine public statement endorsing a nonproliferation agreement.[46]

Despite the disappointing results for nonproliferation, the summit did signal a growing, shared appreciation of the U.S.-Soviet need to cooperate in areas where security interests overlapped. One incident clearly illustrated this new understanding. McNamara, noting the ignorance about nuclear weapons that seemed pervasive in other countries, cited a film of a Chinese nuclear test in which troops charged into the area in the immediate wake of the explosion and described "how the crowd celebrated in some sort of orgiastic ritual way." The Soviets did not dispute this characterization of the Chinese and noted that Russians had much stronger reasons to fear Beijing's nuclear irresponsibility because of their geographic proximity. Johnson simplistically concluded that "Kosygin had an obsession about China, he was scared to death." But U.S.-Soviet Sinophobia did not revive efforts for "parallel action" against Chinese nuclear facilities. The summit ultimately convinced American participants that the Soviets "want a non-proliferation treaty if they can get one." The Soviets did eventually agree to introduce two identical, but separate, partial draft treaties to the ENDC on August 24, 1967. While the nonaligned powers acquainted themselves with the articles already drafted, the two superpowers sought compromise on a safeguards article.[47]

U.S.-Soviet Cooperation

The public unveiling of the draft treaty elicited an avalanche of public comment and proposals for amendment. Articles I and II composed the operative sections of the treaty. In the first article, nuclear states pledged "not to transfer

to any recipient whatsoever nuclear weapons or other nuclear explosive devices or control over such weapons or explosive devices directly or indirectly;
and not in any way assist, encourage, or induce any non–nuclear-weapon
State to manufacture or otherwise acquire nuclear weapons or other nuclear
explosive devices, or control over such weapons or explosive devices." The
second article essentially repeated the language of the first, with non–nuclear
weapons states pledging not to accept nuclear weapons from any "transferor."
As long as the treaty language remained secret, the Western Europeans had
refrained from making public statements, communicating their objections to
Washington privately. Because the United States had failed to address many
of their concerns in the draft treaty, the Europeans turned to the ENDC to
force the changes they desired.[48]

The two superpowers had anticipated many of the objections that arose
during the ENDC discussions. The treaty banned the MLF and prevented
European access to nuclear weapons short of complete political unification of
Europe, at which time the new entity would inherit French or British nuclear
weapons. While France dismissed this agreement "to castrate the impotent,"
Italy and Germany proved to be even more troublesome. Italian diplomats
complained that Washington had left "the best friends of the United States
. . . out on a limb" and still sought to "punish the Axis powers (Germany,
Italy, and Japan) by keeping them from having nuclear weapons, while the
wartime allied powers (the United States, Great Britain, the Soviet Union,
and France) had them." Kiesinger told John McCloy that "the agreement"
seemed "directed primarily against Germany," and even Brandt, who otherwise supported the accord, objected to Bonn's placement "on par with Upper
Volta." Rome and Bonn further balked at the treaty's indefinite duration, arguing that a finite period of twenty years would enable countries to reconsider
their treaty obligations if major shifts in the international balance of power
occurred. To mute the pact's economic effects, they demanded a pledge from
nuclear states to share any technological spin-offs from their military nuclear
programs. As some in Washington had anticipated, PNEs for projects such as
natural gas excavation, canal building, and river diversion emerged among
the specific nonmilitary applications that intrigued both Western and nonaligned non-nuclear countries. The Indian representative to the ENDC, V. M.
Trivedi, underlined these concerns, claiming that "the civil nuclear powers
can tolerate a nuclear weapons apartheid but not an atomic apartheid in their
economic and peaceful development."[49]

Calls for reciprocal sacrifice struck at the heart of the nonproliferation debate. Romania's leader, Nicolae Ceaușescu, blasted the treaty as "even worse

and more dangerous than the 1939 Stalin-Hitler pact" because it "leads to the perpetuation of the atomic monopoly in both the military and political field." All non-nuclear countries—nonaligned and aligned—urged the nuclear powers to pledge substantial progress in disarmament before other countries would agree to forsake the nuclear option. India and Sweden both asked Moscow and Washington to conclude a comprehensive test ban treaty and begin negotiations on reducing their strategic arsenals as signs of good faith. The United States wanted to placate the non-nuclear nations but refused to commit itself to ending underground testing. The Joint Chiefs of Staff, the AEC, and the JCAE remained solidly opposed to a comprehensive test ban. Even without this dedicated domestic opposition, Johnson seemed unlikely to end underground testing, having dismissed the partial test ban treaty's worth as a nonproliferation measure. The Soviets and the Americans, therefore, relegated the nuclear powers' commitments to seek an end to nuclear testing and the nuclear arms race to vague language in the treaty's preamble and a brief passage buried in the middle of the agreement.[50]

The problem of security assurances proved equally complicated. Since the first Chinese nuclear explosion, the United States had displayed willingness to issue positive security assurances, pledging aid to states facing nuclear threats and blackmail. Nonaligned countries also sought promises that nuclear powers would not use nuclear threats and intimidation against them. The United States had consistently resisted such negative security assurances because the Joint Chiefs of Staff reflexively repudiated anything that constrained their ability to use nuclear weapons. Others feared that positive security assurances might drag the United States into numerous international conflicts that did not directly threaten its interests. Having long advocated "ban the bomb" propositions, the Soviets had had little problem with security assurances in earlier versions of the nonproliferation treaty. In the compromise text, both superpowers had agreed to drop all language on the issue. This omission created problems with India and other nonaligned powers that viewed security assurances as the strongest incentives to sign the treaty. Without freedom from nuclear blackmail, the non-nuclear powers would forgo a class of weapons that the nuclear powers could use with impunity for coercive purposes. One Indian official went so far as to suggest that a U.S.-Soviet pledge not to threaten or attack non-nuclear powers could function as a substitute for the nonproliferation treaty. But Rusk dismissed the call for security assurances as compromising U.S. interests, because he "would not care to have a nuclear war with the USSR just to have the Indians sign a nonproliferation treaty."[51]

The developing world's discontent with the treaty mounted. Along with seeking security assurances and expressing concerns that signing a nonproliferation treaty might hinder countries' access to civilian spin-off technology, nonaligned countries believed that the nuclear countries should commit themselves to using money freed from military spending because of arms control and disarmament to aid the economic development of non-nuclear countries. To press their concerns on Washington and Moscow, the non-nuclear states planned to meet on their own in March or April 1968. Should they forge a set of minimum conditions for signing a nonproliferation agreement, they might persuade the United States and the Soviet Union to revise the treaty. The two superpowers now learned that years of delay had come at a high price. Their control over their alliance partners had declined, and they could no longer shape the UN General Assembly debate to conform to their goals and policies. If Moscow and Washington failed to produce a complete nonproliferation text before the non-nuclear states convened their conference, the chance to conclude a nonproliferation treaty acceptable to both nuclear and non-nuclear nations might evaporate.[52]

A window of opportunity opened when the non-nuclear states agreed to postpone their conference until August 1968. Having gained a brief reprieve, the superpowers worked to resolve their remaining differences and construct new language that met some of the non-nuclear states' demands. The Soviets proved receptive to security assurances, and the United States displayed greater openness to other powers' calls for review conferences, limits on the treaty's duration, and requests to mute the discriminatory nature of the safeguards article. Neither superpower, however, would move beyond vague promises regarding future disarmament measures.[53]

The superpowers had clear restrictions on how much they would concede. The Soviets claimed to be willing to meet "the legitimate interests of the non-nuclear powers" but would not "pay a high price for a treaty" because halting proliferation would benefit everyone. This attitude emerged most clearly when the Johnson administration suggested placing U.S. peaceful nuclear facilities under IAEA safeguards as a gesture of goodwill. The Soviets flatly rejected the idea, scoffing that a nonproliferation agreement would be discriminatory by definition and that the non-nuclear powers should reconcile themselves to that fact. Rather than moving forward despite Soviet opposition, the United States held in reserve the offer to open its peaceful facilities to inspection in case the negotiations with both the Soviet and the EURATOM countries became deadlocked. Resistance from the European powers toward IAEA safeguards nonetheless proved overwhelming. They still feared that France's refusal to sign the treaty would exempt Paris from any safeguard arrangements and that IAEA inspection would facilitate industrial espionage by both Washington and Moscow. EURATOM nations tried unsuccessfully to craft alternative language for the safeguards article. On December 2, 1967, despite continued Soviet refusal to reciprocate, President Johnson and British prime minister Wilson announced that they would place all their peaceful uses facilities under IAEA safeguards. The pledge drew praise from West Germany and Italy, both of which soon accepted the most recent U.S. safeguards language to break the stalemate. The administration then commenced wooing the Soviets. On January 15, 1968, Foster told his Soviet counterpart that the new language that allowed the EURATOM countries to negotiate a multilateral safeguards agreement with the IAEA was the best the United States could offer. Moscow reluctantly agreed to the new language, and a complete joint text soon fell into place.[54]

Washington eventually won other important Soviet concessions. Moscow had initially met demands to limit the treaty's duration by sarcastically proposing a term of one thousand years. As a sense of urgency infused the talks in late 1967, the Soviets relented and accepted the U.S. amendment calling for a twenty-five-year duration clause. After that period, a meeting of signatories would debate whether to renew the treaty for another fixed period or indefinitely. Moscow also accepted Britain's proposal to hold a review conference to assess compliance five years after the treaty's ratification. The United States additionally persuaded the Soviets to delete from the text any mention of either positive or negative security assurances, instead substituting a proposed UN Security Council resolution that pledged support for non-nuclear states threatened by nuclear powers and barred nuclear threats and blackmail. After the UN General Assembly had passed a Soviet-sponsored resolution appealing to the ENDC to conclude a treaty banning the use of nuclear weapons, the Johnson administration understood that some type of negative security assurances would be needed to win nonaligned acceptance of the nonproliferation treaty. The United States also made concessions, including revision of amendment procedures so that any alterations to the original text would apply only to those countries that ratified the amendments. In response to both Western and nonaligned demands, the new treaty now included language that promised to share peaceful technology with non-nuclear powers on a nondiscriminatory basis.[55]

Facing Critics

On January 18, 1968, Washington and Moscow finished their draft treaty. But when they presented their new text to the ENDC, it met immediate criticism. German chancellor Kiesinger, who reportedly never abandoned his earlier belief that the treaty was "part of a superpower conspiracy to split and denuclearize Germany forever," pronounced the treaty "unacceptable." Some in the State Department feared that Washington might face "a choice between the NPT and keeping Germany as an ally." The eight nonaligned members of the ENDC immediately called for revisions to the text, including a series of five-year review conferences, a provision allowing non-nuclear powers to develop peaceful nuclear explosives, diversion of savings stemming from disarmament to economic development projects in non-nuclear states, and stronger language on superpower disarmament. In response, Moscow and Washington introduced a new revised treaty on March 11, 1968, which allowed for a series of five-year review conferences if a majority of the signatories requested them and strengthened some language in the preamble and the disarmament article. These changes failed to mute opposition, and the ENDC recessed on March 14 with eleven countries refusing to endorse the joint U.S.-Soviet treaty.[56]

The Johnson administration worked to quell the opposition. U.S. officials contemplated various measures to make the treaty more attractive and did not rule out coercive measures. Although no evidence exists that the administration accepted his advice, James Ramey, an AEC member, suggested making development aid to India conditional on its signature of the NPT. In 1966, the Johnson administration had used economic coercion to force New Delhi to devalue its currency—an act that one Indian official claimed "had castrated India." A repeat effort would likely have failed and deeply damaged U.S.-Indian relations. Others contemplated a nuclear-sharing scheme whereby Washington would earmark tactical nuclear weapons for India if China threatened an attack, but LBJ rejected that option. The administration also tried to ensure Israeli signature of the treaty as part of a quid pro quo that allowed Tel Aviv to purchase F-4 fighter planes. Israel, however, resisted, arguing that it had not been consulted on the treaty text and needed time to assess the impact on its security. Rusk and the new defense secretary, Clark Clifford, also hoped to ease Bonn's resistance by changing U.S.-German nuclear-sharing arrangements to give Bonn a veto over nuclear weapons' use by German troops.[57] Johnson approved this suggestion, with little effect on German attitudes.

Washington also worked to mute agitation for security assurances and nuclear disarmament. Johnson cajoled Kosygin by hinting that announcement of strategic arms limitation talks might convince many non-nuclear states that the superpowers took the disarmament pledge in the treaty seriously. The Soviets did not respond quickly enough to affect the UN nonproliferation debate. Despite the Joint Chiefs' strong objections, the Johnson administration also contemplated a limited no-first-use statement as part of its Security Council resolution on security assurances for non-nuclear powers. The two superpowers could not agree on how to phrase the no-first-use provision, and they dropped it from the final text. Johnson also rejected the advice from subordinates who wanted UN ambassador Arthur Goldberg to make a verbal non-first-use pledge in the General Assembly debate. None of Goldberg's statements went beyond reaffirming U.S. intentions to fulfill its collective security obligations under the UN charter if a non-nuclear power came under threat of nuclear attack.[58]

When the General Assembly debate began on April 24, Moscow and Washington still hoped to have the treaty ready for signature by early summer, before the Conference of Non–Nuclear-Weapon States convened. Johnson also hoped to have a ratified treaty in hand before the presidential election campaign entered its final months. On March 31, LBJ had withdrawn from the presidential race because his tremendously unpopular Vietnam War policies had made it nearly impossible for him to win. As a lame duck president, he would have little influence in Congress if the treaty became a partisan issue. Yet, because the United States wanted as many states as possible to sign the treaty, it would not rush the joint U.S.-Soviet draft through the General Assembly, as the Soviets urged. The Johnson administration instead allowed treaty critics to have their say and then tried to counter their objections.[59]

Feeling pressed for time, both the United States and the Soviet Union discouraged substantive amendments to the treaty text during the General Assembly debate. On May 1, the two countries introduced a UN resolution endorsing the existing draft, but they lacked support from nonaligned countries. No Latin American countries and only two sub-Saharan African states co-sponsored the resolution. Brazil became one of the treaty's most vocal critics, lambasting the U.S.-Soviet draft for not obligating the superpowers to reduce their nuclear arsenals. As debate continued, other states, including Sweden, Japan, Pakistan, India, and South Africa—all of whom the United States believed could soon manufacture nuclear weapons—criticized the treaty and called for changes before the superpowers opened it for signature.

To many, it seemed as if the dominant white nations sought a treaty to deny nuclear weapons to "the developing, mostly dark-skinned world." The U.S. and Soviet General Assembly delegates worked diligently to persuade South Africa, Pakistan, Japan, and Sweden to vote for the General Assembly resolution. Important countries, such as Argentina, Brazil, France, and India, abstained during the final vote. (De Gaulle dismissively compared nonproliferation efforts to a failed ban on crossbows during the Middle Ages, while other French officials disingenuously claimed that the only solution to proliferation was abolition of all nuclear weapons.) Despite such discontent among near-nuclear powers, the two superpowers still wielded enough influence in the General Assembly to earn UN endorsement of their treaty text, with a final vote of 93 in favor, 4 opposed, and 21 abstaining. Walt Rostow found the UN nonproliferation debate "fascinating, in its way, because it shows how intimately the U.S. and the USSR can work when they have isolated an issue in which both countries feel they have a substantial national interest."[60]

But the ability of Moscow and Washington to cooperate meant much less in 1968 than it would have meant earlier. That year has come to symbolize international and domestic challenges to elite hegemony in both the Western and the Soviet alliance systems. The "Third World" contested the United States in the ENDC and on the battlefields of Vietnam. Prague Spring signaled discontent in the communist world, while students rose up in nearly every continent and major country. Many of these young protesters carried banners evoking the images and slogans of Third World leaders. Though local causes cannot be dismissed, the commonalities of transnational dissidence produced crises of legitimacy that taxed both superpowers. The consequences of fractured hegemony became concrete in Saigon, Hue, Prague, Mexico City, Chicago, and Paris.

Amid these extraordinary events, passage of the General Assembly resolution signaled the next phase of nonproliferation negotiations. Many countries voting for the resolution did so aware that it had no bearing on whether they would sign the treaty. Moscow and Washington needed to keep pressure on the near-nuclears to ensure that they would sign and ratify the treaty. The Cold War rivals cooperated to pass a Security Council resolution separate from the treaty that provided positive security assurances to non-nuclear powers. Despite success in the Security Council debate, abstentions by Brazil, India, and Pakistan indicated that non-nuclear states wanted stronger commitments from the nuclear states that they would not be subjected to nuclear blackmail and could count on superpower support if threatened by another nuclear power, such as China. If the United States wanted Asian non-nuclears to sign the treaty, noted Rostow, it could not "pull out of the Far East and go isolationist. It is ironic that some of those who support the non-proliferation treaty most strongly are also for our pulling out of Vietnam." Only if the United States held the line in Southeast Asia would Japan, Korea, Thailand, and Australia ratify the nonproliferation treaty.[61]

Solidifying European support also worried the Johnson administration. Vice President Hubert Humphrey warned that Europeans "resent U.S. power. Détente is what they want." But it soon became clear that they wanted it on their own terms. At the NATO ministerial meeting in June, some delegations worried that the nonproliferation treaty might impair their security if it outlasted NATO defense arrangements. Although on one level European leaders favored reduced tensions between the two blocs, they also feared that amicable U.S.-Soviet relations would endanger the Western alliance system. Détente, moreover, might encourage "isolationist" tendencies in Congress and prompt large American troop reductions. In order to ease European anxiety, Johnson planned to reaffirm the U.S. commitment to NATO at the time he signed the treaty. U.S. attention, as usual, focused on Germany. Whether Bonn would sign the treaty remained an open question throughout summer 1968, in part because mainstream German politicians believed that a hasty signature might embolden the National Democratic Party, an ultranationalist faction that had made significant electoral gains in 1966 and 1968. After Moscow issued a blistering critique of West Germany's foot-dragging on nonproliferation, Washington urged the Soviets to refrain from public statements that might anger the Germans and delay their ratification. The *New York Times* editorialized that "if there is one government on earth that cannot abstain from the treaty, it is the West German government." Kiesinger, however, vowed to withhold a final German position on the treaty until after the Conference of Non–Nuclear-Weapon States in August.[62]

Pyrrhic Victory

Despite failing to win over non-nuclear powers, the United States and the Soviet Union rushed the Nuclear Nonproliferation Treaty to signature on July 1, 1968. In the East Room of the White House, LBJ signed the treaty in front of a crowd that included Rusk, members of Congress, and dignitaries from fifty-five countries. He declared the treaty "the most important international agreement since the beginning of the nuclear age." Sixty-two nations joined Washington and Moscow in giving preliminary approval to the NPT, but few NATO countries and none of the crucial non-nuclears appeared among the initial signatories. Johnson nonetheless remained optimistic.

Although some disarmament advocates viewed the treaty as doing little to slow the arms race, the domestic reaction proved overwhelmingly positive, with 81 percent of the American public in favor and numerous senators and representatives praising it. Johnson transmitted the treaty to the Senate on July 9, expecting quick ratification. Still, one journalist contrasted the muted public reception of the new agreement with the more exuberant reaction to the Limited Test Ban Treaty, an odd response "since the NPT is an infinitely more important measure of disarmament." The *Bulletin of the Atomic Scientists* mirrored this optimism. It had set the Doomsday Clock at seven minutes to midnight earlier in 1968 because of Chinese proliferation and the Arab-Israeli conflict. But when enough countries ratified the NPT in 1969, the editors moved the hands back to ten minutes to midnight.[63]

The need to demonstrate superpower sympathy toward non-nuclear concerns cast a long shadow over the treaty. LBJ believed that many non-nuclears would sign the NPT if the superpowers displayed a firm commitment to nuclear disarmament. He therefore invested substantial energy in scheduling a summit conference with Kosygin at which they would launch negotiations to limit the growth of their nuclear arsenals (a proposal that contained the germ of what became the strategic arms limitation talks [SALT]). On August 20, 1968, Johnson's plans unraveled when the Soviets and their Warsaw Pact allies invaded Czechoslovakia to ensure its loyalty to the communist bloc. Washington immediately withheld announcement of the summit conference, scheduled for the next day. Some circumstantial evidence suggests that Moscow purposely combined efforts to build goodwill in Washington — including the NPT and arms control initiatives — with its preparations to invade Czechoslovakia. Although LBJ remained quiet, Dean Rusk complained to Dobrynin that the Soviet invasion on the eve of the summit announcement "was like throwing a dead fish in the face of the President of the United States." Still, the general inclination of both Rusk and Johnson was "to act as if nothing [had] happened," and their outward demeanor in a meeting with Dobrynin seemed relaxed, with LBJ talking about a recent haircut, congressional drinking habits, and Texas history as all three men sipped cocktails. Rostow warned, however, that although "Czechoslovakia is surely in the Soviet sphere ... that fact hardly justifies murder in broad daylight." Congress concurred, and the NPT and SALT fell victim to postinvasion qualms about détente.[64]

Johnson now had nothing to offer the non-nuclears to prove his willingness to control the arms race, for he had killed all other initiatives besides the NPT and SALT. In July, he had stalled the comprehensive test ban talks, telling subordinates: "Be sure the talks get nowhere." In April, Vice President Humphrey had signed Protocol II of the Latin American denuclearization treaty, which committed the United States to abstain from threatening nuclear attacks against the agreement's signatories. Latin American nations had included two protocols in the treaty. Protocol I asked nuclear states to respect the denuclearization of the region by not transporting or basing nuclear weapons in the area. Protocol II required nuclear states to refrain from encouraging proliferation or from threatening nuclear attacks against Latin American nations. Although the United States favored a Latin American nuclear-free zone, it refused to sign Protocol I in order to preserve its right to transport nuclear weapons through the Panama Canal and to place atomic armaments in Puerto Rico. Unable to get a firm commitment from Latin American countries to respect these qualifications, the Johnson administration delayed submitting Protocol II to the Senate for ratification. When the Conference of Non–Nuclear-Weapon States convened on August 29, neither Moscow nor Washington could demonstrate any recent progress on controlling their bilateral nuclear arms race. The conference's final report ultimately supported the goal of nonproliferation but called for further action by the nuclear powers to correct the imbalances in the treaty. Because neither superpower relished a powerful new forum on nuclear issues, they maneuvered the UN General Assembly vote to make sure the first conference for non-nuclear nations was the last.[65]

Other problems plagued the NPT. The Soviet invasion soured Western European and other U.S. allies' attitudes toward the treaty. Both Italy and Germany reassessed their positions and did not sign in 1968. Although most NATO countries favored the NPT, they did not want to appear too conciliatory toward Moscow following the Czech crisis. Treaty opponents in West Germany welcomed the Soviet invasion as an excuse to delay and eventually scuttle Bonn's agreement to the NPT. Other U.S. allies also proved unwilling to change their stance. In October, Johnson again tried to tie the sale of F-4 fighter planes to Israel's endorsement of the nonproliferation agreement. Tel Aviv bristled at such a quid pro quo and used its influence with Congress to force Johnson to sell Israel the F-4s without signing the NPT. This episode brought to an end a pattern established during the Kennedy years whereby Washington attempted to persuade Tel Aviv to retreat from the nuclear threshold via increased access to advanced conventional weaponry. Hawk surface-to-air missiles, tanks, fighter-bombers, and the F-4s flowed into the

Israeli arsenal in an attempt to assuage security worries and blunt Israel's nuclear ambitions. The strategy failed and actually increased instability in the Middle East by fueling an arms race among regional powers.[66]

American electoral politics may have emboldened allies to resist the Johnson administration's blandishments. Republican presidential nominee Richard M. Nixon had voiced sympathy toward European nuclear ambitions just the year before. On September 11, 1968, Nixon undercut Johnson's non-proliferation efforts when he urged the Senate to postpone treaty ratification until the Czech invasion could be fully assessed. Although the Senate Foreign Relations Committee respected the president's call for early ratification and issued a favorable report on the NPT in late September, the full Senate voted on October 11 to postpone action on the treaty. Johnson did not abandon hope of ratifying the accord before leaving office. He contemplated calling Congress into special session after the election, having received private assurances of Nixon's support for such a move as long as it occurred after the election. But the Senate leaders proved highly resistant and Nixon reneged on his previous promises.[67]

As they prepared to leave office, many Johnson administration officials believed the NPT all but dead. The treaty remained far short of the forty-three ratifications needed to bring it into force. The CIA warned that "the NPT has become so integrally tied to other international issues that to bring it into effect at an early date will be difficult under the best of circumstances." The ACDA agreed and warned that any delay by the new administration could deal U.S. nonproliferation efforts "a serious if not fatal blow." Some administration officials, including Rostow, feared that Nixon and his designated national security adviser, Henry Kissinger, "may let the NPT die" because they failed to "understand the dangers of small nuclear possession" and favored "loose European arrangements." German conservatives, by contrast, hoped that the Republican victory would doom the NPT and revive chances for direct West German access to nuclear weapons.[68]

After his inauguration, Nixon calmed the anxiety of many nonproliferation advocates. After a brief period of deliberation, he decided to submit the treaty for Senate advice and consent on February 5, 1969. After another favorable Foreign Relations Committee vote, the full Senate approved the treaty on March 13, 1969, with 83 votes in favor and only 15 against. Opposition primarily came from nuclear nationalists, who objected to IAEA inspection of U.S. facilities. Nixon held off signing the instruments of ratification until the Soviets had also given final approval to the treaty. The sticking point for

Moscow remained West German agreement. The Social Democratic victory in 1969, and Italy's signature of the NPT in February, transformed Bonn's attitude. When West Germany communicated its intention to sign the treaty by November 28, 1969, it cleared the way for the two superpowers to sign the instruments of ratification on November 24. They waited to deposit those documents, however, until the other requirements for the treaty's enforcement had been met. On March 5, 1970, nearly eight years after President Kennedy had made a nonproliferation treaty a top priority, both superpowers took the last legal steps to bring the treaty into effect.

Any feelings of elation among nonproliferation treaty proponents would have been tempered had they discovered that Rostow had accurately assessed Nixon and Kissinger. The new president and his national security adviser held a dim view of the treaty and took no action to persuade other powers to sign it. Disavowing the treaty would have hurt American standing among disarmament advocates and the non-nuclear nations, so Nixon and Kissinger decided to ratify the treaty and then do nothing to make it effective. One Kissinger aide noted that "Henry believed that it was good to spread nuclear weapons around the world" and that Israel and Japan would be better off with nuclear weapons. Leaders in Tokyo disagreed. In 1967, Japanese prime minister Eisaku Sato announced three non-nuclear principles: His government would not possess, manufacture, or introduce nuclear weapons into its territory. In 1971, Japan's legislature unanimously passed a resolution endorsing these principles. In Israel's case, however, Kissinger got his wish. The Nixon administration learned in early 1969 that Tel Aviv could deploy nuclear weapons in a matter of weeks or days. After several months of internal debate, in September 1969 Nixon brokered a deal with Israeli prime minister Golda Meier whereby her government would not test weapons or publicly declare its status as a nuclear power. In exchange, Washington would not press Israel to sign the NPT or abandon its nuclear arsenal. Even before the NPT went into effect, Nixon had opened the United States to charges of hypocrisy and a blatant double standard.[69]

With the advent of the Nixon administration, the long struggle for a nuclear nonproliferation agreement had culminated in a Pyrrhic victory. Although the administration was publicly committed to refrain from aiding any country whatsoever in manufacturing nuclear weapons, the private attitudes of Nixon policymakers evoked the president's earlier stint in Washington during the Eisenhower administration when selective proliferation reigned as policy. The long delay in concluding the NPT had prevented the more sympathetic Kennedy and Johnson administrations from codifying enforcement procedures for the treaty before the next wave of nuclear-sharing advocates under Nixon took the helm.

But if LBJ lamented his lack of success in nonproliferation matters, he had himself to blame, along with his equally shortsighted Soviet counterparts. Johnson had inherited a strong U.S. commitment to nonproliferation from John F. Kennedy but had squandered the progress the ACDA had already achieved toward agreement. Had Johnson chosen more starkly between the MLF and the NPT, an agreement might have been negotiated as early as 1964 or 1965. The Soviet Union also bears responsibility for important near-nuclear states' rejection of the treaty. By not respecting non-nuclear states' security interests and attempting to force them to sign a discriminatory treaty, Moscow, like Washington, made it more attractive to flout the superpowers than to abstain from nuclear weapons. Both American and Soviet leaders wanted to impede proliferation during the 1960s, but neither desired an agreement enough to pay a high cost to achieve it—either by damaging their alliance relationships or by restricting their own right to produce and deploy nuclear weapons. Instead, the superpowers created a system of nuclear apartheid whereby the European states had access to nuclear weapons via Cold War alliance systems while newly decolonized nations had to abstain from nuclear weapons or risk the ire of Washington and Moscow.

The Legacy of Nuclear Apartheid

Herman Kahn's warning of 1960 that soon even a "Hottentot" would be able to produce nuclear bombs resonated in the decades following the NPT's signature. The treaty's passage seemed a harbinger of a safer world, one wherein the nuclear threat would be regulated and contained. Yet the terms of the accord left untouched incipient nuclear programs in numerous countries, including Israel, India, and South Africa, that anticipated using the threat of going nuclear as leverage in regional power struggles. Two recognized nuclear powers, France and the PRC, refused to sign the treaty and continued providing reactor fuel to non-nuclear nations without implementing international safeguards. U.S. presidents from the 1970s to the early twenty-first century faced the question of whether to coerce holdouts or initiate negotiations to remove the treaty's discriminatory features. New countries did sign the treaty, especially following the Soviet Union's collapse in 1991, but important exceptions remained, most notably Israel, India, and Pakistan. Other countries, such as North Korea and Iran, renounced or threatened to withdraw from the NPT. Despite lip service to the need to halt the spread of nuclear weapons, U.S. nonproliferation policy repeated the pattern of the pretreaty period, remaining selective in enforcement and more concerned with protecting superpower hegemony than with eradicating the deadly threat of indiscriminate nuclear dissemination.[1]

Realist Illusions

The spirit of the NPT dissipated almost immediately after Nixon's inauguration. Nixon and Kissinger refused to pressure Israel, West Germany, or Japan to sign the accord. Both Nixon and Kissinger viewed the treaty as a moralistic endeavor divorced from the reality of power politics. Nations that desired and could afford nuclear weapons would produce them, they assumed. They were not alone in this thinking. Within the State Department and the CIA, many analysts believed that the NPT alone would not and could not prevent proliferation. Even before the treaty opened for signature, the State Department Policy Planning Council predicted that "many nations will develop their peaceful programs to the point where a bomb can be assembled and detonated in short order." Such powers would thus "achieve an advanced state of nuclear 'pregnancy' while remaining within the strictures of the NPT." But Washington could do little more than it had already done to stem the nuclear tide, and State Department analysts saw a robust U.S. military presence around the globe as the best check against proliferation. The Ford presidency also embraced this conclusion. In 1975, a CIA analyst observed that the "Great Powers" could not halt proliferation, which "in its current stage, at least, is largely a political phenomenon and as such is strongly influenced by the growing atmosphere of confrontation between the developed and less-developed countries." The NPT had little effect because it had "become identified with superpower hegemony. And as long as [lesser-developed countries] interpret [it] as an instrument of such hegemony, they will not consider it as a binding international treaty." Washington confronted a world of nuclear powers in various stages of development. The best means to ensure the security of the United States and its allies lay not in treaties but in regional missile defense systems.[2]

It was in such an intellectual atmosphere that Kissinger and Nixon concluded that rather than pursue idealistic disarmament schemes, the United States should seek a favorable balance of power, both globally and regionally. Worldwide stability in a multipolar age could be maintained only if the five great economic powers in the world—the United States, Western Europe, Japan, the Soviet Union, and Communist China—operated as relative equals in global politics. If one or more of these states discerned that the international status quo discriminated against their national interests, war or grave instability could result.

Eisenhower's nuclear legacy loomed over the Nixon presidency. Ike had threatened nuclear strikes to cow China and North Korea in 1953. Nixon utilized the same strategy in 1969 by secretly placing all nuclear forces on alert to signal to Moscow and Hanoi that he might use "excessive force" to end the Vietnam War. This first test of Nixon's "Madman theory," in which he tried to persuade his adversaries that he would abandon rationality to get his way, failed. Neither the North Vietnamese nor the Soviets changed their stance on the conflict, and Moscow may not even have noticed the alert. Late in 1972, Nixon toyed with actually using nuclear weapons in Vietnam, but Kissinger insisted it "would just be too much." Still, these two episodes of nuclear brinksmanship, combined with their lack of attention to proliferation threats, reveal that Kissinger and Nixon viewed nuclear weapons as just one more item in a nation's strategic toolbox.[3]

Nixon and Kissinger's treatment of Japan underscored this pattern. Kissinger privately ridiculed the NPT's exclusion of Tokyo from the nuclear club. In 1969, the Nixon administration quietly assured the Japanese government that it would "understand" if Tokyo decided to go nuclear. Although Japan signed the NPT the next year, Kissinger never stopped believing that Tokyo eventually would produce nuclear weapons. Typical of his Realpolitik style, Kissinger envisioned a nuclear Japan as a check against future Chinese imperialist ambitions. The dangers of an Asian nuclear arms race seemed insignificant to Kissinger even after a Soviet diplomat floated the idea of a joint U.S.-Soviet strike against Chinese nuclear facilities during the Sino-Soviet border conflicts in 1969. Washington flatly refused and offered veiled threats if Moscow acted unilaterally; the Soviet leadership duo Alexei Kosygin and Leonid Brezhnev perhaps regretted the opportunity that had been lost when Khrushchev had spurned Kennedy's anti-Chinese feelers in 1963. Yet, despite Kissinger's fear that Moscow and Beijing might exchange nuclear fire in 1969, his disdain for the NPT remained unshaken.

This dismissive attitude also marked the U.S. response to Israeli and South African nuclear efforts. Kissinger and Nixon tacitly condoned Israel's nuclear program, giving Tel Aviv their full blessing and lying to Congress to preserve Israel's non-nuclear facade. They did, however, stop short of providing direct nuclear aid. The president and his national security adviser learned the costs of this policy during the Yom Kippur War in 1973, when Israel threatened to use nuclear bombs unless Washington furnished it with advanced conventional weapons to repel an Arab offensive.

In South Africa's case, the Nixon administration continued supplying peaceful nuclear aid, despite other powers' warnings that Pretoria harbored nuclear ambitions. In 1974, the United States expanded that aid, in spite of the fact that the South African government had admitted that it had acquired a nuclear weapons capability. Nixon and Kissinger viewed nuclear power production as a legitimate arena of Cold War conflict. If the United States refused to aid countries that harbored military ambitions, Moscow might gain an advantage in the international nuclear trade. The consequences of economic maneuvering divorced from proliferation considerations surfaced in 1977 when American and Soviet intelligence discovered a South African nuclear test site in the Kalahari Desert. Under pressure from Washington and Moscow, Pretoria dismantled the site but continued a program that produced six nuclear weapons by 1993.

The U.S. practice of publicly endorsing nonproliferation while aiding or winking at allied countries' nuclear programs persisted for the remainder of the Cold War. Two decisions near the end of the Nixon presidency set the tone. In June 1973, Kissinger informed French foreign minister Michel Jobert that the United States sought a covert program of U.S.-French nuclear cooperation. Kissinger made the offer despite language in the Atomic Energy Act specifically forbidding the provision of restricted data to any country other than Britain. Patching up Franco-American relations now took precedence over nonproliferation, not to mention the law. By plying Paris with covert aid, Washington succeeded in developing unofficial war plans that required French cooperation with NATO forces in any military conflict with the Soviet Union. This clandestine cooperation continued into the Ford, Carter, and Reagan administrations. Although President Jimmy Carter advocated greater U.S. efforts to stem nuclear dissemination, his administration actually expanded and intensified this illicit nuclear collaboration with the French. Amicable relations with France superseded the need for a consistent proliferation policy. In 1981, Ronald Reagan abandoned any pretense of making a priority of nonproliferation. His administration eagerly built on extant nuclear ties with Paris, finally legitimizing that relationship by drafting an executive order on U.S.-French nuclear cooperation in 1985.[4]

India provided another illustration of American inconstancy in proliferation matters. The Nixon administration viewed the South Asian subcontinent through the prism of its budding relationship with the PRC. Because Pakistan served as a secret go-between to China in 1971, Kissinger and Nixon decided to "tilt" toward Islamabad in its ongoing rivalry with New Delhi. When war erupted between Pakistan and India in 1971, New Delhi seemed poised to deal Islamabad a crushing defeat. In the hope of preventing the complete disintegration of the Muslim country, the Nixon administration moved the aircraft carrier USS *Enterprise* into the Bay of Bengal. The Indian government knew that all American warships could launch a nuclear assault and viewed Nixon's move as both insult and threat, especially given the nonaligned states' long-standing demand that the superpowers refrain from issuing nuclear threats in disputes with non-nuclear powers. Indian nuclear scientists had earlier complained that the Soviets "treated" them "like kings" then "lied" to them "as if we were children" during their visits to the USSR. Now the United States had brandished the implicit threat of its bombs to intervene in a regional conflict, laying bare the condescension that both Moscow and Washington directed toward New Delhi. Momentum within the Indian government quickened to acquire the bomb to protect against future nuclear gunboat diplomacy. This legacy of imperialism, past and future, provided justification for an Indian "peaceful nuclear explosion" (euphemistically code-named "Smiling Buddha") in June 1974. Pakistan rapidly concluded that without nuclear weapons it would be too vulnerable to future Indian attacks and initiated its own clandestine nuclear program in 1972.[5]

After New Delhi's nuclear test, Nixon and Kissinger's disregard for the NPT and nonproliferation stood exposed to the world. Congress blustered as the administration refused to punish India, notwithstanding its already chilly relations with Prime Minister Indira Gandhi's government. Although India's nuclear test raised great fears in Pakistan, Kissinger dismissed congressional calls for action. He made a legalistic claim that New Delhi had not violated any of its nuclear cooperation agreements with the United States by diverting nuclear materials or technology to military uses. The secretary of state's message to the world's near-nuclear nations could not have been starker: If the United States refused to punish an act with grave consequences for the security of one of *its* client states, Washington would surely look the other way if its peaceful uses partners evaded safeguards and developed their own nuclear weapons programs.

In the 1970s, several U.S. clients, including Taiwan, South Korea, Pakistan, and Iran, pushed forward with covert programs, concluding that they would face little, if any, opposition from Washington. Yet U.S. attitudes could change suddenly. Nixon had not taken a clear stance toward a Pakistani military nuclear program, but his successors Gerald Ford and Jimmy Carter pressed Islamabad to suspend its weapons research, especially given rumors of a nuclear alliance between Pakistan and Libya (feared because of the Arab nationalism and anti-Americanism of its leader, Muammar Gadhafi, and his sponsorship of terrorism). Pakistanis, however, resented and resisted such treatment, while U.S.-Indian nuclear cooperation went forward undisturbed. The Carter administration reassessed its approach and switched from coercion to seduction, hoping that generous conventional weapons sales would persuade Pakistan to forgo a nuclear option—a strategy that had failed when previous administrations had tried it with Israel. Even this inconsistent non-proliferation effort evaporated following the Soviet invasion of Afghanistan in 1979. Winning India and Pakistan to the U.S. cause became far more important to the Carter and Reagan administrations than did curbing regional arms races.

The transfer of reactor technology and reactor fuel became the one area wherein Washington made a pretense of curbing nuclear diffusion. Nixon and Kissinger envisioned America's dominance of the international nuclear trade as a check on nuclear programs that threatened U.S. interests. This "free market" approach did not work, however, because French, West German, Swedish, and numerous European multilateral corporations had eliminated the American advantage in peaceful technologies. If the United States refused to provide nuclear reactors, a rejected applicant could easily find a more willing seller. The Indian nuclear explosion of 1974 dealt a clear blow to a unilateral market strategy because Canadian firms had given New Delhi the peaceful technology that it later converted to military purposes. Any nonproliferation effort that used market mechanisms to advance nuclear containment would require the cooperation of all nuclear suppliers.

The need for a multilateral approach gained urgency after West Germany sold Brazil uranium enrichment facilities that could be adapted to either military or peaceful applications. Since the 1950s, the United States had participated in and helped organize meetings of the leading Western uranium suppliers. In light of the increasing proliferation threat, the Ford administration sought to formalize this arrangement through creation of the London Suppliers' Group. This organization included all the major nuclear exporters and worked to coordinate guidelines for technology and fuel transfers, with the goal of reducing negative effects from commercial competition on nonproliferation. The London Suppliers' Group crafted the strictest international safeguards for all nuclear trade agreements. Carter codified some of its recommendations in domestic law through the passage of the Nuclear Nonproliferation Act of 1978, which established rules for sale of peaceful uses technology and reactor fuel to other states.

Given the inconsistency of U.S. nonproliferation policy, the law's attempt to institute a technology control policy divorced from other nonproliferation approaches seemed destined to fail as the Carter administration layered on exception after exception until the policy ultimately collapsed. Few countries took U.S. nonproliferation goals seriously as Washington failed to levy sanctions against Israel, India, and South Korea. When Carter suspended nonproliferation efforts in South Asia after the Soviets invaded Afghanistan, the United States could hardly justify withholding nuclear aid to other near-nuclears, including Argentina, Brazil, and South Africa.

In 1981, the newly elected Ronald Reagan launched an intensified Cold War competition with Moscow and initially abandoned most American arms control goals. A member of the Committee on the Present Danger, which warned of Soviet nuclear superiority and called for an expanded nuclear arsenal, he abandoned even a rhetorical commitment to nonproliferation. He displayed an intense belief in American exceptionalism and technological utopianism, especially in his advocacy of a space-based missile defense program (dubbed "Star Wars" in the press).

Reagan, however, was not a nuclear nationalist but a nuclear absolutist. Notions of mutual destruction disturbed him, so he sought an ability to defend against nuclear attacks and later voiced support for nuclear abolition. Both his Star Wars speech and his negotiations with Soviet leader Mikhail Gorbachev looked backward to a time before nuclear weapons and Pearl Harbor when the United States did not fear a direct attack on its territory. In part inspired by pressure from the international antinuclear movement, he toyed with signing an agreement to abolish nuclear weapons by 2000, eliminated one class of nuclear weapons through the Intermediate Nuclear Forces Treaty (1987), and later proved to be an accommodating partner for Gorbachev in bringing the Cold War to a close.

Still, inconsistency plagued U.S. policy during the Reagan years. Although Washington reaffirmed the American commitment to export controls and to policing by the IAEA, the president made reestablishing the United States as a reliable supplier of nuclear technology and reactor fuel the primary objective of U.S. peaceful uses policy. In practice, the more lax approach allowed many potential proliferators to sign bilateral cooperation agreements with the United States. It also resulted in a Sino-American cooperation arrangement, despite Beijing's aid to South African, Indian, Pakistani, and Argentine nuclear weapons programs. And, by the end of the Reagan administration, the president's laissez-faire approach had allowed Argentina, Brazil, India, Iraq, and Pakistan to obtain large amounts of nuclear aid via covert arrangements with more advanced nuclear countries. Washington gave an even clearer signal of its disinterest in nonproliferation in 1982, when it publicly opposed a comprehensive test ban, reversing a policy that had stood since the Eisenhower presidency. By the time Reagan finally left office, in January 1989, U.S. nonproliferation efforts lacked administrative and intellectual coherence.

Post–Cold War Nonproliferation Efforts

The end of the Cold War, the disintegration of the Soviet Union, and the first Gulf War reenergized U.S. nonproliferation policy. Two Strategic Arms Reduction Treaties, signed in the early 1990s, committed Washington and Moscow to significant reductions in their nuclear arsenals for the first time. The first Persian Gulf War (1991) highlighted the danger that countries could secretly pursue nuclear weapons if IAEA inspection standards remained lax. The disintegration of the Soviet Union raised even more daunting proliferation problems. Where one nuclear power had previously existed, suddenly four new nations — Russia, Belarus, Ukraine, and Kazakhstan — possessed nuclear weapons on their soil. Russia became the acknowledged successor state to the USSR, acquiring a permanent seat on the Security Council and becoming a legitimate nuclear weapons state under the terms of the NPT. The other three republics agreed to transfer their nuclear weapons to Russian control and become non–nuclear weapons states under the NPT.

As both centralized governmental control and the economy began to deteriorate in the former Soviet Union, the proliferation threat only increased. Washington feared that nuclear materials stored under inadequate security might be smuggled out of the former Soviet republics. U.S. leaders also worried that impoverished Soviet physicists might be seduced into helping rogue states, such as Libya, Iran, and Pakistan, produce nuclear arsenals. The United States worked to forestall "nuclear yard sales" and an atomic brain drain by sponsoring joint research centers and projects to keep former Soviet scientists employed and financially stable. Washington also pursued bilateral and multilateral programs to store warheads and nuclear materials more safely. But the U.S. commitment fluctuated as presidential and congressional attention turned to other matters, including global terrorism and domestic financial turmoil.[6]

During the 1990s, the United States led international attempts to secure the NPT's indefinite renewal and to ratify the long-awaited Comprehensive Test Ban Treaty. The questions swirling around the NPT after its initial twenty-five-year term appeared remarkably similar to the problems that had faced its inception in 1968. Both Egypt and India protested the discriminatory aspects of the treaty, calling for nuclear weapons states to announce a timetable for reducing their stockpiles to zero. Many non-nuclear states expressed concern that indefinite renewal would remove their ability to monitor and critique nuclear weapons states' commitment to disarmament, and they called for limited, periodic extensions. Arab states also protested Israel's continued unwillingness to sign the treaty. In May 1995, Washington managed to outmaneuver its critics and win indefinite renewal but at the cost of angering some non-nuclear countries and undeclared nuclear weapons states, especially India. The NPT continued to stand as the apotheosis of U.S. non-proliferation policy, discriminating against non-nuclear countries through its core assumption that only the five recognized nuclear powers could handle nuclear weapons properly. Despite the continuing resentment of some states, the number of NPT signatories expanded from 62 in July 1968 to 178 in early 1997.

In 1996, President Bill Clinton also signed the Comprehensive Test Ban Treaty. After long and complicated negotiations among the nuclear and near-nuclear states, Washington called a special session of the UN General Assembly, which endorsed the treaty, with 158 votes in favor, 3 against, and 5 abstentions. The treaty's fate remains in doubt in 2009, however, because all forty-four countries possessing nuclear reactors must sign and ratify the treaty before it takes effect. Over a decade after its signing, however, it remains far from that goal. The United States dealt an early blow to the Comprehensive Test Ban Treaty when the Senate refused to ratify it in October 1999.

The treaty's failure presaged a retreat from arms control negotiations by the next president, George W. Bush. One Bush official scoffed at past administrations' "fascination with arms control" treaties, claiming that the new president would make up "for decades of stillborn plans, wishful thinking, and irresponsible passivity." Bush initially saw no reason to negotiate a treaty with Russia, claiming he would set U.S. nuclear arsenal limits based on an independent evaluation of American security needs. Under pressure from Russia and Congress, however, Bush reversed course and sought a legally binding treaty setting new limits on U.S. and Russian nuclear arsenals. The two-and-a-half-page Moscow Treaty signed in 2002 fell short of early arms control pacts, containing no verification procedures, no definitions of what would be reduced, and no interim reduction goals to measure compliance, and the agreement's expiration date was the deadline for achieving the arms cuts. The accord called for arsenals limited to 2,200 deployed warheads (and only required their decommissioning, not their destruction). In 2001, moreover, Bush unilaterally abrogated the Anti-Ballistic Missile Treaty (1972) as part of his new policy of "counter-proliferation," which promoted national missile defense systems and viewed military strikes as the best response to countries that attempted, like Iraq, to produce nuclear weapons in secret.[7]

Washington's retreat from arms control coincided with a mounting proliferation threat. India (1998), Pakistan (1998), and North Korea (2006) all declared themselves nuclear powers, and Washington feared that Iraq and Iran would join them. Washington's reactions to these threats proved halting and varied. Federal law forced Clinton to impose sanctions on India and Pakistan in 1998 when they both conducted series of nuclear tests, but in 2001, the new Bush administration quickly reached out to New Delhi, lifting all sanctions and promising to not be a "nagging nanny" in nuclear matters. After the September 11, 2001, terrorist attacks against New York and Washington, a nascent military alliance emerged between the two countries, both of which saw Islamic extremists as their primary national security threat. Building on this relationship, Bush in 2006 signed a nuclear cooperation agreement with India that violated the spirit, and according to some the letter, of U.S. obligations under the NPT. Although nominally limited to civilian nuclear endeavors, decades of experience had shown that no such clear compartmentalization exists. Any nuclear aid to a country with weapons enhances its military program. One expert predicted that the new arrangement would increase Indian bomb production from six to ten bombs annually to several dozen. After contentious debates in both countries, Washington and New Delhi ratified the agreement in late 2008.[8]

U.S.-Pakistan relations proved more complicated. After the September 11 attacks, Washington needed Islamabad's cooperation in its war against the Taliban and the al Qaeda terrorist network in Afghanistan. Washington accordingly lifted the remaining nuclear sanctions. But tensions remained high between the two countries. Connections between Pakistani intelligence, the Taliban, and al Qaeda ran deep, and the United States suspected that Islamabad was contributing only halfhearted support to the Afghan war. Pakistan's standing in the West plummeted in 2004 when its lead nuclear scientist, A. Q. Khan, confessed to giving illegal nuclear aid to Iran, Libya, and North Korea. He claimed that his superiors had no knowledge of his acts, but suspicions to the contrary grew after Pakistan president Pervez Musharraf commuted his sentence to house arrest less than twenty-four hours later. It eventually became clear that Islamabad had had evidence of Khan's guilt for more than three years.

In contrast to India and Pakistan, Clinton and Bush labeled North Korea, Iran, and Iraq nuclear rogues, later to be lumped together as the "axis of evil." The operating assumption behind this approach was that the leaders of all three countries—Kim Jong-Il (North Korea), Mahmoud Ahmadinejad (Iran), and Saddam Hussein (Iraq)—operated outside the bounds of Western rationality and would not be deterred by the much-larger U.S. nuclear arsenal. Although Clinton and Bush both conflated North Korea, Iran, and

Iraq in their rhetoric, they pursued different policies toward the three states. By the time the United States dubbed Iraq a rogue, it had already fought the first Gulf War, in 1991. There followed twelve years of economic sanctions and enforcement of no-fly zones in the north and south of the country. Confrontations ensued over the admittance of UN inspectors to ensure that Iraq had not revived its nuclear, chemical, or biological weapons programs — conflated under the term "weapons of mass destruction" (WMDs). The United States and Britain regularly bombed Iraqi sites to force compliance with the no-fly zones and the weapons inspections. Iraq gave only grudging cooperation to the inspectors, and rumors persisted of clandestine productions and hidden weapons caches.

The pressure to eliminate the Saddam Hussein regime and its WMDs escalated with George W. Bush's entry into the Oval Office. Almost immediately, his national security team called for military action against Baghdad. In 2001, Vice President Dick Cheney and Secretary of Defense Donald Rumsfeld wanted to use the September 11 attacks to justify invasion of Iraq, despite the lack of any evidence of Hussein's complicity. Although the initial U.S. response remained limited to Afghanistan, which harbored al Qaeda camps and refused to turn over al Qaeda's leader, Osama Bin Laden, Cheney and Rumsfeld kept up pressure to attack Iraq, with hidden WMDs now providing the dominant justification. Throughout 2002, Washington built a case against Iraq, demanding undeniable proof that Hussein had no illegal weapons. A rushed series of UN inspections produced no evidence, but Bush, undaunted, attacked Iraq in March 2003. More than six years of war and occupation produced none of the WMDs that Bush and his team had used to frighten the U.S. public and Congress into supporting the invasion.

North Korea's and Iran's nuclear threats did not prompt parallel military action. Reports leaked of U.S. contingency plans for air strikes against both states, but multilateral talks constituted the main response in each case. In North Korea's case, South Korea, Japan, China, and Russia opposed a military response and urged a diplomatic solution to Pyongyang's nuclear threat. Clinton signed a 1994 agreement with North Korea, only to see Kim Jong-Il reverse course in 1998 and revive his nuclear program. He worked to rebuild that relationship, but Bush abandoned negotiations in 2001. North Korea's first nuclear test in October 2006 forced Washington to become more serious about multilateral talks with Pyongyang, and a new agreement emerged in 2007. North Korea would allow IAEA inspection and dismantle its nuclear weapons infrastructure, in return for Washington lifting financial sanctions and removing Pyongyang from its list of states that sponsored terrorism. But this agreement collapsed as Bush left office in 2009, and North Korea once again tested a nuclear weapon, in May 2009.

Iran's nuclear ambitions provoked great outrage in Washington and Europe. In 2003, anxieties flared after the IAEA found evidence that Iran sought nuclear weapons, including the residue of weapons-grade uranium on some equipment. After further study, IAEA inspectors concluded that Iran had purchased nuclear technology on the black market and that the residue predated Iranian acquisition of the equipment. The crisis seemed headed to resolution until American conservatives rejected the IAEA report, while the Iranian election elevated a former student radical, Mahmoud Ahmadinejad, to the presidency. Ahmadinejad halted IAEA inspections and inflamed international opinion with outrageous statements about the Holocaust and Israel. Taking a page from Kim Jong-Il's book, he staged propaganda events that seemed to confirm Washington's charge that he sought nuclear weapons. Despite UN Security Council sanctions levied in December 2006, Ahmadinejad refused to curtail the Iranian nuclear program, claiming it focused on civilian power production. A National Intelligence Estimate clouded the picture further in late 2007 when it concluded that Iran had abandoned its quest for nuclear weapons in 2003. Despite the report, sanctions remained in place, and the Bush administration sent a high-level diplomat to join the European Union's efforts to persuade Iran to resume IAEA inspections. Iranian nuclear development, real or imagined, also threatened to unleash a regional nuclear arms race. Hedging against a nuclear Iran, Turkey, Syria, Saudi Arabia, Kuwait, Egypt, Libya, and Morocco all expressed interest in obtaining nuclear reactors, ostensibly for domestic power production.

Libya emerged as the one rogue who came in from the cold. In December 2003, Washington and London announced that Muammar Gadhafi had agreed to dismantle all of his nuclear, chemical, and biological weapons and facilities. His government also turned over evidence that forced A. Q. Khan's public confession in February 2004. The Bush administration immediately bragged that its tough stance toward Baghdad had brought Libya to the negotiating table. But Gadhafi had approached Britain, not the United States, and he did so before Washington invaded Iraq. Economic inducements, rather than military threats, had convinced him that disarming best served his interests.

Having abandoned arms control and embraced its nuclear arsenal as a check on terrorists and rogue regimes, the Bush administration found itself the focus of harsh criticism at the NPT review conference in 2005, especially after it refused to sign the Comprehensive Test Ban Treaty and the Fissile

Material Cutoff Treaty (the latter an agreement to halt all production of weapons-grade uranium and plutonium). Washington made clear that non-proliferation obligations bound other nations, but not the United States, when it renounced nuclear disarmament under Article IV of the NPT. With Bush displaying so little regard for the conference that he sent only a token delegation, the meeting ended with no major accomplishments. As many non-nuclears had predicted when the NPT had been renewed indefinitely in 1995, they had lost all leverage over the nuclear powers. Some commentators even claimed that the NPT had become obsolete and that the twenty-first-century proliferation threat required new agreements that recognized the existing nuclear powers and guaranteed everyone access to quality nuclear fuels.

The Clinton and Bush administrations, however, made no efforts to strengthen or revise the NPT and instead continued the patterns of the past. Washington persisted in its view that U.S. security rested on a nuclear arsenal numbering thousands of warheads. Policymakers, moreover, still viewed nuclear proliferation from the same discriminatory vantage point that had always allowed them to perceive nuclear danger from others while remaining blind to the threat that American weapons posed to the rest of the world. Even supporters of the Comprehensive Test Ban Treaty claimed that one virtue lay in its ability to preserve U.S. nuclear superiority in perpetuity. Exceptionalist biases and technological utopianism continued to define U.S. policy into the twenty-first century.

Why Has Nonproliferation Failed?

Little good has come from U.S. nonproliferation efforts, and few lessons have been learned. Even in 1945, the United States proved unable to lock the nuclear Pandora's Box. No monopoly over the knowledge required to create atomic weapons ever existed, and the raw materials needed to produce a bomb were then, as now, available throughout the world. The misguided faith in American supremacy in nuclear physics resulted in the wrongheaded policy of selective proliferation in the military and civilian fields. Such an approach served only to speed the acquisition of nuclear weapons by India, South Africa, and Pakistan. When Moscow responded with nuclear aid of its own, China accelerated its nuclear program.

Nonproliferation also failed because both Moscow and Washington subordinated control of nuclear spread to other security considerations. At times, both countries dabbled with nuclear sharing to offset perceived strategic advantages by the other power, exemplified by the United States' basing of Jupiter missiles in Turkey and Moscow's nuclear gambit in Cuba. At other times, the superpowers hesitated to conclude a nonproliferation accord because they feared alienating important allies, such as West Germany and China. U.S. policy proved the most susceptible to alliance pressure. Fear of German nuclear nationalism delayed conclusion of a nonproliferation treaty in the 1960s and prevented the agreement from coming into force during a presidential administration that endorsed its goals. Overall, the subordination of nonproliferation to other security considerations produced vacillation in U.S. policy, which in turn provoked resentment and cries of hypocrisy among non-nuclear nations.

Both superpowers also regarded possession of nuclear weapons as giving them a special status, both within their alliance blocs and in the international system more broadly. This attitude sent a clear message to the rest of the world: Only nuclear powers matter. The superpowers denied that possession of nuclear weapons enhanced a nation's international political status, but their actions contradicted their rhetoric. Nations that sought respect or believed they had a global role to fulfill inevitably sought nuclear leverage.

An ironic example emerged from the Limited Test Ban Treaty negotiations. Great Britain's participation in these talks clearly stemmed from its status as a nuclear weapons state. By measures such as economic strength and conventional military potential, it ranked well behind Germany and France, but the atom gave it a seat at the table. Not wanting matters that affected their own security to be decided without their input, other powers decided to write their own invitation to the negotiating table. The duplication of membership in the legally recognized nuclear club and the permanent membership of the UN Security Council, thus, is hardly coincidental. But the quest for perpetual hegemony sustained by nuclear weapons proved self-defeating. The Cold War arms race drained the treasuries of both Washington and Moscow, while the former Axis powers, Germany and Japan, refrained from nuclear militarism and thrived economically.

The spread of nuclear weapons to France and China—alliance partners who rejected Moscow's and Washington's attempts to dominate the respective blocs—and the emergence of newly decolonized states that refused to embrace either bloc weakened superpower hegemony. To succeed, nondissemination efforts had to embrace conflicting definitions of national security, but Moscow and Washington persisted in prioritizing their own geostrategic interests over those of allied states. In the end, the NPT emerged as an empty pledge not to sin, enforced by sinners. The United States and the Soviet

Union refused to recognize that the only basis for a stable and enforceable agreement rested on mutual respect and sacrifice.

The challenges of the new millennium make prospects for a multinational solution to nuclear proliferation an even more difficult task. In a world confronting such transnational challenges as terrorism, environmental degradation, and competition for scarce resources, nation-states are increasingly unable to control economic activities and information dissemination. This weakening of centralized control has accentuated the difficulties that the major world powers have experienced in adjusting to the post–Cold War international system. A search for global stability and order has taken center stage in many policy debates. Any new nonproliferation effort must accordingly take into account a world in which information regarding weapons of mass destruction can be easily obtained on the World Wide Web. Nonproliferation analysts argue that any effective nonproliferation regime in the future must inspire the cooperation of more than nation-states. Substate groups, such as nationalist movements, nongovernmental organizations, and multinational corporations, must become participants in the nonproliferation dialogue.

The importance of executive action serves as a final lesson from the history of the superpowers' conflicted approach to nuclear containment. Nonproliferation became a mutual goal of Washington and Moscow when both John F. Kennedy and Nikita Khrushchev shared a fear of a multinuclear world. If post–Cold War world leaders also wish to curb the existing proliferation threat, they must be willing to exchange unilateral and bilateral efforts for a concerted multilateral approach. Nuclear apartheid must be brought to an end if its destabilizing spiral of political and economic strife is also to be eradicated. Like Pretoria in the 1990s, the privileged powers must exchange their tiered system of inequality for one based on the principles of openness and democratic ideals that have characterized nonproliferation endeavors at their best. Such an approach necessitates that U.S. and Russian policymakers, along with other international forces, dedicate themselves to a truly transnational effort based on mutual and balanced sacrifice both in disarmament and in the economic realm. Rather than tending to individual plots, the nuclear powers must return to the global commons; only by shifting from competition to cooperation can proliferation be curtailed.

Washington and Moscow should also attempt to persuade the world that cheap and safe nuclear power is a phantasm. Nuclear reactors will always serve as halfway houses toward nuclear bombs, and the nuclear waste that reactors produce constitutes an environmental time bomb. An international effort to produce renewable energy sources that do minimal damage to the environment would complement the arms control element of the new non-proliferation regime. No arrangement will be perfect, but the status quo risks a future in which nuclear weapons become "conventional" armaments and could possibly fall into terrorist hands.

Throughout the nuclear age, the United States has squandered opportunities to forge cooperative ventures to halt proliferation. From the Baruch Plan to national missile defense, Americans have remained infatuated with unilateral and technological solutions to the atomic threat. And they have repeatedly attempted to preserve U.S. nuclear hegemony by undercutting their own professed commitment to nuclear nondissemination. A paradoxical equation derived from this practice. American hegemony, combined with arrogance and a Hobbesian worldview, catalyzed nuclear nationalism in other states and helped break the bonds of Washington's influence. Taught by the superpowers that nuclear weapons equal political power and that warheads prevent wars, other states built the bomb when they could afford to. As the technology became cheaper and more easily available, even states that could not provide their citizenry with a decent standard of living, such as India, Pakistan, North Korea, and the PRC, found the resources to produce limited nuclear arsenals. Since the dawn of the nuclear age, no president has proven capable of producing the right political mixture to yield a viable nonproliferation accord. The superpowers remained so convinced of the correctness of their respective privileged positions in the world system that they refused to make mutual concessions to achieve arms control. Other nations also chose military strength over cooperation and in the process diminished Washington's and Moscow's relative power in the international system.

Actual security priorities alone fail to explain this pattern, especially absent any post–Cold War security threat to the United States comparable to its Cold War rival, the Soviet Union. Culture and ideology have complemented traditional national and hegemonic goals to explain the tenacity of these counterproductive trends in U.S. nonproliferation policies. The persistence of a hegemonic version of American ideology and culture, rooted in beliefs about American exceptionalism, race, gender, and technological utopianism, has continued to spawn nonproliferation failures. At the dawn of the nuclear age, Albert Einstein hoped that the menace of nuclear weapons would "intimidate the human race into bringing order into its international affairs." Einstein's wish remains unfulfilled because entrenched nationalist ideas protected and promulgated by the nuclear guardians blocked any of the new thinking needed to transcend the atomic age.[9]

Notes

OSS	Office of the Staff Secretary
POF	President's Office File
PPOP	*Public Papers of the Presidents of the United States* (Washington, D.C.: Office of the Federal Register)
PRO	British Public Record Office, Kew Gardens, London
PSF	President's Secretary's File
RG	Record Group
SCPC	Swarthmore College Peace Collection, Swarthmore, Pa.
SCS	Selected Correspondence Series
SDDF	State Department Decimal File, RG59, National Archives, College Park, Md.
TCS	Telephone Conversation Series
WHCF	White House Central File
Whitman File	Ann Whitman File, Dwight D. Eisenhower Papers
WHM	White House Memoranda Series
WHO	White House Office Files

Preface

1 Address by President Mandela at the 53rd United Nations General Assembly, September 21, 1998, Nuclear Age Peace Foundation, <http://www.wagingpeace.org> (accessed July 23, 2008).

2 Quoted in Perkovich, *India's Nuclear Bomb*, 138.

Chapter 1

1 Memorandum for the Executive Secretary, NSC, Subject: Meeting of the Special Committee of the National Security Council on Atomic Energy, February 24, 1953, "#16 Special Committee Meetings" folder, ESF, WHO: Box 5, NSCS Records, DDEL. Clinton quoted in Oreskes, "Troubling the Waters of Nuclear Deterrence," *New York Times*, June 4, 2000, Sec. 4, p. 3. For seminal works on U.S. foreign policy and ideology, see Williams, *Tragedy of American Diplomacy*; and Hunt, *Ideology and U.S. Foreign Policy*. See also Hunt, "Ideology."

2 Quoted in Perkovich, *India's Nuclear Bomb*, 138.

3 Quoted in Ribuffo, "What Is Still Living in the Ideas and Example of Williams?" 313.

4 Leffler, "National Security."

5 See Klein, "How the West Was One." For a recent study of U.S. strategic hegemony within NATO, see Johnston, *Hegemony and Culture*.

6 For the creation of the official narrative and its persistence into the present, see Bernstein, "Seizing the Contested Terrain"; Hogan, *Hiroshima in History and Memory*; and Linenthal and Engelhardt, *History Wars*. For the utopian prospects of nuclear energy, see Boyer, *By the Bomb's Early Light*; and Winkler, *Life under a Cloud*.

7   For the power of the bureaucracy, see Clifford, "Bureaucratic Politics."

8   Michael Sherry has explored the faith in technological means of destruction within the military, primarily the air force, in *The Rise of American Air Power*, especially 219–300. He labeled this concept "technological fanaticism," which accurately reflects the irrational and deeply rooted belief in technological means of achieving victory. I, however, see this extreme devotion to progress through technology in both the military and the peace camps during this period and have used the term "technological utopianism." Despite this slight difference in phrasing, the concepts are nearly identical.

9   Stimson quoted in Kuznick, "Prophets of Doom or Voices of Sanity?" 414.

10 Kahn, *On Thermonuclear War*, 491.

11 Myrdal, *Game of Disarmament*, 173.

12 Connelly, "Taking Off the Cold War Lens"; CIA Research Study — Managing Nuclear Proliferation: The Politics of Limited Choice, December 1975, NSA, <www.gwu.edu/~nsarchiv> (accessed July 27, 2006); Mastny, "Was 1968 a Strategic Watershed of the Cold War?" 160; Falk, "Illegitimacy of the Non-Proliferation Regime"; quoted in Cozic, *Nuclear Proliferation*, 12.

13 Ribuffo, "What Is Still Living in the Ideas and Example of Williams?" 314; Lifton, *Superpower Syndrome*; anonymous U.S. official quoted in Keller, "The Thinkable," *New York Times Magazine*, May 4, 2003.

Chapter 2

1   Memorandum from James Franck (Nobel Prize Winner), n.d., "Subject File — NSC — Atomic: Atomic Bomb — Cabinet (Henry Wallace)" folder, PSF, Box 199, HSTL; *PPOP: Harry S. Truman, 1945* (1961), 437.

2   Quoted in Clifford, "Both Ends of the Telescope," 213.

3   Wittner, *One World or None*, 10.

4   Churchill, *Hinge of Fate*, 374–78.

5   *FRUS, Conferences at Washington and Quebec, 1943* (1970), 1117–19.

6   *FRUS, 1944: General; Economic and Social Matters* (1967), 2:1026–28.

7   Quoted in Bundy, *Danger and Survival*, 114; *FRUS, Conference at Quebec, 1944* (1972), 492–93.

8   Diary entries, Friday, January 19, 1945, and Monday, January 22, 1945, Vol. L, Reel 9, pp. 55, 64, Stimson Papers, New Haven, Conn.; *FRUS, 1945: General; Political and Economic Matters* (1967), 2:2–5.

9   Diary entries, Monday, March 5, 1945, Thursday, March 15, 1945, Wednesday, April 4, 1945, and Thursday, April 5, 1945, Vol. L, Reel 9, pp. 164, 189–90, and Vol. LI, Reel 9, pp. 10, 12, Stimson Papers, New Haven, Conn.

10 Lieberman, *The Scorpion and the Tarantula*, 59; Hershberg, *James B. Conant*, 221–22; Williamson and Rearden, *Origins of U.S. Nuclear Strategy*, 8; Bundy, *Danger and Survival*, 120–24; Sherwin, *World Destroyed*, 290–91.

11 Herken, *Winning Weapon*, 125; Sherwin, *World Destroyed*, 62–63; Kimball, *Churchill*

and Roosevelt, 3:319; Williamson and Rearden, *Origins of U.S. Nuclear Strategy,* 9; Hewlett and Anderson, *New World,* 335; Stoler, *Allies and Adversaries,* 213–14.

12 They included Fuchs, David Greenglass (in cooperation with his brother-in-law Julius Rosenberg), Theodore Hall (a young American physicist), and an agent who was first code-named "Fogel" and then "Pers" and "Persian" and who has yet to be identified. For more on these spies, see Weinstein and Vassiliev, *Haunted Wood,* 172–222; Albright and Kunstel, *Bombshell;* and Haynes and Klehr, *Venona,* 287–330.

13 Oral History, R. Gordon Arneson, pp. 24–25, HSTL.

14 Kimball, *Forged in War,* 329.

15 Quoted in Sherwin, *World Destroyed,* 149–50; Truman, *Year of Decisions,* 10–11, 87; Oral History, George M. Elsey, p. 9, HSTL. Byrnes had learned about the bomb project while director of the Office of War Management; see Hewlett and Anderson, *New World,* 343.

16 Memorandum Discussed with the President, April 25, 1945, Stimson diary, Vol. LI, Reel 9, pp. 70–72, Stimson Papers, New Haven, Conn.

17 Offner, "Another Such Victory"; Messer, *End of an Alliance,* 95; Bernstein, "Roosevelt, Truman, and the Atomic Bomb," 35–42.

18 Offner, "Harry S. Truman as Parochial Nationalist," 51–53; Messer, *End of an Alliance,* 6–7; Nye, *American Technological Sublime,* 40, 66, 122; Weart, *Nuclear Fear;* Hofstadter, *Anti-Intellectualism in American Life,* 9, 188–89, 226–27, 285; Memorandum from President Truman to Dean Acheson, May 7, 1946, "Subject File—NSC—Atomic: Atomic Test" folder, PSF, Box 201, HSTL. Despite this outburst, Truman continued to use Oppenheimer as a valued adviser for the rest of his presidency.

19 Rhodes, *Making of the Atomic Bomb,* 500.

20 Diary entry, June 6, 1945, Vol. LI, Reel 9, pp. 159–60, Stimson Papers, New Haven, Conn.

21 *FRUS, Conference at Berlin (Potsdam Conference), 1945* (1960), 2:47, 81–82, 225, 1155–57; quoted in LaFeber, "Comments on Professor Herken's Paper"; Diary entry, July 16, 1945, "Copy—JJM Diary for 1945, April–June" folder, War Department Diaries series, Box DY1, McCloy Papers, Amherst, Mass.

22 Mark, "Today Has Been a Historical One," 323–24; Diary entries, July 23 and July 24, 1945, "Copy—JJM Diary for 1945, April–June" folder, War Department Diaries series, Box DY1, McCloy Papers, Amherst, Mass.; *FRUS, Potsdam,* 2:378–79. For Stalin's comment to Molotov, see Chase, *Acheson,* 117.

23 *FRUS, Potsdam,* 2:1376–79.

24 Wittner, *One World or None,* 55–59, 247; quoted in Boyer, *By the Bomb's Early Light,* 7–8.

25 Wittner, *One World or None,* 56–57; Statement of Purpose, "Correspondence, Subject: 1940–47 Atomic Bomb, August–December 1945" folder, FORUS, Box 12, SCPC; A. J. Muste to President Harry Truman, August 17, 1945, ibid.; Tentative Statement on the Atomic Bomb Prepared by Dorothy Detzer, "Atomic Bomb (1945–1946)" folder, Dorothy Detzer Papers, Box 3, SCPC.

26 Paterson, *On Every Front*, 145–49.

27 Wittner, *One World or None*, 129; *FRUS, 1945*, 2:36–37, 40.

28 Bundy, *Danger and Survival*, 134; Diary entries, August 1, 1945, August 2, 1945, and August 9, 1945, Memorandum of Conversation with President—August 8, 1945, Stimson diary, Vol. LII, Reel 9, pp. 57, 60, 66, 69–71, Stimson Papers, New Haven, Conn.; Lieberman, *The Scorpion and the Tarantula*, 121–22; Groves, *Now It Can Be Told*, 348–52; Ferrell, *Off the Record*, 60; Hershberg, *James B. Conant*, 238.

29 Oral History, George M. Elsey, p. 16, HSTL.

30 Franklin, *War Stars*, 39–44, 50–53; Poen, *Strictly Personal and Confidential*, 31.

31 McLellan, *Dean Acheson*, 64; Wittner, *One World or None*, 80–84, 108–42; Lieberman, *The Scorpion and the Tarantula*, 133–34.

32 Diary entry, August 12–September 3, 1945, Vol. LII, Reel 9, pp. 80, 90, Stimson Papers, New Haven, Conn.

33 Lieberman, *The Scorpion and the Tarantula*, 139–40; Bernstein, "Quest for Security," 1016; *FRUS, 1945*, 2:40–44; Diary entry, September 12, 1945, Vol. LII, Reel 9, pp. 113–14, Stimson Papers, New Haven, Conn.

34 Diary entry, September 12, 1945, Vol. LII, Reel 9, pp. 113–14, Stimson Papers, New Haven, Conn.

35 Diary entry, September 13, 1945, Vol. LII, Reel 9, p. 129, Stimson Papers, New Haven, Conn.; Diary entry, September 17, 1945, ibid., pp. 136–37; McLellan, *Dean Acheson*, 63; Memorandum for Mr. Forrestal from J. H. Vincent, Subject: Atom Bomb, "Forrestal, James Vincent, 1945–72" folder, AECS, Box 28, Strauss Papers, HHL; Millis, *Forrestal Diaries*, 95–96; Hunt, *Ideology and U.S. Foreign Policy*, 69; J. Edgar Hoover to Matthew Connelly, September 12, 1945, "Subject File—FBI: Atomic Bomb" folder, PSF, Box 167, HSTL; J. Edgar Hoover to Matthew J. Connelly, September 18, 1945, ibid.; Oral History, John D. Hickerson, pp. 29–30, HSTL.

36 Acheson, *Present at the Creation*, 123.

37 Quoted in Millis, *Forrestal Diaries*, 94; Diary entry, September 21 (dictated December 11), 1945, Vol. LII, Reel 9, pp. 165–66, Stimson Papers, New Haven, Conn.; Notes of the Cabinet Meeting—Atomic Bomb, September 21, 1945, "Secretary of Defense—Forrestal—Atomic Bomb" folder, PSF, Box 157, HSTL; Memorandum by Lewis L. Strauss, n.d., "Acheson, Dean, 1945–54" folder, AECS, Box 1, Strauss Papers, HHL.

38 Memorandum for the President from Admiral William Leahy, October 23, 1945, Document #6, National Security Archive, *U.S. Nuclear Non-Proliferation*; *FRUS, 1945: Europe* (1967), 5:884–86; J. Edgar Hoover to Brigadier General Harry Hawkins Vaughn (Military Aide to the President), October 5, 1945, "Subject File—FBI: Atomic Bomb" folder, PSF, Box 167, HSTL.

39 *FRUS, 1945*, 2:48–50.

40 Ibid., 2:54–55; Henry A. Wallace to President Truman, September 24, 1945, "Subject File—NSC—Atomic: Atomic Bomb—Cabinet (Henry Wallace)" folder, PSF, Box 199, HSTL; Harold L. Ickes to President Truman, October 24, 1945, "Subject File—

NSC—Atomic: Atomic Bomb—Cabinet (Harold L. Ickes)" folder, ibid.; Major General Philip B. Fleming to President Truman, September 28, 1945, "General Files: Atomic Bomb" folder, PSF, Box 112, HSTL.

41 Clinton Anderson to President Truman, September 25, 1945, "General Files: Atomic Bomb" folder, PSF, Box 112, HSTL.

42 James V. Forrestal to President Truman, October 1, 1945, Document #5, National Security Archive, *U.S. Nuclear Non-Proliferation*; Blum, *Price of Vision*, 485; Culver and Hyde, *American Dreamer*, 400–401; quoted in Bundy, *Danger and Survival*, 141–42; Gaddis, *The United States and the Origins of the Cold War*, 259.

43 Quoted in Bundy, *Danger and Survival*, 142–43.

44 *PPOP: Truman, 1945* (1961), 381–88.

45 Quoted in Herken, *Winning Weapon*, 39, 43–68.

46 *FRUS, 1945*, 2:55–57.

47 Quoted in Offner, *Another Such Victory*, 109; *FRUS, 1945*, 2:58–62.

48 *FRUS, 1945*, 2:63–74; quoted in Gaddis, *The United States and the Origins of the Cold War*, 272.

49 Quoted in Herken, *Winning Weapon*, 63.

50 *FRUS, 1945*, 2:75–76.

51 *Documents on Disarmament, 1945–1959*, 1:1–3.

52 Oral History, R. Gordon Arneson, p. 32, HSTL; Vandenberg, *Private Papers of Senator Vandenberg*, 221; *Congressional Record*, November 28, 1945, 11085–86.

53 Gormly, "Washington Declaration," 137–38; *FRUS, 1945*, 2:77, 593–95, 597–98.

54 *FRUS, 1945*, 2:92–96.

55 Ibid., 2:96–98; Vandenberg, *Private Papers of Senator Vandenberg*, 227–28.

56 Quoted in Herken, *Winning Weapon*, 78; Lieberman, *The Scorpion and the Tarantula*, 205–6.

57 *FRUS, 1945*, 2:609–10, 663–66.

58 Quoted in Hershberg, *James B. Conant*, 252–53; quoted in Gormly, "Washington Declaration," 139–40; Kennan, *Memoirs, 1925–1950*, 286–87.

59 *FRUS, 1945*, 2:750–57; Hershberg, *James B. Conant*, 255.

60 Zubok, "Stalin and the Nuclear Age," 51; Holloway, *Stalin and the Bomb*, 158; *Cold War International History Bulletin* 4 (Fall 1994): 5.

61 *FRUS, 1945*, 5:933–36; quoted in Hershberg, *James B. Conant*, 257.

62 *FRUS, 1945*, 2:815–24.

63 Poen, *Strictly Personal and Confidential*, 41.

Chapter 3

1 Truman, *Years of Trial and Hope*, 11; *FRUS, 1949: National Security Affairs, Foreign Economic Policy* (1976), 1:481–82.

2 Lilienthal, *The Atomic Energy Years*, 10–12.

3 Handwritten notes, "Atomic Bomb and Atomic Energy, 1953–1959" folder, Post-

administrative files, Box 103, Acheson Papers, HSTL; *FRUS, 1946: General; The United Nations* (1972), 1:749–54.

4 Memorandum on "Atomic Explosives," by J. R. Oppenheimer, April 6, 1946, "United States Policy—Toward June 14 Proposal" folder, Unit 10: AECS, Box 52, Baruch Papers, Princeton, N.J.; *FRUS, 1946*, 1:749–54.

5 Lilienthal, *The Atomic Energy Years*, 27.

6 Kennan, *Memoirs, 1925–1950*, 547–59; Millis, *Forrestal Diaries*, 135–40; Isaacson and Thomas, *Wise Men*, 354–56.

7 Leffler, "Negotiating from Strength," 177; Acheson, *Sketches from Life of Men I Have Known*, 103; Blum, *Price of Vision*, 556–57.

8 Hewlett and Anderson, *New World*, 551–52.

9 Lilienthal, *The Atomic Energy Years*, 29; *FRUS, 1946*, 1:761–64.

10 Bush, *Pieces of the Action*, 298; U.S. Atomic Energy Commission, *In the Matter of J. Robert Oppenheimer*, 38; quoted in Herken, *Winning Weapon*, 365.

11 *FRUS, 1946*, 1:738–49, 1197–1203.

12 Leffler, "Negotiating from Strength," 177; Oral History, Dean G. Acheson, pp. 22–23, HSTL.

13 Notes on Bernard M. Baruch, "Atomic Energy—Baruch, B. M.—1946–47–48–49" folder, Unit 10: AEC, Box 58, Baruch Papers, Princeton, N.J.

14 Ferrell, *Off the Record*, 64; Schwarz, *Speculator*, 472, 491; *FRUS, 1946*, 1:757–58.

15 Lilienthal, *The Atomic Energy Years*, 30; quoted in Schrafstetter and Twigge, *Avoiding Armageddon*, 25.

16 Lilienthal, *The Atomic Energy Years*, 30.

17 Ibid., 31–32; *FRUS, 1946*, 1:767–68; quoted in Baruch, *Baruch*, 363; quoted in Lieberman, *The Scorpion and the Tarantula*, 268.

18 Bernard M. Baruch to Secretary of State James F. Byrnes, March 31, 1946, "United States Policy—Toward June 14 Proposal" folder, Unit 10: AECS, Box 52, Baruch Papers, Princeton, N.J.

19 Letter from Marian R. Emerne, Executive Secretary of National Peace Conference, to President Harry S. Truman, May 7, 1946, "OF 85R—United Nations Commission on Atomic Energy" folder, WHCF: Official File, Box 575, HSTL; Lieberman, *The Scorpion and the Tarantula*, 271; Boyer, *By the Bomb's Early Light*, 55.

20 Meeting—April 5, Memorandum by John M. Hancock, April 19, 1946, "United States Policy—Toward June 14 Proposal" folder, Unit 10: AECS, Box 52, Baruch Papers, Princeton, N.J.; Herken, *Winning Weapon*, 367.

21 Lilienthal, *The Atomic Energy Years*, 38–39.

22 Ibid., 39–43.

23 *FRUS, 1946*, 1:777–78, 787–89; Memorandum from John Hancock to Baruch, Searls, Eberstadt, Swope, and Davis, May 3, 1946, "United States Policy—Toward June 14 Proposal" folder, Unit 10: AECS, Box 52, Baruch Papers, Princeton, N.J.

24 Memorandum from John Hancock to Baruch, Searls, Eberstadt, Swope, and Davis, May 3, 1946, "United States Policy—Toward June 14 Proposal" folder, Unit 10:

AECS, Box 52, Baruch Papers, Princeton, N.J.; Lilienthal, *The Atomic Energy Years*, 42–44.

25 Lilienthal, *The Atomic Energy Years*, 49.

26 J. Edgar Hoover to George E. Allen, May 29, 1946, "Subject File — FBI: Atomic Bomb" folder, PSF, Box 167, HSTL.

27 *FRUS, 1946*, 1:802–6, 843–46, 851–56, 1197–1203; Lilienthal, *The Atomic Energy Years*, 58–59; Oral History, R. Gordon Arneson, p. 54, HSTL.

28 Quoted in Broscious, "Looking for International Control, Banking on American Superiority," 26; *FRUS, 1946*, 1:838–40, 846–51; BMB Memorandum of Meeting on June 7, 1946, with the President and J. F. Byrnes, "Atomic Energy — Baruch, B. M., 1946-47-48-49" folder, Unit 10: AECS, Box 58, Baruch Papers, Princeton, N.J.; Truman quoted in Paterson, *On Every Front*, 117; Truman quoted in Bernstein, "Quest for Security," 1042; Biddle, "Handling the Soviet Threat," 287, 300.

29 Address to the Atomic Energy Commission of the United Nations by Bernard M. Baruch, June 14, 1946, "Gen. File — Baruch" folder, PSF, Box 113, HSTL; Churchill quoted in Schrafstetter and Twigge, *Avoiding Armageddon*, 205.

30 Quoted in Winkler, *Life under a Cloud*, 52.

31 Letter from Bourke B. Hickenlooper to General Dwight D. Eisenhower, June 3, 1946, "Eisenhower, Dwight D., 1946-55" folder, JCAE, Box 14, Hickenlooper Papers, HHL; Doenecke, *Not to the Swift*, 68; quoted in Lieberman, *The Scorpion and the Tarantula*, 304. See also "Primer for Peace" leaflet, "Association of Oak Ridge Engineers and Scientists — World Government Committee" folder, Document Group B, SCPC; "The Atomic Bomb — What Are We Going to Do with It?" leaflet, "Leaflets, Files, Etc., 1946-47" folder, FORUS, Box 52, SCPC; Letter from A. J. Muste to Dr. Albert Einstein, May 28, 1946, "Correspondence, Subject, 1940-47 — Atom Bomb, May–December 1946" folder, FORUS, Box 12, SCPC.

32 *FRUS, 1946: Eastern Europe; The Soviet Union* (1969), 6:748–50; Vandenberg, *Private Papers of Senator Vandenberg*, 291 (emphasis in original).

33 *Documents on Disarmament, 1945–59*, 1:17–24; Comparison of the United States and Soviet Proposals as Presented to the First and Second Meetings of the United Nations Atomic Energy Commission, July 1, 1946, "Atomic Energy — Comparison of American and Russian Proposals" folder, Unit 10: AECS, Box 52, Baruch Papers, Princeton, N.J.; Draft Convention on Atomic Weapons and the Control of Atomic Energy, March 14, 1946, Folder 10, Box AT1, McCloy Papers, Amherst, Mass.

34 Gowing, *Independence and Deterrence*, 1:89; *FRUS, 1946*, 1:857–60.

35 Lilienthal, *The Atomic Energy Years*, 62; Letter from Thomas Finletter to Walter Lippmann, July 17, 1946, Folder 760, Series III, Box 70, Lippmann Papers, New Haven, Conn.; Letter to Bernard Baruch from Henry Stimson, June 18, 1946, Reel 115, Stimson Papers, New Haven, Conn.; Letter from Chester I. Barnard to David E. Lilienthal, January 20, 1947, Document #40, National Security Archive, *U.S. Nuclear Non-Proliferation*.

36 Letter to A. J. Muste from John Foster Dulles, June 10, 1946, "Muste, A. J., 1946"

folder, SCS, Box 29, D/E/P; Rosenberg, "U.S. Nuclear Stockpile, 1945 to 1950"; Comments by Franklin A. Lindsay, n.d., "Atomic Energy—Lindsay, Franklin A., 1946–47" folder, Unit 10: AECS, Box 63, Baruch Papers, Princeton, N.J.; Memorandum for the Staff from John M. Hancock, November 21, 1946, "On the Subject of: Bomb Manufacture" folder, Unit 10: AECS, Box 56, Baruch Papers, Princeton, N.J.

37 Quoted in Bundy, *Danger and Survival*, 166; Batyuk, "Baruch Plan and Russia," 18.

38 *FRUS, 1946*, 1:903–5, 907–11.

39 Ibid., 1:881–84; quoted in Hershberg, *James B. Conant*, 275–76.

40 Letter to President Truman from J. Robert Oppenheimer, May 3, 1946, Document #24, National Security Archive, *U.S. Nuclear Non-Proliferation*; Memorandum from President Truman to Dean Acheson, May 7, 1946, "Subject File—NSC—Atomic: Atomic Test" folder, PSF, Box 201, HSTL.

41 Letter from James B. Conant to McGeorge Bundy, November 30, 1946, Reel 116, Stimson Papers, New Haven, Conn. See Hershberg, *James B. Conant*, 291–95.

42 *FRUS, 1946*, 1:906–11, 916–17, 919–29.

43 Blum, *Price of Vision*, 589–603; see also White and Maze, *Henry A. Wallace*, 219–40.

44 *FRUS, 1946*, 1:938–39, 955–60; ibid., 6:806–8.

45 BMB Telephone Conversation with the President, October 28, 1946, "Atomic Energy—Baruch, B. M., 1946–47–48–49" folder, Unit 10: AECS, Box 58, Baruch Papers, Princeton, N.J.; Memorandum to Senator Austin from Bernard M. Baruch, November 2, 1946, "Atomic Energy—Austin, Warren R., 1946–47–48" folder, ibid.; *FRUS, 1946*, 1:982.

46 *FRUS, 1946*, 1:983–88.

47 Ibid., 1:995–96, 1001–5, 1010; Lilienthal, *The Atomic Energy Years*, 69–71, 123–24; quoted in Schwarz, *Speculator*, 505; Oral History, R. Gordon Arneson, p. 55, HSTL; *Documents on Disarmament, 1945–59*, 1:50–59.

48 Lilienthal, *The Atomic Energy Years*, 69–71.

49 *FRUS, 1947: General; The United Nations* (1973), 1:332–36, 381–87; *FRUS, 1949*, 1:36–43.

50 *FRUS, 1947*, 1:555–56; Report by the Joint Strategic Survey Committee, July 14, 1947, Document #44, National Security Archive, *U.S. Nuclear Non-Proliferation*.

51 Oral History, R. Gordon Arneson, pp. 27, 36, HSTL; *FRUS, 1947*, 1:833–34; Memorandum to Senator Hickenlooper, August 29, 1947, "Foreign Exchange of Information, 1947–48" folder, JCAE series, Box 16, Hickenlooper Papers, HHL; Memorandum Summary of General Discussion at Luncheon at Secretary Forrestal's Office, November 16, 1947, ibid.; *FRUS, 1948: General; The United Nations* (1975), 1:677–87.

52 Notes Re Princeton Meeting, January 28, 1949, "Atomic Energy Policies vis-à-vis UK and Canada" folder, Staff Member and Office Files: National Security Council Files, Box 18, HSTL; *FRUS, 1949*, 1:419–28, 441–61; Lilienthal, *The Atomic Energy Years*, 384–85, 457, 463–67; Memorandum for John R. Steelman from the President, January 15, 1949, "Subject File—NSC—Atomic: Atomic Energy—International Control" folder, PSF, Box 200, HSTL.

53 Memorandum Dictated 10:00 A.M. Friday, July 15, 1949, from Penciled Notes Made Approximately 11:00 P.M. on Thursday, July 14, 1949, "Foreign Exchange of Information, 1949" folder, JCAE series, Box 16, Hickenlooper Papers, HHL.

54 *FRUS, 1949,* 1:484–86, 490–98, 505–6; Lilienthal, *The Atomic Energy Years,* 548–52, 556–58.

55 *FRUS, 1949,* 1:558; quoted in Gowing, *Independence and Deterrence,* 1:289.

56 *FRUS, 1951: National Security Affairs; Foreign Economic Policy* (1981), 1:755–68.

57 Meeting with the President, November 7, 1949, "Memoranda of Conversation, October–November 1949" folder, Box 65, Acheson Papers, HSTL; Lilienthal, *The Atomic Energy Years,* 615.

58 *FRUS, 1949,* 1:570–73.

59 Ibid., 1:588–95.

60 Quoted in Bernstein, "Truman and the H-Bomb," 15; *FRUS, 1950: National Security Affairs; Foreign Economic Policy* (1977), 1:513–23.

61 Wittner, *Rebels against War,* 199–201; McLellan, *Dean Acheson,* 179–80; Bernstein, "Truman and the H-Bomb," 17–18.

62 *FRUS, 1949,* 1:191–97, 222–23.

63 *FRUS, 1950,* 1:22–44; quoted in Isaacson and Thomas, *Wise Men,* 489.

64 *FRUS, 1950,* 1:22–44.

65 Ibid., 1:50–52, 66–75; Memorandum for Mr. Murphy, April 19, 1950, "National Defense—Atomic (1950) #2" folder, Box 88, Elsey Papers, HSTL; Letter from Harold Bergman to William Borden, April 25, 1950, Document #63, National Security Archive, *U.S. Nuclear Non-Proliferation;* Letter from Harold Bergman to William Borden, April 29, 1950, Document #64, ibid.

66 *FRUS, 1950,* 1:79–80, 94–100.

67 *FRUS, 1951,* 1:445–48, 450–53, 455–63.

68 *FRUS, 1952–1954: National Security Affairs* (1985), 2:915–24; *FRUS, 1951,* 1:588–89.

69 *FRUS, 1951,* 1:588, 599–600.

70 Bernstein, "Crossing the Rubicon," 141.

71 *FRUS, 1952–1954,* 2:915–24.

72 Ibid., 2:958–63.

73 Ibid., 2:994–1008.

74 Ibid., 2:1033–36.

75 Ibid.

76 Ibid., 2:1038–41.

77 Ibid., 2:1049–55.

78 Quoted in "The Soviet Bombs: Mr. Truman's Doubts," *Bulletin of the Atomic Scientists* 9 (March 1953): 43–45; Memorandum for the President from James C. Hagerty, January 28, 1953, "Atomic Energy Commission: General (1) [January–May 1953]" folder, Subject subseries, Special Assistant series, WHO: Box 1, OSANSA, DDEL.

Chapter 4

1 *FRUS, 1952–1954*, 2:1452–56 (emphasis in original).

2 Ferrell, *Diary of James C. Hagerty*, 69.

3 *FRUS, 1952–1954*, 2:1321–22.

4 Sherry, *In the Shadow of War*, 191; Pells, *Liberal Mind in a Conservative Age*, 232–35.

5 *FRUS, 1952–1954*, 2:1106–9.

6 Ambrose, *The President*, 94; *FRUS, 1952–1954: Eastern Europe; The Soviet Union* (1988), 8:1147–55, 1162–64.

7 *FRUS, 1952–1954*, 2:1150–60, 1160–74; Eisenhower quoted in Jacobs, "Ground Zero," 130.

8 Meeting of the Special Committee of the National Security Council on Atomic Energy, February 24, 1953, "#16 Special Committee Meetings" folder, ESF, WHO: Box 5, NSCS, DDEL.

9 Former member of the AEC quoted in Bird and Sherwin, *American Prometheus*, 362.

10 Memorandum for Files, ca. 7/13/53, "Candor 1953" folder, AECS, Box 14, Strauss Papers, HHL.

11 Quoted in Ambrose, *The President*, 133.

12 *FRUS, 1952–1954*, 2:1213, 1137–39.

13 Stefan T. Possony to Lewis L. Strauss, July 20, 1953, "Atoms for Peace, 1949–1953" folder, AECS, Box 8, Strauss Papers, HHL; Stefan T. Possony to Lewis L. Strauss, August 13, 1953, ibid.

14 Notes on: Control of Atomic Energy, October 13, 1953, "Wheaties, October 3–14" folder, AECS, Box 120, Strauss Papers, HHL; Untitled Memorandum, by LLS [Lewis L. Strauss], November 6, 1953, "Atoms for Peace" folder, Administration series, Box 5, Whitman File, DDEL.

15 Notes on Control of Atomic Energy, October 13, 1953, "Wheaties, October 3–14" folder, AECS, Box 120, Strauss Papers, HHL; Untitled Memorandum by LLS, November 6, 1953, "Atoms for Peace" folder, Administration series, Box 5, Whitman File, DDEL; Rotter, "Gender Relations, Foreign Relations," 523–37.

16 *FRUS, 1952–1954*, 2:1235–40, 1296–97; Chronology — Candor — Wheaties, September 30, 1954, "Atoms for Peace" folder, Administration series, Box 5, Whitman File, DDEL.

17 Diary entry, Speech before the United Nations, December 10, 1953, "DDE Diary — October–December 1953" folder, DDE Diaries, Box 4, Whitman File, DDEL; Memorandum re: The President's United Nations Address, n.d., "PSB [Psychological Strategy Board] 388.3 [Disarmament]" folder, PSB Central File series, WHO: Box 28, NSCS, DDEL; Text of the "Atoms for Peace" Speech Delivered to the United Nations General Assembly by the President, December 8, 1953, Document #141, National Security Archive, *U.S. Nuclear Non-Proliferation*.

18 *FRUS, 1952–1953*, 2:1106–9, 1247–49; Bernard Brodie to Lewis Strauss, October 28, 1953, "Brodie, Bernard, 1953–54" folder, AECS, Box 11, Strauss Papers, HHL; Diary entry, Speech before the United Nations, December 10, 1953, "DDE Diary October–December 1953" folder, DDE Diaries, Box 4, Whitman File, DDEL; Some Final

Observations on the Subject of "Candor," January 15, 1954, "Wheaties, 1954" folder, AECS, Box 120, Strauss Papers, HHL.

19 *FRUS, 1952–1954*, 2:1244–47.

20 Ibid., 5:1750–54; Minutes of the Thirty-eighth Meeting of the General Advisory Committee to the U.S. Atomic Energy Commission, January 6, 7, and 8, 1954, Document #152, National Security Archive, *U.S. Nuclear Non-Proliferation*; *FRUS, 1952–1954*, 2:1296–97.

21 Senator B. B. Hickenlooper's Statement Regarding President Eisenhower's Speech of December 8 before the United Nations, December 1953, "Atoms for Peace, 1949–54" folder, AECS, Box 8, Strauss Papers, HHL; Summary of Reaction to President Eisenhower's Speech before the General Assembly, December 8, 1953, Document #142, National Security Archive, *U.S. Nuclear Non-Proliferation*; quoted in Gerard C. Smith, *Disarming Diplomat*, 29; quoted in Herken, *Counsels of War*, 104.

22 Letter from Stefan T. Possony to Lewis L. Strauss, December 15, 1953, "Atoms for Peace, 1949–54" folder, AECS, Box 8, Strauss Papers, HHL.

23 Thomas E. Murray, "Atoms for Peace: The Challenge to U.S.," *New York Times Magazine*, June 6, 1957.

24 *FRUS, 1952–1954*, 2:1295, 1302–3, 1310–12.

25 Ibid., 2:1314–19, 1323–24; Memorandum of Telephone Conversation with James Hagerty, White House, Folder 6, TCS, Box 10, D/E/P.

26 Divine, *Blowing on the Wind*, 6–8; *FRUS, 1952–1954*, 6:1018–19, 1379–80.

27 Ferrell, *Diary of James C. Hagerty*, 40, 42.

28 *FRUS, 1952–1954: China and Japan* (1985), 14:1643–48.

29 Memorandum for Mr. Strauss's Files, April 1, 1954, "Dulles, John Foster, 1953–54" folder, AECS, Box 26A, Strauss Papers, HHL; *Documents on Disarmament, 1945–59*, 1:408–11.

30 Handwritten memorandum, n.d., "Eisenhower, Dwight D., 1954, January–June" folder, AECS, Box 26D, Strauss Papers, HHL; *FRUS, 1952–1954*, 2:1383; ibid., 5:499–501; Memorandum of Dinner Conversation with Sir Winston Churchill, April 12, 1954, Folder 13, WHM, Box 1, D/E/P; Memorandum of Conference with President Eisenhower, Augusta, Ga., April 19, 1954, Folder 13, WHM, Box 1, D/E/P.

31 *FRUS, 1952–1954: Western European Security* (1983), 5:505–9; ibid., 2:1387–92, 1413–17.

32 Ibid., 2:1413–17.

33 Ibid., 2:1418–19; Memorandum for the Files of Lewis L. Strauss, May 3, 1954, "Memoranda for the Record, 1954" folder, AECS, Box 66, Strauss Papers, HHL.

34 *FRUS, 1952–1954*, 2:1423–29.

35 Ibid., 2:1437–40, 1445–49, 1452–56; Meeting of the Special Committee of the National Security Council on Atomic Energy, February 24, 1953, "#16 Special Committee Meeting" folder, ESF, WHO: Box 5, NSCS, DDEL.

36 *FRUS, 1952–1954*, 2:1457–58, 1463–72.

37 Ibid., 2:1256–85; ibid., 5:449–54, 1767–69, 1771–72; Statement on Proposed Changes in the Atomic Energy Act, n.d., Document #134, National Security Archive, *U.S. Nuclear*

Non-Proliferation; Handwritten Memorandum, December 1953, "C. D. Jackson, 1952–53" folder, AECS, Box 50, Strauss Papers, HHL; quoted in Botti, *Long Wait*, 130.

38 *FRUS, 1952–1954: Western Europe and Canada* (1987), 6:1085–86, 1096–97; Memorandum for Files of Lewis L. Strauss, June 28, 1954, "Cherwell, Lord, 1953–55" folder, AECS, Box 15, Strauss Papers, HHL; Dietl, "Une Déception," 28–35.

39 *FRUS, 1952–1954*, 2:1459–60, 1462–63, 1473–77.

40 Ibid., 2:1477–79; ibid., 3:1508–11; Memorandum from F. Banner Evans to Dr. Horace Craig, Subject: Soviet Propaganda on Atomic Issues, August 9, 1954, "OCB 000.9 [Atomic Energy] (File #1) (9)" folder, OCB [Operations Coordinating Board] Central Files, WHO: Box 8, NSCS, DDEL.

41 *FRUS, 1952–1954*, 2:1482–88, 1488–99.

42 Ibid., 2:1518–19, 1524–25, 1529–31, 1546–47, 1570–76.

43 Ibid., 2:1554–55, 1567–69; Telephone Call to Ambassador Lodge, October 29, 1954, Folder 1, TCS, Box 3, D/E/P.

44 *FRUS, 1952–1954*, 2:1580–82; ibid., 6:1497–98; *FRUS, 1955–1957: Regulation of Armaments; Atomic Energy* (1990), 20:1–7, 15–20.

45 Kirby, "Childe Harold's Pilgrimage," 410; *FRUS, 1955–1957*, 20:60–62.

46 Memorandum: Status of Draft Legislation in West Germany for Future Control of Atomic Energy Matters, July 6, 1954, Document #164, National Security Archive, *U.S. Nuclear Non-Proliferation*; *FRUS, 1952–1954*, 5:1345–66. For Adenauer's questionable version of his exchange with Dulles, see Hans-Peter Schwarz, *Konrad Adenauer*, 122–24. See also Dietl, "Une Déception," 33–35, for evidence that this pledge resulted from British diplomatic maneuverings that the United States did not fully endorse; and Cioc, *Pax Atomica*, xix.

47 Memorandum for the Files of Lewis L. Strauss, January 14, 1955, "Memoranda for the Record, 1955, January–September" folder, AECS, Box 66, Strauss Papers, HHL; Lewis Strauss to President Eisenhower, January 14, 1955, Document #185, National Security Archive, *U.S. Nuclear Non-Proliferation*.

48 *FRUS, 1955–1957*, 20:11–15, 20–34; Divine, *Blowing on the Wind*, 38–41.

49 Intelligence Report by the State Department Estimates Group—Recent Effects of Increasing Nuclear Capabilities on U.S. Allies, February 16, 1955, "Moratorium on Nuclear Tests 1955 (1)" folder, WHO: Box 5, OSD.

50 *FRUS, 1955–1957*, 20:56–57.

51 Memorandum for the Files of Lewis L. Strauss, March 21, 1955, "Memoranda for the Record, 1955, January–September" folder, AECS, Box 66, Strauss Papers, HHL; Memorandum to Mr. Smith from Mr. Key, Subject: Moratorium on Atomic Testing, March 23, 1955, "Moratorium on Nuclear Weapons Tests—1955 (1)" folder, WHO: Box 5, OSD; *FRUS, 1955–1957*, 20:62–64, 76–78, 85–86; Draft Memorandum, Subject: Proposal for Moratorium on Testing of Large Thermonuclear Weapons, April 18, 1955, "#20 Moratorium on Tests (2)" folder, ESF, WHO: Box 6, NSCS, DDEL; *Documents on Disarmament, 1945–59*, 1:456–67; Telegram from the U.S. Embassy in the United Kingdom to the Secretary of State, May 11, 1955, SDDF; Summary and Comments on Soviet Disarmament Proposals of May 1955, May 13, 1955, SDDF.

52 Evangelista, "Cooperation Theory"; Holloway, *Stalin and the Bomb*, 335–41; Richter, *Khrushchev's Double Bind*, 53–76; Larson, *Anatomy of Mistrust*, 64–71; quoted in Pruessen, "From Good Breakfast to Bad Supper," 269; *FRUS, 1955–1957*, 20:136–42.

53 *FRUS, 1955–1957*, 20:73–74, 90–92; Memorandum to the Undersecretary of State (Hoover), May 26, 1955, SDDF; Stephen I. Schwartz, *Atomic Audit*, 422–23. Some within the government had warned of fallout dangers as early as 1947. See Greene, *Eisenhower, Science Advice, and the Nuclear Test Ban Debate*, 11.

54 *FRUS, 1955–1957*, 20:20–34, 46–55, 71–72; Memorandum of Conversation, New York, May 11, 1955, ibid., 81–84; Operation Kremlin Kracks, February 16, 1955, "Jackson, C. D., 1955 (2)" folder, Administration series, Box 22, Whitman File, DDEL; Letter from the President to the Secretary of State, March 7, 1955, "Re Atomic Energy, Atomic Weapons, and Disarmament, 1955" folder, SCS, Box 89, Dulles Papers, DDEL.

55 Stassen and Houts, *Eisenhower*, 299–305; *FRUS, 1955–1957*, 20:93–109.

56 *FRUS, 1955–1957*, 20:109–13, 116–17, 121–25, 136–45; Memorandum for Mr. Anderson, Subject: First Look at the Fundamentals of the Stassen Plan, June 9, 1955, "Disarmament — General (3) (1955–56)" folder, Subject subseries, Special Assistant series, WHO: Box 4, OSANSA, DDEL.

57 Quoted in Appleby, "Eisenhower and Arms Control," 104–5.

58 *FRUS, 1955–1957*, 20:240–50, 255–57, 260–68, 276–79, 307–11, 319–28; Letter from the Atomic Energy Commission to Harold Stassen, December 2, 1955, Document #221, National Security Archive, *U.S. Nuclear Non-Proliferation*; Memorandum for the Secretary of State from the Chairman of the Atomic Energy Commission, December 13, 1955, "Atomic Energy Commission (Accountable Documents) (7)" folder, Alpha subseries, Subject series, WHO: Box 4, Records of the OSS, DDEL; Memorandum for the Secretary of Defense, November 18, 1955, Document #219, National Security Archive, *U.S. Nuclear Non-Proliferation*.

59 Lewis, Wilson, and Xue, *China Builds the Bomb*, 34–72; Chang, "To the Nuclear Brink," 121–22; Khrushchev, *Khrushchev Remembers: The Last Testament*, 268–71; Holloway, *Stalin and the Bomb*, 355; Hersh, *Sampson Option*, 33–46; Pinkus, "Atomic Power to Israel's Rescue."

60 *FRUS, 1955–1957*, 20:198–99.

61 *FRUS, 1955–1957: European Security and Integration* (1986), 4:304–7, 322–23, 355–60, 378–87, 406–7. The French, however, did agree to a two- to three-year moratorium on the production of nuclear weapons as long as research and development were not restricted. See Dietl, "Une Déception," 37.

62 *FRUS, 1955–1957*, 20:355–59; Letter from Lewis Strauss to Harold Stassen, February 7, 1956, "Disarmament — General (1955–56) (2)" folder, Subject subseries, Special Assistant series, WHO: Box 4, OSANSA, DDEL; Telephone Call to Admiral Radford, February 10, 1956, 2:29 P.M., Folder 17, TCS, Box 4, D/E/P; Memorandum for the Files of Lewis L. Strauss, February 10, 1956, "Dulles, J. F., 1956" folder, AECS, Box 26A, Strauss Papers, HHL.

63 *FRUS, 1955–1957: Western Europe and Canada* (1992), 27:629–39, 645–50; *FRUS, 1955–57*, 20:343–46; Telegram from the U.S. Embassy in the United Kingdom to the Department of State, November 30, 1955, Document #220, National Security Archive, *U.S. Nuclear Non-Proliferation*; Memorandum of Conversation with Thomas E. Murray, Atomic Energy Commission, January 10, 1956, "Memos of Conversation — General — L through M (4)" folder, GCM, Box 1, Dulles Papers, DDEL; Position Paper on the Suspension of Experimental Explosions of Nuclear Weapons, February 27, 1956, "DCS [Disarmament Committee Session] Position Papers (9)" folder, WHO: Box 3, OSD.

64 *FRUS, 1955–1957*, 20:360–61.

65 Ibid., 20:366–68, 370, 378–88, 393–400; Telegram from U.S. Delegation Disarmament Subcommittee to Secretary of State, May 5, 1956, "Disarmament Basic Papers (1955–56) (4)" folder, Subject subseries, Special Assistant series, WHO: Box 4, OSANSA, DDEL; Memorandum to the President from Harold Stassen, May 8, 1956, "Stassen, 1956 (3)" folder, Administration series, Box 35, Whitman File, DDEL; Telegram from U.S. Delegation Disarmament Subcommittee to Secretary of State, April 21, 1956, SDDF; Telegram from U.S. Delegation Disarmament Subcommittee to Secretary of State, April 23, 1956, ibid.

66 *FRUS, 1955–1957*, 20:402–8; Revised Outline List of Reasons, Motivations, or Incentives for "Fourth Countries" to Abstain or Not from Nuclear Weapons Fabrication or Possession, June 8, 1956, Document #259, National Security Archive, *U.S. Nuclear Non-Proliferation*.

67 Telephone Call to Admiral Radford, 8:57 A.M., July 20, 1956, Folder 13, TCS, Box 5, D/E/P; Letter from Lewis Strauss to Harold Stassen, July 26, 1956, Document #267, National Security Archive, *U.S. Nuclear Non-Proliferation*; Memorandum of Conference with the President at Gettysburg, July 12, 1956, "Stassen, 1956 (2)" folder, Administrative series, Box 34, Whitman File, DDEL.

68 Diary entry, January 10, 1956, "Diary — Copies of DDE Personal [1955–56] (2)" folder, DDE Diaries series, Box 9, Whitman File, DDEL; Memorandum for the Files of Lewis L. Strauss, August 2, 1956, "Eisenhower, D.D., 1956, July–October" folder, AECS, Box 26E, Strauss Papers, HHL.

69 *FRUS, 1955–1957*, 20:419–27; Memorandum for the Files of Lewis L. Strauss, September 11, 1956, "Dulles, J. F., 1956" folder, AECS, Box 26A, Strauss Papers, HHL; Telephone Call to Mr. Stassen, September 11, 1956, Folder 10, TCS, Box 5, D/E/P; Memorandum of Conference with the President, September 11, 1956, 3:45 P.M., Document #274, National Security Archive, *U.S. Nuclear Non-Proliferation*.

70 Memorandum of Conference with the President, September 11, 1956, 3:45 P.M., Document #274, National Security Archive, *U.S. Nuclear Non-Proliferation*; *FRUS, 1955–1957*, 20:423–28.

71 *FRUS, 1955–1957*, 20:429–32.

72 Walter Johnson, *Papers of Adlai E. Stevenson*, 6:110–21; Memorandum for the Secretary from J. W. Hanes Jr., April 23, 1956, "[Miscellaneous Correspondence, March 3,

1956–May 7, 1956]" folder, GCM, Box 4, Dulles Papers, DDEL; Phone calls—April 23, 1956, "April 1956—Phone Calls" folder, DDE Diaries series, Box 15, Whitman File, DDEL.

73 *FRUS, 1955–1957*, 20:400–402; Memorandum of Conference with the President, May 29, 1956, "May '56 Goodpaster" folder, DDE Diaries, Box 15, Whitman File, DDEL.

74 *FRUS, 1955–1957*, 20:408–9; Handwritten Memorandum by Lewis Strauss, July 9, 1956, "Eisenhower, D. D., 1956, July–October" folder, AECS, Box 26E, Strauss Papers, HHL; quoted in Kimmel, *Manhood in America*, 237; quoted in Hofstadter, *Anti-Intellectualism in American Life*, 9–10, 227; quoted in Divine, *Blowing on the Wind*, 87–88.

75 *Documents on Disarmament, 1945–59*, 1:694–96; Telephone Calls, October 23, 1956, "October 1956 Phone Calls" folder, DDE Diaries, Box 18, Whitman File, DDEL.

76 Memorandum of Conference with the President, September 11, 1956, Document #274, National Security Archive, *U.S. Nuclear Non-Proliferation*.

Chapter 5

1 *FRUS, 1955–1957*, 20:486–90.

2 Newhouse, *War and Peace in the Nuclear Age*, 130–31; Dietl, "Une Déception," 45–52.

3 Clark, *Nuclear Diplomacy and the Special Relationship*, 65–74.

4 *FRUS, 1955–1957: Western Europe and Canada* (1992), 27:733–42, 766; Memorandum of Conversation, March 23, 1957, "Bermuda 1957—Chronology, Saturday, March 23, 1957 (1)" folder, International Trips and Meetings series, WHO: Box 2, Records of the OSS, DDEL.

5 Quoted in Appleby, "Eisenhower and Arms Control," 191.

6 Telephone Call from Admiral Strauss, Folder 7, TCS, Box 6, D/E/P; *FRUS, 1955–1957*, 20:486–90.

7 Telephone Call to the President in Gettysburg, May 13, 1957, Folder 3, TCS, Box 12, D/E/P; Summary Minutes—Meeting of the President's Special Committee on Disarmament Problems, May 1, 1957, "Disarmament Problems Committee—Records of Action (7)" folder, WHO: Box 4, OSD, DDEL.

8 *FRUS, 1955–1957*, 20:532–38.

9 Ibid., 20:539–43, 545–55.

10 Quoted in Hewlett and Holl, *Atoms for Peace and War*, 450.

11 Dietl, "Une Déception," 48–49.

12 Quoted in Gerard C. Smith, *Disarming Diplomat*, 55; Memorandum of Conversation with the President, June 4, 1957, "Meetings with the President 1957 (5)" folder, WHM, Box 6, Dulles Papers, DDEL.

13 Quoted in Wittner, *Resisting the Bomb*, 138, 142.

14 Quoted in ibid., 135, 138, 142; quoted in Hofstadter, *Anti-Intellectualism in American Life*, 10, 227.

15 Newhouse, *War and Peace in the Nuclear Age*, 139; *FRUS, 1955–1957*, 20:638–40; Clean Weapons Effects, n.d., "Clean Weapons, 1956–57 and undated" folder, AECS, Box 16, Strauss Papers, HHL.

16 Hewlett and Holl, *Atoms for Peace and War*, 449; Katz, *Ban the Bomb*, 21–22.

17 Quoted in Hewlett and Holl, *Atoms for Peace and War*, 456.

18 *FRUS, 1955–1957*, 20:638–40, 754–55; Memorandum of Conference with the President, October 29, 1957, Document #348, National Security Archive, *U.S. Nuclear Non-Proliferation*.

19 National Intelligence Estimate 100-6-57: Nuclear Weapons Production in Fourth Countries: Likelihood and Consequences, June 18, 1957, CIA FOIA [Freedom of Information Act] Release, <www.gwu.edu/~nsarchiv> (accessed September 7, 2008).

20 *FRUS, 1958–1960, National Security Policy: Arms Control and Disarmament* (1996), 3:1–3.

21 For the phrase "nuclear flirtation" and further details on the Franco-German nuclear talks, see Kohl, *French Nuclear Diplomacy*, 54–61; Kelleher, *Germany and the Politics of Nuclear Weapons*, 146–53; Ahonen, "Franz-Josef Strauss and the German Nuclear Question," 31–33; and Hans-Peter Schwarz, *Konrad Adenauer*, 317–24; quoted in Dockrill, *Eisenhower's New Look National Security Policy*, 215.

22 Eisenhower quoted in Botti, *Long Wait*, 201.

23 *Amending the Atomic Energy Act of 1954*, Hearings before the Subcommittee on Agreements for Cooperation of the Joint Committee on Atomic Energy, 85th Cong., 2nd Sess. (1958), 453–54; *FRUS, 1958–1960*, 3:259–70.

24 *FRUS, 1952–1954*, 2:1452–56; *FRUS, 1958–1960*, 3:277–91. For Wilson's statement, see Førland, "Selling Firearms to the Indians," 221.

25 *FRUS, 1958–1960*, 3:277–91; Telegram from the United States Delegation to the United Nations to the Department of State, October 4, 1957, RG 59, SDDF; for the text of the lectures, see Kennan, *Russia, the Atom, and the West*.

26 For a full explanation of dual containment, see Hanrieder, *Germany, America, Europe*; quoted in Chase, *Acheson*, 376; Hershberg, *James B. Conant*, 703–4.

27 Ulam, *Rivals*, 290–91.

28 Report on Congressional Hearings, Document #416, National Security Archive, *U.S. Nuclear Non-Proliferation*; Telephone Call to Mr. Farley, May 23, 1958, Folder 5, TCS, Box 8, D/E/P; Botti, *Long Wait*, 224–36.

29 Telephone Call Chronology—May 1, 1958, "Telephone Calls—May 1958" folder, DDE Diaries, Box 33, Whitman File, DDEL.

30 Bozo, *Two Strategies*, 10–11, 40.

31 Memorandum of Conversation, June 9, 1958, Document #431, National Security Archive, *U.S. Nuclear Non-Proliferation*; Telegram from the U.S. Embassy in France to the Secretary of State, June 27, 1958, Document #440, ibid.; Telegram from the U.S. Embassy in France to the Secretary of State, June 28, 1958, Document #441, ibid.; *FRUS, 1958–1960: Western European Integration and Canada* (1993), 7:53–64.

32 *FRUS, 1958–1960*, 7:53–64; ibid., 3:139–45.

33 Record of Meeting in the Palais Schaumburg, October 8, 1958, PREM 11/302, PRO;

Foreign Service Despatch from U.S. Embassy in West Germany to the Department of State, July 31, 1958, Document #448, National Security Archive, *U.S. Nuclear Non-Proliferation.*

34 Quoted in Rusk, *As I Saw It,* 227.

35 Memorandum of Conference with the President, June 16, 1959, Document #562, National Security Archive, *U.S. Nuclear Non-Proliferation.* For a detailed account of the IRBMs' lukewarm reception and Eisenhower's lack of control over the program, see Nash, *Other Missiles of October,* 5–75.

36 Memorandum from Hans Bethe to Dr. James Killian, August 14, 1958, "Arms Control" folder, U.S. President's Science Advisory Committee Records, Box 3, DDEL; Letter to Dr. Ernest Lawrence from Lewis L. Strauss, June 23, 1958, "Lawrence, 1957–58" folder, AECS, Box 59, Strauss Papers, HHL.

37 Memorandum of Conference with the President, August 4, 1958, "Dr. [James R.] Killian (2)" folder, White House subseries, Subject series, WHO: Box 4, Records of the OSS, DDEL; Memorandum by John A. Morse, Special Assistant to the Chairman, June 24, 1958, "Monitoring of Soviet Tests, 1958–71 and undated" folder, AECS, Box 68, Strauss Papers, HHL.

38 Telegram from Secretary of State Dulles to Acting Secretary Herter, August 21, 1958, "Atomic Energy Commission, Vol. II (4)" folder, Alphabetical subseries, Subject series, WHO: Box 3, Records of the OSS, DDEL; Telephone Call to Governor Herter (Washington), August 20, 1958, Folder 4, TCS, Box 9, D/E/P; Telephone Call from Governor Herter, August 21, 1958, Folder 4, TCS, Box 1, D/E/P; National Committee for a Sane Nuclear Policy Executive Committee Meeting, August 22, 1958, "Minutes, Resolutions, Etc.—Executive Committee, 1957–59" folder, Series A: Records of SANE, Inc., Box 4, SCPC.

39 Memorandum for John A. McCone from J. R. Killian Jr., December 5, 1958, "Killian, James R., 1958–59" folder, AECS, Box 55, Strauss Papers, HHL; Memorandum of Conference with the President, January 5, 1959, "Staff Notes—January 1959 (2)" folder, DDE Diaries, Box 38, Whitman File, DDEL; Wadsworth, *Price of Peace,* 24; *FRUS, 1958–1960,* 3:683–87.

40 Letter from Khrushchev to Eisenhower, April 23, 1959, "Khrushchev, April 1959–November 1959 (1)" folder, International series, Box 52, Whitman File, DDEL; *FRUS, 1958–1960,* 3:712–14; Memorandum of Conversation, March 22, 1959, "Disarmament—Nuclear Test Policy [March 1958–September 1959] (3)" folder, WHO: Box 2, OSAST, DDEL; Minutes of Meeting of the Interdepartmental Working Group on Disarmament, Document #539, National Security Archive, *U.S. Nuclear Non-Proliferation;* Risse-Kappen, *Cooperation among Democracies,* 118–21; Ashton, "Harold Macmillan," 697–704; Greene, *Eisenhower, Science Advice, and the Nuclear Test Ban Debate,* 185.

41 Memorandum of Conversation, July 9, 1959, "Disarmament—Nuclear Test Policy [May 1958–October 1960] (3)" folder, WHO: Box 8, OSAST, DDEL; Notes on Pre-Press Conference Briefing, June 3, 1959, "Staff Notes—June 1–15, 1959 (2)" folder,

DDE Diaries, Box 42, Whitman File, DDEL; quoted in Killian, *Sputnik, Scientists, and Eisenhower*, 168.

42 Memorandum of Conversation, September 17, 1959, Document #1657, National Security Archive, *Berlin Crisis, 1958–1962*.

43 Memorandum of Conference with the President, October 16, 1959, "Staff Notes, October 1959 (1)" folder, DDE Diaries, Box 45, Whitman File, DDEL.

44 Letter from Khrushchev to Eisenhower, March 3, 1960, "Khrushchev, November 2, 1959 (2)" folder, International series, Box 3, Whitman File, DDEL; Telegram from President Eisenhower to Soviet premier Nikita Khrushchev, March 12, 1960, Document #1838, National Security Archive, *Berlin Crisis, 1958–1962*; Telegram from Department of State to U.S. Mission to NATO, March 16, 1960, "Atom-NUCL Policy '60 (3)" folder, Box 85, Norstad Papers, DDEL; Letter from President Eisenhower to Soviet premier Khrushchev, April 1, 1960, "Khrushchev, November 2, 1959 (4)" folder, International series, Box 53, Whitman File, DDEL; quoted in Gaddis, *We Now Know*, 229.

45 *FRUS, 1958–1960: Berlin Crisis, 1959–1960; Germany; Austria* (1993), 9:162–65, 321; Memorandum for Brig. Gen. A. J. Goodpaster, March 27, 1960, "Paris — Summit Meeting, May 1960 (4)" folder, International series, Box 13, Whitman File, DDEL; Memorandum — Special Meeting of the National Security Council, February 18, 1960, "Special Meeting of the NSC, 2-18-60" folder, NSC series, Box 12, Whitman File, DDEL.

46 *FRUS, 1958–1960*, 9:426–35.

47 Memorandum of Conference with the President, November 11, 1959, "Atomic Energy Commission, Vol. II (7)" folder, Alphabetical subseries, Subject series, WHO: Box 3, Records of the OSS, DDEL; Kistiakowsky, *Scientist in the White House*, 195; Memorandum to the President from Secretary Herter, November 7, 1959, "Herter, November 1959 (2)" folder, Dulles-Herter series, Box 12, Whitman File, DDEL; Telephone Calls, November 10, 1959, "CAH Telephone Call 5/4/59 to 12/31/59 (1)" folder, Box 12, Herter Papers, DDEL; Memorandum of Conversation, Department of State, December 28, 1959, "Disarmament — Nuclear Test Policy [May 1958–October 1960] (5)" folder, WHO: Box 8, OSAST, DDEL.

48 Memorandum of Conversation with John McCone, December 16, 1959, "Disarmament — Nuclear Test Policy [May 1958–October 1960] (5)" folder, WHO: Box 8, OSAST, DDEL; Memorandum of Conversation, Department of State, January 19, 1960, ibid.; Memorandum of Conversation, Department of State, October 6, 1959, "Disarmament — Nuclear Test Policy [May 1958–October 1960] (4)" folder, WHO: Box 8, OSAST, DDEL.

49 Weart, *Nuclear Fear*, 222–24.

50 Cabinet Agenda for Friday, December 11, 1959, "Cabinet Meeting, December 11, 1959" folder, Cabinet series, Box 15, Whitman File, DDEL; Minutes of the Cabinet Meeting, December 11, 1959, ibid.; "'On the Beach' — Joint USIA-State Information Guidance for Missions Abroad," December 7, 1959, ibid.; *FRUS, 1958–1960*, 3:397–404.

51 Memorandum of Conversation, Department of State, March 23, 1960, "Disarmament—Nuclear Test Policy [May 1958–October 1960] (6)" folder, WHO: Box 8, OSAST, DDEL; Memorandum of Conference, Department of State, August 2, 1960, ibid.; Memorandum of Conference, Department of State, August 11, 1960, ibid.

52 National Intelligence Estimate No. 13-12-60: The Chinese Communist Atomic Energy Program, December 13, 1960, Document #715, National Security Archive, *U.S. Nuclear Non-Proliferation*; Considerations on the Nth Power Problem, April 18, 1960, Document #639, ibid.; Memorandum of Conference with the President, April 22, 1960, "Staff Notes, April 1960 (1)" folder, DDE Diaries, Box 49, Whitman File, DDEL; Memorandum to Goodpaster from McCone, December 1, 1960, "AEC, 1960–61" folder, Administration series, Box 5, Whitman File, DDEL.

53 Telegram from the U.S. Embassy in India to the Department of State, December 24, 1959, Document #612, National Security Archive, *U.S. Nuclear Non-Proliferation*; *FRUS, 1958–1960*, 16:187–90; Perkovich, *India's Nuclear Bomb*, 36–37. Perkovich points out that Bhabha was clearly exaggerating and that India was several years away from being able to produce nuclear explosives.

54 *FRUS, 1958–1960*, 7:203–7, 367–69; Memorandum of Conference with the President, April 22, 1960, "Staff Notes, April 1960 (1)" folder, DDE Diaries, Box 49, Whitman File, DDEL; Hewlett and Holl, *Atoms for Peace and War*, 563; Nuclear Sharing for Defense Purposes, n.d., "O & M 12-1—Cooperation, Coordination, and Liaison—White House [March 1958–June 1960] (1)" folder, Box 3, McCone Papers, DDEL; Memorandum of Conference with the President, November 8, 1960, "Atomic Energy Commission, Vol. III (5)" folder, Alphabetical subseries, Subject series, WHO: Box 4, Records of the OSS, DDEL; Newhouse, *War and Peace in the Nuclear Age*, 133–36.

55 Telegram from the Department of State to U.S. Embassy in France, October 31, 1960, "Atom-NUCL Policy '60 (2)" folder, Box 85, Norstad Papers, DDEL; Telegram from U.S. Embassy in the United Kingdom to Department of State, December 11, 1959, Document #604, National Security Archive, *U.S. Nuclear Non-Proliferation*; Memorandum of Conversation, Department of State, October 4, 1960, Document #683, ibid.; *FRUS, 1958–1960*, 7:608–11, 682–83; Telegram from the Department of State to U.S. Embassy in France, December 13, 1960, "Atom-NUCL '60 (1)" folder, Box 85, Norstad Papers, DDEL.

Chapter 6

1 Kennedy, *Profiles in Courage*, 1, 239; Slotkin, *Gunfighter Nation*, 497–504; Dean, *Imperial Brotherhood*, 43–49; Nevins, *Strategy of Peace*, 23–25; quoted in Seaborg, *Kennedy, Khrushchev, and the Test Ban*, 199.

2 *Cold War International History Project Bulletin* 4 (Fall 1994): 64–67; Beschloss, *Crisis Years*, 40.

3 Beschloss, *Crisis Years*, 45–46; quoted in Bird, *Chairman*, 499.

4 *Documents on Disarmament, 1961,* 1–20; Richter, *Khrushchev's Double Bind,* 138–39; *PPOP: Kennedy, 1961* (1962), 1–3.

5 Quoted in Reeves, *President Kennedy,* 29; FRUS, *1961–1963: Arms Control and Disarmament* (1995), 7:10–14.

6 Quoted in Paterson, *Kennedy's Quest for Victory,* 3; McLellan and Acheson, *Among Friends,* 207.

7 Beschloss, *Crisis Years,* 70–71, 356–60; quoted in Halberstam, *Best and the Brightest,* 79; quoted in Seaborg, *Kennedy, Khrushchev, and the Test Ban,* 38.

8 Quoted in Gardner, "Harry Hopkins with Hand Grenades"; Letter from Grenville Clark to Joseph Clark, January 6, 1961, Clark Papers, Hanover, N.H.; Bird, *Color of Truth,* 189.

9 Naftali, Zelikow, and May, *Presidential Recordings—John F. Kennedy,* 1:47–50; Arthur M. Schlesinger Jr. quoted in Slotkin, *Gunfighter Nation,* 502; Oral History, Chester Bowles, pp. 47, 90, JFKL; Oral History, Roswell L. Gilpatric, p. 76, JFKL.

10 Oral History, Curtis LeMay, p. 7, LBJL.

11 FRUS, *1961–1963: Arms Control and Disarmament* (1995), 7:58–66, 71–78; Oliver, *Kennedy, Macmillan, and the Nuclear Test Ban Debate,* 82.

12 FRUS, *1961–1963,* 7:56–59, 69–71; Record of Actions, May 2, 1961, "National Security Council Meetings 1961—no. 482, 5/2/61" folder, Meetings and Memoranda, NSF, Box 313, JFKL.

13 Quoted in Hersh, *Sampson Option,* 98; National Intelligence Estimate—The Chinese Atomic Energy Program, December 13, 1960, Document #715, National Security Archive, *U.S. Nuclear Non-Proliferation;* Oral History, Walt W. Rostow, p. 63, JFKL; quoted in Kochavi, *Conflict Perpetuated,* 202; Chang, *Friends and Enemies,* 229, 236; Yi, "American Response," 85–88; quoted in Wittner, *Resisting the Bomb,* 162; quoted in Gaddis, *We Now Know,* 218, 252.

14 Executive Sessions of the Senate Foreign Relations Committee (Historical Series), Vol. 13, Pt. 1, 87th Cong., 1st Sess., 1961, p. 8, Document #739, National Security Archive, *U.S. Nuclear Non-Proliferation;* Memorandum on Franco-Israeli Collaboration, April 1961, "Ben-Gurion Visit—The Arab-Israeli Situation" Folder, Country File, NSF, Box 119a, JFKL; Memorandum for President, Subject: Israel's Atomic Energy Activities, January 30, 1961, Document #745, National Security Archive, *U.S. Nuclear Non-Proliferation.*

15 FRUS, *1961–1963: Western Europe and Canada* (1994), 13:283–84, 1035–39; quoted in Thomas Alan Schwartz, "Victories and Defeats," 117.

16 Department of State Report on NATO, n.d., "Department of State 1/61" folder, Department and Agencies series, POF, Box 87, JFKL; Oral History, Paul H. Nitze, pp. 2–3, JFKL; Newhouse, *War and Peace in the Nuclear Age,* 185–86.

17 Quoted in Costigliola, "Pursuit of Atlantic Community," 32; Nash, *Other Missiles of October,* 193; National Security Action Memorandum No. 36, Subject: Improving the Security of Nuclear Weapons in NATO Europe against Unauthorized Use, April 6, 1961, Document #762, National Security Archive, *U.S. Nuclear Non-Proliferation.*

18 Quoted in Costigliola, "Pursuit of Atlantic Community," 36–37; Thomas Alan Schwartz, "Victories and Defeats," 127–33; Trachtenberg, *Constructed Peace*, 284.

19 *FRUS, 1961–1963*, 13:269–72, 654–56; Memorandum on Ambassador-at-Large W. Averell Harriman's Conversation with German Defense Minister Franz Josef Strauss, March 8, 1961, Document #757, National Security Archive, *U.S. Nuclear Non-Proliferation.*

20 *FRUS, 1961–1963*, 13:253–56, 266–69, 654–56; Oral History, Paul H. Nitze, p. 11, JFKL; Memorandum for the Secretary of State and the Secretary of Defense, May 25, 1962, "State 4/62–5/62" folder, Departments and Agencies, POF, Box 88, JFKL.

21 Quoted in Oral History, Eugene V. Rostow, p. 15, LBJL; quoted in Reeves, *President Kennedy*, 113–14.

22 McLellan and Acheson, *Among Friends*, 202; quoted in Trachtenberg, *Constructed Peace*, 306; Policy Directive — Regarding NATO and the Atlantic Nations, April 20, 1961, "National Security Council — 1961 [2 of 2]" folder, Vice Presidential Security File, Box 4, LBJL; Letter from Dean Acheson to General Lauris Norstad, March 23, 1961, Document #761, National Security Archive, *U.S. Nuclear Non-Proliferation*; quoted in Ashton, *Kennedy, Macmillan, and the Cold War*, 137.

23 Brinkley, *Dean Acheson*, 123–24; *Documents on Disarmament, 1961*, 149–51.

24 *FRUS, 1961–1963*, 13:309–16, 662–67; quoted in Bozo, *Two Strategies*, 67; quoted in Beschloss, *Crisis Years*, 185–86.

25 Guthman and Shulman, *Robert Kennedy*, 258–63; quoted in Reeves, *President Kennedy*, 136–37.

26 Quoted in Reeves, *President Kennedy*, 136; Notes to the President from Ambassador Arthur H. Dean, May 24, 1961, "State 4/61–5/61" folder, Departments and Agencies, POF, Box 88, JFKL.

27 Freedman, *Kennedy's Wars*, 53–54; *FRUS, 1961–1963*, 7:83–91; Memorandum of Conversation, Subject: Meeting between the President and Chairman Khrushchev in Vienna, June 4, 1961, "USSR — Kennedy-Khrushchev Talks at Vienna" folder, Country File, NSF, Box 228, LBJL.

28 *FRUS, 1961–1963*, 7:124–27, 134–37; Memorandum to Vice President Johnson from Colonel Burris — re: Nuclear Testing, August 10, 1961, Document #793, National Security Archive, *U.S. Nuclear Non-Proliferation*; Memorandum from Edward R. Murrow to Undersecretary of State Chester Bowles, Subject: The Nuclear Test Ban Issue, June 24, 1961, "Nuclear Weapons Testing 6/61" folder, Subjects, NSF, Box 299, JFKL.

29 Quoted in Beschloss, *Crisis Years*, 278; Wenger and Suri, "At the Crossroads," 8; *Cold War International History Bulletin* 3 (Fall 1993): 58–61; Zubok, "Khrushchev and the Berlin Crisis," 21–24.

30 Quoted in Halberstam, *Best and the Brightest*, 84; quoted in Reeves, *President Kennedy*, 223; *FRUS, 1961–1963*, 7:167–68.

31 Quoted in Reeves, *President Kennedy*, 223, 227; *FRUS, 1961–1963*, 7:149–63; *Documents on Disarmament, 1961*, 351, 355, 403.

32 Master List of Planning Problems, July 31, 1961 (Third Revision), "Key National Security Problems, 3/61–9/61" folder, Meetings and Memoranda, NSF, Box 318, JFKL; Project Pacifica, n.d., Document #799, National Security Archive, *U.S. Nuclear Non-Proliferation*; Memorandum to Secretary of State Rusk from George C. McGhee, State Department Policy Planning Staff, Subject: Anticipatory Action Pending Chinese Communist Demonstration of a Nuclear Capability, September 13, 1961, NSA; *FRUS, 1961–1963*, 7:194.

33 Quoted in Schoenbaum, *Waging Peace and War*, 330; *Documents on Disarmament, 1961*, 465–75.

34 Nevins, *The Burden and the Glory*, 43–44; Record of the Meeting between the Prime Minister and Dr. Adenauer, February 23, 1961, PREM 11/3345, PRO; Hans-Peter Schwarz, *Konrad Adenauer*, 558–62.

35 Quoted in Trachtenberg, *Constructed Peace*, 330; *FRUS, 1961–1963*, 14:493–97, 614–18; *FRUS, 1961–1963: Soviet Union* (1998), Vol. 5, <www.state.gov/www/about_state/history/vol_v/130_139.html> (accessed September 12, 2008).

36 Winand, *Eisenhower, Kennedy, and the United States of Europe*, 231–32; Newhouse, *De Gaulle and the Anglo-Saxons*, 155–61; Oral History, Paul H. Nitze, pp. 7–11, JFKL.

37 *FRUS, 1961–1963*, 7:254–56.

38 Quoted in Wittner, *Resisting the Bomb*, 377.

39 Rose, *One Nation Underground*, 1–10, 78–112; Henriksen, *Dr. Strangelove's America*, 193–239; Jacobs, "There Are No Civilians," 409–11.

40 *FRUS, 1961–1963*, 7:208–9; Memorandum for the President from McGeorge Bundy, October 27, 1961, Document #810, National Security Archive, *U.S. Nuclear Non-Proliferation*.

41 Quoted in Macmillan, *At the End of the Day*, 156. For "emotional blackmail," see Beschloss, *Crisis Years*, 363.

42 *Documents on Disarmament, 1961*, 542–50; Beschloss, *Crisis Years*, 327–32.

43 Quoted in Bradlee, *Conversations with Kennedy*, 61–63.

44 *FRUS, 1961–1963*, 7:141–48, 231–33; *Documents on Disarmament, 1961*, 693–94.

45 *FRUS, 1961–1963: Berlin Crisis, 1961–1962* (1994), 14:808–11; *FRUS, 1961–1963: Berlin Crisis, 1962–1963* (1994), 15:4–6; Hans-Peter Schwarz, *Konrad Adenauer*, 608; Roger Morgan, "Kennedy and Adenauer," 20–21.

46 *FRUS, 1961–1963*, 13:366–68.

47 Wenger, *Living with Peril*, 267–69.

48 *FRUS, 1961–1963*, 13:835–37; Telegram from the U.S. Embassy in France to the Department of State, April 7, 1962, "Atom-NUCL Policy '62 (2)" folder, Box 85, Norstad Papers, DDEL; *FRUS, 1961–1963*, 15:105–9, 125–31; Memorandum of Conversation, Subject: Berlin, May 3, 1962, Berlin Crisis Project, NSA.

49 *FRUS, 1961–1963*, 13:374–80, 1064–69; Oliver, *Kennedy, Macmillan, and the Nuclear Test Ban Debate*, 43.

Chapter 7

1 *PPOP: Kennedy, 1963* (1964), 280; *FRUS, 1961–1963*, 13:487–91.

2 *FRUS, 1961–1963*, 13:694–701.

3 Ibid., 13:702–18; Telegram from the Department of State to the Embassy in France, May 24, 1962, Document #2804, National Security Archive, *Berlin Crisis, 1958–1962*; Trachtenberg, *Constructed Peace*, 338.

4 *FRUS, 1961–1963*, 13:407–8.

5 Quoted in Suri, *Power and Protest*, 54; Bozo, *Two Strategies*, 75.

6 Quoted in Ahonen, "Franz-Josef Strauss and the German Nuclear Question," 37–41; Macmillan, *At the End of the Day*, 334–35; Memorandum for the Record, June 18, 1962, "Department of Defense 6/62" folder, Departments and Agencies, NSF, Box 274, JFKL; Shapley, *Promise and Power*, 144–45; Telegram from the Embassy in the United Kingdom to the Secretary of State, June 19, 1962, "Department of Defense 6/62" folder, Departments and Agencies, NSF, Box 274, JFKL; *FRUS, 1961–1963*, 13:1077–78; Clark, *Nuclear Diplomacy and the Special Relationship*, 334–36.

7 Ashton, "Harold Macmillan," 717–18; Memorandum on Nuclear Weapons from the Minister of Aviation (Thorneycroft) to Prime Minister Macmillan, April 12, 1962, PREM 11/3712, PRO; Minute from Philip de Zulueta to the Prime Minister, April 13, 1962, ibid.; Note of Conversation at the State Department, April 28, 1962, ibid.; Letter from David Ormsby-Gore to the Prime Minister, May 17, 1962, ibid.; Minute from Sir Solly Zuckerman on Anglo/French Cooperation, May 25, 1962, ibid.; Memorandum of Conversation between the Prime Minister and M. Chauvel, April 19, 1962, PREM 11/3792, PRO; Letter from T. J. Bligh (Washington) to P. F. de Zulueta (Prime Minister's Private Secretary), April 27, 1962, ibid.; Note from P. F. de Zulueta to A. A. Auland (Foreign Office), May 3, 1962, ibid.; Minute from Lord Home, the Foreign Secretary, to the Prime Minister, July 13, 1962, PREM 11/3712, PRO; Bozo, *Two Strategies*, 76–77.

8 *FRUS, 1961–1963*, 13:413–19, 718–24; Lewidge, *De Gaulle*, 273.

9 *FRUS, 1961–1963*, 13:419–22; Memorandum of Conversation, Subject: Berlin Discussion, June 22, 1962, Berlin Crisis Project, NSA.

10 *FRUS, 1961–1963*, 13:423–25, 725–27; ibid., 15:200–203.

11 Quoted in Shapley, *Promise and Power*, 145.

12 *FRUS, 1961–1963*, 13:425–30.

13 Quoted in Newhouse, *De Gaulle and the Anglo-Saxons*, 169.

14 *FRUS, 1961–1963*, 7:241–48, 353–55, 358–61, 365–69.

15 Ibid., 7:374–75, 391–93, 395–401, 405–6, 411–14; Oliver, *Kennedy, Macmillan, and the Nuclear Test Ban Debate*, 94.

16 Henriksen, *Dr. Strangelove's America*, 245–65; *FRUS, 1961–1963*, 7:450–52, 458–59, 475, 527–30.

17 *FRUS, 1961–1963*, 7:447–49, 471–72, 476–84.

18 Ibid., 7:493–96.

19 Ibid., 7:499–509; Naftali, Zelikow, and May, *Presidential Recordings—John F. Kennedy*, 1:116–18.

20 *FRUS, 1961–1963,* 7:510–14.

21 Ibid., 7:535–41, 550–51, 559–61; *Documents on Disarmament, 1962,* 792–807.

22 *Documents on Disarmament, 1962,* 820–29; *FRUS, 1961–1963,* 7:561–62, 565–66, 568–69, 572–81, 585–92; Memorandum for Secretary Rusk, n.d., "State 6/62–7/62" folder, Departments and Agencies, POF, Box 88, JFKL; *FRUS, 1961–1963,* 15:359–62; Memorandum for the President, October 1, 1962, "Office of Science and Technology 1962" folder, Departments and Agencies, POF, Box 85, JFKL.

23 *FRUS, 1961–1963,* 7:541–47.

24 Memorandum from Paul H. Nitze, Assistant Secretary of Defense, to McGeorge Bundy, October 5, 1962, "Nuclear Energy Matters: Nuclear Diffusion, 10/62–5/63" folder, Carl Kaysen series, NSF, Box 376, JFKL; Memorandum, Subject: The Diffusion of Nuclear Weapons with and without a Non-Diffusion Agreement: A World-Wide Look, n.d., ibid.; Memorandum, Subject: Comments on Draft Memorandum "Agreement on Non-Diffusion of Nuclear Weapons" from Perspective of NATO and Berlin, n.d., ibid.; Memorandum, Subject: Sino-Soviet Attitudes toward Non-Diffusion of Nuclear Weapons, n.d., ibid.; Memorandum from Carl Kaysen to McGeorge Bundy, October 5, 1962, "Staff Memoranda—Carl Kaysen—8/62–12/62" folder, Meetings and Memoranda, NSF, Box 320, JFKL.

25 Quoted in Beschloss, *Crisis Years,* 4, 6; quoted in Paterson, *Kennedy's Quest for Victory,* 143; *Documents on Disarmament, 1962,* 966–72.

26 Bundy, *Danger and Survival,* 434; Rusk, *As I Saw It,* 238–40; Dobrynin, *In Confidence,* 86–90; Blight and Welch, *On the Brink,* 83–84; Garthoff, "Some Reflections on the History of the Cold War," 1–3.

27 Quoted in Khrushchev, *Khrushchev Remembers,* 494; quoted in Fursenko and Naftali, *One Hell of a Gamble,* 209; Memorandum for Mr. Bundy, Subject: France and a Mediterranean Multilateral MRBM Force, November 23, 1962, "Multilateral Force, General, 7/62–12/62 and undated" folder, Regional Security, NSF, Box 216, JFKL.

28 Zubok, "Unwrapping the Enigma," 160; quoted in Beschloss, *Crisis Years,* 547–49; Oral History, Walt W. Rostow, p. 64, JFKL.

29 *FRUS, 1961–1963,* 7:597–98, 618–19; Memorandum of Conversation between James Reston and W. Averell Harriman, October 30, 1962, "Memcons: R" folder, JFK-LBJ, Special Files: Public Service, Box 588, Harriman Papers, LC; Memorandum of Conversation with Georgi Zhukov, October 31, 1962, "Memcons: Y–Z" folder, ibid.

30 Cousins, *Improbable Triumvirate,* 24–25, 54; Letter to Nikita Khrushchev from Leo Szilard, October 9, 1962, "Disarmament—Szilard, Leo, 1961–1962" folder, Carl Kaysen series, NSF, Box 369, JFKL; Memorandum from Leo Szilard to Carl Kaysen, January 8, 1963, "Disarmament—Szilard, Leo, 1/63" folder, ibid.; Hawkins, Greb, and Szilard, *Toward a Livable World,* 318; Memorandum of Conversation between Mr. Gomulka and Walter Lippmann, November 19, 1962, Folder 902, Series III, Box 74, Lippmann Papers, New Haven, Conn.

31 Quoted in Schlesinger, *Thousand Days,* 896; *FRUS, 1961–1963,* 7:594–95, 623–25; Memorandum for the President, Subject: The Swedish Proposal in the Geneva Test Ban Talks and the United States Position for a Nuclear Test Ban Treaty, Novem-

ber 29, 1962, "National Security Policy—Disarmament Proposals, 2/63" folder, Vice Presidential Security File, Box 7, LBJL.

32 Quoted in Evangelista, *Unarmed Forces*, 79.

33 *FRUS, 1961–1963*, 13:458–60; ibid., 7:601–11; Memorandum of Telecon—McGeorge Bundy/Harriman, January 16, 1963, "January 1963" folder, Chronological File: Telephone Conversations, JFK-LBJ, Special Files: Public Service, Box 581, Harriman Papers, LC; Letter from Assistant Secretary of State W. Averell Harriman to President Kennedy, January 23, 1963, "Harriman, W. Averell" folder, Special Correspondence, POF, Box 30, JFKL.

34 Telegram from the British Attaché (Washington) to Air Ministry, November 13, 1962, PREM 11/3716, PRO; Neustadt, *Report to JFK*, 30–31; *FRUS, 1961–1963: National Security Policy* (1996), 8:390–92; Shapley, *Promise and Power*, 241–43; *FRUS, 1961–1963*, 13:1085–86; Memorandum on Nuclear Aspects of Macmillan Visit, December 15, 1962, "NATO, Weapons, Cables, Skybolt" folder, Regional Security, NSF, Box 227, JFKL; Note to Mr. de Zulueta from Harold Macmillan, December 12, 1962, PREM 11/3716, PRO.

35 Richard E. Neustadt, A Report to the President: "Skybolt and Nassau: American Policy-Making and Anglo-American Relations," November 15, 1963, Document #963, National Security Archive, *U.S. Nuclear Non-Proliferation* (emphasis and ellipsis in original); Record of Conversation at Rambouillet, December 15, 1962, PREM 11/4230, PRO; Summary of Prime Minister's Meeting with General de Gaulle at Rambouillet, December 15/16, 1962, ibid.; Record of Meeting at the Chateau de Rambouillet, December 16, 1962, ibid.; Summary of Prime Minister's Meeting with General de Gaulle at Rambouillet, December 15/16, 1962, ibid.; Record of Meeting at the Chateau de Rambouillet, December 16, 1962, ibid.

36 *FRUS, 1961–1962*, 13:139–41, 439–40, 1088–1108; Richard E. Neustadt, A Report to the President: "Skybolt and Nassau: American Policy-Making and Anglo-American Relations," November 15, 1963, Document #963, National Security Archive, *U.S. Nuclear Non-Proliferation*; Neustadt, *Report to JFK*, 45; quoted in Ashton, "Harold Macmillan," 717; Record of Meeting at Bali-Hali, the Bahamas, December 19, 1962, PREM 11/4229, PRO; Skybolt Briefing Paper, November 19, 1962, PREM 11/3716, PRO.

37 *FRUS, 1961–1962*, 13:1102–8; National Security Action Memorandum No. 215, Subject: Inclusion of Tactical Weapons in the Paragraph 6 Force, January 12, 1963, "NSAM 215" folder, Meetings and Memoranda, NSF, Box 340, JFKL.

38 *FRUS, 1961–1963*, 13:139–41, 467–71, 478–82, 854–57, 1081–82, 1112–15; Letter from Pierson Dixon in Paris Embassy to Patrick Reilly, November 28, 1962, PREM 11/4230, PRO; Summary of Prime Minister's Meeting with General de Gaulle at Rambouillet, December 15/16, 1962, ibid.; Middeke, "Anglo-American Nuclear Weapons Cooperation," 75–82; Memorandum from British Defence Minister Thorneycroft to the Prime Minister, December 19, 1962, PREM 11/4229, PRO; Telegram from First Secretary to the Prime Minister in Nassau, December 21, 1962, ibid.

39 *FRUS, 1961–1963*, 13:475–78, 743–48, 1116–28; quoted in Costigliola, "Kennedy, the

European Allies, and the Failure to Consult," 121; Richard E. Neustadt, A Report to the President: "Skybolt and Nassau: American Policy-Making and Anglo-American Relations," November 15, 1963, Document #963, National Security Archive, *U.S. Nuclear Non-Proliferation*; Memorandum, Subject: Post-Nassau Strategy, December 27, 1962, "NATO, European Nuclear Force, Nassau Agreement, 12/62" folder, Carl Kaysen series, NSF, Box 376, JFKL; *Documents on Disarmament, 1963*, 4–9; Lewidge, *De Gaulle*, 287.

40 Ball, *The Past Has Another Pattern*, 269; Telegram from Ormsby-Gore to Foreign Office, February 9, 1963, FO 371/171147, PRO; quoted in Dallek, *Unfinished Life*, 611; *FRUS, 1961–1963*, 13:487–91, 511–23; Lewidge, *De Gaulle*, 285–86.

41 *FRUS, 1961–1963*, 8:457–62; ibid., 13:156–63, 484–91, 502–6; Summary Record of NSC Executive Committee No. 40, February 5, 1963, "Executive Committee Meetings, Vol. IV" folder, Meetings and Memoranda, NSF, Box 316, JFKL; Trachtenberg, *Constructed Peace*, 377; Memorandum of Conversation in the President's Office, February 18, 1963, "Multilateral Force, General, Merchant (1), 2/21/63 — Instructions" folder, Regional Security, NSF, Box 207, JFKL; Lewidge, *De Gaulle*, 290; Bozo, *Two Strategies*, 106; Giauque, *Grand Designs*, 119, 196–223.

42 *FRUS, 1961–1963*, 13:204–13, 494–502, 509–11, 524, 527–37, 542–46, 551–55, 570–72, 579–82, 871–75; Winand, *Eisenhower, Kennedy, and the United States of Europe*, 346–47; Haftendorn, *NATO and the Nuclear Revolution*, 121.

43 *FRUS, 1961–1963*, 13:582–87.

44 Ibid., 13:592–95, 1132–35; Memorandum for Mr. Bundy from Livingston Merchant, February 15, 1963, "Multilateral Force, General, Merchant, 1/9/63–2/15/63" folder, Regional Security, NSF, Box 217, JFKL; Memorandum for the Record, May 4, 1963, "Meetings with the President, General, 5/63" folder, Meetings and Memoranda, NSF, Box 317a, JFKL; quoted in Costigliola, "Nuclear Family," 178–79.

45 *FRUS, 1961–1963*, 7:640–44, 647–48, 650–52, 674–76, 702–5; Memorandum for Ambassador Bruce from Foy D. Kohler, Subject: Soviet Reaction to Multilateral Force, February 8, 1963, "Test Ban Treaty Background (3)" folder, Trips and Missions, JFK-LBJ, Special Files: Public Service, Box 540, Harriman Papers, LC; *FRUS, 1961–1963*, 13:769–75; Telegram from U.S. Embassy (Paris) to Department of State, January 13, 1962, "Multilateral Force, General, Vol. I, 1961–6/62" folder, Regional Security, NSF, Box 216, JFKL; Letter from Humphrey Trevelyan (British Embassy in Moscow) to A. D. Wilson (Foreign Office), February 21, 1963, FO 371/171147, PRO.

46 Oral History, Walt W. Rostow, p. 67, JFKL; National Security Action Memorandum No. 241, Subject: Report on French Gaseous Diffusion Plant, May 7, 1963, "NSAM 241" folder, Meetings and Memoranda, NSF, Box 341, JFKL; National Security Action Memorandum No. 231, Subject: Middle Eastern Nuclear Capabilities, March 26, 1963, "NSAM 231" folder, Meetings and Memoranda, NSF, Box 340, JFKL; State Department Memorandum on Israel's Atomic Energy Programs, March 15, 1963, Document #944, National Security Archive, *U.S. Nuclear Non-Proliferation*; Memorandum for Mr. Bundy, February 11, 1963, "Bundy, McGeorge, 1/63–6/63" folder, Staff Memoranda, POF, Box 62a, JFKL; Little, "Making of a Special Relationship,"

570–72; Bass, *Support Any Friend*, 228; Cohen, *Israel and the Bomb*, 153–74, 245–51; *FRUS, 1961–1963*, 7:689–91.

47 Burr and Richelson, "Whether to 'Strangle the Baby in the Cradle,'" 68.

48 Voss, *Nuclear Ambush*; Oliver, *Kennedy, Macmillan, and the Nuclear Test Ban Debate*, 153–54, 158; *FRUS, 1961–1963*, 7:637–39, 648–50, 653–54, 668–70, 679–81; Memorandum for the Files of Lewis L. Strauss, May 24, 1963, "Memoranda for the Record, 1963–72 and undated" folder, AECS, Box 67, Strauss Papers, HHL.

49 *FRUS, 1961–1963*, 7:644–46, 653–54.

50 Ibid., 7:685–88, 693–99; Memorandum of Conversation, April 26, 1963, "Harriman, W. Averell" folder, Special Correspondence, POF, Box 30, JFKL.

51 *FRUS, 1961–1963*, 7:734–35, 750–51, 771–72; Briefing Book on U.S.-Soviet Non-Diffusion Agreement for Discussion at the Moscow Meeting, June 12, 1963, "ACDA [Arms Control and Disarmament Agency] — Nuclear Test Ban — Harriman Trip to Moscow — Briefing Book, Vol. 1" folder, Departments and Agencies, NSF, Box 265, JFKL; On Nuclear Diffusion, Vol. II, June 20, 1963, "ACDA — Disarmament — Nuclear Test Ban Trip to Moscow — Briefing Book, Vol. II" folder, ibid.; On Control of Nuclear Weapons, July 2, 1963, "Nuclear Energy Matters: Nuclear Diffusion Briefing Book, Vol. III" folder, Carl Kaysen series, NSF, Box 376, JFKL; Memorandum on Inhibiting Communist China's Making and Exploiting of Nuclear Weapons, June 21, 1963, "Test Ban Treaty Background (1)" folder, Trips and Missions, JFK-LBJ, Special Files: Public Service, Box 539, Harriman Papers, LC; quoted in Oral History, William C. Foster, p. 37, JFKL.

52 Memorandum on Test Ban Treaty from Walt W. Rostow to W. Averell Harriman, July 2, 1963, "Test Ban Treaty Background (3)" folder, Trips and Missions, JFK-LBJ, Special Files: Public Service, Box 540, Harriman Papers, LC; *FRUS, 1961–1963*, 7:747–49, 779–85, 789–90; Memorandum of Telephone Conversation between W. Averell Harriman and Walt W. Rostow, June 19, 1963, "June–July 1963" folder, Chronological File: Telecons, JFK-LBJ, Special Files: Public Service, Box 581, Harriman Papers, LC; quoted in Reeves, *President Kennedy*, 546; Memorandum from Livingston T. Merchant to W. Averell Harriman, June 17, 1963, "Test Ban Treaty Background (1)" folder, Trips and Missions, JFK-LBJ, Special Files: Public Service, Box 539, Harriman Papers, LC; Letter to Livingston T. Merchant from W. Averell Harriman, June 20, 1963, ibid.; Memorandum on the Test Ban Treaty, July 2, 1963, "Test Ban Treaty Background (3)" folder, Box 540, Harriman Papers, LC; Elements for a Package Deal with Moscow, July 3, 1963, ibid.; Memorandum to the President from Walt W. Rostow, Subject: The Harriman Probe, July 8, 1963, "ACDA — Disarmament — Harriman Trip to Moscow, Part III" folder, Departments and Agencies, NSF, Box 265, JFKL.

53 *Documents on Disarmament, 1963*, 244–46; Personal and Confidential Memorandum on Harriman Instructions, n.d., "National Security Council, 1962–63" folder, Vice Presidential Security File, Box 5, LBJL; Memorandum of Conversation, July 5, 1963, "Test Ban Treaty Background (1)" folder, Trips and Missions, JFK-LBJ, Special Files: Public Service, Box 539, Harriman Papers, LC; Memorandum on the Soviet Position in the July 15 Moscow Talks in Light of Khrushchev's Berlin Speech, July 5, 1963,

ibid.; Memorandum of Telephone Conversation between W. Averell Harriman and Marquis Childs, July 4, 1963, "June–July 1963" folder, Chronological File: Telecons, JFK-LBJ, Special Files: Public Service, Box 581, Harriman Papers, LC; Memorandum of Telephone Conversation between W. Averell Harriman and Joseph Alsop, July 3, 1963, ibid.; Memorandum on Allied Attitudes on Linking Test Ban Agreement with a Non-Aggression Pact, July 8, 1963, "ACDA—Disarmament—Harriman Trip to Moscow, Part III" folder, Departments and Agencies, Box 265, JFKL; *FRUS, 1961–1963*, 7:762–64; Letter from Pierson Dixon in Paris Embassy to Lord Home, November 28, 1962, PREM 11/4230, PRO; Points to Be Explored with the Russians, July 9, 1963, "Test Ban Treaty Background (3)" folder, Trips and Missions, JFK-LBJ, Special Files: Public Service, Box 540, Harriman Papers, LC; Memorandum for W. Averell Harriman on the Sino-Soviet Treaty and a Nuclear Test Ban, July 10, 1963, ibid.; Oral History, Llewellyn Thompson, p. 22, JFKL; On Control of Nuclear Weapons, n.d., "Nuclear Energy Matters, Nuclear Diffusion Briefing Book, Vol. II, 7/2/63" folder, Carl Kaysen series, NSF, Box 376, JFKL; Conclusions and Recommendations, ibid.

54 Handling of BAN Series Communications, July 10, 1963, "ACDA—Disarmament—Harriman Trip to Moscow, Part IV" folder, Departments and Agencies, NSF, Box 265, JFKL; *FRUS, 1961–1963*, 7:799–801; Oral History, Llewellyn Thompson, p. 22, JFKL; Burr and Richelson, "Whether to 'Strangle the Baby in the Cradle,'" 71.

55 *FRUS, 1961–1963*, 7:801, 808–9; Telegram from the Department of State to the Embassy in the Soviet Union, July 24, 1963, "Test Ban Treaty (11)" folder, Trips and Missions, JFK-LBJ, Special Files: Public Service, Box 541, Harriman Papers, LC; Tactics and Timing, n.d., "Nuclear Energy Matters, Nuclear Diffusion Briefing Book, Vol. II, 'On Nuclear Diffusion,' 6/20/63" folder, Carl Kaysen series, NSF, Box 376, JFKL.

56 *FRUS, 1961–1963*, 7:804–7, 809–18, 823–24, 831–34, 853–56; Contingency Paper, July 20, 1963, "Test Ban Treaty (8)" folder, Trips and Missions, JFK-LBJ, Special Files: Public Service, Box 541, Harriman Papers, LC; *Documents on Disarmament, 1963*, 291–93; Oral History, Adrian Fisher, p. 37, LBJL.

57 Mastny, "1963 Nuclear Test Ban Treaty," 6; Selvage, "Junior Allies"; Burr and Richelson, "Whether to 'Strangle the Baby in the Cradle,'" 72–74.

58 *FRUS, 1961–1963*, 7:856–63; Memorandum of Telephone Conversation between W. Averell Harriman and Llewellyn Thompson, July 30, 1963, "June–July 1963" folder, Chronological File: Telecons, JFK-LBJ, Special Files: Public Service, Box 581, Harriman Papers, LC; Memorandum from Walt W. Rostow to W. Averell Harriman, July 30, 1963, "USSR, General, 1963" folder, Subject File, JFK-LBJ, Special Files: Public Service, Box 518, Harriman Papers, LC; Department of State Intelligence Note: Moscow Carries Test-Ban Debate to Chinese People, Comments on Non-Diffusion and MLF, August 21, 1963, "Test Ban Treaty (15)" folder, Trips and Missions, JFK-LBJ, Special Files: Public Service, Box 542, Harriman Papers, LC.

59 *FRUS, 1961–1963*, 7:796–98, 821–23, 851–53, 866–69, 877–81, 885–86; Wittner, *Resisting the Bomb*, 430; *FRUS, 1961–1963*, 13:219–23; Telegram from the British Embassy in France to the British Foreign Office, July 16, 1963, "ACDA—Disarmament—Nuclear Test Ban, Harriman Trip to Moscow, Part II" folder, Departments and Agencies,

NSF, Box 265, JFKL; Memorandum for the President from Walt W. Rostow, July 23, 1963, "Disarmament—Nuclear Test Ban Negotiations—7/63, Meeting in Moscow, Part I" folder, Subject File, POF, Box 100, JFKL; Paper from Minister of Defence (Thorneycroft) on Possible Anglo/American Offer to France, n.d., FO 371/173309, PRO; Middeke, "Anglo-American Nuclear Weapons Cooperation," 82–85; Telegram from the Secretary of State to the President and the Acting Secretary, April 8, 1963, "State 4/63–5/63" folder, Departments and Agencies, POF, Box 88a, JFKL; Memorandum on Anglo-French Relations by W. B. J. Lewidge, March 22, 1963, FO 371/171147; Giauque, *Grand Designs*, 118; Suri, *Power and Protest*, 73–79; Wenger and Suri, "At the Crossroads," 7.

60 *FRUS, 1961–1963*, 7:863–64, 870–76; Schrafstetter, "Long Shadow of the Past," 132–33; Hans-Peter Schwarz, *Konrad Adenauer*, 693–98; *FRUS, 1961–1963*, 13:604, 606–7; Memorandum of Conversation, September 20, 1963, Document #961, National Security Archive, *U.S. Nuclear Non-Proliferation*; Letter from Dean Acheson to Robert McNamara, September 16, 1963, Folder 275, Box 22, Acheson Papers, New Haven, Conn.; Memorandum from Walt W. Rostow to Secretary of State Rusk, September 17, 1963, "Rostow, W. W., 8/63–9/63" folder, Staff Memoranda, POF, Box 65, JFKL.

Chapter 8

1 *FRUS, 1964–1968: Arms Control and Disarmament* (1997), 11:134–40.

2 Selvage, "Warsaw Pact," 2–6; *FRUS, 1961–1963*, 7:887–89; ibid., 13:604–24.

3 Schlesinger, *Robert Kennedy*, 222–27; quoted in Newhouse, *War and Peace in the Nuclear Age*, 196; quoted in Fromkin, "Lyndon Johnson and Foreign Policy," 163; Thomas Alan Schwartz, *Lyndon Johnson and Europe*, 28–29, 32; quoted in Chase, *Acheson*, 411; quoted in Colman, *Special Relationship*, 12; Hans-Peter Schwarz, *Konrad Adenauer*, 732.

4 Quoted in Beschloss, *Taking Charge*, 390; Barber, *Presidential Character*, 67; quoted in Dallek, "Lyndon Johnson," 107.

5 Quoted in Goodwin, *Remembering America*, 258; quoted in Beschloss, *Taking Charge*, 388.

6 Quoted in Beschloss, *Crisis Years*, 464; quoted in Beschloss, *Reaching for Glory*, 333; quoted in Beschloss, *Taking Charge*, 248.

7 Quoted in Brinkley, *Dean Acheson*, 221; quoted in Colman, *Special Relationship*, 13.

8 Dallek, *Lone Star Rising*, 9, 275, 293, 382–86, 529–40; H. W. Brands, *Wages of Globalism*, 26–29; Dallek, *Flawed Giant*, 175–76; Beschloss, *Taking Charge*, 297, 465; quoted in Wittner, *Resisting the Bomb*, 431; German and Johnson, *Presidential Recordings—Lyndon B. Johnson*, 3:90–91; Dumbrell, *President Lyndon Johnson and Soviet Communism*, 34, 61.

9 Memorandum of Telephone Conversation between Eugene Rostow and George Ball, November 24, 1963, "(General) US and Europe [11/24/63–5/31/66]" folder, Box 6, Ball Papers, LBJL; *FRUS, 1961–1963*, 13:233–39, 627–29, 631–34, 787–89.

10 H. W. Brands, *Wages of Globalism*, 24; Memorandum from Walt W. Rostow to Dean Rusk, Subject: Congressional Consultation about MLF, December 5, 1963, "Multilateral Force, General, Vol. I" folder, Subject File, NSF, Box 22, LBJL; Schrafstetter, "Long Shadow of the Past," 127; Briefing for the President—Notes on the MLF: Status and Needed Decisions, December 6, 1963, "Multilateral Force, General, Vol. I" folder, Subject File, NSF, Box 22, LBJL.

11 Quoted in Costigliola, "Lyndon B. Johnson, Germany, and 'the End of the Cold War,'" 173; quoted in Fielding, "Coping with Decline," 640; quoted in Colman, *Special Relationship*, 30; Memorandum for the President—re: Meeting on Multilateral Force, December 6, 1963, "McGeorge Bundy, Vol. I" folder, Memos to the President, NSF, Box 1, LBJL; Memorandum for the Record, Subject: Meeting on the MLF at the White House, December 6, 1963, "Multilateral Force, General, Vol. I" folder, Subject File, NSF, Box 22, LBJL; *FRUS, 1964–1968: Western European Region* (1995), 13:7.

12 Priest, "In Common Cause," 759–90.

13 Memorandum of Conversation, December 15, 1963, Nuclear History Collection, NSA; Telegram from U.S. Embassy in France to the Secretary of State, December 16, 1963, "Multilateral Force—Cables, Vol. I" folder, Subject File, NSF, Box 24, LBJL; *FRUS, 1964–1968*, 13:5–7; Documents 87 and 90, *FRUS, 1964–1968: Western Europe*, vol. 12, <www.state.gov> (accessed September 26, 2008); Memorandum for the President from the Secretary of State, Subject: Further Action on the Multilateral Force, April 8, 1964, "Multilateral Force, General, Vol. I" folder, Subject File, NSF, Box 22, LBJL; Telegram from U.S. Embassy in Belgium to the Secretary of State, January 2, 1964, "Multilateral Force—Cables, Vol. I" folder, Subject File, NSF, Box 24, LBJL.

14 *FRUS, 1964–1968*, 13:25–30; Thomas Alan Schwartz, "Victories and Defeats," 134.

15 McLellan and Acheson, *Among Friends*, 275–76; The Multilateral Force: Questions and Answers, n.d., "Time, Inc.—Multilateral Force (MLF)" folder, Box 64, Jackson Papers, DDEL; Memorandum to the Secretary of State from Walt W. Rostow, Subject: Arms Control and the Alliance; Or How to Persuade Allies to Make Peace, April 6, 1964, "Multilateral Force, General, Vol. I" folder, Subject File, NSF, Box 22, LBJL.

16 Telegram from William Foster to the Secretary of State, February 7, 1964, "Disarmament, Vol. I" folder, Subject File, NSF, Box 11, LBJL; Draft Revision of NSC Memorandum of April 24, 1961, entitled "NATO and the Atlantic Nations," January 24, 1964, Nuclear History Collection, NSA.

17 The Multilateral Force: Where It Came From—What It Is—And What It Is Not, June 6, 1963, "Multilateral Force—Bundy Paper" folder, Subject File, NSF, Box 25, LBJL; Memorandum for the President from the Secretary of State, Subject: Further Action on the Multilateral Force, April 8, 1964, "Multilateral Force, General, Vol. I" folder, Subject File, NSF, Box 22, LBJL.

18 Memorandum of Conversation, Subject: Briefing of General Eisenhower on MLF, January 15, 1964, "Multilateral Force, General, Vol. I" folder, Subject File, NSF, Box

22, LBJL; Memorandum for the President from the Secretary of State, Subject: Further Action on the Multilateral Force, April 8, 1964, ibid.; Memorandum of Conversation, Subject: Background on the MLF, January 17, 1964, ibid.; Memorandum for the Secretary of State and the Undersecretary of State, Subject: Congressional Briefings on MLF, February 7, 1964, ibid.; Memorandum to McGeorge Bundy from David Klein, May 20, 1964, ibid.; Memorandum by John Newhouse — Balancing the Risks in the MLF, March 20, 1964, ibid.; Women Strike for Peace Leaflet — Some Questions and Answers on the Multilateral Force and Proliferation of Nuclear Arms through NATO, n.d., "Women's NATO Peace Force Organized by WSP (1964, 1984)" folder, Series A.8, Records of Women Strike for Peace, Box 1, SCPC; SANE's Statement of Policy for 1964, "SANE — 1963-1964 — Statements, Policy Statements, Position Papers, etc." folder, Series A, Records of SANE, Inc., Box 2, SCPC; Memorandum of Conversation between Livingston Merchant, Walt W. Rostow, and Leo Szilard, Subject: MLF, February 20, 1964, "Multilateral Force, General, Vol. I" Subject File, NSF, Box 22, LBJL.

19 Quoted in Oral History, Gerard C. Smith, pp. 6, 12, LBJL; *FRUS, 1964–1968*, 13:35–37.

20 Seaborg, *Stemming the Tide*, 100–101; *FRUS, 1964–1968*, 13:37–41; Telegram from Finletter to Rusk in Manila, April 14, 1964, "Multilateral Force — General" folder, Files of Charles E. Johnson, NSF, Box 3, LBJL.

21 *Documents on Disarmament, 1963*, 651–52; *Documents on Disarmament, 1964*, 53–55; Wandycz, "Adam Rapacki and the Search for European Security," 310–11; Selvage, "Warsaw Pact," 8.

22 *FRUS, 1964–1968*, 11:3–5, 16–18, 29–33, 41–42.

23 Telegram from U.S. Mission in Geneva to the Department of State, February 3, 1964, "Disarmament, Vol. I — Cables" folder, Subject File, NSF, Box 11, LBJL; Telegram from William Foster to Secretary Rusk and Adrian Fisher, February 7, 1964, ibid.

24 Telegram from William Foster to Secretary Rusk and Adrian Fisher, February 7, 1964, ibid.; Telegram from Adrian Fisher to William Foster, February 14, 1964, ibid.; Memorandum for the President from Secretary of State Rusk, April 8, 1964, "Multilateral Force, General, Vol. I" folder, Subject File, NSF, Box 22, LBJL; *Documents on Disarmament, 1964*, 83, 140–44; Telegram from Department of State to Embassy in West Germany, February 8, 1964, "Disarmament, Vol. I — Cables" folder, Subject File, NSF, Box 11, LBJL.

25 *FRUS, 1964–1968*, 13:41–43; Congressional Briefing Paper on Italy, "Multilateral Force, General, Vol. I" folder, Subject File, NSF, Box 22, LBJL; Telegram from Department of State to the U.S. Embassy in France, June 5, 1964, "Multilateral Force — Cables, Vol. II" folder, Subject File, NSF, Box 24, LBJL; Bill, *George Ball*, 115; Memorandum of Conversation, September 28, 1964, "Multilateral Force — General" folder, Files of Charles E. Johnson, NSF, Box 3, LBJL; Costigliola, "Lyndon B. Johnson, Germany, and the End of the 'Cold War,'" 185–86; Rostow, *Diffusion of Power*, 392.

26 Memorandum from David Klein to McGeorge Bundy, May 20, 1964, "Multilateral Force, General, Vol. I" folder, Subject File, NSF, Box 22, LBJL; Memorandum from

David Klein to McGeorge Bundy, June 4, 1964, ibid.; Memorandum from David Klein to McGeorge Bundy, June 20, 1964, ibid.; Letter from Senators Joseph Clark, George McGovern, Lee Metcalf, Eugene McCarthy, Philip Hart, Maurine Neuberger, Gaylord Nelson, and Gale McGee to President Lyndon Johnson, September 7, 1964, Folder 85, Box DA1, McCloy Papers, Amherst, Mass.; Letter from Representative Chet Holifield to President Lyndon Johnson, October 3, 1964, Document #998, National Security Archive, *U.S. Nuclear Non-Proliferation*; Critical Assessment of the Multilateral Force, n.d., Document #997, ibid.; Schrafstetter and Twigge, *Avoiding Armageddon*, 147.

27 Henriksen, *Dr. Strangelove's America*, 307–39; Boyer, *Fallout*, 95–102; Weart, *Nuclear Fear*, 275–80; Biskind, *Seeing Is Believing*, 64–69, 344–46.

28 Quoted in Schrafstetter, "Long Shadow of the Past," 128–29.

29 Soviet Views Private and Public, n.d., "Disarmament, Camp David Conference" folder, Subject File, NSF, Box 12, LBJL.

30 Selvage, "Warsaw Pact," 10–12.

31 *FRUS, 1964–1968*, 11:22–23, 29–34, 47–50, 135–40; Dumbrell, *President Lyndon Johnson and Soviet Communism*, 35; Johnson and Shreve, *Presidential Recordings—Lyndon B. Johnson*, 2:649–53, 659–60.

32 Hersh, *Sampson Option*, 132–36; Cohen, *Israel and the Bomb*, 174–94, 253; quoted in Little, "Making of a Special Relationship," 575.

33 Memorandum for the Record, September 15, 1964, "McGeorge Bundy, Vol. 6" folder, Memos to the President, NSF, Box 2, LBJL; Highlights from Secretary of State Rusk's Policy Planning Meeting, October 15, 1963, Document 191, *FRUS, 1961–1963: Northeast Asia* (1996), vol. 22, <www.state.gov> (accessed September 26, 2008); Documents 14, 25, 29, 30, 50, 63, 64, 66, 68, and 83, *FRUS, 1964–1968: China* (1998), vol. 30, <www.state.gov> (accessed September 26, 2008); Memorandum for the President from Walt W. Rostow, April 17, 1964, "DEF 12-1 Chicom" file, SDDF; China as a Nuclear Power, October 7, 1964, "China" folder, Committee File, NSF, Box 5, LBJL; Burr and Richelson, "Whether to 'Strangle the Baby in the Cradle,'" 76–91.

34 Memorandum for the Record, September 15, 1964, "McGeorge Bundy, Vol. 6" folder, Memos to the President, NSF, Box 2, LBJL; Document 54, *FRUS, 1964–1968*, vol. 30, <www.state.gov> (accessed September 26, 2008); Burr and Richelson, "Whether to 'Strangle the Baby in the Cradle,'" 87–88.

35 *Documents on Disarmament, 1964*, 440–41, 448–52; Document 56, 57, *FRUS, 1964–1968*, vol. 30, <www.state.gov> (accessed September 26, 2008); Circular Telegram from the Department of State, September 29, 1964, Document #995, National Security Archive, *U.S. Nuclear Non-Proliferation*; Department of State Intelligence Note, Subject: Initial World Reaction to the Chinese Communists' Nuclear Detonation, October 28, 1964, "China" folder, Committee File, NSF, Box 5, LBJL; quoted in Perkovich, *India's Nuclear Bomb*, 65; *Documents on Disarmament, 1965*, 462–64; Declaration of Cairo Second Non-Aligned Conference on Non-Dissemination of Nuclear Weapons, Issued at Cairo, October 11, 1964, "Cairo Resolutions" folder, Committee File, NSF, Box 5, LBJL.

36 Quoted in Yi, "American Response," 93–94; Memorandum for the Record, Subject: President's Meeting with Congressional Leadership, October 19, 1964, "Memos for the Record, 1964" folder, Files of McGeorge Bundy, NSF, Box 18–19, LBJL.

37 Oral History, Ray S. Cline, p. 7, LBJL; Circular Telegram from the Department of State, October 21, 1964, Document #1015, National Security Archive, *U.S. Nuclear Non-Proliferation*; Telegram from the U.S. Embassy in India to the Department of State, October 17, 1964, Document #1002, ibid.; Airgram from U.S. Embassy in India to the Department of State, October 23, 1964, Document #1016, ibid.; Telegram from U.S. Embassy in India to the Department of State, October 23, 1964, Document #1018, ibid.; Telegram from U.S. Embassy in India to the Department of State, October 29, 1964, Document #1031, ibid.; Telegram from U.S. Air Force Attaché in India to Department of Air Force, December 7, 1964, "India" folder, Committee File, NSF, Box 6–7, LBJL; Perkovich, *India's Nuclear Bomb*, 65–85.

38 The Indian Nuclear Program: Proposed Course of Action, October 13, 1964, "Disarmament—Committee of Principals, Vol. I" folder, Subject File, NSF, Box 12–13, LBJL; *Documents on Disarmament, 1964*, 465–69; Telegram from U.S. Embassy in Karachi to Department of State, November 18, 1964, "DEF 18-8 US" file, SDDF.

39 Documents 62, 69, 81, 82, and 278, *FRUS, 1964–1968*, vol. 30, <www.state.gov> (accessed September 26, 2008); Destruction of Chinese Nuclear Weapons Capabilities, December 14, 1964, "China" folder, Committee File, NSF, Box 5, LBJL; Burr, "New Evidence on Taiwanese 'Nuclear Intentions,' 1966–1976."

40 Telegram from the U.S. Embassy in the Soviet Union to the Department of State, October 18, 1964, Document #1005, National Security Archive, *U.S. Nuclear Non-Proliferation*; Memorandum of Conversation, Subject: Chinese Nuclear Detonation, October 20, 1964, Document #1014, ibid.; Chang, *Friends and Enemies*, 278; Memorandum of Conversation, October 28, 1964, "ACDA, Vol. I" folder, Agency File, NSF, Box 5, LBJL; Perkovich, *India's Nuclear Bomb*, 86–88.

41 Memorandum for Mr. Bundy from Spurgeon Keeny, October 6, 1964, "Spurgeon Keeny Memos" folder, Name File, NSF, Box 5, LBJL; *FRUS, 1964–1968*, 11:97–120, 127–28, 141–45, 151–52; Memorandum of Conversation between McGeorge Bundy and George Ball, October 20, 1964, "(General) US and Europe" folder, Ball Papers, Box 6, LBJL; National Intelligence Estimate: Prospects for a Proliferation of Nuclear Weapons over the Next Decade, October 21, 1964, "4—Arms and Disarmament" folder, National Intelligence Estimates, NSF, Box 1, LBJL; Memorandum from McNamara to Rusk, October 28, 1964, "DEF 19—US-India" file, SDDF; Memorandum for Bundy from Adam Yarmolinsky—re: Task Force on Non-Proliferation, October 28, 1964, "Presidential Task Force on Nuclear Proliferation" folder, Subject File, NSF, Box 35, LBJL; Memorandum on U.S. Government Committees Considering Implications of Chicom Nuclear Capability, December 31, 1964, Document #1090, National Security Archive, *U.S. Nuclear Non-Proliferation*; Garthoff, *Journey through the Cold War*, 195.

42 Report on Non-Proliferation of Nuclear Weapons, November 9, 1964, Document

#1040, National Security Archive, *U.S. Nuclear Non-Proliferation*; Memorandum of Conversation, November 23, 1964, "Disarmament—Committee of Principals, Vol. I" folder, Subject File, NSF, Box 12–13, LBJL; *FRUS, 1964–1968*, 11:76–82, 122–25; Gavin, "Blast from the Past," 105, 114, 116–17; Program to Limit the Spread of Nuclear Weapons, November 3, 1964, "Presidential Task Force Committee on Nuclear Proliferation" folder, Subject File, NSF, Box 35, LBJL; *FRUS, 1964–1968*, 13:121–22; John McCloy Notes on Conversation with Robert McNamara, n.d., Folder 44, Box DA1, McCloy Papers, Amherst, Mass.; Document 76, *FRUS, 1964–1968*, vol. 30, <www .state.gov> (accessed September 26, 2008).

43 Committee on Nuclear Proliferation—Minutes of Discussion, First Meeting, December 1, 1964, Document #1064, National Security Archive, *U.S. Nuclear Non-Proliferation*; Minutes of Briefing by Hon. William C. Foster to Gilpatric Committee, January 7, 1965, "Briefing" folder, Committee File, NSF, Box 25, LBJL.

44 Program to Limit the Spread of Nuclear Weapons, November 3, 1964, "General Program to Limit the Spread of Nuclear Weapons (State Paper), 11/3/64" folder, Committee File, NSF, Box 7, LBJL; Memorandum of Conversation, Subject: Secretary's Meeting with the Gilpatric Committee on Non-Proliferation, January 7, 1965, "Minutes of Meetings" folder, Committee File, NSF, Box 9, LBJL; Handwritten Notes on Conversation with Dean Rusk by John J. McCloy, n.d., Folder 44, Box DA1, McCloy Papers, Amherst, Mass.; A Way of Thinking about Nuclear Proliferation, November 19, 1964, Document #1046, National Security Archive, *U.S. Nuclear Non-Proliferation*; Committee on Nuclear Proliferation—Minutes of Discussion—Second Meeting, December 13–14, 1964, Document #1087, ibid.; Summary of Statement Made before Gilpatric Committee, December 13, 1964, "Briefing" folder, Committee File, NSF, Box 25, LBJL; Memorandum of Conversation, January 7, 1965, "Presidential Task Force Committee on Nuclear Proliferation" folder, Subject File, NSF, Box 35, LBJL; Memorandum of Conversation, December 15, 1964, "Presidential Task Force Committee Nuclear Proliferation" folder, Subject File, NSF, Box 35, LBJL.

45 Ways of Reconciling the MLF with US, UK, FRG, and Soviet Interests While Leaving Room for Non-Spread Agreements, December 1, 1964, "Collateral Materials, Part II" folder, President's Task Force on Nuclear Proliferation, Box 11, Gilpatric Papers, JFKL; Europe, NATO, Germany, and the MLF, December 12, 1964, "Problem 1: Europe, NATO, Germany, and the MLF" folder, Committee File, NSF, Box 1–2, LBJL; Tentative Thoughts on Certain Proliferation Problems, December 4, 1964, "President's Task Force on Nuclear Proliferation—Major Documents, Tab 1—Notes, Drafts, etc." folder, Box 10, Gilpatric Papers, JFKL; Letter from Roswell Gilpatric to John H. Rubel, December 28, 1964, "Correspondence, November 1964–March 1965" folder, ibid.

46 RLG's [Roswell Gilpatric] Notes on the 12/9/64 Discussion with Messrs. Dean and McCloy on Problems of Europe and NATO, Document #1073, National Security Archive, *U.S. Nuclear Non-Proliferation*; Committee on Nuclear Proliferation—Minutes of Discussion, Third Meeting, January 7–8, 1965, "Minutes of Meetings" folder,

Committee File, NSF, Box 8–9, LBJL; Memorandum of Conversation, January 7, 1965, "Presidential Task Force Committee on Nuclear Proliferation" folder, Subject File, NSF, Box 35, LBJL; Memorandum for the Chairman, January 8, 1965, Folder 87, Box DA1, McCloy Papers, Amherst, Mass.

47 Notes of AHD [Arthur Dean] to R.G. [Roswell Gilpatric], JJM [John McCloy], and AW Jr. [Arthur Watson], Sunday, December 13, 1964, Document #1080, National Security Archive, *U.S. Nuclear Non-Proliferation.*

48 Four Alternatives to Nuclear Proliferation, December 15, 1964, "Alternative Courses of Action" folder, Committee File, NSF, Box 4, LBJL; Problems Concerning Alternative Courses of Action, n.d., "President's Task Force on Nuclear Proliferation — Collateral Materials, Part I — November 1964" folder, Gilpatric Papers, JFKL; RLG's Assessment of End Results of Alternative Courses of Action, December 19, 1964, Document #1083, National Security Archive, *U.S. Nuclear Non-Proliferation.*

49 Destruction of Chinese Nuclear Weapons Capabilities, December 14, 1964, "China" folder, Committee File, NSF, Box 5, LBJL; Memorandum of Conversation, Subject: Non-Proliferation of Nuclear Weapons, December 15, 1964, Nuclear Non-Proliferation Project, NSA; Minutes of Briefing by Secretary McNamara on Issues Relating to Proliferation, January 7, 1965, "Minutes of Meeting" folder, Committee File, NSF, Box 9, LBJL; Effects of the Chinese Bomb on Nuclear Spread, November 2, 1964, "China" folder, Committee File, NSF, Box 5, LBJL; Memorandum for Mr. Gilpatric from Henry Rowen, January 7, 1965, "President's Task Force on Nuclear Proliferation — Meetings Materials, 1/7–8/65" folder, Box 10, Gilpatric Papers, JFKL.

50 A Philosophical Framework for Course III, January 4, 1965, Document #1091, National Security Archive, *U.S. Nuclear Non-Proliferation; FRUS, 1964–1968,* 11:163–68; Memorandum for the Committee on Nuclear Proliferation, January 13, 1965, "Presidential Task Force Committee on Nuclear Proliferation" folder, Subject File, NSF, Box 35, LBJL; President's Committee on Nuclear Proliferation: A Report to the President, n.d., ibid.; Memorandum from Roger Fisher to Gilpatric, A Proposed Decision on the General U.S. Policy toward Nuclear Weapons, December 17, 1964, "President's Task Force on Nuclear Proliferation — Meetings Materials, 1/7–8/65" folder, Box 10, Gilpatric Papers, JFKL; Effects of the Chinese Bomb on Nuclear Spread, November 2, 1964, "China" folder, Committee File, NSF, Box 5, LBJL; Memo on Possible Action — Action Directed against Further French Atmospheric Tests, December 19, 1964, ibid.

51 Memorandum to the Chairman from Arthur Dean, January 18, 1965, "Collateral Materials, Part II" folder, President's Task Force on Nuclear Proliferation, Box 11, Gilpatric Papers, JFKL; Memorandum for the Chairman, January 8, 1965, Folder 87, Box DA1, McCloy Papers, Amherst, Mass.; *FRUS, 1964–1968,* 11:163–68; Memorandum for the Chairman, January 8, 1965, "Presidential Task Force Committee on Nuclear Proliferation" folder, Subject File, NSF, Box 35, LBJL; Memorandum to the Chairman, January 18, 1965, "President's Task Force on Nuclear Proliferation — Collateral

Materials, Part II, December 1964–October 1965" folder, Box 11, Gilpatric Papers, JFKL.

52 Report to the President by the Committee on Nuclear Proliferation, January 21, 1965, "Major Documents, Tab 3, Complete Documents" folder, President's Task Force on Nuclear Proliferation, Box 10, Gilpatric Papers, JFKL; Draft National Security Action Memorandum, Subject: Prevention of the Proliferation of Nuclear Weapons, n.d., "Dr. York Proliferation Committee" folder, Committee File, NSF, Box 8–9, LBJL.

53 Memorandum for the President from McGeorge Bundy, January 21, 1965, "McGeorge Bundy, Vol. 8" folder, Memos to the President, NSF, Box 2, LBJL; Memorandum from Secretary of State Rusk to President Johnson, n.d., "President's Task Force Committee on Nuclear Proliferation" folder, Subject File, NSF, Box 35, LBJL; Hal Brands, "Rethinking Nonproliferation," 101; Memorandum of Telephone Conversation between George Ball and Eugene Rostow, February 3, 1965, "Germany, West, II" folder, Box 4, Ball Papers, LBJL.

54 Seaborg, *Stemming the Tide*, 145, 148–49; Memorandum from McGeorge Bundy to the Secretary of State, the Secretary of Defense, the Director, Arms Control and Disarmament Agency, the Chairman, Atomic Energy Commission, the Chairman, Joint Chiefs of Staff, the Director of Central Intelligence, and the Director of Science and Technology, January 23, 1965, "McGeorge Bundy, Vol. 8" folder, Memos to the President, NSF, Box 2, LBJL; Garthoff, *Journey through the Cold War*, 194; Memorandum of Telephone Conversation between Eugene Rostow and George Ball, February 3, 1965, "Germany, West, II" folder, Ball Papers, Box 4, LBJL.

55 *FRUS, 1964–1968*, 13:64–67.

56 Ibid., 13:79, 82–83, 100–103; quoted in Dallek, *Flawed Giant*, 87.

57 *FRUS, 1964–1968*, 13:92–100, 103–9, 120–22; Telegram from the U.S. Embassy in France to the Department of State, November 19, 1964, "Multilateral Force — Cables, Vol. III" folder, Subject File, NSF, Box 24, LBJL; Memorandum of Telephone Conversation between McGeorge Bundy and George Ball, November 25, 1964, "MLF" folder, Box 5, Ball Papers, LBJL; Bill, *George Ball*, 116–17; Schrafstetter and Twigge, *Avoiding Armageddon*, 148; quoted in Colman, *Special Relationship*, 28–29; Young, "Killing the MLF," 305.

58 Quoted in Geyelin, *Johnson and the World*, 169; quoted in Schrafstetter and Twigge, *Avoiding Armageddon*, 149; *FRUS, 1964–1968*, 13:134–37; quoted in Thomas Alan Schwartz, *Lyndon Johnson and Europe*, 46.

59 *FRUS, 1964–1968*, 13:133–34, 137–39; quoted in Colman, *Special Relationship*, 31; The Nuclear Deterrent, November 1964, "Multilateral Force — General" folder, Files of Charles E. Johnson, NSF, Box 3, LBJL; Young, "Killing the MLF," 306; Schrafstetter and Twigge, *Avoiding Armageddon*, 145.

60 *FRUS, 1964–1968*, 13:141–46; quoted in Thomas Alan Schwartz, *Lyndon Johnson and Europe*, 46.

61 *FRUS, 1964–1968*, 13:133–34, 146–56, 158–60, 165–67; Young, "Killing the MLF," 307.

62 Quoted in Costigliola, "Lyndon B. Johnson, Germany, and 'the End of the Cold War,'" 189; *FRUS, 1964–1968*, 13:169–79; National Security Action Memorandum No. 322, December 17, 1964, "President's Task Force on Nuclear Proliferation—Meetings Materials, 1/7–8/65" folder, Box 10, Gilpatric Papers, JFKL.

63 Memorandum from Adrian Fisher to S. Douglas Carter, June 18, 1962, Document #1118, National Security Archive, *U.S. Nuclear Non-Proliferation*; quoted in Schlesinger, *Robert Kennedy*, 746; Memorandum for McGeorge Bundy from Spurgeon Keeny, Subject: Senator Robert Kennedy's Statement on Nuclear Proliferation, June 22, 1965, Document #1119, National Security Archive, *U.S. Nuclear Non-Proliferation*; United Press International Wire Report on Robert F. Kennedy's Speech, June 23, 1965, "Spurgeon Keeny Memos" folder, Name File, NSF, Box 5, LBJL; Seaborg, *Stemming the Tide*, 149–50; quoted in Goodwin, *Remembering America*, 397; Beschloss, *Reaching for Glory*, 368–70; Memorandum for the President, June 28, 1965, "Luncheons with the President, Vol. I" folder, Files of McGeorge Bundy, NSF, Box 18–19, LBJL; Memorandum for the President, July 3, 1965, "McGeorge Bundy, Vol. 12, July 1965" folder, Memos to the President, Box 4, LBJL.

Chapter 9

1 Quoted in Costigliola, "Lyndon B. Johnson, Germany, and 'the End of the Cold War,'" 201–2; *FRUS, 1964–1968*, 11:558–61; quoted in Perkovich, *India's Nuclear Bomb*, 138; Schrafstetter, "Preventing the 'Smiling Buddha,'" 103.

2 Memorandum for the President, July 1, 1965, "McGeorge Bundy, Vol. 12, July 1965 [2 of 2]" folder, Memos to the President, NSF, Box 4, LBJL; Thomas Alan Schwartz, *Lyndon Johnson and Europe*, 56–57; Beschloss, *Reaching for Glory*, 380; *Documents on Disarmament, 1965*, 265–78; Seaborg, *Stemming the Tide*, 162–64; Memorandum of Conversation, July 9, 1965, Folder 1306, Nuclear Non-Proliferation Project, NSA; Telegram from the Department of State to the U.S. Embassy in West Germany, July 9, 1965, Document #1125, National Security Archive, *U.S. Nuclear Non-Proliferation*; Telegram from U.S. Mission in Geneva to the Department of State, July 30, 1965, "Disarmament—18-Nation Disarmament Conference (ENDC), Vol. I" folder, Subject File, NSF, Box 12–13, LBJL; *FRUS, 1964–1968*, 11:224–28; Memorandum for the Members of the Committee of Principals—Position Paper on a Non-Proliferation Agreement, July 16, 1965, "Treaty—Non-Proliferation—I—1965" folder, Files of Spurgeon Keeny, NSF, Box 8, LBJL; Proposed Program under NSAM #335, July 31, 1965, "Disarmament, Committee of Principals, Vol. II [1 of 2]" folder, Subject File, NSF, Box 14, LBJL; Roger Kelly Smith, "Origins of the Regime," 327–28.

3 *FRUS, 1964–1968*, 11:191–94, 216–17; Memorandum for the President, July 3, 1965, "McGeorge Bundy, Vol. 12, July 1965 [2 of 2]" folder, Memos to the President, NSF, Box 4, LBJL; Memorandum to the President, June 25, 1965, "McGeorge Bundy, Vol. 11, June 1965 [1 of 2]" folder, Memos to the President, NSF, Box 3, LBJL; Memo to the Secretary of State and the Secretary of Defense, March 27, 1965, "Presidential Task Force, Committee on Nuclear Proliferation" folder, Subject File, NSF, Box

35, LBJL (emphasis in original); Memorandum for Bundy from Keeny, March 26, 1965, "Presidential Task Force Committee on Nuclear Proliferation" folder, Subject Files, NSF, Box 35, LBJL; Memorandum for Bundy from Keeny, April 12, 1965, ibid.; Memorandum of the National Security Council Meeting, February 27, 1962, "National Security Council Meetings, 1962—No. 497, 2/27/62" folder, Meetings and Memoranda, NSF, Box 313, JFKL; Memorandum for Bundy and Hornig from Keeny, April 22, 1965, "Disarmament, Committee of Principals, Vol. II [2 of 2]" folder, Subject File, NSF, Box 14, LBJL; Memorandum for Bundy from Keeny, April 12, 1965, "Presidential Task Force Committee on Nuclear Proliferation" folder, Subject File, NSF, Box 35, LBJL; Draft NSAM, April 11, 1965, ibid.; Draft #1—The President's Committee on Nuclear Proliferation—A Report to the President, January 13, 1965, "President's Task Force on Nuclear Proliferation—Meetings Materials" folder, Box 10, Gilpatric Papers, JFKL.

4 *FRUS, 1964–1968*, 11:194–96, 214–24, 229–35; Telegram from the U.S. Embassy in Great Britain to the Department of State, July 16, 1965, "Disarmament—18-Nation Disarmament Conference (ENDC), Vol. I" folder, Subject File, NSF, Box 12–13, LBJL; Memorandum of Conversation, July 19, 1965, Document #1126, National Security Archive, *U.S. Nuclear Non-Proliferation*; Memorandum of Conversation, July 22, 1965, Document #1127, ibid.; Memorandum for McGeorge Bundy, Subject: UK Draft Non-Proliferation Treaty, July 21, 1965, "Non-Proliferation Treaty, Vol. I" folder, Subject File, NSF, Box 26, LBJL; Message from British Foreign Minister Michael Stewart to Secretary of State Dean Rusk, July 23, 1965, "Disarmament—18-Nation Disarmament Conference (ENDC), Vol. I" folder, Subject File, NSF, Box 12–13, LBJL; *Documents on Disarmament, 1965*, 347–49, 362–63, 443–45; Memorandum of Conversation, July 3, 1965, "McGeorge Bundy, Vol. 12, July 1965 [2 of 2]" folder, Memos to the President, Box 4, LBJL.

5 *FRUS, 1964–1968*, 11:170–71, 184, 197–99, 203–5, 237–43; Memorandum for the Committee of Principals, July 16, 1965, "Disarmament—Committee of Principals, Vol. 2" folder, Subject File, NSF, Box 14, LBJL; Memorandum for the Secretary of Defense—The Military Consequences of Alternative Test Ban Proposals, August 21, 1965, ibid.

6 *FRUS, 1964–1968*, 11:289–91.

7 Ibid., 11:309–11, 319–20, 323–25, 330–32, 334–39, 342–45, 348–51, 357–64, 401–4, 425–26; National Intelligence Estimate—Likelihood of Further Nuclear Proliferation, January 26, 1967, "4 Arms and Disarmament" folder, National Intelligence Estimates, NSF, Box 1, LBJL; Proliferation of Missile Delivery Systems for Nuclear Weapons, January 26, 1966, ibid.; Memorandum for President, June 7, 1966, *National Security Archive Electronic Briefing Book No. 6*, <www.gwu.ed/nsarchive/> (accessed October 3, 2008); Telegram from Department of State to U.S. Embassy in New Delhi, March 29, 1966, ibid.; Telegram, Embassy in New Delhi, July 28, 1966, ibid.; Telegram from Department of State to U.S. Embassy in New Delhi, October 27, 1966, ibid.; Memorandum for the President, July 15, 1966, "[Test Ban Treaty]" folder, Intelligence File, NSF, Box 11, LBJL; Proposed U.S. Initiative on Threshold

Test Ban Treaty, July 28, 1966, ibid.; Memorandum for the President, August 3, 1966, ibid.; NSC Discussion of Indian Nuclear Program—A Proposed Sequel, June 7, 1966, ibid.; Memorandum for Mr. Rostow, June 10, 1966, ibid.; Memorandum from McNamara to Rostow, March 18, 1967, "Disarmament, Test Ban Treaty" folder, Subject File, NSF, Box 11, LBJL; Memorandum from Keeny to Rostow, March 22, 1967, ibid.

8 Memorandum for the President from William Foster, Subject: A Time for Decision on Non-Proliferation, October 7, 1965, "Treaty—Non-Proliferation I—1965" folder, Files of Spurgeon Keeny, NSF, Box 8, LBJL; Memorandum to the President from McGeorge Bundy, October 10, 1965, "McGeorge Bundy, Vol. 15" folder, Memos to the President, NSF, Box 5, LBJL.

9 Memorandum of Conversation, March 10, 1965, "ACDA, Vol. I" folder, Agency File, NSF, Box 6, LBJL; *FRUS, 1964–1968*, 13:188–89, 193–95; Schrafstetter and Twigge, *Avoiding Armageddon*, 150; quoted in Dumbrell, *President Lyndon Johnson and Soviet Communism*, 72; Documents 42, 45, *FRUS, 1964–1968: Western Europe* (2001), vol. 12, <www.state.gov> (accessed October 3, 2008); Bozo, *Two Strategies*, 111, 118; Telegram from the U.S. Embassy in France to the Department of State, March 23, 1965, "Multilateral Force—Cables, Vol. 4" folder, Subject File, NSF, Box 25, LBJL; quoted in Colman, *Special Relationship*, 44.

10 *FRUS, 1964–1968*, 13:243–44; Memorandum for the President from McGeorge Bundy, September 12, 1965, "McGeorge Bundy, Vol. 14" folder, Memos to the President, NSF, Box 4, LBJL.

11 Martin Hillenbrand Paper, "The Nuclear Problem of the Alliance," September 21, 1965, "NATO: Atlantic Nuclear Program, September 21, 1965 (Briefing Book)" folder, Agency File, NSF, Box 39–40, LBJL; *FRUS, 1964–1968*, 13:244–47; Memorandum from Martin J. Hillenbrand to the Undersecretary (Ball), Subject: The German Attitude on the Nuclear Problem, September 21, 1965, "NATO: Atlantic Nuclear Program, September 21, 1965 (Briefing Book)" folder, Agency File, NSF, Box 39–40, LBJL; Memorandum from the Assistant Secretary of State for European Affairs (Leddy) to the Acting Secretary of State (Ball), Subject: A Fresh Start on the Collective Nuclear Program, October 7, 1965, Document #1136, National Security Archive, *U.S. Nuclear Non-Proliferation*; Proposal for Collective Nuclear Authority, November 2, 1965, "MLF/ANF" folder, Files of Spurgeon Keeny, NSF, Box 7, LBJL; Telephone Conversation between James Reston and George Ball, September 21, 1965, "(General) US and Europe" folder, Ball Papers, Box 6, LBJL.

12 *FRUS, 1964–1968*, 13:253–57, 261–62; The Case for a Strong American Lead to Establish a Collective Nuclear System That Would Help Save the Western World from Repeating an Old Mistake, n.d., "NATO: George W. Ball Analysis of a Collective Nuclear Force System" folder, Agency File, NSF, Box 39, LBJL; The Dangers from a Psychotic Germany, n.d., ibid.

13 The Case for a Fresh Start on Atlantic Nuclear Defense (with No Mixed Manned Forces or Plans for Such Forces), October 18, 1965, "NSAM 345—Nuclear Planning" folder, National Security Action Memorandums, NSF, Box 8, LBJL; A Phased Ap-

proach to Nuclear Weapons Cooperation, n.d., "MLF/ANF" folder, Files of Spurgeon Keeny, NSF, Box 7, LBJL; *FRUS, 1964–1968*, 13:271–73.

14 Letter from Henry Owen to John McCloy, October 16, 1965, Folder 110, Box DA1, McCloy Papers, Amherst, Mass.; quoted in Gavin, "Blast from the Past," 126.

15 Memorandum of Conversation, Subject: Collective Nuclear Arrangements in NATO, November 8, 1965, Document #1144, National Security Archive, *U.S. Nuclear Non-Proliferation*; Memorandum for the President from Francis Bator, November 17, 1965, Document #1146, ibid.

16 Memorandum from Hayes Redmon to Bill Moyers, November 16, 1965, "BDM Memos" folder, Bill Moyers series, Office Files of the White House Aides, Box 11, LBJL.

17 Quoted in Fielding, "Coping with Decline," 639; Telephone Conversation between McGeorge Bundy and George Ball, January 24, 1966, "USSR III" folder, Ball Papers, Box 6, LBJL.

18 *FRUS, 1964–1968*, 13:289–92.

19 Ibid., 13:295–96, 300–301; David K. E. Bruce quoted in Young, "Killing the MLF," 315.

20 Letter from Sir Frank Roberts, British Embassy in Bonn, to Lord Hood, January 17, 1966, FO 371/190663, PRO; Letter from Patrick Dean, British Embassy in Washington, to Lord Hood, Foreign Office, April 22, 1966, FO 371/190665, PRO.

21 Memorandum of Conversation between Henry Kissinger and Ludwig Erhard, January 28, 1966, Document #1162, National Security Archive, *U.S. Nuclear Non-Proliferation*; Henry Kissinger's Summary of Conversations, January 24–30, 1966, Document #1164, ibid.; Telegram from U.S. Embassy in Bonn to Department of State, April 14, 1966, "INT 2-2" file, SDDF.

22 *FRUS, 1964–1968*, 11:256–57, 259–63, 268–71, 274–75, 277–81, 301–4, 307–8; Memorandum from G. Brennan to William C. Foster, October 18, 1965, "Treaty — Nonproliferation I — 1965" folder, Files of Spurgeon Keeny, NSF, Box 8, LBJL; Central Intelligence Agency Intelligence Information Cable, October 19, 1965, "[MLF] Mr. Bundy: For 6 O'clock Meeting, Monday, 18 October" folder, Subject File, NSF, Box 25, LBJL.

23 Telegram from the U.S. Embassy in France to the Secretary of State, October 1, 1965, Folder 1306, Nuclear Non-Proliferation Project, NSA; Ben-Zvi, *Lyndon B. Johnson*, 33; *FRUS, 1964–1968*, 11:245–56; *Documents on Disarmament, 1965*, 462–64, 532–34, 585.

24 *Documents on Disarmament, 1965*, 555–81; Letter to President Johnson from Representative Chet Holifield, October 26, 1965, "Multilateral Force — General" folder, Files of Charles E. Johnson, NSF, Box 3, LBJL; *FRUS, 1964–1968*, 11:292–95.

25 *Documents on Disarmament, 1966*, 84–96, 159–60; Telegram from the U.S. Mission in Geneva to the Department of State, March 26, 1966, "Disarmament — 18-Nation Disarmament Conference (ENDC), Vol. II" folder, Subject File, NSF, Box 12–13, LBJL.

26 *FRUS, 1964–1968*, 13:314–16.

27 Notes on Conversations with John J. McCloy, January 22, 1966, "McCloy, John J." folder, Subject File, JFK-LBJ, Special Files: Public Service, Box 486, Harriman Papers, LC; Telephone Conversation between John McCloy and George Ball, February 2, 1966, "USSR III" folder, Box 6, Ball Papers, LBJL; Letter from Gerard C. Smith to John J. McCloy, Folder 109, Box DA1, McCloy Papers, Amherst, Mass.; Letter from Henry Owen to John J. McCloy, February 14, 1966, Folder 110, ibid.; Letter from Robert Bowie to John J. McCloy, February 15, 1966, Folder 105, ibid.; Draft speech on nuclear sharing and nonproliferation by John J. McCloy, n.d., Folder 107, ibid.; Letter from John J. McCloy to John Pastore, February 28, 1966, Folder 108, ibid.; Letter from John J. McCloy to Robert F. Kennedy, March 2, 1966, ibid.

28 Thomas Alan Schwartz, *Lyndon Johnson and Europe*, 104; quoted in Chase, *Acheson*, 416; Thomas Alan Schwartz, "Johnson and Europe," 49, 51; Haftendorn, *NATO and the Nuclear Revolution*, 3; *FRUS, 1964–1968*, 13:335–38, 363–65.

29 Quoted in Dobrynin, *In Confidence*, 174; *FRUS, 1964–1968*, 13:374–75, 417–19.

30 *Documents on Disarmament, 1966*, 41–49, 96–102, 253–55, 302–3, 306–7; Memorandum from Walt W. Rostow to President Johnson, May 29, 1966, "NSAM 345 — Nuclear Planning" folder, National Security Action Memorandums, NSF, Box 8, LBJL; quoted in Thomas Alan Schwartz, *Lyndon Johnson and Europe*, 114.

31 Letter from President Johnson to Senator John Pastore, June 13, 1966, "Walt Rostow, Volume 6" folder, Memos to the President, NSF, Box 8, LBJL.

32 Memorandum from George Bunn to William Foster—UK Request to Exclude "European Option"; "Generalized" Version of Draft Non-Proliferation Treaty, June 7, 1966, "Treaty—Non-Proliferation II—1966a" folder, Files of Spurgeon Keeny, NSF, Box 8, LBJL; *FRUS, 1964–1968*, 11:323–26, 333–34; Memorandum from Robert McNamara to Dean Rusk, June 7, 1966, "Treaty—Non-Proliferation II—1966a" folder, Files of Spurgeon Keeny, NSF, Box 8, LBJL.

33 Memorandum for the President from Bill Moyers, July 29, 1966, "BDM Memos, July 12–August 1966" folder, Bill Moyers, Office Files of the White House Aides, Box 12, LBJL; Suggested Changes, n.d., "Treaty—Non-Proliferation II—1966a" folder, Files of Spurgeon Keeny, NSF, Box 8, LBJL; Memorandum for the Secretary of Defense from the Joint Chiefs of Staff, June 29, 1966, Document #1173, National Security Archive, *U.S. Nuclear Non-Proliferation*; Memorandum for Walt Rostow from Henry Owen, July 19, 1966, "Treaty—Non-Proliferation II—1966a" folder, Files of Spurgeon Keeny, NSF, Box 8, LBJL; Memorandum for Walt Rostow from Charles E. Johnson, July 15, 1966, ibid.; Minutes of the Meeting of the Steering Committee of Educational Committee to Halt Atomic Weapons' Spread, July 6, 1966, "Educational Committee to Halt Atomic Weapons Spread (1)" folder, Section VII, Box 11, Papers of Homer A. Jack, SCPC.

34 Seaborg, *Stemming the Tide*, 189–90; Telegram from the U.S. Mission to Geneva to the Secretary of State, July 23, 1966, Document #1182, National Security Archive, *U.S. Nuclear Non-Proliferation*; Telegram from William Foster to Adrian Fisher, July 27, 1966, Document #1185, ibid.; Memorandum for Walt Rostow from Spurgeon Keeny,

July 28, 1966, "Treaty—Non-Proliferation II—1996a" folder, Files of Spurgeon Keeny, NSF, Box 8, LBJL; *Documents on Disarmament, 1966*, 503–5.

35 Memorandum from Walt W. Rostow to President Johnson, August 12, 1966, "Non-Proliferation" folder, Files of Walt W. Rostow, NSF, Box 11, LBJL; Memorandum for the President, Subject: Nonproliferation Treaty, the Organization of the West, and Arms Control, August 8, 1966, "Treaty—Non-Proliferation III—1966b" folder, Files of Spurgeon Keeny, NSF, Box 8, LBJL; A Four-Point Approach to Arms Control, n.d., ibid.; Memorandum to Secretary Rusk from Walt Rostow, September 3, 1966, "Walt W. Rostow, Vol. 12" folder, Memos to the President, NSF, Box 10, LBJL.

36 Working Group Language for the Non-Proliferation Treaty: Relationship to Existing and Possible Allied Nuclear Arrangements, September 30, 1966, "Treaty—Non-Proliferation III—1966b" folder, Files of Spurgeon Keeny, NSF, Box 8, LBJL; Summary—Working Group Language for the Non-Proliferation Treaty: Relationship to Existing and Possible Allied Nuclear Arrangements, September 30, 1966, ibid.

37 Gavin, "Blast from the Past," 127.

38 Gavin, *Gold, Dollars, and the Power*, 135–36, 143–51; Gavin, "Myth of Flexible Response," 867; quoted in Lacouture, *De Gaulle*, 379.

39 Decisions Taken by the President, October 1–2, 1966, "Meetings with the President April–December 1966" folder, Files of Walt Rostow, NSF, Box 1, LBJL; Note Dictated by the Secretary on the President's Views on Nonproliferation, as Set Forth at the Recent Camp David Meeting, October 3, 1966, "The Non-Proliferation Treaty, Vol. II" folder, National Security Council History, NSF, Box 55–56, LBJL; quoted in Oral History, Eugene V. Rostow, p. 15, LBJL; Memorandum of Conversation, Subject: Non-Proliferation, October 10, 1966, "USSR, Gromyko Conversations, Vol. I" folder, Country File, NSF, Box 228, LBJL.

40 *FRUS, 1964–1968*, 11:388–91.

41 Ibid., 13:516–17, 522–23; Memorandum for the President, Subject: Suggested Language for the Non-Proliferation Treaty: Relationship to Existing and Possible Allied Nuclear Arrangements, November 28, 1966, "Walt W. Rostow, Vol. 15" folder, Memos to the President, NSF, Box 11, LBJL; Memorandum for Mr. Robert Kintner from G. William Moser, Subject: Report to the President, December 29, 1966, Document #1204, National Security Archive, *U.S. Nuclear Non-Proliferation*.

42 Wenger, "Crisis and Opportunity," 41–42; *FRUS, 1964–1968*, 13:530–31; quoted in Thomas Alan Schwartz, *Lyndon Johnson and Europe*, 152; quoted in Hanreider, *Germany, America, Europe*, 93.

43 *FRUS, 1964–1968*, 13:538–45; Wenger, "Crisis and Opportunity," 54; Memorandum of Conversation, April 20, 1967, "Walt W. Rostow, Vol. 26" folder, Memos to the President, NSF, Box 15, LBJL; Telegram from Walt Rostow to the President, March 3, 1967, "Walt Rostow, Vol. 22" folder, Memos to the President, NSF, Box 14, LBJL; Text of Cable from Ambassador McGhee, April 21, 1967, "Walt Rostow, Vol. 26" folder, ibid.; Telegram from U.S. Embassy in West Germany to the Secretary of State, April 6, 1967, "Walt Rostow, Vol. 25" folder, ibid.; Memorandum for Mr. Ros-

tow from Spurgeon Keeny, May 9, 1967, "Non-Proliferation Treaty, Vol. I" folder, Subject File, NSF, Box 26, LBJL; *FRUS, 1964–1968*, 11:435–39.

44 Non-Proliferation Treaty Interpretations, April 17, 1967, "Non-Proliferation Treaty, Vol. I" folder, Subject File, NSF, Box 26, LBJL; Memorandum of Conversation, January 18, 1967, "USSR, Dobrynin-Kohler Conversations, Vol. I" folder, Country File, NSF, Box 228, LBJL; *FRUS, 1964–1968*, 11:445–49; Memorandum for Walt Rostow from Spurgeon Keeny, February 27, 1967, "Non-Proliferation Treaty, Vol. I" folder, Subject File, NSF, Box 26, LBJL; Telegram from the U.S. Mission in Geneva to Secretary of State Rusk, February 16, 1967, "Non-Proliferation Treaty, Vol. I" folder, Papers of Francis Bator, Box 31, LBJL; Memorandum for Mr. Bundy from Spurgeon Keeny, June 23, 1967, "Non-Proliferation Treaty, Vol. I" folder, Subject File, NSF, Box 26, LBJL.

45 Letter from Jean Monnet to Eugene Rostow, February 14, 1967, "Non-Proliferation Treaty, Vol. I" folder, Subject File, NSF, Box 26, LBJL; Memorandum from Walt Rostow to President Johnson, February 18, 1967, "Walt Rostow, Vol. 21" folder, Memos to the President, Box 13, NSF, LBJL; *FRUS, 1964–1968*, 11:418–19, 454–65; Bunn, *Arms Control by Committee*, 90–91.

46 The U.S. Arms Control and Disarmament Agency during the Johnson Administration, Vol. 1: I—Summary and Analysis of Principal Developments, n.d., p. 53, Nuclear Non-Proliferation Project, NSA; Memorandum from Walt Rostow to President Johnson, May 16, 1967, "Non-Proliferation Treaty, Vol. I" folder, Subject File, NSF, Box 26, LBJL; Memorandum for the President from Secretary of State Rusk, n.d., "Walt Rostow, Vol. 28" folder, Memos to the President, NSF, Box 16, LBJL; Telegram from U.S. Mission to the United Nations to the Department of State, June 22, 1967, "USSR—Hollybush 6/67, II, President's Mtg. w/Chairman Kosygin" folder, Country File, NSF, Box 230, LBJL; Dumbrell, *President Lyndon Johnson and Soviet Communism*, 47; Lyndon Baines Johnson, *Vantage Point*, 483, 485; Hal Brands, "Progress Unseen," 279; *Documents on Disarmament, 1967*, 268–69.

47 Oral History, Walt W. Rostow, p. 97, LBJL; Dumbrell, *President Lyndon Johnson and Soviet Communism*, 47, 50; Dallek, *Flawed Giant*, 436.

48 *Documents on Disarmament, 1967*, 338–41.

49 Memorandum of Conversation, June 23, 1967, "USSR—Hollybush 6/67, II, President's Mtg. w/Chairman Kosygin" folder, Country File, NSF, Box 230, LBJL; Perkovich, *India's Nuclear Bomb*, 134; Hal Brands, "Progress Unseen," 271; Garthoff, *Journey through the Cold War*, 196; Wenger, "Crisis and Opportunity," 55; Schrafstetter and Twigge, *Avoiding Armageddon*, 175, 183; Status of Non-Proliferation Consultations, March 29, 1967, "Non-Proliferation Treaty" folder, Papers of Francis Bator, Box 31, LBJL; Non-Proliferation Treaty Interpretations, April 17, 1967, ibid.; Memorandum for Mr. Rostow from Spurgeon Keeny, May 9, 1967, ibid.; quoted in Perkovich, *India's Nuclear Bomb*, 138; Memorandum of Conversation between Kurt-Georg Kiesinger and John J. McCloy, June 19, 1967, "Walt Rostow, Vol. 22" folder, Memos to the President, NSF, Box 18, LBJL.

50 Quoted in Mastny, "Was 1968 a Strategic Watershed of the Cold War?" 153; *Documents on Disarmament, 1968,* 1–6.

51 Memorandum of Conversation, March 28, 1967, "Non-Proliferation Treaty" folder, Papers of Francis Bator, Box 31, LBJL; Memorandum for Mr. Rostow, April 19, 1967, ibid.; Dumbrell, *President Lyndon Johnson and Soviet Communism,* 69.

52 Memorandum of Conversation, November 2, 1967, "USSR—Dobrynin Conversations, Vol. I" folder, Country File, NSF, Box 229, LBJL.

53 *Documents on Disarmament, 1967,* 732–33.

54 Memorandum of Conversation, March 28, 1967, "Rostow Memos" folder, Name File, NSF, Box 7, LBJL; *FRUS, 1964–1968,* 11:471–74; Memorandum for the President from Walt Rostow, November 7, 1967, "Non-Proliferation Treaty, Vol. 2" folder, Subject File, NSF, Box 26, LBJL; Note for Walt Rostow, November 9, 1967, ibid.; Memorandum for Walt Rostow from Spurgeon Keeny, November 14, 1967, ibid.; *Documents on Disarmament, 1967,* 613–17; Memorandum of Conversation, December 26, 1967, "USSR—Dobrynin Conversations, Vol. I" folder, Country File, NSF, Box 229, LBJL; The U.S. Arms Control and Disarmament Agency during the Johnson Administration, Vol. 1: I—Summary and Analysis of Principal Developments, n.d., pp. 84–87, Nuclear Non-Proliferation Project, NSA; *FRUS, 1964–1968,* 11:515–16, 520–22, 543–45.

55 *Documents on Disarmament, 1968,* 1–6.

56 Schrafstetter and Twigge, *Avoiding Armageddon,* 191; *FRUS, 1964–1968,* 11:523–24, 539–43; *Documents on Disarmament, 1968,* 162–66; Seaborg, *Stemming the Tide,* 371.

57 Letter from James Ramey to Walt Rostow, March 14, 1968, "Non-Proliferation Treaty, Vol. II" folder, Subject File, NSF, Box 26, LBJL; Perkovich, *India's Nuclear Bomb,* 113, 116–17; *FRUS, 1964–1968,* 13:679–80.

58 *Documents on Disarmament, 1968,* 336–45, 439–40; *FRUS, 1964–1968,* 11:558–61.

59 Memorandum of Conversation, May 17, 1968, "USSR, Dobrynin Conversations, Vol. 2" folder, Country File, NSF, Box 229, LBJL.

60 The U.S. Arms Control and Disarmament Agency during the Johnson Administration, Vol. 1: I—Summary and Analysis of Principal Developments, n.d., p. 97, Nuclear Non-Proliferation Project, NSA; Perkovich, *India's Nuclear Bomb,* 138; Lewidge, *De Gaulle,* 296; Telegram from Paris to Department of State, November 4, 1964, "Multilateral Force—General" folder, Files of Charles E. Johnson, NSF, Box 3, LBJL; *Documents on Disarmament, 1968,* 431–32; Memorandum from Walt W. Rostow to President Johnson, May 21, 1968, "USSR—Dobrynin Conversations, Vol. 2" folder, Country File, NSF, Box 229, LBJL.

61 Memorandum from Walt W. Rostow to President Johnson, May 26, 1968, "Walt Rostow, vol. 79" folder, Memos to the President, NSF, Box 35, LBJL.

62 Quoted in Dumbrell, *President Lyndon Johnson and Soviet Communism,* 25; *FRUS, 1964–1968,* 13:712–16, 722–25, 727–33; *Documents on Disarmament, 1968,* 478–92; Memorandum of Conversation, July 8, 1968, "USSR, Dobrynin Conversations,

Vol. 2" folder, Country File, NSF, Box 229, LBJL; Schrafstetter, "Long Shadow of the Past," 135–36; *FRUS, 1964–1968,* 11:649–51.

63 *Documents on Disarmament, 1968,* 458–65, 871; Thomas Alan Schwartz, *Lyndon Johnson and Europe,* 210, 227.

64 *FRUS, 1964–1968,* 11:583–84, 657–58; Costigliola, "Lyndon B. Johnson, Germany, and 'the End of the Cold War,'" 207–9; Prados, "Prague Spring and SALT," 32; Dumbrell, *President Lyndon Johnson and Soviet Communism,* 170–73; Mastny, "Was 1968 a Strategic Watershed of the Cold War?" 166; Thomas Alan Schwartz, *Lyndon Johnson and Europe,* 216–18.

65 Memorandum of Lunch Meeting, July 24, 1968, "Meetings with the President, July–December 1968" folder, Files of Walt Rostow, NSF, Box 2, LBJL; *Documents on Disarmament, 1968,* 668–87; *FRUS, 1964–1968,* 11:721–22, 762–72.

66 *FRUS, 1964–1968,* 13:744–49, 782–86; Schrafstetter and Twigge, *Avoiding Armageddon,* 187, 192; Cohen, *Israel and the Bomb,* 195–217, 259–76.

67 *Documents on Disarmament, 1968,* 625; Notes on Foreign Policy Meeting, November 7, 1968, "[November 7, 1968, Foreign Policy Meeting—Family Dining Room]" folder, Tom Johnson's Notes of Meetings, Box 4, LBJL; *FRUS, 1964–1968,* 11:739–42; Dallek, *Flawed Giant,* 594–95.

68 CIA Intelligence Memorandum on Prospects for the Nonproliferation Treaty, November 27, 1968, "Non-Proliferation Treaty, Vol. II" folder, Subject File, NSF, Box 26, LBJL; "Ninety-Day" Transition Paper on the Non-Proliferation Treaty, December 10, 1968, ibid.; Notes on the Tuesday Luncheon Meeting, December 3, 1968, "December 3, 1968: 1:29–2:54 P.M. Tuesday Luncheon" folder, Tom Johnson's Notes of Meetings, Box 4, LBJL; Schrafstetter and Twigge, *Avoiding Armageddon,* 193.

69 Quoted in Hersh, *Price of Power,* 148; Wittner, *Resisting the Bomb,* 435; Memorandum on Impact on U.S. Policies of an Israeli Nuclear Weapons Capability, February 7, 1969, *National Security Agency Electronic Briefing Book #189,* <www.gwu.edu/~nsarchiv/> (accessed October 3, 2008); Memorandum for the President, August 1, 1969, ibid.; Memorandum for the President, September 18, 1969, ibid.; Memorandum for Mr. Henry A. Kissinger, September 19, 1969, ibid.; Memorandum from Kissinger to President Nixon, October 8, 1969, ibid.; Memorandum for the President from Kissinger, November 6, 1969, ibid.; Memorandum of Conversation, February 23, 1970, ibid.

Chapter 10

1 Kahn, *On Thermonuclear War,* 491.

2 State Department Policy Planning Council Report: After NPT, What?, May 28, 1968, "Non-Proliferation Treaty, 7/2/67, Vol. 2 [1 of 2]" folder, Subject File, NSF, Box 26, LBJL; CIA Research Study—Managing Nuclear Proliferation: The Politics of Limited Choice, December 1975, NSA website, <www.gwu.edu/~nsarchiv> (accessed October 5, 2008).

3 Burr and Kimball, "Nixon's Nuclear Ploy," 28–37, 72–73; Sagan and Suri, "Madman

Nuclear Alert," 150–83; "Nixon Proposed Using A-Bomb in Vietnam War," *New York Times*, March 1, 2002, A8; Burr and Kimball, "Nixon White House Considered Nuclear Options against North Vietnam, Declassified Documents Reveal."

4 Ullman, "Covert French Connection," 3–33; Costigliola, *France and the United States*, 160–61, 181, 185, 213.

5 Telegram from U.S. Embassy in New Delhi to the Secretary of State, May 7, 1969, *National Security Archive Briefing Book #6*, <www.gwu.edu/~nsarchiv> (accessed October 5, 2008); Assessment of Indian Nuclear Test, June 5, 1974, ibid.; Hersh, *Price of Power*, 444–64; Spector, *Nuclear Ambitions*, 63–65, 90–91; Perkovich, *India's Nuclear Bomb*, 146–89.

6 Weiner, "Preventing Nuclear Entrepreneurship in Russia's Nuclear Cities," 126–58.

7 Michael R. Gordon, "U.S. Weighing Future of Strategic Arms Pacts," *New York Times*, May 9, 2001, A1, A12.

8 Celia W. Dugger, "U.S. Envoy Extols India, Accepting Its Atomic Status," *New York Times*, September 7, 2001, A8.

9 Quoted in Michael Oreskes, "Troubling the Waters of Nuclear Deterrence," *New York Times*, June 4, 2000, Sec. 4, p. 3.

Bibliography

Manuscript Collections

Abilene, Kans.
  Dwight D. Eisenhower Library
    John Foster Dulles Papers
    Dwight D. Eisenhower Papers
      Dwight D. Eisenhower Records as President
      Ann Whitman File
    Christian Herter Papers
    C. D. Jackson Papers
    John McCone Papers
    National Security Council Staff Papers
    Lauris Norstad Papers
    Records of the Office of the Special Assistant for Disarmament
    Records of the Office of the Special Assistant for National Security Affairs
    Records of the Office of the Special Assistant for Science and Technology
    Records of the Office of the Staff Secretary
    Staff Research Group Papers
    U.S. President's Science Advisory Committee Records
    White House Central File
Amherst, Mass.
  Amherst College
    John J. McCloy Papers
Austin, Tex.
  Lyndon B. Johnson Library
    Administrative Histories
    George W. Ball Papers
    Clark Clifford Papers
    Lyndon Johnson Papers

Tom Johnson's Notes of Meetings
National Security File
Office Files of the White House Aides
Vice Presidential Security File
White House Central File
White House Press Office Files

Boston, Mass.
  John F. Kennedy Library
    Roswell L. Gilpatric Papers
    John F. Kennedy Papers
      National Security File
      President's Office File

Hanover, N.H.
  Baker Library of Dartmouth College
    Grenville Clark Papers

Independence, Mo.
  Harry S. Truman Library
    Dean Acheson Papers
    Harry S. Truman Papers
      President's Secretary Files
      White House Central File

London
  Public Record Office, Kew Gardens
    CAB Records
    FO Records
    PREM Records

New Haven, Conn.
  Yale University, Sterling Memorial Library
    Dean Acheson Papers
    Walter Lippmann Papers
    Henry Stimson Papers

Princeton, N.J.
  Princeton University, Seeley Mudd Library
    Bernard Baruch Papers
    John Foster Dulles Papers

Swarthmore, Pa.
  Swarthmore College
    Peace Collection

Washington, D.C.
  Library of Congress
    W. Averell Harriman Papers
  National Archives
    Department of State Records

National Security Archive
    Nuclear History Collection
    Nuclear Non-Proliferation Collection
West Branch, Iowa
  Herbert Hoover Library
    Bourke B. Hickenlooper Papers
    Lewis L. Strauss Papers

Oral Histories

Dwight D. Eisenhower Library, Abilene, Kans.
  Hans A. Bethe
  Richard M. Bissell Jr.
  Robert R. Bowie
  John S. D. Eisenhower
  Andrew J. Goodpaster
  James Hagerty
  Lyman L. Lemnitzer
  John McCone
  White House Staff
Harry S. Truman Library, Independence, Mo.
  Dean G. Acheson
  R. Gordon Arneson
  George Elsey
  John D. Hickerson
John F. Kennedy Library, Boston, Mass.
  Chester Bowles
  McGeorge Bundy
  Adrian Fisher
  William C. Foster
  Roswell L. Gilpatric
  Lord Hailsham
  W. Averell Harriman
  Robert Kennedy
  Nikita Khrushchev
  Robert Lovett
  Robert McNamara
  Paul H. Nitze
  Walt W. Rostow
  Dean Rusk
  Llewellyn Thompson
Lyndon B. Johnson Library, Austin, Tex.
  George W. Ball

Ivan S. Bennet
Clark M. Clifford
Ray S. Cline
John J. Davis
Adrian Fisher
Eilene M. Galloway
W. Averell Harriman
Curtis LeMay
John J. McCloy
Eugene V. Rostow
Walt W. Rostow
Dean Rusk
Gerard C. Smith
Cyrus Vance
Paul C. Warnke

Published Government Records

Public Papers of the Presidents of the United States (1940–70). Washington, D.C.:
Government Printing Office.

U.S. Arms Control and Disarmament Agency. *Documents on Disarmament* (1961–70).
Washington, D.C.: Government Printing Office.

U.S. Atomic Energy Commission. *In the Matter of J. Robert Oppenheimer.* Cambridge,
Mass.: MIT Press, 1970.

U.S. Congress. *Congressional Record.*

U.S. Department of State. *Documents on Disarmament, 1945–59.* Washington, D.C.:
Government Printing Office, 1960.

———. *Documents on Disarmament, 1960.* Washington, D.C.: Government Printing
Office, 1960.

———. *Foreign Relations of the United States* (1940–68). Washington, D.C.:
Government Printing Office.

Published Microfiche Collections

National Security Archive. *The Berlin Crisis, 1958–1962.* Edited by William Burr.
Washington, D.C.: Chadwyck-Healey and National Security Archive, 1990.

———. *U.S. Nuclear Non-Proliferation Policy, 1945–1991.* Edited by Virginia I. Foran.
Washington, D.C.: Chadwyck-Healey and National Security Archive, 1993.

Articles, Books, and Memoirs

Acheson, Dean. *Present at the Creation: My Years in the State Department.* New York:
Norton, 1969.

———. *Sketches from Life of Men I Have Known*. Reprint ed. Westport, Conn.: Greenwood Press, 1974.

Ahonen, Pertti. "Franz-Josef Strauss and the German Nuclear Question, 1956–1962." *Journal of Strategic Studies* 18 (June 1995): 25–51.

Albright, Joseph, and Marcia Kunstel. *Bombshell: The Secret Story of America's Unknown Atomic Spy Conspiracy*. New York: Times Books, 1997.

Ambrose, Stephen E. *The President*. Vol. 2 of *Eisenhower*. New York: Simon and Schuster, 1984.

Appleby, Charles Albert, Jr. "Eisenhower and Arms Control, 1953–1961: A Balance of Risks." Ph.D. diss., Johns Hopkins University, 1987.

Ashton, Nigel J. "Harold Macmillan and the 'Golden Days' of Anglo-American Relations Revisited, 1957–63." *Diplomatic History* 29 (September 2005): 691–723.

———. *Kennedy, Macmillan and the Cold War: The Irony of Interdependence*. New York: Palgrave Macmillan, 2002.

Ball, George W. *The Past Has Another Pattern: Memoirs*. New York: Norton, 1982.

Barber, James David. *The Presidential Character: Predicting Performance in the White House*. 3rd ed. Englewood Cliffs, N.J.: Prentice-Hall, 1985.

Baruch, Bernard. *Baruch: The Public Years*. New York: Holt, Rinehart and Winston, 1960.

Bass, Warren. *Support Any Friend: Kennedy's Middle East and the Making of the U.S.-Israeli Alliance*. New York: Oxford University Press, 2003.

Batyuk, Vladimir. "Baruch Plan and Russia." Unpublished conference paper delivered to the Cold War History Conference, Moscow, January 12–15, 1993.

Ben-Zvi, Abraham. *Lyndon B. Johnson and the Politics of Arms Sales to Israel: In the Shadow of the Hawk*. London: Frank Cass, 2004.

Bernstein, Barton J. "Crossing the Rubicon: A Missed Opportunity to Stop the H-Bomb." *International Security* 14 (Fall 1989): 132–60.

———. "The Quest for Security: American Foreign Policy and International Control of Atomic Energy, 1942–1946." *Journal of American History* 60 (March 1974): 1003–44.

———. "Roosevelt, Truman, and the Atomic Bomb, 1941–1945: A Reinterpretation." *Political Science Quarterly* 90 (Spring 1975): 23–69.

———. "Seizing the Contested Terrain of Early Nuclear History: Stimson, Conant, and Their Allies Explain the Decision to Use the Atomic Bomb." *Diplomatic History* 17 (Winter 1993): 35–72.

———. "Truman and the H-Bomb." *Bulletin of the Atomic Scientists* 40 (March 1984): 12–20.

Beschloss, Michael. *The Crisis Years: Kennedy and Khrushchev, 1960–1963*. New York: Edward Burlingame Books, 1991.

———, ed. *Reaching for Glory: Lyndon Johnson's Secret White House Tapes, 1964–1965*. New York: Simon and Schuster, 2002.

———, ed. *Taking Charge: The Johnson White House Tapes, 1963–1964*. New York: Simon and Schuster, 1997.

Bill, James A. *George Ball: Behind the Scenes in U.S. Foreign Policy*. New Haven: Yale University Press, 1997.

Bird, Kai. *The Chairman: John J. McCloy and the Making of the American Establishment*. New York: Simon and Schuster, 1992.

———. *The Color of Truth: McGeorge Bundy and William Bundy: Brothers in Arms: A Biography*. New York: Simon and Schuster, 1998.

Bird, Kai, and Martin Sherwin. *American Prometheus: The Triumph and Tragedy of J. Robert Oppenheimer*. New York: Knopf, 2005.

Biskind, Peter. *Seeing Is Believing: How Hollywood Taught Us to Stop Worrying and Love the Fifties*. New York: Henry Holt, 1983.

Blight, James G., and David A. Welch. *On the Brink: American and Soviets Reexamine the Cold War*. 2nd ed. New York: Hill and Wang, 1990.

Blum, John Morton, ed. *The Price of Vision: The Diary of Henry A. Wallace, 1942–1946*. Boston: Houghton Mifflin, 1973.

Botti, Timothy J. *The Long Wait: The Forging of the Anglo-American Nuclear Alliance, 1945–1958*. Westport, Conn.: Greenwood Press, 1987.

Boyer, Paul. *By the Bomb's Early Light: American Thought and Culture at the Dawn of the Atomic Age*. New York: Pantheon Books, 1985.

———. *Fallout: A Historian Reflects on America's Half-Century Encounter with Nuclear Weapons*. Columbus: Ohio State University Press, 1998.

Bozo, Frédéric. *Two Strategies for Europe: De Gaulle, the United States, and the Atlantic Alliance*. Lanham, Md.: Rowman & Littlefield, 2001.

Bradlee, Benjamin C. *Conversations with Kennedy*. New York: Norton, 1975.

Brands, Hal. "Progress Unseen: U.S. Arms Control Policy and the Origins of Détente, 1963–1968." *Diplomatic History* 30 (April 2006): 253–85.

———. "Rethinking Nonproliferation: LBJ, the Gilpatric Committee, and U.S. National Security Policy." *Journal of Cold War Studies* 8 (Spring 2006): 83–113.

Brands, H. W. *The Wages of Globalism: Lyndon Johnson and the Limits of American Power*. New York: Oxford University Press, 1995.

Brinkley, Douglas. *Dean Acheson: The Cold War Years, 1953–1971*. New Haven: Yale University Press, 1992.

Broscious, S. David. "Looking for International Control, Banking on American Superiority." In *Cold War Statesmen Confront the Bomb*, edited by John Lewis Gaddis, Philip H. Gordon, Ernest R. May, and Jonathan Rosenberg, 15–38. New York: Oxford University Press, 1999.

Bundy, McGeorge. *Danger and Survival: Choices about the Bomb in the First Fifty Years*. New York: Random House, 1988.

Bunn, George. *Arms Control by Committee: Managing Negotiations with the Russians*. Stanford, Calif.: Stanford University Press, 1992.

Burr, William. "New Evidence on Taiwanese 'Nuclear Intentions,' 1966–1976." <www.gwu.edu/~nsarchiv> (accessed September 26, 2008).

Burr, William, and Jeffrey Kimball. "Nixon's Nuclear Ploy." *Bulletin of the Atomic Scientists* 59 (January/February 2003): 28–37, 72–73.

————, eds. "Nixon White House Considered Nuclear Options against North Vietnam, Declassified Documents Reveal." *National Security Archive Electronic Briefing Book #195*, <www.gwu.edu/~nsarchiv> (accessed October 5, 2008).

Burr, William, and Jeffrey T. Richelson. "Whether to 'Strangle the Baby in the Cradle': The United States and the Chinese Nuclear Program, 1960–1964." *International Security* 25 (Winter 2000/2001): 54–99.

Bush, Vannevar. *Pieces of the Action*. New York: William Morrow, 1970.

Chang, Gordon H. *Friends and Enemies: The United States, China, and the Soviet Union, 1948–1972*. Stanford, Calif.: Stanford University Press, 1990.

————. "To the Nuclear Brink: Eisenhower, Dulles, and the Quemoy-Matsu Crisis." *International Security* 12 (Summer 1988): 96–122.

Chase, James. *Acheson: The Secretary of State Who Created the American World*. New York: Simon and Schuster, 1998.

Churchill, Winston S. *The Hinge of Fate*. Boston: Houghton Mifflin, 1950.

Cioc, Mark. *Pax Atomica: The Nuclear Defense Debate in the Adenauer Era*. New York: Columbia University Press, 1988.

Clark, Ian. *Nuclear Diplomacy and the Special Relationship: Britain's Deterrent and America, 1957–1962*. Oxford: Oxford University Press, 1994.

Clifford, J. Garry. "Both Ends of the Telescope: New Perspectives on FDR and American Entry into World War II." *Diplomatic History* 13 (Spring 1989): 213–30.

————. "Bureaucratic Politics." In *Explaining the History of American Foreign Relations*, edited by Michael J. Hogan and Thomas G. Paterson, 91–102. 2nd ed. New York: Cambridge University Press, 2004.

Cohen, Avner. *Israel and the Bomb*. New York: Columbia University Press, 1998.

Cohen, Avner, and William Burr. "Israel Crosses the Threshold." *Bulletin of the Atomic Scientists* 62 (May/June 2006): 22–30.

Colman, Jonathan. *A "Special Relationship"? Harold Wilson, Lyndon B. Johnson, and Anglo-American Relations "at the Summit," 1964–68*. New York: Palgrave/Manchester University Press, 2004.

Connelly, Matthew. "Taking Off the Cold War Lens: Visions of North-South Conflict during the Algerian War of Independence." *American Historical Review* 105 (June 2000): 739–69.

Costigliola, Frank. *France and the United States: The Cold Alliance since World War II*. New York: Twayne, 1992.

————. "Kennedy, the European Allies, and the Failure to Consult." *Political Science Quarterly* 110, no. 1 (1995): 105–23.

————. "Lyndon B. Johnson, Germany, and 'the End of the Cold War.'" In *Lyndon Johnson Confronts the World*, edited by Warren I. Cohen and Nancy Bernkopf Tucker, 173–210. New York: Cambridge University Press, 1994.

————. "The Nuclear Family: Tropes of Gender and Pathology." *Diplomatic History* 21 (Spring 1997): 163–83.

————. "Pursuit of Atlantic Community." In *Kennedy's Quest for Victory*, edited by Thomas G. Paterson, 24–56. New York: Oxford University Press, 1989.

Cousins, Norman. *The Improbable Triumvirate: John F. Kennedy, Pope John, Nikita Khrushchev.* New York: W. W. Norton, 1972.

Cozic, Charles P., ed. *Nuclear Proliferation: Opposing Viewpoints.* San Diego: Green Haven Press, 1992.

Culver, John C., and John Hyde. *American Dreamer: The Life and Times of Henry A. Wallace.* New York: W. W. Norton, 2000.

Dallek, Robert. *Flawed Giant: Lyndon Johnson and His Times, 1961–1973.* New York: Oxford University Press, 1998.

———. *Lone Star Rising: Lyndon Johnson and His Times.* New York: Oxford University Press, 1991.

———. "Lyndon Johnson, 1963–1969." In *Character Above All: Ten Presidents from FDR to George Bush,* edited by Robert A. Wilson, 105–26. New York: Simon and Schuster, 1995.

———. *An Unfinished Life: John F. Kennedy, 1917–1963.* Boston: Little, Brown, 2003.

Dean, Robert D. *Imperial Brotherhood: Gender and the Making of Cold War Foreign Policy.* Amherst: University of Massachusetts Press, 2001.

Dietl, Ralph. "'Une Déception Amoureuse'? Great Britain, the Continent, and European Nuclear Cooperation, 1953–1957." *Cold War History* 3 (October 2002): 29–66.

Divine, Robert A. *Blowing on the Wind: The Nuclear Test Ban Debate, 1954–1960.* New York: Oxford University Press, 1978.

Dobrynin, Anatoly. *In Confidence: Moscow's Ambassador to America's Six Cold War Presidents (1962–1986).* New York: Times Books, 1995.

Dockrill, Saki. *Eisenhower's New-Look National Security Policy, 1953–1961.* New York: St. Martin's, 1996.

Doenecke, Justus D. *Not to the Swift: The Old Isolationists in the Cold War Era.* Lewisburg, Pa.: Bucknell University Press, 1979.

Dumbrell, John. *President Lyndon Johnson and Soviet Communism.* New York: Palgrave/ Manchester University Press, 2004.

Evangelista, Matthew. "Cooperation Theory and Disarmament Negotiations in the 1950s." *World Politics* 42 (July 1990): 502–28.

———. *Unarmed Forces: The Transnational Movement to End the Cold War.* Ithaca, N.Y.: Cornell University Press, 1999.

Falk, Richard. "Illegitimacy of the Non-Proliferation Regime." In *Predatory Globalization,* 83–91. Malden, Mass.: Blackwell, 1999.

Ferrell, Robert H., ed. *The Diary of James C. Hagerty: Eisenhower in Mid-Course, 1954–55.* Bloomington: Indiana University Press, 1983.

———, ed. *Off the Record: The Private Papers of Harry S. Truman.* New York: Harper & Row, 1980.

Fielding, Jeremy. "Coping with Decline: U.S. Policy toward the British Defense Reviews of 1966." *Diplomatic History* 23 (Fall 1999): 633–56.

Førland, Tor Egil. "'Selling Firearms to the Indians': Eisenhower's Export Control Policy, 1953–1954." *Diplomatic History* 15 (Spring 1991): 221–44.

Franklin, H. Bruce. *War Stars: The Superweapon and the American Imagination.* New York: Oxford University Press, 1988.

Freedman, Lawrence. *Kennedy's Wars: Berlin, Cuba, Laos, and Vietnam.* New York: Oxford University Press, 2000.

Fromkin, David. "Lyndon Johnson and Foreign Policy: What the New Documents Show." *Foreign Affairs* 74 (January/February): 161–70.

Fursenko, Alexandr, and Timothy Naftali. *"One Hell of a Gamble": Khrushchev, Castro, and Kennedy, 1958–1964.* New York: Norton, 1997.

Gaddis, John Lewis. *The United States and the Origins of the Cold War.* New York: Columbia University Press, 1972.

———. *We Now Know: Rethinking Cold War History.* New York: Oxford University Press, 1997.

Gaddis, John Lewis, Philip H. Gordon, Ernest R. May, and Jonathan Rosenberg, eds. *Cold War Statesmen Confront the Bomb: Nuclear Diplomacy since 1945.* New York: Oxford University Press, 1999.

Gardner, Lloyd. "Harry Hopkins with Hand Grenades." In *Behind the Throne*, edited by Thomas J. McCormick and Walter LaFeber, 204–31. Madison: University of Wisconsin Press, 1993.

Garthoff, Raymond L. *A Journey through the Cold War: A Memoir of Containment and Coexistence.* Washington, D.C.: Brookings Institution, 2001.

———. "Some Reflections on the History of the Cold War." *SHAFR Newsletter* 26 (September 1995): 1–16.

Gavin, Francis J. "Blast from the Past: Proliferation Lessons from the 1960s." *International Security* (Winter 2004/2005): 100–135.

———. *Gold, Dollars, and the Power: The Politics of International Monetary Relations, 1958–1971.* Chapel Hill: University of North Carolina Press, 2004.

———. "The Myth of Flexible Response: United States Strategy in Europe during the 1960s." *International History Review* 23 (December 2001): 847–75.

Giauque, Jeffrey Glenn. *Grand Designs and Visions of Unity: The Atlantic Powers and the Reorganization of Europe, 1955–1963.* Chapel Hill: University of North Carolina Press, 2002.

Goodwin, Richard N. *Remembering America: A Voice from the Sixties.* Boston: Little, Brown, 1988.

Gormly, James L. "The Washington Declaration and the 'Poor Relation': Anglo-American Atomic Diplomacy, 1945–46." *Diplomatic History* 8 (Spring 1984): 125–44.

Gowing, Margaret. *Independence and Deterrence: Britain and Atomic Energy, 1945–1952.* 2 vols. New York: Macmillan, 1974.

Greene, Benjamin P. *Eisenhower, Science Advice, and the Nuclear Test Ban Debate, 1945–1963.* Stanford, Calif.: Stanford University Press, 2007.

Groves, Leslie R. *Now It Can Be Told: The Story of the Manhattan Project.* New York: Harper, 1962.

Guthman, Edwin O., and Jeffrey Shulman, eds. *Robert Kennedy: In His Own Words.* New York: Bantam, 1988.

Haftendorn, Helga. *NATO and the Nuclear Revolution: A Crisis of Credibility, 1966–1967*. Oxford: Clarendon Press, 1996.

Halberstam, David. *The Best and the Brightest*. New York: Penguin, 1972.

Hanreider, Wolfram. *Germany, America, Europe: Forty Years of German Foreign Policy*. New Haven: Yale University Press, 1989.

Hawkins, Helen S., G. Allen Greb, and Gertrud Weiss Szilard, eds. *Toward a Livable World: Leo Szilard and the Crusade for Nuclear Arms Control*. Cambridge, Mass.: MIT Press, 1987.

Haynes, John Earl, and Harvey Klehr. *Venona: Decoding Soviet Espionage in America*. New Haven: Yale University Press, 1999.

Henriksen, Margot A. *Dr. Strangelove's America: Society and Culture in the Atomic Age*. Berkeley: University of California Press, 1997.

Herken, Gregg. *Counsels of War*. New York: Knopf, 1985.

———. *The Winning Weapon: The Atomic Bomb in the Cold War, 1945–1950*. New York: Knopf, 1980.

Hersh, Seymour. *The Price of Power: Kissinger in the Nixon White House*. New York: Summit Books, 1983.

———. *The Sampson Option: Israel's Nuclear Arsenal and American Foreign Policy*. New York: Random House, 1991.

Hershberg, James G. *James B. Conant: Harvard to Hiroshima and the Making of the Nuclear Age*. New York: Knopf, 1993.

Hewlett, Richard G., and Oscar Anderson, Jr. *The New World, 1939/1946*. University Park: Pennsylvania State University Press, 1962.

Hewlett, Richard G., and Jack M. Holl. *Atoms for Peace and War, 1953–1961: Eisenhower and the Atomic Energy Commission*. Berkeley: University of California Press, 1989.

Hofstadter, Richard. *Anti-Intellectualism in American Life*. New York: Vintage, 1963.

Hogan, Michael J., ed. *Hiroshima in History and Memory*. New York: Cambridge University Press, 1996.

Holloway, David. *Stalin and the Bomb: The Soviet Union and Atomic Energy, 1939–1956*. New Haven: Yale University Press, 1994.

Hunt, Michael H. "Ideology." In *Explaining the History of American Foreign Relations*, edited by Michael J. Hogan and Thomas G. Paterson, 221–40. 2nd ed. New York: Cambridge University Press, 2004.

———. *Ideology and U.S. Foreign Policy*. New Haven: Yale University Press, 1987.

Isaacson, Walter, and Evan Thomas. *The Wise Men: Six Friends and the World They Made*. New York: Simon and Schuster, 1986.

Jacobs, Robert Alan. "Ground Zero: Nuclear Weapons and Social Transformation." Ph.D. diss., University of Illinois, 2004.

———. "'There Are No Civilians; We Are All at War': Nuclear War Shelter and Survival Narratives during the Early Cold War." *Journal of American Culture* 30 (December 2007): 401–16.

Johnson, Lyndon Baines. *The Vantage Point: Perspectives of the Presidency, 1963–1969*. New York: Holt, Rinehart and Winston, 1971.

Johnson, Walter, ed. *The Papers of Adlai E. Stevenson*. 8 vols. Boston: Little, Brown, 1976.

Johnston, Andrew M. *Hegemony and Culture in the Origins of NATO Nuclear First Use, 1945–1955*. New York: Palgrave, 2005.

Kahn, Herman. *On Thermonuclear War*. Princeton, N.J.: Princeton University Press, 1960.

Katz, Milton S. *Ban the Bomb: A History of SANE, the Committee for a Sane Nuclear Policy, 1957–1985*. Westport, Conn.: Greenwood Press, 1986.

Kelleher, Catherine McArdle. *Germany and the Politics of Nuclear Weapons*. New York: Columbia University Press, 1975.

Kennan, George F. *Memoirs, 1925–1950*. Boston: Little, Brown, 1967.

———. *Russia, the Atom, and the West*. New York: Harper & Row, 1958.

Kennedy, John F. *Profiles in Courage*. New York: Harper, 1956.

Khrushchev, Nikita. *Khrushchev Remembers*. Boston: Little, Brown, 1970.

———. *Khrushchev Remembers: The Last Testament*. Boston: Little, Brown, 1974.

Killian, James R., Jr. *Sputnik, Scientists, and Eisenhower: A Memoir of the First Special Assistant to the President for Science and Technology*. Cambridge, Mass.: MIT Press, 1977.

Kimball, Warren F., ed. *Churchill and Roosevelt: The Complete Correspondence*. 3 vols. Princeton, N.J.: Princeton University Press, 1984.

———. *Forged in War: Roosevelt, Churchill, and the Second World War*. New York: William Morrow, 1997.

Kirby, Alexander B. "Childe Harold's Pilgrimage: A Political Biography of Harold Stassen." Ph.D. diss., George Washington University, 1992.

Kistiakowsky, George B. *A Scientist in the White House: The Private Diary of President Eisenhower's Special Assistant for Science and Technology*. Cambridge, Mass.: Harvard University Press, 1976.

Klein, Bradley S. "How the West Was One: Representational Politics of NATO." *International Studies* 34 (Spring 1990): 311–25.

Kochavi, Noam. *A Conflict Perpetuated: China Policy during the Kennedy Years*. Westport, Conn.: Praeger, 2002.

Kohl, Wilfred L. *French Nuclear Diplomacy*. Princeton, N.J.: Princeton University Press, 1971.

Kuznick, Peter J. "Prophets of Doom or Voices of Sanity? The Evolving Discourse of Annihilation in the First Decade and a Half of the Nuclear Age." *Journal of Genocide Research* 9 (September 2007): 411–41.

Lacouture, Jean. *De Gaulle: The Ruler, 1945–1970*. New York: Norton, 1991.

LaFeber, Walter. "Comments on Professor Herken's Paper." In *James F. Byrnes and the Origins of the Cold War*, edited by Kendrick A. Clements, 99–100. Durham, N.C.: Carolina Academic Press, 1982.

Larson, Deborah Welch. *Anatomy of Mistrust: U.S.-Soviet Relations during the Cold War*. Ithaca, N.Y.: Cornell University Press, 1997.

Leffler, Melvyn P. "National Security." In *Explaining the History of American Foreign*

Relations, edited by Michael J. Hogan and Thomas G. Paterson, 123–36. 2nd ed. New York: Cambridge University Press, 2004.

———. "Negotiating from Strength: Acheson, the Russians, and American Power." In *Dean Acheson and the Making of U.S. Foreign Policy*, edited by Douglas Brinkley, 176–210. New York: St. Martin's, 1993.

Lewidge, Bernard. *De Gaulle*. New York: St. Martin's, 1982.

Lewis, John Wilson, and Xue Litai. *China Builds the Bomb*. Stanford, Calif.: Stanford University Press, 1988.

Lieberman, Joseph I. *The Scorpion and the Tarantula: The Struggle to Control Atomic Weapons, 1945–1949*. Boston: Houghton Mifflin, 1970.

Lifton, Robert Jay. *Superpower Syndrome: America's Apocalyptic Confrontation with the World*. New York: Thunder's Mouth/Nation Books, 2003.

Lilienthal, David. *The Atomic Energy Years, 1945–1960*. Vol. 2 of *The Journals of David Lilienthal*. New York: Harper & Row, 1964.

Linenthal, Edward T., and Tom Engelhardt. *History Wars: The Enola Gay and Other Battles for the American Past*. New York: Metropolitan Books, 1996.

Little, Douglas. "The Making of a Special Relationship: The United States and Israel, 1957–1968." *International Journal of Middle East Studies* 25 (November 1993): 563–85.

Macmillan, Harold. *At the End of the Day, 1961–1963*. New York: Harper, 1973.

Mark, Eduard. "'Today Has Been a Historical One': Harry S Truman's Diary of the Potsdam Conference." *Diplomatic History* 4 (Summer 1980): 317–26.

Mastny, Vojtech. "The 1963 Nuclear Test Ban Treaty: A Missed Opportunity for Détente?" *Journal of Cold War Studies* 10 (Winter 2008): 3–25.

———. "Was 1968 a Strategic Watershed of the Cold War?" *Diplomatic History* 29 (January 2005): 149–77.

McLellan, David. *Dean Acheson: The State Department Years*. New York: Dodd, Mead, 1976.

McLellan, David S., and David C. Acheson. *Among Friends: Personal Letters of Dean Acheson*. New York: Dodd, Mead, 1980.

Messer, Robert L. *The End of an Alliance: James F. Byrnes, Roosevelt, Truman, and the Origins of the Cold War*. Chapel Hill: University of North Carolina Press, 1982.

Middeke, Michael. "Anglo-American Nuclear Weapons Cooperation after the Nassau Conference: The British Policy of Interdependence." *Journal of Cold War Studies* 2 (Spring 2000): 69–96.

Millis, Walter, ed. *The Forrestal Diaries*. New York: Viking, 1951.

Morgan, Roger. "Kennedy and Adenauer." In *John F. Kennedy and Europe*, edited by Douglas Brinkley and Richard T. Griffiths, 16–31. Baton Rouge: Louisiana State University Press, 1999.

Myrdal, Alva. *The Game of Disarmament: How the United States and Russia Run the Arms Race*. New York: Pantheon Books, 1976.

Naftali, Timothy J., Philip Zelikow, and Ernest R. May, eds. *Presidential Recordings — John F. Kennedy: The Great Crises*. 3 vols. New York: Norton, 2001.

Nash, Philip. *The Other Missiles of October: Eisenhower, Kennedy, and the Jupiters, 1957–1963*. Chapel Hill: University of North Carolina Press, 1997.

Neustadt, Richard E. *Report to JFK: The Skybolt Crisis in Perspective*. Ithaca, N.Y.: Cornell University Press, 1999.

Nevins, Allan, ed. *The Burden and the Glory: The Hopes and Purposes of President Kennedy's Second and Third Years in Office as Revealed in His Public Statements and Addresses*. New York: Harper & Row, 1964.

———, ed. *The Strategy of Peace*. New York: Harper & Row, 1960.

Newhouse, John. *De Gaulle and the Anglo-Saxons*. New York: Viking, 1970.

———. *War and Peace in the Nuclear Age*. New York: Knopf, 1989.

Nye, David E. *American Technological Sublime*. Cambridge, Mass.: MIT Press, 1994.

Offner, Arnold A. "'Another Such Victory': President Truman, American Foreign Policy and the Cold War." *Diplomatic History* 23 (Spring 1999): 127–55.

———. *Another Such Victory: President Truman and the Cold War, 1945–1953*. Stanford, Calif.: Stanford University Press, 2002.

———. "Harry S. Truman as Parochial Nationalist." In *The Origins of the Cold War*, edited by Thomas G. Paterson and Robert McMahon, 49–60. 3rd ed. Lexington, Mass.: D. C. Heath, 1991.

Oliver, Kendrick. *Kennedy, Macmillan, and the Nuclear Test Ban Debate, 1961–1963*. New York: St. Martin's, 1998.

Paterson, Thomas G. *On Every Front: The Making and Unmaking of the Cold War*. Rev. ed. New York: Norton, 1992.

———, ed. *Kennedy's Quest for Victory*. New York: Oxford University Press, 1989.

Pells, Richard H. *The Liberal Mind in a Conservative Age: American Intellectuals in the 1940s and 1950s*. 2nd ed. Middletown, Conn.: Wesleyan University Press, 1989.

Perkovich, George. *India's Nuclear Bomb: The Impact on Global Proliferation*. Berkeley: University of California Press, 1999.

Pinkus, Binyamin. "Atomic Power to Israel's Rescue: French-Israeli Nuclear Cooperation, 1949–1957." *Israel Studies* 7 (Spring 2002): 104–38.

Poen, Monte M., ed. *Strictly Personal and Confidential: The Letters Harry Truman Never Mailed*. Boston: Little, Brown, 1982.

Prados, John. "Prague Spring and SALT." In *Foreign Policies of Lyndon Johnson*, edited by H. W. Brands, 19–36. College Station: Texas A&M University Press, 1999.

Priest, Andrew. "'In Common Cause': The NATO Multilateral Force and the Mixed-Manning Demonstration on the USS *Claude V. Ricketts*." *Journal of Military History* 69 (July 2005): 759–90.

Pruessen, Ronald W. "From Good Breakfast to Bad Supper." In *Cold War Respite*, edited by Günter Bischof and Saki Dockrill, 253–70. Baton Rouge: Louisiana University Press, 2000.

Reeves, Richard. *President Kennedy: Profile of Power*. New York: Simon and Schuster, 1993.

Rhodes, Richard. *The Making of the Atomic Bomb*. New York: Simon and Schuster, 1986.

Ribuffo, Leo P. "What Is Still Living in the Ideas and Example of William Appleman Williams? A Comment." *Diplomatic History* 25 (Spring 2001): 309–16.

Richter, James G. *Khrushchev's Double Bind: International Pressures and Domestic Coalition Politics*. Baltimore: Johns Hopkins University Press, 1994.

Risse-Kappen, Thomas. *Cooperation among Democracies: The European Influence on U.S. Foreign Policy*. Princeton, N.J.: Princeton University Press, 1995.

Rose, Kenneth D. *One Nation Underground: The Fallout Shelter in American Culture*. New York: New York University Press, 2001.

Rosenberg, David Alan. "U.S. Nuclear Stockpile, 1945 to 1950." *Bulletin of the Atomic Scientists* 38 (May 1982): 25–30.

Rostow, Walt W. *The Diffusion of Power: An Essay in Recent History*. New York: Macmillan, 1972.

Rotter, Andrew J. "Gender Relations, Foreign Relations: The United States and South Asia, 1947–1964." *Journal of American History* 81 (September 1994): 518–42.

Rusk, Dean (as told to Richard Rusk). *As I Saw It*. Edited by Daniel S. Papp. New York: Norton, 1990.

Sagan, Scott D., and Jeremi Suri. "The Madman Nuclear Alert: Secrecy, Signaling, and Safety in October 1969." *International Security* 27 (Spring 2003): 150–83.

Schlesinger, Arthur M., Jr. *Robert Kennedy and His Times*. New York: Ballantine, 1978.

———. *A Thousand Days: John F. Kennedy in the White House*. Boston: Houghton Mifflin, 1965.

Schoenbaum, Thomas J. *Waging Peace and War: Dean Rusk in the Truman, Kennedy, and Johnson Years*. New York: Simon and Schuster, 1988.

Schrafstetter, Susanna. "The Long Shadow of the Past: History, Memory and the Debates over West Germany's Nuclear Status, 1954–69." *History and Memory* 16 (Spring/Summer 2004): 118–45.

———. "Preventing the 'Smiling Buddha': British-Indian Nuclear Relations and the Commonwealth Nuclear Force, 1964–1968." *Journal of Strategic Studies* 25 (September 2002): 87–108.

Schrafstetter, Susanna, and Stephen Twigge. *Avoiding Armageddon: Europe, the United States, and the Struggle for Nuclear Nonproliferation, 1945–1970*. Westport, Conn.: Praeger, 2004.

Schwartz, Stephen I., ed. *Atomic Audit: The Costs and Consequences of U.S. Nuclear Weapons since 1940*. Washington, D.C.: Brookings Institution Press, 1998.

Schwartz, Thomas Alan. "Lyndon Johnson and Europe: Alliance Politics, Political Economy, and 'Growing Out of the Cold War." In *Foreign Policies of Lyndon Johnson*, edited by H. W. Brands, 37–60. College Station: Texas A&M University Press, 1999.

———. *Lyndon Johnson and Europe: In the Shadow of Vietnam*. Cambridge, Mass.: Harvard University Press, 2003.

———. "Victories and Defeats in the Long Twilight Struggle." In *The Diplomacy of the Crucial Decade*, edited by Diane B. Kunz, 115–48. New York: Columbia University Press, 1994.

Schwarz, Hans-Peter. *Konrad Adenauer: The Statesmen, 1952–1967.* Providence, R.I.: Berghahn Books, 1995.

Schwarz, Jordan A. *The Speculator: Bernard M. Baruch in Washington, 1917–1965.* Chapel Hill: University of North Carolina Press, 1981.

Seaborg, Glenn T. (with Benjamin S. Loeb). *Kennedy, Khrushchev, and the Test Ban.* Los Angeles: University of California Press, 1981.

———. *Stemming the Tide: Arms Control in the Johnson Years.* Lexington, Mass.: Lexington Books, 1987.

Selvage, Douglas. "Junior Allies? Poland, the GDR and Khrushchev's 'Rapallo Policy' (1963–1964)." Unpublished manuscript.

———. "The Warsaw Pact and Nuclear Nonproliferation, 1963–1965." Working Paper No. 32, Cold War International History Project. Washington, D.C.: Woodrow Wilson International Center for Scholars, 2001.

Shapley, Deborah. *Promise and Power: The Life and Times of Robert McNamara.* Boston: Little, Brown, 1993.

Sherry, Michael S. *In the Shadow of War: The United States since the 1930s.* New Haven: Yale University Press, 1995.

———. *The Rise of American Air Power: The Creation of Armageddon.* New Haven: Yale University Press, 1987.

Sherwin, Martin J. *A World Destroyed: The Atomic Bomb and the Grand Alliance.* New York: Knopf, 1975.

Slotkin, Richard. *Gunfighter Nation: The Myth of the Frontier in Twentieth Century America.* New York: Atheneum, 1992.

Smith, Gerard C. *Disarming Diplomat: The Memoirs of Gerard C. Smith, Arms Control Negotiator.* Lanham, Md.: Madison Books, 1996.

Smith, Roger Kelly. "The Origins of the Regime: Nonproliferation, National Interest, and American Decision-Making, 1943–1976." Ph.D. diss., Georgetown University, 1990.

Spector, Leonard S. (with Jaqueline R. Smith). *Nuclear Ambitions: The Spread of Nuclear Weapons, 1989–1990.* Boulder, Colo.: Westview, 1990.

Stassen, Harold, and Marshall Houts. *Eisenhower: Turning the World toward Peace.* St. Paul, Minn.: Merrill-Magnus, 1990.

Stoler, Mark A. *Allies and Adversaries: The Joint Chiefs of Staff, the Grand Alliance, and U.S. Strategy in World War II.* Chapel Hill: University of North Carolina Press, 2000.

Suri, Jeremi. *Power and Protest: Global Revolution and the Rise of Détente.* Cambridge, Mass.: Harvard University Press, 2003.

Trachtenberg, Marc. *A Constructed Peace: The Making of the European Settlement, 1945–1963.* Princeton, N.J.: Princeton University Press, 1999.

Truman, Harry S. *Year of Decisions.* Vol. 1 of *Memoirs.* Garden City, N.Y.: Doubleday, 1955.

Ulam, Adam. *The Rivals: America and Russia since World War II.* New York: Viking, 1971.

Ullman, Richard H. "The Covert French Connection." *Foreign Policy* 75 (Summer 1989): 3–33.

Vandenberg, Arthur H., Jr., ed. *The Private Papers of Senator Vandenberg*. Boston: Houghton Mifflin, 1952.

Voss, Earl H. *Nuclear Ambush: The Test Ban Trap*. Chicago: Regnery, 1963.

Wadsworth, James. *The Price of Peace*. New York: Praeger, 1962.

Wandycz, Piotr. "Adam Rapacki and the Search for European Security." In *The Diplomats, 1939–1979*, edited by Gordon A. Craig and Francis L. Loewenheim, 289–317. Princeton, N.J.: Princeton University Press, 1994.

Weart, Spencer R. *Nuclear Fear: A History of Images*. Cambridge, Mass.: Harvard University Press, 1988.

Weiner, Sharon K. "Preventing Nuclear Entrepreneurship in Russia's Nuclear Cities." *International Security* 27 (Fall 2002): 126–58.

Weinstein, Allen, and Alexander Vassiliev. *The Haunted Wood: Soviet Espionage in America — The Stalin Era*. New York: Random House, 1999.

Wenger, Andreas. "Crisis and Opportunity: NATO's Transformation and the Multilateralization of Détente, 1966–1968." *Journal of Cold War Studies* (Winter 2004): 22–74.

———. *Living with Peril: Eisenhower, Kennedy, and Nuclear Weapons*. Lanham, Md.: Rowman & Littlefield, 1997.

Wenger, Andreas, and Jeremi Suri. "At the Crossroads of Diplomatic and Social History: The Nuclear Revolution, Dissent, and Détente." *Cold War History* 1 (April 2001): 1–42.

White, Graham, and John Maze. *Henry A. Wallace: His Search for a New World Order*. Chapel Hill: University of North Carolina Press, 1995.

Williams, William Appleman. *The Tragedy of American Diplomacy*. New York: World Publishing, 1959.

Williamson, Samuel R., Jr., and Steven L. Rearden. *The Origins of U.S. Nuclear Strategy, 1945–1953*. New York: St. Martin's, 1993.

Winand, Pascaline. *Eisenhower, Kennedy, and the United States of Europe*. New York: St. Martin's, 1993.

Winkler, Allan M. *Life under a Cloud: American Anxiety about the Atom*. New York: Oxford University Press, 1993.

Wittner, Lawrence S. *One World or None: A History of the World Nuclear Disarmament Movement through 1953*. Stanford, Calif.: Stanford University Press, 1993.

———. *Rebels against War: The American Peace Movement, 1933–1983*. 2nd ed. Philadelphia: Temple University Press, 1984.

———. *Resisting the Bomb: A History of the World Nuclear Disarmament Movement, 1954–1970*. Stanford, Calif.: Stanford University Press, 1997.

Yi, Long. "The American Response to the Development of Chinese Nuclear Weapons: A Study in the Evolution of Perception and Policy." Ph.D. diss., University of Hawaii, 1994.

Young, John W. "Killing the MLF? The Wilson Government and Nuclear Sharing in Europe, 1964–66." *Diplomacy & Statecraft* 14 (June 2003): 295–324.

Zubok, Vladislav. "Khrushchev and the Berlin Crisis (1958–1962)." Working Paper No. 6, Cold War International History Project. Washington, D.C.: Woodrow Wilson International Center for Scholars, 1993.

———. "Stalin and the Nuclear Age." In *Cold War Statesmen Confront the Bomb: Nuclear Diplomacy since 1945*, edited by John Lewis Gaddis, Philip H. Gordon, Ernest R. May, and Jonathan Rosenberg, 39–61. New York: Oxford University Press, 1999.

———. "Unwrapping the Enigma." In *The Diplomacy of the Crucial Decade*, edited by Diane B. Kunz, 149–82. New York: Columbia University Press, 1994.

Index

rise of, in Truman administration, 50–51; of Strauss, 86, 121; and test ban proposals, 77–78, 114

Anti-intellectualism, 112–13, 122

Antinuclear movement: anticommunist attacks on, 5, 121, 124; on atmospheric tests, 190; in Britain, 122–23, 169, 170; CIA and FBI investigations of, 121; decline of, 229, 231; Eisenhower's relationship with, 121–23; films in, 6, 94, 140, 229–31; health effects of testing and, 123, 190; Japanese bombings and, 3, 5; Kennedy's relationship with, 169; liberal versus radical, 122, 190; literature in, 140, 190, 229–30; on MLF, 225; peak of, 229; Reagan and, 231, 291. *See also* Peace groups

Apocalypse, nuclear, 5–6

Arab-Israeli conflict, 271, 287

Argentina, 8, 278, 291

Arms control: in Atoms for Peace program, 89; Bohr's model for, through nuclear sharing, 17–18; Kennan on need for, 71, 73–74; in Quebec Agreement, 16–17; after Soviet atomic test, 71; Stimson on need for, 23. *See also* International control; Nonproliferation

Arms Control and Disarmament Agency (ACDA), U.S.: on Chinese nuclear program, 234; on comprehensive test ban, 192–93; containment measures recommended by, 227–28; establishment of, 162; Foster at, 191; on inspections quota, 200; and Johnson's policy reassessment, 239; Kennedy's proposal for, 161–62; on MLF, 221, 224, 264

Arms race: benefits of, 104; economic cost of, as reason for disarmament, 84; proposal for preventing postwar, 17–18; Roosevelt's policies contributing to, 22; Truman on start of, 37

Aron, Raymond, 127, 177–78

Asia: in Afro-Asian nuclear proliferation, 236, 261; racial thinking about people of, 34, 89, 126–27, 153; start of arms race in, 141–42. *See also specific countries*

Atlantic Nuclear Force (ANF): British-German negotiations on, 254–55, 258–60; British proposal of, 247–48; demise of, 262–64; and Johnson's policy reassessment, 240, 243; Soviet opposition to, 217

Atmospheric tests: antinuclear movement on, 190; Eisenhower's proposal for ban on, 135,

160; Geneva Conference of Experts on, 132, 133, 136; health effects of, 120; public opinion on, 190; Soviet resumption of, 199; U.S. resumption of, under Kennedy, 160, 168–71, 189

Atomic bank/pool: Eisenhower's proposal for, 87–90

Atomic bomb: ban of, in Gromyko Plan, 61; political implications of, 23–24; as private property, 33–34; scientists argue against use of, 26–27; Truman's ignorance about science of, 23, 30–31. *See also* Japanese atomic bombings

Atomic bomb development: in Baruch Plan, 62; in Britain, 14–15; international scientists involved in, in U.S., 12–14, 30–31. *See also* Manhattan Project

Atomic Development Authority, 49, 55, 56, 57, 89

Atomic diplomacy, 32–33, 37

Atomic energy. *See* Nuclear energy policy, U.S.

Atomic Energy Act of 1946: Atoms for Peace program and, 90, 96; and British-American nuclear alliance, 63–64, 68, 71, 98; calls for relaxation of, 90, 96, 126; 1954 amendments to, 98, 99–100; 1957 amendments to, 126, 128–29; on nuclear sharing, 63–64, 98, 126; passage of, 63–64; and privatization of energy, 90; provisions of, 63–64

Atomic Energy Commission, UN. *See* United Nations Atomic Energy Commission

Atomic Energy Commission, U.S. (AEC): and antinuclear movement, 123; on British-American alliance, 69; establishment of, 63; General Advisory Committee of, 71, 72, 90–91; McCone as chair of, 133, 135; 1954 thermonuclear test by, 92–94; in Operation Candor, 84, 85, 87; on radioactive isotope export, 86; Seaborg as chair of, 152; Strauss's departure from, 129; Strauss's influence on, 85–86; on test bans, 97, 108, 119; on thermonuclear weapons, 71, 72

Atomic Energy for Military Purposes (Smyth), 30–31, 35

Atomic monopoly. *See* Monopoly, atomic

Atomic power. *See* Nuclear energy policy, U.S.

Atoms for Peace program: Congress on, 99–100; development of, 87–90; Eisenhower's speech announcing, 90; international participation in, 100–101; international reactions to, 90–92; after 1954 thermonuclear test, 95–96; proliferation potential in, 90–91, 96, 99, 111; renewed push for, 99–100; Soviet response to, 92, 95–96, 99

Atoms for Police, 109

Attlee, Clement, 30, 38–39

"Axis of evil," 294–95

Balch, Emily, 29

Baldwin, Hanson, 60

Ball, George: ANF and, 248; and Johnson's policy reassessment, 240, 241, 245, 246; on MLF, 205, 224, 225–26, 245, 255–56, 262, 267; on peaceful nuclear explosions, 254; on West German nuclear ambitions, 156

Bard, Ralph, 24

Barnard, Chester, 49

Baruch, Bernard M., 54–68; announcement of Baruch Plan by, 59–60; chosen as U.S. delegate to UNAEC, 54–55; development of Baruch Plan by, 54–59; health problems of, 54; Lubell's friendship with, 84; Senate confirmation of, 54, 55; staff of, 55; in UNAEC negotiations, 63–67; and vote on Baruch Plan, 65, 66–67; on Wallace's criticism of U.S. policy, 65–66

Baruch Plan, 54–68; Acheson-Lilienthal report and, 54–58; approval by Truman, 58–59; conflicts of interest in, 57; development of, 54–59; at Geneva Summit, 105; media coverage of, 60; nuclear energy in, 90; public announcement of, 59–63; Soviet reaction to, 60–63; as test of Soviet good faith, 58, 64; thermonuclear weapons and, 74–76; UNAEC members' reaction to, 60; UNAEC talks on, 63–68, 75; UNAEC vote on, 65, 66–67; U.S. hopes for Soviet rejection of, 58, 60, 64

Bator, Francis, 264, 267

Bay of Pigs, 157, 159

Beam, Jacob, 127

Belarus, 292

Ben-Gurion, David, 154

Berlin crisis (1961), 131–32, 160–64

Berlin test ban talks: failure of, 173–74; German nuclear program in, 194; indirect proliferation in, 191, 266; MLF in, 191, 194; and NPT drafts, 266, 268; start of, 165–66

Berlin Wall, 162–63

Bermuda Conference: 1953, 98; 1957, 116–18, 125

Bevin, Ernest, 40, 42–43

Bhabha, Homi, 142

Bikini Atoll, 64

Bilateral negotiations: congressional approval required for agreements in, 100; after Cuban Missile Crisis, 181, 196–200; under Eisenhower, 89, 92, 95, 100–101; under Kennedy, 161, 162, 181, 196–200. See also specific agreements and meetings

Bin Laden, Osama, 295

Birrenbach, Kurt, 257–58

Black boxes, 194, 199

Blackmail, nuclear, 273

Blunt, Anthony, 20

Bohlen, Charles, 92, 187

Bohr, Niels, 17–18

Bolshakov, Georgi, 159–60, 163

Bowie, Robert, 143, 175, 262

Bowles, Chester, 147

Bradlee, Ben, 171–72

Brain drain, 13, 292

Brandt, Willy, 269, 272

Bravo bomb test, 92–94

Brazil, 277, 278, 290, 291

Bretton Woods system, 15

Brezhnev, Leonid, 287

Bricker, John W., 100

Britain: antinuclear movement in, 122–23, 169, 170; on ANF, 247–48, 254–55, 258–59; on Baruch Plan, 67; at Bermuda Conference (1957), 116–17; on comprehensive versus limited test ban, 190–91, 193, 208; in ENDC, 188, 189; in EEC, 183, 184–85, 202–3; in international control, 17; in Libya's disarmament, 296; on LTBT, 193, 210, 213, 298; on McNamara's counterforce speech, 184; on MLF, 143, 167, 205, 218, 224, 228–29, 246–47; at Moscow Conference, 40–43; on nontransfer draft agreement, 200; NPT draft by (1965), 252–53; public opinion on Japanese bombings, 32; resistance to U.S. leadership in, 6; sex-for-secrets spy scandal in, 206; Soviet alliance in World War II with, 15–16; Soviet espionage in, 20; 1956 Soviet state visit to, 109; in Stimson's international control plan, 33; as superpower,

15; on test bans, 94–95, 96, 108, 112, 118, 134; on test resumption, 169–70; in Truman's international control proposal, 36–39; at UN Disarmament Subcommittee meetings, 101, 108; U.S. alliance in World War II with, 14–19; U.S.-French-British nonproliferation declaration suggested by, 232. *See also* British nuclear program

British-American nuclear alliance: versus EEC, 183; after Japanese bombings, 30; under Kennedy, 178; in Manhattan Project, 14–19, 23; possibility of termination of, 39; Skybolt crisis in, 201–3; Strauss's opposition to, 69, 86; after Suez crisis, 113, 116; Truman's treatment of, 48, 69–70; U.S. Congress on, 63–64, 68–71, 98; after World War II, 22; in World War II, 14–19, 21

British nuclear program: first atomic test of (1952), x, 3, 21–22, 71; first thermonuclear test of (1957), 120; French alliance with, 183–85, 201–2, 214; independence in, 6; and Nassau agreement, 202–3; 1950s acceleration of, 98; NSC recommendation on, 69; Skybolt crisis and, 201–2; after Suez crisis, 116; U.S. Congress and, 3, 69; U.S. Polaris missiles in, 202–3; U.S. support for, x, 3, 69, 116; before World War II, 13

British-U.S. alliance. *See* British-American nuclear alliance

Bruce, David K. E., 229, 248

Bulganin, Nikolai, 109, 113

Bulletin of the Atomic Scientists, 67, 94, 138, 218, 280

Bundy, McGeorge: on ANF, 248; on Chinese proliferation, 198, 234, 235; in Cuban Missile Crisis, 195; on French nuclear program, 183–84; on Johnson's foreign policy team, 219, 220; and Johnson's policy reassessment, 238, 239, 250, 252; Johnson's relationship with, 220; on Kennedy's foreign policy team, 147, 149–50; on Kennedy's policy-making process, 157; on MLF, 205–6, 222, 225–26, 228, 245–48, 254, 256–57, 259, 263; on problems with war plans, 175; on remote detection techniques, 192; on Rusk, 149

Burgess, Guy, 20, 70

Bush, George W., 293–97

Bush, Vannevar: in Acheson-Lilienthal group, 48, 50, 52; on Baruch as U.S. delegate to UNAEC, 54; and Baruch Plan, 56; on British-American alliance, 15, 16, 18; on Interim Committee, 24, 26; on international control, 18, 19; international control plan by, 38–39; and international control plan by Stimson, 34–35; on Maud Committee, 14; and nuclear secrecy, 18; on Panel of Consultants on Disarmament, 76, 77; on Smyth report, 83–84; on Soviet nuclear capability, 35; on test bans, 77

Byrnes, James F.: in Acheson-Lilienthal group, 48, 52; on Acheson-Lilienthal report publication, 55; and Baruch as U.S. delegate to UNAEC, 54, 59; on Baruch Plan, 58–59, 67; decline of influence of, 44; foreign relations experience of, 24; Groves's influence on, 24–26; on Interim Committee, 24–25, 26; international control opposed by, 32, 34, 35, 37–38; international control plan of, 40–44, 48; on Kennan's "Long Telegram," 50; at Moscow Conference, 40–44; nationalism of, 24, 25; at Paris Peace Conference, 63; at Potsdam Conference, 27; as secretary of state, 24; strategy to prove Soviet intransigence, 45, 47; Truman briefed about Manhattan Project by, 23, 304 (n. 15); Truman's communication problems with, 41, 44; on uranium deposits, 26; uranium-mining investments of, 57; on Wallace's criticism of U.S. policy, 66; at Washington Conference, 38–39

Cadogan, Alexander, 54–55

Cairncross, John, 20

Cambridge Five spy ring, 20

Campaign for Nuclear Disarmament, 122–23

Canada: on Baruch Plan, 67; in ENDC, 188; and Indian nuclear program, 290; in international control, 17; Kennedy's Ottawa speech, 158, 167; in Manhattan Project, 16, 34; in Moscow Conference, 40–41; Soviet espionage in, 34, 51; on test bans, 118; in Truman's international control proposal, 36–39

Candor, Operation, 84, 85, 87–90

Canticle for Leibowitz (Miller), 140

Carnegie Endowment for International Peace, 61

Carter, Jimmy, 288–91

Castro, Fidel, 198

Catch-22 (Heller), 190

Ceaușescu, Nicolae, 272–73

Central Intelligence Agency (CIA): antinuclear groups investigated by, 121; on Cold
War and nonproliferation, 8; in Cuban Missile Crisis, 195; on Kosygin, 271; on nonproliferation accord, 194–95; on NPT, 282, 286;
in Operation Candor, 84; on test bans, 97

"Chance for Peace" speech (Eisenhower),
84–85

Cheney, Dick, 295

Chicago Laboratory of Manhattan Project, 25,
26, 30, 32

Chicago Tribune, 29, 56

Childs, Marquis, 58

China: on Afro-Asian proliferation, 236, 261;
in arms control agreements, 110, 135; Cuban
Missile Crisis and, 198; Indian rivalry with,
141–42, 163; in Korean War, 85; as leader of
African-Asian bloc, 7; in nonproliferation
negotiations, 261; NPT rejected by, 285;
rethinking of U.S. policy toward, 234–35; as
superpower, 15; UN membership of, 234–
35; uranium in, 107; U.S. nuclear threats to,
85, 106. *See also* Sino-Soviet schism

Chinese nuclear program: decision to develop,
106–7; first test of (1964), 7, 217, 235–36;
Gilpatric Committee on, 242; Johnson's
approach to, 234–37; Kennedy's approach
to, 146, 153, 163, 198, 207; in LTBT, 208–14;
progress toward weaponization in, 141, 163,
234; Reagan's approach to, 291; second test
of (1965), 249; Sino-Soviet schism and, 137,
141, 181; Soviet aid to, x, 7, 99, 106–7; Soviet
concerns about, 137, 231–32; U.S. espionage
on, 200, 234; U.S. failure to prevent, 3;
U.S. military action considered against, x,
198, 207, 211, 214, 234, 237, 241; U.S. panels
studying implications of, 163, 238; U.S.-
Soviet joint action considered against, 207,
211, 235, 237, 271, 287

Christmas Island, 170

Churchill, Winston: on Atoms for Peace program, 90; on Baruch Plan, 60; on British-
American alliance, 14–18, 21, 98; on first successful test, 28; on French nuclear program,
18–19; on iron curtain, 50–51; at Potsdam
Conference, 27, 28; on test bans, 95

Civilian deaths: in Japanese bombings, 3; in
nuclear war, 169, 176

Clark, Grenville, 32, 60, 150, 162

Clark, Tom, 34–35

Claude V. Ricketts (destroyer), 223

Clausewitz, Carl von, 82

Clayton, William L., 24

Clean bombs, 122, 123, 124

Cleveland, Harlan, 255

Clifford, Clark, 63, 276

Clifford-Elsey report, 63

Clinton, Bill, 1, 293–95, 297

Cohen, Benjamin V., 76

Cold War: Atoms for Peace program as
weapon in, 89; and decolonization, 8; end
of, 9, 291, 292; impossibility of international
control during, 76; nonproliferation after, 9,
292–97; NSC-68 on, 74; under Reagan, 291;
Soviet leadership transition during, 84–85;
start of, 79

Colonies. *See* Decolonization

Combined Development Trust, 16–17, 22, 39

Combined Policy Committee, 16, 39

Committee for a Sane Nuclear Policy
(SANE): anticommunist attacks on, 121; on
health effects of testing, 190; liberals in, 122;
on MLF, 225; on test bans, 129, 134

Committee for Non-Violent Action, 122

Committee on the Present Danger, 291

Common Market. *See* European Economic
Community

Communists. *See* Anticommunism

Comprehensive disarmament, 75, 95, 101, 108,
112, 118, 151

Comprehensive test ban agreement: British
support for, 190–91, 193, 208; draft treaty
presented to ENDC on, 193; Eisenhower
administration consideration of, 119, 121,
133–36; Gilpatric Committee on, 241–44;
Johnson administration consideration of,
253–54; Johnson's stalling of, 281; Kennedy
administration debate over, x, xi, 191–93;
Reagan's opposition to, 291

Comprehensive Test Ban Treaty (1996): under
Bush (George W.), 296–97; Clinton signing, 293; progress toward ratification of,
293; UN approval of, 293

Compton, Karl, 24, 65

Conant, James: in Acheson-Lilienthal group,

48, 50, 52–53; and Baruch Plan, 56; on British-American alliance, 15, 16, 18; on Interim Committee, 24, 26; on international control, 18, 19; on Japanese bombings, 64–65; at Moscow Conference, 42, 43; on Rapacki Plan, 127; on Smyth's report, 30, 31; on thermonuclear weapons, 72

Conference of Experts (1958). *See* Geneva Conference of Experts

Conference of Non-Aligned Countries, Second (1964), 236

Conference of Non-Nuclear-Weapon States (1968), 274, 277, 279, 281

Congress, U.S.: Arms Control and Disarmament Agency created by, 161–62; on atomic monopoly, 64, 70–71; on Atoms for Peace program, 99–100; and Baruch Plan, 63–64; on British-American alliance, 63–64, 68–71, 98; on Comprehensive Test Ban Treaty, 293; and European proliferation, 155; on IAEA, 100; on Indian nuclear program, 289; on international control, 63–64; Johnson's career in, 219, 220–21; on LTBT, 207, 210, 214; on MLF, 205, 225, 229, 264, 267–68; on need for NPT, 261–62, 264; 1946 elections in, 64; NPT ratification by, 280, 282; nuclear nationalism in, 32, 36, 40; on nuclear sharing, 32, 36, 128; on Quebec Agreement, 69; and selective proliferation, 3; on test resumption, 153; on unilateral nonproliferation, 68; on U.S. forces in Europe, 267; on Vietnam War, 261, 264; on Washington Declaration, 40

Congressional elections, 64

Connally, Thomas, 36, 40, 41–42

Cordier, Andrew, 196

Core values, 2

Corporate control, 143

Council for a Livable World, 225

Council of Foreign Ministers, 32, 34, 51, 63

Counterforce strategy, 175–77, 179, 182, 183–84

Counter-proliferation policy, 293

Cousins, Norman, 29, 121, 198, 199

Couve de Murville, Maurice, 185

Cuba: in LTBT, 213

Cuban Missile Crisis (1962), 195–200; bilateral negotiations after, 181, 196–200; resolution of, 196–97; start of, 195–96

Culture, U.S.: anti-intellectualism in, 112–13,

122; conformity in, 83; and nuclear policy, 300

Custodianship, 30

Cutler, Robert, 99

Czechoslovakia: in nuclear-free zone of Rapacki Plan, 127–28; Soviet invasion of, 280, 281, 282; uranium in, 26, 107

Day, Dorothy, 29

Day After, The (film), 6

Dealey, E. M., 170–71

Dean, Arthur: as chief U.S. negotiator, 152; in Geneva test ban talks, 152, 163, 168; on Gilpatric Committee, 238, 241, 242–43; on inspections, 191, 193, 199–200; on MLF, 241; on remote detection, 191, 192; resignation of, 200

Dean, Gordon, 72

Decolonization: and Cold War, 8; and nuclear apartheid in former colonies, ix, x; in U.S. nonproliferation policy, 2, 7

Defense Department: in Atoms for Peace program, 89, 91; on comprehensive test ban, 192–93; in Operation Candor, 84, 85, 87; on test bans, 96, 97

Defense spending: in Eisenhower's national security policy, 82

Detection: in Geneva Conference of Experts report, 132, 133; on-site stations for, 132, 133; remote, 191, 192, 193, 199. *See also* Inspections

Détente: Kennedy's 1963 speech on, 209; Khrushchev's strategy of, 139, 146, 151, 159, 165, 180, 232; Kosygin on, 265–66; between Soviet Union and West Germany, 232

Deterrence: in Eisenhower's national security policy, 82; joint grand, 155, 156

Detzer, Dorothy, 29

Developing nations: nationalism in, 235–36; U.S. beliefs about, 7

Dewey, John, 32

Dewey, Thomas, 113

Dickey, John, 76

Dimona reactor, 154, 233, 249

Diplomacy: atomic, 32–33, 37; gunboat, 289

Direct Action Committee against Nuclear War, 122–23

Disarmament: in Atoms for Peace program, 88, 89, 91, 92; in Baruch Plan, 57, 59, 61,

62, 66; in Clifford-Elsey report, 63; economic cost of arms race as reason for, 84;
in Eisenhower's national security policy,
82; lack of coherent Eisenhower policy on,
101; Lubell's proposal for, 84; Molotov's
proposal for, 66, 67; NSC hostility toward,
105; Panel of Consultants report on, 76–78,
83–85; peaceful uses linked with, 92, 95–96,
99; proposed treaty on comprehensive, 75,
95, 101, 108, 112, 118, 151; in Rapacki Plan,
127–28; Stassen as presidential assistant
for, 101–2; Stassen's plans for, 105–6, 108–11,
117–24; UN negotiations on, 75, 83. See also
specific agreements and talks

Disarmament Subcommittee, UN. See United
Nations Disarmament Subcommittee

Dobrynin, Anatoly: on Chinese proliferation,
235, 237; in Cuban Missile Crisis, 196; on
MLF, 206, 227, 257; on Soviet interest in
nonproliferation, 191; and Soviet invasion
of Czechoslovakia, 280

Dodd, Thomas, 153, 161, 207

Doomsday Clock, 67, 68, 94, 138, 218, 280

Douglas-Home, Sir Alec, 224

Dr. Strangelove (film), 230–31

Dulles, Allen W., 76, 147, 238

Dulles, John Foster: on acceptability of
nuclear weapons, 1; on Atoms for Peace
program, 95–96, 101; on benefits of arms
race, 104; in Berlin crisis, 131; "Chance for
Peace" speech contradicted by, 85; at Four
Power Conference, 95; on French nuclear
program, 130; at Geneva Conference, 95–
96; on IAEA, 99; on Japanese bombings,
29; on 1954 thermonuclear test, 93, 94; on
nuclear secrecy, 85; on Operation Candor,
85; on Panel of Consultants on Disarmament, 83–84; resignation of, 135; and Soviet
peaceful intentions, 84, 85; Stassen in conflict with, 101–2, 105; on Stassen's disarmament plans, 118–21; on test bans, 95–97, 102,
103, 108, 110–11, 129; at UN Disarmament
Subcommittee meetings, 123

Dylan, Bob, 190

Eastern Europe: iron curtain around, 50–51;
Soviet nuclear aid to, 99; travel bans in, 38.
See also specific countries

East Germany: alternative to MLF proposed

by, 227; in LTBT, 215; in nuclear-free zone
of Rapacki Plan, 127–28; Soviet peace treaty
with, 131, 160

Eastman Kodak Company, 105

Eberstadt, Ferdinand, 55

Economist, 255

Eden, Anthony, 96, 108

Egypt, 207, 233–34, 292

Eighteen-Nation Disarmament Committee
(ENDC) (1962–68): containment measures presented to, 227–28; after Cuban
Missile Crisis, 199–200; draft test ban
treaties presented to, 193, 213; establishment
of, 172–73; Johnson's changes to U.S. position in, 227–28; McCloy-Zorin principles
in, 172; members of, 172; MLF and, 173,
228; NPT drafts presented to, 253, 269, 270,
271–72, 276; pressure for NPT deal in, 262;
pretense of, 7; remote detection and, 191,
199; U.S.-European tensions in, 188; U.S.
test resumption and, 170

Einstein, Albert, 12, 13, 30, 35, 300

Eisenhower, Dwight D., 81–144; anti-
intellectualism of, 122; and antinuclear
movement, 121–23; Atoms for Peace program of, 87–92; and Baruch Plan, 57; at Bermuda Conference (1957), 117; "Chance for
Peace" speech by, 84–85; and comprehensive test ban, 119, 121, 133–36; on Conference
of Experts (1958), 129; at Geneva Summit,
105–6; on IRBM sharing, 132; Khrushchev's
1959 visit to U.S. and, 137; leadership style
of, 82–83; military career of, 82; MLF
proposal of, 115–16, 142–44, 154; on MLF
under Johnson, 225; national security
approach of, 82; 1954 thermonuclear test
under, 92–94; in 1956 presidential election,
110–14; 1960 presidential election and, 141;
Nixon's policies influenced by, 286–87;
nonproliferation policy of, x–xi; nuclear
energy under, 87–92, 96, 99, 107; on nuclear
sharing, 138; Operation Candor under, 84,
85, 87–90; on Panel of Consultants report,
83–85; and Paris Summit, 137–39; resistance
to nonproliferation in administration of, 81,
97; scholarly interpretations of, 82–83; Skybolt under, 201; technological utopianism
of, 90; test ban commitment of, 129, 133–35;
test bans considered by, 95, 96, 111, 113–14,

121, 123–24; test resumption recommended to Kennedy by, 148, 161; on threat of proliferation, 92, 143–44; threshold proposal of, 139–41; on U-2 spy plane incident, 139; on war with Soviet Union, 82

Elsey, George M., 31, 63

Elugelab, 78

Emergency Committee of Atomic Scientists, 60

Energy, renewable, 300. *See also* Nuclear energy policy, U.S.

Engineers: versus scientists, 25

Enterprise, USS, 288–89

Environmental damage, 299–300

Erhard, Ludwig: on ANF, 255, 258–59; collapse of government of, 268, 269; on MLF, 229, 245, 248, 258–60, 266–67; 1965 visit to U.S., 258, 259; 1966 visit to U.S., 266–68

Eshkol, Levi, 233

Espionage, Soviet: accusations of, and Baruch Plan, 58; and British-American alliance, 70; in Canada, 34, 51; at Los Alamos, 20; in Manhattan Project, 19–21, 34; recruitment for, 304 (n. 12); Roosevelt's reaction to, 19–21

Espionage, U.S.: in Chinese nuclear program, 200, 234; in Cuban Missile Crisis, 195; in German nuclear program, 21; and U-2 spy plane incident, 115, 138–39, 148

EURATOM, 107, 270–71, 274–75

Eurocentrism, 126–27

Europe: atomic energy organization of, 107; Kennedy's approach to proliferation in, 146, 154–58; nuclear-free zone of Rapacki Plan in, 127–28; nuclear sharing with, 124–28; resistance to U.S. hegemony, 6, 197; U.S. weapons stockpile in, 98, 102. *See also* NATO; *specific countries*

European Economic Community (EEC): British membership in, 183, 184–85, 202–3

Exceptionalism, American, 2, 4, 291

Executive branch, U.S.: concentration of power in, 4; Congress in conflict with, 3; importance of action by, 299

Export of radioactive isotopes, 86–87

Fail-Safe (film), 229–30

Fallout-free weapons, 122, 123, 124

Fallout shelters, 94, 169

Fanaticism, technological, 303 (n. 8). *See also* Technological utopianism

Farmer, Fyke, 37

Federal Bureau of Investigation (FBI), 35, 121

Federation of Atomic Scientists, 67, 68

Fellowship of Reconciliation, 29, 60

Fermi, Enrico, 12, 13, 72

Films, 6, 94, 140, 229–31

Finletter, Thomas: on MLF, 167, 183–84, 224, 225–26; 1962 speech by, 183–84, 185

Fisher, Adrian: on MLF, 239, 265, 266; on need for NPT, 262, 264

Fissile Material Cutoff Treaty, 297

Fission: discovery of, 12; international research on, 12–13; promise of, 4

Fissionable material cutoff, 138

Flerov, Georgii, 12

Flexible response strategy, 154–56, 167

Fomin, Alexander, 151

Force de frappe: after end of de Gaulle's presidency, 175, 186; and German nuclear program, 156, 167–68; operational readiness achieved by, 263; public opinion on, 175; U.S. monitoring of, 152; U.S. position on, 178, 179, 185

Ford, Gerald, 286–90

Foreign Affairs (journal), 252

Forrestal, James V.: on bomb as private property, 33–34; on Byrnes's international control plan, 41; international control opposed by, 33–36, 37–38; on Kennan's "Long Telegram," 50; Strauss's work with, 86

Foster, William C.: at Arms Control and Disarmament Agency, 191; on comprehensive versus limited test ban, 191–92, 193; on MLF, 225–26, 227, 259; in MLF negotiations, 228, 252; on need for NPT, 252, 254; NPT draft presented to ENDC by, 253; in NPT negotiations, 265, 275; on NPT revised draft, 269

Four Power Conference, 95

Fourth-country problem, 109, 110, 111, 115, 118, 119

France: antinuclear movement in, 169; in ANF, 247–48, 255; on Baruch Plan, 67; at Bermuda Conference (1953), 98; on British membership in EEC, 183, 202–3; in ENDC,

Goldberg, Arthur, 277

Goldwater, Barry, 221

Gomułka, Władysław, 218, 227

Gorbachev, Mikhail, 291

Gordon Walker, Patrick, 255

Gore, Albert, Sr., 153

Grand Coalition, 269

Grand Design, 203, 211

Great Britain. *See* Britain

Greece, 132, 223, 224

Greenglass, David, 304 (n. 12)

Grewe, Wilhelm, 245

Gromyko, Andrei: on Baruch Plan, 61, 62, 68; in Berlin talks with Rusk, 165–66, 173–74, 191, 194, 266, 268; and Geneva test ban talks, 152; Gromyko Plan of, 61; Johnson's pressuring of, 233; on MLF, 218; and 1966 UN nonproliferation resolution, 266; on nuclear freeze proposals, 227; at Vienna summit, 160

Gromyko Plan, 61

Groupthink, 83

Groves, Leslie: in Acheson-Lilienthal group, 48, 49–50, 52–53; and Baruch Plan, 56, 57, 60; on British-American alliance, 16, 39; Byrnes influenced by, 24–26; on Byrnes's international control plan, 41; on Combined Development Trust, 22; on Interim Committee, 24; as media source on Soviet espionage, 51; nuclear nationalism of, 25; on progress of Soviet program, 22; on Smyth's report, 30; on Soviet espionage, 19–20; Truman briefed about Manhattan Project by, 23; Truman influenced by, 4–5, 25; on uranium for Soviet Union, 20

Gruenther, Alfred M., 238

Hagerty, James, 93

Hahn, Otto, 12

Halban, Hans, 13

Hall, Theodore, 304 (n. 12)

Hancock, John M., 55

Harr, Carl, 140

Harriman, W. Averell: on Kennan's "Long Telegram," 50; in LTBT negotiations, 209, 210–13; on Rostow, 263; on Soviet desire for arms control, 146–47

Harrison, George, 24

Hawk missiles, 207

H-bomb. *See* Thermonuclear weapons

Health effects of nuclear tests: AEC on, 123; and antinuclear movement, 123, 190; atmospheric, 120; British report on, 102–3; 1954 thermonuclear test, 93–94; UN study on, 104–5

Hegemony, U.S.: European resistance to, 6, 197; NATO and, 2–3; nonproliferation policy in advancement of, 2–3; NPT and, 286

Heisenberg, Werner, 21

Heller, Joseph, 190

Hersey, John, 5, 64–65

Herter, Christian, 110, 135, 139, 146

Hickenlooper, Bourke: on Baruch Plan, 60; on British-American alliance, 69, 70, 98; on Israeli proliferation, 154; on nuclear sharing, 128; radioactive isotope export and, 86

Hickerson, John, 74

Hierarchy, nuclear, ix, 1

Hillenbrand, Martin, 256

Hiroshima (Hersey), 5; "Hiroshima" (article), 64–65

Hiroshima bombing (1945). *See* Japanese atomic bombings

Holifield, Chet, 124, 128, 229

Hoover, Herbert, 5, 86

Hoover, J. Edgar, 58

House of Representatives, U.S. *See* Congress, U.S.

House Un-American Activities Committee, 77

"Howl" (Ginsberg), 140

Hughes, Donald L., 26

Human experiments, 123

Humphrey, George, 97, 111

Humphrey, Hubert, 124, 279, 281

Hussein, Saddam, 294–95

Hutchins, Robert M., 32

Hydrogen bomb. *See* Thermonuclear weapons

Hypocrisy, 195, 283, 298

Identity, Western: in NATO, 2–3

Ideology: in U.S. nuclear policy, 1–2, 300

India: on Atoms for Peace program, 91; bias in U.S. views of, 89, 126; on Chinese nuclear test, 235–36; Chinese rivalry with, 141–42, 163, 234; currency devaluation in, 276; Gilpatric Committee on, 243; 1971 war between Pakistan and, 288–89; on NPT draft, 272, 273, 276, 277; NPT rejected by, 8, 278, 285; on NPT renewal, 292; on test bans, 95, 99, 118; U.S. sanctions against, 294

Indian nuclear program: Bush's (George W.) approach to, 294; Chinese nuclear program and, 234, 235–36, 249; decision to weaponize, 236–37, 289; development of, 141–42; initial U.S. response to, 8; Johnson's approach to, 236–37, 249, 254; Kennedy's approach to, 146, 163; 1974 test of, 290; 1998 test of, 293, 294; Nixon's approach to, 288–89; no-weapons pledge of, 234, 236; NPT's lack of impact on, 285; peaceful nuclear explosions and, 254, 289; peaceful uses technology used for weapons in, 107, 141–42, 290; Reagan's approach to, 291; U.S. cooperation agreement with, 294

Indirect proliferation: in Berlin talks, 191, 266

Inspections: in Acheson-Lilienthal report, 49, 50, 52–53; aerial, in Open Skies plan, 106; in Baruch Plan, 60, 61; in Byrnes's international control plan, 42; at ENDC meetings, 189, 199; in Geneva Conference of Experts report, 132, 133; in Geneva test ban talks, 151; in Iran, 296; in Iraq, 295; in Israel, 233, 249; in LTBT, 199–200, 208, 253; at Moscow Conference, 42; in North Korea, 295; in Oppenheimer's international control plan, 49; of peaceful use facilities, 274–75; quota on, 135, 199–200; remote detection as substitute for, 191, 193, 199; Soviet travel bans and, 38

Intercontinental ballistic missiles (ICBMs), 125

Interim Committee, 24–27

Intermediate Nuclear Forces Treaty (1987), 291

Intermediate range ballistic missiles (IRBMs): British control of, 116; U.S. production rate of, 130; U.S. sharing with NATO, 126, 128, 130–32, 143; in West Germany, 131, 142, 143

International Atomic Energy Agency (IAEA): Atomic Energy Act and, 100; in Atoms for Peace program, 89, 99–100; Iranian inspections by, 296; negotiations over mission of, 99–100, 106; North Korean inspections by, 295; in NPT drafts, 270–71, 274–75; Persian Gulf War and, 292; proposals for creation

of, 89, 99–100; safeguards in charter of, 107; U.S. reactors inspected by, 232–33

International community: on atmospheric tests, 190; in atomic alliance against Soviet Union, 68; atomic bomb's implications for politics of, 23–24; dissent in, 6; fission research by, 12–13; on Japanese bombings, 32

International control: Acheson-Lilienthal report on, 48–53; Baruch Plan for, 54–68; British-American alliance and, 17, 18; Byrnes's opposition to, 32, 34, 35, 37–38; Byrnes's plan for, 40–44, 48; end of U.S. efforts to establish, 63–68; Forrestal's opposition to, 33–36, 37–38; Gromyko Plan for, 61; impossibility of, during Cold War, 76; Interim Committee recommendations on, 26; Johnson on, 221; at Moscow Conference, 40–44; Oppenheimer's plan for, 49, 52–53, 57, 58; Policy Planning Staff report on, 71–72, 73–74; Roosevelt's opinion of, 17, 18, 19, 23; scientists' support for, 26–27; Stimson's plan for, 23–24, 32–36, 48; thermonuclear weapons and, 73–76; Truman's delay of, 23–24, 31; Truman's proposal on, 4, 6, 36–39; Washington Conference on, 38–39

Internationalism, scientific. See Scientific internationalism

Iran, 294–96; in NPT, 285; Pakistani nuclear aid to, 294; Soviet withdrawal from, 51; U.S. approach to nuclear program of, 294–96

Iraq, 291, 294–95

Iraq war, 295

Ireland, 137, 172–73

Iron curtain, 50–51

Isotopes, radioactive: export of, 86–87

Israel: in Arab-Israeli conflict, 271, 287; on NPT draft, 276; NPT rejected by, 8, 281–82, 283, 285, 292–93; in nuclear hierarchy, 1; U.S. sale of weapons to, 207, 281–82

Israeli nuclear program: Egypt on, 207, 233–34; French aid to, 107, 261; initial U.S. response to, 8, 142; Johnson's approach to, 233–34, 249; Kennedy's approach to, 146, 153, 154, 207; Nixon's approval of, 283, 287; NPT's lack of impact on, 285; U.S. aid to, 207, 233; U.S. discouragement of, 207, 233

Italy: IRBM sharing with, 131–32; on MLF, 177,

205, 223; and Nassau agreement, 203; on NPT, 272, 275, 281, 283; on UN Disarmament Subcommittee, 120

Jackson, C. D.: and Atoms for Peace program, 89–90, 92, 101; in Operation Candor, 87, 89; on Soviet leadership transition, 84

Jackson, Henry "Scoop," 153, 207

Japan: non-nuclear principles of, 283; on NPT draft, 277, 278; on test bans, 95, 102, 118; U.S. occupation of, 25; 1954 U.S. thermonuclear test affects trawler from, 93–94, 102

Japanese atomic bombings (1945), 28–29; civilian deaths in, 3; criticism of, 3, 5; international opinion of, 32; media coverage of, 5, 29, 64–65; official narrative on, 3–4; public reaction to, 28–29, 64; U.S. justification of, 3–4, 5, 65

Japanese nuclear program: after Chinese nuclear test, 239; destruction during U.S. occupation, 25; Nixon's approach to, 287; during World War II, 21

Jiang Jie-Shi, 237

Jobert, Michel, 288

Johnson, Edwin C., 40

Johnson, Louis, 72–73

Johnson, Lyndon B., xi, 217–82; anticommunism of, 220–21; on Chinese proliferation, 234–37; congressional career of, 219, 220–21; foreign policy advisers of, 219–21; German relations with, 222, 245, 251; Gilpatric Committee under, 237–44; Gilpatric report rejected by, 243–44, 250, 252; on international control, 221; leadership style of, 219–20; on LTBT, 221; MLF abandoned by, 245–48, 255; in MLF debate, 221–27; on NATO unity, 221–27; in 1960 presidential election, 219; in 1964 presidential election, 235, 238, 245; in 1968 presidential election, 277; nonproliferation policy reassessed by, 237–44, 250, 252; NPT signed by, 279–80; start of presidency, 217–21; subordinates' relationship with, 219–20; as vice president, 219

Johnston, Joseph E., 76

Joint Chiefs of Staff: Johnson's, 264; Kennedy's, 151, 152, 194, 208, 210; Truman's, 35, 59, 72

Joint Committee on Atomic Energy (JCAE):

on British-American alliance, 69–71; establishment of, 4; on French nuclear program, 130; on MLF, 229; on need for NPT, 264; on Quebec Agreement, 69; on radioactive isotope export, 86–87; on test bans, 108; on thermonuclear weapons, 72

Joint grand deterrent, 155, 156

Joliot-Curie, Frédéric, 12, 18

Jupiter missiles, 126, 177, 196, 197

Kahn, Herman, 7, 230, 285

Kaysen, Carl, 153, 169, 198, 261

Kazakhstan, 292

Kellogg-Briand Pact, 57

Kennan, George F.: on impossibility of agreement with Soviets, 5, 63; "Long Telegram" on Soviet intentions by, 50; on Moscow Conference, 42–43; on need for arms control, 71, 73–74; on Rapacki Plan, 127

Kennedy, John F., x, xi, 145–215; and antinuclear movement, 169; assassination of, 215, 218; on atmospheric tests, 160, 168–71, 189; in Berlin crisis, 160–64; on Chinese proliferation, 146, 153, 163, 198, 207; on comprehensive versus limited test ban, x, xi, 192, 193; conflict between civilian and military officials under, 151; in Cuban Missile Crisis, 195–98; Eisenhower's advice on test resumption to, 148, 161; election of, 141; on European proliferation, 146, 154–58; foreign policy advisers of, 146–50; on French nuclear weapons, 155–59, 164, 167–68, 178; funeral of, 221–22; inconsistency in policy approach of, 164–68, 174; on inspections quota, 199–200; Khrushchev's assessment of, 146–47; Khrushchev's secret letters to, 165, 197, 208; leadership style of, 145, 157, 166; in LTBT, 182, 207–15; on MLF, 143, 154–58, 164, 166–67, 174–75, 178–79, 205; modus vivendi with Khrushchev sought by, 145, 159, 164–65; and Nassau agreement, 202–4; at 1961 NATO meetings, 167; public versus private views of, 147–48; racial thinking of, 153; speeches by, 147, 158, 165, 167, 209; test ban debate in administration of, 148–54, 191–93; test ban supported by, 146; on test resumption, 161, 168–72; on threat of proliferation, 153, 181; on U-2 spy plane

ministration attempts to extend, 253–54; Johnson's views on, 221; Kennedy administration debate over, 192–93, 207–8; MLF in, 211; Moscow Conference on, 209–13; nonaggression treaty combined with, 211–12, 213; reasons for weakness of, 181–82; renewal of negotiations on, 207–13; shortcomings of, 213–15; Soviet openness to, 193–94; U.S. ratification of, 214; withdrawal clause of, 213

Lippmann, Walter, 62, 199

Literature, antinuclear, 140, 190, 229–30

Lodge, Henry Cabot: on Atoms for Peace program, 101; on health effects of fallout, 104–5; on IAEA, 99; and Khrushchev's 1959 visit to U.S., 137; in 1960 presidential election, 122; on test bans, 95, 104

London Conference, 38

London Suppliers' Group, 290

"Long Telegram" (Kennan), 50

Lop Nor test site, 200

Los Alamos: Soviet espionage at, 20

Lovett, Robert, 77–78

Lubell, Samuel, 84

Lucky Dragon (trawler), 93–94, 102

Maclean, Donald, 20, 70

Macmillan, Harold: at Bermuda Conference (1957), 117; and British membership in EEC, 183, 184–85; on comprehensive test ban, 190–91, 208; in ENDC, 189; and Franco-British alliance, 183–85, 214; on LTBT, 193, 210; on McNamara's counterforce speech, 184; and Nassau agreement, 201, 202, 204; on Rapacki Plan, 127; resignation of, 224; sex-for-secrets spy scandal and, 206, 224; and Skybolt crisis, 201–2; on test bans, 118, 135; on test resumption, 170; White Paper on Defence, 167

Madman theory, 287

Makins, Sir Roger, 70

Malenkov, Georgii M., 84, 85, 104

Malraux, André, 182

Mandela, Nelson, ix

Manhattan Project: British participation in, 14–19, 23; Canadian participation in, 16; Chicago Laboratory of, 25, 26, 30, 32; debate over informing Soviets about, 26, 27, 28; foreign scientists in, 12–14, 30–31;

Smyth's report on, 30–31; Soviet espionage on, 19–21, 34; Soviet knowledge of, 20, 21; successful bomb test of, 6, 28; Truman's initial ignorance of, 22–23

Man in the Gray Flannel Suit, The (Wilson), 83

Mann, Thomas, 32

Mansfield, Mike, 225

Mao Ze-dong, 153, 237

Marks, Herbert, 52–53, 58

Marshall Islands, 92–94

Marshall Plan, 69

Masculinity, 220

"Masters of War" (Dylan), 190

Maud Committee, 13, 14, 20

McCarren committee, 77

McCarthy, Joseph, 77, 220

McCloy, John J.: in Acheson-Lilienthal group, 48; and antinuclear movement, 169; and Arms Control and Disarmament Agency, 161–62; and Baruch Plan, 56, 62; in Egypt, 207, 233–34; in ENDC, 172; espionage accusations against, 58; in Geneva test ban talks, 148, 151, 152; on Gilpatric Committee, 238, 240, 242–44; on Kennedy's foreign policy team, 147, 149; and LTBT, 210; on MLF, 224, 240, 257, 258, 262; resignation of, 172; at Ten-Nation Disarmament Conference, 162; on test resumption, 161; on Truman's reaction to successful bomb test, 28

McCone, John: Eisenhower's relationship with, 135; on fallout effects, 140; and French nuclear program, 142; on limited test ban, 208, 209; selection as AEC chair, 133, 135; on test ban negotiations, 189; test bans opposed by, 133–34; on test resumption, 153, 161

McGhee, George, 163, 262, 267, 270

McKellar, Kenneth, 34–35, 60

McMahon, Brien, 57, 72, 73, 74

McNamara, Robert S.: on Chinese proliferation, 234, 271; on comprehensive versus limited test ban, 192; counterforce strategy of, 175–77, 179, 182, 183–84; and *Dr. Strangelove*, 230; evolution of views on proliferation, 175–76; on Gilpatric Committee report, 244; on Johnson's foreign policy team, 219, 220; and Johnson's policy reassessment, 239, 241–42; on Kennedy's foreign policy team, 147, 150; on MLF, 157, 167, 175, 178,

188, 222, 225, 226, 246, 257, 262, 264; at 1962 NATO ministerial meetings, 179; on non-proliferation accord, 195; on NPT revisions, 265; and Skybolt crisis, 201; on test ban negotiations, 152; on underground tests, 161; University of Michigan speech by, 183–84; and U.S.-NATO relations, 183–84

McNaughton, Frank, 51

McNaughton, John, 264

Media coverage: of Acheson-Lilienthal report, 55–56; of Atoms for Peace speech, 89; of Baruch Plan, 60; of Chinese nuclear test, 235–36; of fallout shelters, 169; of French nuclear program, 182; of Japanese bombings, 5, 29, 64–65; of MLF experiment, 223; of 1956 presidential election, 112–13; of Soviet espionage, 51; technological utopianism in, 31; of thermonuclear tests, 93, 103; of UN Disarmament Subcommittee, 109; of Washington Declaration, 40

Medium range ballistic missiles (MRBMs), 142, 164, 177, 195–96

Meier, Golda, 283

Menshikov, Mikhail, 146–47

Middle East: U.S. fears of arms race in, 142, 154, 207, 233–34. *See also specific countries*

Mike device, 78

Military Liaison Committee, 63

Miller, Walter, 140

Missile defense: under Bush (George W.), 293; under Reagan, 291. *See also specific missile types*

Missile gap, 125, 130, 171, 220

"MLF Lullaby" (Lehrer), 231

Molotov, Vyacheslav: atomic bomb development and, 28; on Baruch Plan, 66; disarmament proposal of, 66, 67; at Four Power Conference, 95; at Geneva Conference, 95–96; at Moscow Conference, 40, 43; at Paris Peace Conference, 63; on peaceful uses linked with disarmament, 95–96, 99; and Truman's international control proposal, 38

Monitoring systems: Geneva Conference of Experts on, 132–37. *See also* Detection; Inspections

Monopoly, atomic, 11–45; in Baruch Plan, 60; British-American alliance in World War II and, 14–19; claims about persistence of, 4–5, 25, 26; Congress protects, 64, 70–71; in

energy industry, 88; interwar international research and, 12–14; Roosevelt's faith in, 11–12, 19–22; Soviet espionage and, 19–21; Truman's faith in, ix–x, 4–5, 11–12, 23, 37; warnings about futility of, 11, 18, 21, 23, 26

Moscow Conference: 1945, 40–44, 60; 1963, 209–13

Moscow Treaty (2002), 293

Moyers, Bill, 264, 265, 268

Muller, Hermann, 121

Multilateral force, NATO (MLF): Anglo-German negotiations on, 254–55, 258–60; versus ANF, 247–48, 254–55, 258–59; in Berlin test ban talks, 191, 194; in British NPT draft (1965), 253; Eisenhower's proposal for, 115–16, 142–44, 154; at ENDC, 173, 228; end of, 262–68; Finletter's presentation on U.S. terms for, 183–84; Johnson's abandonment of, 245–48, 255; Johnson's initial approach to, 221–27; and Johnson's policy reassessment, 239–43; Kennedy's consideration of, 154–58, 164, 166–67, 174–75, 178–79; Kennedy's decision to de-emphasize, 178–79, 182, 183–84, 205–6; Kennedy's pessimism regarding, 205; Kennedy's revival of, 185–88; and LTBT, 211; mixed-manned experiment of, 222–23; Nassau agreement and, 202, 203; versus national nuclear forces, 155, 158, 164, 166, 167, 175, 203; at 1962 NATO ministerial meetings, 177–80; nonproliferation accord prevented by, 206–7, 217, 218, 228, 232, 261; in NPT drafts, 265; Soviet opposition to, 143, 174, 206, 217, 218, 228, 231–32, 244, 261; submarines in, 177, 178–79, 187–88, 205; in U.S. NPT draft (1965), 253

Multilateral negotiations, 6–8; current need for, 299; Truman's dismissal of, 47. *See also specific agreements and meetings*

Murphy, Charles J. V., 87

Murray, Thomas, 103, 111, 112

Murrow, Edward R., 29, 163

Musharraf, Pervez, 294

Muste, A. J., 29

Myrdal, Alva, 8

Nagasaki bombing (1945). *See* Japanese atomic bombings

Nassau summit (1962), 201–3

Nasser, Gamal Abdel, 207, 233–34

Nation, The (journal), 56

National Defense Research Committee, U.S., 14

Nationalism: in developing nations, 235–36; German, 156

Nationalism, nuclear: and Atoms for Peace program, 91; and Baruch Plan, 60; in Congress, 32, 36, 40; and failure of nonproliferation, 300; and failure of wartime nuclear projects, 21–22; and Interim Committee, 24; and LTBT, 208; of Roosevelt, 21–22, 44; of Truman, 37, 44; Truman influenced by, 22–25, 28

National nuclear forces: in ANF, 247; versus NATO MLF, 155, 158, 164, 166, 167, 175, 203; in NATO multinational force, 202, 203

National security, U.S.: atomic bomb's effects on, 23; and core values, 2; debate over nuclear sharing and, 7; under Eisenhower, 82; subordination of nonproliferation to other issues and, 297–98; weapons versus treaties and, 47–48

National Security Council (NSC): on Atoms for Peace program, 100; on British-American alliance, 69, 98; disarmament rejected by, 105; on Gilpatric report, 252; on MLF, 177, 221, 224–25; and Operation Candor, 85; on test bans, 96–97; on thermonuclear weapons, 72–73

National Security Council Paper Number 68 (NSC-68), 74

National sovereignty, 49

NATO (North Atlantic Treaty Organization): counterforce strategy and, 176–77, 179; Cuban Missile Crisis and, 196, 200; expanded access to weapons, 97–98, 108; as fourth nuclear power, 143; French withdrawal of forces from, 262–63; Johnson's commitment to unity of, 221–27; and Nassau agreement, 202; national nuclear forces in multinational force of, 202; on 1954 thermonuclear test, 93; 1961 ministerial meetings of, 166–67; 1962 ministerial meetings of, 177–80, 200; 1963 ministerial meetings of, 221; 1968 ministerial meetings of, 279; on nontransfer draft agreement, 200; in nuclear hierarchy, 1; nuclear sharing and, 7, 124–26; and Panel of Consultants

report, 83; and Rapacki Plan, 127–28; rift in U.S. relations with, 177–80, 182–88; U.S. dominance of, 115; and U.S. hegemony, 2–3; U.S. IRBM sharing with, 126, 128, 130–32, 143; U.S. on national nuclear forces within, 155, 158, 164, 166, 167, 175; U.S. weapons sent to, 174; weapons managed by, 126; weapons stockpiles of, 102, 126. *See also* Multilateral force, NATO; Nuclear Planning Group, NATO

Nazi Germany, 12, 13, 21

Negotiating from strength, 51–52

Nehru, Jawaharlal, 95, 142, 236

Neo-imperialism, 6

Neutral countries: bias in U.S. views of, 89; on Chinese nuclear test, 236; on U.S. atmospheric tests, 190

Neutron bomb development, 152

Nevada test site: British use of, 71, 170

Newmont Mining Company, 57

New Republic, 29

New Yorker magazine, 64

New York Times, 55, 60, 279

Nichols, Kenneth, 142

Nickson, J. J., 26

Nimitz, Chester, 57

Nitze, Paul H.: and French nuclear program, 168, 174; on Kennedy's foreign policy team, 150; on MLF, 154, 157; and NSC-68, 74; and Panel of Consultants on Disarmament, 76–77

Nixon, Richard M., 286–89; approach to disarmament negotiations proposed by, 83; Eisenhower's legacy and, 286–87; on MLF, 225; in 1956 presidential election, 110, 113; in 1960 presidential election, 122, 141; NPT enforcement under, 251–52, 283–84, 286–89; on NPT ratification, 282–83; nuclear strikes threatened by, 287; Vietnam War under, 287

Nobel Peace Prize, 89

No-first-use provisions, 277

No-fly zones, 295

Nonaggression treaty: LTBT combined with, 211–12, 213

Nonaligned countries: bias in U.S. views of, 89; on need for NPT, 261; 1964 conference of, 236; on NPT drafts, 273–74, 276, 277; rise of protests by, 7

Non-nuclear nations: 1968 conference of, 274,

277, 279, 281; on NPT, 218, 273–74, 279–81;
nuclear abstinence by, 119, 251
Nonproliferation: future of, 299–300; reasons
for failure of, 297–300; unilateral German
commitment to, 102; U.S.-French-British
proposed agreement on, 232
Nonproliferation negotiations, 7–8; after
Cuban Missile Crisis, 198; faith in atomic
monopoly and, 12; genesis of superpowers'
commitment to, x, 92; Gilpatric Committee
on, 241–44; informal discussions in, 198–99,
265; Johnson administration deadlock over,
227–29, 231–33; Johnson administration
reassessment of, 237–44, 250, 252; Kennedy
administration debate over, 192–93, 194–95;
MLF as barrier in, 206–7, 217, 218, 228, 232,
252, 261; non-nuclear nations' views of,
218; overview of U.S. policy on, 1–7; versus
separate agreement on German nuclear
weapons, 194; U.S. attempts to prove
impossibility of Soviet participation in, 45,
47; West Germany on superpowers in, 251.
See also Nuclear Nonproliferation Treaty;
specific agreements and meetings
Norstad, Lauris, 131, 143, 157, 184, 186–87
North Atlantic Collective Defense Authority,
256
North Atlantic Treaty Organization. *See*
NATO
North Korea, 285, 294–96
North Vietnam, 213, 234, 287
Norway, 118
No-weapons pledges: in EURATOM, 107;
in IAEA, 106; by India, 234, 236; in UN
Disarmament Subcommittee, 120
NSC-68. *See* National Security Council Paper
Number 68
Nth-country problem, 142, 170
Nuclear Ambush (Voss), 207
Nuclear apartheid: codification of, in treaties,
x, 9; evolution of, ix–x; in former colonies,
ix, x; in NPT, 251; origins of term, ix, 1
Nuclear (atomic) energy policy, U.S.: in
Atoms for Peace program, 87–92; under
Eisenhower, 87–92, 96, 99, 107; link be-
tween proliferation and, 90–91, 96, 99, 107;
military control of, 36; misunderstanding
of benefits versus dangers of, 5, 88, 89–91;
Nazi Germany and, 21; opposition to, 32;

postwar options for, 19; presidential au-
thority over, 36; privatization of, 87–88,
90; under Roosevelt, 16, 19, 21–22; under
Truman, 23–24, 29, 31–32, 36–37
Nuclear freeze proposals, 227
Nuclear-free zone: European, 127–28; Latin
American, 198, 218
Nuclear hierarchy, ix, 1
Nuclear nationalism. *See* Nationalism, nuclear
Nuclear Nonproliferation Act (1978), 290
Nuclear Nonproliferation Treaty (NPT)
(1968), 7–8, 251–84; British draft of (1965),
252–53; under Bush (George W.), 296–97;
Chinese participation in, 261, 285; countries
rejecting, 8, 251, 276, 278, 281–83, 285; countries signing, 278–83, 285, 293; duration of,
272, 274, 275; effects on superpowers, 8–9,
251, 298–99; limitations on effectiveness
of, 8, 279–84, 285, 286, 297; MLF in, 265;
Nixon's lack of enforcement of, 251–52,
283–84, 286–89; non-nuclear nations' views
of, 218, 273–74, 279–81; nuclear apartheid
in, 251; objections to drafts of, 272–76, 277;
peaceful nuclear explosions and, 254; presentation at ENDC, 253, 269, 270, 271–72,
276; pressures encouraging, 260–62, 264;
problems after passage of, 279–84; renewal
of, 292–93; review conferences in, 274, 275,
276, 296–97; revisions to drafts of, 265,
268–71, 274–76; Russia under, 292; Soviet
draft of (1965), 253, 260–61; Soviet preconditions for, 261; terms of, 8, 271–72; threshold test ban and, 254; transfer of weapons
in, 265, 268, 269, 270, 271–72; types of
nuclear states in, x, 8; UN debate on, 277–
78; UN endorsement of, 278; U.S. draft of
(1965), 253–54, 260–61, 262; West German
nuclear program in, 262, 266, 269–70
Nuclear Planning Group, NATO: and ANF,
259; establishment of, 255–56; and MLF,
262, 266; Soviet position on, 257, 261, 265;
West Germany in, 266–67
Nuclear power. *See* Nuclear energy policy, U.S.
Nuclear proliferation. *See* Nonproliferation;
Proliferation
Nuclear sharing. *See* Sharing, nuclear
Nuclear states: NPT on types of, x, 8
Nuclear supremacy: U.S. demand for, ix–x, 1–2
Nuclear tests. *See* Tests

Nuclear war. *See* War

Nuclear waste, 299–300

Nuclear weapons: Atoms for Peace program combined with ban on, 92; discussion of ban on, during World War II, 3; national greatness associated with, 6. *See also* Atomic bomb; Tests; Thermonuclear weapons

Nuclear winter, 6

Offset payments, 267

One Flew Over the Cuckoo's Nest (Kesey), 190

On the Beach (film), 6, 140

Open Skies plan, 106, 108

Operation Candor, 84, 85, 87–90

Operation Sunshine, 123

Operation Wheaties, 89

Oppenheimer, J. Robert: in Acheson-Lilienthal group, 49, 52; and Baruch Plan, 56–57, 67; on disarmament, 62; on Interim Committee, 24, 26, 27; international control plan of, 49, 52–53, 57, 58; on nuclear abstinence, 27; on nuclear sharing, 86; on Panel of Consultants on Disarmament, 76–78, 86; on postwar tests, 64; on radioactive isotope export, 87; on Smyth report, 83–84; and Soviet nuclear capability, 35; on Stimson's international control plan, 33; Strauss's campaign against, 86–87; technological utopianism of, 49; on thermonuclear weapons, 72, 73; Truman's dismissal of views of, 25, 64, 304 (n. 18)

"Organization man," 83

Ormsby-Gore, David, 146, 170, 188

Ottawa: Kennedy's speech in, 158, 167

Outer-space tests, 136

Owen, Henry, 257, 262

Oxnam, G. Bromley, 29

Pacifica, Project, 163

Pakistan: Chinese nuclear program and, 234; Chinese rivalry with, 234; on Indian nuclear program, 237; 1971 war between India and, 288–89; Nixon's approach to, 288–89; on NPT draft, 277, 278; NPT rejected by, 8, 285; U.S. sanctions against, 294

Pakistani nuclear program: Bush's (George W.) approach to, 294; Carter's approach to, 289–90; establishment of, 289; 1998 test of,

293, 294; Nixon's approach to, 289; Reagan's approach to, 291

Panama Canal, 281

Panel of Consultants on Disarmament: Eisenhower administration evaluation of, 83–85, 86; publication of declassified version of report of, 87; test ban proposal by, 76–78

Panofsky, Wolfgang, 160–61

Paris Peace Conference (1946), 63, 66

Paris Summit (1960), 137–39

Partial Test Ban Treaty. *See* Limited Test Ban Treaty

Pastore, John, 262, 264

Patterson, Robert: and Baruch Plan, 57; international control opposed by, 33, 34–35, 37–38

Pauling, Linus, 121, 169

Peace: Eisenhower's speech on chance for, 84–85; as goal of Soviet Union, 84–85; Roosevelt's vision for, 15–16, 17; through scientific internationalism, 17; Truman's vision for, 28

Peaceful nuclear explosions (PNEs), 254, 272, 289

Peaceful uses: Congress on, 98; disarmament linked with, 92, 95–96, 99; Indian nuclear weapons produced from, 107, 141–42, 290; inspections of, 274–75; proliferation potential of, 90–91, 96, 99, 107; under Reagan, 291; in Stassen's disarmament plan, 106. *See also* Atoms for Peace program; Nuclear energy policy, U.S.

Peace groups: on Atoms for Peace program, 91; on Baruch Plan, 60; on elimination of atomic bombs, 32; on Japanese bombings, 29. *See also* Antinuclear movement

Peace race, 165

Pearl Harbor, 3

Pearson, Drew, 51

Peierls, Rudolph, 13

People's Republic of China (PRC). *See* China

Pepper, Claude, 32

Perkins, James, 238

Perle, Richard, 231

Permissive action links (PALs), 174, 197

Persian Gulf War (1991), 292, 295

Petrzhak, Konstantin, 12

Philby, Kim, 20

Pius XII, Pope, 95

Plutonium: in Atoms for Peace program, 88,

91; in Fissile Material Cutoff Treaty, 297; reduction in U.S. production of, 232

Poison gas, 3

Poland: on Baruch Plan, 67; on MLF, 218, 227; on nuclear freeze in Central Europe, 227; in nuclear-free zone of Rapacki Plan, 127–28; on Soviet desire for arms control, 199

Polaris missiles: on MLF submarines, 157, 177, 178–79, 187–88, 205; U.S. sale of, in Nassau agreement, 202–3

Policy Planning Staff of State Department: on effectiveness of NPT, 286; international control report by, 71–72, 73–74

Politics: atomic bomb's implications for, 23–24; connection between war and, 82

Pontecorvo, Bruno, 70

Possony, Stefan T., 88, 91

Potsdam Conference (1945), 27, 28

Poverty: disarmament in prevention of, 84

Power, nuclear. *See* Nuclear energy policy, U.S.

Power disparities: in nuclear hierarchy, ix, 1

Powers, Gary Francis, 138

Powers, Thomas, 165

Prague Spring, 278

Presidency, U.S.: authority over atomic energy policy, 36; concentration of power in, 4

Presidential election(s): of 1956, 110–14; of 1960, 122, 141, 146, 219; of 1964, 221, 235, 238, 245; of 1968, 277, 282

President's Special Task Force on Nuclear Proliferation. *See* Gilpatric Committee

Press coverage. *See* Media coverage

Preventive war, 58, 65, 125

Private property: atomic bomb as, 33–34

Privatization: of nuclear energy, 87–88, 90

Profiles in Courage (Kennedy), 145

Profumo affair, 206, 224

Project Pacifica, 163

Proliferation: link between nuclear energy and, 90–91, 96, 99, 107; 1950s rise of, 106–8. *See also* Nonproliferation; Selective proliferation

Proliferation threat: Eisenhower's view of, 92, 143–44; Kennedy's view of, 153, 181; Khrushchev's view of, 137; origins of U.S. and Soviet concerns about, x; Roosevelt's view of, 12, 13, 22; Truman's view of, 45, 48, 92

Propaganda: Atoms for Peace program as, 90,

91, 92, 99; Soviet goal of peaceful coexistence as, 84–85; UNAEC as forum for, 62

Psychological Strategy Board, 84

Psychological warfare: during Soviet leadership transition, 84–85

Public opinion: on Acheson-Lilienthal report, 56; on atmospheric tests, 190; attempts to suppress dissent in, 3–6; on Japanese bombings, 3–4, 28–29, 64; on LTBT, 218; on 1954 thermonuclear test, 93–94; on nuclear war, 6; technological utopianism and, 31–32; on test bans, 102–3, 122; on test resumption, 161; on thermonuclear weapons, 73, 85, 93–94

Pugwash conferences, 169

Qaeda, al, 294, 295

Quarles, Donald, 134

Quebec Agreement (1943), 16–17, 18, 69

Quotas, inspection, 135, 199–200

Rabi, Isidor, 72, 107, 124

Rabinowitch, Eugene, 26

Racial thinking: about Asians, 34, 89, 126–27, 153; of Kennedy, 153; about non-NATO countries, 126–27

Radford, Arthur W., 111

Radiation sickness, 93–94

Radicals, antinuclear, 122

Radioactive isotopes: export of, 86–87

Radioactive material: from 1954 thermonuclear test, 93–94

Ramey, James, 276

Rapacki, Adam, 127

Rapacki Plan, 127–28, 165

Rathjens, George, 241

Raw materials survey: in Baruch Plan, 57, 58, 59

Reactors: future of, 299–300; trade in, 290

Reagan, Ronald, 231, 288, 291

Religious organizations: on Japanese bombings, 29

Remote seismic detection, 191, 192, 193, 199

Research, nuclear: international, 12–13; Soviet, 20; U.S., 13–14

Rickover, Hyman, 205

Roberts, Owen, 32

Rogue nations, 294–95

Rollback policy, 241–42

Romania, 197, 272–73

Roosevelt, Franklin D., 11–22; on atomic monopoly, 11–12, 19–22; on atomic secrecy, 11, 16, 17–19; on British-American alliance, 14–18; Byrnes's relationship with, 24; death of, 19, 22; expansion of research by, 14; on failure of international wartime nuclear programs, 21–22; failure to institutionalize policies, 19, 22, 44; on international control, 17, 18, 19, 23; nationalism of, 21–22, 44; on postwar peace, 15–16, 17; on Soviet espionage, 19–21; on threat of proliferation, 12, 13, 22; Truman insulated by, 22

Rosenberg, Julius, 304 (n. 12)

Roshchin, Alexei, 228

Rostow, Walt W.: on Chinese nuclear program, 234; on Cuban Missile Crisis, 198; and Johnson's policy reassessment, 240; on MLF, 222, 224–25, 229, 263; on NPT, 278–79, 282; on Soviet desire for arms control, 146; on Soviet invasion of Czechoslovakia, 280

Rowen, Henry, 242

Rumsfeld, Donald, 295

Rusk, Dean: on ANF, 255; in Berlin talks with Gromyko, 165–66, 173–74, 191, 194, 266, 268; on Chinese proliferation, 198, 235, 236, 239; on comprehensive versus limited test ban, 192, 253; in Cuban Missile Crisis, 196; on French and German nuclear ambitions, 156, 178; on French-U.S. relations, 182; on Gilpatric Committee report, 243, 244; on Indian nuclear program, 163; on Johnson's foreign policy team, 219; on Kennedy's foreign policy team, 147, 149; on Kennedy's leadership style, 157; Kennedy's nonproliferation approach supported by, 163–64, 178; on MLF, 178, 188, 206, 224–27, 228, 245, 246, 248, 257, 263; at 1962 NATO ministerial meetings, 179–80, 200; 1962 visit to Europe, 185–86; and 1966 UN nonproliferation resolution, 266; in NPT negotiations, 265, 276; at NPT signing, 279; reassessment of nonproliferation by, 239; on security assurances in NPT, 273; on Sino-Soviet schism, 159; on Skybolt crisis, 201; on Soviet invasion of Czechoslovakia, 280; on transfer of weapons, 192, 200, 265

Russell, Richard, 128, 207, 225

Russian nuclear program, 292

Safeguards: in Acheson-Lilienthal report, 50; in Atoms for Peace program, 90, 91; in Byrnes's international control plan, 41, 42, 44; after Cuban Missile Crisis, 197; international conference on (1955), 107; at Moscow Conference, 41, 42, 44; in NPT, 270–71, 274–75; PALs as, 174, 197

Sanctions: UN, 296; U.S., 294, 295

Sato, Eisaku, 283

Sayre, John Nevin, 29

Schweitzer, Albert, 95, 120, 121

Science Advisory Committee, 201

Science fiction, 6

Scientific interchanges: in Byrnes's international control plan, 42, 44; Congress on, 69

Scientific internationalism: Oppenheimer's belief in, 49; peace through, 17; between world wars, 12–13

Scientists, foreign: in Manhattan Project, 12–14, 30–31

Scientists, U.S.: in antinuclear movement, 121–22; on atomic monopoly, 25, 26–27; on Baruch Plan, 60; at Geneva Conference of Experts, 132–33; on Japanese bombings, 29; on nuclear secrecy, 83–84; versus policymakers, 25

Seaborg, Glenn T.: on atomic monopoly, 26; on comprehensive versus limited test ban, 192; on Geneva test ban talks, 152–53; on Gilpatric Committee report, 244; on Israeli nuclear program, 233; selection as AEC chair, 152; on underground tests, 161

Searls, Fred, 55, 57, 58

Secrets, nuclear: Congress on, 32, 36; health effects of fallout as, 105; in Operation Candor, 85; in Panel of Consultants on Disarmament report, 78; public faith in, 31–32; in Quebec Agreement, 17; revealed in Smyth's report, 30, 84; Roosevelt's faith in, 11; in Roosevelt's postwar plans, 16, 17–19; scientists' view of, 83–84; Strauss's commitment to, 85–86; Truman's faith in, 11, 30–31. *See also* Sharing, nuclear

Security. *See* National security, U.S.

Security assurances: in NPT, 273, 275, 277

Seismic decoupling, 136, 139

Seismic recorders: automatic, 194, 199; remote, 191, 192, 193, 199

Seismic research: in threshold treaty, 141

Selective proliferation: definition of, 3; Truman administration support for, 71; U.S. justification for, 3

Senate, U.S.: Baruch confirmed by, 54, 55; on Comprehensive Test Ban Treaty, 293; Johnson's career in, 219; NPT ratification by, 280, 282. See also Congress, U.S.

Senate Special Committee on Atomic Energy, 36, 40, 41, 43, 54, 63

September 11, 2001, terrorist attacks, 294, 295

Seven Days in May (film), 230

Sex-for-secrets spy scandal, 206, 224

Sharing, nuclear: Atomic Energy Act on, 63–64, 98, 126; Bohr's model for arms control through, 17–18; Eisenhower-Khrushchev discussions on, 138; with Europe, 124–28; with France, 142, 164, 168, 174, 176; with Germany, 7; of IRBMs, 128; Kennedy's consideration of, 164; national security debate over, 7; within NATO, 7, 124–26; in Operation Candor, 85; Oppenheimer's support for, 86; origins of, x; with Soviet Union, 17–19, 22, 33–36; after Sputnik launch, 125; on submarines, 125, 126, 157. See also British-American nuclear alliance; Multilateral force, NATO; Secrets, nuclear

Shastri, Lal Bahadur, 236, 237, 249

Sherry, Michael, 303 (n. 8)

Shute, Nevil, 140

Sino-Soviet schism: Chinese nuclear program after, 141, 181; and Geneva test ban talks, 151; and LTBT, 210–11; 1969 border conflicts in, 287; origins of, 137; U.S. underestimation of, 137, 159

Skybolt crisis, 201–3

Smith, Gerard C., 128, 187, 188, 225

Smyth, Henry D.: on Atoms for Peace program, 91; report by, 30–31, 35, 84

Sobolev, Antonin, 66

Sohn, Louis, 162

South Africa: on NPT, 8, 277, 278

South African nuclear program: development of weapons in, 107; Nixon's approach to, 287–88; NPT's lack of impact on, 285

Sovereignty, national, 49

Soviet-Chinese relations. See Sino-Soviet schism

Soviet espionage. See Espionage, Soviet

Soviet nuclear program: aid to China from, x, 7, 99, 106–7; aid to Eastern Europe from, 99; development of, 13; espionage contributing to, 19–21; evolution of, x; first test of (1949), x, 68, 70, 78; fission research in, 12, 13; ICBMs in, 125; after Japanese bombings, 29–30; resource shortage in, 20; Truman's dismissal of, 35; uranium for, 20, 26; U.S. nationalists' dismissal of, 21, 24–25; U.S. scientists' assessment of, 25, 30; after World War II, 21; during World War II, 20, 21

Soviet Union: Acheson's approach to relations with, 51–52, 53; antinuclear movement in, 169; on Atoms for Peace program, 92, 95–96, 99; on Baruch Plan, 60–63, 66, 67, 68; British alliance with, in World War II, 15–16; Byrnes's strategy to prove intransigence of, 45, 47; on Chinese nuclear program, 207, 211, 235, 237; Clifford-Elsey report on, 63; collapse of, 292; in Cuban Missile Crisis, 195–97; East German peace treaty with, 131, 160; in ENDC, 189; genesis of nonproliferation policy in, x; on German rearmament, 104; in IAEA, 99; Kennan's "Long Telegram" on intentions of, 50; leadership transition in, 84–85; on MLF, 143, 174, 206, 217, 218, 228, 231–32, 244, 261; on Nassau agreement, 203–4; NPT draft by (1965), 253, 260–61; NPT signed by, 282–83; peaceful coexistence as goal of, 84–85; postwar rise of tensions with, 50–52, 63; Roosevelt's concerns about, 15–16; Sputnik I launched by, 125, 220; test ban announced by, 129; test bans proposed by, 103–4, 109, 117, 121; 1961 test resumption by, 162–63; on thermonuclear tests, 99; on threshold treaty, 141; UN membership of, 58; uranium in, 26, 107; U.S. debate over informing about atomic bomb, 26, 27, 28; and U.S. 1956 presidential election, 113; U.S. nuclear sharing with proposed, 17–19, 22, 33–36; U.S. views on irrationality of, 5, 34; West German relations with, 232. See also specific agreements, leaders, and meetings

Space: nuclear tests in, 136

Space-based missile defense, 291

Special Committee on Atomic Energy. *See* Senate Special Committee on Atomic Energy

Spock, Benjamin, 190

Sprague, Robert, 125

Sputnik I (satellite), 125, 220

Stalin, Joseph: atomic research under, 20, 30, 43; and Baruch Plan, 60; death of, 84; after Japanese bombings, 30; knowledge of Manhattan Project, 20, 21; at Potsdam Conference, 27, 28; proposal for sharing nuclear secrets with, 19; speeches of, in rise of anticommunism, 50; on Truman's hint about bomb, 28; and UN, 33; on UN Atomic Energy Commission, 43

Standstill agreement, 105

Star Wars, 291

Stassen, Harold: on Baruch Plan, 105; decline in power of, 105–10; disarmament plans of, 105–6, 108–11, 117–24; and Geneva Summit, 105–6; at 1956 Soviet state visit to Britain, 109; on Nixon in 1956 presidential election, 110; as presidential assistant for disarmament, 101–2, 261; resignation of, 124; on Soviet test ban proposal, 104, 117; on test bans, 104, 106, 108, 109; at UN Disarmament Subcommittee meetings, 101–2, 108–9, 117–23

State Department: Byrnes as secretary of, 24; and Johnson's policy reassessment, 239–40; on MLF, 256; in Operation Candor, 84, 87; on test bans, 110–11

Stearns, Joyce C., 26

Stettinius, Edward, 24

Stevenson, Adlai: and Geneva test ban talks, 152; on international opinion of testing, 190; Johnson's opinion of, 220; as Kennedy adviser, 146; in 1956 presidential election, 111–13; on test resumption, 163

Stewart, Jimmy, 231

Stikker, Dirk U., 157, 184, 223

Stimson, Henry: on Baruch Plan, 62; and British-American alliance, 18; on cooperation with Soviet Union, 27; on dangers of bomb, 6; on futility of atomic monopoly, 23; on Interim Committee, 24, 26, 27; on international control, 23–24, 32–36, 48;

justification of Japanese bombings by, 3, 5, 65; Kennedy's foreign policy team influenced by, 149; nationalism of, 23; on nuclear secrecy, 18, 19; on political implications of bomb, 23; resignation of, 32–33, 34; scientists' report on abstinence and, 27; on Smyth's report, 30; on Soviet espionage, 20; on Soviet nuclear capability, 35; Truman briefed about Manhattan Project by, 23

Stockpile, NATO, 102, 126

Stockpile, U.S.: in Atoms for Peace program, 89; in Europe, 98, 108; Gilpatric's 1961 speech on status of, 171; Kennedy's expansion of, 171; military on needed level of, 62; Truman's expansion of, 71

Stone, I. F., 56

Strassmann, Fritz, 12

Strategic arms limitation talks (SALT), 280

Strategic Arms Reduction Treaties, 292

Strauss, Franz Josef, 131, 155, 167, 184, 232, 255, 269

Strauss, Lewis: anticommunism of, 86, 121; on antinuclear movement, 121–22, 124; on Atoms for Peace program, 88–92, 100; on British-American alliance, 69, 86; career of, 85–86; on EURATOM, 107; and Geneva Conference of Experts, 132–33; and health effects of fallout, 105; influence on policy, 85–86; on limited test ban, 207, 208; move to Commerce Department, 129; on 1954 thermonuclear test, 93, 94; on nuclear secrecy, 85–86; on nuclear sharing, 126, 128; on Operation Candor, 85, 87, 88; Oppenheimer in conflict with, 86–87; on privatization of nuclear energy, 87–88, 90; psychosexual language of, 88–89; on radioactive isotope export, 86–87; on Stassen's disarmament plans, 106, 108, 110, 118–19; on test bans, 96, 97, 102, 106, 110–11, 112, 121; on test resumption, 153, 161; on thermonuclear weapons, 71, 72

Strontium-90, 120

Student protests, 278

Submarines, nuclear: in MLF, 177, 178–79, 187–88, 205; sharing information on, 125, 126, 157

Substate groups, 299

Suez crisis, 113, 116

Sulzberger, C. L., 182

194; in NPT drafts, 265, 268, 269, 270; in NPT final version, 271–72. *See also* Sharing, nuclear

Trinity test (1945), 6

Trivedi, V. M., ix, 272

Troika, 151

Truman, Harry S., 22–79; on alliance with Britain, 48; assumption of presidency, 22–23; on atomic monopoly, ix–x, 4–5, 11–12, 23, 37; on atomic secrecy, 11, 30–31; atomic supremacy under, ix–x; and Baruch as delegate to UNAEC, 54, 55; on Baruch Plan, 58–59, 67; on British-American alliance, 48, 69–70; Byrnes's lack of communication with, 41, 44; Clifford-Elsey report to, 63; end of presidency, 78–79; Groves's influence on, 4–5, 25; and Interim Committee, 24–27; international control considered by, 23–24, 32–36; international control delayed by, 23–24, 31; international control proposed by, 4, 6, 36–39; on Japanese bombings, 28; legacy of, 79; major mistakes in beliefs of, 44–45; nationalism of, 37, 44; nationalists' influence on, 22–25, 28; nonproliferation policy of, 71, 78–79; nuclear energy policy of, 23–24, 29, 31–32, 36–37; and nuclear weapons ban, 3; organizational chaos in presidency of, 31; at Potsdam Conference, 27, 28; rise of Soviet tensions with, 50–52; Roosevelt's policy errors inherited by, 22, 44; scientific ignorance of, 23, 30–31; on Smyth report, 30–31, 35; on Soviet atomic test, 68, 71, 78; on Soviet nuclear capability, 35; on start of arms race, 37; successful bomb test and, 28; technological utopianism of, 4–5, 31; on thermonuclear weapons development, 71–73; on threat of proliferation, 45, 48, 92; as vice president, 22; on Wallace's criticism of U.S. policy, 65–66; on war with Soviet Union, 51; at Washington Conference, 38–39; on weapons versus treaties in security, 47–48

Trusteeship, U.S., 31–32, 35, 36

Tsarapkin, Semyon K., 151–52, 168, 228

Tube Alloys, 15

Turkey: in Cuban Missile Crisis, 195, 196, 197; IRBM sharing with, 131–32; on MLF, 223, 224; U.S. missiles in, 195, 196, 197

Twilight Zone, The (television show), 6

Two-key control system, 155

Tydings, Millard, 73, 74

Ukraine, 292

Underground tests: detection of, 191; Geneva Conference of Experts on, 132, 133, 136; Johnson administration on limiting, 253; under Kennedy, 161, 163, 169; in LTBT, 214; U.S. acceleration of, 214

United Nations (UN): as anti-Soviet alliance, 58; atomic bank in, 87; Atoms for Peace speech at, 89, 90; Chinese membership in, 234–35; Comprehensive Test Ban Treaty approved by, 293; in Cuban Missile Crisis, 196; disarmament negotiations in, 75, 83; and ENDC, 172–73; on health effects of fallout, 104–5; influence on Soviet Union, 15; international atomic development agency of, 49; in international control plans, 33, 38; Iraq inspections by, 295; Kennedy's 1961 speech at, 165; Moscow Conference and, 40–43; in political implications of bomb, 23; on thermonuclear tests, 99; U.S. hopes for Soviet withdrawal from, 58; U.S. test resumption and, 161

United Nations Atomic Energy Commission (UNAEC): Baruch as U.S. delegate to, 54–55; Baruch Plan debated in, 63–68, 75; Baruch Plan presented to, 60–62; Baruch Plan voted on by, 65, 66–67; Cadogan as British delegate to, 54–55; development of Baruch Plan for, 54–59; Gromyko as Soviet delegate to, 61; Gromyko Plan presented to, 61; as propaganda forum, 62; Security Council veto power over, 43, 55, 58, 61; Soviet agreement to establish, 42, 43

United Nations Disarmament Commission, 75, 76, 78, 85

United Nations Disarmament Subcommittee: end of, 123; 1954 meetings of, 101; 1955 meetings of, 101–2, 103–4; 1956 meetings of, 106, 108–9; 1957 meetings of, 116–23

United Nations General Assembly: on need for NPT, 261; 1955 meeting of, 104; 1962 meeting of, 194; 1966 nonproliferation resolution in, 266; NPT debate in, 277–78; test ban resolution of, 199; on test bans, 190

United Nations Security Council: on Baruch Plan, 68; sanctions against Iran by, 296; veto power over UNAEC, 43, 55, 58, 61

University of Michigan, 183–84

Uranium: in Atoms for Peace program, 88, 91; in Baruch Plan, 57; claims of U.S. monopoly on, 49–50; Combined Development Trust control of, 22; in Fissile Material Cutoff Treaty, 297; reduction in U.S. production of, 232; under Soviet control, 26; Soviet wartime requests for, 20; Western Suppliers Group control of, 107; West German sale of enrichment facilities to Brazil, 290

Utopianism. *See* Technological utopianism

U-2 spy plane incident, 115, 138–39, 148

Vandenberg, Arthur: on Baruch as U.S. delegate to UNAEC, 54; on Baruch Plan, 60–61; on British-American alliance, 69, 70; on Byrnes's international control plan, 41–42; on Quebec Agreement, 69; on Washington Declaration, 40

Vienna summit (1960), 159–60

Vietnam War: and antinuclear movement, 231; and Chinese proliferation, 234; Congress on, 261, 264; Johnson's preoccupation with, 221, 248, 259, 268; Nixon's threats of excessive force in, 287; and NPT negotiations, 253, 265

Vinson, Fred, 34–35

Von Braun, Werner, 230

Voss, Earl H., 207

Wallace, Henry A.: espionage accusations against, 58; resignation of, 66; on Stimson's international control plan, 34–36; U.S. policy criticized by, 65–66

War: abolition of, in Baruch Plan, 57; connection between politics and, 82; preventive, 58, 65, 125; psychological, 84–85

War, nuclear: civilian deaths in, 169, 176; films about, 6, 94, 140, 229–31; Kennedy on, 165; literature about, 140, 190, 229; nonproliferation policy influenced by fears of, 2, 3; public opinion on, 6; report on effects of fallout from, 140; U.S. planning for, 175–76

War, U.S.-Soviet: Acheson on, 52; Baruch Plan and, 58, 66, 67; Eisenhower on, 82, 105; preventive, 58, 125; Truman on, 51

Warsaw Pact countries, 197

Washington Conference, 38–40

Washington Declaration, 39–40, 42

Washington Post, 151

Waste, nuclear, 299–300

Watson, Arthur K., 238

Weapons of mass destruction (WMDs): in Iraq, 295

Webster, William, 238

Western Suppliers Group, 107

West German nuclear program: ANF and, 247–48; French alliance with, 131, 155–56, 167–68, 203–5, 255; and Johnson's policy reassessment, 240; Kennedy's approach to, 155–56, 165–68; and Nassau agreement, 203; in nonproliferation negotiations, 194, 218; in NPT drafts, 262, 266, 269–70; in Polish plan for nuclear freeze, 227; Soviet desire to contain, 194, 228; U.S. on desire for, 125–26; U.S. sharing with, 7, 128, 131; weapons renounced in, 102, 166

West Germany: antinuclear movement in, 169; on ANF, 247–48, 254–55, 258–59; in Berlin crisis, 131; in Berlin talks, 165–66, 173–74; on counterforce strategy, 184; Erhard government collapse in, 268, 269; Grand Coalition in, 269; Johnson's approach to, 222, 245, 251; in LTBT, 211–12, 215; MLF supported by, 182, 186, 205, 206, 223, 229, 245–46, 252, 256–58, 266–67; NATO weapons in, 102; on nontransfer draft agreement, 200; on NPT drafts, 272, 275, 276, 279; on NPT final version, 281; NPT signed by, 283; in nuclear-free zone of Rapacki Plan, 127–28; resistance to U.S. leadership in, 6; Rusk's 1962 visit to, 186; Soviet attempt at détente with, 232; on superpowers' negotiations, 251; on UN Disarmament Subcommittee, 120; uranium enrichment facilities sold to Brazil by, 290; U.S. IRBMs in, 131, 142, 143; U.S. nuclear weapons in, 108, 124, 131, 142, 143, 197

Wheaties, Operation, 89

White, E. B., 32

White Paper on Defence (Macmillan), 167

Whyte, William, 83